P9-BZI-238

Congratulations!

As a student purchasing Parkin, *Economics, Microeconomics,* or *Macroeconomics,* 5e, you are entitled to a prepaid subscription to *The Economics Place*™, Addison Wesley Longman's premier online resource for students and instructors of economics. *The Economics Place* includes activities, study and testing aids, and a wide range of content to help you succeed in your introductory economics course.

To activate your prepaid subscription:

1. Launch your browser and go to www.economicsplace.com
2. Select the graphic for your book.
3. Enter your pre-assigned Activation ID and Password, exactly as they appear below, in the User ID and Password fields:

Activation ID: ECWNST06020737

Password: contralto

4. Select "Login"
5. Complete the online registration form to establish your personal User ID and Password.
6. Once your personal User ID and Password are confirmed, go to www.economicsplace.com/parkin5 to enter the site with your new User ID and Password.

This Activation ID and Password can be used only once to establish a subscription. This subscription to *The Economics Place* is not transferable.

If you did not purchase this product new and in a shrink-wrapped package, this Activation ID and Password may not be valid. However, if your instructor is recommending or requiring use of *The Economics Place*, you can find information on purchasing a subscription at www.economicsplace.com/parkin5.

Fifth Edition

Microeconomics

MICHAEL PARKIN

The cover depicts dawn at Millennium Island (recently renamed from Caroline Island) in the South Pacific as viewed through the Parkin icon. This is the spot on our planet that many say will see the first dawn of the year 2000. You can look at this cover in many different ways. Here is what I see. ◆ First, this book together with its CD, Web site, and other supplements is the result of an extraordinary publishing effort to guide students into the new millennium and to face the challenges they will encounter armed with a clear and compelling account of the timeless principles of economics illuminated by the issues of our age. ◆ I also see a symbol of what economics (and all scientific endeavor) is about. The Parkin icon is like an economic model. We use models to understand reality. The model is abstract, like the diamond and its hole or aperture. The model distorts our view of the world by omitting some details. But at the same time, it permits us to see the focus of our interest in the brightest and clearest possible light.

Fifth Edition

Microconomics

MICHAEL PARKIN
University of Western Ontario

▲ ADDISON-WESLEY

AN IMPRINT OF ADDISON WESLEY LONGMAN, INC.

READING, MASSACHUSETTS • MENLO PARK, CALIFORNIA • NEW YORK • HARLOW, ENGLAND
DON MILLS, ONTARIO • SYDNEY • MEXICO CITY • MADRID • AMSTERDAM

Executive Editor:	Denise J. Clinton
Senior Editor:	Andrea Shaw
Executive Development Manager:	Sylvia Mallory
Supplements Editor:	Deborah Kiernan
Development Assistant:	Judean Patten
Managing Editor:	James Rigney
Senior Production Supervisors:	Mary Sanger, Lou Bruno
Senior Design Supervisor	Gina Hagen
Technical Illustrator:	Richard Parkin
Photo Researcher:	Beth Anderson
Publishing Technology Manager	Sarah McCracken
Electronic Production Administrator:	Sally Simpson
Copyeditor:	Barbara Willette
Proofreaders:	Kathy Smith, Kris Smead
Indexer:	Robin Bade
Senior Manufacturing Manager:	Ralph Mattivello
Manufacturing Supervisor:	Tim McDonald
Marketing Manager:	Amy Cronin
Marketing Coordinator:	Jennifer Thalmann
Printer:	World Color

Library of Congress Cataloging-in-Publication Data

Parkin, Michael, 1939–
    Economics/Michael Parkin. — 5th ed.
      p.   cm.
    Includes bibliographical references and index.
    ISBN 0-201-47385-2 (softbound)
    1. Microeconomics.   I. Title.
  HB172.P24   1999
  338.5—dc21   98–55283
                                CIP

Copyright © 2000 by Addison-Wesley Publishing Company, Inc.

All rights reserved. No part of this publication may be reproduced, stored in
a retrieval system, or transmitted, in any form or by any means, electronic,
mechanical, photocopying, recording, or otherwise, without the prior written
permission of the publisher.

Printed in the United States of America.

3 4 5 6 7 8 9 – WCT – 03020100

Reprinted with corrections, December 1999

Text and photo credits appear on page xxv, which constitutes a continuation of the
copyright page.

To Robin

About Michael Parkin

Michael Parkin

received his training as an economist at the Universities of Leicester and Essex in England. Currently in the Department of Economics at the University of Western Ontario, Canada, Professor Parkin has held faculty appointments at Brown University, the University of Manchester, the University of Essex, and Bond University. He is a past president of the Canadian Economics Association and has served on the editorial boards of the *American Economic Review* and the *Journal of Monetary Economics* and as managing editor of the *Canadian Journal of Economics*. Professor Parkin's research on macro-economics, monetary economics, and international economics has resulted in over 160 publications in journals and edited volumes, including the *American Economic Review*, the *Journal of Political Economy*, the *Review of Economic Studies*, the *Journal of Monetary Economics*, and the *Journal of Money, Credit and Banking*. He became most visible to the public with his work on inflation that discredited the use of wage and price controls. Michael Parkin also spearheaded the movement toward European monetary union. Professor Parkin is an experienced and dedicated teacher of introductory economics.

Preface

This book presents economics as a serious, lively, and evolving science. Its goal is to help the student to develop the "economic way of thinking" and to gain insights into how the economy works and how it might be made to work better. ◆ My goal is to make economics as accessible as possible yet to provide a thorough and complete coverage of the subject, not a slimmed-down or oversimplified selection. ◆ I am conscious that many students find economics hard, so I place the student at center stage and write for the student. I use a style and language that don't intimidate and that allow the student to concentrate on the substance. ◆ I open each chapter with a clear statement of learning objectives, a real-world student-friendly vignette to grab attention, and a brief preview. I illustrate principles with examples that are selected to hold the student's interest and to make the subject lively. And I put principles to work by using them to illuminate current real-world problems and issues. ◆ I present some new ideas, such as dynamic comparative advantage, game theory, the modern theory of the firm, public choice theory, rational expectations, new growth theory, and real business cycle theory. But I explain these topics with familiar core ideas and tools. ◆ Today's course springs from today's issues—the information revolution, the East Asian recession, and the expansion of global trade and investment. But the principles that we use to understand these issues remain the core principles of our science. ◆ Governments and international agencies place renewed emphasis on long-term fundamentals as they seek to sustain economic growth. This book reflects this emphasis. ◆ To enable students to access the latest information on the national and global economy, I have developed a companion Web site. And to provide active learning opportunities, I have developed the tutorials and quizzes on the accompanying *Economics in Action* CD.

The Fifth Edition Revision

Economics, FIFTH EDITION, RETAINS ALL THE improvements achieved in its predecessor with its emphasis on core principles, coverage of recent economic developments, brief yet accessible explanations, and strong pedagogy. New to this edition are:

- Revised and updated micro content
- In-text review quizzes
- Parallel end-of-chapter problems
- Part wrap-ups

Revised and Updated Micro Content

The six major revisions in the micro chapters are:

1. Elasticity (Chapter 5): A new predictions-oriented treatment of the elasticity of demand and supply.
2. Efficiency and Equity (Chapter 6): A new section on equity and the fairness of market outcomes.
3. Organizing Production (Chapter 10): New look at the issues in industrial and market organization and simplified treatment of cost and profit.
4. Monopoly (Chapter 13): New explanations of single-price and price discriminating monopoly including efficiency and distributional aspects of each type. A section on policy has been added.
5. Monopolistic Competition (Chapter 14): A more extensive discussion of the role and effects of selling costs and advertising.
6. Regulation and Antitrust Law (Chapter 19): A thoroughly revised treatment of the antitrust laws and their application and an updated discussion of the Microsoft and other recent cases.

In-Text Review Quizzes

I have replaced the in-text Reviews of the previous editions with Review Quizzes. These brief quizzes invite students to revisit the material they have just studied with a set of questions in mind. I hope that these quizzes will encourage a more critical and thoughtful rereading of any material that proves difficult for the student. The *Instructor's Manual* provides the answers.

Parallel End-of-Chapter Problems

I have reworked the end-of-chapter problems and created pairs of parallel problems. Robin Bade and I have provided the solutions to the odd-numbered problems at the end of the text, and these solutions together with those to the even-numbered problems provided by Melinda Nish appear in the *Instructor's Manual.* This arrangement provides help to students and flexibility to instructors who want to assign problems for credit.

Part Wrap-Ups

A new feature at the *end* of each part:

- Explains how the chapters relate to each other and fit into the larger picture.
- Provides a biographical sketch of the economist who developed the central idea of that part, and places the original contribution in its historical context.
- Presents an interview with a leading contemporary economist.

Features to Enhance Teaching and Learning

HERE I DESCRIBE THE CHAPTER FEATURES that are designed to enhance the learning process. Each chapter contains the following learning aids.

Chapter Objectives

A list of learning objectives enables students to see exactly where the chapter is going and to set their goals before they begin the chapter. I link these goals directly to the chapter's major headings.

After studying this chapter, you will be able to:

■ Explain the fundamental economic problem

■ Define the production possibility frontier

■ Define and calculate opportunity cost

■ Explain the conditions in which resources are used efficiently

■ Explain how economic growth expands production possibilities

■ Explain how specialization and trade expand production possibilities

Chapter Opener

A one-page student-friendly, attention-grabbing vignette raises questions that both motivate and focus the chapter.

Chapter 3

The Economic Problem

We live in a style that surprises our grandparents and would have astonished our great-grandparents. Most of us live in more spacious homes than they did. We eat more, grow taller, and are even born larger than they were. Video games, cellular phones, gene splices, and personal computers did not exist even 20 years ago. Economic growth has made us richer than our grandparents. And we are not alone in experiencing an expansion in the goods and services that we consume. Many nations around the world are not only sharing our experience: They are setting the pace. Before the recent Asia crisis, Hong Kong, Taiwan, Singapore, Korea, and China expanded at unheard-of rates. But economic growth does not liberate us from scarcity. Why not? Why, despite our immense wealth, must we still make choices and face costs? Why are there no "free lunches"? ◆ We see an incredible amount of specialization and trade in the world. Each one of us specializes in a particular job—as a lawyer, a car maker, a home maker. We have become so specialized that one farm worker can feed 100 people. Less than one sixth of the U.S. work force is employed in manufacturing. More than half of the work force is employed in wholesale and retail trade, banking and finance, government, and other services. Why do we specialize? How do we benefit from specialization and trade? ◆ Over many centuries, institutions and social arrangements have evolved that we take for granted. One of them is property rights and the political and legal system that protects them. Another is markets. Why have these social arrangements evolved? How do they increase production?

◆ These are the questions that we study in this chapter. We begin with the core economic problem: scarcity and choice and the concept of the production possibility frontier. We then learn about the central idea of economics—efficiency. We also discover how we can expand production by accumulating capital and by specializing and trading. ◆ What you will learn in this chapter is the foundation on which all economics is built. You will receive big dividends from a careful study of this material.

Making the Most of It

After studying this chapter, you will be able to:

■ Explain the fundamental economic problem

■ Define the production possibility frontier

■ Define and calculate opportunity cost

■ Explain the conditions in which resources are used efficiently

■ Explain how economic growth expands production possibilities

■ Explain how specialization and trade expand production possibilities

In-Text Review Quizzes

A review quiz at end of most major sections enables students to determine whether a topic needs further study before moving on.

R E V I E W   Q U I Z

- What is scarcity?
- What is the fundamental economic problem?
- Can you provide a definition of economics?
- What are the resources that can be used to produce goods and services?
- How do we cope with the fact that our wants cannot be satisfied with the available resources?

Key Terms

Highlighted terms within the text simplify the student's task of learning the vocabulary of economics. Each highlighted term appears in an end-of-chapter list with page numbers, an end-of-book glossary, boldfaced in the index, in the *Economics in Action* software, and on the Parkin Web site.

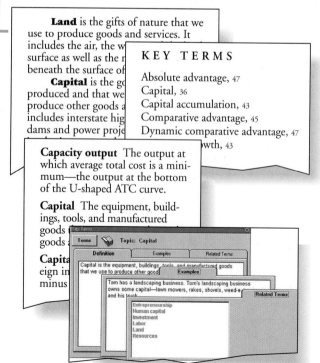

Land is the gifts of nature that we use to produce goods and services. It includes the air, the w... surface as well as the r... beneath the surface of...

Capital is the g... produced and that we... produce other goods a... includes interstate hig... dams and power proj...

Capacity output The output at which average total cost is a minimum—the output at the bottom of the U-shaped ATC curve.

Capital The equipment, buildings, tools, and manufactured goods ... goods a...

Capita... eign in... minus...

KEY TERMS

Absolute advantage, 47
Capital, 36
Capital accumulation, 43
Comparative advantage, 45
Dynamic comparative advantage, 47
...wth, 43

Key Figures and Tables

An icon identifies the most important figures and tables, and the end-of-chapter summary lists them. Instructor's overhead transparencies also contain enlarged and simplified images of most of these key figures.

TABLE 10.3
Efficient Use of Resources

Method	Labor	Capital
a Robot production	1	1,000
b Production line	10	10
c Bench production	100	1
d Hand tool production	1000	1

FIGURE 3.4
Efficient Use of Resources

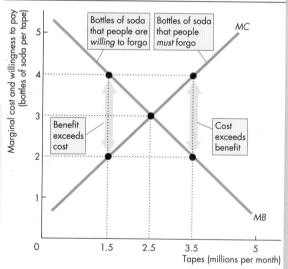

The greater the quantity of tapes produced, the smaller is the marginal benefit (*MB*) from a tape—the fewer bottles of soda people are willing to give up to get an additional tape. But the greater the quantity of tapes produced, the greater is the marginal cost (*MC*) of a tape—the more bottles of soda people must give up to get an additional tape. When marginal benefit equals marginal cost, resources are being used efficiently.

Diagrams That Show the Action

This book has set new standards of clarity in its diagrams. My goal has always been to show "where the economic action is." The diagrams in this book continue to generate an enormously positive response, which confirms my view that graphical analysis is the most important tool available for teaching and learning economics. But many students find graphs hard to work with. For this reason, I have developed the entire art program with the study and review needs of the student in mind. The diagrams feature:

- Shifted curves, equilibrium points, and other important features highlighted in red
- Color-blended arrows to suggest movement
- Graphs paired with data tables
- Diagrams labeled with boxed notes
- Extended captions that make each diagram and its caption a self-contained object for study and review.

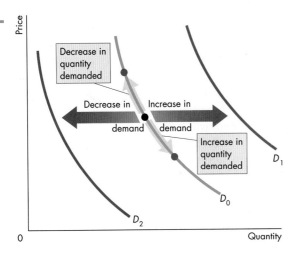

Reading Between the Lines

Each chapter contains an economic analysis of a significant news article from the popular press together with a set of critical thinking questions that relate to the issues raised in the article.

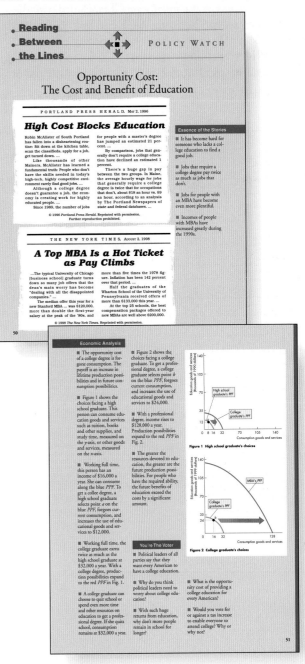

End-of-Chapter Study Material

Each chapter closes with a concise summary organized by major topics; lists of key terms, figures, and tables (all with page references); problems; and critical thinking questions. Items identified by the ⌨ icon link to the *Economics in Action* software CD included with the text. Items identified by the 🌐 icon link to the Parkin Web site at http://www.economicsplace.com. My hope is to encourage students to keep up to date and to become comfortable and efficient in their use of the Internet to access information.

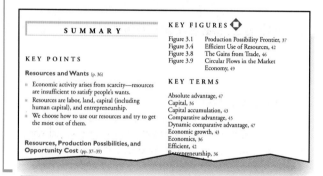

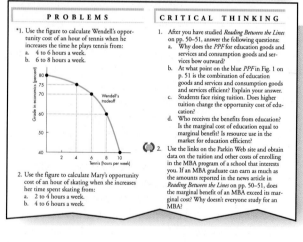

For the Instructor

THIS BOOK ENABLES YOU TO ACHIEVE THREE objectives in your principles course:

- Focus on the core ideas.
- Explain the issues and problems of our time.
- Choose your own course structure.

Focus on the Core Ideas

You know how hard it is to encourage a student to think like an economist. But that is your goal. Consistent with this goal, the text focuses on and repeatedly uses the central ideas: choice; tradeoff; opportunity cost; the margin; incentives; the gains from voluntary exchange; the forces of demand, supply, and equilibrium; the pursuit of economic rent; and the effects of government actions on the economy.

Explain the Issues and Problems of Our Time

Students must *use* the core ideas and tools if they are to begin to understand them. There is no better way to motivate students than by using the tools of economics to explain the issues that confront students in today's world. These issues include the environment, immigration, widening income gaps, the productivity growth slowdown, budget deficits, restraining inflation, watching for the next recession, avoiding protectionism, and the long-term growth of output and incomes.

Choose Your Own Course Structure

You want to teach your own course. I have organized this book to enable you to do so. I demonstrate the book's flexibility in the flexibility chart and alternative sequences table that appear on pp. xxii–xxv. You can use this book to teach a traditional course that blends theory and policy or a current policy issues course. Your micro course can emphasize theory or policy. You can structure your macro course to emphasize long-term growth and supply-side fundamentals. Or you can follow a traditional macro sequence and emphasize short-term fluctuations. The choices are yours.

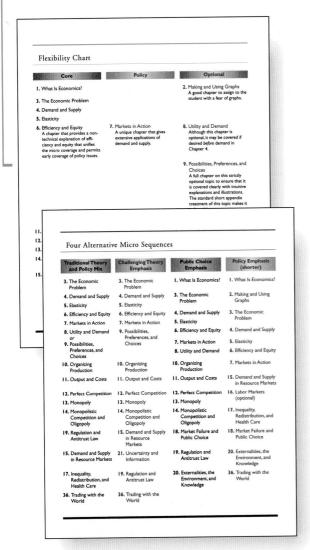

Flexibility Chart

Core	Policy	Optional
1. What Is Economics?		2. Making and Using Graphs A good chapter to assign to the student with a fear of graphs.
3. The Economic Problem		
4. Demand and Supply		
5. Elasticity		
6. Efficiency and Equity A chapter that provides a non-technical explanation of efficiency and equity that unifies the micro coverage and permits early coverage of policy issues.	7. Markets in Action A unique chapter that gives extensive applications of demand and supply.	8. Utility and Demand Although this chapter is optional, it may be covered if desired before demand in Chapter 4.
		9. Possibilities, Preferences, and Choices A full chapter on this strictly optional topic to ensure that it is covered clearly with intuitive explanations and illustrations. The standard short appendix treatment of this topic makes it

Four Alternative Micro Sequences

Traditional Theory and Policy Mix	Challenging Theory Emphasis	Public Choice Emphasis	Policy Emphasis (shorter)
3. The Economic Problem	3. The Economic Problem	1. What Is Economics?	1. What Is Economics?
4. Demand and Supply	4. Demand and Supply	3. The Economic Problem	2. Making and Using Graphs
5. Elasticity	5. Elasticity	4. Demand and Supply	3. The Economic Problem
6. Efficiency and Equity	6. Efficiency and Equity	5. Elasticity	4. Demand and Supply
7. Markets in Action	7. Markets in Action	6. Efficiency and Equity	5. Elasticity
8. Utility and Demand or 9. Possibilities, Preferences, and Choices	9. Possibilities, Preferences, and Choices	7. Markets in Action	6. Efficiency and Equity
		8. Utility and Demand	7. Markets in Action
10. Organizing Production	10. Organizing Production	10. Organizing Production	15. Demand and Supply in Resource Markets
11. Output and Costs	11. Output and Costs	11. Output and Costs	16. Labor Markets (optional)
12. Perfect Competition	12. Perfect Competition	12. Perfect Competition	
13. Monopoly	13. Monopoly	13. Monopoly	17. Inequality, Redistribution, and Health Care
14. Monopolistic Competition and Oligopoly	14. Monopolistic Competition and Oligopoly	14. Monopolistic Competition and Oligopoly	
19. Regulation and Antitrust Law	15. Demand and Supply in Resource Markets	18. Market Failure and Public Choice	18. Market Failure and Public Choice
15. Demand and Supply in Resource Markets	21. Uncertainty and Information	19. Regulation and Antitrust Law	20. Externalities, the Environment, and Knowledge
17. Inequality, Redistribution, and Health Care	19. Regulation and Antitrust Law	20. Externalities, the Environment, and Knowledge	36. Trading with the World
36. Trading with the World	36. Trading with the World		

Instructor's Manual

The Instructor's Manual by Melinda Nish of Salt Lake Community College integrates the teaching and learning package and is a guide to all the supplements. An essay by Dennis Hoffman of Arizona State University explains how to use the *Economics in Action* software as a teaching tool.

Printed Test Banks

We now have three major test banks. Mark Rush of the University of Florida has thoroughly revised the earlier test banks and has coordinated the development of a new 3,000-question test bank written by fifteen outstanding and dedicated principles instructors. They are Sue Bartlett (University of South Florida), Kevin Carey (American University), Leo Chan (University of Kansas), Carol Dole (University of North Carolina, Charlotte), Donald Dutkowsky (Syracuse University), Andrew Foshee (McNeese State University), Jill H. Boylston Herndon (Hamline University), Veronica Kalich (Baldwin-Wallace College), Melinda Nish (Salt Lake Community College), Terry Olson (Truman State University), Rochelle Ruffer (Youngstown State University), Virginia Shingleton (Valparaiso University), Nora Underwood (University of California, Davis), Peter von Allmen (Moravian College), and Peter Zaleski (Villanova University).

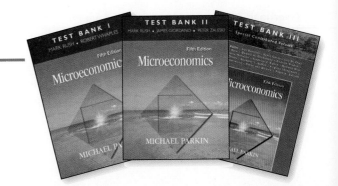

Computerized Test Banks

The test banks are also available in Test Generator Software (TestGen-EQ with QuizMaster-EQ). Version 3.0 of the program, with a wealth of improved features, is now available. This software includes all the questions in the printed test banks. Fully networkable, it is available for Windows and Macintosh. TestGen-EQ's new graphical interface enables instructors easily to view, edit, and add questions; transfer questions to tests; and print different forms of tests. Tests can be formatted by varying fonts and styles, margins, and headers and footers, as in any word-processing document. Search and sort features let the instructor quickly locate questions and arrange them in a preferred order. QuizMaster-EQ, working with your school's computer network, automatically grades the exams, stores the results on disk, and allows the instructor to view or print a variety of reports.

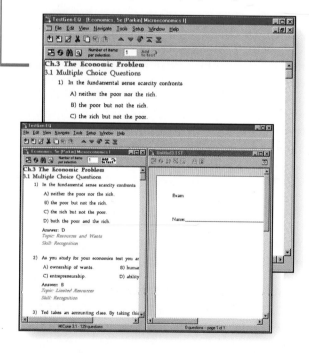

Overhead Transparencies and Overlays

Full-color overhead transparencies (several with overlays) of enlarged and simplified key figures from the text will improve the clarity of your lectures. They are available to qualified adopters of the text (contact your Addison Wesley Longman sales representative).

PowerPoint Lecture Presentations

Charles Pflanz of Scottsdale Community College has developed a full-color Microsoft PowerPoint Lecture Presentation that breaks the chapters into lecture-size bites and includes key figures from the text, animated graphs, and speaking notes. The presentation can be used electronically in the classroom or can be printed to create hard-copy transparency masters. The lecture presentation is available for Macintosh and Windows to qualified adopters of the text (contact your Addison Wesley Longman sales representative).

Economics in Action Software

Instructors can use *Economics in Action* interactive software in the classroom. Its full-screen display option turns its many analytical graphs into "electronic transparencies" for live graph manipulation in lectures. Its real-world data sets and graphing utility bring animated time-series graphs and scatter diagrams to the classroom.

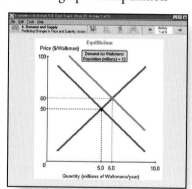

The Parkin Web Site

With the Fifth Edition of the textbook comes the debut of *The Economics Place* at www.economicsplace.com. This Internet-based learning environment contains tools for organizing students' grades from online quizzes, frequent updates of data in the text figures, and news you can use in the classroom. Use the Web site to motivate and organize lectures with electronic *Reading Between the Lines* and *Point-Counterpoint* or to create an online quiz for an in-class review.

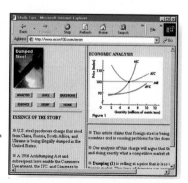

For the Student

Study Guide

The Fifth Edition *Study Guide* by Mark Rush of the University of Florida is carefully coordinated with the main text and the test bank. Each chapter of the Study Guide contains:

- Key concepts
- Helpful hints
- True/false/uncertain questions that ask students to explain their answers
- Multiple-choice questions
- Short-answer questions
- Common questions or misconceptions that the student explains as if he or she were the teacher

Each part allows students to test their cumulative understanding with *Reading Between the Lines* exercises and sample midterm tests.

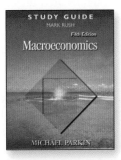

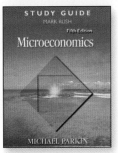

Economics in Action Interactive Software

With *Economics in Action* Release 5.0, which accompanies the Fifth Edition, students will have fun working the tutorials, answering questions that give instant explanations, and testing themselves ahead of their midterm tests. One of my students told me that using *EIA* is like having a private professor in your dorm room!

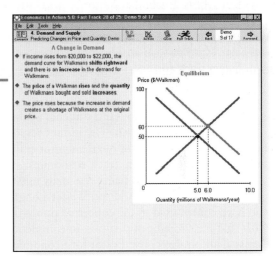

The Parkin Web Site

New for the Fifth Edition, *The Economics Place* Web site provides online quizzes, study tips, office hours, links, electronic *Reading Between the Lines*, a *Point-Counterpoint* feature that encourages students to participate in contemporary policy debates, and much more. You can reach the site at http://www.economicsplace.com.

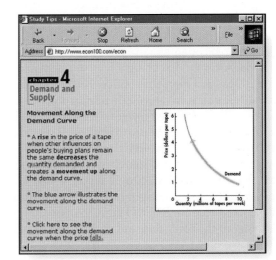

Acknowledgments

I THANK MY CURRENT AND FORMER COLLEAGUES and friends at the University of Western Ontario who have taught me so much. They are Jim Davies, Jeremy Greenwood, Ig Horstmann, Peter Howitt, Greg Huffman, David Laidler, Phil Reny, Chris Robinson, John Whalley, and Ron Wonnacott. I also thank Doug McTaggart and Christopher Findlay, co-authors of the Australian edition, and Melanie Powell and Kent Matthews, co-authors of the European edition. Suggestions arising from their adaptations of earlier editions have been helpful to me in preparing this edition.

I thank the several thousand students whom I have been privileged to teach. The instant response that comes from the look of puzzlement or enlightenment has taught me how to teach economics.

It is an especial joy to thank the many outstanding editors and others at Addison Wesley Longman who have contributed to the concerted publishing effort that has brought this edition to completion. Denise Clinton, Executive Editor for Economics and Finance, has been a constant source of inspiration and encouragement and has provided overall direction. Andrea Shaw, Senior Editor for Economics and my sponsoring editor, has ably coordinated the arrangements for this edition. Sylvia Mallory, Executive Development Manager, has brought her calm, creative, and professional direction to the development effort on this edition. Deborah Kiernan, Senior Supplements Editor, working with the most able team of authors, has managed the creation of a large and complex supplements package. Along with Mark Rush, Sylvia Mallory and Deb Kiernan have pulled together a "dream team" of questions authors and helped to create the best-ever principles of economics test bank. Judean Patten, Editorial Assistant, has cheerfully performed many helpful tasks at a moment's notice. Beth Anderson, Photo Researcher, has diligently persisted in her efforts until the required images were found. Melissa Honig, Senior Project Editor, has directed the development of *Economics in Action* and has been an appreciated and admired source of guidance on many matters relating to the electronic supplements. Amy Cronin, Marketing Manager, has provided inspired marketing direction. Regina Hagen, Senior Designer, has designed the cover, text, and package and surpassed

the challenge of ensuring that we meet the highest design standards. Managing Editor James Rigney and Senior Production Supervisors Mary Sanger and Louis Bruno have worked miracles on a tight production schedule and coped calmly with late-changing content. I thank all of these wonderful people. It has been inspiring to work with them and to share in creating what I believe is a truly outstanding educational tool.

I thank the 17 supplements authors whose names appear on pp. xv and xvi. But I especially thank Mark Rush, who has yet again played a crucial role in creating another edition of this text and package. Mark has been a constant source of good advice and good humor. And I thank Art Woolf for his careful accuracy review of near-final pages.

I am most grateful to the thoughtful news clippers who have greatly helped in the task of writing the *Reading Between the Lines* features. They are Richard Fristensky (Bentley College), Susan Glanz (St. John's University), Jim Lee (Fort Hays State University), Kathryn Nantz (Fairfield University), and Paul Storer (Western Washington University).

I thank the people who work directly with me. Jeannie Gillmore has provided outstanding research assistance. Jane McAndrew has provided excellent library help. Richard Parkin has created the electronic art files for both the text and the CD and offered many ideas that have improved the illustrations. Laurel Davies has helped by creating, editing, and checking the accuracy of the *Economics in Action* database.

As with the previous editions, this one owes an enormous debt to Robin Bade. I dedicate this book to her and again thank her for her work. I could not have written this book without the unselfish help she has given me. My thanks to her are unbounded.

Classroom experience will test the value of this book. I would appreciate hearing from instructors and students about how I can continue to improve it in future editions.

Michael Parkin
London, Ontario, Canada
michael.parkin@ uwo.ca

Reviewers

Tajudeen Adenekan, Bronx Community College
Milton Alderfer, Miami-Dade Community College
William Aldridge, Shelton State Community College
Donald L. Alexander, Western Michigan University
Terence Alexander, Iowa State University
Stuart Allen, University of North Carolina,
    Greensboro
Sam Allgood, University of Nebraska, Lincoln
Neil Alper, Northeastern University
Alan Anderson, Fordham University
Lisa R. Anderson, College of William and Mary
Jeff Ankrom, Wittenberg University
Fatma Antar, Manchester Community Technical
    College
Kofi Apraku, University of North Carolina, Asheville
Moshen Bahmani-Oskooee, University of Wisconsin,
    Milwaukee
Donald Balch, University of South Carolina
Mehmet Balcilar, Wayne State University
A. Paul Ballantyne, University of Colorado
Sue Bartlett, University of South Florida
Valerie R. Bencivenga, University of Texas, Austin
Ben Bernanke, Princeton University
Margot Biery, Tarrant County Community
    College South
John Bittorowitz, Ball State University
Giacomo Bonanno, University of California, Davis
Sunne Brandmeyer, University of South Florida
Audie Brewton, Northeastern Illinois University
Baird Brock, Central Missouri State University
Byron Brown, Michigan State University
Jeffrey Buser, Columbus State Community College
Alison Butler, Florida International University
Tania Carbiener, Southern Methodist University
Kevin Carey, American University
Kathleen A. Carroll, University of Maryland,
    Baltimore County
Michael Carter, University of Massachusetts, Lowell
Adhip Chaudhuri, Georgetown University
Gopal Chengalath, Texas Tech University
Daniel Christiansen, Albion College
John J. Clark, Community College of Allegheny
    County, Allegheny Campus
Meredith Clement, Dartmouth College
Michael B. Cohn, U.S. Merchant Marine Academy
Robert Collinge, University of Texas, San Antonio

Doug Conway, Mesa Community College
Larry Cook, University of Toledo
Bobby Corcoran, Middle Tennessee State University
Kevin Cotter, Wayne State University
James Peery Cover, University of Alabama, Tuscaloosa
Eleanor D. Craig, University of Delaware
Jim Craven, Clark College
Stephen Cullenberg, University of California,
    Riverside
David Culp, Slippery Rock University
Norman V. Cure, Macomb Community College
Dan Dabney, University of Texas, Austin
Andrew Dane, Angelo State University
Joseph Daniels, Marquette University
David Denslow, University of Florida
Mark Dickie, University of Georgia
James Dietz, California State University, Fullerton
Carol Dole, University of North Carolina, Charlotte
Ronald Dorf, Inver Hills Community College
John Dorsey, University of Maryland, College Park
Amrik Singh Dua, Mt. San Antonio College
Thomas Duchesneau, University of Maine, Orono
Lucia Dunn, Ohio State University
Donald Dutkowsky, Syracuse University
John Edgren, Eastern Michigan University
David J. Eger, Alpena Community College
Harry Ellis, Jr., University of North Texas
Ibrahim Elsaify, State University of New York, Albany
Kenneth G. Elzinga, University of Virginia
M. Fazeli, Hofstra University
Philip Fincher, Louisiana Tech University
F. Firoozi, University of Texas, San Antonio
David Franck, University of North Carolina, Charlotte
Roger Frantz, San Diego State University
Alwyn Fraser, Atlantic Union College
Richard Fristensky, Bentley College
Eugene Gentzel, Pensacola Junior College
Andrew Gill, California State University, Fullerton
Robert Giller, Virginia Polytechnic Institute and State
    University
Robert Gillette, University of Kentucky
James N. Giordano, Villanova University
Maria Giuili, Diablo College
Susan Glanz, St. John's University
Richard Gosselin, Houston Community College
John Graham, Rutgers University
John Griffen, Worcester Polytechnic Institute
Robert Guell, Indiana State University
Jamie Haag, University of Oregon
Gail Heyne Hafer, Lindenwood University
Rik W. Hafer, Southern Illinois University

Daniel Hagen, Western Washington University
David R. Hakes, University of Northern Iowa
Craig Hakkio, Federal Reserve Bank, Kansas City
Ann Hansen, Westminster College
Jonathan Haughton, Northeastern University
Randall Haydon, Wichita State University
Jolien A. Helsel, Kent State University
Jill H. Boylston Herndon, Hamline University
John Herrmann, Rutgers University
John M. Hill, Delgado Community College
Lewis Hill, Texas Tech University
Steve Hoagland, University of Akron
Tom Hoerger, Vanderbilt University
Calvin Hoerneman, Delta College
George Hoffer, Virginia Commonwealth University
Dennis L. Hoffman, Arizona State University
Paul Hohenberg, Rensselaer Polytechnic Institute
Jim H. Holcomb, University of Texas, El Paso
Harry Holzer, Michigan State University
Djehane Hosni, University of Central Florida
Harold Hotelling, Jr., Lawrence Technical University
Calvin Hoy, County College of Morris
Julie Hunsaker, Wayne State University
Beth Ingram, University of Iowa
Michael Jacobs, Lehman College
Dennis Jansen, Texas A & M University
Frederick Jungman, Northwestern Oklahoma State University
Paul Junk, University of Minnesota, Duluth
Leo Kahane, California State University, Hayward
Veronica Kalich, Baldwin-Wallace College
John Kane, State University of New York, Oswego
E. Kang, St. Cloud State University
Arthur Kartman, San Diego State University
Manfred W. Keil, Claremont McKenna College
Rose Kilburn, Modesto Junior College
Robert Kirk, Indiana University–Purdue University, Indianapolis
Norman Kleinberg, City University of New York, Baruch College
Robert Kleinhenz, California State University, Fullerton
Joseph Kreitzer, University of St. Thomas
David Lages, Southwest Missouri State University
W. J. Lane, University of New Orleans
Leonard Lardaro, University of Rhode Island
Kathryn Larson, Elon College
Luther D. Lawson, University of North Carolina, Wilmington
Elroy M. Leach, Chicago State University
Jim Lee, Fort Hays State University

Jay Levin, Wayne State University
Arik Levinson, University of Wisconsin, Madison
Tony Lima, California State University, Hayward
William Lord, University of Maryland, Baltimore County
Nancy Lutz, Virginia Polytechnic Institute and State University
K.T. Magnusson, Salt Lake City Community College
Mark Maier, Glendale Community College
Beth Maloan, University of Tennessee, Martin
Jean Mangan, California State University, Sacramento
Michael Marlow, California Polytechnic State University
Akbar Marvasti, University of Houston
Wolfgang Mayer, University of Cincinnati
John McArthur, Wofford College
Amy McCormick, College of William and Mary
Russel McCullough, Iowa State University
Gerald McDougall, Wichita State University
Stephen McGary, Ricks College
Richard D. McGrath, College of William and Mary
Richard McIntyre, University of Rhode Island
John McLeod, Georgia Institute of Technology
Charles Meyer, Iowa State University
Peter Mieszkowski, Rice University
John Mijares, University of North Carolina, Asheville
Richard A. Miller, Wesleyan University
Judith W. Mills, Southern Connecticut State University
Glen Mitchell, Nassau Community College
Jeannette C. Mitchell, Rochester Institute of Technology
Khan Mohabbat, Northern Illinois University
W. Douglas Morgan, University of California, Santa Barbara
William Morgan, University of Wyoming
Joanne Moss, San Francisco State University
Edward Murphy, Southwest Texas State University
Kevin J. Murphy, Oakland University
Kathryn Nantz, Fairfield University
William S. Neilson, Texas A & M University
Bart C. Nemmers, University of Nebraska, Lincoln
Melinda Nish, Salt Lake Community College
Anthony O'Brien, Lehigh University
Mary Olson, Washington University
Terry Olson, Truman State University
James B. O'Niell, University of Delaware
Farley Ordovensky, University of the Pacific
Z. Edward O'Relley, North Dakota State University
Jan Palmer, Ohio University
Michael Palumbo, University of Houston

G. Hossein Parandvash, Western Oregon State College
Randall Parker, East Carolina University
Robert Parks, Washington University
David Pate, St. John Fisher College
Donald Pearson, Eastern Michigan University
Mary Anne Pettit, Southern Illinois University, Edwardsville
Kathy Phares, University of Missouri, St. Louis
William A. Phillips, University of Southern Maine
Dennis Placone, Clemson University
Charles Plot, California Institute of Technology, Pasadena
Mannie Poen, Houston Community College
Kathleen Possai, Wayne State University
Ulrika Praski-Stahlgren, University College in Gavle-Sandviken, Sweden
K.A. Quartey, Talladega College
Herman Quirmbach, Iowa State University
Jeffrey R. Racine, University of South Florida
Peter Rangazas, Indiana University–Purdue University, Indianapolis
Vaman Rao, Western Illinois University
Laura Razzolini, University of Mississippi
J. David Reed, Bowling Green State University
Robert H. Renshaw, Northern Illinois University
W. Gregory Rhodus, Bentley College
John Robertson, Paducah Community College
Malcolm Robinson, University of North Carolina, Greensboro
Richard Roehl, University of Michigan, Dearborn
Thomas Romans, State University of New York, Buffalo
David R. Ross, Bryn Mawr College
Thomas Ross, St. Louis University
Robert J. Rossana, Wayne State University
Rochelle Ruffer, Youngstown State University
Mark Rush, University of Florida
Gary Santoni, Ball State University
John Saussy, Harrisburg Area Community College
David Schlow, Pennsylvania State University

Paul Schmitt, St. Clair County Community College
Martin Sefton, Indianapolis University
Rod Shadbegian, University of Massachusetts, Dartmouth
Gerald Shilling, Eastfield College
Dorothy R. Siden, Salem State College
Scott Simkins, North Carolina Agricultural and Technical State University
Chuck Skoro, Boise State University
Phil Smith, DeKalb College
William Doyle Smith, University of Texas, El Paso
Frank Steindl, Oklahoma State University
Jeffrey Stewart, New York University
Allan Stone, Southwest Missouri State University
Courtenay Stone, Ball State University
Paul Storer, Western Washington University
Mark Strazicich, Ohio State University, Newark
Robert Stuart, Rutgers University
Gilbert Suzawa, University of Rhode Island
David Swaine, Andrews University
Kay Unger, University of Montana
Anthony Uremovic, Joliet Junior College
David Vaughn, City University, Washington
Don Waldman, Colgate University
Francis Wambalaba, Portland State University
Rob Wassmer, Wayne State University
Paul A. Weinstein, University of Maryland, College Park
Lee Weissert, St. Vincent College
Robert Whaples, Wake Forest University
Charles H. Whiteman, University of Iowa
Larry Wimmer, Brigham Young University
Mark Witte, Northwestern University
Willard E. Witte, Indiana University
Mark Wohar, University of Nebraska, Omaha
Cheonsik Woo, Clemson University
Douglas Wooley, Radford University
Arthur G. Woolf, University of Vermont
Ann Al Yasiri, University of Wisconsin, Platteville
John T. Young, Riverside Community College
Michael Youngblood, Rock Valley College.

Microeconomics Flexibility Chart

Core	Policy	Optional

1. What Is Economics?

3. The Economic Problem

4. Demand and Supply

5. Elasticity

6. Efficiency and Equity
A chapter that provides a non-technical explanation of efficiency and equity that unifies the micro coverage and permits early coverage of policy issues.

7. Markets in Action
A unique chapter that gives extensive applications of demand and supply.

2. Making and Using Graphs
A good chapter to assign to the student with a fear of graphs.

8. Utility and Demand
Although this chapter is optional, it may be covered if desired *before* demand in Chapter 4.

9. Possibilities, Preferences, and Choices
A full chapter on this strictly optional topic to ensure that it is covered clearly with intuitive explanations and illustrations. The standard short appendix treatment of this topic makes it indigestible.

10. Organizing Production
This chapter may be skipped or assigned as a reading.

Core	Policy	Optional

11. Output and Costs

12. Perfect Competition

13. Monopoly

14. Monopolistic Competition and Oligopoly

15. Demand and Supply in Resource Markets
Enables you to cover all the resource market issues in a single chapter. Includes an explanation of present value.

16. Labor Markets

17. Inequality, Redistribution, and Health Care

18. Market Failure and Public Choice
Introduces the role of government in the economy and explains the positive theory of government.

19. Regulation and Antitrust Law

20. Externalities, the Environment, and Knowledge

21. Uncertainty and Information

22. Trading with the World

Four Alternative Micro Sequences

Traditional Theory and Policy Mix	Challenging Theory Emphasis	Public Choice Emphasis	Policy Emphasis (shorter)
3. The Economic Problem	**3.** The Economic Problem	**1.** What Is Economics?	**1.** What Is Economics?
4. Demand and Supply	**4.** Demand and Supply	**3.** The Economic Problem	**2.** Making and Using Graphs
5. Elasticity	**5.** Elasticity	**4.** Demand and Supply	**3.** The Economic Problem
6. Efficiency and Equity	**6.** Efficiency and Equity	**5.** Elasticity	
7. Markets in Action	**7.** Markets in Action	**6.** Efficiency and Equity	**4.** Demand and Supply
8. Utility and Demand or	**9.** Possibilities, Preferences, and Choices	**7.** Markets in Action	**5.** Elasticity
9. Possibilities, Preferences, and Choices		**8.** Utility and Demand	**6.** Efficiency and Equity
10. Organizing Production	**10.** Organizing Production	**10.** Organizing Production	**7.** Markets in Action
11. Output and Costs	**11.** Output and Costs	**11.** Output and Costs	**15.** Demand and Supply in Resource Markets
12. Perfect Competition	**12.** Perfect Competition	**12.** Perfect Competition	**16.** Labor Markets (optional)
13. Monopoly	**13.** Monopoly	**13.** Monopoly	
14. Monopolistic Competition and Oligopoly	**14.** Monopolistic Competition and Oligopoly	**14.** Monopolistic Competition and Oligopoly	**17.** Inequality, Redistribution, and Health Care
19. Regulation and Antitrust Law	**15.** Demand and Supply in Resource Markets	**18.** Market Failure and Public Choice	**18.** Market Failure and Public Choice
15. Demand and Supply in Resource Markets	**21.** Uncertainty and Information	**19.** Regulation and Antitrust Law	**20.** Externalities, the Environment, and Knowledge
17. Inequality, Redistribution, and Health Care	**19.** Regulation and Antitrust Law	**20.** Externalities, the Environment, and Knowledge	**22.** Trading with the World
22. Trading with the World	**22.** Trading with the World		

Credits

(continuation from p. IV)

Chapter 1: P. 2 right: PhotoDisc, Inc.; p. 3 top: David Frazier Photolibrary; p. 3 center: George Rose/Gamma Liason; p 3 bottom: Owen Franken/Tony Stone Images; p. 4 top left: MediaFocus International, LLC; p.4 top right: Charles Gupton/The Stock Market; p. 4 bottom left: Chip Henderson/Tony Stone Images; p. 4 bottom right: © Paul Conklin/ PhotoEdit Inc.; p. 5 top: David Joel/Tony Stone Images; p. 5 bottom: PhotoDisc Inc.; p. 6 left: PhotoDisc, Inc.; p. 6 right: © David Young-Wolff/PhotoEdit, Inc.; p. 7: PhotoDisc, Inc.;p. 8 left and right: © David Young-Wolff/PhotoEdit Inc.; p. 9 left: courtesy of Intel Corporation; p. 9 right: PhotoDisc, Inc.; p. 10 top left: Karl Cummels/SuperStock; p. 10 bottom left: PhotoDisc, Inc.; p. 10 top right: © David Young-Wolff/Tony Stone Images; p. 10 bottom right: Bob Sacha/Aurora/PNI; p. 11 top left: © Tony Freeman/PhotoEdit Inc.; p. 11 top right: © R. Crandall/The Image Works; p. 11 bottom: Steven Wernberg/Tony Stone Images; p. 12 top and bottom: Scott Foresman/Addison Wesley Longman, Focus on Sports; p. 13 top: PhotoDisc, Inc.; p. 13 bottom: © M. Reinstein/The Image Works; p. 14 top left: Dick Morton, courtesy of The Weather Channel, Inc. and radar imagery courtesy of WSI Corporation, Inc.; p. 14 bottom left: PhotoDisc, Inc.; p. 14 right: © David Burnett/Contact Press Images/PNI; p. 15 top right: SuperStock; p.15 bottom right: PhotoDisc, Inc.; p. 15 bottom left: PhotoDisc, Inc.; p. 16: AP/Wide World Photos; p. 18: © Jeff Greenberg/PhotoEdit Inc.

Part 1: Adam Smith (p. 56), Corbis-Bettmann. Pin factory (p. 57), Culver Pictures. Silicon wafer (p. 57), Bruce Ando/Tony Stone Images. Douglas North (p. 58), © Bill Stover.

Part 2: Alfred Marshall (p. 150), Stock Montage. Railroad bridge (p.151), National Archives. Airport (p. 151), PhotoDisc, Inc. Paul Milgrom (p. 152), Jenny Thomas.

Part 3: Jeremy Bentham (p. 192), Corbis-Bettmann. Women factory workers (p. 193), Keystone-Mast Collection (V22542) UCR/California Museum of Photography, University of California, Riverside. Man and woman in office (p. 193), PhotoDisc, Inc. Gary Becker (p. 194), Loren Santow.

Chapter 10: Wheatfield (p. 207), PhotoDisc, Inc. Athletic shoe store (p. 207), Dick Morton. Vending machines (p. 207), Dick Morton. Windows 98 display (p. 207), Dick Morton.

Part 4: John von Neumann (p. 312), Stock Montage. Cartoon of the power of monopoly (p. 313), Culver Pictures. Cable worker (p. 313), Don Wilson/West Stock. Avinash K. Dixit (p. 314), Peter Murphy.

Part 5: Thomas Robert Malthus (p. 386), Corbis-Bettmann. Tremont Street, Boston traffic, 1870 (p. 387), courtesy of The Bostonian Society/Old State House. Parking machine (p. 387), Mark E. Gibson. Claudia Goldin (p. 388), Stuart Cohen.

Part 6: Ronald Coase (p. 468), David Joel/David Joel Photography, Inc. Great Lakes pollution (p. 469), Jim Baron/The Image Finders. Fishing boat on Lake Erie (p. 469), Patrick Mullen. Walter E. Williams (p. 470), John Skowronski.

Part 7: David Ricardo (p. 496), Corbis-Bettmann. Clipper ship (p. 497), North Wind Picture Archives. Container ship (p. 497), © M. Timothy O'Keefe/Weststock. Stanley Fisher (p. 498), John Skowronski.

Brief Contents

Contents

Summary (Key Points, Key Figures and Tables, and Key Terms), Problems, and Critical Thinking appear at the end of each chapter.

Chapters marked with this symbol are included on the *Economics in Action* CD.

Fifth Edition

Microeconomics

MICHAEL PARKIN

Chapter 1

What Is Economics?

From the moment you wake up each morning to the moment you fall asleep again each night, your life is filled with *choices*. Your first choice is when to get up. Will you start running the moment the alarm goes off, or will you linger for a few minutes and listen to the radio? What will you wear today? You check the weather forecast and make that decision. Then, what will you have for breakfast? Will you drive to school or take the bus? Which classes will you attend? Which assignments will you complete? What will you do for lunch? Will you play tennis, swim, run, or skate today? How will you spend your evening? Will you study, relax at home with a video, or go to the movies? ◆ You face decisions like these every day. But on some days, you face choices that can change the entire direction of your life.

A Day in Your Life

What will you study? Will you major in economics, business, law, or film? ◆ While you are making your own decisions, other people are making theirs. And some of the decisions that other people make will have an impact on your own subsequent decisions. Your school decides its course offerings for next year. Stephen Spielberg decides what his next movie will be. A team of eye doctors decides on a new experiment that will lead them to a cure for nearsightedness. The U.S. Congress decides to reform Social Security. The Federal Reserve Board decides to cut interest rates. ◆ All these choices and decisions by you and everyone else are all examples of economics in your life.

◆ This chapter takes a first look at the subject you are about to study. It defines economics. Then it expands on that definition with five big questions that economists try to answer and eight big ideas that define the economic way of thinking. These questions and ideas are the foundation on which your course is built. The chapter concludes with a description of how economists go about their work, the scientific method they use, and the pitfalls they try to avoid. When you have completed your study of this chapter, you will have a good sense of what economics is about and you'll be ready to start learning economics and using it to gain a new view of the world.

After studying this chapter, you will be able to:

- Define economics
- Explain the five big questions that economists seek to answer
- Explain eight ideas that define the economic way of thinking
- Describe how economists go about their work

A Definition of Economics

ALL ECONOMIC QUESTIONS AND PROBLEMS ARISE from **scarcity**—they arise because our wants exceed the resources available to satisfy them.

We want good health and long life, material comfort, security, physical and mental recreation, and knowledge. None of these wants is completely satisfied for everyone, and everyone has some unsatisfied wants. While many people have all the material comfort they want, many others do not. And no one feels entirely satisfied with her or his state of health and expected length of life. No one feels entirely secure, even in the post–Cold War era, and no one has enough time for sport, travel, vacations, movies, theater, reading, and other leisure pursuits.

The poor and the rich alike, face scarcity. A child wants a 75¢ can of soft drink and a 50¢ pack of gum but has only $1.00 in her pocket. She experiences scarcity. A student wants to go to a party on Saturday night but also wants to spend that same night catching up on late assignments. He experiences scarcity. A millionaire wants to spend the weekend playing golf *and* attending a business strategy meeting and cannot do both. She experiences scarcity. Even parrots face scarcity—there just aren't enough crackers to go around!

Faced with scarcity, we must *choose* among the available alternatives.

Economics is the *science of choice*—the science that explains the choices that we make and how those choices change as we cope with scarcity.

Not only do I want a cracker—we all want a cracker!

Drawing by Modell; ©1985 *The New Yorker Magazine,* Inc.

Big Economic Questions

ALL ECONOMIC CHOICES CAN BE SUMMARIZED IN big questions about the goods and services we produce. These questions are: What? How? When? Where? Who?

1: What?

What goods and services are produced and in what quantities? **Goods and services** are all the things that we value and are willing to pay for. We produce a dazzling array of goods and services that range from necessities such as houses to leisure items such as camping vehicles and equipment. We build more than a million new homes every year. And these homes are more spacious and better equipped than they were twenty years ago. We make several million new leisure vehicles, tents, microwaves, refrigerators, telephones, television sets, and VCRs, all of which make outdoor living and vacations more attractive and more comfortable.

What determines whether we build more homes or make more camping gear and develop more campsites? How do these choices change over time? And how are they affected by the ongoing changes in technology that make an ever-wider array of goods and services available to us?

2: How?

How are goods and services produced? In a vineyard in France, basket-carrying workers pick the annual grape crop by hand. In a vineyard in California, a huge machine and a few workers do the same job that a hundred French grape harvesters do. Look around you and you will see many examples of this phenomenon—the same job being done in different ways. In some supermarkets, checkout clerks key in

prices. In others, they use a laser scanner. One farmer keeps track of his livestock feeding schedules and inventories by using paper and pencil records, while another uses a personal computer. GM hires workers to weld auto bodies in some of its plants and uses robots to do the job in others.

Why do we use machines in some cases and people in others? Does mechanization and technological change destroy more jobs than it creates? Does it make us better off or worse off?

3: When?

When are goods and services produced? On a building site, there is a surge of production activity and people must work overtime to keep production flowing fast enough. An auto factory closes for the summer, temporarily lays of its workers, and its production dries up.

Sometimes, economy-wide production slackens off and even shrinks in what is called a *recession*. At other times, economy-wide production expands rapidly. We call these ebbs and flows of production the *business cycle*. When production falls, jobs are lost and unemployment climbs. Once, during the Great Depression of the 1930s, production fell so much that one quarter of the workforce was jobless.

During the past few years, production has decreased in Russia and its Central and Eastern European neighbors as these countries try to change the way they organize their economies.

What makes production rise and fall? When will production fall again in the United States? Can the government prevent production from falling?

4: Where?

Where are goods and services produced? The Kellogg Company, of Battle Creek, Michigan, makes breakfast cereals in 20 countries and sells them in 160 countries. Kellogg's business in Japan is so huge that it has a Japanese language Website to promote its products! Honda, the Japanese auto producer, makes cars and motor cycles on most continents. "Globalization through localization" is its slogan. But it produces some cars in one country and ships them for sale in another.

In today's global economy, people who are separated by thousands of miles cooperate to produce many goods and services. Software engineers in Silicon Valley work via the Internet with programmers in India. American Express card charge slips are processed in Barbados. But there is a lot of local concentration of production as well. Most American carpets are made in Dalton, Georgia. And most of our movies are made in Los Angeles.

What determines where goods and services are produced? And how are changing patterns of production location changing the jobs we do and the wages we earn?

5: Who?

Who consumes the goods and services that are produced? Who consumes the goods and services produced depends on the incomes that people earn. Doctors earn much higher incomes than nurses and medical assistants. So doctors get more of the goods and services produced than nurses and medical assistants.

You probably know about many other persistent differences in incomes. Men, on the average, earn more than women. Whites, on the average, earn more than minorities. College graduates, on the average, earn more than high-school graduates do. Americans, on the average, earn more than Europeans, who in turn earn more on the average than Asians and Africans. But there are some significant exceptions. The people of Japan and Hong Kong now earn a similar amount to that of Americans. And there is a lot of income inequality throughout the world.

What determines the incomes we earn? Why do doctors earn larger incomes than nurses? Why do women and minorities earn less than white males?

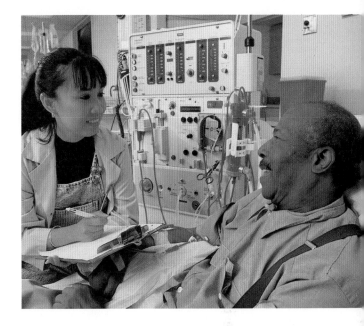

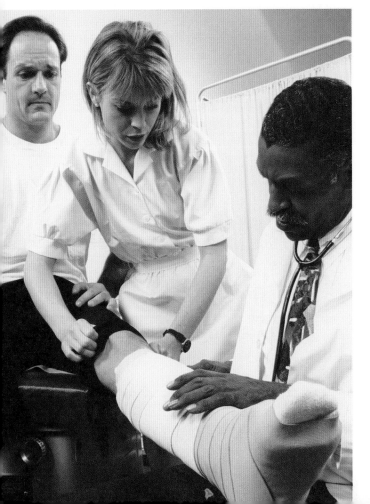

REVIEW QUIZ

- How would you define economics?
- What is scarcity? Give some examples of rich people and poor people facing scarcity.
- Give some examples, different from those in the chapter, of each of the five big economic questions.
- Why do you care about *what* goods and services are produced? Give some examples of goods that you value highly and goods on which you place a low value.
- Why do you care about *how* goods and services are produced? [Hint: Think about cost.]
- Why do you care about *when* or *where* goods and services are produced?
- Why do you care about *who* gets the goods and services that are produced?

These five big economic questions give you a sense of what economics is *about*. They tell you about the *scope of economics*. But they don't tell you what economics *is*. They don't tell you how economists *think* about these questions and seek answers to them. Let's find out how economists approach economic questions by looking at eight big ideas that define the *economic way of thinking*.

Big Ideas of Economics

WE CAN SUMMARIZE THE ECONOMIC WAY OF thinking in eight big ideas. Let's study them.

1: Choice, Tradeoff, and Opportunity Cost

A choice is a tradeoff—we give up something to get something else—and the highest-valued alternative we give up is the opportunity cost of the activity we choose.

Whatever we choose to do, we could have done something else instead. We tradeoff one thing for another. **Tradeoff** means giving up something to get something else. The highest-valued alternative we give up to get something is the **opportunity cost** of the activity chosen. "There's no such thing as a free lunch" is not just a clever throwaway line. It expresses the central idea of economics—that every choice involves a cost.

We use the term *opportunity cost* to emphasize that when we make a choice in the face of scarcity, we give up an opportunity to do something else. The opportunity cost of any action is the highest-valued alternative forgone. The action that you choose not to do—the highest-valued alternative forgone—is the cost of the action that you choose to do.

You can quit school right now or you can remain in school. If you quit and take a job at McDonalds, you might earn enough to buy some CDs, go to the movies, and spend lots of free time with your friends. If you remain in school, you can't afford these things. You will be able to buy these things later, and that is one of the payoffs from being in school. But for now, when you've bought your books, you have nothing left for CDs and movies. And doing assignments means that you've got less time for hanging around with your friends. The opportunity cost of being in school is the alternative things that you would have done if you had quit school.

Opportunity cost is the highest-valued alternative forgone. It is not *all* the possible alternatives forgone. For example, your economics lecture is at 8:30 on a Monday morning. You contemplate two alternatives to the lecture: staying in bed for an hour or jogging for an hour. You can't stay in bed and jog for that same hour. The opportunity cost of attending the lecture is the forgone hour in bed *or* the forgone hour of jogging. If these are the only alternatives you consider, then you have to decide which one you would do if you did not go to the lecture. The opportunity cost of attending a lecture for a jogger is a forgone hour of exercise; the opportunity cost of attending a lecture for a late sleeper is a forgone hour in bed.

2: Margins and Incentives

We make choices in small steps, or at the margin, and choices are influenced by incentives. Everything that we do involves a decision to do a little bit more or a little bit less of an activity. You can allocate the next hour between studying and e-mailing your friends. But the choice is not "all-or-nothing." You must decide how many minutes to allocate to each activity. To make this decision, you compare the benefit of a little bit more study time with its cost—you make your choice at the **margin**.

The mother of a young child must decide how to allocate her time between being with her child and working for an income. Like your decision about study time, this decision too involves comparing the benefit of a little bit more income with the cost of a little bit less time with her child.

The benefit that arises from an increase in an activity is called **marginal benefit**. For example, suppose that a mother is working 2 days a week and is thinking about increasing her work to 3 days. Her marginal benefit is the benefit she will get from the additional day of work. It is *not* the benefit she gets from all 3 days. The reason is that she already has the benefit from 2 days work, so she doesn't count this benefit as resulting from the decision she is now making.

The cost of an increase in an activity is called **marginal cost**. For the mother of the young child, the marginal cost of increasing her work to 3 days a week is the cost of the additional day not spent with her child. It does not include the cost of the 2 days she is already working.

To make her decision, the mother compares the marginal benefit from an extra day of work with its marginal cost. If the marginal benefit exceeds the marginal cost, she works the extra day. If the marginal cost exceeds the marginal benefit, she does not work the extra day.

By evaluating marginal benefits and marginal costs and choosing only those actions that bring greater benefit than cost, we use our scarce resources in the way that makes us as well off as possible.

Our choices respond to incentives. An **incentive** is an inducement to take a particular action. The inducement can be a benefit—a carrot—or a cost—a stick. A change in opportunity cost—in marginal cost—and a change in marginal benefit changes the incentives that we face and leads to changes in our actions.

For example, suppose the daily wage rate rises and nothing else changes. With a higher daily wage rate, the marginal benefit of working increases. For the young mother, the opportunity cost of spending a day with her child has increased. She now has a bigger incentive to work an extra day a week. Whether or not she does so depends on how she evaluates the marginal benefit of the additional income and marginal cost of spending less time with her child.

Similarly, suppose the cost of day care rises and nothing else changes. The higher cost of day care increases the marginal cost of working. For the young mother, the opportunity cost of spending a day with her child has decreased. She now has a smaller incentive to work an extra day a week. Again, whether or not she changes her actions in response to a change in incentives depends on how she evaluates the marginal benefit and marginal cost.

The central idea of economics is that by looking for changes in marginal cost and marginal benefit, we can predict the way choices will change in response to changes in incentives.

3: Voluntary Exchange and Efficient Markets

Voluntary exchange makes both buyers and sellers better off, and markets are an efficient way to organize exchange.

When you shop for food, you give up some money in exchange for a basket of vegetables. But the food is worth the price you have to pay. You are better off having exchanged some of your money for the vegetables. The food store receives a payment that makes its operator happy too. Both you and the food store operator gain from your purchase.

Similarly, when you work at a summer job, you receive a wage that you've decided is sufficient to compensate you for the leisure time you must give up. But the value of your work to the firm that hires you is at least as great as the wage it pays you. So again, both you and your employer gain from a **voluntary exchange**.

You are better off when you buy your food. And you are better off when you sell your labor during the summer vacation. Whether you are a buyer or a seller, you gain from voluntary exchange with others. What is true for you is true for everyone. Everyone gains from voluntary exchange.

In our economy, exchanges take place in **markets** and for money. We sell our labor in exchange for an income in the labor market. And we buy the goods and services we've chosen to consume in a wide variety of markets—markets for vegetables, coffee, movies, videos, muffins, haircuts, and so on. At the other side of these transactions, firms buy our labor and sell us the hundreds of different consumer goods and services we buy.

Markets are **efficient** in the sense that they send resources to the place where they are valued most highly. For example, a frost kills Florida's orange crop and sends the price of orange juice through the roof. This increase in price, with all other prices remaining unchanged, increases the opportunity cost of drinking orange juice. The people who place the highest value on orange juice are the ones who keep drinking it. People who place a lower value on orange juice now have an incentive to substitute other fruit juices.

Markets are not the only way to organize the economy. An alternative is called a command system. In a **command system**, some people give orders (commands) and other people obey those orders. A command system is used in the military and in many firms. And it was used in the former Soviet Union to organize the entire economy. But the market is a superior method of organizing an entire economy.

4: Market Failure

The market does not always work efficiently and sometimes, government action is necessary to make the use of resources efficient.

Market failure is a state in which the market does not use resources efficiently. If you pay attention to the news media, you might get the impression that the market almost never does a good job. It makes credit card interest rates too high. It makes the wages of fast-food workers too low. It causes the price of coffee to go through the ceiling every time Brazil has a serious frost. It increases the world price of oil when political instability threatens the Middle East. These examples are not cases of market failure. They are examples of the market doing its job of helping us to allocate our scarce resources and ensure that they are used in the activities in which they are most highly valued.

Buyers never like it when prices rise. But sellers love it. And sellers never like it when prices fall. But buyers are happy. Rising and falling prices make news because they bring changes in fortunes. Some people win and some lose. Everyone gains from voluntary exchange, as you've just seen, but other things remaining the same, the higher the price, the more the seller gains and the less the buyer gains.

Because a high price brings a bigger gain to the seller, there is an incentive for sellers to try to control a market. When a single producer controls an entire market, the producer can restrict the quantity available and raise the price. This action brings market failure. The quantity of the good available is too small. Some people believe that Intel restricts the quantity of computer chips when it introduces a new design in order to get a high price for it. Eventually, the price falls, but at first, Intel sells its new design for a high price and makes a bigger profit.

Market failure can also arise when producers don't take into account the costs they impose on other people. For example, electric utilities create pollution, such as acid rain, that destroys plants and forests and lowers farm production. If these costs were taken into account, we would produce less electricity.

Market failure can also arise because some goods, such as national defense, must be consumed equally by everyone. None of us has an incentive voluntarily to pay our share of the cost of such a good. Instead, we try to free ride on everyone else. But if everyone tries to free ride, no one gets a ride!

To overcome market failure, governments regulate markets with antitrust laws and environmental protection laws; discourage the production and consumption of some goods and services (tobacco and alcohol for example) by taxing them; encourage the production and consumption of some goods and services (health care and schooling for example) by subsidizing them; and directly provide some goods and services (national defense, for example).

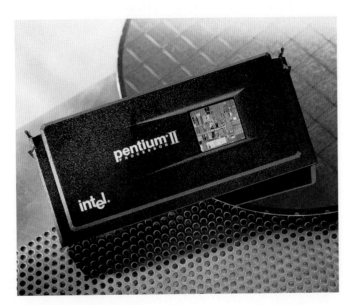

5: Expenditure, Income, and the Value of Production

For the economy as a whole, expenditure *equals* income and *equals* the value of production.

When you buy a coffee milk shake, you spend $2. But what happens to that money? The server gets some of it in wages, the owner of the building gets some of it as rent, and the owner of the milk bar gets some of it as profit. The suppliers of the milk, ice cream, and coffee also get some of your $2. But these suppliers spend part of what they receive on wages and rent. And they keep part of it as profit. Your $2 of **expenditure** creates exactly $2 of **income** for all the people who have contributed to making the milk shake, going all the way back to the farmer in Brazil who grew the coffee beans.

Your expenditure generates incomes of an equal amount. The same is true for everyone else's expenditure. So, for the economy as a whole, total expenditure on goods and services equals total income.

One way to value the things you buy is to use the prices you pay for them. So the value all of the goods and services bought equals total expenditure. Another way to value the items you buy is to use the cost of production. This cost is the total amount paid to the people who produced the items—the total income generated by your expenditure. But we've just seen that total expenditure and total income are equal, so they also equal the **value of production**.

6: Living Standards and Productivity Growth

Living standards improve when production per person increases.

By automating a car production line, one worker can produce a greater output. But if one worker can produce more cars, then more people can enjoy owning a car. The same is true for all goods and services. By increasing output per person, we enjoy a higher standard of living and buy more goods and services.

The dollar value of production can increase for any of three reasons: because prices rise, because production per person—**productivity**—increases, or because the population increases.

But only an increase in productivity brings an improvement in living standards. A rise in prices brings higher incomes, but only in dollars. The extra income is just enough to pay the higher prices, not enough to buy more goods and services. An increase in population brings an increase in *total* production, but not an increase in production per person.

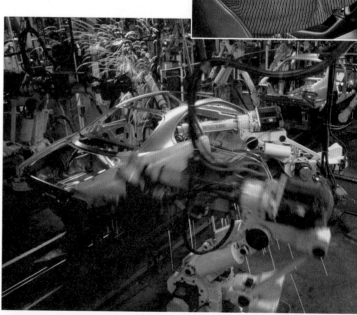

7: Inflation: A Monetary Problem

Prices rise in a process called **inflation** when the quantity of money increases faster than production. This process leads to a situation in which "too much money is chasing too few goods." As people bring more money to market, sellers see that they can raise their prices. But when these sellers go to buy their supplies, they find that the prices they face increase. With too much money around, money starts to lose value.

In some countries, inflation has been rapid. One such country is Poland. Since 1990, prices in Poland have risen more than seven-fold. In the United States, we have moderate inflation of less than 2 percent a year.

Some people say that by increasing the quantity of money, we can create jobs. The idea is that if more money is put into the economy, when it is spent, businesses sell more and so hire more labor to produce more goods and services.

Initially, an increase in money might increase production and create jobs. But eventually, it only increases prices and leaves production and jobs unchanged.

8: Unemployment: Productive and Wasteful

Unemployment can result from market failure and be wasteful. But some unemployment is productive.

Unemployment is ever present. Sometimes its rate is low and sometimes it is high. Also, unemployment fluctuates over the business cycle.

Some unemployment is normal and efficient. We choose to take our time finding a suitable job rather than rushing to accept the first one that comes along. Similarly, businesses take their time in filling vacancies. The unemployment that results from these careful searches for jobs and workers improves productivity because it helps to assign people to their most productive jobs.

Some unemployment results from fluctuations in expenditure and can be wasteful.

R E V I E W   Q U I Z

- Give some examples of *tradeoffs* that you have made and the *opportunity costs* you've incurred today.
- Give some examples of *marginal* cost and *marginal* benefit.
- How do markets enable both buyers and sellers to gain from exchange and why do markets sometimes fail?
- Why for the economy as a whole, does expenditure equal income and the value of production?
- What makes living standards rise?
- What makes prices rise?
- Is unemployment always a problem?

What Economists Do

ECONOMISTS USE THE EIGHT BIG IDEAS THAT YOU have just studied to search for answers to the five big questions that you reviewed at the start of this chapter. But how do they go about their work? What special problems and pitfalls do they encounter? And do they always agree on the answers?

Microeconomics and Macroeconomics

Economists approach their work from either a micro or a macro perspective. These two perspectives define the two major branches of the subject:

- Microeconomics
- Macroeconomics

Microeconomics is the study of the decisions of individual people and businesses and the interaction of those decisions in markets.

Macroeconomics is the study of the national economy and the global economy. It seeks to explain *average* prices and *total* employment, income, and production.

You can take either a micro or a macro view of the spectacular display of national flags in a Korean sports stadium. The micro view is of a single participant and the actions he or she is taking. The macro view is the patterns formed by the joint actions of all the individuals participating in the entire display.

Microeconomics seeks to explain the prices and quantities of individual goods and services. It also

studies the effects of government regulation and taxes on the prices and quantities of individual goods and services. For example, microeconomics studies the forces that determine the prices of cars and the quantities of cars produced and sold. It also studies the effects of regulations and taxes on the prices and quantities of cars.

Macroeconomics studies the effects of taxes, government spending, and the government budget surplus or deficit on total jobs and incomes. It also studies the effects of money and interest rates.

Economic Science

Economics is a social science (along with political science, psychology, and sociology). A major task of economists is to discover how the economic world works. In pursuit of this goal, economists (like all scientists) distinguish between two types of statements:

- What *is*
- What *ought* to be

Statements about what *is* are called *positive* statements. They say what is currently believed about the way the world operates. A positive statement might be right or wrong. And we can test a positive statement by checking it against the facts. When a chemist does an experiment in her laboratory, she is attempting to check a positive statement against the facts.

Statements about what *ought* to be are called *normative* statements. These statements depend on

values and cannot be tested. When Congress debates a motion, it is ultimately trying to decide what ought to be. It is making a normative statement.

To see the distinction between positive and normative statements, consider the controversy over global warming. Some scientists believe that centuries of the burning of coal and oil are increasing the carbon dioxide content of the earth's atmosphere and leading to higher temperatures that eventually will have devastating consequences for life on this planet. "Our planet is warming because of an increased carbon dioxide buildup in the atmosphere" is a positive statement. It can (in principle and with sufficient data) be

tested. "We ought to cut back on our use of carbon-based fuels such as coal and oil" is a normative statement. You may agree with or disagree with this statement, but you can't test it. It is based on values. Health-care reform provides an economic example of the distinction. "Universal health care will cut the amount of work time lost to illness" is a positive statement. "Every American should have equal access to health care" is a normative statement.

The task of economic science is to discover and catalog positive statements that are consistent with what we observe in the world and that enable us to understand how the economic world works. This task is a large one that can be broken into three steps:

- Observation and measurement
- Model building
- Testing models

Observation and Measurement First, economists keep track of the amounts and locations of natural and human resources, of wages and work hours, of the prices and quantities of the different goods and services produced, of taxes and government spending, and of the quantities of goods and services bought from and sold to other countries. This list gives a flavor of the array of things that economists can observe and measure.

Model Building The second step toward understanding how the economic world works is to build a model. An **economic model** is a description of some aspect of the economic world that includes only those features of the world that are needed for the purpose at hand. A model is simpler than the reality it describes. What a model includes and what it leaves out result from *assumptions* about what is essential and what are inessential details.

You can see how ignoring details is useful—even essential—to our understanding by thinking about a model that you see every day, the TV weather map. The weather map is a model that helps to predict the temperature, wind speed and direction, and precipitation over a future period. The weather map shows lines called isobars—lines of equal barometric pressure. It doesn't show the interstate highways. The reason is that our theory of the weather tells us that the pattern of air pressure, not the location of the highways, determines the weather.

An economic model is similar to a weather map. It tells us how a number of variables are determined by a number of other variables. For example, an economic model of the 1994 Los Angeles earthquake might tell us the effects of the earthquake and the government's relief efforts on the number of houses and apartments, rents and prices, jobs, and commuting times.

Testing The third step is testing the model. A model's predictions may correspond to or be in conflict with the facts. By comparing the model's predictions with the facts, we are able to test a model and develop an economic theory. An **economic theory** is a generalization that summarizes what we think we understand about the economic choices that people make and the performance of industries and entire economies. It is a bridge between an economic model and the real economy.

A theory is created by a process of building and testing models. For example, meteorologists have a theory that if the isobars form a particular pattern at a particular time of the year (a model), then it will snow (reality). They have developed this theory by repeated observation and by carefully recording the weather that follows specific pressure patterns.

Economics is a young science. It was born in 1776 with the publication of Adam Smith's *The Wealth of Nations* (see pp. 56–57). Over the past 225 years, economics has dis-

covered many useful theories. But in many areas, economists are still looking for answers. The gradual accumulation of economic knowledge gives most economists some faith that their methods will, eventually, provide usable answers to the big economic questions.

But progress in economics comes slowly. Let's look at some of the obstacles to progress in economics.

Obstacles and Pitfalls in Economics

We cannot easily do economic experiments. And most economic behavior has many simultaneous causes. For these two reasons, it is difficult in economics to unscramble cause and effect.

Unscrambling Cause and Effect By changing one factor at a time and holding all the other relevant factors constant, we isolate the factor of interest and are able to investigate its effects in the clearest possible way. This logical device, that all scientists use to identify cause and effect, is called ***ceteris paribus***. *Ceteris paribus* is a Latin term that means "other things being equal" or "if all other relevant things remain the same." Ensuring that other things are equal is crucial in many activities, including athletic events, and all successful attempts to make scientific progress use this device.

Economic models (like the models in all other sciences) enable the influence of one factor at a time to be isolated in the imaginary world of the model. When we use a model, we are able to imagine what would happen if only one factor changed. But *ceteris paribus* can be a problem in economics when we try to test a model.

Laboratory scientists, such as chemists and physicists, perform experiments by actually holding all the relevant factors constant except for the one under investigation. In the non-experimental sciences such as economics (and astronomy), we usually observe the outcomes of the *simultaneous* operation of many factors. Consequently, it is hard to sort out the effects of each individual factor and to compare the effects with what a model predicts. To cope with this problem, economists take three complementary approaches.

First, they look for pairs of events in which other things were equal (or similar). An example might be to study the effects of unemployment insurance on the unemployment rate by comparing the United States with Canada on the presumption that the people in the two economies are sufficiently similar. Second, economists use statistical tools—called *econometrics*. And third, when they can, they perform experiments. This relatively new approach puts real subjects (usually students) in a decision-making situation and varies their incentives in some way to discover how they respond to one factor at a time.

Economists try to avoid *fallacies*—errors of reasoning that lead to a wrong conclusion. But two fallacies are common, and you need to be on your guard to avoid them. They are the

- Fallacy of composition
- *Post hoc* fallacy

Fallacy of Composition The fallacy of composition is the (false) statement that what is true of the parts is true of the whole or that what is true of the whole is true of the parts. Think of the true statement, "Speed kills," and its implication, going more slowly saves lives. If an entire freeway moves at a lower speed, everyone on the highway has a safer ride.

But suppose that one driver only slows down and all the other drivers try to maintain their original speed. In this situation, there will probably be more accidents because more cars will change lanes to overtake the slower vehicle. So, in this example, what is true for the whole is not true for a part.

The fallacy of composition arises mainly in macroeconomics, and it stems from the fact that the parts interact with each other to produce an outcome for the whole that might differ from the intent of the parts. For example, a firm lays off some workers to cut costs and improve its profits. If all firms take similar actions, incomes fall and so does spending. The firm sells less, and its profits don't improve.

Post Hoc Fallacy Another Latin phrase—*post hoc ergo propter hoc*—means "after this, therefore because of this." The *post hoc* fallacy is the error of reasoning that a first event *causes* a second event because the first occurred before the second. Suppose you are a visitor from a far off world. You observe lots of people shopping in early December and then you see them opening gifts and partying on Christmas day. Does the shopping cause Christmas, you wonder. After a deeper study, you discover that Christmas causes the shopping. A later event causes an earlier event.

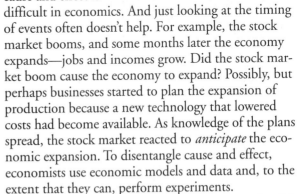

Unraveling cause and effect is difficult in economics. And just looking at the timing of events often doesn't help. For example, the stock market booms, and some months later the economy expands—jobs and incomes grow. Did the stock market boom cause the economy to expand? Possibly, but perhaps businesses started to plan the expansion of production because a new technology that lowered costs had become available. As knowledge of the plans spread, the stock market reacted to *anticipate* the economic expansion. To disentangle cause and effect, economists use economic models and data and, to the extent that they can, perform experiments.

Economics is a challenging science. Does the difficulty of getting answers in economics mean that anything goes and that economists disagree on most questions? Perhaps you've heard the joke: "If you laid all the economists in the world end to end, they still wouldn't reach agreement." Does the joke make a valid point?

Agreement and Disagreement

Economists agree on a remarkably wide range of questions. And surprisingly, the agreed view of economists often disagrees with the popular and sometimes politically correct view. When Fed Chairman Alan Greenspan testifies before the Senate Banking Committee, his words are rarely controversial among economists, even when they generate endless debate in the press and Congress.

Here are twelve propositions[1] with which at least 7 out of every 10 economists broadly agree:

- Tariffs and import restrictions make most people worse off.
- A large federal budget deficit has an adverse effect on the economy.
- Cash payments to welfare recipients make them better off than do transfers-in-kind of equal cash value.
- A minimum wage increases unemployment among young workers and low skilled workers.
- A tax cut can help to lower unemployment when the unemployment rate is high.
- The distribution of income in the United States should be more equal.
- Inflation is primarily caused by a rapid rate of money creation.
- The government should restructure welfare along the lines of a "negative income tax."
- Rent ceilings cut the availability of housing.
- Pollution taxes are more effective than pollution limits.
- The redistribution of income is a legitimate role for the U.S. government.
- The federal budget should be balanced on the average over the business cycle, but not every year.

Which are positive and which are normative? Notice that economists are willing to offer their opinions on normative issues as well as their professional views on positive questions. Be on the lookout for normative propositions dressed up as positive propositions.

---

[1] These are propositions generally supported or supported with provisos by more than 7 out of 10 economists according to a survey by Richard M. Alston, J.R. Kearl, and Michael B. Vaughan, "Is There a Consensus Among Economists," *American Economic Review*, 82 (May 1992), pp. 203–209. I have simplified the language in some cases, and you should check the original for the exact propositions and percentages agreeing.

REVIEW QUIZ

- What is the distinction between microeconomics and macroeconomics? Provide an example (not in the chapter) of a micro issue and a macro issue.
- What is the distinction between a positive statement and a normative statement? Provide an example (different from those in the chapter) of each type of statement.
- What is a model? Can you think of a model that you might use (probably without thinking of it as a model) in your everyday life?
- What is a theory? Why is the statement, "It might work in theory but it doesn't work in practice" a silly statement? [Hint: Think about what a theory is and how it is used.]
- What is the *ceteris paribus* assumption and how is it used?
- Try to think of some everyday examples of fallacies.

You are now ready to start *doing* economics. As you get into the subject, you will see that we rely heavily on graphs. You must be comfortable with this method of reasoning. If you need some help with it, take your time in working carefully through Chapter 2. If you are already comfortable with graphs, then you are ready to jump right into Chapter 3 and begin to study the fundamental economic problem, scarcity.

SUMMARY

KEY POINTS

A Definition of Economics (p. 2)

■ Economics is the *science of choice*—the science that explains the choices that we make to cope with scarcity.

Big Economic Questions (pp. 2–5)

■ Economists try to answer five big questions about goods and services:

1. What?
2. How?
3. When?
4. Where?
5. Who?

What are the goods and services produced, *how*, *when*, and *where* are they produced, and *who* consumes them?

■ These questions interact to determine the standards of living and the distribution of well-being in the United States and around the world.

Big Ideas of Economics (pp. 6–11)

■ A choice is a tradeoff and the highest-valued alternative forgone is the opportunity cost of what is chosen.

■ Choices are made at the margin and are influenced by incentives.

■ Markets enable both buyers and sellers to gain from voluntary exchange.

■ Sometimes government actions are needed to overcome market failure.

■ For the economy as a whole, expenditure equals income and equals the value of production.

■ Living standards rise when production per person increases.

■ Prices rise when the quantity of money increases faster than production.

■ Unemployment can result from market failure but can also be productive.

What Economists Do (pp. 12–16)

■ Microeconomics is the study of individual decisions, and macroeconomics is the study of the economy as a whole.

■ Positive statements are about what *is* and normative statements are about what *ought* to be.

■ To explain the economic world, economists build and test economic models.

■ Economists use the *ceteris paribus* assumption to try to disentangle cause and effect, and they are careful to avoid the fallacy of composition and the *post hoc* fallacy.

■ Economists agree on a wide range of questions about how the economy works.

KEY TERMS

Ceteris paribus, 14
Command system, 8
Economics, 2
Economic model, 13
Economic theory, 13
Efficient, 8
Expenditure, 10
Goods and services, 2
Incentive, 7
Income, 10
Inflation, 11
Macroeconomics, 12
Margin, 7
Marginal benefit, 7
Marginal cost, 7
Market, 8
Market failure, 9
Microeconomics, 12
Opportunity cost, 6
Productivity, 10
Scarcity, 2
Tradeoff, 6
Unemployment, 11
Value of production, 10
Voluntary exchange, 8

PROBLEMS

*1. You plan to go to school this summer. If you do, you won't be able to take your usual job that pays $6,000 for the summer and you won't be able to live at home for free. The cost of your tuition will be $2,000, textbooks $200, and living expenses $1,400. What is the opportunity cost of going to summer school?

2. You plan a major adventure trip for the summer. You won't be able to take your usual summer job that pays $6,000 and you won't be able to live at home for free. The cost of your travel on the trip will be $3,000, film and video tape will cost you $200, and your food will cost $1,400. What is the opportunity cost of taking this trip?

*3. The local mall has free parking, but the mall is always very busy and it usually takes 30 minutes to find a parking space. Today when you found a vacant spot, Harry also wanted it. Is parking really free at this mall? If not, what did it cost you to park today? When you parked your car today, did you impose any costs on Harry? Explain your answers.

4. The university has built a new parking garage. There is always an available parking spot but it costs $1 a day. Before the new garage was built, it usually took 15 minutes of cruising to find a parking space. Compare the opportunity cost of parking in the new garage with that in the old parking lot. Which is less costly and by how much?

CRITICAL THINKING

1. Use the link on the Parkin Web site to visit *Resources For Economists on the Internet.* Scroll down the page and click on General Interest. Visit the "general interest" sites and become familiar with the types of information they contain.

2. Use the link on the Parkin Web site to visit *The Dismal Scientist* ®™—the best free lunch on the Web! In the "Economic Profile" box, enter your zip code and click "Get the profile."
    a.   What is the number of people employed (nonfarm employment) in your area?

b.   Has employment increased or decreased?
c.   What is income per person (per capita income) in your area?

3. This man is homeless, and you can see all his possessions in the photograph.
    Use the five big questions and the eight big ideas of economics to organize a short essay about the economic life of the man in the photograph. Does he face scarcity? Does he make choices? Can you interpret his choices as being in his own best interest? Can either his own choices or the choices of others make this man better off? If so, how?

4. Use the link on the Parkin Web site to visit *CNNfn.*
    a. What is the top economic news story today?
    b. With which of the five big questions does it deal? (Hint: It must deal with at least one of them and might deal with more than one.)
    c. Which of the eight big ideas seem to be relevant to understanding this news item?
    d. Write a brief summary of the news item in a few bulleted points, using as much as possible of the economic vocabulary that you have learned in this chapter and that is in the key terms list on p. 17.

Chapter 2

Making and Using Graphs

British Prime Minister Benjamin Disraeli is reputed to have said that "There are three kinds of lies: lies, damned lies, and statistics." One of the most powerful ways of conveying statistical information is in the form of a graph. And like statistics, graphs can lie. But the right graph does not lie. It reveals a relationship that would otherwise be obscure. ◆ Graphs are a modern invention. They first appeared in the late eighteenth century, long after the discovery of logarithms and calculus. But today, in the age of the personal computer and video display, graphs have become as important as words and numbers. How do economists use graphs? What types of graphs do they use? What do graphs reveal and what can they hide? ◆ The big questions that economics tries to answer—questions that you studied in Chapter 1—are difficult ones. They involve

Three Kinds of Lies

relationships among a large number of variables. Almost nothing in economics has a single cause. Instead, a large number of variables interact with each other. It is often said that in economics, everything depends on everything else. Changes in the quantity of ice cream consumed are caused by changes in the price of ice cream, the temperature, and many other factors. How can we make and interpret graphs of relationships among several variables?

◆ In this chapter, you are going to look at the kinds of graphs that economists use. You are going to learn how to make them and read them. You are also going to learn how to determine the magnitude of the influence of one variable on another by calculating the slope of a line and of a curve. ◆ There are no graphs or techniques used in this book that are more complicated than those described and explained in this chapter. If you are already familiar with graphs, you may want to skip (or skim) this chapter. Whether you study this chapter thoroughly or give it a quick pass, you can use it as a handy reference, returning to it whenever you need extra help in understanding the graphs that you encounter in your study of economics.

After studying this chapter, you will be able to:

■ Make and interpret a time-series graph, a scatter diagram, and a cross-section graph

■ Distinguish between linear and nonlinear relationships and between relationships that have a maximum and a minimum

■ Define and calculate the slope of a line

■ Graph relationships among more than two variables

Graphing Data

GRAPHS REPRESENT A QUANTITY AS A DISTANCE on a line. Figure 2.1 gives two examples. A distance on the horizontal line represents temperature, measured in degrees Fahrenheit. A movement from left to right shows an increase in temperature. A movement from right to left shows a decrease in temperature. The point marked 0 represents zero degrees Fahrenheit. To the right of 0, the temperatures are positive. To the left of 0, the temperatures are negative (as indicated by the minus sign in front of the numbers).

A distance on the vertical line represents altitude or height, measured in thousands of feet above sea level. The point marked 0 represents sea level. Points above 0 represent feet above sea level. Points below 0 (indicated by a minus sign) represent feet below sea level.

There are no rigid rules about the scale for a graph. The scale is determined by the range of the variables being graphed.

The main point of a graph is to enable us to visualize the relationship between two variables. And to accomplish this, we set two scales perpendicular to each other, like those in Fig. 2.1.

The two scale lines are called *axes*. The vertical line is called the *y*-axis, and the horizontal line is called the *x*-axis. The letters *x* and *y* appear on the axes of Fig. 2.1. Each axis has a zero point, which is shared by the two axes. This zero point, common to both axes, is called the *origin*.

To show something in a two-variable graph, we need two pieces of information. We need the value of the variable *x* and the value of the variable *y*. For example, off the coast of Alaska on a winter's day, the temperature is 32 degrees, which we will call the value of *x*. A fishing boat is located at 0 feet above sea level, which we'll call the value of *y*. These two bits of information appear as point *a* in Fig. 2.1. A climber at the top of Mount McKinley on a very cold day is 20,320 feet above sea level and the temperature is 0 degrees. These two pieces of information appear as point *b*. The position of the climber on a warmer day might be at the point marked *c*. This point represents the peak of Mt. McKinley when the temperature is 32 degrees.

Two lines, called coordinates, can be drawn from point *c* in the graph. One of these lines runs from *c* to the horizontal axis. This line is called the *y*-coordinate. Its length is the same as the value marked off on

FIGURE **2.1**

Making a Graph

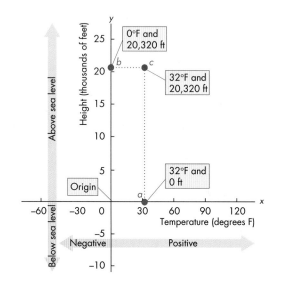

All graphs have axes that measure quantities as distances. Here, the horizontal axis (*x*-axis) measures temperature. A rightward movement shows an increase in temperature. The vertical axis (*y*-axis) measures height. An upward movement shows an increase in height. Point *a* represents a fishing boat at sea level (0 on the *y*-axis) on a day when the temperature is 32° (32° on the *x*-axis). Point *b* represents a climber at the top of Mt. McKinley (20,320 feet above sea level on the *y*-axis) on a day when the temperature on Mt. McKinley is 0° (0° on the *x*-axis). Point *c* represents a climber at the top of Mt. McKinley, 20,320 feet above sea level (on the *y*-axis) on a day when the temperature on Mt. McKinley is 32° (on the *x*-axis).

the *y*-axis. The other of these lines runs from *c* to the vertical axis. This line is called the *x*-coordinate. Its length is the same as the value marked off on the *x*-axis. To describe a point in a graph, we simply use the values of its *x*- and *y*-coordinates.

Graphs like that in Fig. 2.1 can be used to show any type of quantitative data about two variables. Economists use graphs similar to the one in Fig. 2.1 to reveal and describe the relationships among economic variables. To do so, they use three main types of graphs, which we'll now study. They are:

■ Scatter diagrams
■ Time-series graphs
■ Cross-section graphs

Scatter Diagrams

A **scatter diagram** plots the value of one economic variable against the value of another variable. Such a graph is used to reveal whether a relationship exists between two economic variables. It is also used to describe a relationship.

Consumption and Income   Figure 2.2(a) shows a scatter diagram of the relationship between consumption and income. The *x*-axis measures average income, and the *y*-axis measures average consumption. Each point shows consumption per person and income per person (on the average) in the United States in a given year from 1990 to 1997. The points for the eight years are "scattered" within the graph. Each point is labeled with a two-digit number that shows us its year. For example, the point marked 96 shows us that in 1996, income per person was $19,200 and consumption per person was $17,750.

The dots in this graph form a pattern, which reveals that as income increases, consumption also increases.

Phone Calls and Price   Figure 2.2(b) shows a scatter diagram of the relationship between the number of international phone calls made from the United States and the average price per minute.

The dots in this graph reveal that as the price per minute falls, the number of calls increases.

Unemployment and Inflation   Figure 2.2(c) shows a scatter diagram of inflation and unemployment in the United States. The dots in this graph form a pattern that shows us there is no clear relationship between these two variables. By its lack of a distinct pattern, the graph shows us that there is no simple relationship between inflation and unemployment in the United States.

Correlation and Causation   A scatter diagram that shows a clear relationship between two variables, such as Fig. 2.2(a) or Fig. 2.2(b), tells us that the two variables have a high correlation. When a high correlation is present, we can predict the value of one variable from the value of the other variable. But correlation does not imply causation. Sometimes a high correlation is just a coincidence, but sometimes it does

---

FIGURE 2.2

Scatter Diagrams

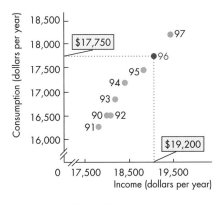

(a) Consumption and income

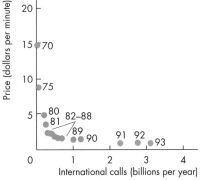

(b) International phone calls and prices

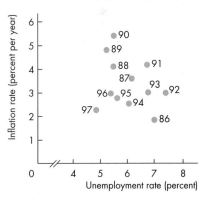

(c) Unemployment and inflation

A scatter diagram reveals the relationship between two variables. Part (a) shows the relationship between consumption and income between 1990 and 1997. Each point shows the values of the two variables in a specific year. For example, in 1996, average income was $19,200 and average consumption was $17,750. The pattern formed by the points shows that as income increases, so does consumption. Part (b) shows the relationship between the price of an international phone call and the number of phone calls made per year between 1970 and 1993. This graph shows that as the price of a phone call has fallen, the number of calls made has increased. Part (c) shows the inflation rate and unemployment rate in the United States between 1986 and 1997. This graph shows that inflation and unemployment are not closely related.

arise from a causal relationship. It is likely, for example, that increasing income causes increasing consumption (Fig. 2.2a) and that falling phone call prices cause more calls to be made (Fig. 2.2b).

Breaks in the Axes   Two of the graphs you've just looked at, Fig. 2.2(a) and Fig. 2.2(c), have breaks in their axes, as shown by the small gaps. The breaks indicate that there are jumps from the origin, 0, to the first values recorded.

In Fig. 2.2(a), the breaks are used because the lowest value of consumption exceeds $15,000 and the lowest value of income exceeds $16,500. With no breaks in the axes of this graph, there would be a lot of empty space, all the points would be crowded into the top right corner, and we would not be able to see whether a relationship exists between these two variables. By breaking the axes, we are able to bring the relationship into view.

Putting a break in the axes is like using a zoom lens to bring the relationship into the center of the graph and magnify it so that it fills the graph.

Misleading Graphs   Breaks can be used to highlight a relationship. But they can also be used to mislead and create a wrong impression—to make a graph that lies. The most common way of making a graph lie is to use axis breaks and to also either stretch or compress a scale. The most effective way to see the power of this kind of lie is to make some graphs that use this technique. For example, redraw Fig. 2.2(a) but make the *y*-axis that measures consumption run from zero to $45,000 and keep the *x*-axis the same as the one shown. The graph will now create the impression that despite huge income growth, consumption has barely changed.

To avoid being misled, it is a good idea to get into the habit of always looking closely at the values and the labels on the axes of a graph before you start to interpret it.

Time-Series Graphs

A **time-series graph** measures time (for example, months or years) on the *x*-axis and the variable or variables in which we are interested on the *y*-axis. Figure 2.3 shows an example of a time-series graph. In this graph, time (on the *x*-axis) is measured in years, which run from 1968 to 1998. The variable that we are interested in is the price of coffee, and it is measured on the *y*-axis.

A time-series graph conveys an enormous amount of information quickly and easily, as this example illustrates. It shows:

1. The *level* of the price of coffee—when it is *high* and *low*. When the line is a long way from the *x*-axis, the price is high. When the line is close to the *x*-axis, the price is low.

2. How the price *changes*—whether it *rises* or *falls*. When the line slopes upward, as in 1976, the price is rising. When the line slopes downward, as in 1978, the price is falling.

3. The *speed* with which the price changes—whether it rises or falls *quickly* or *slowly*. If the line is very steep, then the price rises or falls quickly. If the line is not steep, the price rises or falls slowly. For example, the price rose very quickly in 1976 and 1977. The price went up again in 1993 but slowly. Similarly, when the price was falling in 1978, it fell quickly, but during the early 1980s, it fell more slowly.

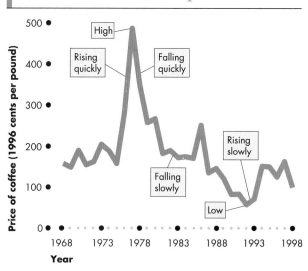

FIGURE 2.3

A Time-Series Graph

A time-series graph plots the level of a variable on the *y*-axis against time (day, week, month, or year) on the *x*-axis. This graph shows the price of coffee (in 1996 cents per pound) each year from 1968 to 1998. It shows us when the price of coffee was *high* and when it was *low*, when the price *increased* and when it *decreased*, and when it changed *quickly* and when it changed *slowly*.

A time-series graph also reveals whether there is a trend. A **trend** is a general tendency for a variable to rise or fall. You can see that the price of coffee had a general tendency to fall from the mid-1970s to the early 1990s. That is, although there were ups and downs in the price, there was a general tendency for it to fall.

A time-series graph also lets us compare different periods quickly. Figure 2.3 shows that the 1980s were different from the 1970s. The price of coffee fluctuated more violently in the 1970s than it did in the 1980s. This graph conveys a wealth of information, and it does so in much less space than we have used to describe only some of its features.

Comparing Two Time Series Sometimes we want to use a time-series graph to compare two different variables. For example, suppose you want to know whether the balance of the government's budget fluctuates with the unemployment rate. You can examine the government's budget balance and the unemployment rate by drawing a graph of each of them on the same time scale. But we can measure the government's budget balance either as a surplus or as a deficit. Figure 2.4(a) plots the budget surplus. The scale of the unemployment rate is on the left side of the figure, and the scale of the government's budget surplus is on the right. The orange line shows unemployment, and the blue line shows the budget surplus. This figure shows that the unemployment rate and the government's budget surplus move in opposite directions. For example, when the unemployment rate decreases, the budget surplus increases.

Figure 2.4(b) uses a scale for the government's budget balance measured as a deficit. That is, we flip the right-side scale over. This figure shows that the unemployment rate and the government's budget deficit move in the same direction. The budget deficit and the unemployment rate increase together and decrease together.

Scatter Diagram for Comparing Two Time Series We can compare two time series in a graph like Fig. 2.4 or in a scatter diagram like Fig. 2.2. Which is better? There is no right answer to this question. If the purpose of the graph is to show *both* the way two variables have changed over time and how they are related to each other, then the time-series graph does the better job. But if the purpose of the graph is to check the strength of the relationship between two variables, then a scatter diagram does a better job. A relationship that looks strong in a time-series graph often looks weak in a scatter diagram.

FIGURE 2.4

Time-Series Relationships

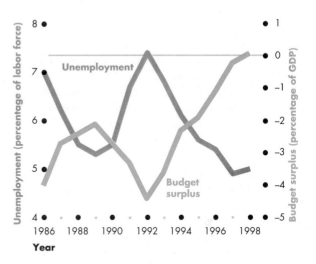

(a) Unemployment and budget surplus

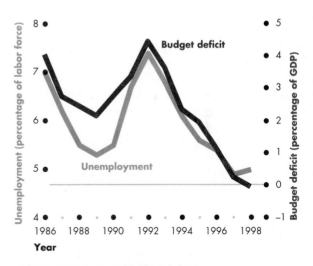

(b) Unemployment and budget deficit

These two graphs show the unemployment rate and the balance of the government's budget. The unemployment line is identical in the two parts. Part (a) shows the budget surplus—*taxes minus spending*—on the right scale. It is hard to see a relationship between the budget surplus and unemployment. Part (b) shows the budget as a deficit—*spending minus taxes*. It inverts the scale of part (a). With the scale for the budget balance inverted, the graph reveals a tendency for unemployment and the budget deficit to move together.

Cross-Section Graphs

A **cross-section graph** shows the values of an economic variable for different groups in a population at a point in time. Figure 2.5 is an example of a cross-section graph. It shows average income per person in the ten largest metropolitan areas in the United States in 1995. This graph uses bars rather than dots and lines, and the length of each bar indicates average income per person. Figure 2.5 enables you to compare the average incomes per person in these ten cities. And you can do so much more quickly and clearly than by looking at a list of numbers.

The cross-section graph in Fig. 2.5 is also an example of a *bar chart*. We often use bars rather than lines in cross-section graphs, but there are no fixed rules about whether to use lines, dots, or bars. It is a matter of taste.

You've now seen how we can use graphs in economics to show economic data and to reveal relationships between variables. Next, we're going to learn how to use graphs in a more abstract way. We'll learn how economists use graphs to construct and display economic models.

FIGURE **2.5**

A Cross-Section Graph

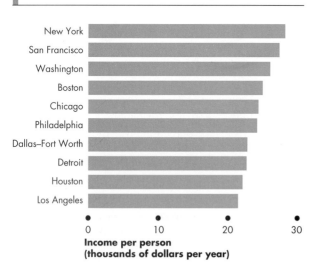

Income per person
(thousands of dollars per year)

A cross-section graph shows the level of a variable across the members of a population. This graph shows the average income per person in each of the ten largest metropolitan areas in the United States in 1995.

Graphs Used in Economic Models

THE GRAPHS USED IN ECONOMICS ARE NOT always designed to show real-world data. Often they are used to show general relationships among the variables in an economic model.

An **economic model** is a stripped down, simplified description of an economy or of a component of an economy such as a business or a household. It consists of statements about economic behavior that can be expressed as equations or as curves in a graph. Economists use models to explore the effects of different policies or other influences on the economy in ways that are similar to the use of model airplanes in wind tunnels and models of the climate.

You will encounter many different kinds of graphs in economic models, but there are some repeating patterns. Once you've learned to recognize these patterns, you will instantly understand the meaning of a graph. Here, we'll look at the different types of curves that are used in economic models, and we'll see some everyday examples of each type of curve. The patterns to look for in graphs are the four cases in which:

- Variables move in the same direction
- Variables move in opposite directions
- Variables have a maximum or a minimum
- Variables are unrelated

Let's look at these four cases.

Variables That Move in the Same Direction

Figure 2.6 shows graphs of the relationships between two variables that move up and down together. A relationship between two variables that move in the same direction is called a **positive relationship** or a **direct relationship**. Such a relationship is shown by a line that slopes upward.

Figure 2.6 shows three types of relationships, one that has a straight line and two that have curved lines. But all the lines in these three graphs are called curves. Any line on a graph—no matter whether it is straight or curved—is called a *curve*.

A relationship shown by a straight line is called a **linear relationship.** Figure 2.6(a) shows a linear

FIGURE 2.6
Positive (Direct) Relationships

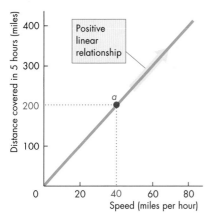

(a) Positive linear relationship

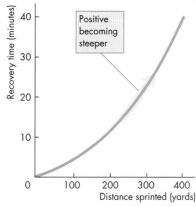

(b) Positive becoming steeper

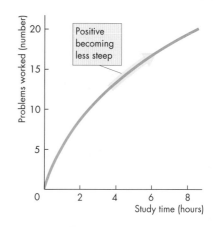

(c) Positive becoming less steep

Each part of this figure shows a positive (direct) relationship between two variables. That is, as the value of the variable measured on the x-axis increases, so does the value of the variable measured on the y-axis. Part (a) shows a linear relationship—as the two variables increase together, we move along a straight line. Part (b) shows a positive relationship such that as the two variables increase together, we move along a curve that becomes steeper. Part (c) shows a positive relationship such that as the two variables increase together, we move along a curve that becomes flatter.

relationship between the number of miles traveled in 5 hours and speed. For example, point *a* shows us that we will travel 200 miles in 5 hours if our speed is 40 miles an hour. If we double our speed to 80 miles an hour, we will travel 400 miles in 5 hours.

Part (b) shows the relationship between distance sprinted and recovery time (the time it takes the heart rate to return to its normal resting rate). This relationship is an upward-sloping one shown by a curved line that starts out fairly flat but then becomes steeper as we move along the curve away from the origin. The reason this curve slopes upward and becomes steeper is because the additional recovery time needed from sprinting an additional 100 yards increases. It takes less than 5 minutes to recover from 100 yards but more than 10 minutes to recover from the third 100 yards.

Part (c) shows the relationship between the number of problems worked by a student and the amount of study time. This relationship is shown by an upward-sloping curved line that starts out fairly steep and becomes flatter as we move away from the origin. Study time becomes less productive as you study for more hours and become more tired.

Variables That Move in Opposite Directions

Figure 2.7 shows relationships between things that move in opposite directions. A relationship between variables that move in opposite directions is called a **negative relationship** or an **inverse relationship**.

Part (a) shows the relationship between the number of hours available for playing squash and the number of hours for playing tennis. One extra hour spent playing tennis means one hour less playing squash and vice versa. This relationship is negative and linear.

Part (b) shows the relationship between the cost per mile traveled and the length of a journey. The longer the journey, the lower is the cost per mile. But as the journey length increases, the cost per mile decreases, and the fall in the cost is smaller, the longer the journey. This feature of the relationship is shown by the fact that the curve slopes downward, starting out steep at a short journey length and then becoming flatter as the journey length increases. This relationship arises because some of the costs are fixed,

FIGURE **2.7**

Negative (Inverse) Relationships

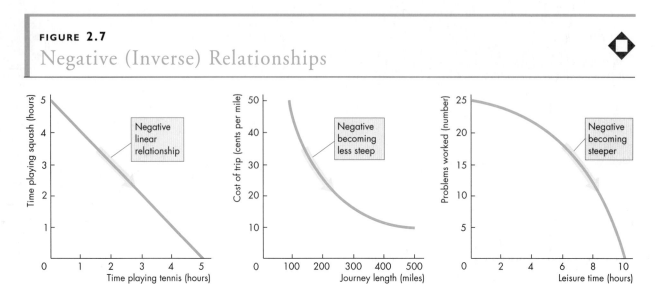

(a) Negative linear relationship   **(b) Negative becoming less steep**   **(c) Negative becoming steeper**

Each part of this figure shows a negative (inverse) relationship between two variables. Part (a) shows a linear relationship—as one variable increases and the other variable decreases, we move along a straight line. Part (b) shows a negative relationship such that as the journey length increases, the curve becomes less steep. Part (c) shows a negative relationship such that as leisure time increases, the curve becomes steeper.

such as auto insurance, and the fixed costs are spread over a longer journey.

Part (c) shows the relationship between the amount of leisure time and the number of problems worked by a student. Increasing leisure time produces an increasingly large reduction in the number of problems worked. This relationship is a negative one that starts out with a gentle slope at a small number of leisure hours and becomes steeper as the number of leisure hours increases. This relationship is a different view of the idea shown in Fig. 2.6(c).

Variables That Have a Maximum or a Minimum

Many relationships in economic models have a maximum or a minimum. For example, firms try to make the maximum possible profit and to produce at the lowest possible cost. Figure 2.8 shows relationships that have a maximum or a minimum.

Part (a) shows the relationship between rainfall and wheat yield. When there is no rainfall, wheat will not grow, so the yield is zero. As the rainfall increases up to 10 days a month, the wheat yield also increases. With 10 rainy days each month, the wheat yield reaches its maximum at 40 bushels an acre (point *a*). Rain in excess of 10 days a month starts to lower the yield of wheat. If every day is rainy, the wheat suffers from a lack of sunshine and the yield falls back to zero. This relationship is one that starts out sloping upward, reaches a maximum, and then slopes downward.

Part (b) shows the reverse case—a relationship that begins sloping downward, falls to a minimum, and then slopes upward. An example of such a relationship is the gasoline cost per mile as the speed of travel increases. At low speeds, the car is creeping along in a traffic snarl-up. The number of miles per gallon is low, so the gasoline cost per mile is high. At very high speeds, the car is traveling faster than its most efficient speed, and again the number of miles per gallon is low and the gasoline cost per mile is high. At a speed of 55 miles an hour, the gasoline cost per mile traveled is at its minimum (point *b*). This relationship is one that starts out sloping downward, reaches a minimum, and then slopes upward.

FIGURE **2.8**

Maximum and Minimum Points

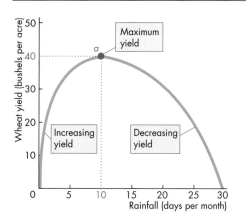

(a) **Relationship with a maximum**

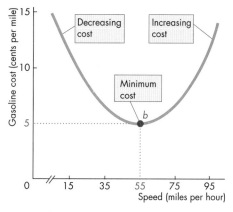

(b) **Relationship with a minimum**

Part (a) shows a relationship that has a maximum point, *a*. The curve slopes upward as it rises to its maximum point, is flat at its maximum, and then slopes downward. Part (b) shows a relationship with a minimum point, *b*. The curve slopes downward as it falls to its minimum, is flat at its minimum, and then slopes upward.

Variables That Are Unrelated

There are many situations in which no matter what happens to the value of one variable, the other variable remains constant. Sometimes we want to show the independence between two variables in a graph, and Fig. 2.9 shows two ways of achieving this.

In describing the graphs in Fig. 2.6 through 2.9, we have talked about the slopes of curves. Let's look more closely at the concept of slope.

FIGURE **2.9**

Variables That Are Unrelated

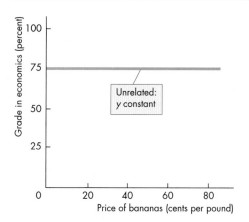

(a) **Unrelated: *y* constant**

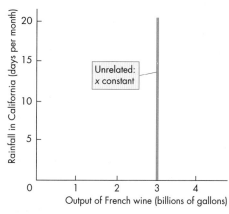

(b) **Unrelated: *x* constant**

This figure shows how we can graph two variables that are unrelated to each other. In part (a), a student's grade in economics is plotted at 75 percent regardless of the price of bananas on the *x*-axis. The curve is horizontal. In part (b), the output of the vineyards of France does not vary with the rainfall in California. The curve is vertical.

The Slope of a Relationship

WE CAN MEASURE THE INFLUENCE OF ONE VARIable on another by the slope of the relationship. The **slope** of a relationship is the change in the value of the variable measured on the *y*-axis divided by the change in the value of the variable measured on the *x*-axis. We use the Greek letter Δ (*delta*) to represent "change in." Thus Δ*y* means the change in the value of the variable measured on the *y*-axis, and Δ*x* means the change in the value of the variable measured on the *x*-axis. Therefore the slope of the relationship is

$$\Delta y\, /\, \Delta x.$$

If a large change in the variable measured on the *y*-axis (Δ*y*) is associated with a small change in the variable measured on the *x*-axis (Δ*x*), the slope is large and the curve is steep. If a small change in the variable measured on the *y*-axis (Δ*y*) is associated with a large change in the variable measured on the *x*-axis (Δ*x*), the slope is small and the curve is flat.

We can make the idea of slope sharper by doing some calculations.

The Slope of a Straight Line

The slope of a straight line is the same regardless of where on the line you calculate it. Thus the slope of a straight line is constant. Let's calculate the slopes of the lines in Fig. 2.10. In part (a), when *x* increases from 2 to 6, *y* increases from 3 to 6. The change in *x* is +4—that is, Δ*x* is 4. The change in *y* is +3—that

---

FIGURE 2.10

The Slope of a Straight Line

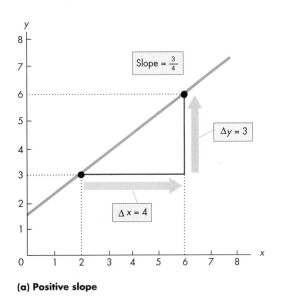

(a) Positive slope

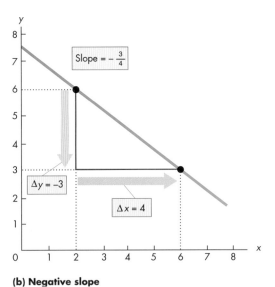

(b) Negative slope

To calculate the slope of a straight line, we divide the change in the value of the variable measured on the *y*-axis (Δ*y*) by the change in the value of the variable measured on the *x*-axis (Δ*x*) as we move along the curve. Part (a) shows the calculation of a positive slope. When *x* increases from 2 to 6, Δ*x* equals 4.

That change in *x* brings about an increase in *y* from 3 to 6, so Δ*y* equals 3. The slope (Δ*y*/Δ*x*) equals $\frac{3}{4}$. Part (b) shows the calculation of a negative slope. When *x* increases from 2 to 6, Δ*x* equals 4. That increase in *x* brings about a decrease in *y* from 6 to 3, so Δ*y* equals −3. The slope (Δ*y*/Δ*x*) equals $-\frac{3}{4}$.

is, Δy is 3. The slope of that line is

$$\frac{\Delta y}{\Delta x} = \frac{3}{4}.$$

In part (b), when x increases from 2 to 6, y decreases from 6 to 3. The change in y is *minus* 3—that is, Δy is –3. The change in x is *plus* 4—that is, Δx is 4. The slope of the curve is

$$\frac{\Delta y}{\Delta x} = \frac{-3}{4}.$$

Notice that the two slopes have the same magnitude (3/4), but the slope of the line in part (a) is positive (+3/+4 = 3/4), while that in part (b) is negative (–3/+4 = –3/4). The slope of a positive relationship is positive; the slope of a negative relationship is negative.

The Slope of a Curved Line

The slope of a curved line is trickier. The slope of a curved line is not constant. Its slope depends on where on the line we calculate it. There are two ways to calculate the slope of a curved line: You can calculate the slope at a point, or you can calculate the slope across an arc of the line. Let's look at the two alternatives.

Slope at a Point   To calculate the slope at a point on a curve, you need to construct a straight line that has the same slope as the curve at the point in question. Figure 2.11 shows how this is done. Suppose you want to calculate the slope of the curve at point *a*. Place a ruler on the graph so that it touches point *a* and no other point on the curve, then draw a straight line along the edge of the ruler. The straight red line is this line, and it is the tangent to the curve at point *a*. If the ruler touches the curve only at point *a*, then the slope of the curve at point *a* must be the same as the slope of the edge of the ruler. If the curve and the ruler do not have the same slope, the line along the edge of the ruler will cut the curve instead of just touching it.

Now that you have found a straight line with the same slope as the curve at point *a*, you can calculate the slope of the curve at point *a* by calculating the slope of the straight line. Along the straight line, as x increases from 0 to 4 ($\Delta x = 4$), y increases from 2 to 5

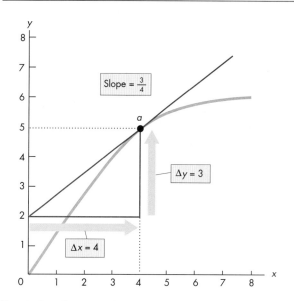

FIGURE **2.11**

Slope at a Point

To calculate the slope of the curve at point *a*, draw the red line that just touches the curve at *a*—the tangent. The slope of this straight line is calculated by dividing the change in y by the change in x along the line. When x increases from 0 to 4, Δx equals 4. That change in x is associated with an increase in y from 2 to 5, so Δy equals 3. The slope of the red line is 3/4. So the slope of the curve at point *a* is 3/4.

($\Delta y = 3$). Therefore the slope of the line is

$$\frac{\Delta y}{\Delta x} = \frac{3}{4}.$$

Thus the slope of the curve at point *a* is 3/4.

Slope Across an Arc   An arc of a curve is a piece of a curve. In Fig. 2.12, you are looking at the same curve as in Fig. 2.11. But instead of calculating the slope at point *a*, we are going to calculate the slope across the arc from *b* to *c*. You can see that the slope at *b* is greater than the slope at *c*. When we calculate the slope across an arc, we are calculating the average slope between two points. As we move along the arc from *b* to *c*, x increases from 3 to 5 and y increases from 4 to 5.5. The change in x is 2 ($\Delta x = 2$), and the

FIGURE 2.12

Slope Across an Arc

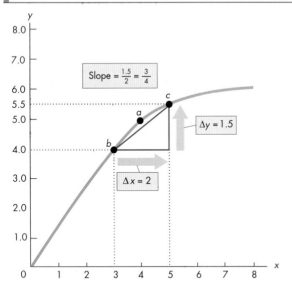

To calculate the average slope of the curve along the arc *bc*, draw a straight line from *b* to *c*. The slope of the line *bc* is calculated by dividing the change in *y* by the change in *x*. In moving from *b* to *c*, Δ*x* equals 2 and Δ*y* equals 1.5. The slope of the line *bc* is 1.5 divided by 2, or ³/₄. So the slope of the curve across the arc *bc* is ³/₄.

---

change in *y* is 1.5 (Δ*y* = 1.5). Therefore the slope of the line is

$$\frac{\Delta y}{\Delta x} = \frac{15}{2} = \frac{3}{4}.$$

Thus the slope of the curve across the arc *bc* is 3/4.

This calculation gives us the slope of the curve between points *b* and *c*. The actual slope calculated is the slope of the straight line from *b* to *c*. This slope approximates the average slope of the curve along the arc *bc*. In this particular example, the slope across the arc *bc* is identical to the slope of the curve at point *a*. But the calculation of the slope of a curve does not always work out so neatly. You might have some fun constructing counterexamples.

You now know how to make and interpret a graph. But so far, we've limited our attention to graphs of two variables. We're now going to learn how to graph more than two variables.

Graphing Relationships Among More Than Two Variables

WE HAVE SEEN THAT WE CAN GRAPH THE RELA-tionship between two variables as a point formed by the *x*- and *y*-coordinates in a two-dimensional graph. You may be thinking that although a two-dimensional graph is informative, most of the things in which you are likely to be interested involve relationships among many variables, not just two. For example, the amount of ice cream consumed depends on the price of ice cream and the temperature. If ice cream is expensive and the temperature is low, people eat much less ice cream than when ice cream is inexpensive and the temperature is high. For any given price of ice cream, the quantity consumed varies with the temperature, and for any given temperature, the quantity of ice cream consumed varies with its price.

Figure 2.13 shows a relationship among three variables. The table shows the number of gallons of ice cream consumed each day at various temperatures and ice cream prices. How can we graph these numbers?

To graph a relationship that involves more than two variables, we use the *ceteris paribus* assumption.

Ceteris Paribus   The Latin phrase **ceteris paribus**, means "other things remaining the same." Every laboratory experiment is an attempt to create *ceteris paribus* and isolate the relationship of interest. We use the same method to make a graph.

Figure 2.13(a) shows an example. There, you can see what happens to the quantity of ice cream consumed when the price of ice cream varies while the temperature is held constant. The line labeled 70°F shows the relationship between ice cream consumption and the price of ice cream if the temperature is 70°F. The numbers used to plot that line are those in the third column of the table in Fig. 2.13. For example, if the temperature is 70°F, 10 gallons are consumed when the price is 60¢ a scoop, and 18 gallons are consumed when the price is 30¢ a scoop. The curve labeled 90°F shows consumption as the price varies if the temperature is 90°F.

We can also show the relationship between ice cream consumption and temperature while the price of ice cream remains constant, as shown in Fig. 2.13(b). The curve labeled 60¢ shows how the consumption

FIGURE 2.13

Graphing a Relationship Among Three Variables

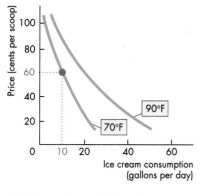

(a) Price and consumption at a given temperature

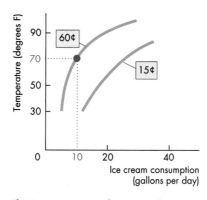

(b) Temperature and consumption at a given price

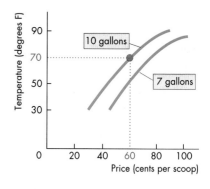

(c) Temperature and price at a given consumption

Price	Ice cream consumption			
(cents per scoop)	(gallons per day)			
	30°F	50°F	70°F	90°F
15	12	18	25	50
30	10	12	18	37
45	7	10	13	27
60	5	7	10	20
75	3	5	7	14
90	2	3	5	10
105	1	2	3	6

The quantity of ice cream consumed depends on its price and the temperature. The table gives some hypothetical numbers that tell us how many gallons of ice cream are consumed each day at different prices and different temperatures. For example, if the price is 60¢ a scoop and the temperature is 70°F, 10 gallons of ice cream are consumed. This set of values is highlighted in the table and each part of the figure. To graph a relationship among three variables, the value of one variable is held constant. Part (a) shows the relationship between price and consumption when temperature is held constant. One curve holds temperature at 90°F and the other at 70°F. Part (b) shows the relationship between temperature and consumption when the price is held constant. One curve holds the price at 60¢ a scoop and the other at 15¢ a scoop. Part (c) shows the relationship between temperature and price when consumption is held constant. One curve holds consumption at 10 gallons and the other at 7 gallons.

of ice cream varies with the temperature when ice cream costs 60¢ a scoop, and a second curve shows the relationship when ice cream costs 15¢ a scoop. For example, at 60¢ a scoop, 10 gallons are consumed when the temperature is 70°F and 20 gallons when the temperature is 90°F.

Figure 2.13(c) shows the combinations of temperature and price that result in a constant consumption of ice cream. One curve shows the combination that results in 10 gallons a day being consumed, and the other shows the combination that results

in 7 gallons a day being consumed. A high price and a high temperature lead to the same consumption as a lower price and a lower temperature. For example, 10 gallons of ice cream are consumed at 90°F and 90¢ a scoop, at 70°F and 60¢ a scoop, and at 50°F and 45¢ a scoop.

◆ With what you have learned about graphs, you can move forward with your study of economics. There are no graphs in this book that are more complicated than those that have been explained here.

SUMMARY

KEY POINTS

Graphing Data (pp. 20–24)

- Time-series graphs show trends, cycles, and other fluctuations in economic data.
- Scatter diagrams show the relationship between two variables. They show whether two variables are positively related, negatively related, or unrelated.
- Cross-section graphs show how variables change across the members of a population.

Graphs Used in Economic Models
(pp. 24–27)

- Graphs are used to show relationships among variables in economic models.
- Relationships can be positive (an upward-sloping curve), negative (a downward-sloping curve), positive and then negative (have a maximum point), negative and then positive (have a minimum point), or unrelated (a horizontal or vertical curve).

The Slope of a Relationship (pp. 28–30)

- The slope of a relationship is calculated as the change in the value of the variable measured on the y-axis divided by the change in the value of the variable measured on the x-axis—that is, $\Delta y/\Delta x$.
- A straight line has a constant slope.
- A curved line has a varying slope. To calculate the slope of a curved line, we calculate the slope at a point or across an arc.

Graphing Relationships Among More Than Two Variables (pp. 30–31)

- To graph a relationship among more than two variables, we hold constant the values of all the variables except two.
- We then plot the value of one of the variables against the value of another.

KEY FIGURES

KEY TERMS

REVIEW QUIZ

- What are the three types of graphs used to show economic data?
- Give an example of a time-series graph.
- List three things that a time-series graph shows quickly and easily.
- Give three examples, different from those in the chapter, of scatter diagrams that show a positive relationship, a negative relationship, and no relationship.
- Draw some graphs to show the relationships between two variables:
  a. That move in the same direction.
  b. That move in opposite directions.
  c. That have a maximum.
  d. That have a minimum.
- Which of the relationships in the previous question is a positive relationship and which a negative relationship?
- What are the two ways of calculating the slope of a curved line?
- How do we graph a relationship among more than two variables?

PROBLEMS

The spreadsheet provides data on the U.S. economy: Column A is the year, column B is the inflation rate, column C is the interest rate, column D is the growth rate, and column E is the unemployment rate. Use this spreadsheet to answer problems 1, 2, 3, and 4.

	A	B	C	D	E
1	1980	13.5	11.9	–0.1	7.1
2	1981	10.3	14.2	0.8	7.6
3	1982	6.2	13.8	–1.1	9.7
4	1983	3.2	12.0	1.5	9.6
5	1984	4.3	12.7	2.8	7.5
6	1985	3.6	11.4	1.4	7.2
7	1986	1.9	9.0	1.2	7.0
8	1987	3.6	9.4	1.5	6.2
9	1988	4.1	9.7	1.9	5.5
10	1989	4.8	9.3	1.1	5.3
11	1990	5.4	9.3	1.2	5.5
12	1991	4.2	7.9	–0.9	6.7
13	1992	3.0	7.0	2.7	7.4
14	1993	3.0	5.8	2.3	6.8
15	1994	2.6	7.1	3.5	6.1
16	1995	2.8	6.6	2.0	5.6
17	1996	3.0	6.4	2.8	5.4
18	1997	2.3	6.4	3.8	4.9
19	1998	2.0	5.5	2.9	5.0

*1. a. Draw a time-series graph of the inflation rate.
   b. In which year(s) (i) was inflation highest, (ii) was inflation lowest, (iii) did it increase, (iv) did it decrease, (v) did it increase most, and (vi) did it decrease most?
   c. What was the main trend in inflation?

2. a. Draw a time-series graph of the interest rate.
   b. In which year(s) (i) was the interest rate highest, (ii) was it lowest, (iii) did it increase, (iv) did it decrease, (v) did it increase most, and (vi) did it decrease most?
   c. What was the main trend in the interest rate?

*3. Draw a scatter diagram to show the relationship between the inflation rate and the interest rate. Describe the relationship.

4. Draw a scatter diagram to show the relationship between the growth rate and the unemployment rate. Describe the relationship.

*5. Draw a graph to show the relationship between the two variables x and y:

x	0	1	2	3	4	5	6	7	8
y	0	1	4	9	16	25	36	49	64

   a. Is the relationship positive or negative?
   b. Does the slope of the relationship increase or decrease as the value of x increases?
   c. Think of some economic relationships that might be similar to this one.

6. Draw a graph that shows the relationship between two variables x and y:

x	0	1	2	3	4	5
y	50	48	44	32	16	0

   a. Is the relationship positive or negative?
   b. Does the slope of the relationship increase or decrease as the value of x increases?
   c. Think of some economic relationships that might be similar to this one.

*7. In problem 5, calculate the slope of the relationship between x and y when x equals 4.

8. In problem 6, calculate the slope of the relationship between x and y when x equals 3.

*9. In problem 5, calculate the slope of the relationship across the arc when x increases from 3 to 4.

10. In problem 6, calculate the slope of the relationship across the arc when x increases from 4 to 5.

*11. Calculate the slope of the relationship shown at point a in the following figure.

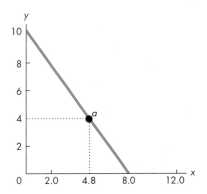

12. Calculate the slope of the relationship shown at point *a* in the following figure.

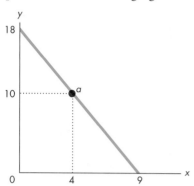

*13. Use the following figure to calculate the slope of the relationship:

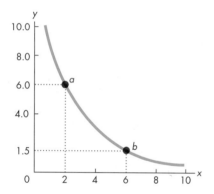

   a.   At points *a* and *b*.
   b.   Across the arc *ab*.

14. Use the following figure to calculate the slope of the relationship:

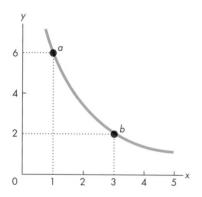

   a.   At points *a* and *b*.
   b.   Across the arc *ab*.

*15. The table gives the price of a balloon ride, the temperature, and the number of rides a day:

Price	Balloon rides (number per day)		
(dollars per ride)	50°F	70°F	90°F
5.00	32	40	50
10.00	27	32	40
15.00	18	27	32
20.00	10	18	27

Draw graphs to show the relationship between
   a.   The price and the number of rides, holding the temperature constant.
   b.   The number of rides and temperature, holding the price constant.
   c.   The temperature and price, holding the number of rides constant.

16. The table gives the price of an umbrella, rainfall, and the number of umbrellas purchased:

Price	Umbrellas (number per day)		
(dollars per umbrella)	0 mm	2 mm	10 mm
10	7	8	12
20	4	7	8
30	2	4	7
40	1	2	4

Draw graphs to show the relationship between
   a.   The price and the number of umbrellas purchased, holding rainfall constant.
   b.   The number of umbrellas purchased and rainfall, holding the price constant.
   c.   Rainfall and the price, holding the number of umbrellas purchased constant.

17. Use the link on the Parkin Web site and find Consumer Price Index (CPI) for the latest 12 months. Make a graph of the CPI. During the most recent month, is the CPI rising or falling? Is the rate of rise or fall increasing or decreasing?

18. Use the link on the Parkin Web site and find the unemployment rate for the latest 12 months. Graph the unemployment rate. During the most recent month, is it rising or falling? Is the rate of rise or fall increasing or decreasing?

3

The Economic Problem

We live in a style that surprises our grandparents and would have astonished our great-grandparents. Most of us live in more spacious homes than they did. We eat more, grow taller, and are even born larger than they were. Video games, cellular phones, gene splices, and personal computers did not exist even 20 years ago. Economic growth has made us richer than our grandparents. And we are not alone in experiencing an expansion in the goods and services that we consume. Many nations around the world are not only sharing our experience: They are setting the pace. Before the recent Asia crisis, Hong Kong, Taiwan, Singapore, Korea, and China expanded at unheard-of rates. But economic growth does not liberate us from scarcity. Why not? Why, despite our immense wealth, must we still make choices and face costs? Why are there no "free lunches"? ◆ We see an incredible amount of specialization and trade in the world. Each one of us specializes in a particular job—as a lawyer, a car maker, a home maker. We have become so specialized that one farm worker can feed 100 people. Less than one sixth of the U.S. work force is employed in manufacturing. More than half of the work force is employed in wholesale and retail trade, banking and finance, government, and other services. Why do we specialize? How do we benefit from specialization and trade? ◆ Over many centuries, institutions and social arrangements have evolved that we take for granted. One of them is property rights and the political and legal system that protects them. Another is markets. Why have these social arrangements evolved? How do they increase production?

◆ These are the questions that we study in this chapter. We begin with the core economic problem: scarcity and choice and the concept of the production possibility frontier. We then learn about the central idea of economics—efficiency. We also discover how we can expand production by accumulating capital and by specializing and trading. ◆ What you will learn in this chapter is the foundation on which all economics is built. You will receive big dividends from a careful study of this material.

Making the Most of It

After studying this chapter, you will be able to:

- Explain the fundamental economic problem
- Define the production possibility frontier
- Define and calculate opportunity cost
- Explain the conditions in which resources are used efficiently
- Explain how economic growth expands production possibilities
- Explain how specialization and trade expand production possibilities

Resources and Wants

TWO FACTS DOMINATE OUR LIVES:

■ We have limited resources.
■ We have unlimited wants.

These two facts define **scarcity**, a condition in which the resources available are insufficient to satisfy people's wants.

Scarcity is a universal fact of life. It confronts each one of us individually, and it confronts our families, local communities, and nations.

The fundamental economic problem is to use our limited resources to produce the items that we value most highly. **Economics** is the study of the *choices* people make to cope with *scarcity*. It is the study of how we each individually try to get the most out of our own limited resources and of how in that endeavor, we interact with each other. Let's look a bit more closely at our limited resources and unlimited wants.

Limited Resources

The resources that can be used to produce goods and services are grouped into four categories:

1. Labor
2. Land
3. Capital
4. Entrepreneurship

Labor is the time and effort that we devote to producing goods and services. It includes the physical and mental work of people who make cars and cola, gum and glue, wallpaper and watering cans.

Land is the gifts of nature that we use to produce goods and services. It includes the air, the water, and the land surface as well as the minerals that lie beneath the surface of the earth.

Capital is the goods that we have produced and that we can now use to produce other goods and services. It includes interstate highways, buildings, dams and power projects, airports and jumbo jets, car production lines, shirt factories, and cookie shops.

Capital also includes **human capital**, which is the knowledge and skill that people obtain from education and on-the-job training. You are building human capital right now as you work on your economics course and other subjects. And your human capital will continue to grow when you get a full-time

job and become better at it. Human capital improves the *quality* of labor.

Entrepreneurship is the resource that organizes labor, land, and capital. Entrepreneurs make business decisions, bear the risks that arise from these decisions, and come up with new ideas about what, how, when, and where to produce.

Our limited resources are converted into goods and services by using the technologies available. These technologies are limited by our knowledge—our human capital—and by our other resources.

Unlimited Wants

Our wants are limited only by our imaginations and are effectively unlimited. We want food and drink, clothing, housing, education, and health care. We want some of these things so badly that we call them *necessities*. But we also want many other things. We want cars and airplanes, movie theaters and videos, popcorn and soda, Walkmans and tapes, books and magazines, restaurant meals, vacations at the beach and in the mountains, music and poetry, and instant telecommunication across the globe.

Some of these wants are less pressing than others, but they are all wants. We even want things that are technologically impossible today but about which we fantasize. We want to live longer and healthier lives. Some of us want to hitchhike the galaxy and be beamed around the universe.

Because our wants exceed our resources, we must make choices. We must rank our wants and decide which wants to satisfy and which to leave unsatisfied. We try to get the most out of our resources.

R E V I E W   Q U I Z

■ What is scarcity?
■ What is the fundamental economic problem?
■ Can you provide a definition of economics?
■ What are the resources that can be used to produce goods and services?
■ How do we cope with the fact that our wants cannot be satisfied with the available resources?

We'll begin our study of the choices people make by looking at the limits to production and at a fundamental implication of choice—opportunity cost.

Resources, Production Possibilities, and Opportunity Cost

EVERY WORKING DAY, IN MINES, FACTORIES, shops, and offices and on farms and construction sites across the United States, 131 million people produce a vast variety of goods and services valued at around $30 billion. The quantities of goods and services that can be produced are limited by our available resources and by technology. That limit is described by the production possibility frontier.

The **production possibility frontier** (*PPF*) is the boundary between those combinations of goods and services that can be produced and those that cannot.

To illustrate the production possibility frontier in a graph, we focus our attention on two goods at a time. In focusing on two goods, we hold the quantities produced of all the other goods and services constant—a device called the *ceteris paribus* assumption. That is, we look at a *model* of the economy in which everything remains the same except for the production of the two goods we are currently considering.

Let's look at the production possibility frontier for two goods that most students buy: bottles of soda and blank audio tapes.

Production Possibility Frontier

The *production possibility frontier* for soda and tapes shows the limits to the production of these two goods, given the total resources available to produce them. Figure 3.1 shows this production possibility frontier. The table lists some combinations of the quantities of tapes and soda that can be produced given the resources available, and the figure graphs these combinations. The quantity of tapes produced is shown on the *x*-axis, and the quantity of soda produced is shown on the *y*-axis. (The numbers are hypothetical.)

Because the *PPF* shows the *limits* to production, we cannot attain the points outside the frontier. They are points that describe wants that cannot be satisfied. We can produce at all the points *inside* the *PPF* and *on* the *PPF*. They are attainable points.

Suppose that in a typical month, 4 million tapes and 5 million bottles of soda are produced. Figure 3.1 shows this combination as point *e* and as possibility *e* in the table. Figure 3.1 also shows other production possibilities. For example, we might stop

FIGURE 3.1

Production Possibility Frontier

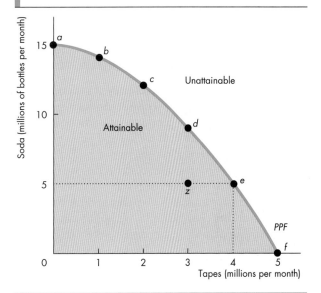

Possibility	Tapes (millions per month)		Soda (millions of bottles per month)
a	0	and	15
b	1	and	14
c	2	and	12
d	3	and	9
e	4	and	5
f	5	and	0

The table lists six points on the production possibility frontier for tapes and soda. Row *a* tells us that if we produce no tapes, the maximum quantity of soda we can produce is 15 million bottles a month. The rows of the table are graphed as points *a, b, c, d, e,* and *f* in the figure. The line passing through these points is the production possibility frontier (*PPF*). It separates the attainable from the unattainable. We can produce at any point inside the orange area or on the frontier. Points outside the frontier are unattainable. Points inside the frontier such as point z are inefficient because it is possible to use the available resources to produce more of either or both goods.

producing tapes and move all the people who produce them into bottling soda. This case is shown as point *a* in the figure and possibility *a* in the table.

The quantity of soda produced increases to 15 million bottles a month, and tape production dries up. Alternatively, we might close down the bottling plants and switch all the resources into producing tapes. In this situation, we produce 5 million tapes a month. This case is shown as point *f* in the figure and possibility *f* in the table.

Production Efficiency

We achieve **production efficiency** if we cannot produce more of one good without producing less of some other good. When production is efficient, we are at a point *on* the *PPF*. If we are at a point *inside* the *PPF*, such as point *z*, production is *inefficient* because we have some *unused* resources or we have some *misallocated* resources or both.

Resources are unused when they are idle but could be working. For example, we might leave some of the bottling plants idle or some workers might be unemployed.

Resources are *misallocated* when they are assigned to tasks for which they are not the best match. For example, we might assign skilled bottling machine operators to work in a tape factory and skilled tape makers to work in a bottling plant. We could get more tapes *and* more bottles of soda from these same workers if we reassigned them to the tasks that more closely match their skills.

If we produce at a point inside the *PPF* such as *z*, we can use our resources more efficiently to produce more tapes, more soda, or more of *both* tapes and soda. But if we produce at a point *on* the *PPF*, we are using our resources efficiently and we can produce more of one good only if we produce less of the other. We face a *tradeoff*.

Tradeoff

On the production possibility frontier, every choice involves a **tradeoff**—we must give up something to get something else. On the *PPF* in Fig. 3.1, we must give up some soda to get more tapes (or give up some tapes to get more soda).

Tradeoffs arise in every imaginable real-world situation. At any given point in time, we have a fixed amount of labor, land, capital, and entrepreneurship. By using our available technologies, we can employ these resources to produce goods and services. But we are limited in what we can produce. This limit defines a boundary between what we can attain and what we

cannot attain. This boundary is the real-world's production possibility frontier, and it defines the tradeoffs that we must make. On our real-world *PPF*, we can produce more of any one good or service only if we produce less of some other goods or services.

When doctors say we must spend more on AIDS and cancer research, they are suggesting a tradeoff: more medical research for less of some other things. When the President says he wants to spend more on education and health care, he is suggesting a tradeoff: more education and health care for less national defense or less private spending (because of higher taxes). When your parents say that you should study more, they are suggesting a tradeoff: more study time for less leisure or less sleep. When an environmental group argues for less logging, it is suggesting a tradeoff: greater conservation of endangered wildlife for less paper.

All tradeoffs involve a cost—an opportunity cost.

Opportunity Cost

The **opportunity cost** of an action is the highest-valued alternative forgone. We can make the concept of opportunity cost more precise by using the production possibility frontier. Along the frontier, there are only two goods, so there is only one alternative forgone—some quantity of the other good. Given our current resources and technology, we can produce more tapes only if we produce fewer bottles of soda. The opportunity cost of producing an additional tape is the number of bottles of soda we must forgo. Similarly, the opportunity cost of producing an additional bottle of soda is the quantity of tapes we must forgo.

For example, at point *c* in Fig. 3.1, we produce fewer tapes and more bottles of soda than we do at point *d*. If we choose point *d* over point *c*, the additional 1 million tapes *cost* 3 million bottles of soda. One tape costs 3 bottles of soda.

We can also work out the opportunity cost of choosing point *c* over point *d* in Fig. 3.1. If we move from point *d* to point *c*, the quantity of soda produced increases by 3 million bottles and the quantity of tapes produced decreases by 1 million. So if we choose point *c* over point *d*, the additional 3 million bottles of soda *cost* 1 million tapes. One bottle of soda costs 1/3 of a tape.

Opportunity Cost Is a Ratio   Opportunity cost is a ratio. It is the decrease in the quantity produced of one good divided by the increase in the quantity produced of another good as we move along the production possibility frontier.

Because opportunity cost is a ratio, the opportunity cost of producing soda is equal to the *inverse* of the opportunity cost of producing tapes. Check this proposition by returning to the calculations we've just worked through. When we move along the *PPF* from *c* to *d*, the opportunity cost of a tape is 3 bottles of soda. The inverse of 3 is 1/3, so if we decrease the production of tapes and increase the production of soda by moving from *d* to *c*, the opportunity cost of a bottle of soda must be 1/3 of a tape. You can check that this number is correct. If we move from *d* to *c*, we produce 3 million more bottles of soda and 1 million fewer tapes. Because 3 million bottles cost 1 million tapes, the opportunity cost of 1 bottle of soda is 1/3 of a tape.

Increasing Opportunity Cost The opportunity cost of a tape increases as the quantity of tapes produced increases. Also, the opportunity cost of soda increases as the quantity of soda produced increases. This phenomenon of increasing opportunity cost is reflected in the *shape* of the *PPF*—it is bowed outward.

When a large quantity of soda and a small quantity of tapes are produced—between points *a* and *b* in Fig. 3.1—the frontier has a gentle slope. A given increase in the quantity of tapes *costs* a small decrease in the quantity of soda, so the opportunity cost of a tape is a small amount of soda.

When a large quantity of tapes and a small quantity of soda are produced—between points *e* and *f* in Fig. 3.1—the frontier is steep. A given increase in the quantity of tapes *costs* a large decrease in the quantity of soda, so the opportunity cost of a tape is a large amount of soda.

The production possibility frontier is bowed outward because resources are not all equally productive in all activities. Production workers with many years of experience working for PepsiCo are very good at producing soda but not very good at making tapes. So if we move these people from PepsiCo to 3M, we get a small increase in the quantity of tapes but a large decrease in the quantity of soda.

Similarly, plastics engineers and production workers who have spent many years working for 3M are good at producing tapes but not so good at bottling soda. So if we move these people from 3M to PepsiCo, we get a small increase in the quantity of soda but a large decrease in the quantity of tapes. The more we try to produce of either good, the less productive are the additional resources we use to

produce that good and the larger is the opportunity cost of a unit of that good.

Increasing Opportunity Costs Are Everywhere Just about every activity that you can think of is one with an *increasing* opportunity cost. Two examples are the production of food and the production of health-care services. We allocate the most skillful farmers and the most fertile land to the production of food. And we allocate the best doctors and least fertile land to the production of health-care services. If we shift fertile land and tractors away from farming to hospitals and ambulances and ask farmers to become hospital porters, the production of food drops drastically and the increase in the production of health-care services is small. The opportunity cost of a unit of health-care services rises. Similarly, if we shift our resources away from health care toward farming, we must use more doctors and nurses as farmers and more hospitals as hydroponic tomato factories. The decrease in the production of health-care services is large, but the increase in food production is small. The opportunity cost of a unit of food rises.

This example is extreme and unlikely, but these same considerations apply to any pair of goods that you can imagine: housing and diamonds, wheelchairs and golf carts, pet food and breakfast cereals.

REVIEW QUIZ

- How does the production possibility frontier illustrate scarcity?
- How does the production possibility frontier illustrate production efficiency?
- How does the production possibility frontier show that every choice involves a tradeoff?
- How does the production possibility frontier illustrate opportunity cost?
- Why is opportunity cost a ratio?
- Why does the *PPF* for most goods bow outward so that opportunity cost increases as the quantity produced of a good increases?

We've seen that production possibilities are limited by the production possibility frontier. And we've seen that production on the *PPF* is efficient. But there are many possible quantities we can produce on the *PPF*. How do we choose among them? How do we know which point on the frontier is the best one?

Using Resources Efficiently

HOW DO WE DECIDE WHETHER TO SPEND MORE on AIDS and cancer research? Whether to vote for an education and health-care package or a tax cut? Whether to join an environmental group and press for a greater conservation of endangered wildlife?

These are big questions that have enormous consequences. But the essence of the answer can be seen by thinking about the simpler question: How do we decide how many tapes and how many bottles of soda to produce?

We decide by calculating and comparing two numbers:

■ Marginal cost
■ Marginal benefit

Marginal Cost

Marginal cost is the opportunity cost of producing *one more unit* of a good or service. You've seen how we can calculate opportunity cost as we move along the production possibility frontier. The marginal cost of a tape is the opportunity cost of *one* tape—the quantity of soda that must be given up to get one more tape—as we move along the *PPF*.

Figure 3.2 illustrates the marginal cost of a tape. If all the available resources are used to produce soda, 15 million bottles of soda and no tapes are produced. If we now decide to produce 1 million tapes, how much soda do we have to give up? You can see the answer in Fig. 3.2(a). To produce 1 million more tapes, we move from *a* to *b* and the quantity of soda decreases by 1 million bottles to 14 million a month. So the opportunity cost of the first 1 million tapes is 1 million bottles of soda.

If we decide to increase the production of tapes to 2 million, how much soda must we give up? This time, we move from *b* to *c* and the quantity of soda decreases by 2 million bottles. So the second million tapes cost 2 million bottles of soda.

You can repeat this calculation for an increase in the quantity of tapes produced from 2 million to 3 million, then to 4 million, and finally to 5 million. Figure 3.2(a) shows these opportunity costs as a series of steps. Each additional million tapes costs more bottles of soda than the preceding million did.

We've just calculated the opportunity cost of tapes in blocks of 1 million at a time and generated

FIGURE 3.2

Opportunity Cost and Marginal Cost

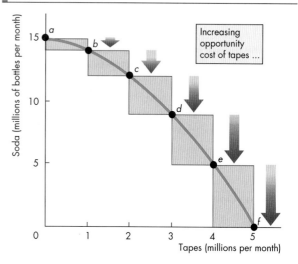

(a) PPF and opportunity cost

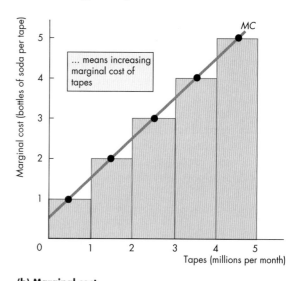

(b) Marginal cost

Opportunity cost is measured along the *PPF* in part (a). If the production of tapes increases from zero to 1 million, the opportunity cost of the first 1 million tapes is 1 million bottles of soda. If the production of tapes increases from 1 million to 2 million, the opportunity cost of the second 1 million tapes is 2 million bottles of soda. The opportunity cost of tapes increases as the production of tapes increases. Marginal cost is the opportunity cost of producing one more unit. Part (b) shows the marginal cost of a tape as the *MC* curve.

the steps in Fig. 3.2(a). If we now calculate the opportunity cost of tapes one at a time, we obtain the *marginal cost* of a tape. In Fig. 3.2(b), the line labeled *MC* shows the marginal cost of a tape. The marginal cost of each additional tape in terms of forgone soda increases, so the marginal cost curve slopes upward.

Marginal Benefit

To use our resources efficiently, we must compare the marginal cost of a tape with its marginal benefit. **Marginal benefit** is the benefit that a person receives from consuming one more unit of a good or service. The marginal benefit from a good or service is measured as the maximum amount that a person is willing to pay for one more unit of it. It is a general principle that the more we have of any good or service, the smaller is our marginal benefit from it—the principle of *decreasing marginal benefit*.

To understand the principle of decreasing marginal benefit, think about your own marginal benefit from tapes. If tapes are very hard to come by and you can buy only one or two a year, you might be willing to pay a high price to get one more tape. But if tapes are readily available and you have as many as you can use, you are willing to pay almost nothing for yet one more tape.

In everyday life, we think of prices as money—as dollars per tape. But you have just been thinking about cost as opportunity cost, which is not a dollar cost but a cost in terms of a forgone alternative. You can also think about prices in the same terms. The price you pay for something is not the number of dollars you give up, but the goods and services that you would have bought with those dollars.

To see this idea more clearly, let's continue with the example we used to study the *PPF* and opportunity cost: tapes and soda. The marginal benefit from a tape can be expressed as the number of bottles of soda that a person is willing to forgo to get a tape. Figure 3.3 illustrates the marginal benefit from tapes. Marginal benefit is the way people feel about different quantities of goods, and we can't derive it from the *PPF*. The numbers in Fig. 3.3 are *assumed*.

In row *a*, 0.5 million tapes a month are available and at that quantity, people are willing to pay 5 bottles of soda for a tape. As the quantity of tapes available increases, the amount that people are willing to pay for a tape falls. When 4.5 million tapes a month are available, people are willing to pay only 1 bottle of soda for a tape.

FIGURE 3.3
Marginal Benefit

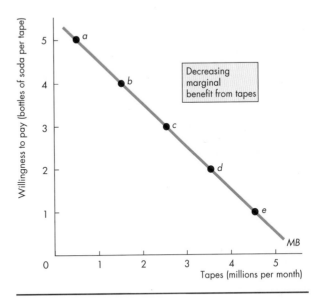

Possibility	Tapes (millions per month)	Willingness to pay (bottles per tape)
a	0.5	5
b	1.5	4
c	2.5	3
d	3.5	2
e	4.5	1

The fewer the number of tapes available, the more soda people are willing to give up to get an additional tape. If only 0.5 million tapes a month are available, people are willing to pay 5 bottles of soda for a tape. But if 4.5 million tapes a month are available, people will pay only 1 bottle of soda for a tape. Decreasing marginal benefit is a universal feature of people's preferences.

The marginal benefit from a tape and the opportunity cost of a tape are both measured in bottles of soda. But they are not the same concept. The *opportunity cost* of a tape is the amount of soda that people *must forgo* to get another tape. The *marginal benefit* from a tape is the amount of soda that people *are willing to forgo* to get another tape.

You now know how to calculate marginal cost and marginal benefit. Let's use these concepts to discover the efficient quantity of tapes to produce.

Efficient Use of Resources

Resource use is **efficient** when we produce the goods and services that we value most highly. That is, when we are using our resources efficiently, we cannot produce more of any good without giving up something that we value even more highly.

We always choose *at the margin*. We compare marginal cost and marginal benefit. If the marginal benefit from a good exceeds the marginal cost of the good, we increase production of that good. If marginal cost exceeds marginal benefit, we decrease production of the good. And if marginal benefit equals marginal cost, we stick with the current production.

This principle is just like the decisions you make when you go shopping. You have $10 to spend and are thinking about buying a CD or a box of floppy disks. You figure that you will get more value from the CD than from the floppy disks, so you spend your $10 on the CD. You have allocated scarce resources to their highest-valued use. The marginal benefit from a CD is greater than (or equal to) its marginal cost, the box of floppy disks. The marginal benefit from a box of floppy disks is less than its marginal cost. No matter what the good or service, if you can afford it and you think it is worth the price, you buy it. If you think it not worth its price, you pass it up.

We can illustrate an efficient use of resources by continuing to use the example of soda and tapes. Figure 3.4 shows the marginal cost and marginal benefit of tapes. Suppose we produce 1.5 million tapes a month. The marginal cost of a tape is 2 bottles of soda. But the marginal benefit from a tape is 4 bottles of soda. Because someone values an additional tape more highly than it costs to produce, we can get more value from our resources by moving some of them out of soda production and into tape production.

Now suppose we produce 3.5 million tapes a month. The marginal cost of a tape is now 4 bottles of soda. But the marginal benefit from a tape is only 2 bottles of soda. Because an additional tape costs more to produce than anyone thinks it is worth, we can get more value from our resources by moving some of them away from tape production and into soda production.

But suppose we produce 2.5 million tapes a month. Marginal cost and marginal benefit are now equal at 3 bottles of soda. This allocation of resources between tapes and soda is efficient. If more tapes are produced, the forgone soda is worth more than the additional tapes. If fewer tapes are produced, the forgone tapes are worth more than the additional soda.

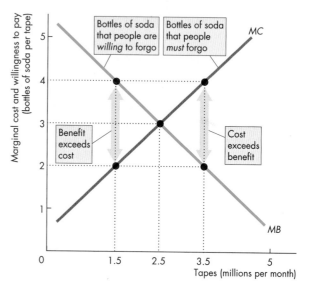

FIGURE 3.4

Efficient Use of Resources

The greater the quantity of tapes produced, the smaller is the marginal benefit (*MB*) from a tape—the fewer bottles of soda people are willing to give up to get an additional tape. But the greater the quantity of tapes produced, the greater is the marginal cost (*MC*) of a tape—the more bottles of soda people must give up to get an additional tape. When marginal benefit equals marginal cost, resources are being used efficiently.

REVIEW QUIZ

- What is marginal cost and how is it measured?
- What is the relationship between marginal cost and the production possibility frontier?
- What is marginal benefit and how is it measured?
- How does the marginal benefit from a good change as the quantity of that good increases? Why?
- What conditions must be satisfied if resources are used efficiently? Why?

You now understand the limits to production and the conditions under which resources are used efficiently. Your next task is to study the expansion of production possibilities.

Economic Growth

DURING THE PAST 30 YEARS, PRODUCTION IN THE United States has expanded by 80 percent. Such an expansion of production is called **economic growth**. Can economic growth enable us to overcome scarcity and avoid opportunity cost? You are going to see that economic growth does not overcome scarcity and avoid opportunity cost. You are also going to see that the faster we make production grow, the greater is the opportunity cost of economic growth.

The Cost of Economic Growth

Two key factors influence economic growth: technological change and capital accumulation. **Technological change** is the development of new goods and of better ways of producing goods and services. **Capital accumulation** is the growth of capital resources.

As a consequence of technological change and capital accumulation, we have an enormous quantity of cars that enable us to produce more transportation than when we had only horses and carriages; we have satellites that make global communications possible on a scale that is much larger than that produced by the earlier cable technology. But new technologies and new capital have an opportunity cost. To use resources in research and development and to produce new capital, we must decrease our production of consumption goods and services. Let's look at this opportunity cost.

Instead of studying the *PPF* of tapes and soda, we'll hold the quantity of soda produced constant and examine the *PPF* for tapes and tape-making machines. Figure 3.5 shows this *PPF* as the blue curve *abc*. If we devote no resources to producing tape-making machines, we produce at point *a*. If we produce 3 million tapes a month, we can produce 6 tape-making machines at point *b*. If we produce no tapes, we can produce 10 tape-making machines a month at point *c*.

The amount by which our production possibilities expand depends on the resources we devote to technological change and capital accumulation. If we devote no resources to this activity (point *a*), the frontier remains at *abc*—the blue curve in Fig. 3.5. If we cut the current production of tapes and produce 6 machines a month (point *b*), then in the future, we'll have more capital and our *PPF* rotates outward to the

FIGURE 3.5

Economic Growth

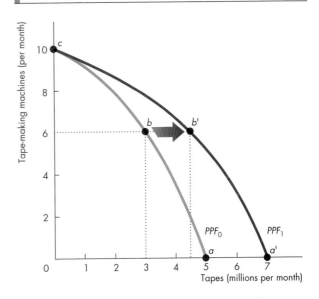

PPF_0 shows the limits to the production of tapes and tape-making equipment, with the production of all other goods and services remaining constant. If we devote no resources to producing tape-making machines and produce 5 million tapes a month, we remain stuck at point *a*. But if we decrease tape production to 3 million a month and produce 6 tape-making machines a month, at point *b*, our production possibilities will expand. After a year, the production possibility frontier shifts outward to PPF_1 and we can produce at point *b'*, a point outside the original *PPF*. We can shift the *PPF* outward, but we cannot avoid opportunity cost. The opportunity cost of producing more tapes in the future is fewer tapes today.

position shown by the red curve. The fewer resources we devote to producing tapes and the more resources we devote to producing machines, the greater is the expansion of our production possibilities.

Economic growth is not free. To make it happen, we devote resources to producing new machines and fewer resources to producing tapes. In Fig. 3.5, we move from *a* to *b*. There is no free lunch. The opportunity cost of more tapes in the future is fewer tapes today. Also, economic growth is no magic formula for abolishing scarcity. On the new production possibility frontier, we continue to face opportunity costs.

The ideas about economic growth that we have explored in the setting of the audio tape industry also apply to nations. Let's look at two examples.

Economic Growth in the United States and Hong Kong

If as a nation we devote all our resources to producing consumer goods and none to research and capital accumulation, our production possibilities in the future will be the same as they are today. To expand our production possibilities in the future, we must devote fewer resources to producing consumption goods and some resources to accumulating capital and developing technologies so we can produce more consumption goods in the future. The decrease in today's consumption is the opportunity cost of an increase in future consumption.

The experiences of the United States and Hong Kong make a striking example of the effects of our choices on the rate of economic growth. In 1960, the production possibilities per person in the United States were more than four times those in Hong Kong (see Fig. 3.6). The United States devoted one fifth of its resources to accumulating capital and the other four fifths to consumption. In 1960, the United States was at point *a* on its *PPF*. Hong Kong devoted one third of its resources to accumulating capital and two thirds to consumption. In 1960, Hong Kong was at point *a* on its *PPF*.

Since 1960, both countries have experienced economic growth, but growth in Hong Kong has been more rapid than in the United States. Because Hong Kong devoted a bigger fraction of its resources to accumulating capital, its production possibilities have expanded more quickly.

In 1998, the *PPF* per person in the United States and Hong Kong were similar. If Hong Kong continues to devote more resources to accumulating capital than we do (at point *b* on its 1998 *PPF*), it will continue to grow more rapidly than the United States and its frontier will move out beyond our own. But if Hong Kong increases consumption and decreases capital accumulation (moving to point *c* on its 1998 *PPF*), then its rate of economic growth will slow.

The United States is typical of the rich industrial countries, which include the United States, Western Europe, and Japan. Hong Kong is typical of the fast-growing Asian economies, which include Taiwan, Thailand, South Korea, and China. Growth in these countries has slowed during the past two years, but before the slowdown, these countries expanded production by between 5 percent and almost 10 percent a year. If these high growth rates are restored, these other countries will eventually

FIGURE 3.6

Economic Growth in the United States and Hong Kong

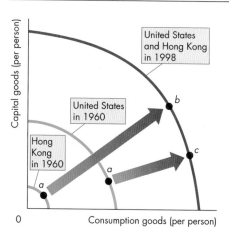

In 1960, the production possibilities per person in the United States were much larger than those in Hong Kong. But Hong Kong devoted more of its resources to accumulating capital than did the United States, so its production possibility frontier has shifted outward more quickly than has that of the United States. In 1998, the two production possibilities per person were similar.

close the gap on the United States as Hong Kong has done.

REVIEW QUIZ

- What are the two key factors that generate economic growth?
- How does economic growth influence the production possibility frontier?
- What is the opportunity cost of economic growth?
- Why has Hong Kong experienced faster economic growth than the United States has?

Next, we're going to study another way we expand our production possibilities—the amazing fact that buyers and sellers gain from specialization and trade.

Gains from Trade

PEOPLE CAN PRODUCE FOR THEMSELVES ALL THE goods that they consume, or they can concentrate on producing one good (or perhaps a few goods) and then trade with others—exchange some of their own goods for those of others. Concentrating on the production of only one good or a few goods is called *specialization*. We are going to discover how people gain by specializing in the production of the good in which they have a *comparative advantage* and trading with each other.

Comparative Advantage

A person has a **comparative advantage** in an activity if that person can perform the activity at a lower opportunity cost than anyone else. Differences in opportunity costs arise from differences in individual abilities and from differences in the characteristics of other resources.

No one excels at everything. One person is an outstanding pitcher but a poor catcher; another person is a brilliant lawyer but a poor teacher. In almost all human endeavors, what one person does easily, someone else finds difficult. The same applies to land and capital. One plot of land is fertile but has no mineral deposits; another plot of land has outstanding views but is infertile. One machine has great precision but is difficult to operate; another machine is fast but often breaks down.

Although no one excels at everything, some people excel and can outperform others in many activities. But such a person does not have a *comparative* advantage in every activity. For example, John Grisham is a better lawyer than most people. But he is an even better writer of fast-paced thrillers. His *comparative* advantage is in writing.

Because people's abilities and the quality of their resources differ, they have different opportunity costs of producing various goods. Such differences give rise to comparative advantage. Let's explore the idea of comparative advantage by looking at two audio cassette factories, one operated by Tom and the other operated by Nancy.

Tom's Factory   To simplify the story quite a lot, suppose that audio cassettes have just two components: a length of tape and a plastic case. Tom has two production lines, one for tape and one for cases.

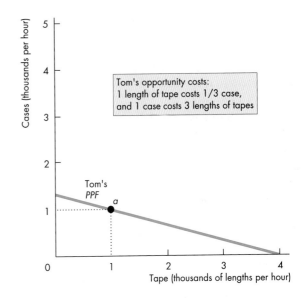

FIGURE 3.7

Production Possibilities
in Tom's Factory

> Tom's opportunity costs:
> 1 length of tape costs 1/3 case,
> and 1 case costs 3 lengths of tapes

Tom can produce tape and cassette cases along the production possibility frontier *PPF*. For Tom, the opportunity cost of 1 length of tape is ¹/₃ of a case and the opportunity cost of 1 case is 3 lengths of tape. If Tom produces at point *a*, he can produce 1,000 cassette cases and 1,000 lengths of tape an hour.

Figure 3.7 shows Tom's production possibility frontier for tape and cases. It tells us that if Tom uses all his resources to make tape, he can produce 4,000 lengths of tape an hour. The *PPF* in Fig. 3.7 also tells us that if Tom uses all his resources to make cases, he can produce 1,333 cases an hour. But to produce cases, Tom must decrease his production of tape. For each 1 case produced, he must decrease his production of tape by 3 lengths.

Tom's opportunity cost of producing 1 case is 3 lengths of tape.

Similarly, if Tom wants to increase his production of tape, he must decrease his production of cases. For each 1,000 lengths of tape produced, he must decrease his production of cases by 333. So

Tom's opportunity cost of producing 1 length of tape is 0.333 case.

Nancy's Factory   The other factory, operated by Nancy, can also produce cases and tape. But Nancy's factory has machines that are custom made for case production, so they are more suitable for producing cases than tape. Also, Nancy's work force is more skilled in making cases.

This difference between the two factories means that Nancy's production possibility frontier—shown along with Tom's *PPF* in Fig. 3.8—is different from Tom's. If Nancy uses all her resources to make tape, she can produce 1,333 lengths an hour. If she uses all her resources to make cases, she can produce 4,000 an hour. To produce tape, Nancy must decrease her production of cases. For each 1,000 additional lengths of tape produced, she must decrease her production of cases by 3,000.

Nancy's opportunity cost of producing 1 length of tape is 3 cases.

Similarly, if Nancy wants to increase her production of cases, she must decrease her production of tape. For each 1,000 additional cases produced, she must decrease her production of tape by 333 lengths. So

Nancy's opportunity cost of producing 1 case is 0.333 length of tape.

Suppose that Tom and Nancy produce both tapes and cases and that each produces 1,000 lengths of tape and 1,000 cases—1,000 cassettes—an hour. That is, each produces at point *a* on their production possibility frontiers. Total production is 2,000 cassettes an hour.

In which of the two goods does Nancy have a comparative advantage? Recall that comparative advantage is a situation in which one person's opportunity cost of producing a good is lower than another person's opportunity cost of producing that same good. Nancy has a comparative advantage in producing cases. Nancy's opportunity cost of a case is 0.333 length of tape, whereas Tom's is 3 lengths of tape.

You can see her comparative advantage by looking at the production possibility frontiers for Nancy and Tom in Fig. 3.8. Nancy's production possibility frontier is steeper than Tom's. To produce one more case, Nancy gives up less tape than Tom. Hence Nancy's opportunity cost of a case is less than Tom's. This means that Nancy has a comparative advantage in producing cases.

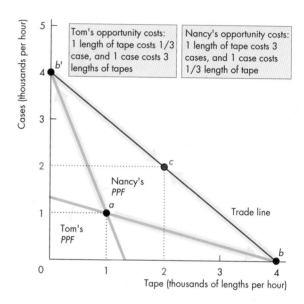

FIGURE 3.8

The Gains from Trade

Tom and Nancy each produce at point *a* on their respective *PPF*s. Nancy has a comparative advantage in cases, and Tom has a comparative advantage in tape. If Nancy specializes in cases, she produces at point *b'* on her *PPF*. If Tom specializes in tape, he produces at point *b* on his *PPF*. They then exchange cases for tape along the red "Trade line." Nancy buys tape from Tom for less than her opportunity cost of producing it, and Tom buys cases from Nancy for less than his opportunity cost of producing them. Each goes to point *c*—a point outside his or her *PPF*—where each has 2,000 cassettes an hour. Tom and Nancy double their rate of production with no change in resources.

Tom's comparative advantage is in producing tape. His production possibility frontier is less steep than Nancy's. This means that Tom gives up fewer cases to produce one more length of tape than Nancy does. Tom's opportunity cost of producing a length of tape is 0.333 case, which is less than Nancy's 3 cases. So Tom has a comparative advantage in producing tape.

Because Nancy has a comparative advantage in cases and Tom in tape, they can both gain from specialization and exchange.

Achieving the Gains from Trade

If Tom, who has a comparative advantage in tape production, puts all his resources into that activity, he can produce 4,000 lengths of tape an hour—point *b* on his *PPF*. If Nancy, who has a comparative advantage in producing cases, puts all her resources into that activity, she can produce 4,000 cases an hour—point *b* on her *PPF*. By specializing, Tom and Nancy together can produce 4,000 cases and 4,000 lengths of tape an hour, double their total production without specialization. By specialization and exchange, Tom and Nancy can get *outside* their production possibility frontiers.

To achieve the gains from specialization, Tom and Nancy must trade with each other. Suppose they agree to the following deal: Each hour, Nancy produces 4,000 cases, Tom produces 4,000 lengths of tape, and Nancy supplies Tom with 2,000 cases in exchange for 2,000 lengths of tape. With this deal in place, Tom and Nancy move along the red "Trade line" to point *c*. At this point, each produces 2,000 cassettes an hour—double their previous production rate. These are the gains from specialization and trade.

Both parties to the trade share the gains. Nancy, who can produce tape at an opportunity cost of 3 cases per length of tape, can buy tape from Tom for a price of 1 case per length. Tom, who can produce cases at an opportunity cost of 3 lengths of tape per case, can buy cases from Nancy at a price of 1 length per case. Nancy gets her tape more cheaply, and Tom gets his cases more cheaply.

Absolute Advantage

Suppose that Nancy invents and patents a production process that makes her *four* times as productive as she was before in the production of both cases and tape. With her new technology, Nancy can produce 16,000 cases an hour (4 times the original 4,000) if she puts all her resources into that activity. Alternatively, she can produce 5,332 lengths of tape (4 times the original 1,333) if she puts all her resources into that activity. Nancy now has an **absolute advantage** in producing *both* goods—using the same quantity of resources as Tom, she can produce more of both goods than Tom can produce.

But Nancy does not have a *comparative* advantage in both goods. She can produce four times as much of *both* goods as before, but her *opportunity cost* of

1 length of tape is still 3 cases. And this opportunity cost is higher than Tom's. So Nancy can still get tape at a lower cost by exchanging cases for tape with Tom.

A key point to recognize is that it is *not* possible for *anyone* to have a comparative advantage in *everything*. So gains from specialization and trade are always available when opportunity costs diverge.

Dynamic Comparative Advantage

At any given point in time, the available resources and technologies determine the comparative advantages that individuals and nations have. But just by repeatedly producing a particular good or service, people become more productive in that activity, a phenomenon called **learning-by-doing**. Learning-by-doing is the basis of *dynamic* comparative advantage. **Dynamic comparative advantage** is a comparative advantage that a person (or country) possesses as a result of having specialized in a particular activity and, as a result of learning-by-doing, having become the producer with the lowest opportunity cost.

Hong Kong and Singapore are examples of countries that have pursued dynamic comparative advantage vigorously. They have developed industries in which initially they did not have a comparative advantage but, through learning-by-doing, became low opportunity cost producers in those industries. A specific example is the decision to develop a genetic engineering industry in Singapore. Singapore probably did not have a comparative advantage in genetic engineering initially. But it might develop one as its scientists and production workers become more skilled in this activity.

REVIEW QUIZ

- What gives a person a comparative advantage in producing a good?
- Why is it not possible for anyone to have a comparative advantage at everything?
- What are the gains from specialization and trade?
- Explain the source of the gains from specialization and trade.
- Distinguish between comparative advantage and absolute advantage.
- What is dynamic comparative advantage and how does it arise?

The Market Economy

INDIVIDUALS AND COUNTRIES GAIN BY SPECIALIZ-
ing in the production of those goods and services in
which they have a comparative advantage and trading
with each other. This source of economic wealth was
identified by Adam Smith in his *Wealth of Nations,*
published in 1776—see pp. 56–57.

To enable billions of people who specialize in
producing millions of different goods and services to
reap these gains, trade must be organized. But trade
need not be *planned* or *managed* by a central authority. In fact, when such an arrangement has been tried,
as it was for 60 years in Russia, the result has been
less than dazzling.

Trade is organized by using social institutions.
The two key ones are:

- Property rights
- Markets

Property Rights

Property rights are social arrangements that govern the ownership, use, and disposal of resources,
goods, and services. *Real property* includes land and
buildings—the things we call property in ordinary
speech—and durable goods such as plant and equipment. *Financial property* includes stocks and bonds
and money in the bank. *Intellectual property* is the
intangible product of creative effort. This type of
property includes books, music, computer programs,
and inventions of all kinds and is protected by copyrights and patents.

If property rights are not enforced, the incentive
to specialize and produce the goods in which each
person has a comparative advantage is weakened, and
some of the potential gains from specialization and
trade are lost. If people can easily steal the production
of others, then time, energy, and resources are devoted
not to production, but to protecting possessions.

Establishing property rights is one of the greatest
challenges facing Russia and other Eastern European
nations as they seek to develop market economies.
Even in countries where property rights are well
established, such as the United States, protecting
intellectual property is proving to be a challenge in
the face of modern technologies that make it relatively easy to copy audio and video material, computer programs, and books.

Markets

In ordinary speech, the word *market* means a place
where people buy and sell goods such as fish, meat,
fruits, and vegetables. In economics, a *market* has a
more general meaning. A **market** is any arrangement that enables buyers and sellers to get information and to do business with each other. An example
is the market in which oil is bought and sold—the
world oil market. The world oil market is not a place.
It is the network of oil producers, oil users, whole-
salers, and brokers who buy and sell. In the world oil
market, decision makers do not meet physically. They
make deals throughout the world by telephone, fax,
and direct computer link.

In the example we've just studied, Nancy and
Tom get together and do a deal. They agree to
exchange cassette cases for lengths of tape. But in a
market economy, Nancy sells cassette cases to a dealer
in plastic products and buys lengths of tape from a
dealer in electronic recording media. Similarly, Tom
buys cassette cases and sells lengths of tape in these
same two markets. Tom can use Nancy's cases and
Nancy can use Tom's lengths of tape and yet be
unaware of each other's existence.

Circular Flows in the Market Economy

Figure 3.9 identifies two types of markets: goods
markets and resource markets. *Goods markets* are
those in which goods and services are bought and
sold. *Resource markets* are those in which productive
resources are bought and sold.

Households decide how much of their labor,
land, capital, and entrepreneurship to sell or rent in
resource markets. They receive incomes in the form
of wages, rent, interest, and profit. Households also
decide how to spend their incomes on goods and services produced by firms. Firms decide the quantities
of resources to hire, how to use them to produce
goods and services, what goods and services to
produce, and in what quantities.

Figure 3.9 shows the flows that result from these
decisions by households and firms. The red flows
are the resources that go from households through
resource markets to firms and the goods and services
that go from firms through goods markets to households. The green flows in the opposite direction are
the payments made in exchange for these items.

How do markets coordinate all these decisions?

FIGURE 3.9

Circular Flows in the Market Economy

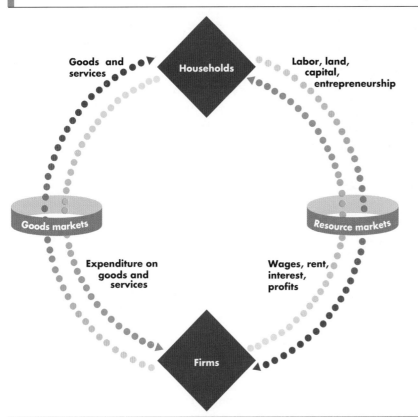

Households and firms make economic choices. Households choose the quantities of labor, land, capital, and entrepreneurship to sell or rent to firms in exchange for wages, rent, interest, and profits. Households also choose how to spend their incomes on the various types of goods and services available. Firms choose the quantities of resources to hire and the quantities of the various goods and services to produce. Goods markets and resource markets coordinate these choices of households and firms. Resources and goods flow clockwise (red), and money payments flow counterclockwise (green).

Coordinating Decisions

Markets coordinate individual decisions through price adjustments. To see how, think about your local market for hamburgers. Suppose that some people who want to buy hamburgers are not able to do so. To make the choices of buyers and sellers compatible, buyers must scale down their appetites or more hamburgers must be offered for sale (or both must happen). A rise in the price of hamburgers produces this outcome. A higher price encourages producers to offer more hamburgers for sale. It also curbs the appetite for hamburgers and changes some lunch plans. Fewer people buy hamburgers, and more buy hot dogs. More hamburgers (and more hot dogs) are offered for sale.

Alternatively, suppose that more hamburgers are available than people want to buy. In this case, to make the choices of buyers and sellers compatible, more hamburgers must be bought or fewer hamburgers must be offered for sale (or both). A fall in the price of hamburgers achieves this outcome. A lower price encour-

ages firms to produce a smaller quantity of hamburgers. It also encourages people to buy more hamburgers.

R E V I E W Q U I Z

- Why are social arrangements such as markets and property rights necessary?
- What are the main functions of markets?

◆ You have now begun to see how economists approach economic questions. Scarcity, choice, and divergent opportunity cost explain why we specialize and trade and why property rights and markets have developed. You can see the lessons you've learned in this chapter all around you. *Reading Between the Lines* on pp. 50–51 gives an example. It explores the *PPF* of a student like you and the choices that students must make that influence their own economic growth—the growth of their incomes.

Opportunity Cost:
The Cost and Benefit of Education

PORTLAND PRESS HERALD, MAY 2, 1996

High Cost Blocks Education

Robin McAlister of South Portland has fallen into a disheartening routine: Sit down at the kitchen table, scan the classifieds, apply for a job, get turned down. ...

Like thousands of other Mainers, McAlister has learned a fundamental truth: People who don't have the skills needed in today's high-tech, highly competitive environment rarely find good jobs. ...

Although a college degree doesn't guarantee a job, the economy is creating work for highly educated people. ...

Since 1989, the number of jobs for people with a master's degree has jumped an estimated 21 percent. ...

By comparison, jobs that generally don't require a college education have declined an estimated 1 percent.

There's a huge gap in pay between the two groups. In Maine, the average hourly wage for jobs that generally require a college degree is twice that for occupations that don't, about $18 an hour vs. $9 an hour, according to an analysis by The Portland Newspapers of state and federal databases. ...

© 1996 *Portland Press Herald*. Reprinted with permission. Further reproduction prohibited.

THE NEW YORK TIMES, AUGUST 2, 1998

A Top MBA Is a Hot Ticket as Pay Climbs

...The typical University of Chicago [business school] graduate turns down so many job offers that the dean's main worry has become "dealing with all the disappointed companies." ...

The median offer this year for a new Stanford MBA ... was $120,000, more than double the first-year salary at the peak of the '80s, and more than five times the 1978 figure. Inflation has been 142 percent over that period. ...

Half the graduates of the Wharton School of the University of Pennsylvania received offers of more than $133,000 this year. ...

At the top 25 schools, the best compensation packages offered to new MBAs are well above $200,000.

© 1998 *The New York Times*. Reprinted with permission. Further reproduction prohibited.

Essence of the Stories

■ It has become hard for someone who lacks a college education to find a good job.

■ Jobs that require a college degree pay twice as much as jobs that don't.

■ Jobs for people with an MBA have become even more plentiful.

■ Incomes of people with MBAs have increased greatly during the 1990s.

■ The opportunity cost of a college degree is forgone consumption. The payoff is an increase in lifetime production possibilities and in future consumption possibilities.

■ Figure 1 shows the choices facing a high school graduate. This person can consume education goods and services such as tuition, books and other supplies, and study time, measured on the *y*-axis, or other goods and services, measured on the *x*-axis.

■ Working full time, this person has an income of $16,000 a year. She can consume along the blue *PPF*. To get a collee degree, a high school graduate selects point *a* on the blue *PPF*, forgoes current consumption, and increases the use of educational goods and services to $12,000.

■ Working full time, the college graduate earns twice as much as the high school graduate at $32,000 a year. With a college degree, production possibilities expand to the red *PPF* in Fig. 1.

■ A college graduate can choose to quit school or spend even more time and other resources on education to get a professional degree. If she quits school, consumption remains at $32,000 a year.

■ Figure 2 shows the choices facing a college graduate. To get a professional degree, a college graduate selects point *b* on the blue *PPF*, forgoes current consumption, and increases the use of educational goods and services to $24,000.

■ With a professional degree, income rises to $128,000 a year. Production possibilities expand to the red *PPF* in Fig. 2.

■ The greater the resources devoted to education, the greater are the future production possibilities. For people who have the required ability, the future benefits of education exceed the costs by a significant amount.

■ Political leaders of all parties say that they want every American to have a college education.

■ Why do you think political leaders need to worry about college education?

■ With such huge returns from education, why don't more people remain in school for longer?

■ What is the opportunity cost of providing a college education for every American?

■ Would you vote for or against a tax increase to enable everyone to attend college? Why or why not?

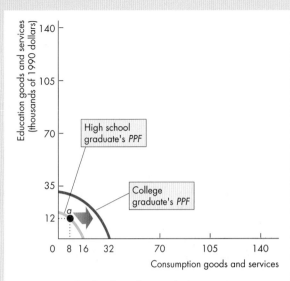

Figure 1 High school graduate's choices

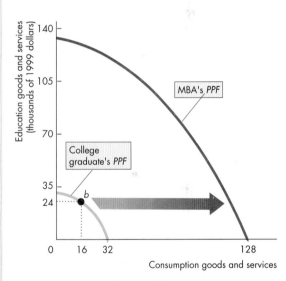

Figure 2 College graduate's choices

51

SUMMARY

KEY POINTS

Resources and Wants (p. 36)

- Economic activity arises from scarcity—resources are insufficient to satisfy people's wants.
- Resources are labor, land, capital (including human capital), and entrepreneurship.
- We choose how to use our resources and try to get the most out of them.

Resources, Production Possibilities, and Opportunity Cost (pp. 37–39)

- The production possibility frontier, *PPF*, is the boundary between production levels that are attainable and those that are not attainable when all the available resources are used to their limit.
- Production efficiency occurs at points on the *PPF*.
- Along the *PPF*, the opportunity cost of producing more of one good is the amount of the other good that must be given up.
- The opportunity cost of a good increases as the production of the good increases.

Using Resources Efficiently (pp. 40–42)

- The marginal cost of a good is the opportunity cost of producing one more unit.
- The marginal benefit from a good is the maximum amount of another good that a person is willing to forgo to obtain more of the first good.
- The marginal benefit of a good decreases as the amount available increases.
- Resources are used efficiently when the marginal cost of each good is equal to its marginal benefit.

Economic Growth (pp. 43–44)

- Economic growth, which is the expansion of production possibilities, results from capital accumulation and technological change.
- The opportunity cost of economic growth is forgone current consumption.

Gains from Trade (pp. 45–47)

- A person has a comparative advantage in producing a good if that person can produce the good at a lower opportunity cost than everyone else can.
- It is *not* possible for *anyone* to have a comparative advantage at *everything*.
- People gain by specializing in the activity in which they have a comparative advantage and trading with others.

The Market Economy (pp. 48–49)

- Property rights and markets enable people to gain from specialization and trade.
- Markets coordinate decisions and help to allocate resources to *higher*-valued uses.

KEY FIGURES

KEY TERMS

PROBLEMS

*1. Use the figure to calculate Wendell's opportunity cost of an hour of tennis when he increases the time he plays tennis from:
   a.   4 to 6 hours a week.
   b.   6 to 8 hours a week.

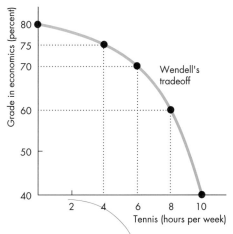

2. Use the figure to calculate Mary's opportunity cost of an hour of skating when she increases her time spent skating from:
   a.   2 to 4 hours a week.
   b.   4 to 6 hours a week.

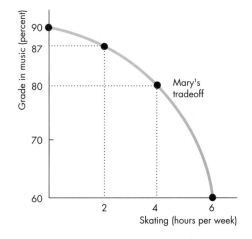

*3. In problem 1, describe the relationship between the time Wendell spends playing tennis and the opportunity cost of an hour of tennis.

4. In problem 2, describe the relationship between the time Mary spends skating and the opportunity cost of an hour of skating.

*5. Wendell, in problem 1, has the following marginal benefit curve:

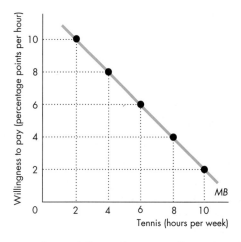

a.   If Wendell uses his time efficiently, what grade will he get?
b.   Why would Wendell be worse off getting a higher grade?

6. Mary, in problem 2, has the following marginal benefit curve:

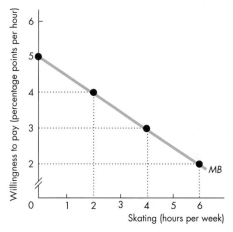

a.   If Mary uses her time efficiently, how much skating will she do?
b.   Why would Mary be worse off spending fewer hours skating?

*7. Leisureland's production possibilities are:

Food (pounds per month)		Sunscreen (gallons per month)
300	and	0
200	and	50
100	and	100
0	and	150

a.   Draw a graph of Leisureland's production possibility frontier.

b. What are Leisureland's opportunity costs of producing food and sunscreen at each output in the table?

8. Jane's Island's production possibilities are:

Corn (pounds per month)		Cloth (yards per month)
3.0	and	0
2.0	and	2
1.0	and	4
0	and	6

a. Draw a graph of the *PPF* on Jane's Island.
b. What are Jane's opportunity costs of producing corn and cloth at each output in the table?

*9. In problem 7, to get a gallon of sunscreen the people of Leisureland are willing to give up 5 pounds of food if they have 25 gallons of sunscreen; 2 pounds of food if they have 75 gallons of sunscreen; and 1 pound of food if they have 125 gallons of sunscreen.
a. Draw a graph of Leisureland's marginal benefit from sunscreen.
b. What is the efficient quantity of sunscreen?

10. In problem 8, to get a yard of cloth Jane is willing to give up 0.75 pound of corn if she has 2 yards of cloth; 0.50 pound of corn if she has 4 yards of cloth; and 0.25 pound of corn if she has 6 yards of cloth.
a. Draw a graph of Jane's marginal benefit from cloth.
b. What is Jane's efficient quantity of cloth?

*11. Busyland's production possibilities are:

Food (pounds per month)		Sunscreen (gallons per month)
150	and	0
100	and	100
50	and	200
0	and	300

Calculate Busyland's opportunity costs of food and sunscreen at each output in the table.

12. Joe's production possibilities are:

Corn (pounds per month)		Cloth (yards per month)
6	and	0.0
4	and	1.0
2	and	2.0
0	and	3.0

What are Joe's opportunity costs of producing corn and cloth at each output in the table?

*13. In problems 7 and 11, Leisureland and Busyland each produce and consume 100 pounds of food and 100 gallons of sunscreen per month; and they do not trade. Now the countries begin to trade with each other.
a. What good does Leisureland sell to Busyland and what good does it buy from Busyland?
b. If Leisureland and Busyland divide the total output of food and sunscreen equally, what are the gains from trade?

14. In problems 8 and 12, Jane's Island produces and consumes 1 pound of corn and 4 yards of cloth. Joe's Island produces and consumes 4 pounds of corn and 1 yard of cloth. Now the islands begin to trade.
a. What good does Jane sell to Joe and what good does Jane buy from Joe?
b. If Jane and Joe divide the total output of corn and cloth equally, what are the gains from trade?

CRITICAL THINKING

1. After you have studied *Reading Between the Lines* on pp. 50–51, answer the following questions:
a. Why does the *PPF* for education goods and services and consumption goods and services bow outward?
b. At what point on the blue *PPF* in Fig. 1 on p. 51 is the combination of education goods and services and consumption goods and services efficient? Explain your answer.
c. Students face rising tuition. Does higher tuition change the opportunity cost of education?
d. Who receives the benefits from education? Is the marginal cost of education equal to marginal benefit? Is resource use in the market for education efficient?

2. Use the links on the Parkin Web site and obtain data on the tuition and other costs of enrolling in the MBA program of a school that interests you. If an MBA graduate can earn as much as the amounts reported in the news article in *Reading Between the Lines* on pp. 50–51, does the marginal benefit of an MBA exceed its marginal cost? Why doesn't everyone study for an MBA?

Understanding the Scope of Economics

PART 1

Your Economic Revolution

You are making progress in your study of economics. You've already encountered the big questions and big ideas of economics. And you've learned about the key insight of Adam Smith, the founder of economics: specialization and exchange create economic wealth. ◆ You are studying economics at a time that future historians will call the *Information Revolution*. We reserve the word 'Revolution' for big events that influence all future generations. ◆ During the *Agricultural Revolution*, which occurred 10,000 years ago, people learned to domesticate animals and plant crops. They stopped roaming in search of food and settled in villages and eventually towns and cities, where they developed markets in which to exchange their products. ◆ During the *Industrial Revolution*, which began 240 years ago, people used science to create new technologies. This revolution brought extraordinary wealth for some but created conditions in which others were left behind. It brought social and political tensions that we still face today. ◆ During today's *Information Revolution*, people who have the ability and opportunity to embrace the new technologies are prospering on an unimagined scale. But the incomes and living standards of the less educated are falling behind, and social and political tensions are increasing. Today's revolution has a global dimension. Some of the winners live in previously poor countries in Asia, and some of the

losers live here in the United States. ◆ So you are studying economics at an interesting time. Whatever *your* motivation is for studying economics, *my* objective is to help you do well in your course, to enjoy it, and to develop a deeper understanding of the economic world around you. ◆ There are three reasons why I hope that we both succeed: First, a decent understanding of economics will help you to become a full participant in the Information Revolution. Second, an understanding of economics will help you play a more effective role as a citizen and voter and enable you to add your voice to those who are looking for solutions to our social and political problems. Third, you will enjoy the sheer fun of *understanding* the forces at play and how they are shaping our world. ◆ If you are finding economics interesting, think seriously about majoring in the subject. A degree in economics gives the best training available in problem solving, offers lots of opportunities to develop conceptual skills, and opens doors to a wide range of graduate courses, including the MBA, and to a wide range of jobs. You can read more about the benefits of an economics degree in Robert Whaples's essay in your *Study Guide*. ◆ Economics was born during the Industrial Revolution. We'll look at its birth and meet its founder, Adam Smith. Then we'll talk about economic revolutions and other matters with one of today's leading economists, Nobel Laureate, Professor Douglass North of Washington University in St. Louis.

Probing the Ideas

The Sources of Economic Wealth

The Father of Economics

Adam Smith *was a giant of a scholar who contributed to ethics and jurisprudence as well as economics. Born in 1723 in Kirkcaldy, a small fishing town near Edinburgh, Scotland, Smith was the only child of the town's customs officer (who died before Adam was born).*

His first academic appointment, at age 28, was as Professor of Logic at the University of Glasgow. He subsequently became tutor to a wealthy Scottish duke, whom he accompanied on a two-year grand European tour, following which he received a pension of £300 a year—ten times the average income at that time.

With the financial security of his pension, Smith devoted ten years to writing An Inquiry into the Nature and Causes of **The Wealth of Nations**, *which was published in 1776. Many people had written on economic issues before Adam Smith, but he made economics a science. Smith's account was so broad and authoritative that no subsequent writer on economics could advance ideas without tracing their connections to those of Adam Smith.*

> "It is not from the benevolence of the butcher, the brewer, or the baker that we expect our dinner, but from their regard to their own interest."
>
> ADAM SMITH
> *The Wealth of Nations*

The Issues

Why are some nations wealthy while others are poor? This question lies at the heart of economics. And it leads directly to a second question: What can poor nations do to become wealthy?

Adam Smith, who is regarded by many scholars as the founder of economics, attempted to answer these questions in his book *The Wealth of Nations*, published in 1776. Smith was pondering these questions at the height of the Industrial Revolution. During these years, new technologies were invented and applied to the manufacture of cotton and wool cloth, iron, transportation, and agriculture.

Smith wanted to understand the sources of economic wealth, and he brought his acute powers of observation and abstraction to bear on the question. His answer:

- The division of labor
- Free markets

The division of labor—breaking tasks down into simple tasks and becoming skilled in those tasks—is the source of "the greatest improvement in the productive powers of labor," said Smith. The division of labor became even more productive when it was applied to creating new technologies. Scientists and engineers, trained in extremely narrow fields, became specialists at inventing. Their powerful skills accelerated the advance of technology, so by the 1820s, machines could make consumer goods faster and more accurately than any craftsman could. And by the 1850s, machines could make other machines that labor alone could never have made.

But, said Smith, the fruits of the division of labor are limited by the extent of the market. To make the market as large as possible, there must be no impediments to free trade both within a country and among countries. Smith argued that when each person makes the best possible economic choice, that choice leads as if by "an invisible hand" to the best outcome for society as a whole. The butcher, the brewer, and the baker each pursue their own interests but, in doing so, also serve the interests of everyone else.

Then

Adam Smith speculated that one person, working hard, using the hand tools available in the 1770s, might possibly make 20 pins a day. Yet, he observed, by using those same hand tools but breaking the process into a number of individually small operations in which people specialize—by the **division of labor**—ten people could make a staggering 48,000 pins a day. One draws out the wire, another straightens it, a third cuts it, a fourth points it, a fifth grinds it. Three specialists make the head, and a fourth attaches it. Finally, the pin is polished and packaged. But a large market is needed to support the division of labor: One factory employing ten workers would need to sell more than 15 million pins a year to stay in business.

Now

If Adam Smith were here today, the computer chip would fascinate him. He would see it as an extraordinary example of the productivity of the division of labor and of the use of machines to make machines that make other machines. From a design of a chip's intricate circuits, cameras transfer an image to glass plates that work like stencils. Workers prepare silicon wafers on which the circuits are printed. Some slice the wafers, others polish them, others bake them, and yet others coat them with a light-sensitive chemical. Machines transfer a copy of the circuit onto the wafer. Chemicals then etch the design onto the wafer. Further processes deposit atom-sized transistors and aluminum connectors. Finally, a laser separates the hundreds of chips on the wafer. Every stage in the process of creating a computer chip uses other computer chips. And like the pin of the 1770s, the computer chip of the 1990s benefits from a large market—a global market—to buy chips in the huge quantities in which they are produced efficiently.

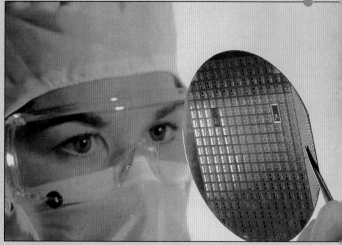

Many economists have worked on the big themes that Adam Smith began. One of these economists is Douglass North, of Washington University, whom you can meet on the following pages.

Douglass North, *who teaches economics and economic history at Washington University in St. Louis, was born in Cambridge, Massachusetts, in 1920. He was an undergraduate and graduate student at the University of California, Berkeley, where he earned his Ph.D. in 1952. Professor North has pioneered the study of economic institutions such as stable government, the rule of law, and private property rights and the role these institutions play in fostering economic development and sustained income growth. He has used his ideas to explain why the United States and*

Douglass North

Western Europe have evolved from low-income agricultural societies 200 years ago into high-income complex societies today. In 1993, Professor North was awarded the Nobel Prize for Economic Science for this work. Michael Parkin talked with Professor North about his work and its relevance to today's—and tomorrow's—world.

Professor North, what attracted you to economics?

I grew up during the Great Depression, and when I was a student at the University of California at Berkeley, I became a Marxist. I thought that Marxists had the answers to the economic concerns that were so prevalent during the Depression. If the market economy of capitalism was replaced by the planned economy of socialism, the Depression and other economic ills could, I then believed, be cured.

At Berkeley, I looked for courses that would enable me to understand why some countries were rich and some poor. That is how I was drawn toward economic history.

After I graduated, World War II broke out, and I spent four years in the Merchant Marine. During those years, I read a whole slew of books. I decided that I wanted to save the world—like any good Marxist wanted to—and I decided that the way to save it was to understand what made economies work badly and work well. And I've been pursuing that utopian goal ever since.

How did you abandon your Marxist beginning? Was there a sudden revelation or was it a gradual process?

Converting from Marxism was a very slow process. My first teaching job was at the University of Washington in Seattle in 1950. I used to play chess every day with my colleague, Donald Gordon. He was a good economist, and over three years of playing chess every day and talking economics, I gradually evolved away from Marxism and became a mainstream economist.

What are the key economic principles that guide your work—the principles and perspectives the economist brings to a study of long-term historical processes?

There are two. The first is the importance of transactions costs—the costs that people incur in order to do business with each other.

Economics attempts to understand how societies cope with the problem of scarcity—with the fact that people's wants always outstrip their limited resources. Traditionally, economists have focused on how resources are allocated at a moment of time—what determines today's allocation of spending between high schools and hospitals, computers and cars. Economic history deals with how societies evolve over time and tries to discover why some societies become wealthy while others remain poor. I became convinced that the economic way of reasoning underlying the economic principles is the right way to understand how societies evolve over time. But this conviction led me on a long trail.

Back in the days when I was learning economics, economic theories were based on the *assumption* that people could specialize and exchange their products in markets that function efficiently. They ignored transaction costs—the costs that people incur when they do business with each other and the costs that governments and firms incur to make markets work. So the first problem was to think about how exchange takes place in the face of large transactions costs.

And the second principle?
The second principle is that transactions costs depend crucially on the way that human beings structure the economic order—on their institutions. And this fact gave me my second problem, to think about how institutions evolve to make markets work better over time.

When an economist talks about economic institutions, what exactly is he or she talking about? What are these institutions?
Institutions are rules of the society that structure the interaction among people. Institutions are made up of formal rules, like constitutions and statute law, and common rules and regulations. But they're also more than that. They are the informal ways by which people deal with each other every day, which you could think of as norms of behavior.

Institutions are the framework within which all of human interaction—political, social, and economic—takes place. And so, understanding how those work, why they work well in some circumstances, and why they work badly in others is the key, really, to the wealth of nations. Some examples of economic institutions include antitrust laws, patent laws, and bankruptcy laws.

Can economists explain the radically different institutional evolution of the United States and Russia?
This question is at the very heart of what economic history should be about. The United States inherited a set of institutions—among them common law and property rights—from Great Britain. These institutions had made Britain the world's leading nation by the end of the eighteenth century. The United States modified Britain's institutions and elaborated on them. The result has been two and a half centuries of economic growth. Much of the rest of the world, and Russia in particular,

evolved institutions that didn't work very well.

In Britain and the United States, the governments evolved a set of rules that provided a lot of freedom and latitude for people to make contracts and agreements among themselves. These rules produced economic efficiency on an unparalleled scale and led to sustained economic growth.

Russia, as well as some other Eastern European and Third World countries, chose a different economic path based on Communism, which turned out to be an institution that could not sustain economic growth.

The goal of research in economic development and economic history is to understand exactly what led to this very different process of change among countries such as the United States and Russia.

> To have efficient markets, a country needs rules and regulations that provide incentives for people to be creative and become increasingly productive.

How do you explain the economic success of China and economic failure of Russia?
China had political authoritarianism at the top, and those authorities have either deliberately or accidentally loosened control in the provinces. The result has made for a very lucrative combination of local Communist Party officials teaming up with entrepreneurs, who got their capital and sometimes their training from the

governments of Hong Kong and Taiwan, being let loose to pursue business ventures. And that's a unique situation. This certainly doesn't appear likely to happen in the former Soviet Union.

I think the biggest economic lessons are from successful Asian economies. Despite recent setbacks, countries such as South Korea and Taiwan show us that a proper dose of government can accelerate the process of creating efficient markets. To have efficient markets, a country needs rules and regulations that provide incentives for people to be creative and to become increasingly productive. We also learn from the Asian crisis and recession of 1998 that the conditions for efficient markets change over time as technologies and market conditions change. This ongoing change requires continual updating of the rules to maintain efficient conditions. It doesn't happen automatically. Asia has shown us that while governments can sometimes hasten the evolution of efficient markets, they can also sometimes thwart the continuation of efficient markets.

How would you characterize the changes that are taking place in today's global and national economy?

I look at economic revolutions as changes in knowledge that fundamentally changed the whole economic social organization of societies. The origin and development of agriculture were the first economic revolution. This economic revolution probably occurred in the eighth millennium

B.C. Agriculture completely altered the pace of economic and all other kinds of human change. Human beings settled down into villages and towns. This eventually led to the growth of exchange and to the whole basis for civilization. Agriculture enormously increased productivity potential and the potential for human progress.

The next real fundamental economic change was the application of science to technology. I would say there's never been a time in human history in which there's been as dramatic a setting of change as we're seeing in the world we live in today. I think it's extraordinary. It's a very exciting world to live in, particularly for an economic historian. I have argued that something happened in the nineteenth century, which I call the Second Economic Revolution: There was a systematic wedding of science to technology that led to the development of the disciplines of physics, chemistry, genetics, and biology. This revolution has completely changed the way in which all of modern economic activity takes place and the way that human beings live and interact.

The personal and social implications of that revolution are enormous. As a result of this revolution, we live packed together in huge cities, many of which are plagued by crime on a scale that frightens us, and we depend for our economic well-being on millions of people we do not know. Many people have benefited from the advances in technology and enjoy unimagined high living standards, while many others have

been left behind and are not sharing in the prosperity that the second economic revolution has created. So, combined with the prosperity of this economic revolution, we've created a set of social, political, and economic problems that we haven't figured out how to solve. And they may overwhelm us down the road.

> I think the most important thing in the world is to have a creative, stimulating, exciting life. . . . Find out what things excite you, and pursue them all your life.

What is your advice to a student who is just setting out to become an economist? How should the student approach his or her work? What are the things to study?

You should find excitement and challenge in the things you do and pursue them. At a university, this means that you ought to bug your professors. You should be continually trying to get a lot out of them. I think most university students don't get out of school what they could. Both in and out of class, you should ask questions and pursue the answers to those questions. I think that's terribly important.

I think the most important thing in the world is to have a creative, stimulating, exciting life. Everybody can do that in their own way, depending on their own curiosities, interests, and talents. Find out what things excite you, and pursue them all your life.

Chapter 4

Demand and Supply

Slide, rocket, and roller coaster—
Disneyland rides? No. Commonly
used descriptions of price changes. ◆ CD
players have taken a price slide from around
$1,100 (in today's money) in 1983 to less than
$100 today. And during these years, the quantity of
CD players bought has increased steadily. What caused
this price slide? Why didn't brisk buying keep the
price high? ◆ The price of health care has rocketed. Yet despite
rocketing prices, people buy more health services every year. Why?
◆ The prices of bananas, coffee, and other agricultural commodities
follow a roller coaster. Why does the price of bananas roller-coaster
even when people's tastes for bananas barely change? ◆ The prices of
many things we buy are remarkably steady. For example, the price of an

Slide, Rocket, and Roller Coaster

audio cassette tape has not changed much.
But despite its steady price, the number of
tapes people buy increases each year. Why do
people buy more tapes even though their
price is no lower than it was a decade ago?
And why do firms sell more tapes even
though they can't get higher prices for them?
◆ Economics is about the choices people
make to cope with scarcity. These choices are guided by costs and benefits and are coordinated through markets. ◆ The tool that explains how
markets work is demand and supply. It is central to the whole of economics. It is used to study issues as diverse as wages and jobs, rents and
housing, pollution, crime, consumer protection, education, welfare,
health care, the value of money, and interest rates.

◆ Your careful study of this topic will bring big rewards both in
your further study of economics and in your everyday life. Once you
understand demand and supply, you will view the world through new
eyes. When you have completed your study of demand and supply,
you will be able to explain how prices are determined and make predictions about price slides, rockets, and roller coasters. But first, we're
going to take a closer look at the idea of price. Just what is a price?

After studying this chapter, you will be able to:

- Distinguish between a money price and a relative price
- Explain the main influences on demand
- Explain the main influences on supply
- Explain how prices and quantities bought and sold are determined by demand and supply
- Explain why some prices fall, some rise, and some fluctuate
- Use demand and supply to make predictions about price changes

Price and Opportunity Cost

ECONOMIC ACTIONS ARISE FROM SCARCITY—WANTS exceed the resources available to satisfy them. Faced with *scarcity*, we must make choices. And to make choices, we compare *costs* and *benefits*. Choices are influenced by opportunity costs. Producers offer items for sale only if the price is high enough to cover their opportunity cost. And consumers respond to changing opportunity cost by seeking cheaper alternatives to expensive items.

We are going to study the way people respond to *prices* and the forces that determine prices. But to pursue these tasks, we need to understand the relationship between a price and an opportunity cost.

In everyday life, the *price* of an object is the number of dollars that must be given up in exchange for it. Economists refer to this price as the *money price*.

The *opportunity cost* of an action is the highest-valued alternative forgone. If, when you buy a cup of coffee, the highest-valued thing you forgo is some gum, then the opportunity cost of buying a coffee is the *quantity* of gum forgone. We can calculate this quantity from the money prices of coffee and gum.

If the money price of coffee is $1 a cup and the money price of gum is 50¢ a pack, then the opportunity cost of one cup of coffee is two packs of gum. To calculate this opportunity cost, we divide the price of a cup of coffee by the price of a pack of gum and find the *ratio* of one price to the other. The ratio of one price to another is called a **relative price**, and a *relative price is an opportunity cost.*

We can express the relative price of coffee in terms of gum or any other good. The normal way of expressing a relative price is in terms of a "basket" of all goods and services. To calculate this relative price, we divide the money price of a good by the money price of a "basket" of all goods (called a *price index*). The resulting relative price is expressed in the buying power of money in a particular year. It tells us the opportunity cost of an item in terms of how much of the "basket" we must give up to buy it.

Figure 4.1 shows the money price and the relative price of wheat. The money price (green) has fluctuated but has tended to rise. The relative price (red) peaked in 1974 and has tended to fall since that year.

The theory of demand and supply that we are about to study determines *relative prices,* and the word "price" means *relative* price. When we predict that a price will fall, we do not mean that its *money*

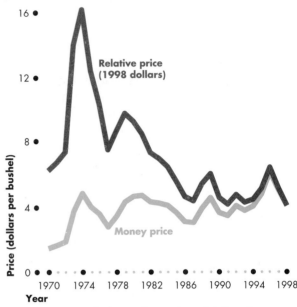

FIGURE 4.1

The Price of Wheat

The money price of wheat—the number of dollars that must be given up for a bushel of wheat—has fluctuated between $1.50 and $6.20. But the *relative* price or *opportunity cost* of wheat, expressed in 1998 dollars, has fluctuated between $4.10 and $16.25 and has tended to fall. The fall in the relative price of wheat is obscured by the behavior of the money price.

Sources: International Financial Statistics, International Monetary Fund, Washington, DC, 1999.

price will fall—although it might. We mean that its *relative* price will fall. That is, its price will fall *relative* to the average price of other goods and services.

R E V I E W   Q U I Z

- Explain the distinction between a money price and a relative price.
- Why is a relative price an opportunity cost?
- Can you think of an example of a good whose money price and relative price have risen?
- Can you think of an example of a good whose money price and relative price have fallen?

Let's now begin our study of demand and supply, starting with demand.

Demand

IF YOU DEMAND SOMETHING, THEN YOU

1. Want it,
2. Can afford it, and
3. Have made a definite plan to buy it.

Wants are the unlimited desires or wishes that people have for goods and services. How many times have you thought that you would like something "if only you could afford it" or "if it weren't so expensive"? Scarcity guarantees that many—perhaps most—of our wants will never be satisfied. Demand reflects a decision about which wants to satisfy.

The **quantity demanded** of a good or service is the amount that consumers plan to buy during a given time period at a particular price. The quantity demanded is not necessarily the same amount as the quantity actually bought. Sometimes the quantity demanded is greater than the amount of goods available, so the quantity bought is less than the quantity demanded.

The quantity demanded is measured as an amount per unit of time. For example, suppose that you consume one cup of coffee a day. The quantity of coffee that you demand can be expressed as 1 cup a day or 7 cups a week or 365 cups a year. Without a time dimension, we cannot tell whether a particular quantity demanded is large or small.

What Determines Buying Plans?

The amount of any particular good or service that consumers plan to buy depends on many factors. The main ones are:

1. The price of the good
2. The prices of related goods
3. Expected future prices
4. Income
5. Population
6. Preferences

We first look at the relationship between the quantity demanded and the price of a good. To study this relationship, we hold constant all other influences on consumers' planned purchases and ask: How does the quantity demanded of the good vary as its price varies, other things remaining the same?

The Law of Demand

The law of demand states:

Other things remaining the same, the higher the price of a good, the smaller is the quantity demanded.

Why does a higher price reduce the quantity demanded? For two reasons:

1. Substitution effect
2. Income effect

Substitution Effect   When the price of a good rises, other things remaining the same, its *relative* price—its opportunity cost—rises. Although each good is unique, it has *substitutes*—other goods that can be used in its place. As the opportunity cost of a good rises, people buy less of that good and more of its substitutes.

Income Effect   When a price changes and all other influences on buying plans remain unchanged, the price rises *relative* to people's incomes. So faced with a higher price and an unchanged income, people cannot afford to buy all the things they previously bought. The quantities demanded of at least some goods and services must be decreased. Normally, the good whose price has increased is one of those bought in a smaller quantity.

To see the substitution effect and the income effect at work, think about the effects of changes in the price of blank audio cassette tapes. Many different goods provide a service similar to that provided by a tape. For example, a compact disc, a prerecorded tape, a radio or television broadcast, and a live concert all provide similar services to a tape. Suppose that tapes initially sell for $3 each and then the price doubles to $6. People now substitute compact discs and prerecorded tapes for blank tapes—the substitution effect. And faced with a tighter budget, they buy fewer tapes as well as less of other goods and services—the income effect. The quantity of tapes demanded decreases for these two reasons.

Now suppose the price of a tape falls to $1. People now substitute blank tapes for compact discs and prerecorded tapes—the substitution effect. And with a budget that now has some slack from the lower price of tapes, people buy more tapes as well as more of other goods and services—the income effect. The quantity of tapes demanded increases for these two reasons.

Demand Curve and Demand Schedule

You are now about to study one of the two most used curves in economics, the demand curve. And you are going to encounter one of the most critical distinctions: the distinction between *demand* and *quantity demanded*.

The term **demand** refers to the entire relationship between the quantity demanded and the price of a good, and it is illustrated by the demand curve and the demand schedule. The term *quantity demanded* refers to a point on a demand curve—the quantity demanded at a particular price.

Figure 4.2 shows the demand curve for tapes. A **demand curve** shows the relationship between the quantity demanded of a good and its price when all other influences on consumers' planned purchases remain the same.

The table in Fig. 4.2 is the demand schedule for tapes. A *demand schedule* lists the quantities demanded at each different price when all the other influences on consumers' planned purchases—such as income, population, preferences, and future prices—remain the same. For example, if the price of a tape is $1, the quantity demanded is 9 million tapes a week. If the price of a tape is $5, the quantity demanded is 2 million tapes a week. The other rows of the table show the quantities demanded at prices of $2, $3, and $4.

We graph the demand schedule as a demand curve with the quantity demanded on the horizontal axis and the price on the vertical axis. The points on the demand curve labeled *a* through *e* represent the rows of the demand schedule. For example, point *a* on the graph represents a quantity demanded of 9 million tapes a week at a price of $1 a tape.

Willingness and Ability to Pay   Another way of looking at the demand curve is as a willingness-and-ability-to-pay curve. And the willingness-and-ability-to-pay is a measure of *marginal benefit.*

If a small quantity is available, the highest price that someone is willing and able to pay for one more unit is high. But as the quantity available increases, the marginal benefit of each additional unit falls and the highest price that someone is willing and able to pay for it also falls along the demand curve.

In Fig. 4.2, if 2 million tapes are available each week, the highest price that someone is willing to pay for the 2 millionth tape is $5. But if 9 million tapes are available each week, someone is willing to pay only $1 for the last tape bought.

FIGURE 4.2

The Demand Curve

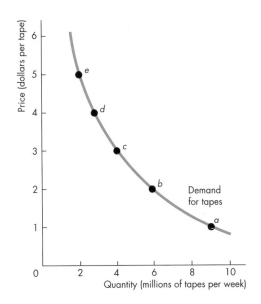

	Price (dollars per tape)	Quantity (millions of tapes per week)
a	1	9
b	2	6
c	3	4
d	4	3
e	5	2

The table shows a demand schedule listing the quantity of tapes demanded at each price if all other influences on buyers' plans remain the same. At a price of $1 a tape, 9 million tapes a week are demanded; at a price of $3 a tape, 4 million tapes a week are demanded. The demand curve shows the relationship between quantity demanded and price, everything else remaining the same.

The demand curve slopes downward: As price decreases, the quantity demanded increases. The demand curve can be read in two ways. For a given price, it tells us the quantity that people plan to buy. For example, at a price of $3 a tape, the quantity demanded is 4 million tapes a week. For a given quantity, the demand curve tells us the maximum price that consumers are willing and able to pay for the last tape available. For example, the maximum price that consumers will pay for the 6 millionth tape is $2.

A Change in Demand

When any factor that influences buying plans other than the price of the good changes, there is a **change in demand**. Figure 4.3 illustrates an increase in demand. When demand increases, the demand curve shifts rightward and the quantity demanded is greater at each and every price. For example, at a price of $5, on the original (blue) demand curve, the quantity demanded is 2 million tapes a week. On the new (red) demand curve, the quantity demanded is 6 million tapes a week. Look closely at the numbers in the table in Fig. 4.3 and check that the quantity demanded is higher at each price.

Let's look at the factors that bring a change in demand. There are five key factors to consider.

1. Prices of Related Goods　The quantity of tapes that consumers plan to buy depends in part on the prices of substitutes for tapes. A **substitute** is a good that can be used in place of another good. For example, a bus ride is a substitute for a train ride; a hamburger is a substitute for a hot dog, and a compact disc is a substitute for a tape. If the price of a substitute for a tape increases, people buy less of the substitute and more tapes. For example, if the price of a CD rises, people buy fewer CDs and more tapes. The demand for tapes increases.

The quantity of tapes that people plan to buy also depends on the prices of complements of tapes. A **complement** is a good that is used in conjunction with another good. Hamburgers and fries are complements. So are spaghetti and meat sauce, and so are tapes and Walkmans. If the price of a Walkman falls, people buy more Walkmans *and more tapes*. It is a fall in the price of a Walkman that increases the demand for tapes in Fig. 4.3.

2. Expected Future Prices　If the price of a good is expected to rise in the future and if the good can be stored, the opportunity cost of obtaining the good for future use is lower now than it will be when the price has increased. So people retime their purchase—they substitute over time. They buy more of the good now before its price is expected to rise (and less after), so the current demand for the good increases.

For example, suppose that Florida is hit by a severe frost that damages the season's orange crop. You expect the price of orange juice to soar. So, anticipating the higher price, you fill your freezer with enough frozen juice to get you through the next six months. Your current demand for frozen orange juice has increased (and your future demand has decreased).

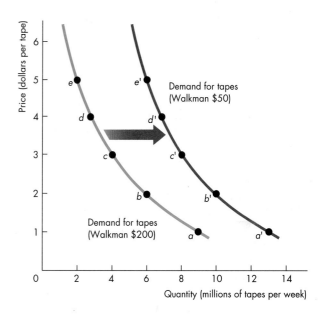

FIGURE 4.3

An Increase in Demand

Original demand schedule Walkman $200			New demand schedule Walkman $50		
	Price (dollars per tape)	Quantity (millions of tapes per week)		Price (dollars per tape)	Quantity (millions of tapes per week)
a	1	9	a'	1	13
b	2	6	b'	2	10
c	3	4	c'	3	8
d	4	3	d'	4	7
e	5	2	e'	5	6

A change in any influence on buyers' plans other than the price of the good itself results in a new demand schedule and a shift of the demand curve. A change in the price of a Walkman changes the demand for tapes. At a price of $3 a tape (row *c* of the table), 4 million tapes a week are demanded when the Walkman costs $200 and 8 million tapes a week are demanded when the Walkman costs only $50. A *fall* in the price of a Walkman *increases* the demand for tapes because the Walkman is a complement of tapes. When demand *increases,* the demand curve shifts *rightward,* as shown by the shift arrow and the resulting red curve.

Similarly, if the price of a good is expected to fall in the future, the opportunity cost of buying the good in the present is high relative to what it is expected to be in the future. So again, people retime their purchases. They buy less of the good now before its price is expected to fall (and more after), so the current demand for the good decreases.

Computer prices are constantly falling, and this fact poses a dilemma. Will you buy a new computer now, in time for the start of the school year, or will you wait until the price has fallen some more? Because people expect computer prices to keep falling, the current demand for computers is less (the future demand is greater) than it otherwise would be.

3. Income   Another influence on demand is consumer income. When income increases, consumers buy more of most goods, and when income decreases, they buy less of most goods. Although an increase in income leads to an increase in the demand for *most* goods, it does not lead to an increase in the demand for *all* goods. A **normal good** is one for which demand increases as income increases. An **inferior good** is one for which demand decreases as income increases. Long-distance transportation has examples of both normal goods and inferior goods. As incomes increase, the demand for air travel (a normal good) increases and the demand for long-distance bus trips (an inferior good) decreases.

4. Population   Demand also depends on the size and the age structure of the population. The larger the population, the greater is the demand for all goods and services. And the smaller the population, the smaller is the demand for all goods and services.

For example, the demand for car parking spaces or movies or tapes or just about anything you can imagine is much greater in New York City (population 7.5 million) than it is in Boise, Idaho (population 150,000).

Also, the larger the proportion of the population in a given age group, the greater is the demand for the types of goods and services used by that age group.

For example, between 1988 and 1998, the number of 20–24 year olds in the United States decreased by 2 million. As a result, the demand for college places decreased during those years. During those same years, the number of Americans aged 85 years and over increased by more than 1 million. As a result, the demand for nursing home services increased.

TABLE 4.1

The Demand for Tapes

The Law of Demand

The quantity of tapes demanded

Decreases if:	*Increases if:*
■ The price of a tape rises	■ The price of a tape falls

Changes in Demand

The demand for tapes

Decreases if:	*Increases if:*
■ The price of a substitute falls	■ The price of a substitute rises
■ The price of a complement rises	■ The price of a complement falls
■ The price of a tape is expected to fall in the future	■ The price of a tape is expected to rise in the future
■ Income falls*	■ Income rises*
■ The population decreases	■ The population increases

*A tape is a normal good.

---

5. Preferences   Demand depends on preferences. *Preferences* are an individual's attitudes toward goods and services. For example, a rock music fanatic has a much greater taste for tapes than does a tone-deaf workaholic. As a consequence, even if they have the same incomes, their demands for tapes will be very different.

Table 4.1 summarizes the influences on demand and the direction of those influences.

A Change in the Quantity Demanded Versus a Change in Demand

Changes in the factors that influence buyers' plans cause either a change in the quantity demanded or a change in demand. Equivalently, they cause either a movement along the demand curve or a shift of the demand curve.

The distinction between a change in the quantity demanded and a change in demand is the same as that between a movement along the demand curve and a shift of the demand curve.

A point on the demand curve shows the quantity demanded at a given price. So a movement along the demand curve shows a **change in the quantity demanded**. The entire demand curve shows demand. So a shift of the demand curve shows a **change in demand**. Figure 4.4 illustrates and summarizes these distinctions.

Movement Along the Demand Curve   If the price of a good changes but everything else remains the same, there is a movement along the demand curve. The negative slope of the demand curve reveals that a decrease in the price of a good or service increases the quantity demanded—the law of demand.

In Fig. 4.4, if the price of a good falls when everything else remains the same, the quantity demanded of that good increases and there is a movement down the demand curve D_0. If the price rises when everything else remains the same, the quantity demanded decreases and there is a movement up the demand curve D_0.

A Shift of the Demand Curve   If the price of a good remains constant but some other influence on buyers' plans changes, there is a change in demand for that good. We illustrate a change in demand as a shift of the demand curve. For example, a fall in the price of the Walkman—a complement of tapes—increases the demand for tapes. We illustrate this increase in the demand for tapes with a new demand schedule and a new demand curve. If the price of the Walkman falls, consumers buy more tapes regardless of whether the price of a tape is high or low. That is what a rightward shift of the demand curve shows—that more tapes are bought at each and every price.

In Fig. 4.4, when any influence on buyers' planned purchases changes, other than the price of the good, the demand curve shifts and there is a *change* (an increase or a decrease) *in demand*. A rise in income (for a normal good), in population, in the price of a substitute, or in the expected future price of the good or a fall in the price of a complement shifts the demand curve rightward (to the red demand curve D_1). This represents an *increase in demand*. A fall in income (for a normal good), in population, in the price of a substitute, or in the expected future price of the good or a rise in the price of a complement shifts the demand curve leftward (to the red demand curve D_2). This represents a *decrease in demand*. (For an inferior good, the effects of changes in income are in the direction opposite to those described above.)

FIGURE 4.4

A Change in the Quantity Demanded Versus a Change in Demand

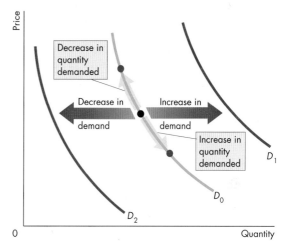

When the price of the good changes, there is a movement along the demand curve and a *change in the quantity demanded*, shown by the blue arrows on demand curve D_0. When any other influence on buying plans changes, there is a shift of the demand curve and a *change in demand*. An increase in demand shifts the demand curve rightward (from D_0 to D_1). A decrease in demand shifts the demand curve leftward (from D_0 to D_2).

REVIEW QUIZ

- Can you define the *quantity demanded* of a good or service?
- What is the *law of demand* and how do we illustrate it?
- If a fixed amount of a good is available, what does the demand curve tell us about the price that consumers are willing to pay for that fixed quantity?
- Can you list all the influences on buying plans that *change demand* and for each influence say whether it increases demand or decreases demand?
- What happens to the quantity of CDs demanded and the demand for CDs if the price of a CD falls and all other influences on buying plans remain the same?

Supply

IF A FIRM SUPPLIES A GOOD OR SERVICE, THE FIRM

1. Has the resources and technology to produce it,
2. Can profit from producing it, and
3. Has made a definite plan to produce it and sell it.

A supply is more that just having the *resources* and the *technology* to produce something. *Resources and technology* are the constraints that limit what is possible.

Many useful things can be produced, but they are not produced unless it is profitable to do so. Supply reflects a decision about which technologically feasible items to produce.

The **quantity supplied** of a good or service is the amount that producers plan to sell during a given time period at a particular price. The quantity supplied is not necessarily the same amount as the quantity actually sold. Sometimes the quantity supplied is greater than the quantity demanded, so the quantity bought is less than the quantity supplied.

Like the quantity demanded, the quantity supplied is measured as an amount per unit of time. For example, suppose that GM produces 1,000 cars a day. The quantity of cars supplied by GM can be expressed as 1,000 a day or 7,000 a week or 365,000 a year. Without the time dimension, we cannot tell whether a particular number is large or small.

What Determines Selling Plans?

The amount of any particular good or service that producers plan to sell depends on many factors. The main ones are:

1. The price of the good
2. The prices of resources used to produce the good
3. The prices of related goods produced
4. Expected future prices
5. The number of suppliers
6. Technology

Let's first look at the relationship between the price of a good and the quantity supplied. To study this relationship, we hold constant all the other influences on the quantity supplied. We ask: How does the quantity supplied of a good vary as its price varies?

The Law of Supply

The law of supply states:

Other things remaining the same, the higher the price of a good, the greater is the quantity supplied.

Why does a higher price increase the quantity supplied? It is because of *increasing marginal cost*. As the quantity produced of any good increases, the marginal cost of producing the good increases. (You can refresh your memory of increasing marginal cost in Chapter 3, p. 40.)

It is never worth producing a good if the price received for it does not at least cover marginal cost. So when the price of a good rises, other things remaining the same, producers are willing to incur the higher marginal cost and increase production. The higher price brings forth an increase in the quantity supplied.

Let's now illustrate the law of supply with a supply curve and a supply schedule.

Supply Curve and Supply Schedule

You are now going to study the second of the two most used curves in economics, the supply curve. And you're going to learn about the critical distinction between *supply* and *quantity supplied*.

The term **supply** refers to the entire relationship between the quantity supplied and the price of a good, and it is illustrated by the supply curve and the supply schedule. The term *quantity supplied* refers to a point on a supply curve—the quantity supplied at a particular price.

Figure 4.5 shows the supply curve of tapes. A **supply curve** shows the relationship between the quantity supplied of a good and its price when all other influences on producers' planned sales remain the same. It is a graph of a supply schedule.

The table in Fig. 4.5 sets out the supply schedule for tapes. A *supply schedule* lists the quantities supplied at each different price when all the other influences on producers' planned sales remain the same. For example, if the price of a tape is $1, the quantity supplied is zero—on row *a* of the table. If the price of a tape is $2, the quantity supplied is 3 million tapes a week—on row *b*. The other rows of the table show the quantities supplied at prices of $3, $4, and $5.

FIGURE 4.5

The Supply Curve

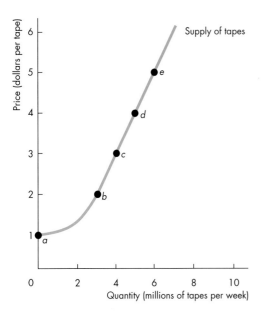

To make a supply curve, we graph the quantity supplied on the horizontal axis and the price on the vertical axis, just as in the case of the demand curve. The points on the supply curve labeled *a* through *e* represent the rows of the supply schedule. For example, point *a* on the graph represents a quantity supplied of zero at a price of $1 a tape.

Minimum Supply Price   Just as the demand curve has two interpretations, so too does the supply curve. The demand curve can be interpreted as a willingness-and-ability-to-pay curve. The supply curve can be interpreted as a minimum-supply-price curve. It tells us the lowest price at which someone can profitably sell another unit.

If a small quantity is produced, the lowest price at which someone can profitably sell one more unit is low. But if a large quantity is produced, the lowest price at which someone can profitably sell one more unit is high.

In Fig. 4.5, if 6 million tapes are produced each week, the lowest price that a producer is willing to accept for the 6 millionth tape is $5. But if only 4 million tapes are produced each week, the lowest price that a producer is willing to accept for the 4 millionth tape is $3.

	Price (dollars per tape)	Quantity (millions of tapes per week)
a	1	0
b	2	3
c	3	4
d	4	5
e	5	6

The table shows the supply schedule of tapes. For example, at $2 a tape, 3 million tapes a week are supplied; at $5 a tape, 6 million tapes a week are supplied. The supply curve shows the relationship between the quantity supplied and price, everything else remaining the same. The supply curve usually slopes upward: As the price of a good increases, so does the quantity supplied.

A supply curve can be read in two ways. For a given price, its tells us the quantity that producers plan to sell. And for a given quantity, it tells us the minimum price that producers are willing to accept for that quantity.

A Change in Supply

When any factor that influences selling plans other than the price of the good changes, there is a **change in supply**. Let's look at the five key factors that change supply.

1. Prices of Productive Resources   The prices of productive resources influence supply. The easiest way to see this influence is to think about the supply curve as a minimum-supply-price curve. If the prices of productive resources rise, the lowest price a producer is willing to accept rises so supply decreases. For example, during 1996, the price of jet fuel increased and the supply of air transportation decreased. Similarly, a rise in the minimum wage decreased the supply of hamburgers. If the wages of tape producers rise, the supply of tapes decreases.

2. Prices of Related Goods Produced   The prices of related goods and services that firms produce influence supply. For example, if the price of prerecorded tapes rises, the supply of blank tapes decreases. Blank tapes and prerecorded tapes are *substitutes in produc-*

tion—goods that can be produced by using the same resources. If the price of beef rises, the supply of cowhide increases. Beef and cowhide are *complements in production*—goods that must be produced together.

3. Expected Future Prices   If the price of a good is expected to rise, the return from selling the good in the future is higher than it is in the present. So the current supply decreases.

4. The Number of Suppliers   Supply also depends on the number of suppliers. The larger the number of firms that produce a good, the greater is the supply of the good. As firms enter an industry, the supply in that industry increases. As firms leave an industry, the supply in that industry decreases. For example, over the past two years, there has been a huge increase in the number of firms that produce and manage World Wide Web sites. As a result, the supply of Internet and World Wide Web services has increased enormously.

5. Technology   New technologies create new products and lower the costs of producing existing products. As a result they change supply. For example, the development of a new technology for tape production by Sony and Minnesota Mining and Manufacturing (3M) has lowered the cost of producing tapes and increased the supply of tapes.

Figure 4.6 illustrates an increase in supply. When supply increases, the supply curve shifts rightward and the quantity supplied is larger at each and every price. For example, at a price of $2, on the original (blue) supply curve, the quantity supplied is 3 million tapes a week. On the new (red) supply curve, the quantity supplied is 6 million tapes a week. Look closely at the numbers in the table in Fig. 4.6 and check that the quantity supplied is larger at each price.

Table 4.2 summarizes the influences on supply and the directions of those influences.

A Change in the Quantity Supplied Versus a Change in Supply

Changes in the factors that influence producers' planned sales cause either a change in the quantity supplied or a change in supply. Equivalently, they cause either a movement along the supply curve or a shift of the supply curve.

A point on the supply curve shows the quantity supplied at a given price. So a movement along the

FIGURE **4.6**

An Increase in Supply

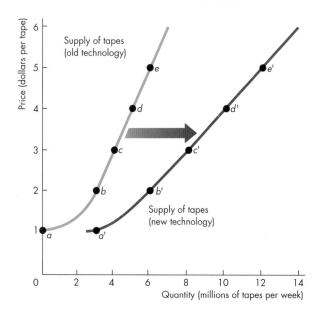

Original supply schedule Old technology		New supply schedule New technology	
Price (dollars per tape)	**Quantity** (millions of tapes per week)	**Price** (dollars per tape)	**Quantity** (millions of tapes per week)
a 1	0	*a'* 1	3
b 2	3	*b'* 2	6
c 3	4	*c'* 3	8
d 4	5	*d'* 4	10
e 5	6	*e'* 5	12

A change in any influence on sellers' plans other than the price of the good itself results in a new supply schedule and a shift of the supply curve. For example, if Sony and 3M invent a new, cost-saving technology for producing tapes, the supply of tapes changes.

At a price of $3 a tape, 4 million tapes a week are supplied when producers use the old technology (row *c* of the table) and 8 million tapes a week are supplied when producers use the new technology. An advance in technology *increases* the supply of tapes and shifts the supply curve *rightward*, as shown by the shift arrow and the resulting red curve.

supply curve shows a **change in the quantity supplied**. The entire supply curve shows supply. So a shift of the supply curve shows a **change in supply**.

Figure 4.7 illustrates and summarizes these distinctions. If the price of a good falls and everything else remains the same, the quantity supplied of that good decreases and there is a movement down the supply curve S_0. If the price of a good rises and everything else remains the same, the quantity supplied increases and there is a movement up the supply curve S_0. When any other influence on selling plans changes, the supply curve shifts and there is a change in supply. If the supply curve is S_0 and if production costs fall supply increases and the supply curve shifts to the red supply curve S_1. If production costs rise, supply decreases and the supply curve shifts to the red supply curve S_2.

TABLE 4.2

The Supply of Tapes

The Law of Supply

The quantity of tapes supplied

Decreases if:

- The price of a tape falls

Increases if:

- The price of a tape rises

Changes in Supply

The supply of tapes

Decreases if:

- The price of a resource used to produce tapes rises
- The price of a substitute in production rises
- The price of a complement in production falls
- The price of a tape is expected to rise in the future
- The number of tape producers decreases

Increases if:

- The price of a resource used to produce tapes falls
- The price of a substitute in production falls
- The price of a complement in production rises
- The price of a tape is expected to fall in the future
- The number of tape producers increases
- More efficient technologies for producing tapes are discovered

---

FIGURE 4.7

A Change in the Quantity Supplied Versus a Change in Supply

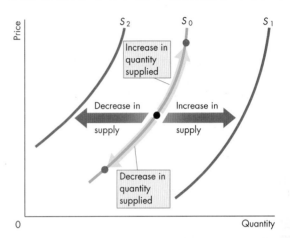

When the price of the good changes, there is a movement along the supply curve and a *change in the quantity supplied*, shown by the blue arrows on supply curve S_0. When any other influence on selling plans changes, there is a shift of the supply curve and a *change in supply*. An increase in supply shifts the supply curve rightward (from S_0 to S_1). A decrease in supply shifts the supply curve shifts leftward (from S_0 to S_2).

R E V I E W   Q U I Z

- Can you define the *quantity supplied* of a good or service?
- What is the *law of supply* and how do we illustrate it?
- If consumers are willing to buy only a given quantity, what does the supply curve tell us about the price at which firms will supply that quantity?
- Can you list all the influences on selling plans that *change supply* and for each influence say whether it increases supply or decreases supply?

Your next task is to use what you've learned about demand and supply and learn how prices and quantities are determined.

Market Equilibrium

WE HAVE SEEN THAT WHEN THE PRICE OF A GOOD rises, the quantity demanded decreases and the quantity supplied increases. We are now going to see how prices coordinate the plans of buyers and sellers and achieve an equilibrium.

An *equilibrium* is a situation in which opposing forces balance each other. Equilibrium in a market occurs when the price balances the plans of buyers and sellers. The **equilibrium price** is the price at which the quantity demanded equals the quantity supplied. The **equilibrium quantity** is the quantity bought and sold at the equilibrium price. A market moves toward its equilibrium because:

■ Price regulates buying and selling plans
■ Price adjusts when plans don't match

Price as a Regulator

The price of a good regulates the quantities demanded and supplied. If the price is too high, the quantity supplied exceeds the quantity demanded. If the price is too low, the quantity demanded exceeds the quantity supplied. There is one price at which the quantity demanded equals the quantity supplied. Let's work out what that price is.

Figure 4.8 shows the market for tapes. The table shows the demand schedule (from Fig. 4.2) and the supply schedule (from Fig. 4.5). If the price of a tape is $1, the quantity demanded is 9 million tapes a week, but no tapes are supplied. The quantity demanded exceeds the quantity supplied by 9 million tapes a week. In other words, at a price of $1 a tape, there is a shortage of 9 million tapes a week. This shortage is shown in the final column of the table. At a price of $2 a tape, there is still a shortage, but only of 3 million tapes a week. If the price of a tape is $5, the quantity supplied exceeds the quantity demanded. The quantity supplied is 6 million tapes a week, but the quantity demanded is only 2 million. There is a surplus of 4 million tapes a week. The one price at which there is neither a shortage nor a surplus is $3 a tape. At that price, the quantity demanded is equal to the quantity supplied: 4 million tapes a week. The equilibrium price is $3 a tape, and the equilibrium quantity is 4 million tapes a week.

Figure 4.8 shows that the demand curve and supply curve intersect at the equilibrium price of $3 a

FIGURE 4.8
Equilibrium

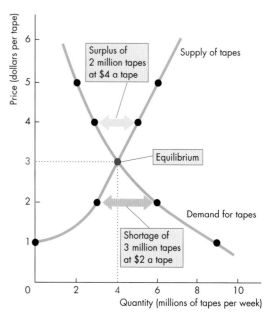

Price (dollars per tape)	Quantity demanded	Quantity supplied	Shortage (–) or surplus (+)
	(millions of tapes per week)		
1	9	0	–9
2	6	3	–3
3	4	4	0
4	3	5	+2
5	2	6	+4

The table lists the quantities demanded and quantities supplied as well as the shortage or surplus of tapes at each price. If the price is $2 a tape, 6 million tapes a week are demanded and 3 million are supplied. There is a shortage of 3 million tapes a week, and the price rises. If the price is $4 a tape, 3 million tapes a week are demanded and 5 million are supplied. There is a surplus of 2 million tapes a week, and the price falls. If the price is $3 a tape, 4 million tapes a week are demanded and 4 million are supplied. There is neither a shortage nor a surplus. Neither buyers nor sellers have any incentive to change the price. The price at which the quantity demanded equals the quantity supplied is the equilibrium price.

tape. At each price *above* $3 a tape, there is a surplus of tapes. For example, at $4 a tape, the surplus is 2 million tapes a week, as shown by the blue arrow. At each price *below* $3 a tape, there is a shortage of tapes. For example, at $2 a tape, the shortage is 3 million tapes a week, as shown by the red arrow.

Price Adjustments

You've seen that if the price is below equilibrium there is a shortage and if the price is above equilibrium there is a surplus. But can we count on the price to change and eliminate a shortage or surplus? We can, because such price changes are mutually beneficial to both buyers and sellers. Let's see why the price changes when there is a shortage or a surplus.

A Shortage Forces the Price Up   Suppose the price of a tape is $2. Consumers plan to buy 6 million tapes a week, and producers plan to sell 3 million tapes a week. Consumers can't force producers to sell more than they plan, so the quantity actually offered for sale is 3 million tapes a week. In this situation, powerful forces operate to increase the price and move it toward the equilibrium price. Some producers, noticing lines of unsatisfied consumers, move their prices up. Some producers increase their output. As producers push their prices up, the price rises toward its equilibrium. The rising price reduces the shortage because it decreases the quantity demanded and increases the quantity supplied. When the price has increased to the point at which there is no longer a shortage, the forces moving the price stop operating and the price comes to rest at its equilibrium.

A Surplus Forces the Price Down   Suppose the price of a tape is $4. Producers plan to sell 5 million tapes a week, and consumers plan to buy 3 million tapes a week. Producers cannot force consumers to buy more than they plan, so the quantity that is actually bought is 3 million tapes a week. In this situation, powerful forces operate to lower the price and move it toward the equilibrium price. Some producers, unable to sell the quantities of tapes they planned to sell, cut their prices. In addition, some producers scale back production. As producers cut prices, the price falls toward its equilibrium. The falling price decreases the surplus because it increases the quantity demanded and decreases the quantity supplied. When the price has fallen to the point at which there is no longer a surplus, the forces moving the price

stop operating, and the price comes to rest at its equilibrium.

The Best Deal Available for Buyers and Sellers

When the price is below equilibrium, it is forced upward toward the equilibrium. Why don't buyers resist the increase and refuse to buy at the higher price? Because they value the good more highly than the current price and they cannot satisfy all their demands at the current price. In some markets—an example is the market for rental accommodation in Atlanta during the 1996 Olympic Games—the buyers might even be the ones who force the price upward by offering higher prices to divert the limited quantities away from other buyers.

When the price is above equilibrium, it is bid downward toward the equilibrium. Why don't sellers resist this decrease and refuse to sell at the lower price? Because their minimum supply price is below the current price and they cannot sell all they would like to at the current price. Normally, it is the sellers who force the price downward by offering lower prices to gain market share from their competitors.

At the price at which the quantity demanded and the quantity supplied are equal, neither buyers nor sellers can do business at a better price. Buyers pay the highest price they are willing to pay for the last unit bought, and sellers receive the lowest price at which they are willing to supply the last unit sold.

When people freely make offers to buy and sell, and when demanders try to buy at the lowest possible price and suppliers try to sell at the highest possible price, the price at which trade takes place is the equilibrium price—the price at which the quantity demanded equals the quantity supplied. The price coordinates the plans of buyers and sellers.

R E V I E W   Q U I Z

- What is the *equilibrium price* of a good or service?
- Over what range of prices does a shortage arise?
- Over what range of prices does a surplus arise?
- What happens to the price when there is a shortage?
- What happens to the price when there is a surplus?
- Why is the price at which the quantity demanded equals the quantity supplied the equilibrium price?
- Why is the equilibrium price the best deal available for both buyers and seller?

Predicting Changes in Price and Quantity

THE DEMAND AND SUPPLY THEORY WE HAVE JUST studied provides us with a powerful way of analyzing influences on prices and the quantities bought and sold. According to the theory, a change in price stems from either a change in demand or a change in supply or a change in both. Let's look first at the effects of a change in demand.

A Change in Demand

What happens to the price and quantity of tapes if the demand for tapes increases? We can answer this question with a specific example. Suppose the price of a Walkman falls from $200 to $50. Because the Walkman and tapes are complements, the demand for tapes increases, as is shown in the table in Fig. 4.9. The original demand schedule and the new one are set out in the first three columns of the table. The table also shows the supply schedule for tapes.

The original equilibrium price is $3 a tape. At that price, 4 million tapes a week are demanded and supplied. When demand increases, the price that makes the quantity demanded equal the quantity supplied is $5 a tape. At this price, 6 million tapes are bought and sold each week. When demand increases, both the price and the quantity increase.

Figure 4.9 shows these changes. The figure shows the original demand for and supply of tapes. The original equilibrium price is $3 a tape, and the quantity is 4 million tapes a week. When demand increases, the demand curve shifts rightward. The equilibrium price rises to $5 a tape, and the quantity supplied increases to 6 million tapes a week, as highlighted in the figure. There is an *increase in the quantity supplied* but *no change in supply*—a movement along, but no shift of, the supply curve.

We can reverse the exercise that we've just conducted. We can work out what happens if we start at a price of $5 a tape with 6 million tapes a week being bought and sold and then demand decreases to its original level. Such a decrease in demand might arise from a fall in the price of CDs or CD players (both substitutes for tapes). The decrease in demand shifts the demand curve leftward. The equilibrium price falls to $3 a tape, and the equilibrium quantity decreases to 4 million tapes a week.

FIGURE 4.9

The Effects of a Change in Demand

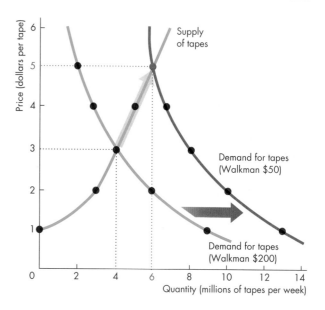

| Price | Quantity demanded | | Quantity supplied |
| (dollars per tape) | (millions of tapes per week) | | (millions of tapes per week) |
	Walkman $200	Walkman $50	
1	9	13	0
2	6	10	3
3	4	8	4
4	3	7	5
5	2	6	6

With the price of a Walkman at $200, the demand for tapes is the blue curve. The equilibrium price is $3 a tape, and the equilibrium quantity is 4 million tapes a week. When the price of a Walkman falls from $200 to $50, the demand for tapes increases and the demand curve shifts rightward to become the red curve.

At $3 a tape, there is now a shortage of 4 million tapes a week. The price of a tape rises to a new equilibrium of $5 a tape. As the price rises to $5, the quantity supplied increases—shown by the blue arrow on the supply curve—to the new equilibrium quantity of 6 million tapes a week. Following an increase in demand, the quantity supplied increases but supply does not change—the supply curve does not shift.

We can now make our first two predictions:

1. When demand increases, both the price and the quantity increase.
2. When demand decreases, both the price and the quantity decrease.

A Change in Supply

Suppose that Sony and 3M introduce a new cost-saving technology in their tape production plants. The new technology increases the supply of tapes. The new supply schedule (the same one that was shown in Fig. 4.6) is presented in the table in Fig. 4.10. What are the new equilibrium price and quantity? The answer is highlighted in the table: The price falls to $2 a tape, and the quantity increases to 6 million a week. You can see why by looking at the quantities demanded and supplied at the old price of $3 a tape. The quantity supplied at that price is 8 million tapes a week, and there is a surplus of tapes. The price falls. Only when the price is $2 a tape does the quantity supplied equal the quantity demanded.

Figure 4.10 illustrates the effect of an increase in supply. It shows the demand curve for tapes and the original and new supply curves. The initial equilibrium price is $3 a tape and the quantity is 4 million tapes a week. When the supply increases, the supply curve shifts rightward. The equilibrium price falls to $2 a tape, and the quantity demanded increases to 6 million tapes a week, highlighted in the figure. There is an *increase in the quantity demanded* but *no change in demand*—a movement along, but no shift of, the demand curve.

The exercise that we've just conducted can be reversed. If we start out at a price of $2 a tape with 6 million tapes a week being bought and sold, we can work out what happens if supply decreases to its original level. Such a decrease in supply might arise from an increase in the cost of labor or raw materials. The decrease in supply shifts the supply curve leftward. The equilibrium price rises to $3 a tape, and the equilibrium quantity decreases to 4 million tapes a week.

We can now make two more predictions:

1. When supply increases, the quantity increases and the price falls.
2. When supply decreases, the quantity decreases and the price rises.

FIGURE 4.10

The Effects of a Change in Supply

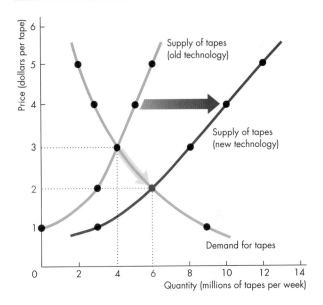

Price (dollars per tape)	Quantity demanded (millions of tapes per week)	Quantity supplied (millions of tapes per week)	
		old technology	new technology
1	9	0	3
2	6	3	6
3	4	4	8
4	3	5	10
5	2	6	12

With the old technology, the supply of tapes is shown by the blue supply curve. The equilibrium price is $3 a tape, and the equilibrium quantity is 4 million tapes a week. When the new technology is adopted, the supply of tapes increases and the supply curve shifts rightward to become the red curve.

At $3 a tape, there is now a surplus of 4 million tapes a week. The price of a tape falls to a new equilibrium of $2 a tape. As the price falls to $2, the quantity demanded increases—shown by the blue arrow on the demand curve—to the new equilibrium quantity of 6 million tapes a week. Following an increase in supply, the quantity demanded increases but demand does not change—the demand curve does not shift.

A Change in Both Demand and Supply

You can now predict the effects of a change in either demand or supply on the price and the quantity. But what happens if *both* demand and supply change together? To answer this question, we look first at the case in which demand and supply move in the same direction—either both increase or both decrease. Then we look at the case in which they move in opposite directions—demand decreases and supply increases or demand increases and supply decreases.

Demand and Supply Change in the Same Direction

We've seen that an increase in the demand for tapes increases the price of tapes and increases the quantity bought and sold. And we've seen that an increase in the supply of tapes lowers the price of tapes and increases the quantity bought and sold. Let's now examine what happens when both of these changes occur together.

The table in Fig. 4.11 brings together the numbers that describe the original quantities demanded and supplied and the new quantities demanded and supplied after the fall in the price of the Walkman and the improved tape production technology. These same numbers are illustrated in the graph. The original (blue) demand and supply curves intersect at a price of $3 a tape and a quantity of 4 million tapes a week. The new (red) supply and demand curves also intersect at a price of $3 a tape but at a quantity of 8 million tapes a week.

An increase in either demand or supply increases the quantity. So when both demand and supply increase, so does quantity.

An increase in demand raises the price, and an increase in supply lowers the price, so we can't say whether the price will rise or fall when demand and supply increase together. In this example, the price does not change. But notice that if demand increases by slightly more than the amount shown in the figure, the price will rise. And if supply increases by slightly more than the amount shown in the figure, the price will fall.

We can now make two more predictions:

1. When *both* demand and supply increase, the quantity increases and the price increases, decreases, or remains constant.

2. When *both* demand and supply decrease, the quantity decreases and the price increases, decreases, or remains constant.

FIGURE 4.11

The Effects of an Increase in Both Demand and Supply

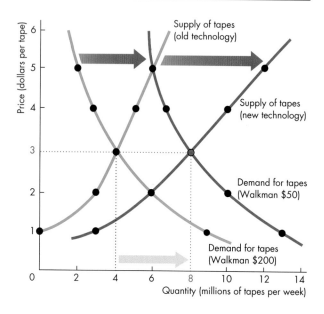

Price (dollars per tape)	Original quantities (millions of tapes per week)		New quantities (millions of tapes per week)	
	Quantity demanded Walkman $200	Quantity supplied old technology	Quantity demanded Walkman $50	Quantity supplied new technology
1	9	0	13	3
2	6	3	10	6
3	4	4	8	8
4	3	5	7	10
5	2	6	6	12

When a Walkman costs $200 and the old technology is used to produce tapes, the price of a tape is $3 and the quantity is 4 million tapes a week. A fall in the price of a Walkman increases the demand for tapes, and improved technology increases the supply of tapes. The new supply curve intersects the new demand curve at $3 a tape, the same price as before, but the quantity increases to 8 million tapes a week. These increases in demand and supply increase the quantity but leave the price unchanged.

Demand and Supply Change in Opposite Directions

Let's now see what happens when demand and supply change together but move in *opposite* directions. An improved production technology increases the supply of tapes as before. But now the price of CD players falls. A CD player is a *substitute* for tapes. With less costly CD players, more people buy them and switch from buying tapes to buying discs, and the demand for tapes decreases.

The table in Fig. 4.12 describes the original and new demand and supply schedules. These schedules are shown as the original (blue) and new (red) demand and supply curves in the graph. The original demand and supply curves intersect at a price of $5 a tape and a quantity of 6 million tapes a week. The new supply and demand curves intersect at a price of $2 a tape and at the original quantity of 6 million tapes a week.

A decrease in demand or an increase in supply lowers the price. So when a decrease in demand and an increase in supply occur together, the price falls.

A decrease in demand decreases the quantity, and an increase in supply increases the quantity, so we can't say for sure which way the quantity will change when demand decreases and supply increases at the same time. In this example, the decrease in demand and the increase in supply are such that the increase in quantity brought about by an increase in supply is offset by the decrease in quantity brought about by a decrease in demand—so the quantity does not change. But notice that if demand had decreased by slightly more, the quantity would have decreased. And if supply had increased by slightly more, the quantity would have increased.

We can now make two more predictions:

1. When demand decreases and supply increases, the price falls and the quantity increases, decreases, or remains constant.
2. When demand increases and supply decreases, the price rises and the quantity increases, decreases, or remains constant.

R E V I E W   Q U I Z

- What is the effect on the price of a tape and the quantity of tapes if (a) the price of a CD rises or (b) the price of a Walkman rises or (c) more firms start to produce tapes or (d) tape producers' wages rise or (e) any pair of these events occur at the same time? (Draw the diagrams!)

FIGURE 4.12

The Effects of a Decrease in Demand and an Increase in Supply

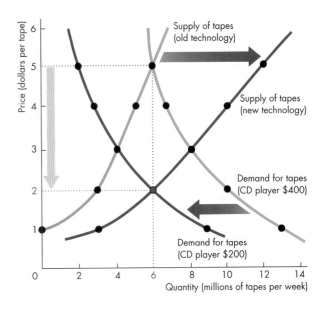

	Original quantities (millions of tapes per week)		**New quantities** (millions of tapes per week)	
Price (dollars per tape)	**Quantity demanded** CD player $400	**Quantity supplied** old technology	**Quantity demanded** CD player $200	**Quantity supplied** new technology
1	13	0	9	3
2	10	3	6	6
3	8	4	4	8
4	7	5	3	10
5	6	6	2	12

When a CD player costs $400 and the old technology is used to produce tapes, the price of a tape is $5 and the quantity is 6 million tapes a week. A fall in the price of a CD player decreases the demand for tapes, and improved technology increases the supply of tapes. The new supply curve intersects the new demand curve at $2 a tape, a lower price, but in this case the quantity remains constant at 6 million tapes a week. The decrease in demand and increase in supply lower the price but leave the quantity unchanged.

CD Players, Health Care, and Bananas

Earlier in this chapter, we looked at some facts about prices and quantities of CD players, health care, and bananas. Let's use the theory of demand and supply that we have just studied to explain the movements in the prices and quantities of those goods.

A Price Slide: CD Players   Figure 4.13(a) shows the market for CD players. In 1983, when CD players were first manufactured, very few producers made them and the supply was small. The supply curve was S_0. In 1983, there weren't many titles on CDs and the demand for CD players was small. The demand curve was D_0. The quantities supplied and demanded in 1983 were equal at Q_0, and the price was $1,100 (1994 dollars). As the technology for making CD players improved and as more and more factories began to produce CD players, the supply increased by a large amount and the supply curve shifted rightward from S_0 to S_1. At the same time, increases in incomes, a decrease in the price of CDs, and an increase in the number of titles on CDs increased the demand for CD players. But the increase in demand was much smaller than the increase in supply. The demand curve shifted rightward from D_0 to D_1. With the new demand curve D_1 and the new supply curve S_1, the equilibrium price fell to $170 in 1994 and the quantity increased to Q_1. The large increase in supply combined with a smaller increase in demand resulted in an increase in the quantity of CD players and a dramatic fall in the price. Figure 4.13(a) shows the CD player price slide.

A Price Rocket: Health Care   Figure 4.13(b) shows the market for health-care services. In 1980, the supply curve for health-care services was S_0. Advances in medical technology have greatly increased the range and complexity of conditions that can be treated and have increased the supply of health-care services. But large increases in doctors' compensation and costs have escalated the cost of providing health care and have decreased supply. The net change in supply resulting from these two opposing forces has been an increase. The supply curve has shifted rightward from S_0 to S_1. At the same time that supply increased by a relatively modest amount, the demand for health care increased enormously. Some of the increase resulted from higher incomes, some from an aging population, and some from a demand for newly available treatments. The combination of these influences on demand resulted in the demand curve shifting from D_0 to D_1. The combined effect of a large increase in demand and a small increase in supply was an increase in the quantity from Q_0 to Q_1 and an increase in price from 100 (an index number) in 1980 to 167 in 1998. Figure 4.13(b) shows the health-care price rocket.

A Price Roller Coaster: Bananas   Figure 4.13(c) shows the market for bananas. The demand for bananas—curve D—does not change much over the years. But the supply of bananas, which depends mainly on the weather, fluctuates between S_0 and S_1. With good growing conditions, the supply curve is S_1. With bad growing conditions, supply decreases and the supply curve is S_0. As a consequence of fluctuations in supply, the quantity fluctuates between Q_0 and Q_1. The price of bananas fluctuates between 33 cents per pound (1995 cents), the maximum price, and 20 cents per pound, the minimum price. Figure 4.13(c) shows the banana price roller coaster.

The Invisible Hand   Adam Smith said that each buyer and seller in a market "is led by an invisible hand to promote an end which was no part of his intention." What did he mean? He meant that when each one of us makes decisions to buy or sell to achieve the best outcome for ourselves and when our decisions are coordinated in free markets, we end up achieving the best outcome for everyone.

Although markets are amazing instruments, it turns out that they do not always work quite as perfectly as Adam Smith imagined. If you go on to study *micro*economics, you will discover the conditions under which markets are efficient and why they sometimes fail to achieve the best possible outcome for everyone. If you go on to study *macro*economics, you will discover the reasons why the market economy produces fluctuations in output and employment and sometimes creates persistent unemployment.

◆ You now know the basic theory of demand and supply. By using this theory, you can explain past price and quantity fluctuations and make predictions about future fluctuations. *Reading Between the Lines* on pp. 80–81 shows you the theory in action in the market for oranges. You will see many news articles that you can better understand by using your knowledge of demand and supply. Watch for stories about frosts, droughts, and floods and their effects on the prices of many crops and other items.

FIGURE 4.13

Price Slide, Rocket, and Roller Coaster

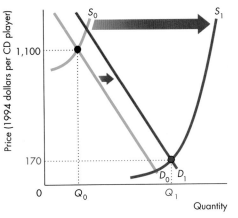

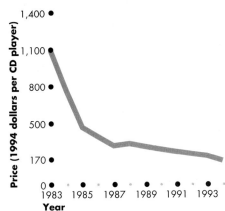

A large increase in the supply of CD players, from S_0 to S_1 combined with a small increase in demand, from D_0 to D_1, resulted in an increase in the quantity of CD players bought and sold from Q_0 to Q_1. The average price of CD players fell from $1,100 in 1983 to $170 in 1994—a price slide.

Source: U.S. Bureau of the Census, Statistical Abstract of the United States: 1994 (114th edition). Washington, D.C., 1994.

(a) Price slide: CD players

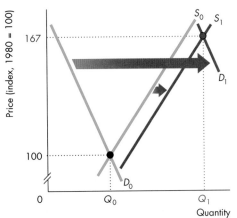

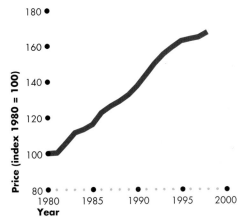

A large increase in demand for health care, from D_0 to D_1, combined with a small increase in the supply, from S_0 to S_1, has resulted in an increase in the quantity of health care, from Q_0 to Q_1 and a rise in the price of health care from 100 in 1980 to 167 in 1998—a price rocket.

Source: Economic Report of the President, 1999.

(b) Price rocket: health care

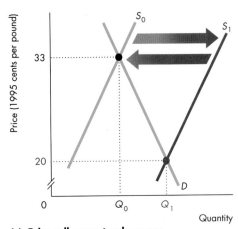

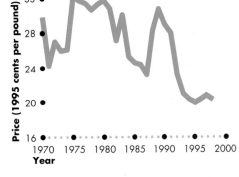

The demand for bananas remains constant at D. But supply fluctuates between S_0 and S_1. As a result, the price of bananas has fluctuated between 20 cents per pound and 33 cents per pound—a price roller coaster.

Source: International Financial Statistics, International Monetary Fund, Washington, D.C., February, 1999.

(c) Price roller coaster: bananas

Demand and Supply:
The Price of Oranges

USA TODAY, JANUARY 4, 1999

Orange Prices Start to Rise after Calif. Freeze

LOS ANGELES—Consumers will pay dramatically more for fresh oranges, the result of a killer freeze in California that has already doubled wholesale prices.

The coming price rise is the last in a string of calamities that struck agriculture in 1998.

California navel oranges "will be in very limited quantities," and "what is available will be higher in price," said Paul Bernish, spokesman for Kroger, the nation's largest supermarket chain.

"So far, at least, price increases for citrus products have not been passed along to consumers," Bernish said.

Food Lion, with 1,208 stores mostly in the Southeast, said store prices on fresh oranges will rise 20% to 30% this week, less than the 100% increase it's paying at wholesale. "We're trying to absorb as much of that (the price increase) as we can," spokeswoman Chris Ahearn said.

California supplies about 80% of the nation's eating oranges and lemons. Four days of freezing temperatures in the Central Valley last month caused about $530 million in damage. ...

For fresh oranges, the prices are already rising. A standard 37½-pound box of oranges is selling at wholesale for $20 to $24 depending on size and quality, double the price before the frost, the California Farm Bureau Federation reported. ...

© 1999 USA Today. Reprinted with permission. Further reproduction prohibited.

Essence of the Story

■ In December 1998, four days of freezing temperatures destroyed a large part of the California crop of navel oranges.

■ During early January 1999, the wholesale price of navel oranges doubled.

■ At the same time, the store price of navel oranges increased by 20 percent to 30 percent.

■ Orange growers sell their production to major supermarket chains in a **wholesale market**.

■ Supermarket chains sell oranges to consumers in a **retail market**.

■ A serious 4-day freeze in California wiped out a large quantity of navel oranges and led to a rise in their price. The wholesale price increased by more than the retail price.

■ Why did the retail price rise? Why did the wholesale price rise by a larger percentage than the retail price?

■ Figure 1 shows the wholesale market for California navel oranges. The demand curve is *D*. Before the freeze, the supply curve was S_{98}. The price was $11 a box, and 2 million boxes a week were bought.

■ In December 1998, freezing temperatures destroyed a large quantity of oranges and the supply of oranges decreased. The supply curve shifted leftward to S_{99}.

■ The price increased to $22 a box (a 100 percent increase, as reported in the news article).

■ The increase in price did not change demand. The demand curve did not shift. But the increase in price brought a *decrease in the quantity*

demanded, which is shown by a *movement along the demand curve*.

■ Figure 2 shows the retail market for California navel oranges. The demand curve is *D*. Before the freeze, the supply curve was S_{98}. The price was 50 cents a pound, and 2 million boxes a week were bought.

■ The decrease in supply shifted the supply curve leftward to S_{99}.

■ The price increased to 65 cents a pound (a 30 percent increase, as reported in the news article).

■ The wholesale price increased by a larger percentage than the retail price, and the profits of supermarkets were squeezed.

■ The percentage rise in the wholesale price exceeded the percentage rise in the retail price because of the way the quantity demanded responds to a price change.

■ A supermarket must stock navel oranges if it is to attract customers who want to buy the oranges even at a higher-than-normal price.

■ A supermarket that does not stock navel oranges loses customers, and its sales of a wide range of items decrease.

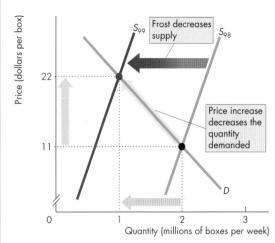

Figure 1 The wholesale market

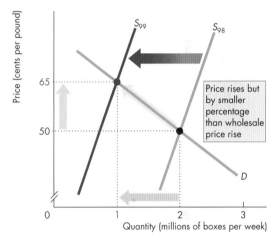

Figure 2 The retail market

■ So a relatively large price rise is needed to allocate the smaller quantity of oranges to the supermarkets.

■ Consumers have many alternatives to navel oranges. When the price of navel oranges rises, some consumers switch to grapefruit and other types of fruit and stop buying oranges. So the quantity of oranges demanded decreases sharply.

■ So a relatively small price rise is sufficient to allocate the smaller quantity of oranges to consumers.

■ In the news article, Chris Ahearn says that Food Lion is trying to absorb the price rise. But the forces of demand and supply prevent super-markets from raising the retail price by as much as the rise in the wholesale price.

MATHEMATICAL NOTE
Demand, Supply, and Market Equilibrium

Demand Curve

The law of demand says that as the price of a good or service falls, the quantity demanded of it increases. We illustrate the law of demand by setting out a demand schedule, by drawing a graph of the demand curve, or by writing down an equation. When the demand curve is a straight line, a linear equation describes it. The equation that describes a downward-sloping demand curve is

$$P = a - bQ_D,$$

where P is the price and Q_D is the quantity demanded. The a and b are positive constants.

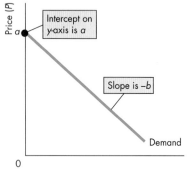

This equation tells us three things:
1. The price at which no one is willing to buy the good (Q_D is zero). That is, if the price is a, then the quantity demanded is zero. You can see the price a on the graph. It is the price at which the demand curve hits the y-axis—what we call the demand curve's "intercept on the y-axis."
2. That as the price falls, the quantity demanded increases. If Q_D is a positive number, then the price P must be less than a. And as Q_D gets larger, the price P becomes smaller. That is, as the quantity increases, the maximum price that buyers are willing to pay for the good falls.
3. The constant b tells us how fast the maximum price that someone is willing to pay for the good falls as the quantity increases. That is, the constant b tells us about the steepness of the demand curve. The equation tells us that the slope of the demand curve is $-b$.

Supply Curve

The law of supply says that as the price of a good or service rises, the quantity supplied of it increases. We illustrate the law of supply by setting out a supply schedule, by drawing a graph of the supply curve, or by writing down an equation. When the supply curve is a straight line, a linear equation describes the supply curve. The equation that describes an upward-sloping supply curve is

$$P = c + dQ_S,$$

where P is the price and Q_S the quantity supplied. The c and d are positive constants.

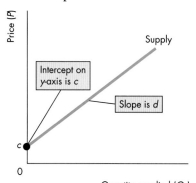

This equation tells us three things:
1. The price at which no one is willing to sell the good (Q_S is zero) That is, if the price is c, then the quantity supplied is zero. You can see the price c on the graph. It is the price at which the supply curve hits the y-axis—what we call the supply curve's "intercept on the y-axis."
2. That as the price rises, the quantity supplied increases. If Q_S is a positive number, then the price P must be greater than c. And as Q_S increases, the price P gets larger. That is, as the quantity increases, the minimum price that sellers are willing to accept rises.
3. The constant d tells us how fast the minimum price at which someone is willing to sell the good rises as the quantity increases. That is, the constant d tells us about the steepness of the supply curve. The equation tells us that the slope of the supply is d.

Market Equilibrium

Demand and supply determine market equilibrium. The figure shows the equilibrium price (P^*) and equilibrium quantity (Q^*) at the intersection of the demand curve and the supply curve.

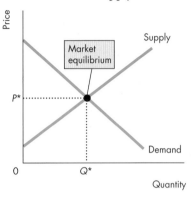

We can use the equations to find the equilibrium price and equilibrium quantity. The price of a good will adjust until the quantity demanded equals the quantity supplied. That is,

$$Q_D = Q_S.$$

So at the equilibrium price (P^*) and equilibrium quantity (Q^*),

$$Q_D = Q_S = Q^*.$$

To find the equilibrium price and equilibrium quantity:

First substitute Q^* for Q_D in the demand equation and Q^* for Q_S in the supply equation. Then the price is the equilibrium price (P^*), which gives

$$P^* = a - bQ^*,$$
$$P^* = c + dQ^*.$$

Notice that,

$$a - bQ^* = c + dQ^*$$

Now, solve for Q^*

$$a - c = bQ^* + dQ^*$$
$$a - c = (b + d)Q^*$$
$$Q^* = \frac{a - c}{b + d}.$$

To find the equilibrium price (P^*), substitute for Q^* in either the demand equation or the supply equation.

Using the demand equation,

$$P^* = a - b\left(\frac{a - c}{b + d}\right)$$

$$P^* = \frac{a(b + d) - b(a - c)}{b + d}$$

$$P^* = \frac{ad + bc}{b + d}.$$

Alternatively, using the supply equation,

$$P^* = c + d\left(\frac{a - c}{b + d}\right)$$

$$P^* = \frac{c(b + d) + d(a - c)}{b + d}$$

$$P^* = \frac{cb + da}{b + d}$$

$$P^* = \frac{ad + bc}{b + d}.$$

An Example

The demand for ice cream cones is
$$P = 800 - 2Q_D.$$
The supply of ice cream cones is
$$P = 200 + 1Q_S.$$
The price of a cone is expressed in cents, and the quantities are expressed in cones per day.

To find the equilibrium price (P^*) and equilibrium quantity (Q^*), substitute Q^* for Q_D and Q_S and P^* for P.

That is,

$$P^* = 800 - 2Q^*$$
$$P^* = 200 + 1Q^*$$

Now solve for Q^*:

$$800 - 2Q^* = 200 + 1Q^*$$
$$600 = 3Q^*$$
$$Q^* = 200$$

And

$$P^* = 800 - 2Q^*$$
$$= 800 - 2(200)$$
$$= 400$$

The equilibrium price is $4 a cone, and the equilibrium quantity is 200 cones per day.

SUMMARY

KEY POINTS

Price and Opportunity Cost (p. 62)

- Opportunity cost is a relative price. We measure relative price by dividing the price of one good by the price (index) of a basket of all goods.
- Demand and supply determines relative prices.

Demand (pp. 63–67)

- Demand is the relationship between the quantity demanded of a good and its price when all other influences on buying plans remain the same.
- The higher the price of a good, other things remaining the same, the smaller is the quantity demanded.
- Demand depends on the prices of substitutes and complements, expected future prices, income, population, and preferences.

Supply (pp. 68–71)

- Supply is the relationship between the quantity supplied of a good and its price when all other influences on selling plans remain the same.
- The higher the price of a good, other things remaining the same, the greater is the quantity supplied.
- Supply depends on the prices of resources used to produce a good, the prices of related goods produced, expected future prices, the number of producers, and technology.

Market Equilibrium (pp. 72–73)

- At the equilibrium price, the quantity demanded equals the quantity supplied.
- At prices above equilibrium, there is a surplus and the price falls.
- At prices below equilibrium, there is a shortage and the price rises.

Predicting Changes in Price and Quantity (pp. 74–79)

- An increase in demand brings a rise in price and an increase in the quantity supplied. (A decrease in demand brings a fall in price and a decrease in the quantity supplied.)
- An increase in supply brings a fall in price and an increase in the quantity demanded. (A decrease in supply brings a rise in price and a decrease in the quantity demanded.)
- An increase in demand and an increase in supply bring an increased quantity but an ambiguous price change. An increase in demand and a decrease in supply raise the price and bring an ambiguous quantity change.

KEY FIGURES

KEY TERMS

PROBLEMS

*1. What is the effect on the price of a tape and the quantity of tapes sold if:
   a. The price of a CD rises?
   b. The price of a Walkman rises?
   c. The supply of CD players increases?
   d. Consumers' incomes increase?
   e. Workers who make tapes get a pay raise?
   f. The price of a Walkman rises at the same time as the workers who make tapes get a pay raise?

2. What is the effect on the price of hotdogs and the quantity of hotdogs sold if:
   a. The price of a hamburger rises?
   b. The price of a hotdog bun rises?
   c. The supply of hotdog sausages increases?
   d. Consumers' incomes decrease?
   e. The wage rate of a hotdog seller increases?
   f. If the wage rate of the hotdog seller rises and at the same time prices of ketchup, mustard, and relish fall?

*3. Suppose that one of the following events occurs:
   a. The price of crude oil rises.
   b. The price of a car rises.
   c. All speed limits on highways are abolished.
   d. Robot technology cuts car production costs.
   Which of the above events increases or decreases (state which):
      (i) The demand for gasoline.
      (ii) The supply of gasoline.
      (iii) The quantity of gasoline demanded.
      (iv) The quantity of gasoline supplied.

4. Suppose that one of the following events occurs:
   a. The price of wool rises.
   b. The price of sweaters falls.
   c. A close substitute for wool is invented.
   d. A new high-speed loom is invented.
   Which of the above events increases or decreases (state which):
      (i) The demand for wool.
      (ii) The supply of wool.
      (iii) The quantity of wool demanded.
      (iv) The quantity of wool supplied.

*5. The figure illustrates the market for pizza.
   a. Label the curves in the figure.
   b. What are the equilibrium price of a pizza and the equilibrium quantity of pizza?

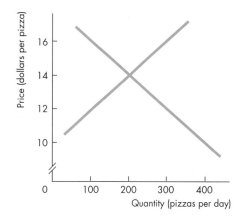

6. The figure illustrates market for bread.
   a. Label the curves in the figure.
   b. What are the equilibrium price of bread and the equilibrium quantity of bread?

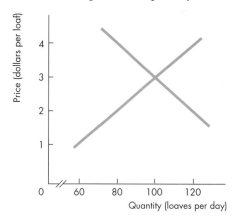

*7. The demand and supply schedules for gum are:

Price (cents per pack)	Quantity demanded	Quantity supplied
	(millions of packs a week)	
20	180	60
30	160	80
40	140	100
50	120	120
60	100	140
70	80	160
80	60	180

   a. What are the equilibrium price and equilibrium quantity of gum?
   b. If gum was 70 cents a pack, describe the situation in the gum market and explain what would happen to the price of gum.

8. The demand and supply schedules for potato chips are:

Price (cents per bag)	Quantity demanded	Quantity supplied
	(millions of bags per week)	
40	170	90
50	160	100
60	150	110
70	140	120
80	130	130
90	120	140
100	110	150
110	100	160

   a.   What are the equilibrium price and equilibrium quantity of potato chips?
   b.   If chips were 60 cents a bag, describe the situation in the market for potato chips and explain what would happen to the price of a bag of chips.

*9. In problem 7, suppose that a fire destroys some gum-producing factories and the supply of gum decreases by 40 million packs a week.
   a.   Has there been a shift in or a movement along the supply curve of gum?
   b.   Has there been a shift in or a movement along the demand curve for gum?
   c.   What is the new equilibrium price and quantity of gum?

10. In problem 8, suppose a new snack food comes onto the market and as a result the demand for potato chips decreases by 40 million bags per week.
   a.   Has there been a shift in or a movement along the supply curve of chips?
   b.   Has there been a shift in or a movement along the demand curve for chips?
   c.   What is the new equilibrium price and quantity of chips?

*11. In problem 9, suppose an increase in the teenage population increases the demand for gum by 40 million packs per week at the same time as the fire occurs. What is the new equilibrium price and quantity of gum?

12. In problem 10, suppose that a flood destroys several potato farms and as a result supply decreases by 20 million bags a week at the same time as the new snack food comes onto the market. What is the new equilibrium price and quantity of chips?

CRITICAL THINKING

1. After you have studied *Reading Between the Lines* on pp. 80–81, answer the following questions:
   a.   Why does the supply of oranges decrease but the demand for oranges not change? How can the demand not change when the quantity available decreases?
   b.   Explain to Chris Ahearn and Paul Bernish (the spokespeople for Food Lion and Kroger) why the retail price of oranges is out of their control. How would you explain the forces that determine the prices in both the wholesale market and the retail market?
   c.   Gray Davis, the governor of California, wants your advice on what to do about the effects of the freeze on the orange market. In particular, he wants to know what can be done to keep the price of oranges down and the incomes of the orange growers up. Write a brief report to Mr. Davis outlining his options, if he has any, or explaining why there is nothing he can do, if that is your opinion.
   d.   Use the links on the Parkin Web site and obtain the latest data on the quantities of oranges produced in the United States.

2. Use the links on the Parkin Web site and obtain data on the prices and quantities of wheat.
   a.   Make a figure similar to Fig. 1 on page 81 to illustrate the market for wheat in 1998.
   b.   Show the changes in demand and supply and the changes in the quantity demanded and the quantity supplied that are consistent with the price and quantity data.

3. Use the link on the Parkin Web site and read the story about the prices of millennium cruises.
   a.   Describe how the millennium changes the price of a cruise.
   b.   Use the demand and supply model to explain what happens to the price when there is an increase in demand and no change in supply.
   c.   What do you predict would happen to the price of a cruise if air fares to Australia and the South Pacific decreased?
   d.   What do you predict would happen to the price of a cruise if the price of oil increased?

Chapter 5

Elasticity

Your pizza business is earning you a good profit but you are worried. You've just learned that a major pizza franchise is planning a big expansion in your neighborhood. You know that the resulting increase in supply will lower the price of pizza and bring tough competition for you. But how big a price fall will you have to cope with? Will there be little change in pizza consumption and a large fall in price? Or will there be a huge increase in pizza consumption and little change in price? To answer these questions, you need a measure of the responsiveness of the quantity of pizza demanded to the price of pizza. ◆ Faced with tough competition from your pizzeria, the burger shop next door has cut its prices. How will the lower price of burgers affect the demand for your pizza? Will it wipe you out of business or make only a small dent in your sales? To answer this question, you need a measure of the responsiveness of the demand for your pizza to the price of burgers, a substitute for pizza. ◆ The economy is booming, and people's incomes are rising. You know that with more income to spend, people will buy more pizza. But how much more pizza will people buy? Will the higher incomes bring a large increase in your sales or will they make only a small difference? To answer this question, you need a measure of the responsiveness of the demand for pizza to consumers' incomes. ◆ As incomes increase, you expect the demand for pizza to increase. But will the increase in demand bring a rise in price with little change in the quantity bought? Or will it bring a huge increase in pizza consumption with little change in price? To answer this question, you need a measure of the responsiveness of the quantity of pizza supplied to a change in the price of pizza.

◆ In this chapter, you will learn how to answer questions like the ones just posed. You will learn about elasticity, a measure of the responsiveness of quantities bought and sold to changes in prices and other influences on buyers' and sellers' plans.

Predicting Prices

After studying this chapter, you will be able to:

■ Define and calculate the price elasticity of demand

■ Use a total revenue test and an expenditure test to estimate the price elasticity of demand

■ Explain the factors that influence the price elasticity of demand

■ Define and calculate the cross elasticity of demand

■ Define and calculate the income elasticity of demand

■ Define and calculate the elasticity of supply

The Price Elasticity of Demand

YOU KNOW THAT WHEN SUPPLY INCREASES, THE equilibrium price falls and the equilibrium quantity increases. But does the price fall by a large amount and the quantity increase by a little? Or does the price barely fall and the quantity increase by a large amount?

The answer depends on the responsiveness of the quantity demanded to a change in price. You can see why by studying Fig. 5.1, which shows two possible scenarios in a local pizza market. Fig. 5.1(a) shows one scenario, and Fig. 5.1(b) shows the other.

In both cases, supply is initially S_0. In part (a), the demand for pizza is shown by the demand curve D_a. In part (b), the demand for pizza is shown by the demand curve D_b. Initially, in both cases, the price is $20 a pizza and the quantity of pizza produced and consumed is 10 pizzas an hour.

Now a large pizza franchise opens up and the supply of pizza increases. The supply curve shifts rightward to S_1. In case (a), the price of a pizza falls by an enormous $15 to $5 and the quantity increases by only 3 to 13 pizzas an hour. In contrast, in case (b), the price falls by only $5 to $15 a pizza and the quantity increases by 7 to 17 pizzas an hour.

The different outcomes arise from differing degrees of responsiveness of the quantity demanded to a change in price. But what do we mean by responsiveness? One possible answer is slope. The slope of demand curve D_a is steeper than the slope of demand curve D_b.

In this example, we can compare the slopes of the two demand curves. But we can't always do so. The reason is that the slope of a demand curve depends on the units in which we measure the price and quantity. And we often must compare the demand curves for different goods and services that are measured in unrelated units. For example, a pizza producer might want to compare the demand for pizza with the demand for soda. Which quantity demanded is more responsive to a price change? This question can't be answered by comparing the slopes of two demand curves. The units of measurement of pizza and soda are unrelated. The question can be answered with a measure of responsiveness that is independent of units of measurement. Elasticity is such a measure.

The **price elasticity of demand** is a units-free measure of the responsiveness of the quantity demanded of a good to a change in its price when all other influences on buyers' plans remain the same.

FIGURE **5.1**

How a Change in Supply Changes Price and Quantity

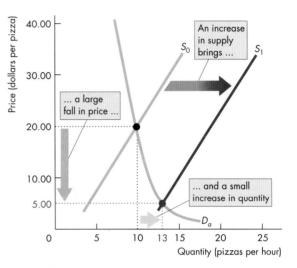

(a) Large price change and small quantity change

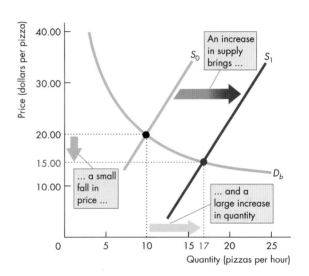

(b) Small price change and large quantity change

Initially, the price is $20 a pizza and the quantity sold is 10 pizzas an hour. Then supply increases from S_0 to S_1. In part (a), the price falls by $15 to $5 a pizza and the quantity increases by only 3 to 13 pizzas an hour. In part (b), the price falls by only $5 to $15 a pizza and the quantity increases by 7 to 17 pizzas an hour. This price change is smaller and quantity change is larger than in case (a). The quantity demanded is more responsive to price in case (b) than in case (a).

Calculating Elasticity

We calculate the *price elasticity of demand* by using the formula

$$\text{Price elasticity of demand} = \frac{\text{Percentage change in quantity demanded}}{\text{Percentage change in price}}.$$

To use this formula, we need to know the quantities demanded at different prices when all other influences on buyers' plans remain the same. Suppose we have the data on prices and quantities demanded of pizza and calculate the price elasticity of demand for pizza.

Figure 5.2 zooms in on the demand curve for pizza and shows how the quantity demanded responds to a small change in price. Initially, the price is $20.50 a pizza and 9 pizzas an hour are sold—the original point in the figure. The price then falls to $19.50 a pizza and the quantity demanded increases to 11 pizzas an hour—the new point in the figure. When the price falls by $1 a pizza, the quantity demanded increases by 2 pizzas an hour.

To calculate the price elasticity of demand, we express the changes in price and quantity demanded as percentages of the *average price* and the *average quantity*. By using the average price and average quantity, we calculate the elasticity at a point on the demand curve midway between the original point and the new point. The original price is $20.50 and the new price is $19.50, so the average price is $20. The $1 price decrease is 5 percent of the average price. That is,

$$\Delta P/P_{ave} = (\$1/\$20)\times 100 = 5\%.$$

The original quantity demanded is 9 pizzas and the new quantity demanded is 11 pizzas, so the average quantity demanded is 10 pizzas. The 2 pizza increase in the quantity demanded is 20 percent of the average quantity. That is,

$$\Delta Q/Q_{ave} = (2/10)\times 100 = 20\%.$$

So the price elasticity of demand, which is the percentage change in the quantity demanded (20 percent) divided by the percentage change in price (5 percent), is 4. That is,

$$\begin{aligned} \text{Price elasticity of demand} &= \frac{\%\Delta Q}{\%\Delta P} \\ &= \frac{20\%}{5\%} = 4. \end{aligned}$$

FIGURE 5.2

Calculating the Elasticity of Demand

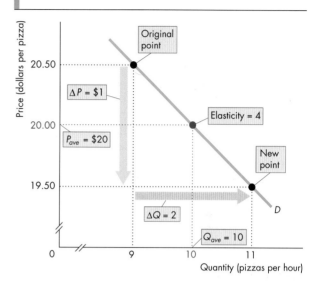

The elasticity of demand is calculated by using the formula*

$$\begin{aligned} \text{Price elasticity of demand} &= \frac{\text{Percentage change in quantity demanded}}{\text{Percentage change in price}} \\ &= \frac{\%\Delta Q}{\%\Delta P} \\ &= \frac{\Delta Q/Q_{ave}}{\Delta P/P_{ave}} \\ &= \frac{2/10}{1/20} \\ &= 4. \end{aligned}$$

This calculation measures the elasticity at an average price of $20 a pizza and an average quantity of 10 pizzas an hour.

*In the formula, the Greek letter delta (Δ) stands for "change in" and %Δ stands for "percentage change in."

Average Price and Quantity   Notice that we use the *average* price and *average* quantity. We do this because it gives the most precise measurement of elasticity—at the midpoint between the original price and the new price. If the price falls from $20.50 to $19.50, the $1 price change is 4.9 percent of $20.50. The 2 pizza change in quantity is 22.2 percent of 9, the original quantity. So if we use these numbers, the elasticity of demand is 22.2 divided by 4.9, which equals 4.5. If the price rises from $19.50 to $20.50, the $1 price change is 5.1 percent of $19.50. The 2 pizza change in quantity is 18.2 percent of 11, the original quantity. So if we use these numbers, the elasticity of demand is 18.2 divided by 5.1, which equals 3.6.

By using percentages of the *average* price and *average* quantity, we get the same value for the elasticity regardless of whether the price falls from $20.50 to $19.50 or rises from $19.50 to $20.50.

Percentages and Proportions   Elasticity is the ratio of the *percentage* change in the quantity demanded to the percentage change in the price. It is also, equivalently, the proportionate change in the quantity demanded divided by the proportionate change in the price. The proportionate change in price is $\Delta P/P_{ave}$, and the proportionate change in quantity demanded is $\Delta Q/Q_{ave}$. The percentage changes are the proportionate changes multiplied by 100. So when we divide one percentage change by another, the 100s cancel and the result is the same as we get by using the proportionate changes.

A Units-Free Measure   Now that you've calculated a price elasticity of demand, you can see why it is a *units-free measure*. Elasticity is a units-free measure because the percentage change in each variable is independent of the units in which the variable is measured. And the ratio of the two percentages is a number without units.

Minus Sign and Elasticity   When the price of a good *rises*, the quantity demanded *decreases* along the demand curve. Because a *positive* change in price brings a *negative* change in the quantity demanded, the price elasticity of demand is a negative number. But it is the magnitude, or *absolute value*, of the price elasticity of demand that tells us how responsive—how elastic—demand is. To compare elasticities, we use the magnitude of the price elasticity of demand and ignore the minus sign.

Inelastic and Elastic Demand

Figure 5.3 shows three demand curves that cover the entire range of possible elasticities of demand. In Fig. 5.3(a), the quantity demanded is constant regardless of the price. If the quantity demanded remains constant when the price changes, then the price elasticity of demand is zero and the good is said to have **perfectly inelastic demand.** One good that has a very low price elasticity of demand (perhaps zero over some price range) is insulin. Insulin is of such

importance to some diabetics that if the price rises or falls, they do not change the quantity they buy.

If the percentage change in the quantity demanded equals the percentage change in price, then the price elasticity equals 1 and the good is said to have **unit elastic demand**. The demand in Fig. 5.3(b) is an example of unit elastic demand.

Between the cases shown in parts (a) and (b) of Fig. 5.3 is the general case in which the percentage change in the quantity demanded is less than the percentage change in price. In this case, the price elasticity of demand is between zero and 1, and the good is said to have **inelastic demand.** Food and housing are examples of goods with inelastic demand.

If the quantity demanded changes by an infinitely large percentage in response to a tiny price change, then the price elasticity of demand is infinity, and the good is said to have **perfectly elastic demand.** Fig. 5.3(c) shows perfectly elastic demand. An example of a good that has a very high elasticity of demand (almost infinite) is soda from two campus machines located side by side. If the two machines offer soda for the same price, some people buy from one and some from the other. But if one machine's price is higher than the other's price, even by a small amount, no one will buy from the machine with the higher price. Sodas from the two machines are perfect substitutes.

Between the cases in parts (b) and (c) of Fig. 5.3 is the general case in which the percentage change in the quantity demanded exceeds the percentage change in price. In this case, the price elasticity is greater than 1 and the good is said to have **elastic demand**. Automobiles and furniture are examples of goods that have elastic demand.

Elasticity Along a Straight-Line Demand Curve

Along a straight-line demand curve like the one shown in Fig. 5.4, the elasticity varies. At high prices and small quantities, the elasticity is large and at low prices and large quantities, the elasticity is small. To convince yourself of this fact, calculate the elasticity at three different average prices.

First, suppose the price falls from $25 to $15 a pizza. The quantity demanded increases from zero to 20 pizzas an hour. The average price is $20, so the percentage change in price is $10 divided by $20 multiplied by 100, which equals 50. The average quantity is 10 pizzas, so the percentage change in quantity is 20 pizzas divided by 10 pizzas multiplied

FIGURE 5.3

Inelastic and Elastic Demand

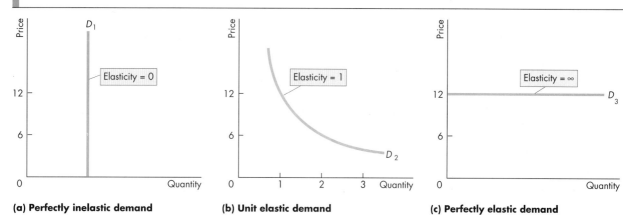

(a) Perfectly inelastic demand　　**(b) Unit elastic demand**　　**(c) Perfectly elastic demand**

Each demand illustrated here has a constant elasticity. The demand curve in part (a) illustrates the demand for a good that has a zero elasticity of demand. The demand curve in part (b) illustrates the demand for a good with a unit elasticity of demand. And the demand curve in part (c) illustrates the demand for a good with an infinite elasticity of demand.

by 100, which equals 200. So dividing the percentage change in the quantity demanded (200) by the percentage change in price (50), you see that the elasticity of demand at an average price of $20 is 4.

Next, suppose that the price falls from $15 to $10 a pizza. The quantity demanded increases from 20 to 30 pizzas an hour. The average price is now $12.50, so the percentage change in price is $5 divided by $12.50 multiplied by 100, which equals 40 percent. The average quantity is 25 pizzas an hour, so the percentage change in the quantity demanded is 10 pizzas divided by 25 pizzas multiplied by 100, which also equals 40 percent. So dividing the percentage change in the quantity demanded (40) by the percentage change in price (40), you see that the elasticity of demand at an average price of $12.50 is 1. The elasticity of demand is always equal to one at the midpoint of a straight-line demand curve.

Finally, suppose that the price falls from $10 to zero. The quantity demanded increases from 30 to 50 pizzas an hour. The average price is now $5, so the percentage change in price is $10 divided by $5 multiplied by 100, which is 200 percent. The average quantity is 40 pizzas, so the percentage change in the quantity demanded is 20 pizzas divided by 40 pizzas multiplied by 100, which is 50 percent. So dividing the percentage change in the quantity demanded (50) by the percentage change in price (200), the elasticity of demand at an average price of $5 is ¼.

FIGURE 5.4

Elasticity Along a
Straight-Line Demand Curve

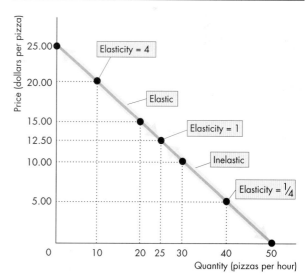

On a straight-line demand curve, elasticity decreases as the price falls and the quantity demanded increases. Demand is unit elastic at the midpoint of the demand curve (elasticity is 1). Above the midpoint, demand is elastic; and below the midpoint, demand is inelastic.

Total Revenue and Elasticity

The **total revenue** from the sale of a good equals the price of the good multiplied by the quantity sold. When a price changes, total revenue also changes. But a rise in price does not always increase total revenue. The change in total revenue depends on the elasticity of demand in the following way:

■ If demand is elastic, a 1 percent price cut increases the quantity sold by more than 1 percent and total revenue increases.
■ If demand is unit elastic, a 1 percent price cut increases the quantity sold by 1 percent and so total revenue does not change.
■ If demand is inelastic, a 1 percent price cut increases the quantity sold by less than 1 percent and total revenue decreases.

We can use this relationship between elasticity and total revenue to estimate elasticity using the total revenue test. The **total revenue test** is a method of estimating the price elasticity of demand by observing the change in total revenue that results from a price change (with all other influences on the quantity sold remaining unchanged).

■ If a price cut increases total revenue, demand is elastic.
■ If a price cut decreases total revenue, demand is inelastic.
■ If a price cut leaves total revenue unchanged, demand is unit elastic.

Figure 5.5 shows the connection between the elasticity of demand and total revenue. In part (a), over the price range from $25 to $12.50, demand is elastic. Over the price range from $12.50 to zero, demand is inelastic. At a price of $12.50, demand is unit elastic.

Figure 5.5(b) shows total revenue. At a price of $25, the quantity sold is zero, so total revenue is also zero. At a price of zero, the quantity demanded is 50 pizzas an hour but total revenue is again zero. A price cut in the elastic range brings an increase in total revenue—the percentage increase in the quantity demanded is greater than the percentage decrease in price. A price cut in the inelastic range brings a decrease in total revenue—the percentage increase in the quantity demanded is less than the percentage decrease in price. At a unit elasticity, total revenue is at a maximum.

FIGURE **5.5**

Elasticity and Total Revenue

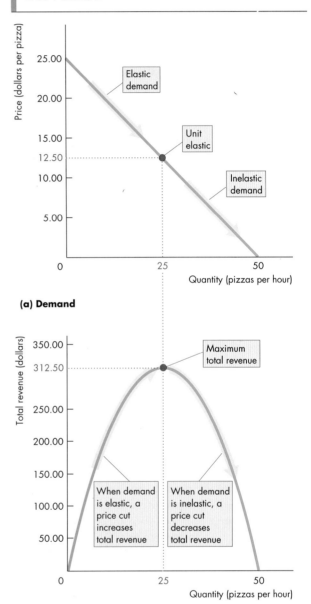

(a) Demand

(b) Total revenue

When demand is elastic, in the price range from $25 to $12.50, a decrease in price (part a) brings an increase in total revenue (part b). When demand is inelastic, in the price range from $12.50 to zero, a decrease in price (part a) brings a decrease in total revenue (part b). When demand is unit elastic, at a price of $12.50 (part a), total revenue is at a maximum (part b).

Your Expenditure and Your Elasticity

When a price changes, the change in your expenditure on the good depends on *your* elasticity of demand.

- If your demand is elastic, a 1 percent price cut increases the quantity you buy by more than 1 percent and your expenditure on the item increases.
- If your demand is unit elastic, a 1 percent price cut increases the quantity you buy by 1 percent and so your expenditure on the item does not change.
- If your demand is inelastic, a 1 percent price cut increases the quantity you buy by less than 1 percent and your expenditure on the item decreases.

So if when the price of an item falls, you spend more on it, your demand for that item is elastic; if you spend the same amount, your demand is unit elastic; and if you spend less, your demand is inelastic.

The Factors That Influence the Elasticity of Demand

Table 5.1 lists some estimates of actual elasticities in the United States. You can see that these real-world elasticities of demand range from 1.52 for metals, the good with the most elastic demand in the table, to 0.12 for food, the good with the most inelastic demand in the table. What makes the demand for some goods elastic and the demand for others inelastic?

Elasticity depends on three main factors:

- The closeness of substitutes
- The proportion of income spent on the good
- The time elapsed since a price change

Closeness of Substitutes The closer the substitutes for a good or service, the more elastic is the demand for it. For example, oil has substitutes but none that are very close (imagine a steam-driven, coal-fueled car or a nuclear-powered jetliner). So the demand for oil is inelastic. Metals have substitutes such as plastics, so the demand for metals is elastic.

The degree of substitutability between two goods also depends on how narrowly (or broadly) we define them. For example, the elasticity of demand for meat is low, but the elasticity of demand for beef, lamb, or chicken is high. The elasticity of demand for personal computers is low, but the elasticity of demand for a Compaq, Dell, or IBM is high.

TABLE 5.1
Some Real-World Price Elasticities of Demand

Good or Service	Elasticity
Elastic Demand	
Metals	1.52
Electrical engineering products	1.39
Mechanical engineering products	1.30
Furniture	1.26
Motor vehicles	1.14
Instrument engineering products	1.10
Professional services	1.09
Transportation services	1.03
Inelastic Demand	
Gas, electricity, and water	0.92
Oil	0.91
Chemicals	0.89
Beverages (all types)	0.78
Clothing	0.64
Tobacco	0.61
Banking and insurance services	0.56
Housing services	0.55
Agricultural and fish products	0.42
Books, magazines, and newspapers	0.34
Food	0.12

Sources: Ahsan Mansur and John Whalley, "Numerical Specification of Applied General Equilibrium Models: Estimation, Calibration, and Data," in *Applied General Equilibrium Analysis*, eds. Herbert E. Scarf and John B. Shoven (New York: Cambridge University Press, 1984), 109, and Henri Theil, Ching-Fan Chung, and James L. Seale, Jr., *Advances in Econometrics, Supplement 1, 1989, International Evidence on Consumption Patterns* (Greenwich, Conn: JAI Press, Inc., 1989). Reprinted with permission.

In everyday language, we call some goods, such as food and housing, *necessities* and other goods, such as exotic vacations, *luxuries*. A necessity is a good that has poor substitutes and that is crucial for our well-being. So generally, a necessity has an inelastic demand. A luxury is a good that usually has many substitutes, one of which is not buying it. So a luxury generally has an elastic demand.

Proportion of Income Spent on the Good   Other things remaining the same, the greater the proportion of income spent on a good, the more elastic is the demand for it.

Think about your own elasticity of demand for chewing gum and housing. If the price of chewing gum doubles, you consume almost as much gum as before. Your demand for gum is inelastic. If apartment rents double, you shriek and look for more students to share accommodation with you. Your demand for housing is more elastic than your demand for gum. Why the difference? Housing takes a large proportion of your budget and gum takes only a tiny proportion. You don't like either price increase, but you hardly notice the higher price of gum, while the higher rent puts your budget under severe strain.

Figure 5.6 shows the proportion of income spent on food and the price elasticity of demand for food in 10 countries. This figure confirms the gen-

eral tendency we have just described. The larger the proportion of income spent on food, the larger is the price elasticity of demand for food. For example, in Tanzania, a nation where average incomes are 3.3 percent of incomes in the United States and where 62 percent of income is spent on food, the price elasticity of demand for food is 0.77. In contrast, in the United States, where 12 percent of income is spent on food, the elasticity of demand for food is 0.12.

Time Elapsed Since a Price Change   The longer the time that has elapsed since a price change, the more elastic is demand. When a price rises, consumers often continue to buy similar quantities of a good for a while. But given enough time, they find acceptable and less costly substitutes. As this process of substitution occurs, the quantity purchased of a good or service that has become more expensive gradually decreases. When a price falls, consumers buy more of the good. But as time passes, they find ever more creative ways of using inexpensive items and demand becomes more elastic. For example, some Japanese farmers have discovered that they can use an inexpensive pager to tell their cows when it is milking time!

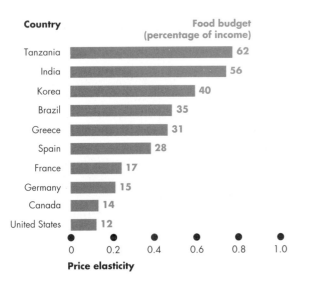

FIGURE 5.6

Price Elasticities in 10 Countries

As income increases and the proportion of income spent on food decreases, the demand for food becomes less elastic.

Source: Henri Theil, Chung-Fan Chung, and James L. Seale, Jr., *Advances in Econometrics, Supplement I, 1989, International Evidence on Consumption Patterns* (Greenwich, Conn.: JAI Press, Inc., 1989).

REVIEW QUIZ

- Why do we need a units-free measure of the responsiveness of the quantity demanded of a good or service to a change in its price?
- Can you define and calculate the price elasticity of demand?
- Why, when we calculate the price elasticity of demand, do we express the change in price as a percentage of the *average* price and the change in quantity as a percentage of the *average* quantity?
- What is the total revenue test and why does it work?
- What are the main influences on the elasticity of demand that make the demand for some goods elastic and the demand for other goods inelastic?

You've now completed your study of the *price* elasticity of demand. Two other elasticity concepts tell us the effects of other influences on demand. Let's look at these other elasticities of demand.

More Elasticities of Demand

BACK AT THE PIZZERIA, YOU ARE TRYING TO WORK out how a price cut by the burger shop next door will affect the demand for your pizza. You know that pizzas and burgers are substitutes. And you know that when the price of a substitute for pizza falls, the demand for pizza decreases. But by how much?

You also know that pizza and soda are complements. And you know that if the price of a complement of pizza falls, the demand for pizza increases. So you wonder whether you might keep your customers by cutting the price you charge for soda. But you want to know by how much you must cut the price of soda to hold onto your customers in the face of the cheaper burgers next door.

To answer these questions, you need to calculate the cross elasticity of demand. Let's examine this elasticity measure.

Cross Elasticity of Demand

We measure the influence of a change in the price of substitutes or complements by using the concept of the cross elasticity of demand. The **cross elasticity of demand** is a measure of the responsiveness of the demand for a good to a change in the price of a substitute or complement, other things remaining the same. It is calculated by using the formula

$$\text{Cross elasticity of demand} = \frac{\text{Percentage change in quantity demanded}}{\text{Percentage change in price of a substitute or complement}}.$$

The cross elasticity of demand can be positive or negative. It is positive for a substitute and negative for a complement.

Figure 5.7 illustrates the cross elasticity of demand. Pizza and burgers are substitutes. Because they are substitutes, when the price of a burger falls, the demand for pizza decreases. The demand curve for pizza shifts leftward from D_0 to D_1. Because a *fall* in the price of a burger brings a *decrease* in the demand for pizza, the cross elasticity of demand for pizza with respect to the price of a burger is *positive*. Both the price and the quantity change in the same direction.

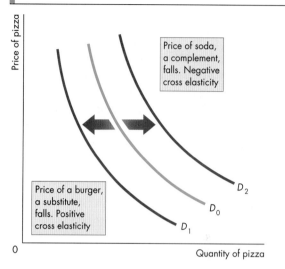

FIGURE 5.7
Cross Elasticity of Demand

A burger is a *substitute* for pizza. When the price of a burger falls, the demand for pizza decreases and the demand curve for pizza shifts leftward from D_0 to D_1. The cross elasticity of the demand for pizza with respect to the price of a burger is *positive*. Soda is a *complement* of pizza. When the price of soda falls, the demand for pizza increases and the demand curve for pizza shifts rightward from D_0 to D_2. The cross elasticity of the demand for pizza with respect to the price of soda is *negative*.

Pizza and soda are complements. Because they are complements, when the price of soda falls, the demand for pizza increases. The demand curve for pizza shifts rightward from D_0 to D_2. Because a *fall* in the price of soda brings an *increase* in the demand for pizza, the cross elasticity of demand for pizza with respect to the price of soda is *negative*. The price and quantity change in *opposite* directions.

The magnitude of the cross elasticity of demand determines how far the demand curve shifts. The larger the cross elasticity (absolute value), the greater is the change in demand and the larger is the shift in the demand curve.

If two items are very close substitutes, such as two brands of spring water, the cross elasticity is large. If two items are close complements, such as movies and popcorn, the cross elasticity is large.

If two items are somewhat unrelated to each other, such as newspapers and orange juice, the cross elasticity is small, and perhaps zero.

Income Elasticity of Demand

The economy is expanding and people are enjoying rising incomes. This prosperity is bringing an increase in the demand for all types of goods and services. But by how much will the demand for pizza increase?

The answer depends on the income elasticity of demand for the good. The **income elasticity of demand** is a measure of the responsiveness of the demand for a good or service to a change in income, other things remaining the same. It is calculated by using the formula

$$\text{Income elasticity of demand} = \frac{\text{Percentage change in quantity demanded}}{\text{Percentage change in income}}.$$

Income elasticities of demand can be positive or negative and fall into three interesting ranges:

1. Greater than 1 (*normal* good, income elastic)
2. Between zero and 1 (*normal* good, income inelastic)
3. Less than zero (*inferior* good)

Figure 5.8(a) shows an income elasticity of demand that is greater than 1. As income increases, the quantity demanded increases, but the quantity demanded increases faster than income. Examples of goods in this category are ocean cruises, international travel, jewelry, and works of arts.

Figure 5.8(b) shows an income elasticity of demand that is between zero and 1. In this case, the quantity demanded increases as income increases, but income increases faster than the quantity demanded. Examples of goods in this category are food, clothing, newspapers, and magazines.

Figure 5.8(c) shows an income elasticity of demand that eventually becomes negative. In this case, the quantity demanded increases as income increases until it reaches a maximum at income *m*. As income continues to increase above *m*, the quantity demanded decreases. The elasticity of demand is positive but less than 1 up to income *m*. Beyond income *m*, the income elasticity of demand is negative. Examples of goods in this category are small motorcycles, potatoes, and rice. Low-income consumers buy most of these goods. At low income levels, the demand for such goods increases as income increases. But as income increases above *m*, consumers replace these goods with superior alternatives. For example, a small car replaces the motorcycle; fruit, vegetables, and meat begin to appear in a diet that was heavy in rice or potatoes.

FIGURE 5.8

Income Elasticity of Demand

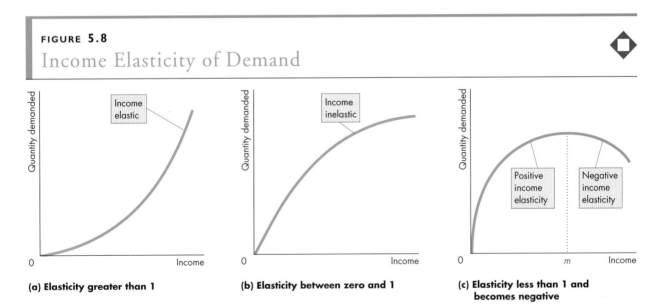

(a) Elasticity greater than 1

(b) Elasticity between zero and 1

(c) Elasticity less than 1 and becomes negative

Income elasticity of demand has three ranges of values. In part (a), income elasticity of demand is greater than 1. As income increases along the x-axis, the quantity demanded increases but by a bigger percentage than the increase in income. In part (b), income elasticity of demand is between zero and 1. As income increases, the quantity demanded increases but by a smaller percentage than the increase in income. In part (c), the income elasticity of demand is positive at low incomes but becomes negative as income increases above level *m*. Maximum consumption of this good occurs at the income *m*.

Real-World Income Elasticities of Demand

Table 5.2 shows estimates of some income elasticities in the United States. Necessities such as food and clothing are income inelastic, while luxuries such as airline and foreign travel are income elastic.

But what is a necessity and what is a luxury depend on the level of income. For people with a low income, food and clothing can be luxuries. So the *level* of income has a big effect on income elasticities of demand. Figure 5.9 shows this effect on the income elasticity of demand for food in 10 countries. In countries with low incomes, such as Tanzania and India, the income elasticity of demand for food is high. In countries with high incomes, such as the United States, it is low.

TABLE 5.2

Some Real-World Income Elasticities of Demand

Elastic Demand

Airline travel	5.82
Movies	3.41
Foreign travel	3.08
Electricity	1.94
Restaurant meals	1.61
Local buses and trains	1.38
Haircuts	1.36
Cars	1.07

Inelastic Demand

Tobacco	0.86
Alcoholic beverages	0.62
Furniture	0.53
Clothing	0.51
Newspapers and magazines	0.38
Telephone	0.32
Food	0.14

Sources: H.S. Houthakker and Lester D. Taylor, *Consumer Demand in the United States* (Cambridge, Mass.: Harvard University Press, 1970), and Henri Theil, Ching-Fan Chung, and James L. Seale, Jr., *Advances in Econometrics, Supplement 1, 1989, International Evidence on Consumption Patterns* (Greenwich, Conn: JAI Press, Inc., 1989). Reprinted with permission.

FIGURE 5.9

Income Elasticities in 10 Countries

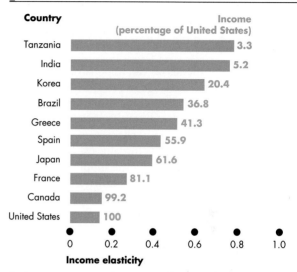

As income increases, the income elasticity of demand for food decreases. For low-income consumers, a larger percentage of any increase in income is spent on food than for high-income consumers.

Source: Henri Theil, Ching-Fan Chung, and James L. Seale, Jr., *Advances in Econometrics, Supplement 1, 1989, International Evidence on Consumption Patterns* (Greenwich, Conn: JAI Press, Inc., 1989).

REVIEW QUIZ

- What does the cross elasticity of demand measure?
- What does the sign (positive versus negative) of the cross elasticity of demand tell us about the relationship between two goods?
- What does the income elasticity of demand measure?
- What does the sign (positive versus negative) of the income elasticity of demand tell us about a good?
- Why does the level of income influence the magnitude of the income elasticity of demand?

You've now completed your study of the *cross elasticity* of demand and the *income elasticity* of demand. Let's look at the other side of a market and examine the elasticity of supply.

Elasticity of Supply

YOU KNOW THAT WHEN DEMAND INCREASES, THE equilibrium price rises and the equilibrium quantity increases. But does the price rise by a large amount and the quantity increase by a little? Or does the price barely rise and the quantity increase by a large amount?

The answer depends on the responsiveness of the quantity supplied to a change in price. You can see why by studying Fig. 5.10, which shows two possible scenarios in a local pizza market. Fig. 5.10(a) shows one scenario, and Fig. 5.10(b) shows the other.

In both cases, demand is initially D_0. In part (a), the supply of pizza is shown by the supply curve S_a. In part (b), the supply of pizza is shown by the supply curve S_b. Initially, in both cases, the price is $20 a pizza and the quantity produced and consumed is 10 pizzas an hour.

Now an increase in income and population increases the demand for pizza. The demand curve shifts rightward to D_1. In case (a), the price rises by $10 to $30 a pizza and the quantity increases by only 3 to 13 an hour. In contrast, in case (b), the price rises by only $1 to $21 a pizza and the quantity increases by 10 to 20 pizzas an hour.

The different outcomes arise from differing degrees of responsiveness of the quantity supplied to a change in price. We measure the degree of responsiveness by using the concept of the elasticity of supply.

Calculating the Elasticity of Supply

The **elasticity of supply** measures the responsiveness of the quantity supplied to a change in the price of a good when all other influences on selling plans remain the same. It is calculated by using the formula

$$\frac{\text{Elasticity}}{\text{of supply}} = \frac{\text{Percentage change in quantity supplied}}{\text{Percentage change in price}}.$$

We use the same method that you learned when you studied the elasticity of demand. Let's calculate the elasticity of supply for the supply curves in Fig. 5.10.

In Fig. 5.10(a), when the price rises from $20 to $30, the price rise is $10 and the average price is $25, so the price rises by 40 percent of the average price. The quantity increases from 10 to 13, so the increase

FIGURE 5.10

How a Change in Demand Changes Price and Quantity

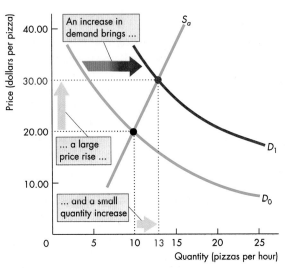

(a) Large price change and small quantity change

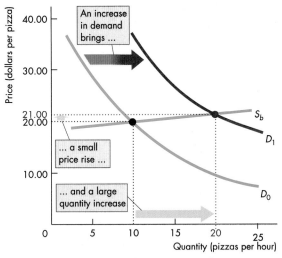

(b) Small price change and large quantity change

Initially, the price is $20 a pizza and the quantity sold is 10 pizzas an hour. Then incomes and population increase and demand increases from D_0 to D_1. In part (a), the price rises by $10 to $30 a pizza and the quantity increases by only 3 to 13 pizzas an hour. In part (b), the price rises by only $1 to $21 a pizza and the quantity increases by 10 to 20 pizzas an hour. The quantity supplied is more responsive to price in case (b) than in case (a).

is 3, the average quantity is 11.5, and the quantity increases by 26 percent. The elasticity of supply is equal to 26 percent divided by 40 percent, which equals 0.65.

In Fig. 5.10(b), when the price rises from $20 to $21, the price rise is $1 and the average price is $20.50, so the price rises by 4.9 percent of the average price. The quantity increases from 10 to 20, so the increase is 10, the average quantity is 15, and the quantity increases by 67 percent. The elasticity of supply is equal to 67 percent divided by 4.9 percent, which equals 13.67.

Figure 5.11 shows the range of supply elasticities. If the quantity supplied is fixed regardless of the price, the supply curve is vertical and the elasticity of supply is zero. Supply is perfectly inelastic. This case is shown in Fig. 5.11(a). A special intermediate case occurs when the percentage change in price equals the percentage change in quantity. Supply is then unit elastic. This case is shown in Fig. 5.11(b). No matter how steep the supply curve is, if it is linear and passes through the origin, supply is unit elastic. If there is a price at which sellers are willing to offer any quantity for sale, the supply curve is horizontal and the elasticity of supply is infinite. Supply is perfectly elastic. This case is shown in Fig. 5.11(c).

The Factors That Influence the Elasticity of Supply

The magnitude of the elasticity of supply depends on:
- Resource substitution possibilities
- Time frame for the supply decision

Resource Substitution Possibilities   Some goods and services can be produced only by using unique or rare productive resources. These items have a low, and perhaps a zero, elasticity of supply. Other goods and services can be produced by using commonly available resources that could be allocated to a wide variety of alternative tasks. Such items have a high elasticity of supply.

A van Gogh painting is an example of a good with a vertical supply curve and an elasticity of supply of zero. At the other extreme, wheat can be grown on land that is almost equally good for growing corn. So it is just as easy to grow wheat as corn, and the opportunity cost of wheat in terms of forgone corn is almost constant. As a result, the supply curve of wheat is almost horizontal and its elasticity of supply is very large. Similarly, when a good is produced in many different countries (for example, sugar and beef), the supply of the good is highly elastic.

FIGURE 5.11
Inelastic and Elastic Supply

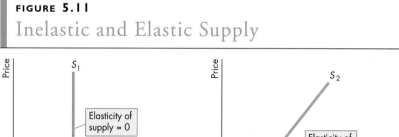
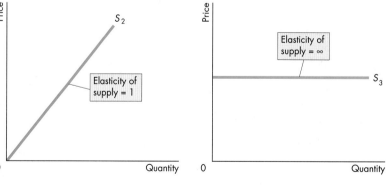

(a) Perfectly inelastic supply   (b) Unit elastic supply   (c) Perfectly elastic supply

Each supply illustrated here has a constant elasticity. The supply curve in part (a) illustrates the supply of a good that has a zero elasticity of supply. The supply curve in part (b) illustrates the supply for a good with a unit elasticity of supply. All linear supply curves that pass through the origin have a unit elasticity. The supply curve in part (c) illustrates the supply for a good with an infinite elasticity of supply.

The supply of most goods and services lies between the two extremes. The quantity produced can be increased but only by incurring higher cost. If a higher price is offered, the quantity supplied increases. Such goods and services have an elasticity of supply between zero and infinity.

Time Frame for the Supply Decision   To study the influence of the length of time elapsed since a price change, we distinguish three time frames of supply:

- Momentary supply
- Long-run supply
- Short-run supply

When the price of a good rises or falls, the *momentary supply curve* shows the response of the quantity supplied immediately following a price change.

Some goods, such as fruits and vegetables, have a perfectly inelastic momentary supply—a vertical supply curve. The quantities supplied depend on crop-planting decisions made earlier. In the case of oranges, for example, planting decisions have to be made many years in advance of the crop being available. The momentary supply curve is vertical because, on a given day, no matter what the price of oranges, producers cannot change their output. They have picked, packed, and shipped their crop to market, and the quantity available for that day is fixed.

In contrast, some goods have a perfectly elastic momentary supply. Long-distance phone calls are an example. When many people simultaneously make a call, there is a big surge in the demand for telephone cables, computer switching, and satellite time, and the quantity supplied increases (up to the physical limits of the telephone system). But the price remains constant. Long-distance carriers monitor fluctuations in demand and reroute calls to ensure that the quantity supplied equals the quantity demanded without changing the price.

The *long-run supply curve* shows the response of the quantity supplied to a change in price after all the technologically possible ways of adjusting supply have been exploited. In the case of oranges, the long run is the time it takes new plantings to grow to full maturity—about 15 years. In some cases, the long-run adjustment occurs only after a completely new production plant has been built and workers have been trained to operate it—typically a process that might take several years.

The *short-run supply curve* shows how the quantity supplied responds to a price change when only some of the technologically possible adjustments to production have been made. The first adjustment that is usually made is in the amount of labor employed. To increase output in the short run, firms work their labor force overtime and perhaps hire additional workers. To decrease their output in the short run, firms lay off workers or reduce their hours of work. With the passage of time, firms can make additional adjustments, perhaps training additional workers or buying additional tools and other equipment. The short-run response to a price change, unlike the momentary and long-run responses, is not a unique response but a sequence of adjustments.

The short-run supply curve slopes upward because producers can take actions quite quickly to change the quantity supplied in response to a price change. For example, if the price of oranges falls, growers can stop picking and leave oranges to rot on the tree. Or if the price rises, they can use more fertilizer and improved irrigation to increase the yields of their existing trees. In the long run, they can plant more trees and increase the quantity supplied even more in response to a given price rise.

R E V I E W   Q U I Z

- Why do we need to measure of the responsiveness of the quantity supplied of a good or service to a change in its price?
- Can you define and calculate the elasticity of supply?
- What are the main influences on the elasticity of supply that make the supply of some goods elastic and the supply of other goods inelastic?
- Can you provide examples of goods or services whose elasticity of supply are (a) zero, (b) greater than zero but less than infinity, and (c) infinity?
- How does the time frame over which a supply decision is made influence the elasticity of supply?

◆ You have now studied the theory of demand and supply, and you have learned how to measure the elasticities of demand and supply. Table 5.3 summarizes all the elasticities that you've met in this chapter. In the next chapter, we are going to study the efficiency of competitive markets. But before we do that, take a look at *Reading Between the Lines* on pp. 102–103 to see elasticity in action.

TABLE 5.3
A Compact Glossary of Elasticities

Price Elasticities of Demand

A relationship is described as	When its magnitude is	Which means that
Perfectly elastic or infinitely elastic	Infinity	The smallest possible increase in price causes an infinitely large decrease in the quantity demanded*
Elastic	Less than infinity but greater than 1	The percentage decrease in the quantity demanded exceeds the percentage increase in price
Unit elastic	1	The percentage decrease in the quantity demanded equals the percentage increase in price
Inelastic	Greater than zero but less than 1	The percentage decrease in the quantity demanded is less than the percentage increase in price
Perfectly inelastic or completely inelastic	Zero	The quantity demanded is the same at all prices

Cross Elasticities of Demand

A relationship is described as	When its value is	Which means that
Perfect substitutes	Infinity	The smallest possible increase in the price of one good causes an infinitely large increase in the quantity demanded of the other good
Substitutes	Positive, less than infinity	If the price of one good increases, the quantity demanded of the other good also increases
Independent	Zero	The quantity demanded of one good remains constant, regardless of the price of the other good
Complements	Less than zero	The quantity demanded of one good decreases when the price of the other good increases

Income Elasticities of Demand

A relationship is described as	When its value is	Which means that
Income elastic (normal good)	Greater than 1	The percentage increase in the quantity demanded is greater than the percentage increase in income
Income inelastic (normal good)	Less than 1 but greater than zero	The percentage increase in the quantity demanded is less than the percentage increase in income
Negative income elastic (inferior good)	Less than zero	When income increases, quantity demanded decreases

Elasticities of Supply

A relationship is described as	When its magnitude is	Which means that
Perfectly elastic	Infinity	The smallest possible increase in price causes an infinitely large increase in the quantity supplied
Elastic	Less than infinity but greater than 1	The percentage increase in the quantity supplied exceeds the percentage increase in the price
Inelastic	Greater than zero but less than 1	The percentage increase in the quantity supplied is less than the percentage increase in the price
Perfectly inelastic	Zero	The quantity supplied is the same at all prices

*In each description, the directions of change may be reversed. For example, in this case: The smallest possible *decrease* in price causes an infinitely large *increase* in the quantity demanded.

Elasticity in Action:
The Market for Gas

USA TODAY, FEBRUARY 4, 1999

Gas Wars Send Prices Plummeting

Gas wars across the nation are driving already-low fuel costs to their cheapest levels in more than two decades.

Prices have plummeted into the 70-cents-a-gallon range at some warring stations from Hawaii to Pennsylvania.

Some stations in Virginia and New Jersey are selling fuel for 57 to 59 cents a gallon to lure motorists from rival dealers across the street. Not since the 1960s and '70s has competition between stations made gas such a bargain.

"Let the wars rage on," says Eric Pressman, who filled his Toyota MR2 for $7 in Dale City, Va.

The average national price of self-serve, unleaded gas dropped to 97.9 cents a gallon last month. That's the lowest since 1979 and 18 cents cheaper than the same time last year, according to AAA.

When adjusted for inflation, prices are the lowest in history. ...

A glut of crude oil and improvements in manufacturing have created a gas surplus. As a result, oil prices fell to an average of $12 a barrel last month, down from $15 in January 1998. That's the lowest level in a quarter century. ...

Motorists should enjoy cheap driving all year. Good summer driving weather probably will increase fuel demands and could bump prices 5 to 10 cents a gallon. But analysts don't expect dramatic price increases.

Reprinted by permission of *USA Today*
February 4, 1999

Essence of the Story

■ The national average price of self-serve unleaded gas was 97.9 cents a gallon in January 1999, down 18 cents a gallon from its January 1998 level.

■ Prices in some Virginia and New Jersey gas stations were 57 to 59 cents a gallon, and many gas stations across the nation had prices in the 70-cents-a-gallon range.

■ These gas prices are the lowest in 20 years; adjusted for inflation, they are the lowest ever.

■ The price of crude oil fell from $15 in January 1998 to $12 a barrel in January 1999, its lowest level in 25 years.

■ If good summer driving weather increases the demand for gasoline, the price could rise by 5 to 10 cents a gallon.

■ Figure 1 shows the price of gasoline since 1959. The green line is the money price, and the red line is the relative price (the price adjusted for inflation)—see Chapter 4, p. 62.

■ As the news article reports, adjusted for inflation, the price in January 1999 was the lowest ever.

■ The money price is the lowest since 1979 except for 1986-1989, when the price was also roughly the same as in 1999 (a slight error in the news article).

■ The price of gasoline has fallen because the supply of gasoline has increased. And the fall in price is relatively large because the *demand for gasoline is inelastic*.

■ Figure 2 illustrates the effects of an increase in supply. The demand for gasoline is D. Initially, the supply of gasoline is S_{98}, and the price is $1.26 (126 cents) a gallon.

■ The supply of gasoline increases to S_{99}. In Fig. 2, the elasticity of demand for gasoline is (approximately) 0.5. So the price falls to 98 cents a gallon, and the quantity increases from 7 million barrels a day to 8 million barrels a day.

■ If the demand for gasoline were elastic, the increase in supply would bring only a small fall in price. Its main effect would be to bring a relatively large increase in the equilibrium quantity.

■ Figure 3 illustrates the effect of an increase in the demand for gasoline during the summer. Demand increases from D_{Jan} to D_{Jul}. The price rise is the upper end of the range predicted in the news article. The elasticity of supply is (approximately) 0.9.

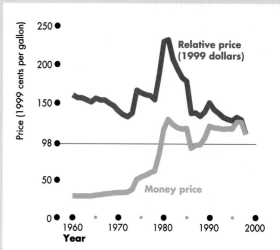

Figure 1 The price of gasoline

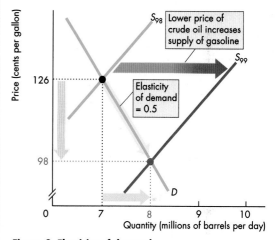

Figure 2 Elasticity of demand

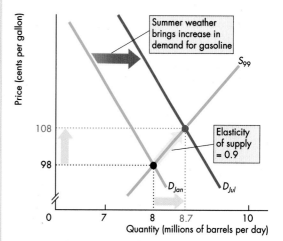

Figure 3 Elasticity of supply

SUMMARY

KEY POINTS

The Price Elasticity of Demand (pp. 88–94)

- Elasticity is a measure of the responsiveness of the quantity demanded of a good to a change in its price.
- Price elasticity of demand equals the percentage change in the quantity demanded divided by the percentage change in price.
- The larger the magnitude of the elasticity of demand, the greater is the responsiveness of the quantity demanded to a given change in price.
- Price elasticity of demand depends on how easily one good serves as a substitute for another, the proportion of income spent on the good, and the length of time elapsed since the price change.
- If demand is elastic, a decrease in price leads to an increase in total revenue. If demand is unit elastic, a decrease in price leaves total revenue unchanged. And if demand is inelastic, a decrease in price leads to a decrease in total revenue.

More Elasticities of Demand (pp. 95–97)

- Cross elasticity of demand measures the responsiveness of demand for one good to a change in the price of a substitute or a complement.
- The cross elasticity of demand with respect to the price of a substitute is positive. The cross elasticity of demand with respect to the price of a complement is negative.
- Income elasticity of demand measures the responsiveness of demand to a change in income. For a normal good, the income elasticity of demand is positive. For an inferior good, the income elasticity of demand is negative.
- When the income elasticity is greater than 1, as income increases, the percentage of income spent on the good increases.
- When the income elasticity is less than 1 but greater than zero, as income increases, the percentage of income spent on the good decreases.

Elasticity of Supply (pp. 98–100)

- Elasticity of supply measures the responsiveness of the quantity supplied of a good to a change in its price.
- Elasticities of supply range between zero (vertical supply curve) and infinity (horizontal supply curve).
- Supply decisions have three time frames: momentary, long run, and short run.
- Momentary supply refers to the response of sellers to a price change at the instant that the price changes.
- Long-run supply refers to the response of sellers to a price change when all the technologically feasible adjustments in production have been made.
- Short-run supply refers to the response of sellers to a price change after some adjustments in production have been made.

KEY FIGURES AND TABLE

KEY TERMS

PROBLEMS

*1. Rain spoils the strawberry crop. As a result, the price rises from $4 to $6 a box and the quantity demanded decreases from 1,000 to 600 boxes a week. Over this price range,
   a. What is the price elasticity of demand?
   b. Describe the demand for strawberries.

2. Good weather brings a bumper tomato crop. The price of tomatoes falls from $6 to $4 a basket and the quantity demanded increases from 200 to 400 baskets a day. Over this price range,
   a. What is the price elasticity of demand?
   b. Describe the demand for tomatoes.

*3. The figure shows the demand for videotape rentals.

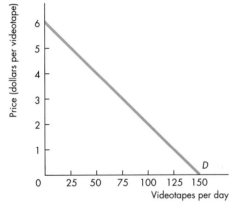

   a. Calculate the elasticity of demand for a rise in rental price from $3 to $5.
   b. At what price is the elasticity of demand equal to 1, infinity, and zero?

4. The figure shows the demand for pens.

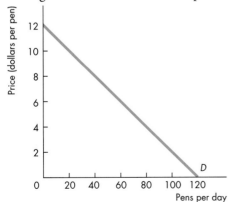

   a. Calculate the elasticity of demand for a rise in price from $2 to $4.

b. At what prices is the elasticity of demand equal to 1, greater than 1, and less than 1?

*5. If the quantity of dental services demanded increases by 10 percent when the price of dental services falls by 10 percent, is the demand for dental service inelastic, elastic, or unit elastic?

6. If the quantity of fish demanded decreases by 5 percent when the price of fish rises by 10 percent, is the demand for fish elastic, inelastic, or unit elastic?

*7. The demand schedule for computer chips is:

Price (dollars per chip)	Quantity demanded (millions of chips per year)
200	50
250	45
300	40
350	35
400	30

   a. What happens to total revenue if the price of a chip falls from $400 to $350?
   b. What happens to total revenue if the price of a chip falls from $350 to $300?
   c. At what price is total revenue a maximum?
   d. What quantity of chips will be sold at the price that answers problem 7(c)?
   e. At an average price of $350, is the demand for chips elastic or inelastic? Use the total revenue test to answer this question.

8. The demand schedule for coffee is:

Price (dollars per pound)	Quantity demanded (millions of pounds per year)
10	30
15	25
20	20
25	15

   a. What happens to total revenue if the price of coffee rises from $10 to $20 per pound?
   b. What happens to total revenue if the price rises from $15 to $25 per pound?
   c. What price will maximize total revenue?
   d. What quantity of coffee will be sold at the price that answers problem 8(c)?
   e. At an average price of $15 a pound, is the demand for coffee elastic or inelastic? Use the total revenue test to answer this question.

*9. In problem 7, at $250 a chip, is the demand for chips elastic or inelastic? Use the total revenue test to answer this question.

10. In problem 8, at $15 a pound, is the demand for coffee elastic or inelastic? Use the total revenue test to answer this question.

*11. If a 12 percent rise in the price of orange juice decreases the quantity of orange juice demanded by 22 percent and increases the quantity of apple juice demanded by 14 percent, calculate the cross elasticity of demand between orange juice and apple juice.

12. If a 10 percent fall in the price of beef increases the quantity of beef demanded by 15 percent and decreases the quantity of chicken demanded by 20 percent, calculate the cross elasticity of demand between beef and chicken.

*13. Last year, Alex's income increased from $3,000 to $5,000. Alex increased his consumption of bagels from 4 to 8 a month and decreased his consumption of donuts from 12 to 6 a month. Calculate Alex's income elasticity of demand for i) bagels, and ii) donuts.

14. Last year Judy's income increased from $10,000 to $12,000. Judy increased her demand for concert tickets by 10 percent and decreased her demand for bus rides by 5 percent. Calculate Judy's income elasticity of demand for i) concert tickets and ii) bus rides.

*15. The table gives the supply schedule for long-distance phone calls:

Price (cents per minute)	Quantity supplied (millions of minutes per day)
10	200
20	400
30	600
40	800

Calculate the elasticity of supply when
a. The price falls from 40 cents to 30 cents a minute.
b. The price is 20 cents a minute.

16. The table gives the supply schedule for shoes.

Price (dollars per pair)	Quantity supplied (millions of pairs per year)
120	1200
125	1400
130	1600
135	1800

Calculate the elasticity of supply when
a. The price rises from $125 to $135 a pair.
b. The price is $125 a pair.

CRITICAL THINKING

1. According to the news article in *Reading Between the Lines* on pp. 102–103, a glut of crude oil caused the supply of gasoline to increase during 1998 and early 1999:
   a. What do you think the article means by "a glut of crude oil"? Answer this question by using the concepts of demand, supply, quantity demanded, and quantity supplied.
   b. Why do you think the reported glut of crude oil caused the price of crude oil to fall? Use the concept of elasticity in your answer to this question.
   c. Calculate the elasticity of demand implied by the data and curves in Fig. 2 on p. 103.
   d. Calculate by approximately how much the price of gasoline would have fallen if the elasticity of demand for gasoline was 2 and the quantity of gasoline increased from 7 million barrels a day to 8 million barrels a day.
   e. Calculate the elasticity of supply implied by the data and curves in Fig. 3 on p. 103.

2. Use the link on the Parkin Web site and:
   a. Find the price of gasoline in the summer of 1999. Did the predictions of the news article occur?
   b. Use the tools of demand and supply and the concept of elasticity to explain the recent changes in the price of gasoline.
   c. Find the latest price of crude oil.
   d. Use the tools of demand and supply and the concept of elasticity to explain the recent changes in the price of crude oil.

3. Use the link on the Parkin Web site and:
   a. Find the number of gallons in a barrel.
   b. What is the cost of the crude oil in one gallon of gasoline?
   c. What are the other costs that make up the total cost of a gallon of gasoline?
   d. If the price of crude oil falls by 10 percent, by what percentage would you expect the price of gasoline to change, other things remaining the same?
   e. In light of your answer to part (d), do you think the elasticity of demand for crude oil is greater than, less than, or equal to the elasticity of demand for gasoline?

6

Efficiency and Equity

People constantly strive to get more
for less. As consumers, we love a bargain. We enjoy telling our friends about
the great deal we got on CDs or some other
item we bought at a surprisingly low price.
Every time we buy something or decide *not* to buy
something, we express our view about how scarce
resources should be used. We try to spend our incomes in
ways that get the most out of our scarce resources. For example, we balance the pleasure we get from our expenditure on
movies against that we get from our textbooks. ◆ Is the allocation of
our resources between leisure and education, pizza and submarine
sandwiches, roller blades and squash balls, and all the other things we
buy the right one? Could we get more out of our resources if we spent
more on some goods and services and less on
others? ◆ Scientists and engineers devote
enormous efforts to finding new technologies
for producing goods and services. Workers in
factories and on assembly lines make suggestions that increase productivity. Is our economy efficient at producing goods and services? Do we get the most out of our scarce
resources in our factories, offices, and shops?
◆ Some firms make huge profits year after year. Microsoft, for example, has generated enough profit over the past ten years to rocket Bill
Gates, one of its founders, into the position of being one of the richest
people in the world. Is that kind of business success a sign of efficiency?
◆ And is it fair that Bill Gates is so incredibly rich while others live in
miserable poverty?

◆ These are the kinds of questions you'll explore in this chapter. You
will first learn some concepts that enable you to think about efficiency
more broadly than the everyday use of that word. You will discover that
competitive markets can be efficient. But you will also discover some
sources of inefficiency that can be addressed with government action.
And you will discover that firms that make huge profits, while efficient
in one sense, might be inefficient in a broader sense.

More for Less

After studying this chapter, you will be able to:

- ■ **Define efficiency**

- ■ **Distinguish between value and price and define consumer surplus**

- ■ **Distinguish between cost and price and define producer surplus**

- ■ **Explain the conditions in which competitive markets move resources to their highest-valued uses**

- ■ **Explain the obstacles to efficiency in our economy**

- ■ **Explain the main ideas about fairness and evaluate claims that competitive markets result in unfair outcomes**

Efficiency: A Refresher

IT IS HARD TO TALK ABOUT EFFICIENCY IN ORDI-
nary conversation without generating both disagreement and misunderstanding. Many people see efficiency as a clearly desirable goal. To an engineer, an
entrepreneur, a politician, a working mother, or
an economist, getting more for less seems like an
obviously sensible thing to aim for. But some people
think that the pursuit of efficiency conflicts with
other goals. And they believe the other goals are
more worthy of pursuit. Environmental protection
groups worry about contamination from "efficient"
nuclear power plants. And car producers worry about
competition from "efficient" foreign producers.

Economists use the idea of efficiency in a way
that avoids these conflicts. Resource use is **efficient**
when we produce the goods and services that people
value most highly (see Chapter 3, pp. 40-42). Equivalently, resource use is efficient when we cannot produce more of a good or service without giving up
some other good or service that we value more highly.

If people value a nuclear-free environment more
highly than they value cheap electric power, it is efficient to use higher-cost, nonnuclear technologies to
produce electricity. Efficiency is not a cold, mechanical concept. It is a concept based on value, and value
is based on people's feelings.

Think about the efficient quantity of pizza. To
produce more pizza, we must give up some other
goods and services. For example, we might give up
some submarine sandwiches. To get more pizzas, we
forgo submarine sandwiches. If we produce fewer
pizzas, we can produce more submarine sandwiches.
What is the efficient quantity of pizza to produce? The
answer depends on marginal benefit and marginal cost.

Marginal Benefit

If we consume one more pizza, we receive a marginal
benefit. **Marginal benefit** is the benefit that a person receives from consuming one more unit of a good
or service. The marginal benefit from a good or service
is measured as the maximum amount that a person is
willing to pay for one more unit of it. So the marginal
benefit from a pizza is the maximum amount of other
goods and services that people are willing to give up to
get one more pizza. The marginal benefit from pizza
decreases as the quantity of pizza consumed increases—
the principle of *decreasing marginal benefit*.

We can express the marginal benefit from a pizza
as the number of submarine sandwiches that people
are willing to forgo to get one more pizza. But we can
also express marginal benefit as the dollar value of
other goods and services that people are willing to
forgo. Figure 6.1 shows the marginal benefit from
pizza expressed in this way. As the quantity of pizza
increases, the value of other items that people are
willing to forgo to get yet one more pizza decreases.

Marginal Cost

If we produce one more pizza, we incur a marginal
cost. **Marginal cost** is the opportunity cost of producing *one more unit* of a good or service. The marginal cost of a good or service is measured as the

---

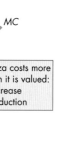

FIGURE 6.1

The Efficient Quantity of Pizza

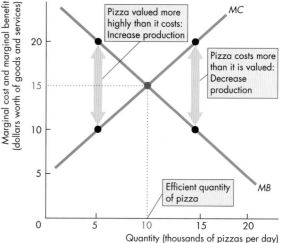

The marginal benefit curve (MB) shows what people *are willing
to* forgo to get one more pizza. The marginal cost curve (MC)
shows what people *must* forgo to get one more pizza. If fewer
than 10,000 pizzas a day are produced, marginal benefit exceeds
marginal cost. Greater value can be obtained by producing
more pizzas. If more than 10,000 pizzas a day are produced,
marginal cost exceeds marginal benefit. Greater value can be
obtained by producing fewer pizzas. If 10,000 pizzas a day are
produced, marginal benefit equals marginal cost and the efficient quantity of pizza is available.

value of the best alternative forgone. So the marginal cost of a pizza is the value of the best alternative forgone to get one more pizza. The marginal cost of a pizza increases as the quantity of pizza produced increases—the principle of *increasing marginal cost*.

We can express marginal cost as the number of submarine sandwiches we must forgo to get one more pizza. But we can also express marginal cost as the dollar value of other goods and services we must forgo. Figure 6.1 shows the marginal cost of pizza expressed in this way. As the quantity of pizza produced increases, the value of other items we must forgo to get yet one more pizza increases.

Efficiency and Inefficiency

To determine the efficient quantity of pizza, we compare the marginal cost of a pizza with the marginal benefit from a pizza. There are three possible cases:

- Marginal benefit exceeds marginal cost.
- Marginal cost exceeds marginal benefit.
- Marginal benefit equals marginal cost.

Marginal Benefit Exceeds Marginal Cost Suppose the quantity of pizza produced is 5,000 a day. Figure 6.1 shows that at this quantity, the marginal benefit of a pizza is $20. That is, when the quantity of pizza available is 5,000 a day, people are willing to pay $20 for the 5,000th pizza.

Figure 6.1 also shows that the marginal cost of the 5,000th pizza is $10. That is, to produce one more pizza, the value of other goods and services that we must forgo is $10. If pizza production increases from 4,999 to 5,000, the value of the additional pizza is $20 and its marginal cost is $10. By producing this pizza, the value of the pizza produced exceeds the value of the goods and services forgone by $10. Resources are used more efficiently—they create more value—if we produce an extra pizza and fewer other goods and services. This same reasoning applies all the way up to the 9,999th pizza. Only when we get to the 10,000th pizza does marginal benefit not exceed marginal cost.

Marginal Cost Exceeds Marginal Benefit Suppose the quantity of pizza produced is 15,000 a day. Figure 6.1 shows that at this quantity, the marginal benefit of a pizza is $10. That is, when the quantity of pizza available is 15,000 a day, people are willing to pay $10 for the 15,000th pizza.

Figure 6.1 also shows that the marginal cost of the 15,000th pizza is $20. That is, to produce one

more pizza, the value of the other goods and services that we must forgo is $20.

If pizza production decreases from 15,000 to 14,999, the value of the one pizza forgone is $10 and its marginal cost is $20. So by not producing this pizza, the value of the other goods and services produced exceeds the value of the pizza forgone by $10. Resources are used more efficiently—they create more value—if we produce one fewer pizza and more other goods and services. This same reasoning applies all the way down to the 10,001st pizza. Only when we get to the 10,000th pizza does marginal cost not exceed marginal benefit.

Marginal Benefit Equals Marginal Cost Suppose the quantity of pizza produced is 10,000 a day. Figure 6.1 shows that at this quantity, the marginal benefit of a pizza is $15. That is, when the quantity of pizza available is 10,000 a day, people are willing to pay $15 for the 10,000th pizza.

Figure 6.1 also shows that the marginal cost of the 10,000th pizza is $15. That is, to produce one more pizza, the value of other goods and services that we must forgo is $15.

In this situation, we cannot increase the value of the goods and services produced by either increasing or decreasing the quantity of pizza. If we increase the quantity of pizza, the 10,001st pizza costs more to produce than it is worth. If we decrease the quantity of pizza produced, the 9,999th pizza is worth more than it costs to produce. So when marginal benefit equals marginal cost, resource use is efficient.

R E V I E W   Q U I Z

- If the marginal benefit of pizza exceeds the marginal cost of pizza, are we producing too much pizza and too little of other goods, or are we producing too little pizza and too much of other goods?
- If the marginal cost of pizza exceeds the marginal benefit of pizza, are we producing too much pizza and too little of other goods, or are we producing too little pizza and too much of other goods?
- What is the relationship between the marginal benefit of pizza and the marginal cost of pizza when we are producing the efficient quantity of pizza?

Does a competitive pizza market produce the efficient quantity of pizza? Let's answer this question.

Value, Price, and Consumer Surplus

TO INVESTIGATE WHETHER A COMPETITIVE MARKET is efficient, we need to learn about the connection between demand and marginal benefit and supply and marginal cost.

Value, Willingness to Pay, and Demand

In everyday life, we talk about "getting value for money." When we use this expression we are distinguishing between *value* and *price*. Value is what we get, and price is what we pay.

The **value** of one more unit of a good or service is its *marginal benefit*. Marginal benefit can be expressed as the maximum price that people are willing to pay for another unit of the good or service. The willingness to pay for a good or service determines the demand for it.

In Fig. 6.2(a), the demand curve shows the quantity demanded at each price. For example, when the price of a pizza is $15, the quantity demanded is 10,000 pizzas a day. In Fig. 6.2(b), the demand curve shows the maximum price that people are willing to pay when there is a given quantity. For example, when 10,000 pizzas a day are available, the most that people are willing to pay for a pizza is $15. This interpretation means that the marginal benefit from the 10,000th pizza is $15.

When we draw a demand curve, we use a *relative price*, not a *money price*. A relative price is expressed in dollar units, but it measures the number of dollars worth of other goods and services forgone to obtain one more unit of the good in question (see Chapter 4, p. 62). So a demand curve tells us the quantity of other goods and services that people are willing to forgo to get an additional unit of a good. But this is what a marginal benefit curve tells us, too. So:

A demand curve is a marginal benefit curve.

We don't always have to pay the maximum price that we are willing to pay. When we buy something, we often get a bargain. Let's see how.

FIGURE 6.2

Demand, Willingness to Pay, and Marginal Benefit

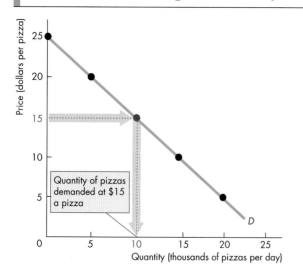

(a) Price determines quantity demanded

The demand curve for pizza, D, shows the quantity of pizza demanded at each price, other things remaining the same. It also shows the maximum price that consumers are willing to pay if a given quantity of pizza is available. At a price of $15,

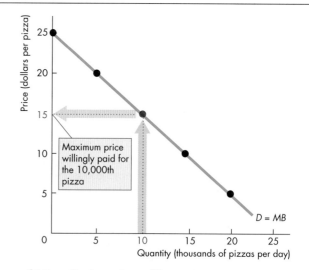

(b) Quantity determines willingness to pay

the quantity demanded is 10,000 pizzas a day (part a). If 10,000 pizzas a day are available, the maximum price that consumers are willing to pay for the 10,000th pizza is $15 (part b).

Consumer Surplus

When people buy something for less than it is worth to them, they receive a consumer surplus. A **consumer surplus** is the value of a good minus the price paid for it.

To understand consumer surplus, let's look at Lisa's demand for pizza, which is shown in Fig. 6.3. Lisa likes pizza, but the marginal benefit she gets from it decreases quickly as her consumption increases.

To keep things simple, suppose Lisa can buy pizza by the slice and that there are 10 slices in a pizza. If a pizza costs $2.50 a slice (or $25 a pizza), Lisa spends her fast food budget on items that she values more highly than pizza. At $2 a slice (or $20 a pizza), she buys 10 slices (one pizza) a week. At $1.50 a slice, she buys 20 slices a week; at $1 a slice, she buys 30 slices a week; and at 50 cents a slice ($5 a pizza), she eats nothing but pizza and buys 40 slices a week.

Lisa's demand curve for pizza in Fig. 6.3 is also her *willingness-to-pay* or marginal benefit curve. It tells us that if Lisa can have only 10 slices a week, she is willing to pay $2 a slice. Her marginal benefit from the 10th slice is $2. If she can have 20 slices a week, she is willing to pay $1.50 for the 20th slice. Her marginal benefit from the 20th slice is $1.50.

Figure 6.3 also shows Lisa's consumer surplus from pizza when the price of pizza is $1.50 a slice. At this price, she buys 20 slices a week. A price of $1.50 a slice is the most she is willing to pay for the 20th slice, so its marginal benefit is exactly the price she pays for it.

But Lisa is willing to pay almost $2.50 for the first slice. So the marginal benefit from this slice is close to $1 more than she pays for it. She receives a *consumer surplus* of almost $1 from her first slice of pizza. At a quantity of 10 slices of pizza a week, Lisa's marginal benefit is $2 a slice. So on this slice, she receives a consumer surplus of 50 cents. To calculate Lisa's consumer surplus, we must find the consumer surplus on each slice and add these surpluses together. This sum is the area of the green triangle in Fig. 6.3. This area is equal to the base of the triangle (20 slices of pizza per week) multiplied by the height of the triangle ($1) divided by 2, or $10 a week.

The blue rectangle in Fig. 6.3 is the amount that Lisa pays for pizza, which is $30 a week—20 slices at $1.50 a slice.

All goods and services are like the pizza example you've just studied. Because of decreasing marginal benefit, people receive more benefit from their consumption than the amount they pay.

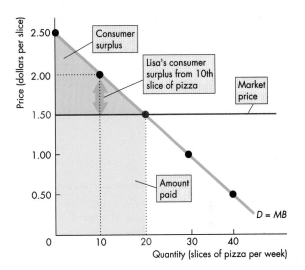

FIGURE 6.3

A Consumer's Demand and Consumer Surplus

Lisa's demand curve for pizza tells us that at $2.50 a slice, she does not buy pizza. At $2 a slice, she buys 10 slices a week; at $1.50 a slice, she buys 20 slices a week. Lisa's demand curve also tells us that she is willing to pay $2 for the 10th slice and $1.50 for the 20th. She actually pays $1.50 a slice—the market price—and buys 20 slices a week. Her consumer surplus from pizza is $10—the area of the green triangle.

REVIEW QUIZ

- How do we measure the value or marginal benefit of a good or service?
- Can you explain the relationship between marginal benefit and the demand curve?
- What is consumer surplus and how do we measure it?

You've seen how we distinguish between value—marginal benefit—and price. And you've seen that buyers receive a consumer surplus because marginal benefit exceeds price. Next, we're going to study the connection between supply and marginal cost and learn about producer surplus.

Cost, Price, and Producer Surplus

WHAT YOU ARE NOW GOING TO LEARN ABOUT cost, price, and producer surplus parallels the related ideas about value, price, and consumer surplus that you've just studied.

Firms are in business to make a profit. To do so, they must sell their output for a price that exceeds the cost of production. Let's look at the relationship between cost and price.

Cost, Minimum Supply-Price, and Supply

Firms undertake the most elaborate schemes to earn profits. Earning a profit means receiving more (or at least receiving no less) for the sale of a good or service than the cost of producing it. Just as consumers distinguish between *value* and *price*, so producers

distinguish between *cost* and *price*. Cost is what a producer gives up, and price is what a producer receives.

The cost of producing one more unit of a good or service is its *marginal cost*. Marginal cost is the minimum price that producers must receive to induce them to produce another unit of the good or service. This minimum acceptable price determines supply.

In Fig. 6.4(a), the supply curve shows the quantity supplied at each price. For example, when the price of a pizza is $15, the quantity supplied is 10,000 pizzas a day. In Fig. 6.4(b), the supply curve shows the minimum price that producers must be offered to produce a given quantity of pizza. For example, if 10,000 pizzas a day are to be produced, the minimum price that producers must be offered is $15 a pizza. This second view of the supply curve means that the marginal cost of the 10,000th pizza is $15.

Because the price is a relative price, a supply curve tells us the quantity of other goods and services that *sellers must forgo* to produce one more unit of the good. But a marginal cost curve also tells us the quantity of other goods and services that we must

---

FIGURE 6.4

Supply, Minimum Supply-Price, and Marginal Cost

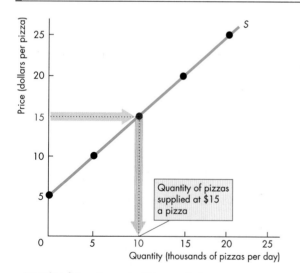

(a) Price determines quantity supplied

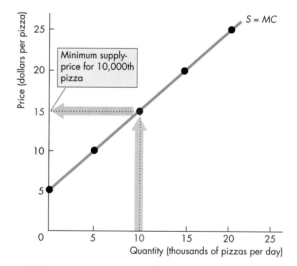

(b) Quantity determines minimum supply-price

The supply curve of pizza, S, shows the quantity of pizza supplied at each price, other things remaining the same. It also shows the minimum price that producers must be offered if a given quantity of pizza is to be produced. At a price of $15,

the quantity supplied is 10,000 pizzas a day (part a). If 10,000 pizzas a day are produced, the minimum price that producers must be offered for the 10,000th pizza is $15 (part b).

forgo to get one more unit of the good. So:

A supply curve is a marginal cost curve.

Producers don't always wind up receiving their minimum supply-price. If the price they receive exceeds the cost they incur, they earn a surplus. This surplus earned by producers is analogous to consumer surplus. Let's look at producer surplus.

Producer Surplus

When a firm sells something for more than it costs to produce, the firm obtains a producer surplus. A **producer surplus** is the price of a good minus the opportunity cost of producing it. To understand producer surplus, let's look at Max's supply of pizza in Fig. 6.5.

Max can produce pizza or bake bread that people like a lot. The more pizza he bakes, the less bread he can bake. His opportunity cost of pizza is the value of the bread he must forgo. This opportunity cost increases as Max increases his production of pizza. If a pizza sells for only $5, Max produces no pizza. He uses his kitchen to bake bread. Pizza just isn't worth producing. But at $10 a pizza, Max produces 50 pizzas a day, and at $15 a pizza, he produces 100 a day.

Max's supply curve is also his *minimum supply-price* curve. It tells us that if Max can sell only one pizza a day, the minimum that he must be paid for it is $5. If he can sell 50 pizzas a day, the minimum that he must be paid for the 50th pizza is $10, and so on.

Figure 6.5 also shows Max's producer surplus. If the price of pizza is $15, Max plans to sell 100 pizzas a day. The minimum that he must be paid for the 100th pizza is $15. So its opportunity cost is exactly the price he receives for it. But his opportunity cost of the first pizza is only $5. So this first pizza costs $10 less to produce than he receives for it. Max receives a *producer surplus* from his first pizza of $10. He receives a slightly smaller producer surplus on the second pizza, less on the third, and so on until he receives no producer surplus on the 100th pizza.

Figure 6.5 shows Max's producer surplus as the blue triangle formed by the area above the supply curve and beneath the price line. This area is equal to the base of the triangle ($10 a pizza) multiplied by the height (100 pizzas a week) divided by 2, or $500 a week. Figure 6.5 also shows Max's opportunity costs of production as the red area beneath the supply curve.

FIGURE 6.5

A Producer's Supply and Producer Surplus

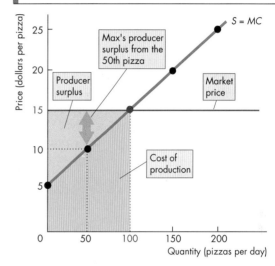

Max's supply curve of pizza tells us that at a price of $5, Max plans to sell no pizza. At a price of $10, he plans to sell 50 pizzas a day; and at a price of $15, he plans to sell 100 pizzas a day. Max's supply curve also tells us that the minimum he must be offered is $10 for the 50th pizza a day and $15 for the 100th pizza a day. If the market price is $15 a pizza, he sells 100 pizzas a day and receives $1,500. The red area shows Max's cost of producing pizza, which is $1,000 a day, and the blue area shows his producer surplus, which is $500 a day.

R E V I E W   Q U I Z

- What is the relationship between the marginal cost or opportunity cost of producing a good or service and the minimum supply-price—the minimum price that producers must be offered?
- Can you explain the relationship between marginal cost and the supply curve?
- What is producer surplus and how do we measure it?

Consumer surplus and producer surplus can be used to measure the efficiency of a market. Let's see how we can use these concepts to study the efficiency of a competitive market.

Is the Competitive Market Efficient?

Figure 6.6 shows the market for pizza. The demand for pizza is shown by the demand curve, *D*. The supply of pizza is shown by the supply curve *S*. The equilibrium price is $15 a pizza, and the equilibrium quantity is 10,000 pizzas a day.

The market forces that you studied in Chapter 4 (pp. 72–73) will pull the pizza market to this equilibrium. If the price is greater than $15, a surplus will force the price down. If the price is less than $15, a shortage will force the price up. Only if the price is $15 is there neither a surplus nor a shortage and no forces operating to change the price.

So the market price and quantity are pulled toward their competitive equilibrium values. But is a competitive market efficient? Does it produce the efficient quantity of pizza?

Efficiency of a Competitive Market

The equilibrium in Fig. 6.6 is efficient. Resources are being used to produce the quantity of pizza that people value most highly. It is not possible to produce more pizza without giving up some other good or service that is valued more highly. And if a smaller quantity of pizza is produced, resources are used to produce some other good that is not valued as highly as the pizza forgone.

To see why the equilibrium in Fig. 6.6 is efficient, think about the interpretation of the demand curve as a marginal benefit curve and the supply curve as a marginal cost curve. The demand curve tells us the marginal benefit from pizza. The supply curve tells us the marginal cost of pizza. So where the demand curve and the supply curve intersect, marginal benefit equals marginal cost.

But this condition—marginal benefit equals marginal cost—is the condition that delivers an efficient use of resources. It puts resources to work in the activities that create the greatest possible value. So a competitive market is efficient.

If production is less than 10,000 pizzas a day, the marginal pizza is valued more highly that its opportunity cost. If production exceeds 10,000 pizzas a day, the marginal pizza costs more to produce than the value that consumers place on it. Only when 10,000

FIGURE 6.6

An Efficient Market for Pizza

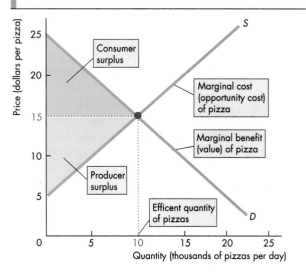

Resources are used efficiently when the sum of consumer surplus and producer surplus is maximized. Consumer surplus is the area below the demand curve and above the market price line—the green triangle. Producer surplus is the area below the price line and above the supply curve—the blue triangle. Here consumer surplus is $50,000, and producer surplus is also $50,000. The total surplus is $100,000. This surplus is maximized when the willingness to pay equals the opportunity cost. The efficient quantity of pizza is 10,000 pizzas per day.

pizzas a day are produced is the marginal pizza worth exactly what it costs. The competitive market pushes the quantity of pizza produced to its efficient level of 10,000 a day. If production is less than 10,000 a day, a shortage raises the price, which stimulates an increase in production. If production exceeds 10,000 a day, a surplus lowers the price, which decreases production.

When the market is using resources efficiently at a competitive equilibrium, the sum of consumer surplus and producer surplus is maximized. At this equilibrium, resources are used in the activities in which they are valued most highly.

Buyers and sellers each attempt to do the best they can for themselves, and no one plans for an efficient outcome for society as a whole. Buyers seek the lowest possible price, and sellers seek the highest possible price. And the market comes to an equilibrium in which the gains from trade are as large as possible.

The Invisible Hand

Writing in his *Wealth of Nations* in 1776, Adam Smith (see pp. 56–57) was the first to suggest that competitive markets send resources to the uses in which they have the highest value. Smith believed that each participant in a competitive market is "led by an invisible hand to promote an end [the efficient use of resources] which was no part of his intention."

You can see the invisible hand at work in the cartoon. The cold drinks vendor has both cold drinks and shade. He has an opportunity cost of each and a minimum supply-price of each. The park-bench reader has a marginal benefit from a cold drink and from shade. You can see that the marginal benefit from shade exceeds the marginal cost, but the marginal cost of a cold drink exceeds its marginal benefit. The transaction that occurs creates gains from trade. The vendor obtains a producer surplus from selling the shade for more than its opportunity cost, and the reader obtains a consumer surplus from buying the shade for less than its marginal benefit. In the third frame of the cartoon, both the consumer and the producer are better off than they were in the first frame. The umbrella has moved to its highest-valued use.

The Invisible Hand at Work Today

The market economy relentlessly performs the activity illustrated in the cartoon and in Fig. 6.6 to achieve an efficient use of resources. And rarely has the market been working as hard as it is today. Think about a few of the changes taking place in our economy that the market is guiding toward an efficient use of resources.

New technologies have cut the cost of producing computers. As these advances have occurred, supply has increased and the price has fallen. Lower prices have encouraged an increase in the quantity demanded of this now less costly tool. The marginal benefit from computers is brought to equality with their marginal cost.

A Florida frost cuts the supply of oranges. With fewer oranges available, the marginal benefit from an orange increases. A shortage of oranges raises their price to allocate the smaller quantity available to the people who value them most highly.

Market forces persistently bring marginal cost and marginal benefit to equality and maximize value.

Drawing by M. Twohy; © 1985 The New Yorker Magazine, Inc.

Obstacles to Efficiency

ALTHOUGH MARKETS GENERALLY DO A GOOD JOB at sending resources to where they are most highly valued, they do not always get the correct answer. Sometimes markets overproduce a good or service, and sometimes they underproduce. The most significant obstacles to achieving an efficient allocation of resources in the market economy are

- Price ceilings and floors
- Taxes, subsidies, and quotas
- Monopoly
- Public goods
- External costs and external benefits

Price Ceilings and Floors   A price ceiling is a regulation that makes it illegal to charge a higher price than a specified level. An example is a ceiling on apartment rents, which some cities impose. A price floor is a regulation that makes it illegal to pay a lower price than a specified level. An example is the minimum wage. (We study both of these restrictions on buyers and sellers in Chapter 7.)

The presence of a price ceiling or a price floor blocks the forces of demand and supply, resulting in a level of production that might exceed or fall short of the quantity determined in an unregulated market.

Taxes, Subsidies, and Quotas   Taxes increase the prices paid by buyers and lower the prices received by sellers. Taxes decrease the quantity produced (for reasons that are explained in Chapter 7, on p. 135). All kinds of goods and services are taxed, but the goods with the highest taxes are on gasoline, alcohol, and tobacco.

Subsidies, which are payments by the government to producers, decrease the prices paid by buyers and increase the prices received by sellers. Subsidies increase the quantity produced.

Quotas, which are limits to the quantity that a firm is permitted to produce, restrict output below the level that a competitive market produces. Farms are sometimes subject to quotas.

Monopoly   A **monopoly** is a firm that has sole control of a market. For example, Microsoft has a near monopoly on operating systems for personal computers. Although monopolies earn large profits, they prevent markets from achieving an efficient use of resources. The goal of a monopoly is to maximize profit; to achieve this goal, it restricts production and raises price. (We study monopoly in Chapter 13.)

Public Goods   A **public good** is a good or service that is consumed simultaneously by everyone, even if they don't pay for it. Examples are national defense and the enforcement of law and order. Competitive markets would produce too small a quantity of public goods because of a *free-rider problem*: It is not in each person's interest to buy her or his share of a public good. So a competitive market produces less than the efficient quantity. (We study public goods in Chapter 18.)

External Costs and External Benefits   An **external cost** is a cost not borne by the producer but borne by other people. The cost of pollution is an example of an external cost. When an electric power utility burns coal to generate electricity, it puts sulfur dioxide into the atmosphere. This pollutant falls as acid rain and damages vegetation and crops. The utility does not consider the cost of pollution when it decides the quantity of electric power to supply. Its supply is based on its own costs, not on the costs that it inflicts on others. As a result, the utility produces more power than the efficient quantity.

An **external benefit** is a benefit that accrues to people other than the buyer of a good. An example is when someone in a neighborhood paints her home or landscapes her yard. The homeowner does not consider her neighbor's marginal benefit when she decides whether to do this type of work. So the demand curve for house painting and yard improvement does not include all the benefits that accrue. In this case, the quantity falls short of the efficient quantity. (We study externalities in Chapter 20.)

The impediments to efficiency that we've just reviewed and that you will study in greater detail in later chapters result in two possible outcomes:

- Underproduction
- Overproduction

Underproduction

Suppose that one firm owned all the pizza outlets in a city and that it restricted the quantity of pizzas produced to 5,000 a day. Figure 6.7(a) shows that at this quantity, consumers are willing to pay $20 for the marginal pizza—marginal benefit is $20. The marginal cost of a pizza is only $10. So there is a gap between what people are willing to pay and what producers must be offered—between marginal benefit and marginal cost.

The sum of consumer surplus and producer surplus is decreased by the amount of the gray triangle in Fig. 6.7(a). This triangle is called deadweight loss. **Deadweight loss** is the decrease in consumer surplus and producer surplus that results from an inefficient level of production.

The 5,000th pizza brings a benefit of $20 and costs only $10 to produce. If we don't produce this pizza, we are wasting almost $10. Similar reasoning applies all the way up to the 9,999th pizza. By producing more pizza and less of other goods and services, we get more value from our resources.

The deadweight loss is borne by the entire society. It is not a loss for the consumers and a gain for the producer. It is a *social* loss.

FIGURE **6.7**

Underproduction and Overproduction

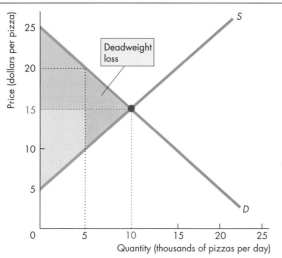

(a) Underproduction

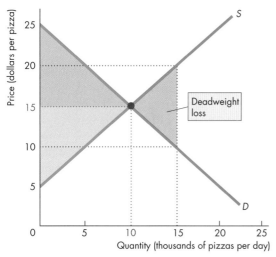

(b) Overproduction

If production is restricted to 5,000 a day, a deadweight loss (the gray triangle) arises. Consumer surplus and producer surplus are reduced to the green and blue areas. At 5,000 pizzas, the benefit of one more pizza exceeds its cost. The same is true for all levels of production up to 10,000 pizzas a day. If production increases to 15,000, a deadweight loss arises. At 15,000 pizzas a day, the cost of the 15,000th pizza exceeds its benefit. The cost of each pizza above 10,000 exceeds its benefit. Consumer surplus plus producer surplus equals the green and blue area minus the deadweight loss.

Overproduction

Suppose the pizza lobby gets the government to pay the pizza producers a fat subsidy and that production increases to 15,000 a day. Figure 6.7(b) shows that at this quantity, consumers are willing to pay only $10 for that marginal pizza but the opportunity cost of that pizza is $20. It now costs more to produce the marginal pizza than consumers are willing to pay for it. The gap gets smaller as production approaches 10,000 pizzas a day, but it is present at all quantities greater than 10,000 a day.

Again, deadweight loss is shown by the gray triangle. This loss must be subtracted from the producer and consumer surplus to calculate the gains from trade. The 15,000th pizza brings a benefit of only $10 but costs $20 to produce. If we produce this pizza, we are wasting almost $10. Similar reasoning applies all the way down to the 10,001st pizza. By producing less pizza and more of other goods and services, we get more value from our resources.

R E V I E W   Q U I Z

- Do competitive markets use resources efficiently? Explain why or why not.
- Do markets with a price ceiling or price floor, taxes, subsidies, quotas, monopoly power, public goods, or externalities result in the quantity produced being the efficient quantity?
- What is deadweight loss and in what conditions does it occur?
- Does a deadweight loss occur in a competitive market when the quantity produced equals the competitive equilibrium quantity and the resource allocation is efficient?

You now know the conditions under which the resource allocation is efficient. You've seen how a competitive market can be efficient, and you've seen some impediments to efficiency.

But is an efficient allocation of resources fair? Does the competitive market provide people with fair incomes for their work? And do people always pay a fair price for the things they buy? Don't we need the government to step into some competitive markets to prevent the price from rising too high or falling too low? Let's now study these questions.

Is the Competitive Market Fair?

WHEN A NATURAL DISASTER STRIKES, SUCH AS A severe winter storm or a hurricane, the prices of many essential items jump. The reason the prices jump is that some people have a greater demand and greater willingness to pay while the items are in limited supply. So the higher prices achieve an efficient allocation of scarce resources. News reports of these price hikes almost never talk about efficiency. Instead, they talk about fairness, or more particularly, unfairness. The claim is that it is unfair for profit-seeking dealers to cheat the victims of natural disaster.

Similarly, when low-skilled people work for a wage that is below what most would regard as a "living wage," the media and politicians talk of employers taking unfair advantage of their workers.

How do we decide if something is fair or unfair? You know when *you* think something is unfair. But how do you know? What are the *principles* of fairness?

Philosophers have tried for centuries to answer this question. Economists have offered their answers too. But before we look at the proposed answers, you should know that there is no universally agreed answer.

Economists agree about efficiency. That is, they agree that it makes sense to make the economic pie as large as possible and to bake it at the lowest possible cost. But they do not agree about fairness. That is, they do not agree about what are fair shares of the economic pie for all the people who make it. The reason is that ideas about fairness are not exclusively economic ideas. They touch on politics, ethics, and religion. Nevertheless, economists have thought about these issues and have a contribution to make. So let's examine the views of economists on this topic.

To think about fairness, think of economic life as a game—a serious game. All ideas about fairness can be divided into two broad groups. They are:

■ It's not fair if the *result* isn't fair

■ It's not fair if the *rules* aren't fair

It's Not Fair If the *Result* Isn't Fair

The earliest efforts to establish a principle of fairness were based on the view that the result is what matters. And the general idea was that it is unfair if people's incomes are too unequal. It is unfair that bank chairpersons earn millions of dollars a year while bank tellers earn only thousands of dollars a year. It is unfair that a storeowner enjoys a larger profit and her customers pay higher prices in the aftermath of a winter storm.

There was a lot of excitement during the nineteenth century when economists thought they had made the incredible discovery that efficiency requires equality of incomes. To make the economic pie as large as possible, it must be cut into equal pieces, one for each person. This idea turns out to be wrong, but there is a lesson in the reason that it is wrong. So this nineteenth century idea is worth a closer look.

Utilitarianism The nineteenth century idea that only equality brings efficiency is called utilitarianism. **Utilitarianism** is a principle that states that we should strive to achieve "the greatest happiness for the greatest number." The people who developed this idea were known as utilitarians. They included the most eminent minds, such as David Hume, Adam Smith, Jeremy Bentham, and John Stuart Mill.

Utilitarians argued that to achieve "the greatest happiness for the greatest number," income must be transferred from the rich to the poor up to the point of complete equality—to the point at which there are no rich and no poor.

They reasoned in the following way: First, everyone has the same basic wants and a similar capacity to enjoy life. Second, the greater a person's income, the smaller is the marginal benefit of a dollar. The millionth dollar spent by a rich person brings a smaller marginal benefit to that person than the marginal benefit of the thousandth dollar spent by a poorer person. So by transferring a dollar from the millionaire to the poorer person, more is gained than is lost and the two people added together are better off.

Figure 6.8 illustrates this utilitarian idea. Tom and Jerry each have the same marginal benefit curve, *MB*. (Marginal benefit is measured on the same scale of 1 to 3 for both Tom and Jerry.) Tom is at point *a*. He earns $5,000 a year, and his marginal benefit of a dollar of income is 3. Jerry is at point *b*. He earns $45,000 a year, and his marginal benefit of a dollar of income is 1. If a dollar is transferred from Jerry to Tom, Jerry loses 1 unit of marginal benefit and Tom gains 3 units. So together Tom and Jerry are better off. They are sharing the economic pie more efficiently. If a second dollar is transferred, the same thing happens: Tom gains more than Jerry loses. And the same is true for every dollar transferred until they each reach point *c*. At point *c*, Tom and Jerry each

FIGURE 6.8

Utilitarian Fairness

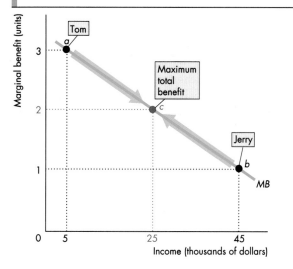

Tom earns $5,000 and has 3 units of marginal benefit at point *a*. Jerry earns $45,000 and has 1 unit of marginal benefit at point *b*. If income is transferred from Jerry to Tom, Jerry's loss is less than Tom's gain. Only when each of them has $25,000 and 2 units of marginal benefit (at point *c*) can the sum of their total benefit increase no further.

have $25,000 and each have a marginal benefit of 2 units. Now they are sharing the economic pie in the most efficient way. It is bringing the greatest attainable happiness to Tom and Jerry.

The Big Tradeoff One big problem with the utilitarian ideal of complete equality is that it ignores the costs of making income transfers. Recognizing the cost of making income transfers leads to what is called "the **big tradeoff**," which is a tradeoff between efficiency and fairness.

The big tradeoff is based on the following facts. Income can be transferred from people with high incomes to people with low incomes only by taxing incomes. Taxing people's income from employment makes them work less. It results in the quantity of labor being less than the efficient quantity. Taxing people's income from capital makes them save less. It results in the quantity of capital being less than the efficient quantity. With smaller quantities of both labor and capital, the quantity of goods and services produced is less than the efficient quantity. The economic pie shrinks.

The tradeoff is between the size of the economic pie and the degree of equality with which it is shared. The greater the amount of income redistribution through income taxes, the greater is the inefficiency—the smaller is the economic pie.

There is a second source of inefficiency. A dollar taken from a rich person does not end up as a dollar in the hands of a poorer person. Some of it is spent on administration of the tax and transfer system. The cost of tax-collecting agencies, such as the IRS, and welfare-administering agencies, such as Health Care Financing Administration that administers Medicaid and Medicare, must be paid with some of the taxes collected. Also, taxpayers hire accountants, auditors, and lawyers to help them ensure that they pay the correct amount of tax. These activities use skilled labor and capital resources that could otherwise be used to produce goods and services that people value.

You can see that when all these costs are taken into account, transferring a dollar from a rich person does not give a dollar to a poor person. It is even possible that with high taxes, those with low incomes end up being worse off. Suppose, for example, that highly taxed entrepreneurs decide to work less hard and shut down some of their businesses. Low-income workers get fired and must seek other, perhaps even lower-paid work.

Because of the big tradeoff, those who say that fairness is equality propose a modified version of utilitarianism.

Make the Poorest as Well Off as Possible A Harvard philosopher, John Rawls, proposed a modified version of utilitarianism in a classic book entitled *A Theory of Justice*, published in 1971. Rawls says that, after counting all the costs of income transfers, the fair distribution of the economic pie is the one that makes the poorest person as well off as possible. The incomes of rich people should be taxed and, after paying the costs of administering the tax and transfer system, what is left should be transferred to the poor. But the taxes must not be so high that they make the economic pie shrink to the point at which the poorest person ends up with a smaller piece. A bigger share of a smaller pie can be less than a smaller share of a bigger pie. The goal is to make the piece enjoyed by the poorest person as big as possible. Most likely, this piece will not be an equal share.

The "fair results" ideas require a change in the results after the game is over. Some economists say that these changes are themselves unfair and propose a different way of thinking about fairness.

It's Not Fair If the *Rules* Aren't Fair

The idea that it's not fair if the rules aren't fair is based on a fundamental principle that seems to be hard wired into the human brain. It is the symmetry principle. The **symmetry principle** is the requirement that people in similar situations be treated similarly. It is the moral principle that lies at the center of all the major religions and that says, in some form or other, "Behave toward other people in the way you expect them to behave toward you."

In economic life, this principle translates into *equality of opportunity*. But equality of opportunity to do what? This question is answered by another Harvard philosopher, Robert Nozick, in a book entitled *Anarchy, State, and Utopia,* published in 1974.

Nozick argues that the idea of fairness as an outcome or result cannot work and that fairness must be based on the fairness of the rules. He suggests that fairness obeys two rules:

1. The state must enforce laws that establish and protect private property.
2. Private property may be transferred from one person to another only by voluntary exchange.

The first rule says that everything that is valuable must be owned by individuals and that the state must ensure that theft is prevented. The second rule says that the only legitimate way a person can acquire property is to buy it in exchange for something else that the person owns. If these rules, which are the only fair rules, are followed, the result is fair. It doesn't matter how unequally the economic pie is shared provided that it is baked by people each one of whom voluntarily provides services in exchange for the share of the pie offered in compensation.

These rules satisfy the symmetry principle. And if these rules are not followed, the symmetry principle is broken. You can see these facts by imagining a world in which the laws are not followed.

First, suppose that some resources or goods are not owned. They are common property. Then everyone is free to participate in a grab to use these resources or goods. The strongest will prevail. But when the strongest prevails, the strongest effectively *owns* the resources or goods in question and prevents others from enjoying them.

Second, suppose that we do not insist on voluntary exchange for transferring ownership of resources from one person to another. The alternative is *involuntary* transfer. In simple language, the alternative is theft.

Both of these situations violate the symmetry principle. Only the strong get to acquire what they want. The weak end up with only the resources and goods that the strong don't want.

In contrast, if the two rules of fairness are followed, everyone, strong and weak, is treated in a similar way. All are free to use their resources and human skills to create things that are valued by themselves and others and to exchange the fruits of their efforts with each other. This is the only set of arrangements that obeys the symmetry principle.

Fairness and Efficiency   If private property rights are enforced and if voluntary exchange takes place in a competitive market, resources will be allocated efficiently if there are no:

- Price ceilings and price floors
- Taxes, subsidies, and quotas
- Monopolies
- Public goods
- External costs and external benefits

And according to the Nozick rules, the resulting distribution of income and wealth will be fair. Let's study a concrete example to examine the claim that if resources are allocated efficiently, they are also allocated fairly.

A Price Hike in a Natural Disaster   An earthquake has broken the pipes that deliver drinking water to a city. The price of bottled water jumps from $1 to $8 a bottle in the 30 or so shops that have water for sale.

First, let's agree that the water is being used *efficiently*. There is a fixed amount of bottled water in the city and, given the quantity available, some people are willing to pay $8 to get a bottle. The water goes to the people who value it most highly. Consumer surplus and producer surplus are maximized.

So the water resources are being used efficiently. But are they being used fairly? Shouldn't people who can't afford to pay $8 a bottle get some of the available water for a lower price that they can afford? Isn't the fair solution for the shops to sell water for a lower price that people can afford? Or perhaps it might be fairer if the government bought the water and then made it available to people through a government store at a "reasonable" price. Let's think about these alternative solutions to the water problem of this city.

The first answer that jumps into your mind is that the water should somehow be made available at a more reasonable price. But is this the correct answer?

Shop Offers Water for $5 Suppose that Chip, a shop owner, offers water at $5 a bottle. Who will buy it? There are two types of buyers. Chuck is an example of one type. He values water at $8—is willing to pay $8 a bottle. Recall that, given the quantity of water available, the equilibrium price is $8 a bottle. If Chuck buys the water, he consumes it. Chuck ends up with a consumer surplus of $3 on the bottle, and Chip receives $3 *less* of producer surplus.

Mitch is an example of the second type of buyer. Mitch would not pay $8 for a bottle. In fact, he wouldn't even pay $5 to consume a bottle of water. But he buys a bottle for $5. Why? Because he plans to sell the water to someone who is willing to pay $8 to consume it. When Mitch buys the water, Chip again receives a producer surplus of $3 *less* than he would receive if he charged the going market price. Mitch now becomes a water dealer. He sells the water for the going price of $8 and earns a producer surplus of $3.

So by being public spirited and offering water for less than the market price, Chip ends up $3 a bottle worse off, and the buyers end up $3 a bottle better off. The same people consume the water in both situations. They are the people who value the water at $8 a bottle. But the distribution of consumer surplus and producer surplus is different in the two cases. When Chip offers the water for $5 a bottle, he ends up with a smaller producer surplus and Chuck and Mitch end up with a larger consumer surplus and producer surplus.

So which is the fair arrangement? The one that favors Chip or the one that favors Chuck and Mitch? The fair-rules view is that both arrangements are fair. Chip voluntarily sells the water for $5, so in effect, he is helping the community to cope with its water problem. It is fair that he should help. But the choice is his. He owns the water. It is not fair that he should be compelled to help.

Government Buys Water Now suppose instead that the government buys all the water. The going price is $8 a bottle, so that's what the government pays. Now they offer the water for sale for $1 a bottle, its "normal" price.

The quantity of water supplied is exactly the same as before. But now, at $1 a bottle, the quantity demanded is much larger than the quantity supplied. There is a shortage of water.

Because there is a large water shortage, the government decides to ration the amount that anyone may buy. Everyone is allocated one bottle. So everyone lines up to collect his or her bottle. Two of these people are Chuck and Mitch. Chuck, you'll recall, is willing to pay $8 a bottle. Mitch is willing to pay less than $5. But they both get a bargain. Chuck drinks his $1 bottle and enjoys a $7 consumer surplus. What does Mitch do? Does he drink his bottle? He does not. He sells it to another person who values the water at $8. And he enjoys a $7 producer surplus from his temporary water trading business.

So the people who value the water most highly consume it. But the consumer and producer surpluses are distributed in a different way from what the free market would have delivered. Again, the question arises, which arrangement is fair?

The main difference between the government scheme and Chip's private charitable contributions lies in the fact that to buy the water for $8 and sell it for $1, the government must tax someone $7 for each bottle sold. So whether this arrangement is fair depends on whether the taxes are fair.

Taxes are an involuntary transfer of private property, so according to the fair-rules view, they are unfair. But most economists, and most other people, think that there is such a thing as a fair tax. So it seems that the fair-rules view needs to be weakened a bit. Agreeing that there is such a thing as a fair tax is the easy part. Agreeing on what is a fair tax brings endless disagreement and debate.

REVIEW QUIZ

- What are the two big approaches to thinking about fairness?
- What is the utilitarian idea of fairness and what is wrong with it?
- What is the big tradeoff and what idea of fairness has been developed to deal with it?
- What is the main idea of fairness based on fair rules?

◆ You've now studied the two biggest issues that run right through the whole of economics: efficiency and equity, or fairness. In the next chapter, we study some sources of inefficiency and unfairness. And at many points throughout this book—and in your life—you will return to and use the ideas about efficiency and equity that you've learned in this chapter. *Reading Between the Lines* on pp. 122-123 looks at an example of an inefficiency—and, some would argue, an inequity—in our economy today.

Efficiency and Equity in Agriculture

THE NEW YORK TIMES, OCTOBER 16, 1998

Congress Disregards Free Market With Farm Bill

BY DIRK JOHNSON

CHICAGO—The agreement to spend $6 billion on the nation's farmers marks a departure, at least in spirit, from a landmark 1996 measure intended to move agriculture into a free market economy.

The aid, which comes in addition to the more than $5 billion that has already been appropriated for farmers this year, is intended to salve agricultural economy that has been hurt by weather disasters, crop disease and falling commodity prices.

The bid to rescue farmers is a contrast to the 1996 law, under which subsidies will be phased out by 2002.

"Congress is demonstrating an unwillingness to let the free market control the agricultural economy—at least in an election year," said Neil Harl, an agricultural economist at Iowa State University. "There is a big upside to the market approach. And there's a big downside. And that downside causes pain."

... In the view of some critics of the 1996 measure, including the more liberal National Farmers Union, the free market approach has led to overproduction of some crops, causing prices to fall.

"We've seen what happens when the market takes over—prices drop through the floor," said Marilyn Wentz, a spokeswoman for the National Farmers Union. ...

Critics of subsidies have long complained that farmers have no special right to a safety net. Unsuccessful farms should fail, just like unsuccessful drug stores and auto repair shops, critics say.

But Brent Kleinsasser, a grain farmer in Huron, South Dakota, said farmers were not the only ones who gained from aid to agriculture.

"The more farms there are, the longer food will stay cheap," he said. "When you get a handful of big corporations that control food production, the prices would go way up."

© 1998 *The New York Times*. Reprinted with permission.
Further reproduction prohibited.

Essence of the Story

■ In 1996, Congress enacted a law to phase out farm subsidies by 2002.

■ Because of bad weather, crop diseases, and falling prices, Congress decided in 1998 to provide $6 billion for farmers in addition to $5 billion that it had provided earlier that year.

■ The National Farmers Union says that the free market approach to farming leads to overproduction of some crops and causes their prices to fall.

■ A South Dakota farmer says that everyone gains from aid to farmers because it prevents the control of food production from falling into the hands of big corporations that would raise prices.

■ Critics of farm subsidies say that unsuccessful farms, like unsuccessful drug stores and auto repair shops, should be allowed to fail.

Economic Analysis

■ Figure 1 shows the market for wheat. The demand curve, which is also the marginal benefit curve, is $D = MB$. The supply curve, which is also the marginal cost curve, is $S = MC$.

■ If the wheat market is competitive—what the news article calls a *free market*—equilibrium occurs at a price of $4 a bushel and 20 billion bushels a year—at the intersection of the demand curve and the supply curve. (The numbers are just an example.)

■ At the equilibrium, production is efficient— marginal benefit equals marginal cost. The green area is consumer surplus, and the blue area is producer surplus.

■ Figure 2 shows the outcome for an individual farmer when the price is $4 and the farmer's marginal cost is MC_0. The farmer produces 10,000 bushels, and the producer surplus is the sum of the blue triangles.

■ Figure 2 also shows what happens to an individual farmer when:
   (i) Competition in the world economy lowers the price from $4 to $3 a bushel and
   (ii) Bad weather lowers crop yields and increases marginal cost from MC_0 to MC_1.

■ The farmer cuts production to 2,000 bushels, where marginal cost equals price. Producer surplus shrinks to the small darker blue triangle. The farmer is in distress. But production is efficient.

■ Figure 3 shows what happens if Congress helps the farmer in distress by paying a subsidy on each unit of production. The subsidy lowers the farm's cost per unit, so marginal cost falls by the amount the subsidy.

■ In Fig. 3, the subsidy is $2 a bushel. It is equal to the vertical distance between the two MC curves. The farmer produces the quantity at which *marginal cost minus the subsidy* equals the price. So production increases to 10,000 bushels.

■ At this quantity, marginal cost is $5 a bushel and marginal benefit is $3 a bushel. Because marginal cost exceeds marginal benefit, over-production of wheat occurs and a deadweight loss arises.

■ Subsidizing farmers helps farmers but is inefficient.

■ Because of global competition, there is little chance of markets for farm products being dominated by a small number of firms that could cut production and raise price.

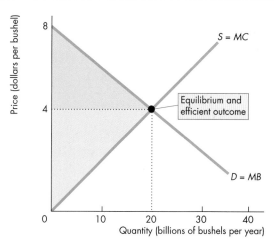

Figure 1 A free market in wheat

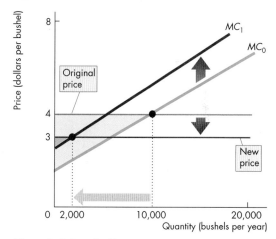

Figure 2 A farm in distress

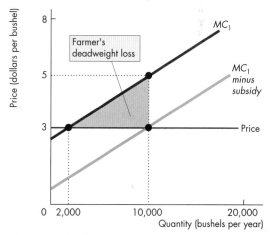

Figure 3 Subsidy and efficiency

S U M M A R Y

KEY POINTS

Efficiency: A Refresher (pp. 108–109)

- The marginal benefit received from a good or service—the benefit of consuming one additional unit—is the *value* of the good or service to its consumers.
- The marginal cost of a good or service—the cost of producing one additional unit—is the *opportunity* cost of one more unit to its producers.
- Resource allocation is efficient when marginal benefit equals marginal cost.
- If marginal benefit exceeds marginal cost, an increase in production uses resources more efficiently.
- If marginal cost exceeds marginal benefit, a decrease in production uses resources more efficiently.

Value, Price, and Consumer Surplus (pp. 110–111)

- Marginal benefit is measured by the maximum price that consumers are willing to pay for a good or service.
- Marginal benefit determines demand, and a demand curve is a marginal benefit curve.
- Value is what people are *willing to* pay; price is what people *must* pay.
- Consumer surplus equals value minus price, summed over the quantity consumed.

Cost, Price, and Producer Surplus (pp. 112–113)

- Marginal cost is measured by the minimum price producers must be offered to increase production by one unit.
- Marginal cost determines supply, and a supply curve is a marginal cost curve.
- Opportunity cost is what producers pay; price is what producers receive.
- Producer surplus equals price minus opportunity cost, summed over the quantity produced.

Is the Competitive Market Efficient? (pp. 114–115)

- In a competitive equilibrium, marginal benefit equals marginal cost and resource allocation is efficient.

Obstacles to Efficiency (pp. 115–117)

- Monopoly restricts production and creates deadweight loss.
- A competitive market provides too small a quantity of public goods because of the free-rider problem.
- A competitive market provides too large a quantity of goods and services that have external costs and too small a quantity of goods and services that have external benefits.

Is the Competitive Market Fair? (pp. 118–121)

- Ideas about fairness divide into two groups: fair *results* or fair *rules*.
- Fair-results ideas require income transfers from the rich to the poor.
- Fair-rules ideas require property rights and voluntary exchange.

KEY FIGURES ◆

KEY TERMS

PROBLEMS

*1. The figure shows the demand for and supply of floppy disks.

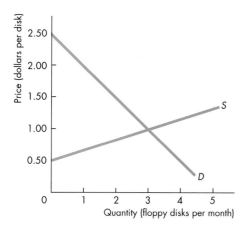

a. What are the equilibrium price and equilibrium quantity of floppy disks?
b. What is the consumer surplus?
c. What is the producer surplus?
d. What is the efficient quantity of floppy disks?

2. The figure shows the demand for and supply of cans of beans.

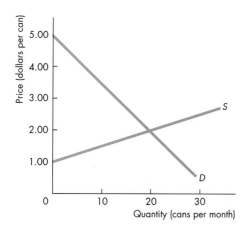

a. What are the equilibrium price and equilibrium quantity of cans of beans?
b. What is the consumer surplus?
c. What is the producer surplus?
d. What is the efficient quantity of beans?

*3. The table gives the demand and supply schedules for sandwiches:

Price (dollars per sandwich)	Quantity demanded	Quantity supplied
	(sandwiches per hour)	
0	400	0
1	350	50
2	300	100
3	250	150
4	200	200
5	150	250
6	100	300
7	50	350
8	0	400

a. What is the maximum price that consumers are willing to pay for the 250th sandwich?
b. What is the minimum price that producers are willing to accept for the 250th sandwich?
c. Are 250 sandwiches an hour less than or greater than the efficient quantity?
d. What is the consumer surplus if the efficient quantity of sandwiches is produced?
e. What is the producer surplus if the efficient quantity of sandwiches is produced?
f. What is the deadweight loss if 250 sandwiches are produced?

4. The table gives the demand and supply schedules for spring water:

Price (dollars per bottle)	Quantity demanded	Quantity supplied
	(bottles per day)	
0	80	0
0.50	70	10
1.00	60	20
1.50	50	30
2.00	40	40
2.50	30	50
3.00	20	60
3.50	10	70
4.00	0	80

a. What is the maximum price that consumers are willing to pay for the 30th bottle?
b. What is the minimum price that producers are willing to accept for the 30th bottle?
c. Are 30 bottles a day less than or greater than the efficient quantity?
d. What is the consumer surplus if the efficient quantity of spring water is produced?

e. What is the producer surplus if the efficient quantity of spring water is produced?
f. What is the deadweight loss if 30 bottles are produced?

*5. The table gives the demand and supply schedules for train travel for Ben, Beth, and Bo:

Price (cents per passenger mile)	Quantity demanded (passenger miles)		
	Ben	Beth	Bo
10	500	300	60
20	450	250	50
30	400	200	40
40	350	150	30
50	300	100	20
60	250	50	10
70	200	0	0

a. If the price of train travel is 40 cents a passenger mile, what is the consumer surplus of each consumer?
b. Which consumer has the largest consumer surplus? Explain why.
c. If the price of train travel rises to 50 cents a passenger mile, what is the change in consumer surplus of each consumer?

6. The table gives the demand and supply schedules for bus travel for Joe, Jean, and Joy:

Price (cents per passenger mile)	Quantity demanded (passenger miles)		
	Joe	Jean	Joy
10	50	600	300
20	45	500	250
30	40	400	200
40	35	300	150
50	30	200	100
60	25	100	50
70	20	0	0

a. If the price of bus travel is 50 cents a passenger mile, what is the consumer surplus of each passenger?
b. Which passenger has the largest consumer surplus? Explain why.
c. If the price of bus travel falls to 30 cents a passenger mile, what is the change in consumer surplus of each passenger?

CRITICAL THINKING

1. Study *Reading Between the Lines* on pp. 122–123 on farm subsidies and then answer the following questions:
    a. Is the quantity of farm output in the United States greater than, less than, or equal to the efficient quantity? Explain your answer by using the concepts of marginal benefit, marginal cost, price, consumer surplus, and producer surplus.
    b. What, if anything, do you think Congress should do to make the farm sector efficient?
    c. Explain what Professor Neil Harl means when he says, "There is a big upside to the market approach. And there's a big downside. And that downside causes pain."
    d. Explain what Marilyn Wentz, spokeswoman for the National Farmers Union, means when she says, "We've seen what happens when the market takes over—prices drop through the floor." Do you agree with her? Why?
    e. Do you agree or disagree with Brent Kleinsasser that everyone gains from aid to agriculture because it prevents a few big corporations from controlling production and raising prices? Why?

2. Use the link on the Parkin Web site to visit the U.S. Department of Agriculture and read the remarks President Clinton made when he signed the 1996 Farm Act. Do you agree or disagree with President Clinton? Why?

3. How would you set about determining whether the allocation of your time between studying different subjects is efficient? In what units would you measure marginal benefit and marginal cost? Explain your answer by using the concepts of marginal benefit, marginal cost, price, consumer surplus, and producer surplus.

Chapter 7

Markets in Action

In 1906, San Francisco suffered a devastating earthquake that destroyed more than half the city's homes but killed few people. How did San Francisco's housing market cope with this enormous shock? Did rents have to be controlled to keep housing affordable? Were scarce housing resources allocated to their highest-valued uses? ◆ Almost every day, a new machine is invented that saves labor and increases productivity. How do labor markets cope with labor-saving technological change? Do the wages of low-skilled workers fall? Do we need minimum wage laws to prevent wages from falling? Do minimum wages enable us to use labor efficiently? ◆ Almost everything we buy is taxed. How do taxes affect prices? Do they increase by the full amount of the tax so that we, the buyers, pay all the tax? Or does the seller pay part of the tax? Do

Turbulent Times

taxes help or hinder the market in its attempt to move resources to where they are valued most highly? ◆ Trade in items such as drugs, automatic firearms, and enriched uranium is illegal. What are the effects of laws that make trading in a good or service illegal on the amounts of such items consumed? And how do these laws affect the prices paid by those who trade illegally? ◆ In 1991, ideal conditions brought high grain yields. But in 1996, crops were devastated by drought and grain yields were low. How do farm prices and revenues react to such output fluctuations? And how do the actions of speculators and government agencies influence farm revenues?

◆ In this chapter, we study a variety of markets. We use the theory of demand and supply (Chapter 4) and the concepts of elasticity (Chapter 5) and efficiency (Chapter 6) to answer the questions just posed. We'll begin by studying two markets that have the biggest impacts on our lives: the housing market and the labor market. Governments often intervene in these markets to try to control prices. They impose rent ceilings and minimum wages. To set the scene for each, we're going to see how a market responds to turbulent events. We'll begin by seeing how a housing market copes with an extremely severe supply shock.

After studying this chapter, you will be able to:

- Explain how housing markets work and how price ceilings create housing shortages and inefficiency
- Explain how labor markets work and how minimum wage laws create unemployment and inefficiency
- Explain the effects of the sales tax
- Explain how markets for illegal goods work
- Explain why farm prices and revenues fluctuate
- Explain how speculation limits price fluctuations

Housing Markets and Rent Ceilings

TO SEE HOW A MARKET COPES WITH A SUPPLY shock, let's transport ourselves to San Francisco in April 1906, as the city is suffering from a massive earthquake and fire. You can sense the enormity of San Francisco's problems by reading a headline from the *New York Times* on one of the first days of the crisis, April 19, 1906:

Over 500 Dead, $200,000,000 Lost in San Francisco Earthquake
Nearly Half the City Is in Ruins and 50,000 Are Homeless

The commander of federal troops in charge of the emergency described the magnitude of the problem:

> Not a hotel of note or importance was left standing. The great apartment houses had vanished . . . two hundred-and-twenty-five thousand people were . . . homeless.[1]

Almost overnight, more than half the people in a city of 400,000 had lost their homes. Temporary shelters and camps alleviated some of the problem, but it was also necessary to utilize the apartment buildings and houses left standing. As a consequence, they had to accommodate 40 percent more people than they had before the earthquake.

The *San Francisco Chronicle* was not published for more than a month after the earthquake. When the newspaper reappeared on May 24, 1906, the city's housing shortage—what would seem to be a major news item that would still be of grave importance—was not mentioned. Milton Friedman and George Stigler describe the situation:

> *There is not a single mention of a housing shortage*! The classified advertisements listed sixty-four offers of flats and houses for rent, and nineteen of houses for sale, against five advertisements of flats or houses wanted. Then and thereafter a considerable number of all types of accommodation except hotel rooms were offered for rent.[2]

How did San Francisco cope with such a devastating reduction in the supply of housing?

[1]Reported in Milton Friedman and George J. Stigler, "Roofs or Ceilings? The Current Housing Problem," in *Popular Essays on Current Problems*, vol. 1, no. 2 (New York: Foundation for Economic Education, 1946), 3–159.
[2]*Ibid.*, 3.

The Market Response to a Decrease in Supply

Figure 7.1 shows the market for housing in San Francisco. The demand curve for housing is *D*. There is a short-run supply curve, labeled *SS*, and a long-run supply curve, labeled *LS*.

The short-run supply curve shows the change in the quantity of housing supplied as the price (rent) changes while the number of houses and apartments remains constant. The short-run supply response arises from changes in the intensity with which existing buildings are used. The quantity of housing supplied increases if families rent out rooms that they previously used themselves, and it decreases if families use rooms that they previously rented out to others.

The long-run supply curve shows how the quantity of housing supplied responds to a change in price after enough time has elapsed for new apartments and houses to be erected or for existing ones to be destroyed. In Fig. 7.1, the long-run supply curve is *perfectly elastic*. We do not actually know that the long-run supply curve is perfectly elastic, but it is a reasonable assumption. It implies that the cost of building an apartment is much the same regardless of the numbers of apartments in existence.

The equilibrium price (rent) and quantity are determined at the point of intersection of the *short-run* supply curve and the demand curve. Before the earthquake, the equilibrium rent is $16 a month and the quantity is 100,000 units of housing.

Figure 7.1(a) shows the situation immediately after the earthquake. The destruction of buildings decreases the supply of housing and shifts the short-run supply curve *SS* leftward to *SS$_A$*. With no change in the population, the demand for housing is unchanged. If the rent remains at $16 a month, only 44,000 units of housing are available. But with only 44,000 units of housing available, the maximum rent that someone is willing to pay for the last available apartment is $24 a month. So rents rise. In Fig. 7.1(a), the rent rises to $20 a month.

As the rent rises, the quantity of housing demanded decreases and the quantity supplied increases to 72,000 units. These changes occur because people economize on their use of space and make spare rooms, attics, and basements available to others. The higher rent allocates the scarce housing to those people who value it most highly and are willing to pay most for it.

But the higher rent has other, long-run effects. Let's look at these long-run effects.

FIGURE 7.1

The San Francisco Housing Market in 1906

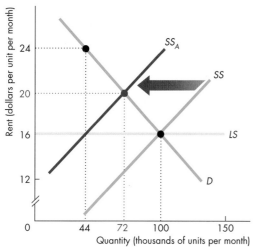

(a) After earthquake

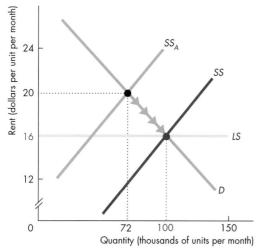

(b) Long-run adjustment

Part (a) shows that before the earthquake, 100,000 housing units were rented at $16 a month. After the earthquake, the short-run supply curve shifts from SS to SS_A. The rent rises to $20 a month, and the quantity of housing decreases to 72,000 units.

With rent at $20 a month, there is profit in building new apartments and houses. As the building program proceeds, the short-run supply curve shifts rightward (part b). The rent gradually falls to $16 a month, and the quantity of housing increases to 100,000 units—as the arrowed line shows.

Long-Run Adjustments

With sufficient time for new apartments and houses to be constructed, supply increases. The long-run supply curve in Fig. 7.1(a) tells us that in the long run, housing is supplied at a rent of $16 a month. Because the rent of $20 a month exceeds the long-run supply price, there is a building boom. More apartments and houses are built, and the short-run supply curve shifts gradually rightward.

Figure 7.1(b) shows the long-run adjustment. As more housing is built, the short-run supply curve shifts rightward and intersects the demand curve at lower rents and larger quantities. The market equilibrium follows the arrows down the demand curve. When the process ends, there is no further profit in building. The rent is back at $16 a month, and 100,000 units of housing are available.

A Regulated Housing Market

We've just seen how a housing market responds to a decrease in supply. And we've seen that a key part of the adjustment process is a rise in the rent.

Suppose the government passes a law to stop the rent from rising. Such a law is called a price ceiling. A **price ceiling** is a regulation that makes it illegal to charge a price higher than a specified level. When a price ceiling is applied to housing markets, it is called a **rent ceiling**. How does a rent ceiling affect the housing market?

The effect of a price (rent) ceiling depends on whether it is imposed at a level that is above or below the equilibrium price (rent). A price ceiling set above the equilibrium price has no effect. The reason is that the price ceiling does not constrain the market forces. The force of the law and the market forces are not in conflict. But a price ceiling set below the equilibrium price has powerful effects on a market. The reason is that it attempts to prevent the price from regulating the quantities demanded and supplied. The force of the law and the market forces are in conflict, and one (or both) of these forces must yield to some degree. Let's study the effects of a price ceiling set below the equilibrium price by returning to San Francisco. What would have happened in San Francisco if a rent ceiling of $16 a month—the rent before the earthquake—had been imposed after the earthquake?

This question and some answers are illustrated in Fig. 7.2. At a rent of $16 a month, the quantity of housing supplied is 44,000 units and the quantity

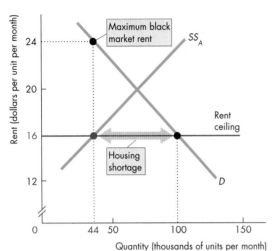

If there had been a rent ceiling of $16 a month, then the quantity of housing supplied after the earthquake would have been stuck at 44,000 units. People would willingly have paid $24 a month for the 44,000th unit. Because the last unit of housing available is worth more than the rent ceiling, frustrated renters will spend time searching for housing and frustrated renters and landlords will make deals in a black market.

demanded is 100,000 units. So there is a shortage of 56,000 units of housing.

But the story does not end here. Somehow, the 44,000 units of available housing must be allocated among people who demand 100,000 units. How is this allocation achieved? When a rent ceiling creates a housing shortage, two developments occur. They are:

- Search activity
- Black markets

Search Activity

The time spent looking for someone with whom to do business is called **search activity**. We spend some time in search activity almost every time we buy something. You want the latest hot CD, and you know 4 stores that stock it. But which store has the best deal? You need to spend a few minutes on the telephone finding out. In some markets, we spend

a lot of time searching. An example is the used car market. People spend a lot of time checking out alternative dealers and cars.

But when a price is regulated and there is a shortage, search activity increases. In rent-controlled housing markets, frustrated would-be renters scan the newspapers, not only for housing ads but also for death notices! Any information about newly available housing is useful. And they race to be first on the scene when news of a possible supplier breaks.

The *opportunity cost* of a good includes not only its price but also the value of the search time spent finding the good. So the opportunity cost of housing is equal to the rent (a regulated price) plus the time and other resources spent searching for the restricted quantity available. Search activity is costly. It uses time and other resources, such as telephones, cars, and gasoline, that could have been used in other productive ways. A rent ceiling controls the rent portion of the cost of housing, but it does not control the opportunity cost, which might even be *higher* than the rent would be if the market were unregulated.

Black Markets

A **black market** is an illegal market in which the price exceeds the legally imposed price ceiling. Black markets occur in rent-controlled housing, and scalpers run black markets in tickets for major sporting events and rock concerts.

When rent ceilings are in force, frustrated renters and landlords constantly seek ways to increase rents. One common way is for a new tenant to pay a high price for worthless fittings, such as $2,000 for threadbare drapes. Another is for the tenant to pay an exorbitant price for new locks and keys—called "key money."

The level of a black market rent depends on how tightly the rent ceiling is enforced. With loose enforcement, the black market rent is close to the unregulated rent. But with strict enforcement, the black market rent is equal to the maximum price that renters are willing to pay.

With strict enforcement of the rent ceiling in the San Francisco example shown in Fig. 7.2, the quantity of housing available remains at 44,000 units. A small number of people offer housing for rent at $24 a month—the highest rent that someone is willing to pay—and the government detects and punishes some of these black market traders.

Inefficiency of Rent Ceilings

In an unregulated market, the market determines the rent at which the quantity demanded equals the quantity supplied. In this situation, scarce housing resources are allocated efficiently. The sum of *consumer surplus* and *producer surplus*—the gains from trade—is maximized (see Chapter 6, pp. 110–111).

Figure 7.3 shows the inefficiency of a rent ceiling. If the rent is fixed at $16 per unit per month, 44,000 units are supplied. The producer surplus is shown by the blue triangle above the supply curve and below the rent line. Because the quantity of housing is less than the competitive quantity, there is a deadweight loss shown by the gray triangle. This loss is borne by the consumers who can't find housing and the producers who can't supply housing at the new lower price. Consumers who do find housing at the controlled rent gain. If no one incurs search cost, consumer surplus is shown by the sum of the green triangle and the red rectangle. But search costs might eat up part of the consumer surplus, possibly as much as the entire amount that consumers are willing to pay for the available housing, which is shown by the red rectangle.

So rent ceilings prevent scarce resources from flowing to their highest-valued use. But don't they ensure that scarce housing goes to the people whose need is greatest? The idea of need is complex. Who is to determine whether one person's "need" is greater than another person's? The unregulated market respects everyone's assessment of "need" by permitting each person's willingness to pay to allocate scarce resources.

When the law prevents rents from adjusting to bring the quantity demanded into equality with the quantity supplied, factors other than rent allocate the scarce housing. One of these factors is discrimination on the basis of race, ethnicity, or sex.

There are many modern examples of rent ceilings, but the best is New York City. One consequence of New York's rent ceilings is that families that have lived in the city for a long time—including some rich and famous ones—enjoy low rents, while newcomers pay high rents for hard-to-find apartments. At the same time, landlords in rent-controlled Harlem abandon entire city blocks to rats and drug dealers.

The effects of rent ceilings have led Assar Lindbeck, chairman of the economic science Nobel Prize committee, to suggest that rent ceilings are the most effective means yet for destroying cities, even more effective than the hydrogen bomb.

FIGURE 7.3

The Inefficiency of a Rent Ceiling

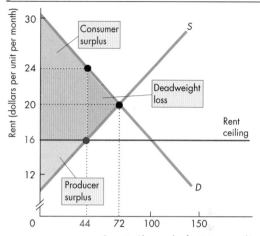

A rent ceiling of $16 a month decreases the quantity of housing supplied to 44,000 units. Producer surplus shrinks to the blue triangle and a deadweight loss (the gray triangle) arises. If people use no resources in search activity, consumer surplus is shown by the green triangle plus the red rectangle. But people might use resources in search activity equal to the amount they are willing to pay for the available housing, the red rectangle.

REVIEW QUIZ

- How does a decrease in the supply of housing change the equilibrium rent in the short run? Who gets to consume the scarce housing resources?
- What are the long-run effects of higher rents following a decrease in the supply of housing?
- What is a rent ceiling and what are the effects of a rent ceiling set above the equilibrium rent?
- What are the effects of a rent ceiling set below the equilibrium rent?
- How do scarce housing resources get allocated when a rent ceiling is in place?

You now know how a price ceiling (rent ceiling) works. Next, we'll learn about the effects of a price floor by studying minimum wages in the labor market.

The Labor Market and the Minimum Wage

FOR EACH ONE OF US, THE LABOR MARKET IS THE most important market in which we participate. It is the market that influences the jobs we get and the wages we earn. Firms decide how much labor to demand, and the lower the wage rate, the greater is the quantity of labor demanded. Households decide how much labor to supply, and the higher the wage rate, the greater is the quantity of labor supplied. The wage rate adjusts to make the quantity of labor demanded equal to the quantity supplied.

But the labor market is constantly hit by shocks, and wages and employment prospects constantly change. The most pervasive source of these shocks is the advance of technology.

New labor-saving technologies become available every year. As a result, the demand for some types of labor, usually the least skilled types, decreases. During the 1980s and 1990s, for example, the demand for telephone operators and television repair persons has decreased. Throughout the past 200 years, the demand for low-skilled farm laborers has steadily decreased.

How does the labor market cope with this continuous decrease in the demand for low-skilled labor? Doesn't it mean that the wages of low-skilled workers are constantly falling?

To answer these questions, we must study the market for low-skilled labor. And just as we did when we studied the housing market, we must look at both the short run and the long run.

In the short run, there is a given number of people who have a given skill, training, and experience. The short-run supply of labor describes how the number of hours of labor supplied by this given number of workers changes as the wage rate changes. To get workers to work more hours, they must be offered a higher wage rate.

In the long run, people can acquire new skills and find new types of jobs. The number of people in the low-skilled labor market depends on the wage rate in this market compared with other opportunities. If the wage rate of low-skilled labor is high enough, people will enter this market. If the wage rate is too low, people will leave it. Some will seek training to enter higher-skilled labor markets, and others will stop working and stay at home or retire.

The long-run supply of labor is the relationship between the quantity of labor supplied and the wage rate after enough time has passed for people to enter or leave the low-skilled labor market. If people can freely enter and leave the low-skilled labor market, the long-run supply of labor is *perfectly elastic.*

Figure 7.4 shows the market for low-skilled labor. Other things remaining the same, the lower the wage rate, the greater is the quantity of labor demanded by firms. The demand curve for labor, D in part (a), shows this relationship between the wage rate and the quantity of labor demanded. Other things remaining the same, the higher the wage rate, the greater is the quantity of labor supplied by households. But the longer the period of adjustment, the greater is the *elasticity of supply* of labor. The short-run supply curve is SS, and the long-run supply curve is LS. In the figure, long-run supply is assumed to be perfectly elastic (the LS curve is horizontal). This market is in equilibrium at a wage rate of $5 an hour and with 22 million hours of labor employed.

What happens if a labor-saving invention decreases the demand for low-skilled labor? Figure 7.4(a) shows the short-run effects of such a change. The demand curve before the new technology is introduced is the curve labeled D. After the introduction of the new technology, the demand curve shifts leftward to D_A. The wage rate falls to $4 an hour, and the quantity of labor employed decreases to 21 million hours. This short-run effect on the wage rate and employment is not the end of the story.

People who are now earning only $4 an hour look around for other opportunities. They see many other jobs (in markets for other types of skills) that pay more than $4 an hour. One by one, workers decide to go back to school or take jobs that pay less but offer on-the-job training. As a result, the short-run supply curve begins to shift leftward.

Figure 7.4(b) shows the long-run adjustment. As the short-run supply curve shifts leftward, it intersects the demand curve D_A at higher wage rates and lower levels of employment. The process ends when workers have no incentive to leave the market for low-skilled labor and the short-run supply curve has shifted all the way to SS_A. At this point, the wage rate has returned to $5 an hour and employment has decreased to 20 million hours a year.

Sometimes, the adjustment process that we've just described is rapid. At other times, it is slow and wages remain low for a long period. To boost the incomes of the lowest-paid workers, the government intervenes in the labor market and sets the minimum wage that employers are required to pay. Let's look at the effects of the minimum wage.

FIGURE **7.4**
A Market for Low-Skilled Labor

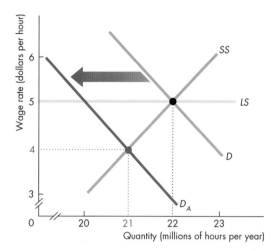

(a) After invention

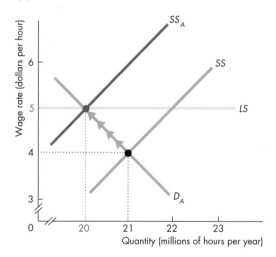

(b) Long-run adjustment

Part (a) shows the immediate effect of a labor-saving invention on the market for low-skilled labor. Initially, the wage rate is $5 an hour and 22 million hours of labor a year are employed. A labor-saving invention shifts the demand curve from D to D_A. The wage rate falls to $4 an hour, and employment decreases to 21 million hours a year. With the lower wage rate, some workers leave this market, and the short-run supply curve starts to shift gradually to SS_A (part b). The wage rate gradually increases, and the employment level decreases. In the long run, the wage rate returns to $5 an hour, and employment falls to 20 million hours a year.

The Minimum Wage

A **minimum wage law** is a regulation that makes hiring labor for less than a specified wage illegal. Figure 7.5 shows how a minimum wage law works. With no minimum wage, the equilibrium wage is $4 an hour. If the equilibrium wage *exceeds* the minimum wage, the law and market forces are not in conflict and the minimum wage has no effect. But if the equilibrium wage is *below* the minimum wage, the minimum wage is in conflict with the market forces and does have some effects on the labor market.

Suppose the government sets a minimum wage at $5 an hour. The horizontal red line in Fig. 7.5 shows this minimum wage. At $5 an hour, 20 million hours of labor are demanded (point *a*) and 22 million hours of labor are supplied (point *b*). There are 2 million hours of available labor that go unemployed.

With only 20 million hours demanded, some workers are willingly to supply that 20 millionth hour for $3. Frustrated unemployed workers spend time and other resources searching for a hard-to-find job.

FIGURE **7.5**
Minimum Wage and Unemployment

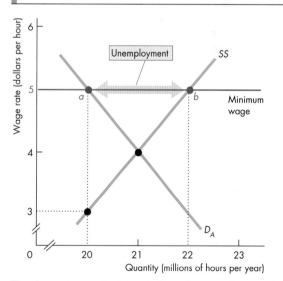

The demand curve for labor is D_A, and the supply curve is SS. In an unregulated market, the wage rate is $4 an hour and 21 million hours of labor a year are employed. If a minimum wage of $5 an hour is imposed, only 20 million hours are hired but 22 million hours are available. Unemployment—*ab*—of 2 million hours a year is created.

The Minimum Wage in Practice

The minimum wage in the United States is set by the federal government's Fair Labor Standards Act. Some state governments have passed state minimum wage laws that exceed the federal minimum. In 1998, the minimum wage is $5.15 an hour. The minimum has been increased from time to time and has fluctuated between 35 percent and more than 50 percent of the average wage of production workers.

You saw in Fig. 7.5 that the minimum wage brings unemployment. But how much unemployment does it bring? Economists do not agree on the answer to this question. Until recently, most economists believed that the minimum wage was a big contributor to high unemployment among low-skilled young workers. But recently this view has been challenged and the challenge rebutted.

David Card, a Canadian economist who works at the University of California at Berkeley, and Alan Krueger of Princeton University say that increases in the minimum wage have not decreased employment and created unemployment. Studying minimum wages in California, New Jersey, and Texas, they say that the employment rate of low-income workers increased following an increase in the minimum wage. They suggest three reasons why higher wages might increase employment. First, workers become more conscientious and productive. Second, workers are less likely to quit, so labor turnover, which is costly, is reduced. Third, managers make a firm's operations more efficient.

Most economists are skeptical about the suggestions by Card and Krueger. They ask two questions. First, if higher wages make workers more productive and reduce labor turnover, why don't firms freely pay the wage rates above the equilibrium wage to encourage more productive work habits? Second, are there other explanations for the employment responses that Card and Krueger have found?

Card and Krueger have got the timing wrong according to Daniel Hamermesh of the University of Texas at Austin. He says that firms cut employment *before* the minimum wage is increased in anticipation of the increase. If he is correct, looking for the effects of an increase *after* it has occurred misses its main effects. Finis Welch of Texas A&M University and Kevin Murphy of the University of Chicago say the employment effects that Card and Krueger found are caused by regional differences in economic growth, not changes in the minimum wage.

One effect of the minimum wage, according to Fig. 7.5, is an increase in the quantity of labor supplied. If this effect occurs, it might show up as an increase in the number of people who quit school before completing high school to look for work. Some economists say this response does occur.

Inefficiency of the Minimum Wage

An unregulated labor market allocates scarce labor resources to the jobs in which they are valued most highly. The minimum wage frustrates the market mechanism and results in unemployment—wasted labor resources—and an inefficient amount of job search.

In Fig. 7.5, with firms employing only 20 million hours of labor at the minimum wage, many people who are willing to supply labor are unable to get hired. You can see that the 20 millionth hour of labor is available for $3. That is, the lowest wage at which someone is willing to supply the 20 millionth hour—read off from the supply curve—is $3. Someone who manages to find a job earns $5 an hour—$2 an hour more than the lowest wage rate at which someone is willing to work. So it pays unemployed people to spend time and effort looking for work. Even though only 20 million hours of labor actually get employed, each person spends time and effort searching for one of the scarce jobs.

R E V I E W   Q U I Z

- How does a decrease in the demand for low-skilled labor change the wage rate in the short run?
- What are the long-run effects of a falling wage rate on the supply of low-skilled labor?
- What is a minimum wage law and what is the effect of a minimum wage that is set below the equilibrium wage?
- What is the effect of a minimum wage that is set above the equilibrium wage?

Next we're going to study a more widespread government intervention in markets: taxes, such as the state sales tax. We'll see how taxes change prices and quantities. We'll discover that the sales tax is not paid entirely by the consumer. And we'll see that usually, taxes create a deadweight loss.

Taxes

ALMOST EVERYTHING YOU BUY IS TAXED. But who really pays the tax? Because the sales tax is added to the price of a good or service when it is sold, isn't it obvious that *you*, the buyer, pay the tax? Isn't the price higher than it otherwise would be by an amount equal to the tax? It can be, but usually it isn't. And it is even possible that you actually pay none of the tax! Let's see how we can make sense of these apparently absurd statements.

Who Pays the Sales Tax?

Suppose the government puts a $10 sales tax on CD players. What are the effects of the sales tax on the price and quantity of CD players? To answer this question, we need to work out what happens to demand and supply in the market for CD players.

Figure 7.6 shows this market. The demand curve is *D*, and the supply curve is *S*. With no sales tax, the equilibrium price is $100 per CD player and 5,000 players are bought and sold each week.

When a good is taxed, it has two prices: a price that excludes the tax and a price that includes the tax. Buyers respond only to the price that includes the tax, because that is the price they pay. Sellers respond only to the price that excludes the tax, because that is the price they receive. The tax is like a wedge between these two prices.

Think of the price on the vertical axis of Fig. 7.6 as the price paid by buyers—the price that *includes* the tax. When a tax is imposed and the price changes, there is a change in the quantity demanded but no change in demand. That is, there is a movement along the demand curve and no shift of the demand curve.

But the supply changes and the supply curve shifts. The sales tax is like an increase in cost, so supply decreases and the supply curve shifts leftward to *S* + *tax*. To determine the position of this new supply curve, we add the tax to the minimum price that sellers are willing to accept for each quantity sold. For example, with no tax, sellers are willing to offer 5,000 players a week for $100 a player. So with a $10 tax, they will supply 5,000 players a week for $110—a price that includes the tax. The curve *S* + *tax* describes the terms on which sellers are willing to offer players for sale now that there is a $10 tax.

Equilibrium occurs where the new supply curve intersects the demand curve—at a price of $105 and

FIGURE 7.6
The Sales Tax

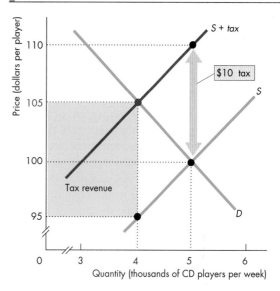

With no sales tax, 5,000 players a week are bought and sold at $100 each. A sales tax of $10 a player is imposed, and the supply curve shifts leftward to *S* + *tax*. In the new equilibrium, the price rises to $105 a player and the quantity decreases to 4,000 CD players a week. The sales tax raises the price by less than the tax, lowers the price received by the seller, and decreases the quantity. The sales tax brings in revenue to the government equal to the blue rectangle.

a quantity of 4,000 CD players a week. The $10 sales tax increases the price paid by the buyer by $5 a player. And it decreases the price received by the seller by $5 a player. So the buyer and the seller pay the $10 tax equally.

The tax brings in tax revenue to the government equal to the tax per item multiplied by the number of items sold. The blue area in Fig. 7.6 illustrates the tax revenue. The $10 tax on CD players brings in a tax revenue of $40,000 a week.

In this example, the buyer and the seller split the tax equally: The buyer pays $5 a player, and so does the seller. This equal sharing of the tax is a special case and does not usually occur. But some split of the tax between the buyer and seller is usual. Also, there are other special cases in which either the buyer or the seller pays the entire tax. The division of the tax between the buyer and the seller depends on the elasticities of demand and supply.

Tax Division and Elasticity of Demand

The division of the tax between the buyer and the seller depends, in part, on the elasticity of demand. There are two extreme cases:

- Perfectly inelastic demand—buyer pays.
- Perfectly elastic demand—seller pays.

Perfectly Inelastic Demand Figure 7.7(a) shows the market for insulin, a vital daily medication of diabetics. Demand is perfectly inelastic at 100,000 doses a day, regardless of the price as shown by the vertical curve D. That is, a diabetic would sacrifice all other goods and services rather than not consume the insulin dose that provides good health. The supply curve of insulin is S. With no tax, the price is $2 a dose and the quantity is 100,000 doses a day.

If insulin is taxed at 20¢ a dose, we must add the tax to the minimum price at which drug companies are willing to sell insulin. The result is a new supply curve $S + tax$. The price rises to $2.20 a dose, but the quantity does not change. The buyer pays the entire sales tax of 20¢ a dose.

Perfectly Elastic Demand Figure 7.7(b) shows the market for pink marker pens. Demand is perfectly elastic at $1 a pen as shown by the horizontal curve D. If pink pens are less expensive than the others, everyone uses pink. If pink pens are more expensive than the others, no one uses them. The supply curve is S. With no tax, the price of a pink marker is $1, and the quantity is 4,000 pens a week.

If a sales tax of 10¢ a pen is imposed on pink marker pens, we add the tax to the minimum price at which sellers are willing to offer them for sale and the new supply curve is $S + tax$. The price remains at $1 a pen, and the quantity decreases to 1,000 a week. The 10¢ sales tax leaves the price paid by the buyer unchanged but lowers the amount received by the seller by the full amount of the sales tax. As a result, sellers decrease the quantity offered for sale.

We've seen that when demand is perfectly inelastic, the buyer pays the entire tax, and when demand is perfectly elastic, the seller pays it. In the usual case, demand is neither perfectly inelastic nor perfectly elastic, and the tax is split between the buyer and the seller. But the division depends on the elasticity of demand. The more inelastic the demand, the larger is the amount of the tax paid by the buyer.

FIGURE 7.7

Sales Tax and the Elasticity of Demand

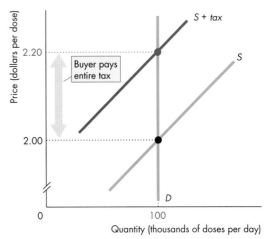

(a) Inelastic demand

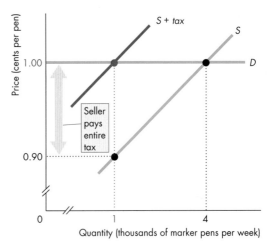

(b) Elastic demand

Part (a) shows the market for insulin. The demand for insulin is perfectly inelastic. With no tax, the price is $2 a dose and the quantity is 100,000 doses a day. A sales tax of 20¢ a dose shifts the supply curve to $S + tax$. The price rises to $2.20 a dose, but the quantity bought does not change. Buyers pay the entire tax. Part (b) shows the market for pink marker pens. The demand for pink pens is perfectly elastic. With no tax, the price is $1 a pen and the quantity is 4,000 pens a week. A sales tax of 10¢ a pink pen shifts the supply curve to $S + tax$. The price remains at $1 a pen, and the quantity of pink markers sold decreases to 1,000 a week. Sellers pay the entire tax.

Tax Division and Elasticity of Supply

The division of the tax between the buyer and the seller also depends, in part, on the elasticity of supply. Again, there are two extreme cases:

■ Perfectly inelastic supply—seller pays.
■ Perfectly elastic supply—buyer pays.

Perfectly Inelastic Supply Figure 7.8(a) shows the market for water from a mineral spring that flows at a constant rate that can't be controlled. Supply is perfectly inelastic at 100,000 bottles a week as shown by the supply curve S. The demand curve for the water from this spring is D. With no tax, the price is 50¢ a bottle and the 100,000 bottles that flow from the spring are bought.

Suppose this spring water is taxed at 5¢ a bottle. The supply curve does not change because the spring owners still produce 100,000 bottles a week even though the price they receive falls. But buyers are willing to buy the 100,000 bottles only if the price is 50¢ a bottle. So the price remains at 50¢ a bottle, and the seller pays the entire tax. The sales tax reduces the price received by sellers to 45¢ a bottle.

Perfectly Elastic Supply Figure 7.8(b) shows the market for sand from which computer-chip makers extract silicon. Supply of this sand is perfectly elastic at a price of 10¢ a pound as shown by the supply curve S. The demand curve for sand is D. With no tax, the price is 10¢ a pound and 5,000 pounds a week are bought.

If this sand is taxed at 1¢ a pound, we must add the tax to the minimum supply-price. Sellers are now willing to offer any quantity at 11¢ a pound along the curve $S + tax$. A new equilibrium is determined where the new supply curve intersects the demand curve—at a price of 11¢ a pound and a quantity of 3,000 pounds a week. The sales tax has increased the price paid by the buyer by the full amount of the tax—1¢ a pound—and has decreased the quantity sold.

We've seen that when supply is perfectly inelastic, the seller pays the entire tax, and when supply is perfectly elastic, the buyer pays it. In the usual case, supply is neither perfectly inelastic nor perfectly elastic, and the tax is split between the buyer and the seller. But the division between the buyer and the seller depends on the elasticity of supply. The more elastic the supply, the larger is the amount of the tax paid by the buyer.

FIGURE 7.8

Sales Tax and the Elasticity of Supply

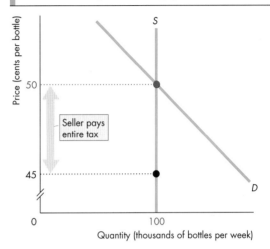

(a) Inelastic supply

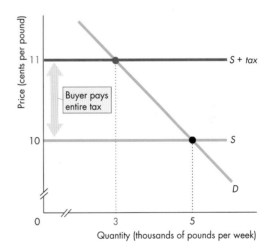

(b) Elastic supply

Part (a) shows the market for water from a mineral spring. Supply is perfectly inelastic. With no tax, the price is 50¢ a bottle. With a sales tax of 5¢ a bottle, the price remains at 50¢ a bottle. The number of bottles bought remains the same, but the price received by the seller decreases to 45¢ a bottle. The seller pays the entire tax. Part (b) shows the market for sand. Supply is perfectly elastic. With no tax, the price is 10¢ a pound and 5,000 pounds a week are bought. The sales tax of 1¢ a pound increases the minimum supply-price to 11¢ a pound. The supply curve shifts to $S + tax$. The price increases to 11¢ a pound. The buyer pays the entire tax.

Sales Taxes in Practice

Heavily taxed items such as alcohol, tobacco, and gasoline have a low elasticity of demand. So the buyer pays most of the tax. Also, because demand is inelastic, the quantity bought does not decrease much and the government collects a large tax revenue.

But sometimes, the government makes a mistake. In 1991, the federal government was scraping around for every dollar it could find to cut its deficit. It came up with a plan to put a 10 percent "luxury tax" on pleasure boats, private airplanes, high-priced cars, furs, and jewelry, which it estimated would bring in $300 million a year. But the government did not reckon on the high elasticity of demand for these items. The quantities of pleasure boats and other luxury items bought decreased by up to 90 percent, and the tax revenue collected was only one tenth the amount expected. The luxury tax was quickly abandoned.

This short-lived experiment with a luxury tax explains why the items that are taxed are those that have inelastic demands and why, in practice, buyers pay most of the taxes.

Taxes and Efficiency

You've seen that a sales tax places a wedge between the price paid by buyers and the price received by sellers. The price paid by buyers is also the buyers' willingness to pay, which measures marginal benefit. And the price received by sellers is the sellers' minimum supply-price, which equals marginal cost.

So, because a tax places a wedge between the buyers' price and the sellers' price, it also puts a wedge between marginal benefit and marginal cost and creates inefficiency. With a higher buying price and a lower selling price, the tax decreases the quantity produced and consumed and a deadweight loss arises. Figure 7.9 shows the inefficiency of taxes. Both the consumer surplus and producer surplus shrink. Part of each of these surpluses goes to the government in tax revenue—the light blue area in the figure. And part of the surpluses becomes a deadweight loss—the gray area.

In the extreme cases of perfectly inelastic demand and perfectly inelastic supply, the quantity does not change and there is no deadweight loss. The more inelastic is either demand or supply, the smaller is the decrease in quantity and the smaller is the deadweight loss. When demand or supply is perfectly inelastic, the quantity remains constant and there is no deadweight loss.

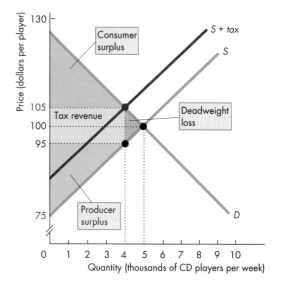

FIGURE 7.9

Taxes and Efficiency

With no sales tax, 5,000 players a week are bought and sold at $100 each. With a sales tax of $10 a player, the buyers' price rises to $105 a player, the sellers' price falls to $95, and the quantity decreases to 4,000 CD players a week. Consumer surplus shrinks to the green area, and producer surplus shrinks to the dark blue area. Part of the loss of consumer surplus and producer surplus goes to the government as tax revenue, which is shown as the light blue area. A deadweight loss also arises, which is shown by the gray area.

REVIEW QUIZ

- How does the elasticity of demand influence the effect of a sales tax on the price paid by the buyer, the price received by the seller, the quantity, the tax revenue, and the deadweight loss?
- How does the elasticity of supply influence the effect of a sales tax on the price paid by the buyer, the price received by the seller, the quantity, the tax revenue, and the deadweight loss?
- Why do taxes create a deadweight loss?

Governments make the trading of some types of goods, such as drugs illegal. Let's see how the market works when trade in an illegal good takes place.

Markets for Illegal Goods

THE MARKETS FOR MANY GOODS AND SERVICES are regulated, and the buying and selling of some goods are illegal—the goods and services are illegal. The best-known examples of such goods are drugs, such as marijuana, cocaine, and heroin.

Despite the fact that these drugs are illegal, trade in them is a multibillion-dollar business. This trade can be understood by using the same economic model and principles that explain trade in legal goods. To study the market for illegal goods, we're first going to examine the prices and quantities that would prevail if these goods were not illegal. Next, we'll see how prohibition works. Then we'll see how a tax might limit consumption of these goods.

A Free Market for Drugs

Figure 7.10 shows the market for drugs. The demand curve, *D,* shows that, other things remaining the same, the lower the price of drugs, the larger is the quantity of drugs demanded. The supply curve, *S,* shows that, other things remaining the same, the lower the price of drugs, the smaller is the quantity supplied. If drugs were not illegal, the quantity bought and sold would be Q_c and the price would be P_c.

A Market for Illegal Drugs

When a good is illegal, the cost of trading in the good increases. By how much the cost increases and on whom the cost falls depend on the penalties for violating the law and the effectiveness with which the law is enforced. The larger the penalties and the more effective the policing, the higher are the costs. Penalties might be imposed on sellers, buyers, or both.

Penalties on Sellers   Drug dealers in the United States face large penalties if their activities are detected. For example, a marijuana dealer could pay a $200,000 fine and serve a 15-year prison term. A heroin dealer could pay a $500,000 fine and serve a 20-year prison term. These penalties are part of the cost of supplying illegal drugs, and they bring a decrease in supply—a leftward shift in the supply curve. To determine the new supply curve, we add the cost of breaking the law to the minimum price

FIGURE 7.10

A Market for an Illegal Good

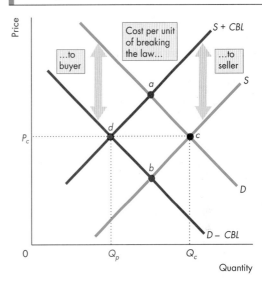

The demand curve for drugs is *D,* and the supply curve is *S.* If drugs are not illegal, the quantity bought and sold is Q_c at a price of P_c—point c. If selling drugs is illegal, the cost of breaking the law by selling drugs (*CBL*) is added to the minimum supply-price and supply decreases to *S* + *CBL*. The price rises, and the quantity bought decreases—point a. If buying drugs is illegal, the cost of breaking the law is subtracted from the maximum price that buyers are willing to pay, and demand decreases to *D* − *CBL*. The price falls, and the quantity bought decreases—point b. If both buying and selling are illegal, both the supply and demand curves shift, the quantity bought decreases even more, but (in this example) the price remains at its unregulated level—point d.

that drug dealers are willing to accept. In Fig. 7.10, the cost of breaking the law by selling drugs (*CBL*) is added to the minimum price that dealers will accept, and the supply curve shifts leftward to *S* + *CBL*. If penalties are imposed only on sellers, the market moves from point *c* to point *a*. The price increases, and the quantity bought decreases.

Penalties on Buyers   In the United States, it is illegal to *possess* drugs such as marijuana, cocaine, and heroin. For example, possession of marijuana can bring a prison term of 1 year and possession of heroin can bring a prison term of 2 years. Penalties fall on buyers, and the cost of breaking the law must be subtracted from the value of the good to determine the maximum price buyers are willing to pay for the drugs. Demand decreases, and the demand curve shifts leftward. In Fig. 7.10, the demand curve shifts to $D - CBL$. With penalties imposed only on buyers, the market moves from point c to point b. The price and the quantity bought decrease.

Penalties on Both Sellers and Buyers   If penalties are imposed on sellers *and* buyers, both supply and demand decrease, and both the supply curve and the demand curve shift leftward. In Fig. 7.10, the costs of breaking the law are the same for both buyers and sellers, so both curves shift leftward by the same amount. The market moves to point d. The price remains at P_c, but the quantity bought decreases to Q_p.

The larger the penalties and the greater the degree of law enforcement, the larger is the decrease in demand and/or supply and the greater is the shift of the demand and/or supply curve. If the penalties are heavier on sellers, the supply curve shifts farther than the demand curve and the price rises above P_c. If the penalties are heavier on buyers, the demand curve shifts farther than the supply curve and the price falls below P_c. In the United States, the penalties on sellers are larger than those on buyers, so the quantity of drugs traded decreases and the price increases compared with an unregulated market.

With high enough penalties and effective law enforcement, it is possible to decrease demand and/or supply to the point at which the quantity bought is zero. But in reality, such an outcome is unusual. It does not happen in the case of illegal drugs. The key reason is the high cost of law enforcement and insufficient resources for the police to achieve effective enforcement. Because of this situation, some people suggest that drugs (and other illegal goods) should be legalized and sold openly but also be taxed at a high rate in the same way that legal drugs such as alcohol are taxed. How would such an arrangement work?

Legalizing and Taxing Drugs

From your study of the effects of taxes, it is easy to see that the quantity of drugs bought could be decreased if drugs were legalized and taxed. A sufficiently high tax could be imposed to decrease supply, raise the price, and achieve the same decrease in the quantity bought as with a prohibition on drugs. The government would collect a large tax revenue.

Illegal Trading to Evade the Tax   It is likely that an extremely high tax rate would be needed to cut the quantity of drugs bought to the level prevailing with a prohibition. It is also likely that many drug dealers and consumers would try to cover up their activities to evade the tax. If they did act in this way, they would face the cost of breaking the law—the tax law. If the penalty for tax law violation is as severe and as effectively policed as drug-dealing laws, the analysis we've already conducted applies also to this case. The quantity of drugs bought would depend on the penalties for law breaking and on the way in which the penalties are assigned to buyers and sellers.

Taxes Versus Prohibition: Some Pros and Cons
Which is more effective, prohibition or taxes? In favor of taxes and against prohibition is the fact that the tax revenue can be used to make law enforcement more effective. It can also be used to run a more effective education campaign against drugs. In favor of prohibition and against taxes is the fact that a prohibition sends a signal that might influence preferences, decreasing the demand for drugs. Also, some people intensely dislike the idea of the government profiting from trade in harmful substances.

REVIEW QUIZ

- How does the imposition of a penalty for selling a drug influence demand, supply, price, and the quantity of the drug consumed?
- How does the imposition of a penalty for buying a drug influence demand, supply, price, and the quantity of the drug consumed?
- How does the imposition of a penalty for selling *or* buying a drug influence demand, supply, price, and the quantity of the drug consumed?
- Is there any case for legalizing drugs?

You've seen how government intervention in markets in the form of price ceilings, price floors, and taxes limits the quantity and creates inefficient resource use. You've also seen how in a market for an illegal good, the quantity can be decreased by imposing penalties on either buyers or sellers or by legalizing and taxing the good. In the next and final section of this chapter, we look at agricultural markets and see how governments try to stabilize farm revenues.

Stabilizing Farm Revenues

WHEN FLOODS COVERED VAST TRACTS OF THE Midwest in the summer of 1993, many farmers saw their crops wiped out. Farm output fluctuates a great deal because of fluctuations in the weather. How do changes in farm output affect farm prices and farm revenues? And how might farm revenues be stabilized? Let's begin to answer these questions by looking at an agricultural market.

An Agricultural Market

Figure 7.11 shows the market for wheat. In both parts, the demand curve for wheat is *D*. Once farmers have harvested their crop, they have no control over the quantity supplied, and supply is inelastic along a *momentary supply curve*. In normal climate conditions, the momentary supply curve is MS_0 (in both parts of the figure).

The price is determined at the point of intersection of the momentary supply curve and the demand curve. In normal conditions, the price is $4 a bushel. The quantity of wheat produced is 20 billion bushels, and farm revenue is $80 billion. Suppose the opportunity cost to farmers of producing wheat is also $80 billion. Then in normal conditions, farmers just cover their opportunity cost.

Poor Harvest Suppose there is a bad growing season, resulting in a poor harvest. What happens to the price of wheat and the revenue of farmers? These questions are answered in Fig. 7.11(a). Supply decreases, and the momentary supply curve shifts leftward to MS_1, where 15 billion bushels of wheat are produced. With a decrease in supply, the price increases to $6 a bushel.

What happens to total farm revenue? It *increases* to $90 billion. A decrease in supply has brought an increase in price and an increase in farm revenue. It does so because the demand for wheat is *inelastic*. The percentage decrease in the quantity demanded is less than the percentage increase in price. You can verify this fact by noticing in Fig. 7.11(a) that the increase in revenue from the higher price ($30 billion light blue area) exceeds the decrease in revenue from the smaller quantity ($20 billion red area). Farmers are now making a revenue in excess of their opportunity cost.

Although total farm revenue increases when there is a poor harvest, some farmers, whose entire crop is

FIGURE 7.11

Harvests, Farm Prices, and Farm Revenue

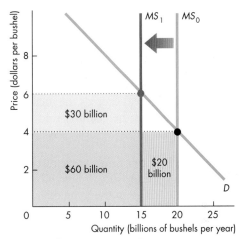

(a) Poor harvest: revenue increases

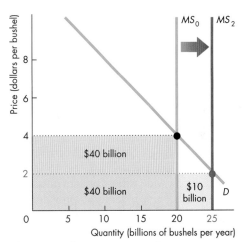

(b) Bumper harvest: revenue decreases

The demand curve for wheat is *D*. In normal times, the supply curve is MS_0 and 20 million bushels are sold for $4 a bushel. In part (a), a poor harvest decreases supply to MS_1. The price rises to $6 a bushel, and farm revenue increases to $90 billion—the $30 billion increase from the higher price (light blue area) exceeds the $20 billion decrease from the smaller quantity (red area). In part (b), a bumper harvest increases supply to MS_2. The price falls to $2 a bushel, and farm revenue decreases to $50 billion—the $40 billion decrease from the lower price (red area) exceeds the $10 billion increase from the increase in the quantity sold (light blue area).

wiped out, suffer a decrease in revenue. Others, whose crop is unaffected, make an enormous gain.

Bumper Harvest   Figure 7.11(b) shows what happens in the opposite situation, when there is a bumper harvest. Now supply increases to 25 billion bushels, and the momentary supply curve shifts rightward to MS_2. With the increased quantity supplied, the price falls to $2 a bushel. Farm revenue decreases to $50 billion. It does so because the demand for wheat is inelastic. To see this fact, notice in Fig. 7.11(b) that the decrease in revenue from the lower price ($40 billion red area) exceeds the increase in revenue from the increase in the quantity sold ($10 billion light blue area).

Elasticity of Demand   In the example we've just worked through, demand is inelastic. If demand is elastic, the price fluctuations go in the same directions as those we've worked out, but revenue fluctuates in the opposite direction. Bumper harvests increase revenue, and poor harvests decrease it. But the demand for most agricultural products is inelastic, and the case we've studied is the relevant one.

Because farm prices fluctuate, institutions have evolved to stabilize them. There are two types of institutions:

- Speculative markets in inventories
- Farm price stabilization policy

Speculative Markets in Inventories

Many goods, including a wide variety of agricultural products, can be stored. These inventories provide a cushion between production and consumption. If production decreases, goods can be sold from inventory; if production increases, goods can be put into inventory.

In a market that has inventories, we must distinguish production from supply. The quantity produced is not the same as the quantity supplied. The quantity supplied exceeds the quantity produced when goods are sold from inventory. And the quantity supplied is less than the quantity produced when goods are put into inventory. Supply therefore depends on the behavior of inventory holders.

The Behavior of Inventory Holders   Inventory holders speculate. They hope to buy at a low price and sell at a high price. That is, they hope to buy goods and put them into inventory when the price is low and

sell them from inventory when the price is high. They make a profit or incur a loss equal to their selling price minus their buying price and minus the cost of storage.

But how do inventory holders know when to buy and when to sell? How do they know whether the price is high or low? To decide whether a price is high or low, inventory holders forecast future prices. If the current price is above the forecasted future price, inventory holders sell goods from inventory. If the current price is below the forecasted future price, inventory holders buy goods to put into inventory. This behavior by inventory holders makes the supply perfectly elastic at the price forecasted by inventory holders.

Let's work out what happens to price and quantity in a market in which inventories are held when production fluctuates. Let's look again at the wheat market.

Fluctuations in Production   In Fig. 7.12 the demand curve for wheat is D. Inventory holders expect the future price to be $4 a bushel. The supply curve is S—supply is perfectly elastic at the price expected by inventory holders. Production fluctuates between Q_1 and Q_2.

When production fluctuates and there are no inventories, the price and the quantity fluctuate. We saw this result in Fig. 7.11. But if there are inventories, the price does not fluctuate. When production decreases to Q_1, or 15 billion bushels, inventory holders sell 5 billion bushels from inventory and the quantity bought by consumers is 20 billion bushels. The price remains at $4 a bushel. When production increases to Q_2, or 25 billion bushels, inventory holders buy 5 billion bushels and consumers continue to buy 20 billion bushels. Again, the price remains at $4 a bushel. Inventories reduce price fluctuations. In Fig. 7.12, the price fluctuations are entirely eliminated. When there are costs of carrying inventories and when inventories become almost depleted, some price fluctuations do occur, but these fluctuations are smaller than those occurring in a market without inventories.

Farm Revenue   Even if inventory speculation succeeds in stabilizing prices, it does not stabilize farm revenue. With the price stabilized, farm revenue fluctuates as production fluctuates. But now bumper harvests always bring larger revenues than poor harvests do because the price is now constant and only the quantity fluctuates.

FIGURE 7.12

How Inventories Limit
Price Changes

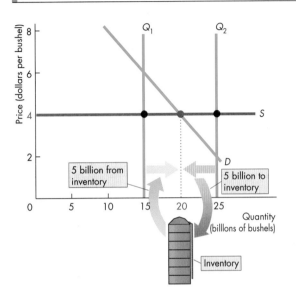

Inventory holders sell wheat from inventory if a poor harvest causes the price to rise above $4 a bushel and buy wheat to hold in inventory if a bumper harvest causes the price to fall below $4 a bushel, making supply (S) perfectly elastic. When production decreases to Q_1, 5 billion bushels are sold from inventory; when production increases to Q_2, 5 billion bushels are added to inventory. The price remains at $4 a bushel.

Farm Price Stabilization Policy

Most governments intervene in agricultural markets. The most extensive such intervention occurs in the European Union and Japan. Farm price intervention is not so extensive in the United States. But U.S. government regulations influence the prices of some items, examples of which are sugar and peanuts.

Governments intervene in agricultural markets in three ways. They:

1. Set production limits
2. Set price floors
3. Hold inventories

Production limits, which are called *quotas,* restrict the quantity produced and can result in the price exceeding the price in an unregulated market. Farmers benefit from quotas because the price rises above the minimum supply-price. But consumers lose, and quotas create deadweight loss. Quotas exist mainly because of the power of the farm lobby.

Price floors, which are set above the equilibrium price, create surpluses. They work in a similar way to the minimum wage that we studied earlier. The minimum wage creates unemployment and price floors in agricultural markets create surpluses of food products. To make a price floor work, the government's price stabilization agency must buy the persistent surpluses. If the price is persistently greater than the equilibrium price, the government agency buys more than it sells and ends up with large inventory. Such has been the outcome in Europe, where they have "mountains" of butter and "lakes" of wine! The cost of buying and storing the inventory falls on taxpayers, and the main gainers are large, low-cost farms.

If the government price stabilization agency operates like a private inventory holder, it maintains the price close to the equilibrium price. It sells from inventory when price is above normal, and it buys for inventory when the price is below normal. But this type of intervention is not necessary because private trading can achieve the same outcome.

R E V I E W   Q U I Z

- Can you explain how poor harvests and bumper harvests influence farm prices and farm revenues?
- Can you explain how the existence of inventories and speculation influence farm prices and farm revenues?
- What are the main actions that governments take in farm markets and how do these actions influence farm prices and farm revenues?

You now know how to use the demand and supply model to predict prices, to study government intervention in markets, and to study the sources and costs of inefficiency. Before you leave this topic, take a look at *Reading Between the Lines* on pp. 144–145 and see what is happening in the market for cigarettes in Michigan today.

Taxes and Illegal Activities

ECONOMIC TIMES, OCTOBER 7, 1999

Cigarette Stamp Tax Raises Revenue

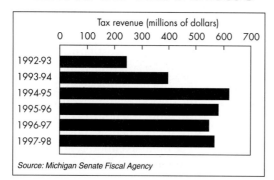

Tax revenue (millions of dollars)

	0	100	200	300	400	500	600	700

1992-93
1993-94
1994-95
1995-96
1996-97
1997-98

Source: Michigan Senate Fiscal Agency

Michigan increased the tax on cigarettes from 25 cents a pack to 75 cents a pack in 1994. At this level, the Michigan cigarette tax became the seventh highest in the nation and around twice the national average rate. At the opposite end of the tax scale are Kentucky at 3 cents a pack, North Carolina at 5 cents a pack, and South Carolina at 7cents a pack.

After the increase in the tax rate in 1994, tax revenues increased. Total tobacco and cigarette tax revenues were up by 56 percent between fiscal year 1993–94 and fiscal year 1994–95.

But between 1994-95 and 1996-97, the revenue from the tobacco and cigarette tax decreased by 12 percent, or by $73 million. The Michigan Motor Fuel and Tobacco Tax Division of the Treasury Department attributed the decrease in tax revenue to an increase in smuggling.

In an attempt to control smuggling and increase state revenue, the Michigan legislature introduced a cigarette tax stamp in 1998. The stamp makes it harder to sell illegally imported cigarettes from low-tax states and makes it more obvious whether the Michigan state tax has been paid on a pack of cigarettes.

After the introduction of the tax stamp, tax revenue began to increase again. The Michigan state Attorney General, Jennifer Granholm, says that the tax stamp has reduced the smuggling of cigarettes into Michigan but she also says that criminals are making counterfeit tobacco stamps.

Despite the remaining problems, other states have noticed the relative success of the Michigan experiment and introduced their own version of the tax stamp. The low-tax state of Alabama made such a move in 1999.

© 1999 Economic Times. Reprinted with permission. Further reproduction prohibited.

Essence of the Story

■ In 1994, Michigan increased its tax on cigarettes from 25 cents to 75 cents per package

■ The cigarette tax per package is 3 cents in Kentucky, 5 cents in North Carolina, and 7 cents in South Carolina.

■ The Michigan cigarette tax is about twice the national average.

■ Michigan's cigarette tax revenue increased in the first year of the higher tax but then began to decrease.

■ The state tax administrator says that tax revenue decreased because of smuggling.

■ In 1998, Michigan introduced a cigarette tax stamp that decreased smuggling and increased the state's tax revenue.

■ Figure 1 shows the market for cigarettes in Michigan before the 1994 tax increase.

■ The demand for cigarettes is D. This demand curve *assumes* an elasticity of demand equal to 0.61, which is the estimated price elasticity of demand for tobacco for the United States. (See Table 5.1, p. 93.)

■ The supply of cigarettes in Michigan is perfectly elastic. The reason is that the tobacco companies can sell their products anywhere in the world at the going before-tax price, so they are willing to sell any quantity in Michigan at that price.

■ With no cigarette tax, the equilibrium price is $2.75 per pack and 1,028 million packs a year are bought.

■ With a tax of 25 cents per pack, the supply curve shifts to $S + tax_0$. The price rises to $3.00 per pack, and the quantity bought decreases to 975 million packs per year. The state collects $244 million in tax, and there is a small deadweight loss.

■ Figure 2 shows the situation after the tax increased to 75 cents a pack but before the tax stamp law was introduced.

■ The supply curve shifts to $S + tax_1$. The price rises to $3.50 per pack, and the quantity bought decreases to 887 million packs per year. This decrease in the quantity bought is predicted by the assumed elasticity of demand of 0.61.

■ Michigan collected $562 million in tax revenue (average for 1995–1998). So at 75 cents a pack, the tax was paid on only 750 million packs.

■ If the elasticity of demand assumption is correct, 137 million packs of cigarettes per year are smuggled into Michigan. The smugglers collect $103 million a year that the state treasury loses.

■ So the tax stamp seems to have decreased smuggling but not eliminated it.

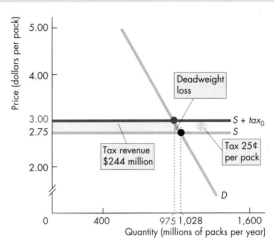

Figure 1 Before the tax increase

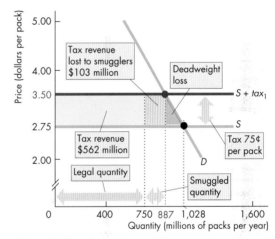

Figure 2 After the tax increase

You're The Voter

■ Would you vote for a law that taxes cigarettes in your state at a higher rate than the national average? Explain why.

■ Would you vote for a cigarette stamp tax law? Why or why not?

■ What other measures would you recommend the government take to deter smuggling? (Hint: Think about the analysis in this chapter of markets for illegal goods.)

SUMMARY

KEY POINTS

Housing Markets and Rent Ceilings (pp. 128–131)

- A decrease in the supply of housing decreases short-run supply and increases the equilibrium rent.
- The higher rent increases the quantity of housing supplied in the short run and stimulates building in the long run. The rent decreases, and the quantity of housing increases.
- If a rent ceiling prevents the rent from increasing, the quantity supplied remains constant and there is a housing shortage, which creates wasteful search and black markets.

The Labor Market and the Minimum Wage (pp. 132–134)

- A decrease in the demand for low-skilled labor lowers the wage rate and reduces employment.
- The lower wage rate encourages people with low skill to acquire more skill, which decreases the supply of low-skilled labor. The wage rises gradually to its original level, and employment decreases.
- Imposing a minimum wage above the equilibrium wage creates unemployment and an increase in the amount of time people spend searching for a job.
- Minimum wages hit young people who have the fewest skills hardest.

Taxes (pp. 135–138)

- When a good or service is taxed, usually the price increases and the quantity bought decreases but the price increases by less than the tax. The buyer pays part of the tax, and the seller pays part of the tax.
- The portion of the tax paid by the buyer and by the seller depends on the elasticity of demand and the elasticity of supply.
- The less elastic the demand and the more elastic the supply, the greater is the price increase, the smaller is the quantity decrease, and the larger is the portion of the tax paid by the buyer.

- If demand is perfectly elastic or supply is perfectly inelastic, the seller pays the entire tax. If demand is perfectly inelastic or supply is perfectly elastic, the buyer pays the entire tax.

Markets for Illegal Goods (pp. 139–140)

- Penalties on sellers of an illegal good increase the cost of selling the good and decrease its supply. Penalties on buyers decrease their willingness to pay and decrease the demand for the good.
- The higher the penalties and the more effective the law enforcement, the smaller is the quantity bought. The price is higher or lower than the unregulated price, depending on whether the penalties on sellers or buyers are higher.
- A tax set at a sufficiently high rate will decrease the quantity of a drug consumed, but there will be a tendency for the tax to be evaded.

Stabilizing Farm Revenues (pp. 141–143)

- Farm revenues fluctuate because supply fluctuates.
- The demand for most farm products is inelastic, so a decrease in supply increases the price and increases farm revenue, while an increase in supply decreases price and decreases farm revenue.
- Inventory holders and government agencies act to stabilize farm prices and revenues.

KEY FIGURES

KEY TERMS

PROBLEMS

*1. The figure shows the demand for and supply of rental housing in Village:

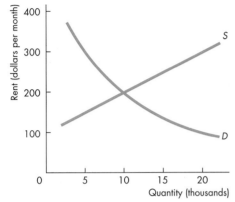

a. What are the equilibrium rent and equilibrium quantity of rented housing?

If a rent ceiling is set at $150 a month, what is:
b. The quantity of housing rented?
c. The shortage of housing?
d. The maximum price that someone is willing to pay for the last unit of housing available?

2. The figure shows the demand for and supply of rental housing in Township:

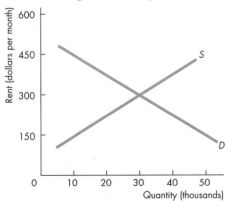

a. What are the equilibrium rent and equilibrium quantity of rented housing?

If a rent ceiling is set at $150 a month, what is:
b. The quantity of housing rented?
c. The shortage of housing?
d. The maximum price that someone is willing to pay for the last unit available?

*3. The table gives the demand for and supply of teenage labor:

Wage rate (dollars per hour)	Quantity demanded	Quantity supplied
	(hours per month)	
2	3,000	1,000
3	2,500	1,500
4	2,000	2,000
5	1,500	2,500
6	1,000	3,000

a. What are the equilibrium wage rate and level of employment?
b. What is the quantity of unemployment?
c. If a minimum wage of $3 an hour is set for teenagers, how many hours do they work?
d. If a minimum wage of $3 an hour is set for teenagers, how many hours of their labor is unemployed?
e. If a minimum wage is set at $5 an hour for teenagers, what are the quantities of employment and unemployment?
f. If a minimum wage is set at $5 an hour and demand increases by 500 hours a month, what is the wage rate paid to teenagers and how many hours of their labor is unemployed?

4. The table gives the demand for and supply of high school graduates:

Wage rate (dollars per hour)	Quantity demanded	Quantity supplied
	(hours per month)	
6	9,000	4,000
7	8,000	5,000
8	7,000	6,000
9	6,000	7,000
10	5,000	8,000

a. What are the equilibrium wage rate and level of employment?
b. What is the level of unemployment?
c. If a minimum wage is set at $7 an hour, how many hours do high school graduates work?
d. If a minimum wage is set at $7 an hour, how many hours of labor are unemployed?
e. If a minimum wage is set at $9 an hour, what are employment and unemployment?
f. If the minimum wage is $9 an hour and demand increases by 500 hours a month, what is the wage rate paid to high school graduates and how many hours of their labor are unemployed?

*5. The table gives the demand and supply schedules for chocolate brownies:

Price (cents per brownie)	Quantity demanded	Quantity supplied
	(millions per day)	
50	5	3
60	4	4
70	3	5
80	2	6
90	1	7

a. If brownies are not taxed, what is the price of a brownie and how many are consumed?
b. If brownies are taxed at 20¢ each, what is the price and how many brownies are consumed? Who pays the tax?

6. The demand and supply schedules for coffee are:

Price (dollars per cup)	Quantity demanded	Quantity supplied
	(cups per hour)	
1.50	90	30
1.75	70	40
2.00	50	50
2.25	30	60
2.75	10	70

a. If there is no tax on coffee, what is the price and how much coffee is consumed?
b. If a tax of 75¢ a cup is introduced, what is the price and how much coffee is consumed? Who pays the tax?

*7. The demand for and supply of rice is:

Price (dollars per box)	Quantity demanded	Quantity supplied
	(boxes per week)	
1.20	3,000	500
1.30	2,750	1,500
1.40	2,500	2,500
1.50	2,250	3,500
1.60	2,000	4,500

A storm destroys part of the crop and decreases supply by 500 boxes a week.
a. What do inventory holders do?
b. What is the price and what is farm revenue?

8. In problem 7 instead of a storm, perfect weather increases supply by 500 boxes a week.
a. What do inventory holders do?
b. What is the price and what is farm revenue?

CRITICAL THINKING

1. Study *Reading Between the Lines* on the market for cigarettes in Michigan on pp. 144–145 and answer the following questions.
   a. Suppose that the Michigan police steps up its rate of detecting smuggling. And suppose the demand and supply curves shown in Fig. 1 on p. 145 correctly describe the market for cigarettes in Michigan. Show in the figure the changes that result from the efforts of the Michigan police.
   b. Suppose that the Michigan treasury's loss from smuggling is not the amount suggested in the analysis on p. 145 but instead is the $73 million decrease in revenue that occurred between 1994–95 and 1996–97. Draw a new version of Fig. 1 and Fig. 2 that is consistent with this view. What is the implied elasticity of demand? Which case do you think is more likely?
   c. Suppose that the people of Michigan want to decrease the amount of cigarette smoking. What level of tax per pack would be needed to achieve a 10 percent and a 20 percent decrease in smoking? What special problems would arise with taxes set at these levels?
   d. How other than by increasing the cigarette tax might we reduce the amount of cigarette smoking?

2. Use the links on the Parkin Web site to obtain information about cigarette tax rates, tax revenues, purchases, population, and income in the 50 states. Then answer the following questions about the relationship between the number of packs of cigarettes purchased and the price of a pack across the states.
   a. How would you describe the relationship?
   b. What does the relationship tell you about the demand for cigarettes?
   c. What does the relationship tell you about the amount of cigarette smuggling?

3. Use the links on the Parkin Web site to obtain information about farm programs in the United States. What are the main programs and what are their effects on the quantities of farm products, their prices, and economic efficiency?

Understanding How Markets Work

PART 2

The four chapters that you've just studied explain how markets work. The market is an amazing instrument. It enables people who have never met and who know nothing about each other to interact and do business. It also enables us to allocate our scarce resources to the uses that we value most highly. Markets can be very simple or highly organized.

The Amazing Market

◆ A simple market is one that the American historian Daniel J. Boorstin describes in *The Discoverers* (p. 161). In the late fourteenth century,

The Muslim caravans that went southward from Morocco across the Atlas Mountains arrived after twenty days at the shores of the Senegal River. There the Moroccan traders laid out separate piles of salt, of beads from Ceutan coral, and cheap manufactured goods. Then they retreated out of sight. The local tribesmen, who lived in the strip mines where they dug their gold, came to the shore and put a heap of gold beside each pile of Moroccan goods. Then they, in turn, went out of view, leaving the Moroccan traders either to take the gold offered for a particular pile or to reduce the pile of their merchandise to suit the offered price in gold. Once again the Moroccan traders withdrew, and the process went on. By this system of commercial etiquette, the Moroccans collected their gold.

An organized market is the New York Stock Exchange, which trades many millions of stocks each day. Another is an auction at which the U.S. government sells rights to broadcasters and cellular telephone companies for the use of the airwaves. ◆ All of these markets determine the prices at which

exchanges take place and enable both buyers and sellers to benefit. ◆ Everything and anything that can be exchanged is traded in markets. There are markets for goods and services; for resources such as labor, capital, and raw materials; for dollars, pounds, and yen; for goods to be delivered now and for goods to be delivered in the future. Only the imagination places limits on what can be traded in markets. ◆ You began your study of markets in Chapter 4, by learning about the laws of demand and supply. There, you discovered the forces that make prices adjust to coordinate buying plans and selling plans. In Chapter 5, you learned how to calculate and use the concept of elasticity to predict the responsiveness of prices and quantities to changes in supply and demand. In Chapter 6, you studied efficiency and discovered the conditions under which a competitive market sends resources to uses in which they are valued most highly. And finally, in Chapter 7, you studied markets in action. There, you learned how markets cope with change and discovered how they operate when governments intervene to fix prices, impose taxes, or make some goods illegal. ◆ The laws of demand and supply that you've learned and used in these four chapters were discovered during the nineteenth century by some remarkable economists. We conclude our study of demand and supply and markets by looking at the lives and times of some of these economists and by talking to one of today's most influential economists who studies and creates sophisticated auction markets.

149

Discovering the Laws of Demand and Supply

Alfred Marshall

(1842–1924) grew up in an England that was being transformed by the railroad and by the expansion of manufacturing. Mary Paley was one of Marshall's students at Cambridge, and when Alfred and Mary married, in 1877, celibacy rules barred Alfred from continuing to teach at Cambridge. By 1884, with more liberal rules, the Marshalls returned to Cambridge, where Alfred became Professor of Political Economy.

Many others had a hand in refining the theory of demand and supply, but the first thorough and complete statement of the theory as we know it today was set out by Alfred Marshall, with the acknowledged help of Mary Paley Marshall. Published in 1890, this monumental treatise, The Principles of Economics, *became the textbook on economics on both sides of the Atlantic for almost half a century. Marshall was an outstanding mathematician, but he kept mathematics and even diagrams in the background. His supply and demand diagram appears only in a footnote.*

"The forces to be dealt with are . . . so numerous, that it is best to take a few at a time. . . . Thus we begin by isolating the primary relations of supply, demand, and price"

ALFRED MARSHALL
The Principles of Economics

The Issues

The laws of demand and supply that you studied in Chapter 4 were discovered during the 1830s by Antoine-Augustin Cournot (1801–1877), a professor of mathematics at the University of Lyon, France. Although Cournot was the first to use demand and supply, it was the development and expansion of the railroads during the 1850s that gave the newly emerging theory its first practical applications. Railroads then were at the cutting edge of technology just as airlines are today. And as in the airline industry today, competition among the railroads was fierce.

Dionysius Lardner (1793–1859), an Irish professor of philosophy at the University of London, used demand and supply to show railroad companies how they could increase their profits by cutting rates on long-distance business on which competition was fiercest and by raising rates on short-haul business on which they had less to fear from other transportation suppliers. Today, economists use the principles that Lardner worked out during the 1850s to calculate the freight rates and passenger fares that will give airlines the largest possible profit. And the rates calculated have a lot in common with the railroad rates of the nineteenth century. On local routes on which there is little competition, fares per mile are highest, and on long-distance routes on which the airlines compete fiercely, fares per mile are lowest.

Known satirically among scientists of the day as "Dionysius Diddler," Lardner worked on an amazing range of problems from astronomy to railway engineering to economics. A colorful character, he would have been a regular guest of David Letterman if late-night talk shows had been around in the 1850s. Lardner visited the École des Ponts et Chaussées (School of Bridges and Roads) in Paris and must have learned a great deal from Jules Dupuit.

In France, Jules Dupuit (1804–1866), a French engineer/ economist, used demand to calculate the benefits from building a bridge and, once the bridge was built, for calculating the toll to charge for its use. His work was the forerunner of what is today called *cost-benefit analysis*. Working with the principles invented by Dupuit, economists today calculate the costs and benefits of highways and airports, dams, and power stations.

Then

Dupuit used the law of demand to determine whether a bridge or canal would be valued enough by its users to justify the cost of building it. Lardner first worked out the relationship between the cost of production and supply and used demand and supply theory to explain the costs, prices, and profits of railroad operations. He also used the theory to discover ways of increasing revenue by raising rates on short-haul business and lowering them on long-distance freight.

Now

Today, using the same principles that Dupuit devised, economists calculate whether the benefits of expanding airports and air-traffic control facilities are sufficient to cover their costs. Airline companies use the principles developed by Lardner to set their prices and to decide when to offer "seat sales." Like the railroads before them, the airlines charge a high price per mile on short flights, for which they face little competition, and a low price per mile on long flights, for which competition is fierce.

Markets do an amazing job. And the laws of demand and supply help us to understand how markets work. But in some situations, a market must be designed and institutions must be created to enable the market to operate. In recent years, economists have begun to use their tools to design and create markets. And one of the chief architects of new style markets is Paul Milgrom, whom you can meet on the following pages.

Paul R. Milgrom

is Professor of Economics at Stanford University and an Associate Editor of the American Economic Review, *the leading journal that publishes economic research. He is founder and president of Market Design, Inc., a young company that designs new auction and market rules for businesses and governments. Born in Detroit, Michigan, in 1948, Professor Milgrom was an undergraduate at the University of Michigan and a graduate student at Stanford University (Ph.D. 1979). He taught at Northwestern University and Yale University before returning to Stanford in 1987.*

Paul R. Milgrom

Professor Milgrom is an economic theorist, which means that he uses mathematical techniques to study economic behavior. His work on auctions has been especially influential and has found practical applications in auctioning items ranging from radio spectrum (used in paging and cellular telephones) to mining rights.

Michael Parkin talked with Professor Milgrom about his work and how it connects with the theory of demand and supply developed by Cournot and Marshall.

Professor Milgrom, how did you become an economist?

I came into the house of economics through an unmarked side door, not knowing where I was until I was well inside. The main entrance is through a graduate degree in economics, but I have no university degree in economics at any level. My undergraduate studies were in mathematics and statistics, and my graduate studies were in business. It was in graduate school that I stumbled across a brilliant study of auction theory by William Vickrey—work for which he was awarded the Nobel Prize 21 years later, in 1996. Vickrey's work surprised me and convinced me that mathematical analysis could help me to understand auctions and could even point the way to new, improved types of auctions.

Auctions, like all market arrangements, bring buyers and sellers together. Doesn't the supply and demand model explain how auctions work?

The supply and demand model is the economist's workhorse for day-to-day market analysis. It provides a wonderful way to summarize some of the main factors affecting prices and quantities and to explain how prices guide important choices.

But the model is silent about how the rules that govern trade are set or how they affect economic outcomes. Also, it is not very helpful for thinking about technology decisions that can have a huge impact on economic outcomes. For example, the way standards are set for cellular telephone systems determines whether the same phone will work on different systems in different parts of the nation and the world. In Europe, a single standard allows a consumer to go from country to country and still have a working telephone. In the United States, where no single standard exists, a consumer may find that her telephone fails to

The supply and demand model is the economist's workhorse for day-to-day market analysis.

operate even with the system in the next town.

Obviously, that failure depresses the sales of cellular phone service, although it has nothing to do with the consumer preferences for communications or with the cost or availability of the cellular telephone technology.

So institutions influence prices and quantities and the kinds of plans that people make. And sometimes, institutions such as standards-setting bodies can solve problems that a market guided only by prices can't deal with effectively.

Let's return to auctions. What is auction theory? How does it relate to supply and demand?

Auctions are institutions that determine the prices and other terms at which buyers and sellers will trade. Auction theory explains how the rules of an auction affect its outcome.

Sellers want auctions that generate the highest price. Buyers want auctions that generate the lowest price. Auction houses want auctions that balance the interests of buyers and sellers and ensure a continuing flow of customers for future auctions.

In the U.S. auctions of radio spectrum, the government's main objective was to assign spectrum efficiently.

The supply and demand model does not include a place for auction rules. It supposes that buyers and sellers know all the relevant prices

when they make their decisions. In reality, that is not always true.

Often in an auction, bidders must make a choice without knowing all the relevant prices.

What are the main types of auctions and why are there so many different types? Why isn't one type best?

An auction may be either sealed or open. In a sealed auction, the bids are written and the best bids win. In open auctions, there is usually a sequence of bids with each bidder getting an opportunity to respond to the bids of others. Within these two auction types, there is great variety.

The sealed bid has two advantages over the open auction. First, the bidders don't have to be gathered together physically at one time to conduct the auction. In bidding at a used car warehouse, for example, the bidders (usually used car dealers) examine the cars at times that are convenient for themselves and leave behind a sealed envelope with their bids. There is a deadline for bids. When the deadline passes, the bids are opened and the bidders are notified of the results.

Second, it is harder for bidders to collude and depress the price received by the seller. With sealed bids, a member of a ring of buyers who agree to keep prices low might be tempted to submit a slightly higher bid and take advantage of the low bids by other ring members. The temptation to cheat in an open auction is much less, because the other ring members can punish the cheater by driving up the price when the member violates the agreement.

Open auctions have advantages, too. When a single item is being sold and price is the key factor, an open auction eliminates the guesswork of sealed bids. The bidder with the highest value can outbid the competitors. Also, when a large number of items are to be sold and the bidders are present for an open auction, the items can be sold quickly in sequence.

What advances have we made in auction theory?

Since Vickrey initiated auction theory some 35 years ago, we have improved our ability to predict how different types of auctions perform. And we've learned how to design auctions with particular objectives in mind. We even have developed mathematical descriptions of "optimal auctions," which are theoretically the best auction designs for achieving particular objectives.

We still haven't implemented an optimal auction in a real situation, but a small group of economists have used auction theory to design significant new auctions. Recently, I was among a group that proposed a brand-new auction design called a "simultaneous ascending auction." This type of auction is an open auction of many different items, all of which can be bid for simultaneously.

The U.S. Federal Communications Commission used such an auction to sell licenses to use radio spectrum for telecommunications services. The auction was the largest in history and generated gross revenues of $24 billion.

More important to me, the new auction design performed as predicted and led to much more efficient license assignments than other kinds of auctions could have achieved.

The radio spectrum auctions have shaped competition in wireless communications and have determined which firms will operate businesses in which parts of the country.

Why did selling the frequency spectrum need a simultaneous ascending bid auction? And how does such an auction work?

Bidders want to acquire licenses to provide a wireless communications service covering certain geographic areas. A bidder might want to use one of two available bands of spectrum to provide services in, say, Los Angeles County. If either spectrum band will do and the bidder needs just one, then the licenses to use these bands are economic substitutes.

But a bidder might also be willing to pay more to acquire a license covering southern California if he or she could also acquire a license covering northern California. These licenses are complements. One reason why licenses might be complements is that the two areas can share some facilities and lower costs. Another reason is that an owner of both licenses might be able to provide a more valuable service to consumers and so charge a higher price for it.

The simultaneous ascending bid auction handles both situations well. In such an auction, the bid-

ding for the northern and southern California licenses, and in fact *all* the licenses, goes on at the same time, and bidding remains open on all the individual licenses until bidding for all licenses is complete. In an auction like this, a bidder who is interested in the California licenses can bid for both and can cease bidding when the combination price gets too high. This is a far from perfect solution, but it is much better than any of the traditional alternatives and seems to have performed well in the sale of spectrum licenses in the United States.

What differences are today's information technologies making to the problems of auction design?

Without modern information technology, the simultaneous ascending auction of radio spectrum licenses couldn't have been conducted. In a large version of the auction, both the auctioneer and the bidders need to keep track of bids on hundreds or even thousands of licenses simultaneously. Software programs have been created to facilitate submitting bids and tracking the auction results.

> The best economists are technically able, curious about the world, concerned about human welfare, flexible in their perspectives, and dedicated to clear, analytical thinking.

How do you advise today's undergraduate to prepare for a career in economics? What besides economics should he or she study?

The best economists are technically able, curious about the world, concerned about human welfare, flexible in their perspectives, and dedicated to clear, analytical thinking. Courses can help with some of these things. Students can certainly learn mathematical and statistical concepts as undergraduates.

To enjoy a career as an economist, you have to go beyond the academic abstractions and incorporate elements that excite you. Many students study economics because of their specific social concerns, for example, wanting to understand the sources of poverty in their home countries and to discern the paths out of poverty. For those students, I recommend reading widely and studying other social sciences to learn about the culture and politics of poverty and the kinds of barriers they create to good economic policies. There are so many ways to incorporate one's pleasures in an economics career! I have friends and colleagues who've studied the economics of sports, of wine prices, of the performing arts, and of the Internet. By weaving their personal and professional interests together, they eliminate the sharp divide between their career and their leisure. These are the folks I hold up as role models.

Chapter 8

Utility and Demand

We need water to live. We don't need diamonds for much besides decoration. If the benefits of water far outweigh the benefits of diamonds, why, then, does water cost practically nothing while diamonds are terribly expensive? ◆ When the Organization of Petroleum Exporting Countries (OPEC) restricted its sale of oil in 1973, it created a dramatic rise in price, but people continued to use almost as much oil as they had before. Our demand for oil was price inelastic. But why? ◆ When the CD player was introduced in 1983, it cost more than $1,000, and consumers didn't buy very many. Since then, the price has decreased dramatically, and people are buying CD players in enormous quantities. Our demand for CD players is price elastic. What makes the demand for some things price elastic while the demand for others is price inelastic? ◆ Over the past 20 years, after the effects of inflation are removed, incomes in the United States have increased by 40 percent. Over that same period, expenditure on electricity has increased by more than 60 percent, while expenditure on transportation has increased by less than 20 percent. Thus the proportion of income spent on electricity has increased, and the proportion spent on transportation has decreased. Why, as incomes rise, does the proportion of income spent on some goods rise and that spent on others fall?

Water, Water, Everywhere

◆ In the preceding four chapters, we saw that demand has an important effect on the price of a good. But we did not analyze what exactly shapes a person's demand. This chapter examines household behavior and its influence on demand. It explains why demand for some goods is elastic and demand for other goods is inelastic. It also explains why the prices of some things, such as diamonds and water, are so out of proportion to their total benefits.

After studying this chapter, you will be able to:

- Explain the household's budget constraint
- Define total utility and marginal utility
- Explain the marginal utility theory of consumer choice
- Use marginal utility theory to predict the effects of changing prices and incomes
- Explain the connection between individual demand and market demand
- Explain the paradox of value

Household Consumption Choices

A HOUSEHOLD'S CONSUMPTION CHOICES ARE determined by many factors, but we can summarize all of these factors under two concepts:

■ Consumption possibilities
■ Preferences

Consumption Possibilities

A household's consumption choices are constrained by the household's income and by the prices of the goods and services it buys. The household has a given amount of income to spend and cannot influence the prices of the goods and services it buys.

The limits to a household's consumption choices are described by its *budget line*. Let's consider Lisa's household. Lisa has an income of $30 a month, and she plans to buy only two goods: movies and soda. Movies cost $6 each; soda costs $3 a six-pack. If Lisa spends all her income, she will reach the limits to her consumption of movies and soda.

Figure 8.1 illustrates Lisa's possible consumption of movies and soda. Rows *a* through *f* in the table show six possible ways of allocating $30 to these two goods. For example, Lisa can see 2 movies for $12 and buy 6 six-packs for $18 (row *c*). Points *a* through *f* in the figure illustrate the possibilities presented in the table. The line passing through these points is Lisa's budget line.

Lisa's budget line is a constraint on her choices. It marks the boundary between what she can afford and what she can not afford. She can afford all the points on the line and inside it. She cannot afford the points outside the line. The constraint on her consumption depends on prices of movies and soda and on her income. The constraint changes when the price of movies or soda changes or her income changes.

Preferences

How does Lisa divide her $30 between these two goods? The answer depends on her likes and dislikes—her *preferences*. Economists use the concept of utility to describe preferences. The benefit or satisfaction that a person gets from the consumption of a good or service is called **utility**. But what exactly is utility and in what units can we measure it? Utility is an abstract concept, and its units are arbitrary.

FIGURE 8.1
Consumption Possibilities

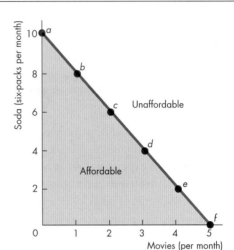

Possibility	Movies		Soda	
	Quantity	Expenditure (dollars)	Six-packs	Expenditure (dollars)
a	0	0	10	30
b	1	6	8	24
c	2	12	6	18
d	3	18	4	12
e	4	24	2	6
f	5	30	0	0

Rows *a* through *f* in the table show six possible ways that Lisa can allocate $30 to movies and soda. For example, Lisa can buy 2 movies and 6 six-packs (row *c*). The combination in each row costs $30. These possibilities are points *a* through *f* in the figure. The line through those points is a boundary between what Lisa can afford and what she cannot afford. Her choices must lie along the line *af* or inside the orange area.

Temperature—An Analogy   Temperature is an abstract concept, and the units of temperature are arbitrary. You know when you feel hot, and you know when you feel cold. But you can't *observe* temperature. You can observe water turning to steam if it is hot enough or turning to ice if it is cold enough. And you can construct an instrument, called a thermometer, which can help you to predict when such changes will occur. The scale on the thermometer is what we call temperature. But the units in which we measure temperature are arbitrary. For example, we can accurately predict that when a Celsius thermometer shows a temperature of 0, water will turn to ice. But the units of measurement do not matter because this same event also occurs when a Fahrenheit thermometer shows a temperature of 32.

The concept of utility helps us to make predictions about consumption choices in much the same way that the concept of temperature helps us to make predictions about physical phenomena. Admittedly, marginal utility theory is not as precise as the theory that enables us to predict when water will turn to ice or steam.

Let's now see how we can use the concept of utility to describe preferences.

Total Utility

Total utility is the total benefit that a person gets from the consumption of goods and services. Total utility depends on the level of consumption—more consumption generally gives more total utility. Table 8.1 shows Lisa's total utility from movies and soda. If she sees no movies, she gets no utility from movies. If she sees 1 movie in a month, she gets 50 units of utility. As the number of movies she sees in a month increases, her total utility increases; if she sees 10 movies a month, she gets 250 units of total utility. The other part of the table shows Lisa's total utility from soda. If she drinks no soda, she gets no utility from soda. As the amount of soda she drinks increases, her total utility increases.

Marginal Utility

Marginal utility is the change in total utility that results from a one-unit increase in the quantity of a good consumed. The table in Fig. 8.2 shows the calculation of Lisa's marginal utility of movies. When the number of movies she sees increases from 4 to 5 a month, her total utility from movies increases from 150 units to 175 units. Thus for Lisa, the marginal utility of seeing a fifth movie each month is 25 units. Notice that marginal utility appears midway between the quantities of movies. It does so because it is the *change* in consumption from 4 to 5 movies that produces the *marginal* utility of 25 units. The table displays calculations of marginal utility for each number of movies seen.

TABLE 8.1

Lisa's Total Utility from Movies and Soda

Movies		Soda	
Quantity per month	Total utility	Six-packs per month	Total utility
0	0	0	0
1	50	1	75
2	88	2	117
3	121	3	153
4	150	4	181
5	175	5	206
6	196	6	225
7	214	7	243
8	229	8	260
9	241	9	276
10	250	10	291
11	256	11	305
12	259	12	318
13	261	13	330
14	262	14	341

Figure 8.2(a) illustrates the total utility that Lisa gets from movies. The more movies Lisa sees in a month, the more total utility she gets. Figure 8.2(b) illustrates her marginal utility. This graph tells us that as Lisa sees more movies, the marginal utility that she gets from watching movies decreases. For example, her marginal utility decreases from 50 units from the first movie to 38 units from the second and 33 units from the third. We call this decrease in marginal utility as the quantity of the good consumed increases the principle of **diminishing marginal utility**.

Marginal utility is positive but diminishes as the consumption of a good increases. Why does marginal utility have these two features? In Lisa's case, she likes movies, and the more she sees the better. That's why marginal utility is positive. The benefit that Lisa gets from the last movie seen is its marginal utility. To see why marginal utility diminishes, think about the following two situations: In one, you've

FIGURE 8.2
Total Utility and Marginal Utility

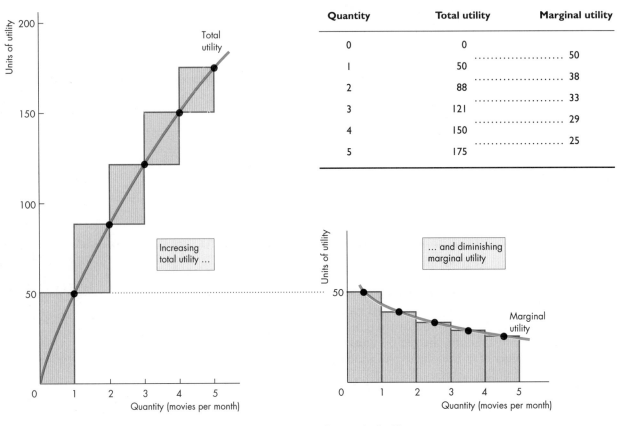

Quantity	Total utility	Marginal utility
0	0	
		50
1	50	
		38
2	88	
		33
3	121	
		29
4	150	
		25
5	175	

(a) Total utility

The table shows that as Lisa sees more movies her total utility from movies increases. The table also shows her marginal utility—the change in total utility resulting from seeing one additional movie. Marginal utility declines as consumption increases. The figure graphs Lisa's total utility and marginal

(b) Marginal utility

utility from movies. Part (a) shows her total utility. It also shows as a bar the extra total utility she gains from each additional movie—her marginal utility. Part (b) shows how Lisa's marginal utility from movies diminishes by placing the bars shown in part (a) side by side as a series of declining steps.

just been studying for 29 evenings. An opportunity arises to see a movie. The utility you get from seeing that movie is the marginal utility from seeing one movie in a month. In the second situation, you've been on a movie binge. For the past 29 nights, you have not even seen an assignment. You are up to your eyeballs in movies. You are happy enough to go to a movie once more. But the thrill that you get out of that thirtieth movie in 30 days is not very large. It is the marginal utility of the thirtieth movie in a month.

R E V I E W   Q U I Z

- Explain how a consumer's income and the prices of goods limit consumption possibilities.
- What is utility and how do we use the concept of utility to describe a consumer's preferences?
- What is the distinction between total utility and marginal utility?
- What is the key assumption about marginal utility?

Maximizing Utility

L A HOUSEHOLD'S INCOME AND THE PRICES THAT it faces limit the household's consumption choices, and the household's preferences determine the utility that it can obtain from each consumption possibility. Marginal utility theory assumes that the household chooses the consumption possibility that maximizes its total utility. This assumption of utility maximization is a way of expressing the fundamental economic problem—scarcity. People's wants exceed the resources available to satisfy those wants, so they must make hard choices. In making choices, they try to get the maximum attainable benefit—they try to maximize total utility.

Let's see how Lisa allocates $30 a month between movies and soda to maximize her total utility. We'll continue to assume that movies cost $6 each and soda costs $3 a six-pack.

The Utility-Maximizing Choice

The most direct way of calculating how Lisa spends her income to maximize her total utility is by making a table like Table 8.2. The rows of the table show the affordable combinations of movies and soda that lie along her budget line in Fig. 8.1. The table records three things: first, the number of movies seen and the total utility derived from them (the left side of the table); second, the number of six-packs consumed and the total utility derived from them (the right side of the table); and third, the total utility derived from both movies and soda (the center column).

The first row of Table 8.2 records the situation when Lisa watches no movies and buys 10 six-packs. In this case, Lisa gets no utility from movies and 291 units of total utility from soda. Her total utility from movies and soda (the center column) is 291 units. The rest of the table is constructed in the same way.

The consumption of movies and soda that maximizes Lisa's total utility is highlighted in the table. When Lisa sees 2 movies and buys 6 six-packs of soda, she gets 313 units of total utility. This is the best Lisa can do, given her preferences, given that she has only $30 to spend, and given the prices of movies and six-packs. If she buys 8 six-packs of soda, she can see only 1 movie. She gets 310 units of total utility, 3 less than the maximum attainable. If she sees 3 movies, she can drink only 4 six-packs. She gets 302 units of total utility, 11 less than the maximum attainable.

TABLE 8.2
Lisa's Affordable Combinations

| | Movies | | Total utility from movies and soda | Soda | |
	Quantity per month	Total utility		Total utility	Six-packs per month
a	0	0	291	291	10
b	1	50	310	260	8
c	2	88	313	225	6
d	3	121	302	181	4
e	4	150	267	117	2
f	5	175	175	0	0

We've just described Lisa's consumer equilibrium. A **consumer equilibrium** is a situation in which a consumer has allocated all his or her available income in the way that, given the prices of goods and services, maximizes his or her total utility. Lisa's consumer equilibrium is 2 movies and 6 six-packs.

In finding Lisa's consumer equilibrium, we measured her *total* utility from movies and soda. But there is a better way of determining a consumer equilibrium—one that does not involve measuring total utility at all. Let's look at this alternative.

Equalizing Marginal Utility per Dollar Spent

Another way to find out the allocation that maximizes a consumer's total utility is to make the marginal utility per dollar spent on each good equal for all goods. The **marginal utility per dollar spent** is the marginal utility obtained from the last unit of a good consumed divided by the price of the good. For example, Lisa's marginal utility from seeing the first movie is 50 units of utility. The price of a movie is $6, which means that when Lisa sees one movie the marginal utility per dollar spent on movies is 50 units divided by $6, or 8.33 units of utility per dollar.

Total utility is maximized when all the consumer's available income is spent and when the marginal utility per dollar spent is equal for all goods.

Lisa maximizes total utility when she spends all her income and consumes movies and soda such that

$$\frac{\text{Marginal utility from movies}}{\text{Price of a movie}} = \frac{\text{Marginal utility from soda}}{\text{Price of soda}}.$$

Call the marginal utility from movies MU_m, the marginal utility from soda MU_s, the price of a movie P_m, and the price of soda P_s. Then Lisa maximizes her utility when she spends all her income and when

$$\frac{MU_m}{P_m} = \frac{MU_s}{P_s}.$$

Let's use this formula to find Lisa's utility-maximizing consumption choice. In Table 8.3, each row exhausts Lisa's income of $30. The table sets out Lisa's marginal utilities (which are calculated from Table 8.1) and her marginal utility per dollar spent on each good. For example, in row b, Lisa's marginal utility from movies is 50 units, and since movies cost $6 each, her marginal utility per dollar spent on movies is 8.33 units per dollar (50 units divided by $6). You can see that Lisa's marginal utility per dollar spent on each good, like marginal utility itself, decreases as more of the good is consumed.

Lisa maximizes her total utility when the marginal utility per dollar spent on movies is equal to the marginal utility per dollar spent on soda—possibility c. Lisa consumes 2 movies and 6 six-packs.

TABLE 8.3
Equalizing Marginal Utilities per Dollar Spent

	Movies ($6 each)			Soda ($3 per six-pack)		
	Quantity	Marginal utility	Marginal utility per dollar spent	Six-packs	Marginal utility	Marginal utility per dollar spent
a	0			10	15	5.00
b	1	50	8.33	8	17	5.67
c	2	38	6.33	6	19	6.33
d	3	33	5.50	4	28	9.33
e	4	29	4.83	2	42	14.00
f	5	25	4.17	0		

Figure 8.3 shows why the rule "equalize marginal utility per dollar spent on all goods" works. Suppose that instead of 2 movies and 6 six-packs (possibility c), Lisa consumes 1 movie and 8 six-packs (possibility b). She then gets 8.33 units of utility per dollar spent on movies and 5.67 units per dollar spent on soda. Lisa can increase her total utility by buying less soda and seeing more movies. If she spends less on soda and more on movies, her total utility from soda decreases by 5.67 units per dollar and her total utility from movies increases by 8.33 units per dollar. Her total utility increases by 2.66 units per dollar.

FIGURE 8.3
Equalizing Marginal Utilities per Dollar Spent

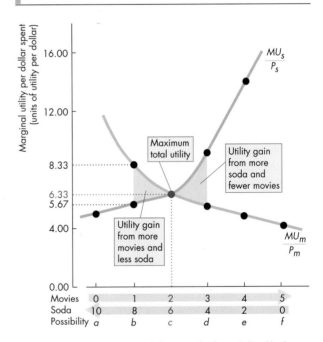

If Lisa consumes 1 movie and 8 six-packs (possibility b), she gets 8.33 units of utility from the last dollar spent on movies and 5.67 units of utility from the last dollar spent on soda. She can get more total utility by seeing one more movie. If she consumes 4 six-packs and 3 movies (possibility d), she gets 5.50 units of utility from the last dollar spent on movies and 9.33 units of utility from the last dollar spent on soda. She can increase her total utility by seeing one fewer movie. When Lisa's marginal utility per dollar spent on both goods is equal, her total utility is maximized.

Or suppose that Lisa consumes 3 movies and 4 six-packs (possibility *d*). In this situation, her marginal utility per dollar spent on movies (5.50) is less than her marginal utility per dollar spent on soda (9.33). Lisa can now increase her total utility by spending less on movies and more on soda.

The Power of Marginal Analysis   The method we've just used to find Lisa's utility-maximizing choice of movies and soda is an example of the power of marginal analysis. By comparing the marginal gain from having more of one good with the marginal loss from having less of another good, Lisa is able to ensure that she gets the maximum attainable utility.

In the example, Lisa chooses the combination in which the marginal utilities per dollar spent on movies and soda are equal. Because we buy goods and services in indivisible lumps, the numbers don't always work out so precisely. But the basic approach always works.

The rule to follow is very simple: If the marginal utility per dollar spent on movies exceeds the marginal utility per dollar spent on soda, see more movies and buy less soda; if the marginal utility per dollar spent on soda exceeds the marginal utility per dollar spent on movies, buy more soda and see fewer movies.

More generally, if the marginal gain from an action exceeds the marginal loss, take the action. You have met this principle before, and you will meet it time and again in your study of economics. And you will find yourself using it when you make your own economic choices, especially when you must make a big decision.

Units of Utility   In calculating Lisa's utility-maximizing choice in Table 8.3 and Fig. 8.3, we have not used the concept of total utility at all. All our calculations use marginal utility and price. By making the marginal utility per dollar spent equal for both goods, we know that Lisa maximizes her total utility.

This way of viewing maximum utility means that the units in which utility is measured do not matter. We could double or halve all the numbers measuring utility, or multiply them by any other positive number, or square them, or take their square roots. None of these transformations of the units used to measure utility makes any difference to the outcome. It is in this respect that utility is analogous to temperature. Our prediction about the freezing of water does not depend on the temperature scale; our prediction about the household's consumption choice does not depend on the units of utility.

REVIEW QUIZ

- What is Lisa's goal when she chooses the quantities of movies and soda to consume?
- What two conditions are met if a consumer is maximizing utility?
- Explain why equalizing the marginal utility of each good does *not* maximize utility.
- Explain why equalizing the marginal utility per dollar spent on each good *does* maximize utility.

Predictions of Marginal Utility Theory

LET'S NOW USE MARGINAL UTILITY THEORY TO make some predictions. What happens to Lisa's consumption of movies and soda when their prices change and when her income changes?

To work out the effect of a change in price or income on the consumption choice: First, determine the combinations of movies and soda that just exhaust the new income at the new prices. Second, calculate the new marginal utilities per dollar spent. Third, determine the combination that makes the marginal utilities per dollar spent on movies and soda equal.

A Fall in the Price of Movies

Suppose that the price of a movie falls from $6 to $3. The rows of Table 8.4 show the combinations of movies and soda that exactly exhaust Lisa's $30 of income when movies cost $3 each and soda costs $3 a six-pack. Lisa's preferences do not change when prices change, so her marginal utility schedule remains the same as before. Now divide her marginal utility from movies by $3 to get the marginal utility per dollar spent on movies.

To find how Lisa responds to the fall in the price of a movie, compare her new utility-maximizing choice (Table 8.4) with her original choice (Table 8.3). Lisa sees more movies (up from 2 to 5 a month) and drinks less soda (down from 6 to 5 six-packs a month). That is, Lisa *substitutes* movies for soda. Figure 8.4 shows these effects. The fall in the price of a movie produces a movement along Lisa's demand curve for movies (part a) and shifts her demand curve for soda (part b).

TABLE 8.4

How a Change in Price of Movies Affects Lisa's Choices

Movies ($3 each)		Soda ($3 per six-pack)	
Quantity	Marginal utility per dollar spent	Six-packs	Marginal utility per dollar spent
0		10	5.00
1	16.67	9	5.33
2	**12.67**	8	5.67
3	11.00	7	6.00
4	9.67	**6**	**6.33**
5	**8.33**	5	**8.33**
6	7.00	4	9.33
7	6.00	3	12.00
8	5.00	2	14.00
9	4.00	1	25.00
10	3.00	0	

A Rise in the Price of Soda

Now suppose that the price of soda rises from $3 to $6 a six-pack. The rows of Table 8.5 show the combinations of movies and soda that exactly exhaust Lisa's $30 of income when movies cost $3 each and soda costs $6 a six-pack. Lisa's preferences don't change when the price of soda changes. Now divide Lisa's marginal utility from soda by $6 to get her marginal utility per dollar spent on soda.

To find the effect of the rise in the price of soda on Lisa's utility-maximizing choice, compare her new choice (Table 8.5) with her previous choice (Table 8.4). When the price of soda increases, Lisa drinks less soda (down from 5 to 2 six-packs a month) and sees more movies (up from 5 to 6 a month). That is, Lisa *substitutes* movies for soda. Figure 8.5 shows these effects. The rise in the price of soda produces a movement along Lisa's demand curve for soda (part a) and shifts her demand curve for movies (part b).

FIGURE 8.4

A Fall in the Price of Movies

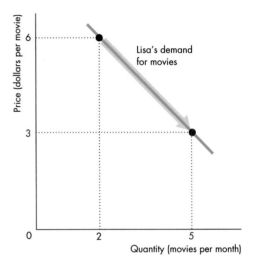

(a) Movies

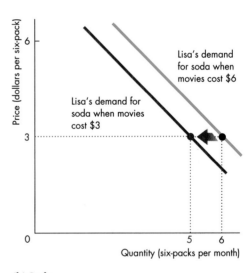

(b) Soda

When the price of a movie falls and the price of soda remains the same, the quantity of movies demanded by Lisa increases and, in part (a), Lisa moves along her demand curve for movies. Also, Lisa decreases her demand for soda and, in part (b), her demand curve for soda shifts leftward.

TABLE 8.5

How a Change in Price of Soda Affects Lisa's Choices

Movies ($3 each)		Soda ($6 per six-pack)	
Quantity	Marginal utility per dollar spent	Six-packs	Marginal utility per dollar spent
0		5	4.17
2	12.67	4	4.67
4	9.67	3	6.00
6	7.00	2	7.00
8	5.00	1	12.50
10	3.00	0	

Marginal utility theory predicts these two results:

1. When the price of a good rises, the quantity demanded of that good decreases.
2. If the price of one good rises, the demand for another good that can serve as a substitute increases.

Does this sound familiar? It should. These predictions of marginal utility theory correspond to the assumptions that we made about demand in Chapter 4. There we *assumed* that the demand curve for a good slopes downward, and we *assumed* that a rise in the price of a substitute increases demand.

We have now seen that marginal utility theory predicts how the quantities of goods and services that people demand respond to price changes. The theory helps us to understand both the shape and the position of the demand curve and how the demand curve for one good shifts when the price of another good changes. Marginal utility theory also helps us to understand one further thing about demand: how it changes when income changes. Let's study the effects of a change in income on consumption.

FIGURE 8.5

A Rise in the Price of Soda

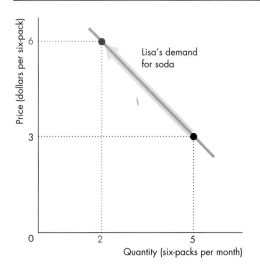

(a) Soda

When the price of soda rises and the price of movies remains the same, the quantity of soda demanded by Lisa decreases and, in part (a), Lisa moves along her demand curve for soda.

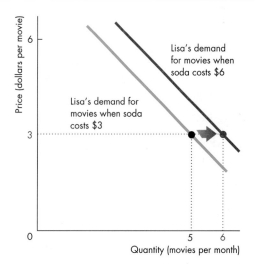

(b) Movies

Also, Lisa increases her demand for movies and, in part (b), her demand curve for movies shifts rightward.

A Rise in Income

Let's suppose that Lisa's income increases to $42 a month and that a movie costs $3 and a six-pack costs $3. We saw in Table 8.4 that with these prices and with an income of $30 a month, Lisa sees 5 movies and drinks 5 six-packs a month. We want to compare this choice of movies and soda with Lisa's choice when her income is $42. Table 8.6 shows the calculations needed to make the comparison. With $42, Lisa can see 14 movies a month and buy no soda or buy 14 six-packs a month and see no movies or choose any combination of the two goods in the rows of the table. We calculate the marginal utility per dollar spent in exactly the same way as we did

before and find the quantities at which the marginal utilities per dollar spent on movies and on soda are equal. With an income of $42, the marginal utility per dollar spent on each good is equal when Lisa sees 7 movies and drinks 7 six-packs of soda a month.

By comparing this situation with that in Table 8.4, we see that with an additional $12 a month, Lisa buys 2 more six-packs and sees 2 more movies a month. Lisa's response arises from her preferences, as described by her marginal utilities. Different preferences would produce different quantitative responses. With a larger income, the consumer always buys more of a *normal* good and less of an *inferior* good. For Lisa, soda and movies are normal goods. When her income increases, Lisa buys more of both goods.

You have now completed your study of the marginal utility theory of a household's consumption choices. Table 8.7 summarizes the key assumptions, implications, and predictions of the theory.

TABLE 8.6

Lisa's Choices with an Income of $42 a Month

Movies ($3 each)		Soda ($3 per six-pack)	
Quantity	Marginal utility per dollar spent	Six-packs	Marginal utility per dollar spent
0		14	3.67
1	16.67	13	4.00
2	12.67	12	4.33
3	11.00	11	4.67
4	9.67	10	5.00
5	**8.33**	9	5.33
6	7.00	8	5.67
7	6.00	7	6.00
8	5.00	6	6.33
9	4.00	**5**	**8.33**
10	3.00	4	9.33
11	2.00	3	12.00
12	1.00	2	14.00
13	0.67	1	25.00
14	0.33	0	

TABLE 8.7

Marginal Utility Theory

Assumptions

- A consumer derives utility from the goods consumed.

- Each additional unit of consumption yields additional total utility; marginal utility is positive.

- As the quantity of a good consumed increases, marginal utility decreases.

- A consumer's aim is to maximize total utility.

Implication

Total utility is maximized when all the available income is spent and when the marginal utility per dollar spent is equal for all goods.

Predictions

- Other things remaining the same, the higher the price of a good, the smaller is the quantity demanded of it (the law of demand).

- The higher the price of a good, the greater is the quantity demanded of substitutes for that good.

- The higher the consumer's income, the greater is the quantity demanded of normal goods.

Individual Demand and Market Demand

Marginal utility theory explains how an individual household spends its income and enables us to derive an individual household's demand curve. In earlier chapters, we used *market* demand curves. We can derive a *market* demand curve from individual demand curves. Let's see how.

The relationship between the total quantity demanded of a good and its price is called **market demand**. The market demand curve is what you studied in Chapter 4. The relationship between the quantity demanded of a good by a single individual and its price is called *individual demand*.

Figure 8.6 illustrates the relationship between individual demand and market demand. In this example, Lisa and Chuck are the only people. The market demand is the total demand of Lisa and Chuck. At $3 a movie, Lisa demands 5 movies a month and Chuck demands 2, so the total quantity demanded by the market is 7 movies a month. Lisa's demand curve for movies in part (a) and Chuck's in part (b) sum *horizontally* to give the market demand curve in part (c).

The market demand curve is the horizontal sum of the individual demand curves and is formed by adding the quantities demanded by each individual at each price.

Because marginal utility theory predicts that individual demand curves slope downward, it also predicts that market demand curves slope downward.

FIGURE 8.6

Individual and Market Demand Curves

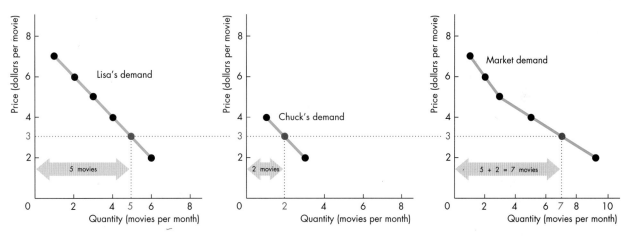

(a) Lisa's demand   **(b) Chuck's demand**   **(c) Market demand**

Price	Quantity of movies demanded		
(dollars per movie)	Lisa	Chuck	Market
7	1	0	1
6	2	0	2
5	3	0	3
4	4	1	5
3	5	2	7
2	6	3	9

The table and the figure illustrate how the quantity of movies demanded varies as the price of a movie varies. In the table, the market demand is the sum of the individual demands. For example, at a price of $3, Lisa demands 5 movies and Chuck demands 2 movies, so the total quantity demanded in the market is 7 movies. In the figure, the market demand curve is the horizontal sum of the individual demand curves. Thus when the price is $3, the market demand curve shows that the quantity demanded is 7 movies, the sum of the quantities demanded by Lisa and Chuck.

Marginal Utility and the Real World

Marginal utility theory can be used to answer a wide range of questions about the real world. The theory sheds light on why the demand for CD players is price elastic while the demand for oil is price inelastic and why the demand for electricity is income elastic while the demand for transportation is income inelastic. Elasticities are determined by preferences. The feature of our preferences that determines elasticity is the step size with which marginal utility declines—the steepness of the marginal utility steps in Fig. 8.2(b).

If marginal utility declines in big steps, a small change in the quantity bought brings a big change in the marginal utility per dollar spent. So it takes a big change in price or income to bring a small change in the quantity demanded—demand is inelastic. Conversely, if marginal utility diminishes slowly, even a large change in the quantity bought brings a small change in the marginal utility per dollar spent. So it takes only a small change in price or income to bring a large change in quantity—demand is elastic.

But marginal utility theory can do much more than explain households' *consumption* choices. It can be used to explain *all* the choices made by households. One of these choices, the allocation of time between work in the home, office, or factory and leisure is the theme of issues and ideas on pp. 192–193.

R E V I E W   Q U I Z

- When the price of a good falls and the prices of other goods and a consumer's income remain the same, what happens to the consumption of the good whose price has fallen and to the consumption of other goods?
- Elaborate on your answer to the previous question by using demand curves. For which good is there a change in demand and for which is there a change in the quantity demanded?
- If a consumer's income increases and if all goods are normal goods, how does the quantity bought of each good change?

We're going to end this chapter by returning to a recurring theme throughout your study of economics: the concept of efficiency and the distinction between price and value.

Efficiency, Price, and Value

MARGINAL UTILITY THEORY HELPS US TO DEEPEN our understanding of the concept of efficiency and also helps us to see more clearly the distinction between *value* and *price*. Let's see how.

Consumer Efficiency and Consumer Surplus

When Lisa allocates her limited budget to maximize utility, she is using her resources efficiently. Any other allocation of her budget wastes some resources.

But when Lisa has allocated her limited budget to maximize utility, she is *on* her demand curve for each good. A demand curve is a description of the quantity demanded at each price when utility is maximized. When we studied efficiency in Chapter 6, we learned that a demand curve is also a willingness-to-pay curve. It tells us a consumer's *marginal benefit*—the benefit from consuming an additional unit of a good. You can now give the idea of marginal benefit a deeper meaning:

Marginal benefit is the maximum price that a consumer is willing to pay for an extra unit of a good or service when utility is maximized.

The Paradox of Value

For centuries, philosophers have been puzzled by a paradox that we raised at the start of this chapter. Water, which is essential to life itself, costs little, but diamonds, which are useless compared to water, are expensive. Why? Adam Smith tried to solve this paradox. But not until the theory of marginal utility had been developed could anyone give a satisfactory answer.

You can solve this puzzle by distinguishing between *total* utility and *marginal* utility. The total utility that we get from water is enormous. But remember, the more we consume of something, the smaller is its marginal utility. We use so much water that its marginal utility—the benefit we get from one more glass of water—diminishes to a small value. Diamonds, on the other hand, have a small total utility relative to water, but because we buy few diamonds, they have a high marginal utility. When a household has maximized its total utility, it has allocated its

FIGURE 8.7
The Paradox of Value

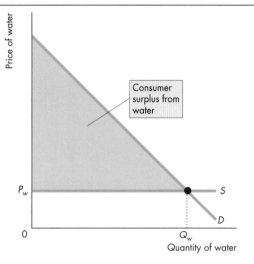

(a) Water

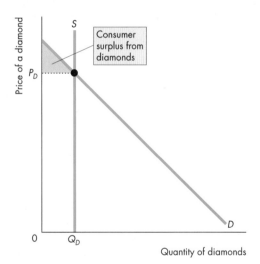

(b) Diamonds

Part (a) shows the demand for water, D, and the supply of water, S. The supply is (assumed to be) perfectly elastic at the price P_W. At this price, the quantity of water consumed is Q_W and the consumer surplus from water is the large green triangle. Part (b) shows the demand for diamonds, D, and the supply of diamonds, S. The supply is (assumed to be) perfectly inelastic at the quantity Q_D. At this quantity, the price of a diamond is P_D and the consumer surplus from diamonds is the small green triangle. Water is valuable—has a large consumer surplus—but is cheap. Diamonds are less valuable than water—have a smaller consumer surplus—but are expensive.

budget in the way that makes the marginal utility per dollar spent equal for all goods. That is, the marginal utility from a good divided by the price of the good is equal for all goods. This equality of marginal utilities per dollar spent holds true for diamonds and water: Diamonds have a high price and a high marginal utility. Water has a low price and a low marginal utility. When the high marginal utility of diamonds is divided by the high price of diamonds, the result is a number that equals the low marginal utility of water divided by the low price of water. The marginal utility per dollar spent is the same for diamonds as for water.

Another way to think about the paradox of value uses *consumer surplus*. Figure 8.7 explains the paradox of value by using this idea. The supply of water (part a) is assumed to be perfectly elastic at price P_W, so the quantity of water consumed is Q_W and the consumer surplus from water is the large green area. The supply of diamonds (part b) is perfectly inelastic at the quantity Q_D, so the price of diamonds is P_D and the consumer surplus from diamonds is the small green area. Water is cheap but brings a large consumer surplus; diamonds are expensive but bring a small consumer surplus.

R E V I E W   Q U I Z

- Can you explain why, along a demand curve, a consumer's choices are efficient?
- Can you explain the paradox of value?
- Does water or diamonds have the greater marginal utility? Does water or diamonds have the greater total utility? Does water or diamonds have the greater consumer surplus?

◇ We've now completed our study of the marginal utility theory. And we've seen how the theory can be used to explain our real-world consumption choices. You can see the theory in action once again in *Reading Between the Lines* on pp. 168–169, where it is used to interpret some recent trends in the things that we drink.

The next chapter presents an alternative theory of household behavior. To help you see the connection between the two theories of consumer behavior, we'll continue with the same example. We'll meet Lisa again and discover another way of understanding how she gets the most out of her $30 a month.

Marginal Utility in Action

THE DETROIT NEWS, FEBRUARY 20, 1999

Coca-Cola Will Sell Bottled Water in U.S.

BY DAN SEWELL, AP BUSINESS WRITER

ATLANTA—Water. It's the real thing.

Coca-Cola Co. will begin selling bottled water in the United States this year.

It will be called Dasani (pronounced duh-SAW-nee), which doesn't mean anything in particular but is meant to convey "a clean, fresh taste."

"Suffice it to say, we think this is the right time for us to get into this market," said Coke spokesman Scott Jacobson. Bottled water is hot these days, outstripping soft drinks in sales growth.

Dasani is expected to be available nationwide and in Canada before this summer in a light blue plastic bottle.

"If it's a Coke brand, it's going to sell. Why they waited five or six years to get into it, I don't know," said Steve Tessereau, manager of a busy Texaco station in suburban Atlanta.

The maker of the world's most popular soft drink sells a brand of bottled water called BonAqua overseas but has been reluctant to get into the business in the United States, preferring instead to encourage people to drink Coke, Sprite and its other sodas.

To meet increased demand among health- and weight-conscious Americans, Coke in recent years has begun offering sports drinks and juices.

But as recently as last month, M. Douglas Ivester, chairman and chief executive, said Coke was leery of water: "There's an awful lot of water sold in the world. There's not an awful lot of money made selling water."

Bottled water sales have jumped from $2.65 billion in 1990 to $4.3 billion in 1998. Sales grew nearly 10 percent over 1997. The $56.3 billion carbonated soft drink market grew by only 3 percent last year.

Pepsi-Cola Co. started selling bottled water five years ago. Aquafina has since become the leading water brand in convenience stores.

© 1999 *The Detroit News*. Reprinted with permission. Further reproduction prohibited.

Essence of the Story

■ Bottled water sales grew from $2.65 billion in 1990 to $4.3 billion in 1998. They grew by almost 10 percent during 1998.

■ Soda sales were $56.3 billion in 1998 but grew by only 3 percent during the year.

■ Pepsi-Cola Co. started selling bottled water in 1993 and became the market leader.

■ Coca-Cola Co. traditionally has tried to encourage people to drink Coke, Sprite, and its other sodas.

■ But to meet the increased demand for non-soda beverages, Coke offers sports drinks and juices and began selling bottled water in the United States in 1999.

■ Consumption patterns change over time. Figure 1 shows some trends in the consumption of beverages in the United States during the 1990s.

■ The quantity of bottled water consumed and the quantity of soda consumed have increased.

■ The quantities of coffee and beer consumed have decreased.

■ You can understand these trends by using the marginal utility theory.

■ People receive utility from consuming bottled water, soda, coffee, and beer.

■ To maximize utility, people make the marginal utility per dollar spent equal for all goods. So people consume bottled water, soda, coffee, and beer in quantities that make the marginal utilities per dollar spent on each of them equal, as shown by the equation displayed below.

■ If the price of a good rises, other things remaining the same, the marginal utility of that good must increase to maintain maximum possible utility.

■ But marginal utility increases as the quantity consumed of the good decreases. So other things remaining the same, when the price of a good rises, the quantity consumed of that good decreases.

■ If prices explain the consumption trends in Fig. 1, then it must be that the prices of water and soda have fallen relative to the prices of beer and coffee.

■ The price of bottled water has fallen as high-cost spring water has been replaced with lower-cost water purified by reverse osmosis and carbon filtering.

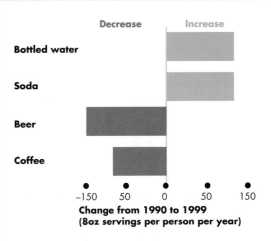

Figure 1 Trends in beverage consumption

■ The price of bottled water has also fallen as more firms have entered the water market, as Coca Cola is doing according to the news article.

■ Similarly, the price of soda has also fallen as more firms have entered the soda market and sales of generic sodas have taken off.

■ The price of coffee has increased through the 1990s because of low crop yields in some growing regions (Brazil experienced a very severe frost and drought in 1994) and because of export restrictions by major producers.

■ The true price, or opportunity cost, of beer has also increased. The money price of beer has not changed much. But improved policing and stiffer penalties for drunk driving have increased the opportunity cost of drinking beer.

■ You can see that the trends in drinking can be understood as the responses to changes in prices. The trends are not a mystery or a social phenomenon. They are the consequence of people trying to get the highest value from their scarce resources.

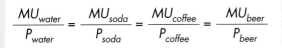

$$\frac{MU_{water}}{P_{water}} = \frac{MU_{soda}}{P_{soda}} = \frac{MU_{coffee}}{P_{coffee}} = \frac{MU_{beer}}{P_{beer}}$$

SUMMARY

KEY POINTS

Household Consumption Choices (pp. 156–158)

- A household's choices are determined by its consumption possibilities and preferences.
- A household's consumption possibilities are constrained by its income and by prices. Some combinations of goods are affordable, and some are not affordable.
- A household's preferences can be described by marginal utility.
- The key assumption of marginal utility theory is that the marginal utility of a good or service decreases as consumption of the good or service increases.

Maximizing Utility (pp. 159–161)

- Marginal utility theory assumes that people buy the affordable combination of goods and services that maximizes total utility.
- Total utility is maximized when all the available income is spent and when the marginal utility per dollar spent on each good is equal.
- If the marginal utility per dollar spent on good *A* exceeds that on good *B*, the consumer can increase total utility by buying more of good *A* and less of good *B*.

Predictions of Marginal Utility Theory (pp. 161–166)

- Marginal utility theory predicts the law of demand. That is, other things remaining the same, the higher the price of a good, the smaller is the quantity demanded of that good.
- Marginal utility theory also predicts that other things remaining the same, the higher the income of a consumer, the larger is the quantity demanded of a normal good.
- Market demand is the sum of all individual demands, and the market demand curve is found by summing horizontally all the individual demand curves.

Efficiency, Price, and Value (pp. 166–167)

- When a consumer maximizes utility, he or she is using resources efficiently.
- Marginal utility theory resolves the paradox of the relative value of water and diamonds.
- When we talk loosely about value, we are thinking of *total* utility or consumer surplus. But price is related to *marginal* utility.
- Water, which we consume in large amounts, has a high total utility and a large consumer surplus but a low price and low marginal utility.
- Diamonds, which we consume in small amounts, have a low total utility and a small consumer surplus but a high price and a high marginal utility.

KEY FIGURES AND TABLE ◆

KEY TERMS

PROBLEMS

*1. Jason enjoys rock CDs and spy novels and spends $60 a month on them. The table shows the utility he gets from each good:

Quantity per month	Utility from rock CDs	Utility from spy novels
1	60	20
2	110	38
3	150	53
4	180	64
5	200	70
6	206	75

a. Draw graphs showing Jason's utility from rock CDs and from spy novels.

b. Compare the two utility graphs. Can you say anything about Jason's preferences?

c. Draw graphs that show Jason's marginal utility from rock CDs and from spy novels.

d. What do the two marginal utility graphs tell you about Jason's preferences?

e. If rock CDs and spy novels both cost $10 each, how does Jason spend the $60?

2. Mary enjoys classical CDs and travel books and spends $50 a month on them. The table shows the utility she gets from each good:

Quantity per month	Utility from classical CDs	Utility from travel books
1	30	30
2	40	38
3	48	44
4	54	46
5	58	47

a. Draw graphs showing Mary's utility from classical CDs and from travel books.

b. Compare the two utility graphs. Can you say anything about Mary's preferences?

c. Draw graphs that show Mary's marginal utility from classical CDs and from travel books.

d. What do the two marginal utility graphs tell you about Mary's preferences?

e. If a classical CD and a travel book cost $10 each, how does Mary spend the $50 a month?

*3. Max enjoys windsurfing and snorkeling. The table shows Max's utility from each sport:

Hours per day	Utility from windsurfing	Utility from snorkeling
1	120	40
2	220	76
3	300	106
4	360	128
5	400	140
6	412	150
7	422	158

Max has $35 to spend, and he can spend as much time as likes on his leisure pursuits. Windsurfing equipment rents for $10 an hour, and snorkeling equipment rents for $5 an hour.

a. Draw a graph that shows Max's budget line.

b. How long does he spend windsurfing and how long does he spend snorkeling?

4. Rob enjoys rock concerts and the opera. The table shows the utility he gets from each activity:

Concerts per month	Utility from rock concerts	Utility from operas
1	100	60
2	180	110
3	240	150
4	280	180
5	300	200
6	310	210

Rob has $100 a month to spend on concerts. A rock concert ticket is $20, and an opera ticket is $10.

a. Draw a graph that shows Rob's budget line.

b. How many rock concerts and how many operas does he attend?

*5. In problem 3, Max's sister gives him $20 to spend on his leisure pursuits, so he now has $55.

a. Draw a graph that shows Max's budget line.

b. How many hours does Max choose to windsurf and how many hours does he choose to snorkel now that he has $55 to spend?

6. In problem 4, Rob's uncle gives him $30 to spend on concert tickets, so he now has $130.

a. Draw a graph that shows Rob's budget line.

b.   How many rock concerts and how many operas does he attend now that he has $130 to spend?

*7. In problem 5, if the rent on windsurfing equipment decreases to $5 an hour, how many hours does Max now windsurf and how many hours does he snorkel?

8. In problem 4, if the price of a rock concert decreases to $10, how many rock concerts and operas will Rob attend?

*9. Max takes a Club Med vacation, the cost of which includes unlimited sports activities. There is no extra charge for equipment. If Max windsurfs and snorkels for 6 hours a day, how many hours does he windsurf and how many hours does he snorkel?

10. Rob wins a lottery and has more than enough money to satisfy his desires for rock concerts and opera. He decides that he would like to see 5 concerts each month. How many rock concerts and how many operas does he now attend?

*11. Shirley's and Dan's demand schedules for popcorn are:

| Price (cents per carton) | Quantity demanded by | |
| | Shirley | Dan |
	(cartons per week)	
10	12	6
30	9	5
50	6	4
70	3	3
90	1	2

If Shirley and Dan are the only two individuals, what is the market demand for popcorn?

12. Ben's and Jerry's demand schedules for ice cream cones are:

| Price (dollars per cone) | Quantity demanded by | |
| | Ben | Jerry |
	(cones per week)	
1.00	8	10
1.30	7	8
1.50	6	6
1.70	5	4
1.90	4	2

If Ben and Jerry are the only two individuals, what is the market demand for ice cream cones?

CRITICAL THINKING

1. Study *Reading Between the Lines* on pp. 168–169 on beverage consumption in the United States during the 1990s and then answer the following questions:
    a.   What facts about bottled water consumption are reported in the news article?
    b.   How can we account for the increasing quantity of bottled water consumed using marginal utility theory?
    c.   Use marginal utility theory to predict what will happen to bottled water consumption if its price rises sharply.
    d.   Use marginal utility theory to predict what will happen to bottled water consumption as incomes rise.
    e.   Do you think price changes and the marginal utility theory can explain all of the changes in beverage consumption in the United States during the 1990s, or do you think there are some other factors at work? If so, what are they?

2. Use the links on the Parkin Web site and read what Henry Schimberg, CEO of Coca-Cola Enterprises, says about the market for bottled water. Use the marginal utility theory you have learned in this chapter to interpret and explain Mr. Schimberg's remarks about the bottled water market.

3. Why do you think the percentage of income spent on food has decreased while the percentage of income spent on cars has increased during the past 50 years? Use the marginal utility theory to explain these trends.

4. Smoking is banned on all airline flights in the United States and on most international flights. Use marginal utility theory to explain your answers to the following questions:
    a.   What effect does this ban have on the utility of (i) smokers and (ii) nonsmokers?
    b.   How do you expect the ban to influence the decisions of (i) smokers and (ii) non-smokers? In your answer to this question, consider decisions about smoking, flying, and the willingness to pay for a flight.

Chapter 9

Possibilities, Preferences, and Choices

Like the continents floating on the earth's mantle, our spending patterns change steadily over time. On such subterranean movements, business empires rise and fall. Goods such as home videos and microwave popcorn now appear on our shopping lists, while 78 rpm phonograph records and horse-drawn carriages have disappeared. Miniskirts appear, disappear, and reappear in cycles of fashion. ◆ But the glittering surface of our consumption obscures deeper and slower changes in how we spend. In the last few years, we've seen a proliferation of gourmet food shops and designer clothing boutiques. Yet we spend a

Subterranean Movements

smaller percentage of our income today on food and clothing than we did in 1950. At the same time, the percentage of our income spent on vacations and medical care has grown steadily. Why does consumer spending change over the years? How do people react to changes in income and changes in the prices of the things they buy? ◆ Similar subterranean movements govern the way we spend our time. For example, the average workweek has fallen steadily from 70 hours a week in the nineteenth century to 35 hours a week today. Although the average workweek is now much shorter than it once was, far more people now have jobs. This change has been especially dramatic for women, who are much more likely to work outside the home than they were in previous generations. Why has the average workweek declined? And why do more women work?

◆ In this chapter, we're going to study a model of choice that predicts the effects of changes in prices and incomes on what people buy and how much work they do.

After studying this chapter, you will be able to:

- Calculate and graph a household's budget line
- Work out how the budget line changes when prices or income changes
- Make a map of preferences by using indifference curves
- Explain the choices that households make
- Predict the effects of price and income changes on consumption choices
- Predict the effects of wage changes on work-leisure choices

Consumption Possibilities

CONSUMPTION CHOICES ARE LIMITED BY INCOME and by prices. A household has a given amount of income to spend and cannot influence the prices of the goods and services it buys. The limits to a household's consumption choices are described by its **budget line**.

Let's look at Lisa's budget line.[1] Lisa has an income of $30 a month to spend. She buys two goods—movies and soda. Movies cost $6 each; soda costs $3 for a six-pack. Figure 9.1 shows alternative affordable ways for Lisa to consume movies and soda. Row *a* says that she can buy 10 six-packs of soda and see no movies, a combination of movies and soda that exhausts her monthly income of $30. Row *f* says that Lisa can watch 5 movies and drink no soda—another combination that exhausts the $30 available. Each of the other rows in the table also exhausts Lisa's income. (Check that each of the other rows costs exactly $30.) The numbers in the table define Lisa's consumption possibilities. We can graph Lisa's consumption possibilities as points *a* through *f* in Fig. 9.1.

Divisible and Indivisible Goods   Some goods—called divisible goods—can be bought in any quantity desired. Examples are gasoline and electricity. We can best understand household choice if we suppose that all goods and services are divisible. For example, Lisa can consume a half a movie a month *on the average* by seeing one movie every two months. When we think of goods as being divisible, the consumption possibilities are not just the points *a* through *f* shown in Fig. 9.1, but those points plus all the intermediate points that form the line running from *a* to *f*. Such a line is a budget line.

Lisa's budget line is a constraint on her choices. It marks the boundary between what is affordable and what is unaffordable. She can afford any point on the line and inside it. She cannot afford any point outside the line. The constraint on her consumption depends on prices and her income, and the constraint changes when prices or her income changes. Let's see how by studying the budget equation.

---

[1] If you have read the preceding chapter on marginal utility theory, you have already met Lisa. This tale of her thirst for soda and zeal for movies will sound familiar to you—up to a point. But in this chapter, we're going to use a different method for representing preferences—one that does not require us to resort to the idea of utility.

FIGURE 9.1

The Budget Line

Income	$30
Movies	$6
Soda	$3

Consumption possibility	Movies (per month)	Soda (six-packs per month)
a	0	10
b	1	8
c	2	6
d	3	4
e	4	2
f	5	0

Lisa's budget line shows the boundary between what she can and cannot afford. The rows of the table list Lisa's affordable combinations of movies and soda when her income is $30, the price of soda is $3 a six-pack, and the price of a movie is $6. For example, row *a* tells us that Lisa exhausts her $30 income when she buys 10 six-packs and sees no movies. The figure graphs Lisa's budget line. Points *a* through *f* on the graph represent the rows of the table. For divisible goods, the budget line is the continuous line *af*. To calculate the equation for Lisa's budget line, start with expenditure equal to income:

$$\$3Q_s + \$6Q_m = \$30.$$

Divide by $3 to obtain

$$Q_s + 2Q_m = 10.$$

Subtract $2Q_m$ from both sides to obtain

$$Q_s = 10 - 2Q_m.$$

The Budget Equation

We can describe the budget line by using a *budget equation*. The budget equation starts with the fact that

$$\text{Expenditure} = \text{Income}.$$

Expenditure is equal to the sum of the price of each good multiplied by the quantity bought. For Lisa,

$$\text{Expenditure} = (\text{Price of soda} \times \text{Quantity of soda})$$
$$+ (\text{Price of movie} \times \text{Quantity of movies}).$$

Call the price of soda P_s, the quantity of soda Q_s, the price of a movie P_m, the quantity of movies Q_m, and income y. Using these symbols, Lisa's budget equation is

$$P_s Q_s + P_m Q_m = y.$$

Or, using the prices Lisa faces, $3 for a six-pack and $6 for a movie, and Lisa's income, $30, we get

$$\$3 Q_s + \$6 Q_m = \$30.$$

Lisa can choose any quantities of soda (Q_s) and movies (Q_m) that satisfy this equation. To find the relationship between these quantities, first divide both sides of the equation by the price of soda (P_s) to get

$$Q_s + \frac{P_m}{P_s} \times Q_m = \frac{y}{P_s}.$$

Now subtract the term $(P_m/P_s) \times Q_m$ from both sides of this equation to give

$$Q_s = \frac{y}{P_s} - \frac{P_m}{P_s} \times Q_m.$$

For Lisa, income (y) is $30, the price of a movie (P_m) is $6, and the price of a six-pack (P_s) is $3. So Lisa must choose the quantities of movies and soda to satisfy the equation

$$Q_s = \frac{\$30}{\$3} - \frac{\$6}{\$3} \times Q_m$$

or

$$Q_s = 10 - 2 Q_m.$$

To interpret the equation, go back to the budget line of Fig. 9.1 and check that the equation delivers that budget line. First set Q_m equal to zero. In this case, the budget equation tells us that Q_s, the quantity of soda, is y/P_s, which is 10 six-packs. This combination of Q_m and Q_s is the same as that shown in row *a* of the table in Fig. 9.1. Next set Q_m equal to 5.

Q_s is now equal to zero (row *f* of the table). Check that you can derive the other rows.

The budget equation contains two variables chosen by the household (Q_m and Q_s) and two variables (y/P_s and P_m/P_s) that the household takes as given. Let's look more closely at these variables.

Real Income A household's **real income** is the household's income expressed not as money but as a quantity of goods the household can afford to buy. Expressed in terms of soda, Lisa's real income is y/P_s. This quantity is the maximum number of six-packs that she can buy. It is equal to her money income divided by the price of soda. Lisa's income is $30 and the price of soda is $3 a six-pack, so her real income in terms of soda is 10 six-packs, which is shown in Fig. 9.1 as the point at which the budget line intersects the y-axis.

Relative Price A **relative price** is the price of one good divided by the price of another good. In Lisa's budget equation, the variable P_m/P_s is the relative price of a movie in terms of soda. For Lisa, P_m is $6 a movie and P_s is $3 a six-pack, so P_m/P_s is equal to 2 six-packs per movie. That is, to see one more movie, Lisa must give up 2 six-packs.

You've just calculated Lisa's opportunity cost of a movie. Recall that the opportunity cost of an action is the best alternative forgone. For Lisa to see 1 more movie a month, she must forgo 2 six-packs. You've also calculated Lisa's opportunity cost of soda. For Lisa to consume 2 more six-packs a month, she must give up seeing 1 movie. So her opportunity cost of 2 six-packs is 1 movie.

The relative price of a movie in terms of soda is the magnitude of the slope of Lisa's budget line. To calculate the slope of the budget line, recall the formula for slope (Chapter 2): Slope equals the change in the variable measured on the y-axis divided by the change in the variable measured on the x-axis as we move along the line. In Lisa's case (Fig. 9.1), the variable measured on the y-axis is the quantity of soda, and the variable measured on the x-axis is the quantity of movies. Along Lisa's budget line, as soda decreases from 10 to 0 six-packs, movies increase from 0 to 5. Therefore the magnitude of the slope of the budget line is 10 six-packs divided by 5 movies, or 2 six-packs per movie. The magnitude of this slope is exactly the same as the relative price we've just calculated. It is also the opportunity cost of a movie.

A Change in Prices When prices change, so does the budget line. The lower the price of the good

FIGURE 9.2

Changes in Prices and Income

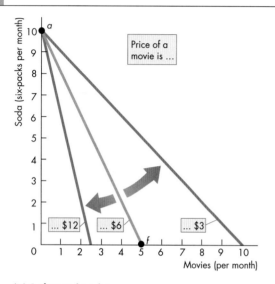

(a) A change in price

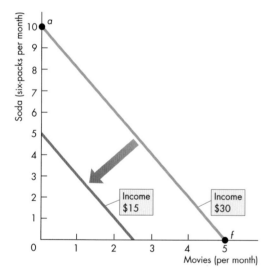

(b) A change in income

In part (a), the price of a movie changes. A fall in the price from $6 to $3 rotates the budget line outward and makes it flatter. A rise in the price from $6 to $12 rotates the budget line inward and makes it steeper.

In part (b), income falls from $30 to $15 while the prices of movies and soda remain constant. The budget line shifts leftward, but its slope does not change.

measured on the horizontal axis, other things remaining the same, the flatter is the budget line. For example, if the price of a movie falls from $6 to $3, real income in terms of soda does not change but the relative price of a movie falls. The budget line rotates outward and becomes flatter, as shown in Fig. 9.2(a). The higher the price of the good measured on the horizontal axis, other things remaining the same, the steeper is the budget line. For example, if the price of a movie rises from $6 to $12, the relative price of a movie increases. The budget line rotates inward and becomes steeper, as shown in Fig. 9.2(a).

A Change in Income   A change in *money income* changes real income but does not change the relative price. The budget line shifts, but its slope does not change. The bigger a household's money income, the bigger is real income and the farther to the right is the budget line. The smaller a household's money income, the smaller is real income and the farther to the left is the budget line. Figure 9.2(b) shows the effect of a change in money income on Lisa's budget line. The initial budget line is the same one that we began with in Fig. 9.1 when Lisa's income is $30. The new budget line shows the limits to Lisa's consumption if her income falls to $15 a month. The two budget lines have the same slope because they have the same relative price. The new budget line is closer to the origin than the initial one because Lisa's real income has decreased.

R E V I E W   Q U I Z

- What does a household's budget line show?
- How do a household's real income and the relative price that it faces influence its budget line?
- If a household has an income of $40 and consumes only bus rides at $4 each and magazines at $2 each, what is the equation that describes its budget line?
- If the price of one good changes, what happens to the relative price and to the slope of the budget line?
- If a household's money income changes and no prices change, what happens to the household's real income and its budget line?

We've studied the limits to what a household can consume. Let's now learn how we can describe preferences and make a map that contains a lot of information about a household's preferences.

Preferences and Indifference Curves

YOU ARE GOING TO DISCOVER A VERY NEAT IDEA— that of drawing a map of a person's preferences. A preference map is based on the intuitively appealing assumption that people can sort all the possible combinations of goods into three groups: preferred, not preferred, and indifferent. To make this idea more concrete, let's ask Lisa to tell us how she ranks various combinations of movies and soda.

Figure 9.3(a) shows part of Lisa's answer. She tells us that she currently consumes 2 movies and 6 six-packs a month at point *c*. She then lists all the combinations of movies and soda that she says are equally acceptable to her as 2 movies and 6 six-packs a month are. When we plot these combinations of movies and soda, we get the green curve in Fig. 9.3(a). This curve is the key element in a map of preferences and is called an indifference curve.

An **indifference curve** is a line that shows combinations of goods among which a consumer is *indifferent*. The indifference curve in Fig. 9.3(a) tells us that Lisa is just as happy to consume 2 movies and 6 six-packs a month at point *c* as to consume the combination of movies and soda at point *g* or at any other point along the curve.

Lisa also says that she prefers any combination of movies and soda in the yellow area above the indifference curve in Fig. 9.3(a) to any combination on the indifference curve. And she prefers any combination on the indifference curve to any combination in the gray area below the indifference curve.

The indifference curve in Fig. 9.3(a) is just one of a whole family of such curves. This indifference curve appears again in Fig. 9.3(b) labeled I_1. The curves labeled I_0 and I_2 are two other indifference curves. Lisa prefers any point on indifference curve I_2 to any point on indifference curve I_1, and she prefers any point on I_1 to any point on I_0. We refer to I_2 as being a higher indifference curve than I_1 and I_1 as being higher than I_0.

A preference map is a series of indifference curves that resemble the contour lines on a map. By looking at the shape of the contour lines on a map, we can draw conclusions about the terrain. Similarly, by looking at the shape of indifference curves, we can draw conclusions about a person's preferences.

Let's learn how to "read" a preference map.

FIGURE 9.3

A Preference Map

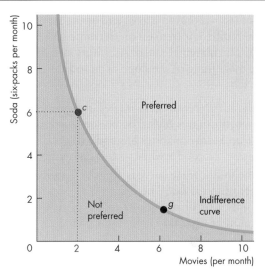

(a) An indifference curve

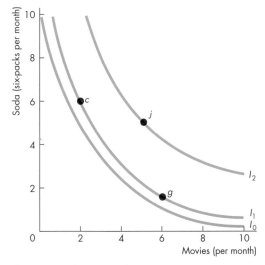

(b) Lisa's preference map

In part (a), Lisa consumes 6 six-packs of soda and 2 movies a month at point *c*. She is indifferent between all the points on the green indifference curve, such as *c* and *g*. She prefers any point above the indifference curve (yellow area) to any point on it, and she prefers any point on the indifference curve to any point below it (gray area). A preference map is a number of indifference curves. Part (b) shows three—I_0, I_1, and I_2— that are part of Lisa's preference map. She prefers point *j* to point *c* or *g*, so she prefers any point on I_2 to any point on I_1.

Marginal Rate of Substitution

The **marginal rate of substitution** (*MRS*) is the rate at which a person will give up good *y* (the good measured on the *y*-axis) to get more of good *x* (the good measured on the *x*-axis) and at the same time remain indifferent (remain on the same indifference curve). The marginal rate of substitution is measured by the magnitude of the slope of an indifference curve.

- If the indifference curve is *steep*, the marginal rate of substitution is *high*. The person is willing to give up a large quantity of good *y* to get a small quantity of good *x* while remaining indifferent.

- If the indifference curve is *flat*, the marginal rate of substitution is *low*. The person is willing to give up only a small amount of good *y* to get a large amount of good *x* to remain indifferent.

Figure 9.4 shows you how to calculate the marginal rate of substitution. Suppose that Lisa consumes 6 six-packs and 2 movies at point *c* on indifference curve I_1. Her marginal rate of substitution is calculated by measuring the magnitude of the slope of the indifference curve at point *c*. To measure this magnitude, place a straight line against, or tangent to, the indifference curve at point *c*. Along that line, as soda consumption decreases by 10 six-packs, movie consumption increases by 5. So at point *c*, Lisa is willing to give up soda for movies at the rate of 2 six-packs per movie. Her marginal rate of substitution is 2.

Now, suppose that Lisa consumes 6 movies and $1\frac{1}{2}$ six-packs at point *g* in Fig. 9.4. Her marginal rate of substitution is now measured by the slope of the indifference curve at point *g*. That slope is the same as the slope of the tangent to the indifference curve at point *g*. Here, as soda consumption decreases by 4.5 six-packs, movie consumption increases by 9. So at point *g*, Lisa is willing to give up soda for movies at the rate of $\frac{1}{2}$ six-pack per movie. Her marginal rate of substitution is $\frac{1}{2}$.

As Lisa's consumption of movies increases and her consumption of soda decreases, her marginal rate of substitution diminishes. Diminishing marginal rate of substitution is the key assumption of consumer theory. The assumption of **diminishing marginal rate of substitution** is a general tendency for the marginal rate of substitution to diminish as the consumer moves along an indifference curve, increasing consumption of the good measured on the *x*-axis and decreasing consumption of the good measured on the *y*-axis.

FIGURE 9.4
The Marginal Rate of Substitution

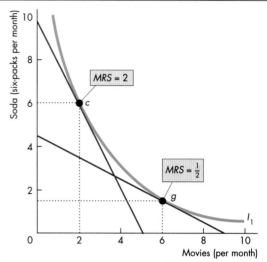

The magnitude of the slope of an indifference curve is called the marginal rate of substitution (*MRS*). The red line at point *c* tells us that Lisa is willing to give up 10 six-packs to see 5 movies. Her marginal rate of substitution at point *c* is 10 divided by 5, which equals 2. The red line at point *g* tells us that Lisa is willing to give up 4.5 six-packs to see 9 movies. Her marginal rate of substitution at point *g* is 4.5 divided by 9, which equals $\frac{1}{2}$.

Your Own Diminishing Marginal Rate of Substitution
You may be able to appreciate why we assume the principle of a diminishing marginal rate of substitution by thinking about your own preferences. Imagine that in a week, you consume 10 six-packs of soda and no movies. Most likely, you are willing to give up a lot of soda so that you can go to the movies just once. But now imagine that in a week, you consume 1 six-pack and 6 movies. Most likely you will now be willing to give up only a little soda to see a seventh movie. As a general rule, the greater the number of movies you see, the smaller is the quantity of soda you are willing to give up to see one additional movie.

The shape of a person's indifference curves incorporates the principle of the diminishing marginal rate of substitution because the curves are bowed toward the origin. The tightness of the bend of an indifference curve tells us how willing a person is to substitute one good for another while remaining indifferent. Let's look at some examples that make this point clear.

Degree of Substitutability

Most of us would not regard movies and soda as being close substitutes for each other. We probably have some fairly clear ideas about how many movies we want to see each month and how many cans of soda we want to drink. Nevertheless, to some degree, we are willing to substitute between these two goods. No matter how big a soda freak you are, there is surely some increase in the number of movies you can see that will compensate you for being deprived of a can of soda. Similarly, no matter how addicted you are to the movies, surely some number of cans of soda will compensate you for being deprived of seeing one movie. A person's indifference curves for movies and soda might look like those shown in Fig. 9.5(a).

Close Substitutes   Some goods substitute so easily for each other that most of us do not even notice which we are consuming. The different brands of personal computers are an example. As long as it has an "Intel inside" and runs Windows, most of us don't care whether our PC is a Dell, a Compaq, a Toshiba, or any of a dozen other brands. The same holds true for marker pens. Most of us don't care whether we use a marker pen from the campus bookstore or the local supermarket. When two goods are perfect substitutes for each other, their indifference curves are straight lines that slope downward, as Fig. 9.5(b) illustrates. The marginal rate of substitution is constant.

Complements   Some goods cannot substitute for each other at all. Instead, they are complements. The complements in Fig. 9.5(c) are left and right running shoes. Indifference curves of perfect complements are L-shaped. One left running shoe and one right running shoe are as good as one left shoe and two right ones. Having two of each is preferred to having one of each, but having two of one and one of the other is no better than having one of each.

The extreme cases of perfect substitutes and perfect complements shown here don't often happen in reality. They do, however, illustrate that the shape of the indifference curve shows the degree of substitutability between two goods. The more perfectly substitutable

---

FIGURE 9.5

The Degree of Substitutability

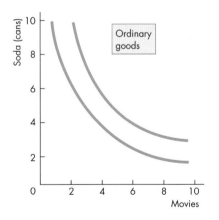

(a) Ordinary goods

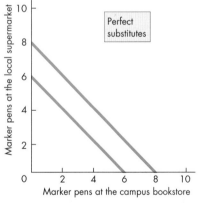

(b) Perfect substitutes

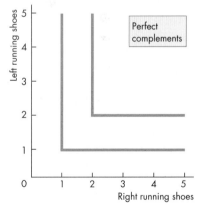

(c) Perfect complements

The shape of the indifference curves reveals the degree of substitutability between two goods. Part (a) shows the indifference curves for two ordinary goods: movies and soda. To consume less soda and remain indifferent, one must see more movies. The number of movies that compensates for a reduction in soda increases as less soda is consumed. Part (b) shows the indifference curves for two perfect substitutes. For the consumer to remain indifferent, one fewer marker pen from the local supermarket must be replaced by one extra marker pen from the campus bookstore. Part (c) shows two perfect complements—goods that cannot be substituted for each other at all. Having two left running shoes with one right running shoe is no better than having one of each. But having two of each is preferred to having one of each.

"With the pork I'd recommend an Alsatian white or a Coke."

Drawing by Weber; © 1988 *The New Yorker Magazine,* Inc.

the two goods, the more nearly are their indifference curves straight lines and the less quickly does the marginal rate of substitution fall. Poor substitutes for each other have tightly curved indifference curves, approaching the shape of those shown in Fig. 9.5(c)

As you can see in the cartoon, according to the waiter's preferences, Coke and Alsatian white wine are perfect substitutes and each is a complement with pork. We hope the customers agree with him.

R E V I E W   Q U I Z

- What is an indifference curve and how does an indifference map show preferences?
- Why does an indifference curve slope downward and why is it bowed toward the origin?
- What do we call the magnitude of the slope of an indifference curve?
- What is the key assumption about a consumer's marginal rate of substitution?

The two components of the model of household choice are now in place: the budget line and the preference map. We will now use these components to work out the household's choice and to predict how choices change when prices and income change.

Predicting Consumer Behavior

WE ARE NOW GOING TO PREDICT THE QUANTITIES of movies and soda that Lisa *chooses* to buy. Figure 9.6 shows Lisa's budget line from Fig. 9.1 and her indifference curves from Fig. 9.3(b). We assume that Lisa consumes at her best affordable point, which is 2 movies and 6 six-packs—at point *c*. Here, Lisa:

- Is on her budget line
- Is on her highest attainable indifference curve
- Has a marginal rate of substitution between movies and soda equal to the relative price of movies and soda.

For every point inside the budget line, such as point *i*, there are points *on* the budget line that Lisa

FIGURE 9.6

The Best Affordable Point

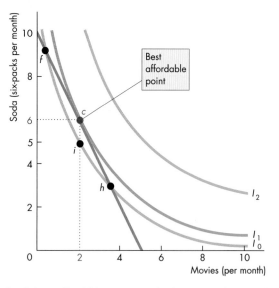

Lisa's best affordable point is *c*. At that point, she is on her budget line and also on the highest attainable indifference curve. At a point such as *h*, Lisa is willing to give up more movies in exchange for soda than she has to. She can move to point *i*, which is just as good as point *h*, and have some unspent income. She can spend that income and move to *c*, a point that she prefers to point *i*.

prefers. For example, she prefers all the points on the budget line between *f* and *h* to point *i*. So she chooses a point on the budget line.

Every point on the budget line lies on an indifference curve. For example, point *h* lies on the indifference curve I_0. At point *h*, Lisa's marginal rate of substitution is less than the relative price. Lisa is willing to give up more movies in exchange for soda than the budget line says she must give up. So she moves along her budget line from *h* toward *c*. As she does so, she passes through a number of indifference curves (not shown in the figure) located between indifference curves I_0 and I_1. All of these indifference curves are higher than I_0, and therefore Lisa prefers any point on them to point *h*. But when Lisa gets to point *c*, she is on the highest attainable indifference curve. If she keeps moving along the budget line, she starts to encounter indifference curves that are lower than I_1. So Lisa chooses point *c*.

At the chosen point, the marginal rate of substitution (the magnitude of the slope of the indifference curve) equals the relative price (the magnitude of the slope of the budget line).

Let's use this model of household choice to predict the effects on consumption of changes in prices and income. We'll begin by studying the effect of a change in price.

A Change in Price

The effect of a change in price on the quantity of a good consumed is called the **price effect**. We will use Fig. 9.7(a) to work out the price effect of a fall in the price of a movie. We start with movies costing $6 each, soda costing $3 a six-pack, and Lisa's income at $30 a month. In this situation, she consumes 6 six-packs and 2 movies a month at point *c*.

Now suppose that the price of a movie falls to $3. With a lower price of a movie, the budget line rotates outward and becomes flatter. (Check back to Fig. 9.2(a) for a refresher on how a price change affects the budget line.) The new budget line is the dark orange one in Fig. 9.7(a).

Lisa's best affordable point is now point *j*, where she consumes 5 movies and 5 six-packs of soda. Lisa drinks less soda and watches more movies now that movies cost less. She cuts her soda consumption from 6 to 5 six-packs and increases the number of movies she sees from 2 to 5 a month. Lisa substitutes movies for soda when the price of a movie falls and the price of soda and her income remain constant.

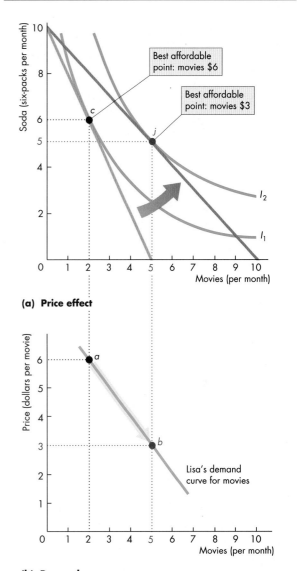

FIGURE 9.7

Price Effect and Demand Curve

(a) Price effect

(b) Demand curve

Initially, Lisa consumes at point *c* (part a). If the price of a movie falls from $6 to $3, she consumes at point *j*. The move from *c* to *j* is the price effect.

At a price of $6 a movie, Lisa sees 2 movies a month, at point *a* (part b). At a price of $3 a movie, she sees 5 movies a month, at point *b*. Lisa's demand curve traces out her best affordable quantity of movies as the price of a movie varies.

The Demand Curve   In Chapter 4, we asserted that the demand curve slopes downward. We can now derive a demand curve from a consumer's budget line and indifference curves. By doing so, we can see that the law of demand and the downward-sloping demand curve are consequences of the consumer's choosing his or her best affordable combination of goods.

To derive Lisa's demand curve for movies, lower the price of a movie and find her best affordable point at different prices. We've just done this for two movie prices in Fig. 9.7(a). Figure 9.7(b) highlights these two prices and two points that lie on Lisa's demand curve for movies. When the price of a movie is $6, Lisa sees 2 movies a month at point *a*. When the price falls to $3, she increases the number of movies she sees to 5 a month at point *b*. The demand curve is made up of these two points plus all the other points that tell us Lisa's best affordable consumption of movies at each movie price, given the price of soda and Lisa's income. As you can see, Lisa's demand curve for movies slopes downward. The lower the price of a movie, the more movies she watches each month. This is the law of demand.

Next, let's examine how Lisa changes her consumption of movies and soda when her income changes.

A Change in Income

The effect of a change in income on consumption is called the **income effect**. Let's work out the income effect by examining how consumption changes when income changes and prices remain constant. Figure 9.8(a) shows the income effect when Lisa's income falls. With an income of $30 and with a movie costing $3 and soda $3 a six-pack, she consumes at point *j*—5 movies and 5 six-packs. If her income falls to $21, she consumes at point *k*—consuming 4 movies and 3 six-packs. When Lisa's income falls, she consumes less of both goods. Movies and soda are normal goods.

The Demand Curve and the Income Effect   A change in income leads to a shift in the demand curve, as shown in Fig. 9.8(b). With an income of $30 and a movie costing $3, Lisa is at point *b* on demand curve D_0, the same curve as in Fig. 9.7. But when her income falls to $21, Lisa sees only 4 movies at point *c*. With less income, she plans to see fewer movies at each price, so her demand curve shifts leftward to D_1.

FIGURE 9.8

Income Effect and Change in Demand

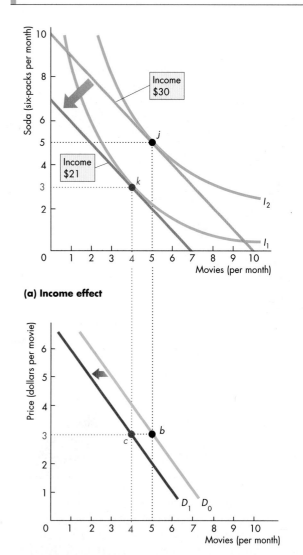

(a) Income effect

(b) Demand curve

A change in income shifts the budget line and changes the best affordable point and changes consumption. In part (a), when Lisa's income decreases from $30 to $21, she consumes less of both movies and soda. In part (b), Lisa's demand curve for movies when her income is $30 is D_0. When Lisa's income decreases to $21, her demand curve for movies shifts leftward to D_1. Lisa's demand for movies decreases because she now sees fewer movies at each price.

Substitution Effect and Income Effect

For a normal good, a fall in price *always* increases the quantity bought. We can prove this assertion by dividing the price effect into two parts:

■ Substitution effect
■ Income effect

Figure 9.9(a) shows the price effect, and Fig. 9.9(b) divides that price effect into its two parts.

Substitution Effect The **substitution effect** is the effect of a change in price on the quantity bought when the consumer (hypothetically) remains indifferent between the original and the new situation. To work out Lisa's substitution effect, we imagine that when the price of a movie falls, we cut Lisa's income by enough to keep her on the same indifference curve as before.

When the price of a movie falls from $6 to $3, suppose (hypothetically) that we cut Lisa's income to $21. What's special about $21? It is the income that is just enough, at the new price of a movie, to keep Lisa's best affordable point on the same indifference curve as her original consumption point *c*. Lisa's budget line is now the light orange line shown in Fig. 9.9(b). With the lower price of a movie and the smaller income, Lisa's best affordable point is *k* on indifference curve I_1. The move from *c* to *k* isolates the substitution effect of the price change. The substitution effect of the fall in the price of a movie is an increase in the consumption of movies from 2 to 4. The direction of the substitution effect never varies: When the relative price of a good falls, the consumer substitutes more of that good for the other good.

Income Effect To calculate the substitution effect, we gave Lisa a $9 pay cut. Now let's give Lisa her $9 back. The $9 increase in income shifts Lisa's budget line outward, as shown in Fig. 9.9(b). The slope of the budget line does not change because both prices remain constant. This change in Lisa's budget line is similar to the one illustrated in Fig. 9.8. As Lisa's budget line shifts outward, her best affordable point becomes *j* on indifference curve I_2. The move from *k* to *j* isolates the income effect of the price change. The income effect of the fall of the price of movies is the increase in the quantity of movies consumed from 4 to 5. As Lisa's income increases, she increases her consumption of movies. For Lisa, movies are a normal good. For a normal good, the income effect reinforces the substitution effect.

FIGURE 9.9

Substitution Effect and Income Effect

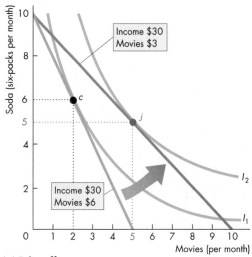

(a) Price effect

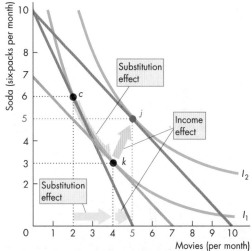

(b) Substitution effect and income effect

The price effect in part (a) can be separated into a substitution effect and an income effect in part (b). To isolate the substitution effect, we confront Lisa with the new price but keep her on her original indifference curve, I_1. The substitution effect is the move from *c* to *k*. To isolate the income effect, we confront Lisa with the new price of movies but increase her income so that she can move from the original indifference curve, I_1, to the new one, I_2. The income effect is the move from *k* to *j*.

Inferior Goods   The example that we have just studied is that of a change in the price of a normal good. The effect of a change in the price of an inferior good is different. Recall that an inferior good is one whose consumption decreases as income increases. For an inferior good, the income effect is negative. Thus for an inferior good, a lower price does not always lead to an increase in the quantity demanded. The lower price has a substitution effect that increases the quantity demanded. But the lower price also has a negative income effect that reduces the demand for the inferior good. Thus the income effect offsets the substitution effect to some degree. If the negative income effect exceeded the positive substitution effect, the demand curve would slope upward. This case does not appear to occur in the real world.

Back to the Facts

We started this chapter by observing how consumer spending has changed over the years. The indifference curve model explains those changes. Spending patterns are determined by best affordable choices. Changes in prices and incomes change the best affordable choice and change consumption patterns.

R E V I E W   Q U I Z

- When a consumer chooses the combination of goods and services to buy, what is she or he trying to achieve?
- Explain the conditions that are met when a consumer has found the best affordable combination of goods to buy. (Use the terms "budget line," "marginal rate of substitution," and "relative price" in your explanation.)
- If the price of a normal good falls, what happens to the quantity demanded of that good?
- Into what two effects can we divide the effect of a price change?
- For a normal good, does the income effect reinforce the substitution effect or does it partly offset the substitution effect?

The model of household choice can explain many other household choices. Let's look at one of them.

Work-Leisure Choices

HOUSEHOLDS MAKE MANY CHOICES OTHER THAN those about how to spend their income on the various goods and services available. We can use the model of consumer choice to understand many other household choices. Some of these are discussed on pp. 192–196. Here we'll study a key choice: how much labor to supply.

Labor Supply

Every week, we allocate our 168 hours between working—called *labor*—and all other activities—called *leisure*. How do we decide how to allocate our time between labor and leisure? We can answer this question by using the theory of household choice.

The more hours we spend on *leisure,* the smaller is our income. The relationship between leisure and income is described by an *income-time budget line.* Figure 9.10(a) shows Lisa's income-time budget line. If Lisa devotes the entire week to leisure—168 hours—she has no income and is at point *z*. By supplying labor in exchange for a wage, she can convert hours into income along the income-time budget line. The slope of that line is determined by the hourly wage rate. If the wage rate is $5 an hour, Lisa faces the flatest budget line. If the wage rate is $10 an hour, she faces the middle budget line. And if the wage rate is $15 an hour, she faces the steepest budget line.

Lisa buys leisure by not supplying labor and by forgoing income. The opportunity cost of an hour of leisure is the hourly wage rate forgone.

Figure 9.10(a) also shows Lisa's indifference curves for income and leisure. Lisa chooses her best attainable point. This choice of income and time allocation is just like her choice of movies and soda. She gets onto the highest possible indifference curve by making her marginal rate of substitution between income and leisure equal to her wage rate. Lisa's choice depends on the wage rate she can earn. At a wage rate of $5 an hour, Lisa chooses point *a* and works 20 hours a week (168 minus 148) for an income of $100 a week. At a wage rate of $10 an hour, she chooses point *b* and works 35 hours a week (168 minus 133) for an income of $350 a week. And at a wage rate of $15 an hour, she chooses point *c* and works 30 hours a week (168 minus 138) for an income of $450 a week.

FIGURE 9.10

The Supply of Labor

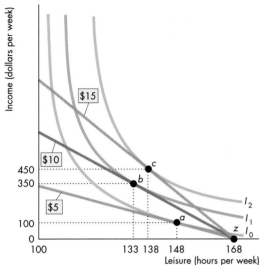

(a) Time allocation decision

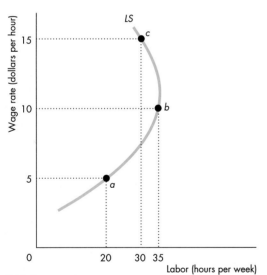

(b) Labor supply curve

In part (a), at a wage rate of $5 an hour, Lisa takes 148 hours of leisure and works 20 hours a week at point *a*. If the wage rate increases from $5 to $10, she decreases her leisure to 133 hours and increases her work to 35 hours a week at point *b*. But if the wage rate increases from $10 to $15, Lisa *increases* her leisure to 138 hours and *decreases* her work to 30 hours a week at point *c*. Part (b) shows Lisa's labor supply curve. Points *a*, *b*, and *c* on the supply curve correspond to Lisa's choices on her income-time budget lines in part (a).

The Labor Supply Curve

Figure 9.10(b) shows Lisa's labor supply curve. This curve shows that as the wage rate increases from $5 an hour to $10 an hour, Lisa increases the quantity of labor supplied from 20 hours a week to 35 hours a week. But when the wage rate increases to $15 an hour, she decreases her quantity of labor supplied to 30 hours a week.

Lisa's supply of labor is similar to that described for the economy as a whole at the beginning of this chapter. As wage rates have increased, work hours have decreased. At first, this pattern seems puzzling. We've seen that the hourly wage rate is the opportunity cost of leisure. So a higher wage rate means a higher opportunity cost of leisure. This fact on its own leads to a decrease in leisure and an increase in work hours. But instead, we've cut our work hours. Why? Because our incomes have increased. As the wage rate increases, incomes increase, so people demand more of all normal goods. Leisure is a normal good, so as incomes increase, people demand more leisure.

The higher wage rate has both a *substitution effect* and an *income effect.* The higher wage rate increases the opportunity cost of leisure and so leads to a substitution effect away from leisure. And the higher wage rate increases income and so leads to an income effect toward more leisure.

This theory of household choice can explain the facts about work patterns described at the beginning of this chapter. First, it can explain why the average workweek has fallen steadily from 70 hours in the nineteenth century to 35 hours today. The reason is that as wage rates have increased, although people have substituted work for leisure, they have also decided to use their higher incomes in part to consume more leisure. Second, the theory can explain why more women now have jobs in the labor market. The reason is that increases in their wage rates and improvements in their job opportunities have led to a substitution effect away from working at home and toward working in the labor market.

This theory of household choice can also explain trends in vacation services, as you can see in *Reading Between the Lines* on pp. 186–187. In the chapters that follow, we're going to study the choices made by firms. We'll see how, in the pursuit of profit, firms make choices that determine the supply of goods and services and the demand for productive resources.

Indifference Curves in Action

THE LOS ANGELES TIMES, NOVEMBER 23, 1998

Pushing High End at Sea Level

BY E. SCOTT RECKARD, TIMES STAFF WRITER

Breakers toss salt into the breeze as a beachcomber eyes a tide pool. A skim-boarder shoots skyward, then plunges into the foam. On this warm fall day, in a Laguna Beach cove with surf-sculpted rock arches and bougainvillea-draped bluffs, just two sunbathers share the sand with the darting seabirds.

In the past, the few visitors here mostly scrambled down from Treasure Island, a bluff-top trailer park looking out to Santa Catalina Island. Retirees and middle-class families shared paradise with part-time residents such as John Wayne's widow, Pilar, and weekend fugitives from inland heat and smog. In the future, far more visitors will stroll down from the trailer park's replacement: a 275-room resort hotel, 18 estate homes and 19 condos for the wealthy, with beach trails, scenic overlooks and 70 parking slots for everyone else.

Here and at choice coastal sites from San Diego County to Santa Barbara, four- and five-star resorts will proliferate in the coming decades, along with upgrades of older hotels. At least 14 such projects are in various stages of development in Southern California, motivated by a web of economic, demographic and political factors. ...

Underlying these factors are prosperous times and the powerful demographics of an aging population. Analysts say millions of baby boomers in their peak earning years are demanding high-end recreation, often several short getaways a year instead of the long summer vacations of their childhoods.

As always, standing in between developers and the coastline are powerful and vocal environmental interests such as the Sierra Club, which has been adept at delaying big coastal projects for years. ...

© 1996 *The Los Angeles Times*. Reprinted with permission. Further reproduction prohibited

Essence of the Story

■ Aging baby boomers in their peak earning years are demanding high-quality recreation facilities for several short vacations a year instead of a single long summer vacation.

■ To meet this demand, at least 14 projects to replace trailer parks with luxury resorts are in various stages of development on Southern California's choice coastal sites.

■ Environmental interests oppose and delay these big coastal projects.

■ A luxury resort is a normal good. A trailer park is an inferior good. (The quantity consumed of a normal good increases as income increases. The quantity consumed of an inferior good *decreases* as income *increases*.)

■ Figure 1 shows the *income effect* on the quantities consumed of trailer parks and luxury resorts. (Think of this consumer as the "average" consumer.)

■ At today's income and prices, we can consume either 30 trailer parks or 30 luxury resorts or any combination of the two along the budget line *ab*.

■ The best affordable point is where 20 trailer parks and 10 luxury resorts are consumed.

■ Suppose that in the future, incomes double. We can now consume either 60 trailer parks or 60 luxury resorts or any combination of the two along the budget line *cd*.

■ Now the best afford-able point is where 10 trailer parks and 50 lux-ury resorts are consumed. Because a trailer park is an inferior good, when income increases, the quantity of trailer parks consumed decreases *if prices do not change.*

■ But prices are likely to change.

■ As more luxury resorts are built, environmental interests begin to block further development. This action increases the cost of building luxury resorts, which limits their supply and increases the prices that people must pay to use them.

■ At the same time, technological advances lower the relative price of trailers, so the cost of using trailer parks falls.

■ Instead of shifting outward to *cd*, the bud-get line shifts outward *and becomes less steep.* It shifts to *ef* in Figure 2.

■ Along the budget line *ef*, the relative price of trailer parks in terms of luxury resorts is lower than along budget lines *ab* and *cd*.

■ In this example, the consumer can just reach indifference curve I_1 on budget line *cd* and bud-get line *ef*.

■ With the prices and income that generate the budget line *ef*, the best affordable point is where 50 trailer parks and 20 luxury resorts are con-sumed.

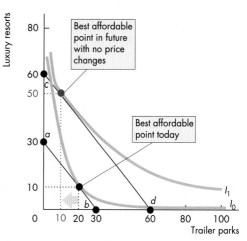

Figure 1 An income effect

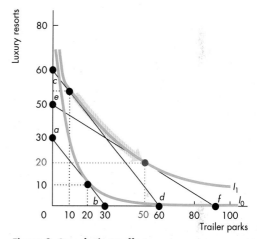

Figure 2 An substitute effect

■ The increase in trailer parks from 10 to 50 and the decrease in luxury resorts from 50 to 20 along I_1 is a *substitution effect.*

■ This analysis shows how changes in prices allocate scarce resources and prevent the over-development of ocean-side sites when they have a high environmental value.

187

SUMMARY

KEY POINTS

Consumption Possibilities (pp. 174–176)

- The budget line is the boundary between what the household can and cannot afford given its income and the prices of goods.
- The point at which the budget line intersects the *y*-axis is the household's real income in terms of the good measured on that axis.
- The magnitude of the slope of the budget line is the relative price of the good measured on the *x*-axis in terms of the good measured on the *y*-axis.
- A change in price changes the slope of the budget line. A change in income shifts the budget line but does not change its slope.

Preferences and Indifference Curves (pp. 177–180)

- A consumer's preferences can be represented by indifference curves. An indifference curve joins all the combinations of goods among which the consumer is indifferent.
- A consumer prefers any point above an indifference curve to any point on it and any point on an indifference curve to any point below it.
- The magnitude of the slope of an indifference curve is called the marginal rate of substitution.
- The marginal rate of substitution diminishes as consumption of the good measured on the *y*-axis decreases and consumption of the good measured on the *x*-axis increases.

Predicting Consumer Behavior (pp. 180-184)

- A household consumes at its best affordable point. This point is on the budget line and on the highest attainable indifference curve and has a marginal rate of substitution equal to relative price.
- The effect of a price change (the price effect) can be divided into a substitution effect and an income effect.
- The substitution effect is the effect of a change in price on the quantity bought when the consumer (hypothetically) remains indifferent between the original and the new situation.

- The substitution effect always results in an increase in consumption of the good whose relative price has fallen.
- The income effect is the effect of a change in income on consumption.
- For a normal good, the income effect reinforces the substitution effect. For an inferior good, the income effect works in the opposite direction to the substitution effect.

Work-Leisure Choices (pp. 184–185)

- The indifference curve model of household choice enables us to understand how a household allocates its time between work and leisure.
- Work hours have decreased and leisure hours have increased because the income effect on the demand for leisure has been greater than the substitution effect.

KEY FIGURES ◆

KEY TERMS

PROBLEMS

*1. Sara has an income of $12 a week. Popcorn costs $3 a bag, and cola costs $3 a can.
   a. What is Sara's real income in terms of cola?
   b. What is her real income in terms of popcorn?
   c. What is the relative price of cola in terms of popcorn?
   d. What is the opportunity cost of a can of cola?
   e. Calculate the equation for Sara's budget line (placing bags of popcorn on the left side).
   f. Draw a graph of Sara's budget line with cola on the x-axis.
   g. In part (f), what is the slope of Sara's budget line? What is it equal to?

2. Marc has an income of $20 per week. CDs cost $10 each, and root beer costs $5 a can.
   a. What is Marc's real income in terms of root beer?
   b. What is his real income in terms of CDs?
   c. What is the relative price of root beer in terms of CDs?
   d. What is the opportunity cost of a can of root beer?
   e. . Calculate the equation for Marc's budget line (placing cans of root beer on the left side).
   f. Draw a graph of Marc's budget line with CDs on the x-axis.
   g. In part (f), what is the slope of Marc's budget line? What is it equal to?

*3. Sara's income and the prices she faces are the same as in problem 1. The figure illustrates Sara's preferences.

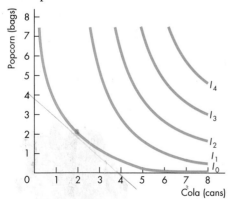

   a. What are the quantities of popcorn and cola that Sara buys?
   b. What is Sara's marginal rate of substitution of popcorn for cola at the point at which she consumes?

4. Marc's income and the prices he faces are the same as in problem 2. The figure illustrates his preferences.

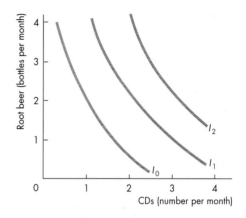

   a. What are the quantities of root beer and CDs that Marc buys?
   b. What is Marc's marginal rate of substitution of CDs for root beer at the point at which he consumes?

*5. Now suppose that in problem 3, the price of cola falls to $1.50 per can and the price of popcorn and Sara's income remain constant.
   a. Find the new quantities of cola and popcorn that Sara buys.
   b. Find two points on Sara's demand curve for cola.
   c. Find the substitution effect of the price change.
   d. Find the income effect of the price change.
   e. Is cola a normal good or an inferior good for Sara?
   f. Is popcorn a normal good or an inferior good for Sara?

6. Now suppose that in problem 4, the price of a CD falls to $5, the price of root beer and income remain constant.
   a. Find the new quantities of root beer and CDs that Marc buys.
   b. Find two points on Marc's demand curve for CDs.
   c. Find the substitution effect of the price change.

d. Find the income effect of the price change.
e. Are CDs a normal good or an inferior good for Marc?
f. Is root beer a normal good or an inferior good for Marc?

*7. Pam buys cookies and comic books. The price of a cookie is $1, and the price of a comic book is $2. Each month, Pam spends all of her income and buys 30 cookies and 5 comic books. Next month, the price of a cookie will fall to 50¢ and the price of a comic book will rise to $5. Assume that Pam's preference map is similar to that in Fig. 9.3(b).
a. Will Pam be able to buy 30 cookies and 5 comic books next month?
b. Will Pam want to buy 30 cookies and 5 comic books?
c. Which situation does Pam prefer: cookies at $1 and comic books at $2 or cookies at 50¢ and comic books at $3?
d. If Pam changes the quantities that she buys, which good will she buy more of and which will she buy less of?
e. When the prices change next month, will there be an income effect and a substitution effect at work or just one of them?

8. Pete buys tuna and golf balls. The price of tuna is $2.00 a can, and the price of golf balls is $1.00 each. Each month, Pete spends all of his income and buys 20 cans of tuna and 40 golf balls. Next month, the price of tuna will rise to $3.00 a can and the price of golf balls will fall to 50¢ each. Assume that Pete's preference map is similar to that in Fig. 9.3(b).
a. Will Pete be able to buy 20 cans of tuna and 40 golf balls next month?
b. Will Pete want to buy 20 cans of tuna and 40 golf balls?
c. Which situation does Pete prefer: tuna at $2 a can and golf balls at $1 each or tuna at $3 a can and golf balls at 50¢ each?
d. If Pete changes the quantities that he buys, which good will he buy more of and which will he buy less of?
e. When the prices change next month, will there be an income effect and a substitution effect at work or just one of them?

CRITICAL THINKING

1. Study *Reading Between the Lines* about trailer parks and luxury resorts on pp. 186–187, and then:
a. Provide a demographic and economic profile of the people who buy the services of luxury resorts based on the information given in the news article.
b. Discuss the alternative uses of the sites on which luxury resorts might be developed.
c. Use the indifference curve model to explain the changes in buying patterns that the news article predicts will occur in the markets for trailer parks and luxury resorts.

2. Use the links on the Parkin Web site to obtain prices for luxury condominiums and trailer park accommodation. Draw a diagram that shows the budget line of a family that has $2,000 a month to spend.

3. Some people say that increasing the tobacco tax can help to limit smoking. Suppose the tobacco tax currently is 75 cents a pack and that a pack of cigarettes costs $3.50. If the tobacco tax doubled to $1.50:
a. What would happen to the relative price of cigarettes and other goods and services?
b. What would happen to the budget line showing the quantities of cigarettes and other goods and services that a person could afford to buy?
c. How would a typical person change her or his purchases of cigarettes? Use a figure to show your answer to this question and separately identify the substitution effect and the income effect.

4. Jim spends his income on apartment rent, food, clothing, and vacations. He gets a pay raise from $3,000 a month to $4,000 a month. At the same time, airfares and other vacation-related costs increase by 50 percent while other prices remain unchanged.
a. How do you think Jim will change his spending pattern as a result of the changes in his income and prices?
b. Is Jim better off or worse off in his new situation? Why or why not?
c. If *all* prices rise by 50 percent, how does Jim change his purchases? Is he now better off or worse off? Why?

Understanding Households' Choices

Making the Most of Life

The powerful forces of demand and supply shape the fortunes of families, businesses, nations, and empires in the same unrelenting way that the tides and winds shape rocks and coastlines. You saw in Chapters 4 through 7 how these forces raise and lower prices, increase and decrease quantities bought and sold, cause revenues to fluctuate, and send resources to their most valuable uses. ◆ These powerful forces begin quietly and privately with the choices that each one of us makes. Chapters 8 and 9 probe these individual choices. Chapter 8 explores the marginal utility theory of human decisions. This theory explains people's consumption plans. It also explains people's consumption of leisure time and its flip side, the supply of work time. Marginal utility theory can even be used to explain "non-economic" choices, such as whether to marry and how many children to have. In a sense, there are no non-economic choices. If there is scarcity, there must be choice. And economics studies all such choices. Chapter 9 describes a tool that enables us to make a map of people's likes and dislikes, a tool called an *indifference curve*. Indifference curves are considered an advanced topic, so this chapter is *strictly optional*. But the presentation of indifference curves in Chapter 9 is the clearest and most straightforward available, so if you want to learn about this tool, this chapter is the place to do so. ◆ The earliest economists (Adam Smith and his contemporaries) did not have a very deep understanding of households' choices. It was not until the nineteenth century that progress was made in this area. On the following pages, you can spend some time with Jeremy Bentham, the person who pioneered the use of the concept of utility to study of human choices, and with Gary Becker of the University of Chicago, who is one of today's most influential students of human behavior.

People as Rational Decision Makers

The Economist

Jeremy Bentham

(1748–1832), who lived in London, was the son and grandson of a lawyer and was himself trained as a barrister. But he rejected the opportunity to maintain the family tradition and, instead, spent his life as a writer, activist, and Member of Parliament in the pursuit of rational laws that would bring the greatest happiness to the greatest number of people.

Bentham, whose embalmed body is preserved to this day in a glass cabinet in the University of London, was the first person to use the concept of utility to explain human choices. But in Bentham's day, the distinction between explaining and prescribing was not a sharp one, and Bentham was ready to use his ideas to tell people how they ought to behave. He was one of the first to propose pensions for the retired, guaranteed employment, minimum wages, and social benefits such as free education and free medical care.

> "... It is the greatest happiness of the greatest number that is the measure of right and wrong."
>
> JEREMY BENTHAM
> *Fragment on Government*

The Issues

The economic analysis of human behavior in the family, the workplace, the markets for goods and services, the markets for labor services, and financial markets is based on the idea that our behavior can be understood as a response to scarcity. Everything we do can be understood as a choice that maximizes total benefit subject to the constraints imposed by our limited resources and technology. If people's preferences are stable in the face of changing constraints, then we have a chance of predicting how they will respond to an evolving environment.

The economic approach explains the incredible change that has occurred during the past 100 years in the way women allocate their time as the consequence of changing constraints, not of changing attitudes. Technological advances have equipped the nation's farms and factories with machines that have increased the productivity of both women and men, thereby raising the wages they can earn. The increasingly technological world has increased the return to education for both women and men and has led to a large increase in high school and college graduates of both sexes. And equipped with an ever-widening array of gadgets and appliances that cut the time taken to do household jobs, an increasing proportion of women have joined the labor force.

The economic explanation might not be correct, but it is a powerful one. And if it is correct, the changing attitudes are a consequence, not a cause, of the economic advancement of women.

Economists explain people's actions as the consequences of choices that maximize total utility subject to
constraints. In the 1890s, fewer than 20 percent of
women chose market employment, and most of those
who did had low-paying and unattractive jobs. The other
80 percent of women chose nonmarket work in the
home. What constraints led to these choices?

By 1997, more than 60 percent of women were in the
labor force, and although many had low-paying jobs,
women were increasingly found in the professions and in
executive positions. What brought about this dramatic
change compared with 100 years earlier? Was it a
change in preferences or a change in the constraints that
women face?

Today, one economist who stands out above all
others and who stands on the shoulders of
Jeremy Bentham is Gary Becker of the University
of Chicago. Professor Becker has transformed
the way we think about human choices. You
can meet him on the following pages.

Talking with

Gary S. Becker

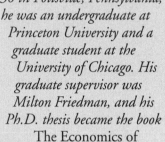

is Professor of Economics and Sociology at the University of Chicago. Born in 1930 in Pottsville, Pennsylvania, he was an undergraduate at Princeton University and a graduate student at the University of Chicago. His graduate supervisor was Milton Friedman, and his Ph.D. thesis became the book The Economics of Discrimination, *a work that profoundly changed the way we think about discrimination and economic ways of reducing it.*

Gary S. Becker

Professor Becker's other major book, Human Capital, *first published in 1964, has become a classic and has influenced the thinking of the Clinton Administration on education issues. In 1992 he was awarded the Nobel Prize for Economic Science for his work on human capital.*

Professor Becker has revolutionized the way we think about human decisions in all aspects of life. Michael Parkin talked with Professor Becker about his work and how it uses and builds on the work of Jeremy Bentham.

Why are you an economist?

When I went to Princeton, I was interested in mathematics, but I wanted to do something for society. I took economics in my freshman year by accident, and it was a lucky accident. I found economics

to be tremendously exciting intellectually because it could be used to understand the difference between capitalism and socialism, what determined wages, and how people are taxed. This was so exciting to me that I didn't even worry about job opportunities at the time.

Can we really hope to explain all human choices by using models that were invented initially to explain and predict choices about the allocation of income among alternative consumer goods and services?

I think we can hope to explain all human choices. All choices involve making comparisons and assessing how to allocate our time between work, leisure, and taking care of children. These are choices that are not in principle very different from the type of choices involved in allocating income. Whether economists succeed at the goal of explaining everything, of course, remains to be seen. We certainly haven't done that yet, but I think we've made considerable progress in expanding our horizons with the theory of choice.

You are a professor of both economics and sociology. Do you see these same techniques that we've developed in economics being used to address questions that are the traditional domain of the sociologist? Or is sociology just a totally different discipline?

Sociology is a discipline with many different approaches. There is a small but growing and vocal group of sociologists who believe in what they call *rational choice theory*, which is the theory economists have used to explain choices in markets. My late colleague, James Coleman, was the leader of that group. One of the issues they deal with is the influence of peers on behavior. For example, imagine that I am a teenager facing choices of getting involved with drugs or heavy drinking or smoking because of peer pressure. How would rational choice theorists incorporate this peer pressure into an analysis of these choices? The simple approach they take is that my utility, or pleasure, depends not only on what I'm consuming but also on what my peers are doing. If they're doing something very different from what I'm doing, that reduces my utility partly because I receive less respect from them and feel less part of the group.

Therefore when I am trying to get as much utility as possible, I take into account what my peers are doing. But since we're all doing that, this leads to some equilibrium in this peer market. Instead of us all behaving independently, we are all behaving interdependently. I think economists have given social structures such as peer pressure far too little attention. One of the things I learned during my association with Coleman and other sociologists is a better appreciation of the importance of social factors in individual behavior.

Can you identify the historical figures that have been most influential to your thinking and your career?
Economics is a cumulative field in which we build on the giants who went earlier, and we try to add a little bit. And then other people build on our generation's contributions. The view I take of the broad scope of the economic approach has had a number of major practitioners,

including Jeremy Bentham, who stated and applied a very general view of utility-maximizing behavior to many problems, such as the factors that reduce crime.

Other nineteenth century people like Wicksteed and Marshall highlighted the rational choice aspect of economics. In the eighteenth century, Adam Smith already applied economic reasoning to political behavior. My work on human capital was very much influenced by Irving Fisher, Alfred Marshall, Milton Friedman, and Ted Schultz. Very few people's work, certainly not mine, spring out of nowhere. They have continuity with the past. What we do is try to build on the work of past economists and do a little more and a little better than what they did.

> Very few people's work, certainly not mine, spring out of nowhere. They have continuity with the past. What we do is try to build on the work of past economists and do a little more and a little better than what they did.

How would you characterize the major achievements of the economics of human behavior? What questions, for example, would have convincing answers?
The area of law and economics has been very successful in analyzing criminal behavior. Work by many lawyers and economists, particularly Judge Richard Posner and William Landes of the University of Chicago Law School, has produced

many successful applications. The question that economics of crime seeks to answer is: What determines the amount of crime that we have and how effective are various actions that governments can take in reducing the amount of crime? This analysis discusses apprehending and punishing criminals, giving better education to people who might commit crimes, reducing unemployment, and so on. They have basically said that fundamentally, the factors determining criminal behavior are not so different from the factors determining whether people become professors or not. People make choices, and these choices are conditional on their expected benefits and the cost. You can affect the number of people who decide to enter criminal activities by affecting the benefits and costs. To the extent that people make these calculations, they are more likely to enter crime when benefits are high relative to the cost.

One way to affect costs is to make it more likely that if somebody commits a crime they'll be captured, apprehended, convicted, and punished. That raises the cost and reduces crime. I think now that people accept this conclusion for most crimes.

But the economic approach is not simply a law and order approach. It also says that if you can increase the attractiveness to people of working at legal activities rather than illegal or criminal activities, you will also have less crime. One way to increase the attractiveness is to make it easier for people to find jobs and to earn more by improving their skills, their education, and their training and also by improving the functioning of labor markets.

You've made a significant contribution to demographic economics. Nearly 40 years ago, you introduced the idea of children being durable goods. Can you talk about the evolution of this idea?
Demographers initially were extremely hostile to my point of view. However, I recently received the Irene Taeuber Award from the Population Association of America, their most prestigious demographic award. It was given to me in recognition of the value of the economic way of looking at demographic questions, including birth and marriage rates. Over time, the cumulative work of many economists working on population problems around the world made an impact.

The main payoffs from this work have been in our understanding of fertility. The conclusions from the economic approach are that the number of children people have is very much a function of two variables: costs and choices. Costs depend not only on how much food and shelter you give children, but also on the time of parents. In most societies, most of that time is the mother's time, which has a value. As we have become richer, and as women have become better educated and are working outside the home more, the cost to them of spending time on children has risen. As these costs have risen, families are deterred from having as many children as they had in the past. So one of the factors explaining the big decline in birth rates is the increasing costs of children.

The second variable that economists recognize is that families are making choices about the quality of children's lives in terms of their education, training, and health. In modern economies, this quality component has become very important because the emphasis in modern economies is on knowledge, technology, and skills. But there is a tradeoff. If you spend more on each child's skills, education, and training, you make children more costly and you are likely to have fewer children. Over the past 30 years, birth rates have been decreasing in most countries of the world, including India, China, parts of Asia, Latin America, some parts of Africa, Europe, and the United States.

> There are about 15 countries of the world that now have birth rates well below replacement levels. If families continue with these rates, the populations will eventually decline—and decline rapidly.

How do you respond to people who feel that explaining choices such as how many children to raise is deeply personal and that it is therefore immoral to think of children in these terms?
I think morality is misplaced in this area. We are trying to understand very major changes in the world. There are about 15 countries of the world that now have birth rates well below replacement levels. If families continue with these rates, these populations will eventually decline—and decline rapidly. This includes Germany, Italy, Spain, Portugal, France, and Japan. It is important to understand why birth rates are going down. If this way of looking at it is a powerful tool for understanding why families have made these choices, then it would be immoral, I believe, to neglect this approach. If we are concerned about low birth rates, how can we go about raising them? Or if we want to understand what to expect in other countries that are experiencing significant economic development, we will miss out if we neglect an important set of considerations that help us to understand what's going on.

Is economics a subject that a young person can happily enter today? What are the major incentives for pursuing economics as an undergraduate?
I would certainly encourage a young person to enter economics for several reasons. There are many employment opportunities in economics, and it is also valuable if you decide to go into other areas such as the law, business, or even medicine. Economic issues, including the budget deficit, entitlement programs, minimum wages, and how to subsidize the elderly, are extremely important public policy issues.

I want also to stress that economics is a wonderful intellectual activity. To be able to take this very mysterious world we live in and to illuminate parts of it, important parts of it, through the use of economics is enormously intellectually satisfying and challenging for an undergraduate or for anybody else. So I would say it's both practical and satisfying. Who can ask for a better combination?

Chapter 10

Organizing Production

In the fall of 1990, a British scientist named Tim Berners-Lee invented the World Wide Web. This remarkable idea paved the way for the creation and growth of thousands of profitable businesses. One of these businesses is Netscape, which was founded by Marc Andreessen, the author of the now famous Navigator Web browser, and entrepreneur Jim Clark. ◆ How do Netscape and the other 20 million firms that operate in the United States make their business decisions? How do they operate efficiently? ◆ Businesses range from multinational giants, such as Microsoft, to small family restaurants and local Internet service providers. Three quarters of all firms are operated by their owners. But corporations (such as Netscape and Microsoft) account for 86 percent of all business sales. What are the different forms a firm can take? Why

Spinning a Web

do some firms remain small while others become giants? Why are most firms owner-operated? ◆ Many businesses operate in a highly competitive environment and struggle to make a profit. Others, such as Microsoft, seem to have cornered the market on their products and make a large profit. What are the different types of market in which firms operate, and why is it harder to make a profit in some markets than others? ◆ Most of the components of an IBM personal computer are made by other firms. Microsoft created its Windows operating system, and Intel makes its processor chip. Other firms make hard drives and modems, and yet others make CD drives, sound cards, and so on. Why doesn't IBM make all its own computer components? Why does it leave these activities to other firms and buy from them in markets? How do firms decide what to make themselves and what to buy in the marketplace from other firms?

◆ In this chapter, we are going to learn about firms and the choices they make to cope with scarcity. We begin by studying the economic problems and choices that *all* firms face.

After studying this chapter, you will be able to:

■ Explain what a firm is and describe the economic problems that *all* firms face

■ Distinguish between technological efficiency and economic efficiency

■ Define and explain the principal-agent problem

■ Describe and distinguish between different types of business organization

■ Describe and distinguish between different types of markets in which firms operate

■ Explain why firms coordinate some economic activities and markets coordinate others

The Firm and Its Economic Problem

THE 20 MILLION FIRMS IN THE UNITED STATES differ in size and in the scope of what they do. But they all perform the same basic economic functions. Each **firm** is an institution that hires productive resources and that organizes those resources to produce and sell goods and services.

Our goal is to predict firm behavior. To do so, we need to know a firm's goals and the constraints it faces. We begin with the goals.

The Firm's Goal

If you asked a group of entrepreneurs what they are trying to achieve, you would get many different answers. Some would talk about making a quality product, others about business growth, others about market share, and others about job satisfaction of their work force. All of these goals might be pursued, but they are not the fundamental goal. They are means to a deeper goal.

A firm's goal is to *maximize profit*. A firm that does not seek to maximize profit is either eliminated or bought out by firms that do seek to maximize profit.

What exactly is the profit that a firm seeks to maximize? To answer this question, let's look at Sidney's Sweaters.

Measuring a Firm's Profit

Sidney runs a successful business that makes sweaters. Sidney's Sweaters receives $400,000 a year for the sweaters it sells. Its expenses are $80,000 a year for wool, $20,000 for utilities, $120,000 for labor, and $10,000 in interest on a bank loan. With receipts of $400,000 and expenses of $230,000, Sidney's Sweaters' annual surplus is $170,000.

Sidney's accountant lowers this number by $20,000, which he says is the depreciation (fall in value) of the firm's buildings and knitting machines during the year. (Accountants use Internal Revenue Service rules based on standards established by the Financial Accounting Standards Board to calculate the depreciation.) So the accountant reports that the profit of Sidney's Sweaters is $150,000 a year.

Sidney's accountant measures cost and profit to ensure that the firm pays the correct amount of income tax and to show the bank how its loan has been used. But we want to predict the decisions that a firm makes. These decisions respond to *opportunity cost* and *economic profit*.

Opportunity Cost

The **opportunity cost** of any action is the highest-valued alternative forgone. The action that you choose not to take—the highest-valued alternative forgone—is the cost of the action that you choose to take. For a firm, the opportunity cost of production is the value of the firm's best alternative use of its resources.

Opportunity cost is a real alternative forgone. But so that we can compare the cost of one action with that of another action, we express opportunity cost in money units. A firm's opportunity costs are:

- Explicit costs
- Implicit costs

Explicit Costs Explicit costs are paid in money. The amount paid for a resource could have been spent on something else, so it is the opportunity cost of using the resource. For Sidney, his expenditures on wool, utilities, wages, and bank interest are explicit costs.

Implicit Costs A firm incurs implicit costs when it forgoes an alternative action but does not make a payment. A firm incurs implicit costs when it:

1. Uses its own capital
2. Uses its owner's time or financial resources.

The cost of using its own capital is an implicit cost —and an opportunity cost—because the firm could rent the capital to another firm. The rental income forgone is the firm's opportunity cost of using its own capital. This opportunity cost is called the **implicit rental rate** of capital.

People rent houses, apartments, cars, telephones, and videotapes. And firms rent photocopiers, earth-moving equipment, satellite-launching services, and so on. If a firm rents capital, it incurs an *explicit* cost. If a firm buys the capital it uses, it incurs an *implicit* cost. The implicit rental rate of capital is made up of:

1. Economic depreciation
2. Interest forgone

Economic depreciation is change in the *market* value of capital over a given period. It is calculated as the market price of the capital at the beginning of the period minus its market price at the end of the period. For example, suppose that Sidney could have sold his buildings and knitting machines on December 31, 1998, for $400,000. If he can sell the same capital on December 31, 1999, for $375,000, his economic depreciation during 1999 is $25,000—the fall in the market value of the machines. This $25,000 is an implicit cost of using the capital during 1999.

The funds used to buy capital could have been used for some other purpose. And in their next best use, they would have yielded a return—an interest income. This forgone interest is part of the opportunity cost of using the capital. For example, Sidney's Sweaters could have bought government bonds instead of a knitting factory. The interest forgone on the government bonds is an implicit cost of operating the knitting factory.

Cost of Owner's Resources A firm's owner often supplies *entrepreneurial ability*—the resource that organizes the business, makes business decisions, innovates, and bears the risk of running the business. The return to entrepreneurship is profit, and the *average* return for supplying entrepreneurial ability is called **normal profit**. Normal profit is part of a firm's opportunity cost, because it is the cost of a forgone alternative—running another firm. If normal profit in the textile business is $50,000 a year, this amount must be added to Sidney's costs to determine his opportunity cost.

The owner of a firm also can supply labor (in addition to entrepreneurship). The return to labor is a wage. And the opportunity cost of the owner's time spent working for the firm is the wage income forgone by not working in the best alternative job. Suppose that Sidney could take another job that pays $40,000 a year. By working for his knitting business and forgoing this income, Sidney incurs an opportunity cost of $40,000 a year.

Economic Profit

What is the bottom line—the profit or loss of the firm? A firm's **economic profit** is equal to its total revenue minus its opportunity cost. The firm's opportunity cost is the sum of its explicit costs and implicit costs. And the implicit costs, remember, include *normal profit*. The return to entrepreneurial ability is greater than normal

in a firm that makes a positive economic profit. And the return to entrepreneurial ability is less than normal in a firm that makes a negative economic profit—a firm that incurs an economic loss.

Economic Accounting: A Summary

Table 10.1 summarizes the economic accounting concepts that you've just studied. Sidney's Sweaters' total revenue is $400,000. Its opportunity cost is $365,000. And its economic profit is $35,000.

To achieve the objective of maximum profit—maximum economic profit—a firm must make five basic decisions:

1. What goods and services to produce and in what quantities
2. How to produce—the technology to use
3. How to organize and compensate its managers and workers
4. How to market and price its products
5. What to produce itself and what to buy from other firms

In all these decisions, a firm's actions are limited by the constraints that it faces. Our next task is to learn about these constraints.

TABLE 10.1

Economic Accounting

Item		Amount
Total revenue		**$400,000**
Opportunity Costs		
Wool	$80,000	
Utilities	20,000	
Wages paid	120,000	
Bank interest paid	10,000	
Total Explicit Costs		$230,000
Sidney's wages forgone	40,000	
Sidney's interest forgone	20,000	
Economic depreciation	25,000	
Normal profit	50,000	
Total Implicit Costs		$135,000
Total Cost		**$365,000**
Economic Profit		**$35,000**

The Firm's Constraints

Three features of its environment limit the maximum profit a firm can make. They are:

- Technology constraints
- Information constraints
- Market constraints

Technology Constraints Economists define technology broadly. A **technology** is any method of producing a good or service. Technology includes the detailed designs of machines. It also includes the layout of the workplace. And it includes the organization of the firm. For example, the shopping mall is a technology for producing retail services. It is a different technology from the catalog store, which in turn is different from the downtown store.

It might seem surprising that a firm's profits are limited by technology because technological advances are constantly increasing profit opportunities. Almost every day, we learn about some new technological advance that amazes us. With computers that speak and recognize our own speech and cars that can find the address we need in a city we've never visited before, we are able to accomplish ever more.

Technology is advancing. But at each point in time, to produce more output and gain more revenue, a firm must hire more resources and incur greater costs. The increase in profit that the firm can achieve is limited by the technology available for transforming resources into output. For example, using its current plant and work force, Ford can produce some maximum number of cars per day. To produce more cars per day, Ford must hire more resources and incur greater costs, which limits the increase in profit that Ford can make by selling the additional cars.

Information Constraints We never possess all the information we would like to have to make decisions. We lack information about both the future and the present. For example, suppose you plan to buy a new computer. When should you buy it? The answer depends on how the price is going to change in the future. Where should you buy it? The answer depends on the prices at hundreds of different computer shops. To get the best deal, you must compare the quality and prices in every shop. But the opportunity cost of this comparison exceeds the cost of the computer!

Similarly, a firm is constrained by limited information about the quality and effort of its work force,

the current and future buying plans of its customers, and the plans of its competitors. Workers slacken off when managers believe they are working hard. Customers switch to competing suppliers. Firms must compete against competition from a new firm.

Firms try to create incentive systems for workers to ensure that they work hard even when no one is monitoring their efforts. And firms spend millions of dollars on market research. But none of these efforts and expenditures eliminates the problems of incomplete information and uncertainty. And the cost of coping with limited information itself limits profit.

Market Constraints What each firm can sell and the price it can obtain are constrained by the willingness to pay of its customers and by the prices and marketing efforts of other firms. Similarly, the resources that each firm can buy and the prices it must pay are limited by the willingness of people to work for and invest in the firm. Firms spend billions of dollars a year marketing and selling their products. Some of the most creative minds strive to find the right message that will produce a knockout television advertisement. Market constraints and the expenditures firms make to overcome them limit the profit a firm can make.

R E V I E W   Q U I Z

- Why do firms seek to maximize profit? What happens to firms that don't pursue this goal?
- Why do accountants and economists calculate a firm's cost and profit in different ways?
- What are the items that make opportunity cost depart from the accountant's measure of cost?
- Why is normal profit an opportunity cost?
- What are the three types of constraint that firms face? How does each constraint limit the profit that a firm can make?

In the rest of this chapter and in Chapters 11 through 14, we study the decisions that firms make. We're going to learn how we can predict a firm's behavior as the response to the constraints that it faces and to changes in those constraints. We begin by taking a closer look at the technology constraints, information constraints, and market constraints that firms face.

Technology and Economic Efficiency

MICROSOFT EMPLOYS A LARGE WORK FORCE. And most Microsoft workers possess a large amount of human capital, but the firm uses a small amount of physical capital. In contrast, a coal-mining company employs a huge amount of mining equipment (physical capital) and almost no labor. Why? The answer lies in the concept of efficiency. There are two concepts of production efficiency: technological efficiency and economic efficiency. **Technological efficiency** occurs when the firm produces a given output by using the least inputs. **Economic efficiency** occurs when the firm produces a given output at least cost. Let's explore the two concepts of efficiency by studying an example.

Suppose that there are four alternative techniques for making TV sets:

a. *Robot production.* One person monitors the entire computer-driven process.

b. *Production line.* Workers specialize in a small part of the job as the emerging TV set passes them on a production line.

c. *Bench production.* Workers specialize in a small part of the job but walk from bench to bench to perform their tasks.

d. *Hand-tool production.* A single worker uses a few hand tools to make a TV set.

Table 10.2 sets out the amounts of labor and capital that each of these four methods require to make 10 TV sets a day. Which of these alternative methods are technologically efficient?

Technological Efficiency

Recall that technological efficiency occurs when the firm produces a given output by using the least inputs. Inspect the numbers in the table and notice that method *a* uses the most capital but the least labor. Method *d* uses the most labor but the least capital. Methods *b* and *c* lie between the two extremes. They use less capital but more labor than method *a* and less labor but more capital than method *d*. Compare methods *b* and *c*. Method *c* requires 100 workers and 10 units of capital to produce 10 TV sets. Those same 10 TV sets can be produced by

method *b* with 10 workers and the same 10 units of capital. Because method *c* uses the same amount of capital and more labor than method *b*, method *c* is not technologically efficient.

Are any of the other methods not technologically efficient? The answer is no. Each of the other methods is technologically efficient. Method *a* uses more capital but less labor than method *b*, and method *d* uses more labor but less capital than method *b*.

Which of the methods are economically efficient?

Economic Efficiency

Recall that economic efficiency occurs when the firm produces a given output least cost. Suppose that labor costs $75 per person-day and that capital costs $250 per machine-day. Table 10.3(a) calculates the costs of using the different methods. By inspecting the table, you can see that method *b* has the lowest cost. Although method *a* uses less labor, it uses too much expensive capital. And although method *d* uses less capital, it uses too much expensive labor.

Method *c*, which is technologically inefficient, is also economically inefficient. It uses the same amount of capital as method *b* but 10 times as much labor, so it costs more. A technologically inefficient method is never economically efficient.

Although *b* is the economically efficient method in this example, method *a* or *d* could be economically efficient with different input prices.

First, suppose that labor costs $150 a person-day and capital costs only $1 a machine-day. Table 10.3(b)

TABLE 10.2

Four Ways of Making 10 TV Sets a Day

		Quantities of inputs	
	Method	**Labor**	**Capital**
a	Robot production	1	1,000
b	Production line	10	10
c	Bench production	100	10
d	Hand-tool production	1,000	1

TABLE 10.3

The Costs of Different Ways of Making 10 TV Sets a Day

(a) Four ways of making TVs

Method	Labor cost ($75 per day)		Capital cost ($250 per day)		Total cost	Cost per TV set
a	$75	+	$250,000	=	$250,075	$25,007.50
b	750	+	2,500	=	3,250	325.00
c	7,500	+	2,500	=	10,000	1,000.00
d	75,000	+	250	=	75,250	7,525.00

(b) Three ways of making TVs: High labor costs

Method	Labor cost ($150 per day)		Capital cost ($1 per day)		Total cost	Cost per TV set
a	$150	+	$1,000	=	$1,150	$115.00
b	1,500	+	10	=	1,510	151.00
d	150,000	+	1	=	150,001	15,000.10

(c) Three ways of making TVs: High capital costs

Method	Labor cost ($1 per day)		Capital cost ($1,000 per day)		Total cost	Cost per TV set
a	$1	+	$1,000,000	=	$1,000,001	$100,000.10
b	10	+	10,000	=	10,010	1,001.00
d	1,000	+	1,000	=	2,000	200.00

---

now shows the costs of making a TV set. In this case, method *a* is economically efficient. Capital is now so cheap relative to labor that the method that uses the most capital is the economically efficient method.

Second, suppose that labor costs only $1 a person-day while capital costs $1,000 a machine-day. Table 10.3(c) shows the costs in this case. Method *d*, which uses a lot of labor and little capital, is now the least-cost method and economically efficient method.

From these examples, you can see that while technological efficiency depends only on what is feasible, economic efficiency depends on the relative costs of resources. The economically efficient method is the one that uses the smaller amount of a more expensive resource and a larger amount of a less expensive resource.

A firm that is economically efficient maximizes profit. Natural selection favors efficient firms and opposes inefficient firms. Inefficient firms go out of business or are taken over by firms that lower costs. Profit-maximizing firms are better able to survive temporary adversity than are inefficient ones.

R E V I E W   Q U I Z

- How do we define technological efficiency? Is a firm technologically efficient if it uses the latest technology? Why?
- How do we define economic efficiency? Is a firm economically inefficient if it can cut costs by producing less? Why?
- Explain the key distinction between technological efficiency and economic efficiency.
- Why do some firms use large amounts of capital and small amounts of labor while others use small amounts of capital and large amounts of labor?

You've now seen how the technology constraints that a firm faces influence the amounts of capital and labor that it employs. Next we study information constraints and the diversity of organization structures they generate.

Information and Organization

EACH FIRM ORGANIZES THE PRODUCTION OF goods and services by combining and coordinating the productive resources it hires. But there is variety across firms in how they organize production. Firms use a mixture of two systems:

- Command systems
- Incentive systems

Command Systems

A **command system** is a method of organizing production that uses a managerial hierarchy. Commands pass downward through the managerial hierarchy, and information passes upward. Managers spend most of their time collecting and processing information about the performance of the people under their control and making decisions about commands to issue and how best to get those commands implemented.

The military uses the purest form of command system. A commander-in-chief (in the United States, the President) makes the big decisions about strategic objectives. Beneath this highest level, generals organize their military resources. Beneath the generals, successively lower ranks organize smaller and smaller units but pay attention to ever increasing degrees of detail. At the bottom of the managerial hierarchy are the people who operate weapons systems.

Command systems in firms are not as rigid as they are in the military. But they share some similar features. A chief executive officer (CEO) sits at the top of a firm's command system. Senior executives who report to and receive commands from the CEO specialize in managing production, marketing, finance, personnel, and perhaps other aspects of the firm's operations. Beneath these senior managers might be several tiers of middle management ranks that stretch downward to the managers who supervise the day-to-day operations of the business. Beneath these managers are the people who operate the firm's machines and who make and sell goods and services.

Small firms have one or two layers of managers, while large firms have several layers. As production processes have become ever more complex, management ranks have swollen. Today, more people have management jobs than ever before. But the information revolution of the 1990s slowed the growth of management, and in some industries, it decreased the number of layers of managers and brought a shakeout of middle managers.

Managers make enormous efforts to be well informed. And they try hard to make good decisions and to issue commands that end up using resources efficiently. But managers always have incomplete information about what is happening in the divisions of the firm for which they are responsible. It is for this reason that firms use incentive systems as well as command systems to organize production.

Incentive Systems

An **incentive system** is a method of organizing production that uses a market-like mechanism inside the firm. Instead of issuing commands, senior managers create compensation schemes that will induce workers to perform in ways that maximize the firm's profit.

Selling organizations use incentive systems most extensively. Sales representatives who spend most of their working time alone and unsupervised are induced to work hard by being paid a small salary and a large performance-related bonus.

But incentive systems operate at all levels in a firm. A CEO's compensation plan includes a share in the firm's profit, and factory floor workers sometimes receive compensation based on the quantity they produce.

Mixing the Systems

Firms use a mixture of commands and incentives, and they choose the mixture to maximize profit. They use commands when it is easy to monitor performance or when a small deviation from an ideal performance is very costly. They use incentives when monitoring performance is either not possible or too costly to be worth doing.

For example, it is easy and not very costly to monitor the performance of workers on a production line. And if one person works too slowly, the entire line slows. So a production line is organized with a command system.

In contrast, it is costly to monitor a CEO. What, for example, did John Sculley (a former president of Apple Computer) contribute to the success and subsequent problems faced by Apple? This question cannot be answered with certainty, yet Apple must put someone in charge of operations and provide this person the *incentive* to be efficient. Incentives and the contracts that create them are an attempt to cope with a general problem called the principal-agent problem.

The Principal-Agent Problem

The **principal-agent problem** is the problem of devising compensation rules that induce an *agent* to act in the best interest of a *principal*. For example, the stockholders of Chase Manhattan Bank are *principals*, and the bank's managers are *agents*. The stockholders (the principals) must induce the managers (agents) to act in the stockholders' best interest. Similarly, Bill Gates (a principal) must induce the programmers developing Windows 2000 (agents) to work efficiently.

Agents, whether they are managers or workers, pursue their own goals and often impose costs on a principal. For example, the goal of a stockholder of the Chase Manhattan (a principal) is to maximize the bank's profit. But the bank's profit depends on the actions of its managers (agents) who have their own goals. Perhaps a manager takes a customer to a ball game on the pretense that she is building customer loyalty, when in fact she is simply taking on-the-job leisure. This same manager is also a principal, and her tellers are agents. The manager wants the tellers to work hard and attract new customers so that she can meet her operating targets. But the tellers enjoy conversations with each other and keep customers waiting in line. Nonetheless, the bank constantly strives to find ways of improving performance and increasing profits.

Coping with the Principal-Agent Problem

Issuing commands does not address the principal-agent problem. In most firms, the shareholders can't monitor the managers and often the managers can't monitor the workers. Each principal must create incentives that induce each agent to work in the interests of the principal. Three ways of attempting to cope with the principal-agent problem are:

■ Ownership
■ Incentive pay
■ Long-term contracts

Ownership By assigning ownership (or part-ownership) of a business to the manager or workers, the principal can sometimes induce a job performance that increases the firm's profits. Part-ownership schemes for senior managers are quite common, but they are less common for workers. When United Airlines ran into problems a few years ago, it made all its employees owners of the company.

Incentive Pay Incentive pay schemes—pay related to performance—are very common. They are based on a variety of performance criteria such as profits or production or sales targets. Promoting an employee for good performance is another example of an incentive pay scheme.

Long-term Contracts Long-term contracts tie the long-term fortunes of managers and workers (agents) to the success of the principal(s)—the owner(s) of the firm. For example, a multiyear employment contract for a CEO encourages that person to take a long-term view and devise strategies that achieve maximum profit over a sustained period.

These three ways of coping with the principal-agent problem give rise to different types of business organization. Each type of business organization is a different response to the principal-agent problem. Each uses ownership, incentives, and long-term contracts in different ways. Let's look at the main types of business organization.

Types of Business Organization

The three main types of business organization are:

■ Proprietorship
■ Partnership
■ Corporation

Proprietorship A *proprietorship* is a firm with a single owner—a proprietor—who has unlimited liability. *Unlimited liability* is the legal responsibility for all the debts of a firm up to an amount equal to the entire wealth of the owner. If a proprietorship cannot pay its debts, those to whom the firm owes money can claim the personal property of the owner. Corner stores, computer programmers, and artists are all examples of proprietorships.

The proprietor makes management decisions, receives the firm's profits, and is responsible for its losses. Profits from a proprietorship are taxed at the same rate as other sources of the proprietor's personal income.

Partnership   A *partnership* is a firm with two or more owners who have unlimited liability. Partners must agree on an appropriate management structure and on how to divide the firm's profits among themselves. The profits of a partnership are taxed as the personal income of the owners. But each partner is legally liable for all the debts of the partnership (limited only by the wealth of an individual partner). Liability for the full debts of the partnership is called *joint unlimited liability*. Most law firms are partnerships.

Corporation   A *corporation* is a firm owned by one or more limited liability stockholders. *Limited liability* means that the owners have legal liability only for the value of their initial investment. This limitation of liability means that if the corporation becomes bankrupt, its owners are not required to use their personal wealth to pay the corporation's debts.

Corporation profits are taxed independently of stockholders' incomes. Because stockholders pay taxes on the income they receive as dividends on stocks,

corporate profits are taxed twice. The stockholders also pay capital gains tax on the profit they earn by selling a stock for a higher price than they paid for it. Corporate stocks generate capital gains when a corporation retains some of its profit and reinvests it in profitable activities. So even retained earnings are taxed twice because the capital gains they generate are taxed.

Pros and Cons of Different Types of Firms

The different types of business organization arise as different ways of trying to cope with the principal-agent problem. Each has advantages in particular situations. And because of its special advantages, each type continues to exist. Each type also has its disadvantages, which explain why it has not driven out the other two.

Table 10.4 summarizes these pros and cons of the different types of firm.

TABLE 10.4
Pros and Cons of Different Types of Firms

Proprietorship	Pros	Cons
	■ Easy to set up	■ Bad decisions not checked by need for consensus
	■ Simple decision making	■ Owner's entire wealth at risk
	■ Profits taxed only once as owner's income	■ Firm dies with owner
		■ Capital is expensive
		■ Labor is expensive
Partnership	■ Easy to set up	■ Achieving consensus may be slow and expensive
	■ Diversified decision making	■ Owners' entire wealth at risk
	■ Can survive withdrawal of partner	■ Withdrawal of partner may create capital shortage
	■ Profits taxed only once as owners' incomes	■ Capital is expensive
Corporation	■ Owners have limited liability	■ Complex management structure can make decisions slow and expensive
	■ Large-scale, low-cost capital available	■ Profits taxed twice as company profit and as stockholders' income
	■ Professional management not restricted by ability of owners	
	■ Perpetual life	
	■ Long-term labor contracts cut labor costs	

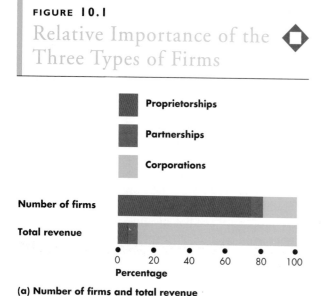

FIGURE 10.1

Relative Importance of the
Three Types of Firms

(a) Number of firms and total revenue

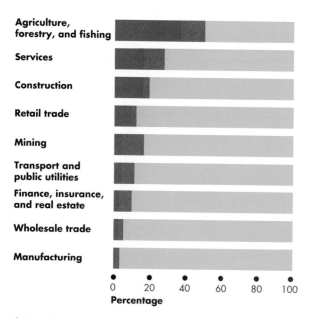

(b) Total revenue in various industries

Three quarters of all firms are proprietorships, almost one fifth are corporations, and only one twentieth are partnerships. Corporations account for 89 percent of business revenue (part a). But proprietorships and partnerships account for a significant percentage of business revenue in some industries (part b).

Source: U.S. Bureau of the Census *Statistical Abstract of the United States: 1998,* 118th ed. (Washington, DC: 1998): Tables 855, 856, and 1103.

Relative Importance of Different Types of Firms

Figure 10.1(a) shows the relative importance of the three main types of firms in the U.S. economy. The figure also shows that the revenue of corporations is much larger than that of the other types of firms. Although only 19 percent of all firms are corporations, they generate 89 percent of revenue.

Figure 10.1(b) shows the percentage of revenue generated by the different types of firms in various industries. Proprietorships in agriculture, forestry, and fishing generate about 36 percent of the total revenue in those sectors. Proprietorships in the service sector, construction, and retail trades also generate a large percentage of total revenue. Partnerships in agriculture, forestry, and fishing generate about 14 percent of total revenue. Partnerships are more prominent in services; mining; and finance, insurance, and real estate than in other sectors. Corporations are important in all sectors, and in manufacturing, corporations have the field almost to themselves.

Why do corporations dominate the business scene? Why do the other types of business survive? And why are proprietorships and partnerships more prominent in some sectors? The answers to these questions lie in the pros and cons of the different types of business organization that are summarized in Table 10.4. Corporations dominate where a large amount of capital is used. But proprietorships dominate where flexibility in decision making is critical.

REVIEW QUIZ

- Explain the distinction between a command system and an incentive system.
- What is the principal-agent problem and what are the three ways in which firms try to cope with it?
- What are the three types of firm? Explain the major advantages and disadvantages of each type.
- Why do all three types of firm survive and in which sectors are the three types most prominent?

You've now seen how technology constraints influence a firm's use of capital and labor and how information constraints influence a firm's organization. We'll now look at market constraints and see how they influence the environment in which firms compete for business.

Markets and the Competitive Environment

THE MARKETS IN WHICH FIRMS OPERATE VARY A great deal. Some are highly competitive, with profits hard to come by. Some appear to be almost free from competition and have firms that earn large profits. Some markets are dominated by fierce advertising campaigns in which each firm seeks to persuade buyers that it has the best products. And some markets display a warlike character.

Economists identify four market types:

1. Perfect competition
2. Monopolistic competition
3. Oligopoly
4. Monopoly

Perfect competition arises when there are many firms, each selling an identical product; many buyers; and no restrictions on the entry of new firms into the industry. The many firms and buyers are all well informed about the prices of the products of each firm in the industry. The worldwide markets for corn, rice, and other grain crops are examples of perfect competition.

Monopolistic competition is a market structure in which a large number of firms compete by making similar but slightly different products. Making a product slightly different from the product of a competing firm is called **product differentiation**. Product differentiation gives a monopolistically competitive firm an element of monopoly power. The firm is the sole producer of the particular version of the good in question. For example, in the market for running shoes, Nike, Reebok, Fila, and Asics all make their own version of the perfect shoe. Each of these firms has a monopoly on a particular brand of shoe. Differentiated products are not necessarily different products. What matters is that consumers *perceive* them to be different. For example, various brands of aspirin are chemically identical (salicylic acid) and differ only in their packaging.

Oligopoly is a market structure in which a small number of firms compete. Computer software, airplane manufacture, and international air transportation are examples of oligopolistic industries. Oligopolies might produce almost identical products, such as the colas produced by Coke and Pepsi. Or they might produce differentiated products such as Chevrolet's Lumina and Ford's Taurus.

A **monopoly** is an industry that produces a good or service for which no close substitute exists and in which there is one supplier that is protected from competition by a barrier preventing the entry of new firms. In some places, the phone, gas, electricity, and water suppliers are local monopolies—monopolies that are restricted to a given location. Microsoft Corporation, the software developer that created Windows, the operating system used by PCs, is an example of a global monopoly.

Perfect competition is the most extreme form of competition. Monopoly is the most extreme absence of competition. The other two market types fall between these extremes.

Many factors must be taken into account to determine which market structure describes a particular real-world market. One of these factors is the extent to which the market is dominated by a small number of firms. To measure this feature of a market, economists use indexes called measures of concentration. Let's look at these measures.

Measures of Concentration

Economists use two measures of concentration:

1. The four-firm concentration ratio
2. The Herfindahl-Hirschman Index

The Four-Firm Concentration Ratio The **four-firm concentration ratio** is the percentage of the value of sales accounted for by the four largest firms in an industry. The range of the concentration ratio is from almost zero for perfect competition to 100 percent for monopoly. This ratio is the main measure used to assess market structure.

Table 10.5 shows two calculations of the four-firm concentration ratio, one for tires and one for printing. In this example, 14 firms produce tires. The largest four have 80 percent of the sales, so the four-firm concentration ratio is 80 percent. In the printing industry, with 1,004 firms, the largest four firms have only 0.5 percent of the sales, so the four-firm concentration ratio is 0.5 percent.

A low concentration ratio indicates a high degree of competition, and a high concentration ratio indicates an absence of competition. A monopoly has a concentration ratio of 100 percent—the largest (and only) firm has 100 percent of the sales. A four-firm concentration ratio that exceeds 60 percent is regarded as an indication of a market that is highly concentrated and dominated by a few firms in an oligopoly. A ratio of less than 40 percent is regarded as an indication of a competitive market.

The Herfindahl-Hirschman Index The **Herfindahl-Hirschman Index**—also called the HHI—is the square of the percentage market share of each firm summed over the largest 50 firms (or summed over all the firms if there are fewer than 50) in a market. For example, if there are four firms in a market and the market shares of the firms are 50 percent, 25 percent, 15 percent, and 10 percent, the Herfindahl-Hirschman Index is

$$HHI = 50^2 + 25^2 + 15^2 + 10^2 = 3,450.$$

In perfect competition, the HHI is small. For example, if each of the largest 50 firms in an industry

---

TABLE 10.5

Concentration Ratio Calculations

Tiremakers		Printers	
Firm	**Sales** (millions of dollars)	**Firm**	**Sales** (millions of dollars)
Top, Inc.	200	Fran's	2.5
ABC, Inc.	250	Ned's	2.0
Big, Inc.	150	Tom's	1.8
XYZ, Inc.	100	Jill's	1.7
Largest 4 firms	700	Largest 4 firms	8.0
Other 10 firms	175	Other 1,000 firms	1,592.0
Industry	875	Industry	1,600.0

Four-firm concentration ratios:

Tiremakers: $\dfrac{700}{875} \times 100 = 80\%$

Printers: $\dfrac{8}{1,600} \times 100 = 0.5\%$

has a market share of 0.1 percent, the HHI is $0.1^2 \times 50 = 0.5$. In a monopoly, the HHI is 10,000—the firm has 100 percent of the market: $100^2 = 10,000$.

The HHI became a popular measure of the degree of competition during the 1980s, when the Federal Trade Commission (FTC) used it to classify markets. A market in which the HHI is less than 1,000 is regarded as being competitive. A market in which the HHI lies between 1,000 and 1,800 is regarded as being moderately competitive. But a market in which the HHI exceeds 1,800 is regarded as being uncompetitive. The FTC scrutinizes any merger of firms in a market in which the HHI exceeds 1,000 and is likely to challenge a merger if the HHI exceeds 1,800.

Concentration Measures for the U.S. Economy

Figure 10.2 shows a selection of concentration ratios and HHIs for the United States calculated by the Department of Commerce.

Industries that produce chewing gum, household laundry equipment, light bulbs, breakfast cereals, and motor vehicles have a high degree of concentration and are oligopolies. The milk, ice cream, and commercial printing industries have low concentration measures and are highly competitive. Industries that produce pet food and cookies and crackers are moderately concentrated. These industries are examples of monopolistic competition.

Concentration measures are a useful indicator of the degree of competition in a market. But they must be supplemented by other information to determine a market's structure. Table 10.6 summarizes the range of other information along with the measures of concentration that determine which market structure describes a particular real-world market.

Limitations of Concentration Measures

The three main limitations of concentration measures alone as determinants of market structure are their failure to take proper account of:

- The geographical scope of the market
- Barriers to entry and firm turnover
- The correspondence between a market and an industry

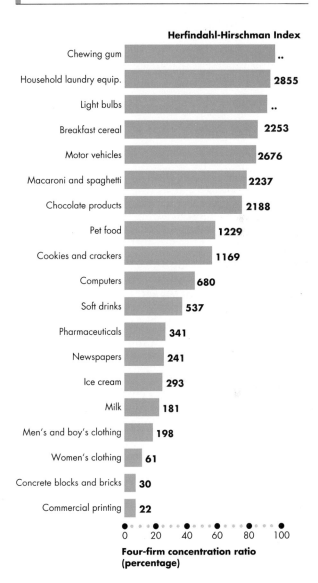

FIGURE 10.2

Concentration Measures in the United States

The industries that produce chewing gum, household laundry equipment, light bulbs, and motor vehicles are highly concentrated, while those that produce milk, ice cream, and commercial printing are highly competitive. The industries that produce pet foods and cookies and crackers have an intermediate degree of concentration.

Source: U.S. Department of Commerce, *Concentration Ratios in Manufacturing,* Washington D.C., 1996.

TABLE 10.6
Market Structure

Characteristics	Perfect competition	Monopolistic competition	Oligopoly	Monopoly
Number of firms in industry	Many	Many	Few	One
Product	Identical	Differentiated	Either identical or differentiated	No close substitutes
Barriers to entry	None	None	Moderate	High
Firm's control over price	None	Some	Considerable	Considerable or regulated
Concentration ratio	0	Low	High	100
HHI (approx. ranges)	Less than 100	101 to 999	More than 1,000	10,000
Examples	Wheat, corn	Food, clothing	Automobiles, cereals	Local water supply

---

Geographical Scope of Market Concentration measures take a national view of the market. Many goods are sold in a *national* market, but some are sold in a *regional* market and some in a *global* one. The newspaper industry consists of local markets. The concentration measures for newspapers are low, but there is a high degree of concentration in the newspaper industry in most cities. The auto industry has a global market. The biggest three U.S. car producers account for 92 percent of cars sold by U.S. producers, but they account for a smaller percentage of the total U.S. car market (including imports) and a smaller percentage of the global market for cars.

Barriers to Entry and Turnover Concentration measures don't measure barriers to entry. Some industries are highly concentrated but have easy entry and an enormous amount of turnover of firms. For example, many small towns have few restaurants but there are no restrictions on opening a restaurant and many firms attempt to do so.

Also, an industry might be competitive because of *potential entry*—because a few firms in a market face competition from many firms that can easily enter the market and will do so if economic profits are available.

Market and Industry To calculate concentration ratios, the Department of Commerce classifies each firm as being in a particular industry. But markets do not always correspond closely to industries for three reasons: First, markets are often narrower than industries. For example, the pharmaceutical industry, which has a low concentration ratio, operates in many separate markets for individual products—for example, measles vaccine and AIDS fighting drugs. These drugs do not compete with each other, so this industry, which looks competitive, includes firms that are monopolies (or near monopolies) in markets for individual drugs.

Second, most firms make several products. For example, Westinghouse makes electrical equipment and, among other things, gas-fired incinerators and plywood. So this one firm operates in at least three separate markets. But the Department of Commerce classifies Westinghouse as being in the electrical goods and equipment industry. The fact that Westinghouse competes with other producers of plywood does not show up in the concentration numbers for the plywood market.

Third, firms switch from one market to another depending on profit opportunities. For example, Motorola, which today produces cellular telephones and other communications products, has diversified from being a TV and computer chip maker. Motorola produces no TVs today. Publishers of newspapers, magazines, and textbooks are today rapidly diversifying into Internet and multimedia products. These switches among industries show that there is much scope for entering and exiting an industry and so measures of concentration have limited usefulness.

Despite their limitations, concentration measures do provide a basis for determining the degree of competition in an industry when they are combined with information about the geographical scope of the market, barriers to entry, and the extent to which large, multiproduct firms straddle a variety of markets.

Market Structures in the U.S. Economy

How competitive are the markets of the United States? Do most U.S. firms operate in competitive markets or in markets with monopoly elements?

Figure 10.3 provides part of the answer to these questions. It shows the market structure of the U.S. economy and the trends in market structure between 1939 and 1980. (Unfortunately, comparable data for the 1980s and 1990s are not available.)

In 1980, three quarters of the value of goods and services bought and sold in the United States was traded in markets that are essentially competitive—markets that have almost perfect competition or monopolistic competition. Monopoly and the dominance of a single firm accounted for about 5 percent of sales. Oligopoly, which is found mainly in manufacturing, accounted for about 18 percent of sales.

Over the period covered by the data in Fig. 10.3, the U.S. economy became increasingly competitive. You can see that the competitive markets have expanded most (the blue areas) and the oligopoly markets have shrunk most (the red areas).

But also, during the past decade, the U.S. economy has become much more exposed to competition from the rest of the world. Figure 10.3 does not capture this international competition.

FIGURE 10.3

The Market Structure of the U.S. Economy

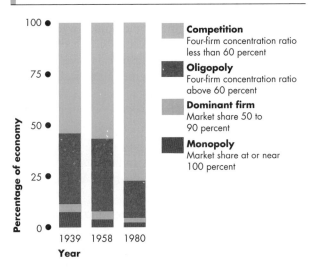

Competition
Four-firm concentration ratio less than 60 percent

Oligopoly
Four-firm concentration ratio above 60 percent

Dominant firm
Market share 50 to 90 percent

Monopoly
Market share at or near 100 percent

Three quarters of the U.S. economy is effectively competitive (perfect competition or monopolistic competition), one fifth is oligopoly, and the rest is monopoly. The economy became more competitive between 1939 and 1980. (Professor Shepherd, whose 1982 study remains the latest word on this topic, suspects that although some industries have become more concentrated, others have become less concentrated, so the net picture has probably not changed much since 1980.)

Source: William G. Shepherd, "Causes of Increased Competition in the U.S. Economy, 1939–1980," *Review of Economics and Statistics,* November 1982, pp. 613–626.

R E V I E W   Q U I Z

- What are the four market types? Explain the distinguishing characteristics of each.
- What are the two measures of concentration? Explain how each measure is calculated.
- Under what conditions do the measures of concentration give a good indication of the degree of competition in a market?
- Is our economy competitive? Is it becoming more competitive or less competitive?

You now know the variety of market structures in our economy and you know how we classify different types of firms and industries into these market types. Our final question in this chapter is what determines the things that firms decide to buy from other firms rather than produce for themselves?

Firms and Markets

AT THE BEGINNING OF THIS CHAPTER, WE DEFINED a firm as an institution that hires productive resources and organizes them to produce and sell goods and services. To organize production, firms coordinate the economic decisions and activities of many individuals. But firms are not the only coordinators of economic decisions. You learned in Chapter 4 that markets also coordinate decisions. By adjusting prices, markets make the decisions of buyers and sellers consistent—make the quantities demanded equal to the quantities supplied for different goods and services.

Markets can coordinate production. An example of market coordination versus firm coordination is the production of a rock concert. A promoter hires a stadium, some stage equipment, audio and video recording engineers and technicians, some rock groups, a superstar, a publicity agent, and a ticket agent—all market transactions—and sells tickets to thousands of rock fans, audio rights to a recording company, and video and broadcasting rights to a television network—another set of market transactions. If rock concerts were produced like corn flakes, the firm producing them would own all the capital used (stadiums, stage, sound and video equipment) and would employ all the labor needed (singers, engineers, salespeople, and so on).

Another example of market coordination versus firm coordination is *outsourcing*. A firm uses outsourcing when it buys parts or products from another firm rather than making them itself. The major automakers use outsourcing for windshields and windows, gearboxes, tires, and many other car parts.

What determines whether a firm or markets coordinate a particular set of activities? How does a firm decide whether to buy from another firm or to make an item itself? The answer is cost. Taking account of the opportunity cost of time as well as the costs of the other inputs, people use the method that costs least. In other words, they use the economically efficient method.

Firms coordinate economic activity when they can perform a task more efficiently than markets can. In such a situation, it is profitable to set up a firm. If markets can perform a task more efficiently than a firm can, people will use markets and any attempt to set up a firm to replace such market coordination will be doomed to failure.

Why Firms?

There are four key reasons why, in many instances, firms are more efficient than markets as coordinators of economic activity. Firms can achieve:

- Lower transactions costs
- Economies of scale
- Economies of scope
- Economies of team production

Transactions Costs The idea that firms exist because there are activities in which they are more efficient than markets was first suggested by University of Chicago economist and Nobel Laureate Ronald Coase. Coase focused on the firm's ability to reduce or eliminate transactions costs. **Transactions costs** are the costs arising from finding someone with whom to do business, of reaching an agreement about the price and other aspects of the exchange, and of ensuring that the terms of the agreement are fulfilled. *Market* transactions require buyers and sellers to get together and to negotiate the terms and conditions of their trading. Sometimes, lawyers have to be hired to draw up contracts. A broken contract leads to still more expenses. A *firm* can lower such transactions costs by reducing the number of individual transactions undertaken.

Consider, for example, two ways of getting your creaking car fixed.

Firm coordination: You take the car to the garage. The garage owner coordinates parts and tools as well as the mechanic's time, and your car gets fixed. You pay one bill for the entire job.

Market coordination: You hire a mechanic who diagnoses the problems and makes a list of the parts and tools needed to fix them. You buy the parts from the local wrecker's yard and rent the tools from ABC Rentals. You hire the mechanic again to fix the problems. You return the tools and pay your bills—wages to the mechanic, rental to ABC, and the cost of the parts used to the wrecker.

What determines the method that you use? The answer is cost. Taking account of the opportunity cost of your own time as well as the costs of the other inputs that you would have to buy, you will use the method that costs least. In other words, you will use the economically efficient method.

The first method requires that you undertake only one transaction with one firm. It's true that the firm has to undertake several transactions—hiring the labor and buying the parts and tools required to do the job. But the firm doesn't have to undertake those transactions simply to fix your car. One set of such transactions enables the firm to fix hundreds of cars. Thus there is an enormous reduction in the number of individual transactions that take place if people get their cars fixed at the garage rather than going through an elaborate sequence of market transactions.

Economies of Scale When the cost of producing a unit of a good falls as its output rate increases, economies of scale exist. Car makers, for example, experience economies of scale because as the scale of production increases, the firm can use cost-saving equipment and highly specialized labor. A car maker that produces only a few cars a year must use costly hand-tool methods. Economies of scale arise from specialization and the division of labor that can be reaped more effectively by firm coordination rather than market coordination.

Economies of Scope A firm experiences **economies of scope** when it uses specialized (and often expensive) resources to produce a *range of goods and services*. For example, Microsoft hires specialist programmers, designers, and marketing experts and uses their skills across a range of software products. As a result, Microsoft coordinates the resources that produce software at a lower cost than an individual can who buys all these services in markets.

Economies of Team Production A production process in which the individuals in a group specialize in mutually supportive tasks is *team production*. Sport provides the best example of team activity. Some team members specialize in pitching and some in batting, some in defense and some in offense. The production of goods and services offers many examples of team activity. For example, production lines in car and TV-manufacturing plants work most efficiently when individual activity is organized in teams, each specializing in a small task. You can also think of an entire firm as being a team. The team has buyers of raw material and other inputs, production workers, and salespeople. There are even specialists within these various groups. Each individual member of the team specializes, but the value of the output of the team and the profit that it earns depend on the coordinated activities of all the team's members. The idea that firms arise as a consequence of the economies of team production was first suggested by Armen Alchian and Harold Demsetz of the University of California at Los Angeles.

Because firms can economize on transactions costs, reap economies of scale, and organize efficient team production, it is firms rather than markets that coordinate most economic activity. But there are limits to the economic efficiency of firms. If a firm becomes too big or too diversified in the things that it seeks to do, the cost of management and monitoring per unit of output begins to rise, and at some point, the market becomes more efficient at coordinating the use of resources. IBM is an example of a firm that became too big to be efficient. In an attempt to restore efficient operations, IBM split up its large organization into a number of "Baby Blues," each of which specializes in a segment of the computer market.

Sometimes, firms enter into long-term relationships with each other that effectively cut out ordinary market transactions and make it difficult to see where one firm ends and another begins. For example, GM has long-term relationships with suppliers of windows, tires, and other parts. Wal-Mart has long-term relationships with suppliers of the goods it sells in its stores. Such relationships make transactions costs lower than they would be if GM or Wal-Mart went shopping on the open market each time it wanted new supplies.

R E V I E W   Q U I Z

- What are the two ways in which economic activity can be coordinated?
- What determines whether a firm or markets coordinate production?
- What are the main reasons why firms can often coordinate production at a lower cost than markets?

Reading Between the Lines on pp. 214–215 explores the economic problem faced by Levi Strauss, the firm that produces denim jeans. We continue to study firms and their decisions in the next four chapters. In Chapter 11, we learn about the relationships between cost and output at different output levels. These cost-output relationships are common to all types of firms in all types of markets. We then turn to problems that are special to firms in different types of markets—perfect competition in Chapter 12, monopoly in Chapter 13, and monopolistic competition and oligopoly in Chapter 14.

Levi Strauss's Economic Problem

THE WALL STREET JOURNAL, FEBRUARY 23, 1999

Levi Strauss to Close One-Half of Plants in North America, Cut Staff in Area

BY REBECCA QUICK

Taking the ax to its operations for the second time in just over a year, Levi Strauss and Co. said it will close half of its 22 manufacturing plants in North America, laying off about 5,900 employees, or 30% of its total in the U.S. and Canada. ...

The ... denim empire has seen sales of its pioneering jeans shrink, caught in a market squeeze between trendy, expensive jeans from designers like Ralph Lauren, and cheaper brands from department stores like J.C. Penney. Since 1990, Levi's market share of men's jeans dropped to 25% from 48%, according to Tactical Retail Solutions, a market-research firm in New York. And last week, Levi Strauss said its sales slumped 13% in 1998, to $6 billion from $6.9 billion a year earlier. ...

But the company said the latest round of closings wouldn't lower its production because it intends to shift much of the work to independent contractors in other countries. Many of Levi Strauss's competitors, including Guess and Tommy Hilfiger, have most if not all of their jeans produced overseas. There, labor costs are frequently much lower than the $10.12 an hour in wages and benefits paid to the average U.S. garment worker.

Aside from chopping its labor bills, Levi Strauss said it will also be able to reduce the time it takes to get apparel into stores. "The drawback to owning your own plant is that changing the line a plant produces is very time- and cost-consuming," said Clarence Grebey, a spokesman for Levi Strauss. "If we go to contractors to do that, we can get our consumers into the product more quickly." ...

Copyright © 1999 Dow Jones & Company, Inc. Reprinted with permission. Further reproduction prohibited.

Essence of the Story

- Since 1990, Levi Strauss and Company's share of the market for men's jeans has shrunk from 48 percent to 25 percent as the market shares of designer and department store brands have expanded.

- Most of Levi's competitors produce their jeans overseas, where labor costs are lower than those in the United States.

- Levi plans to cut production in North America and transfer the work to independent contractors in other countries.

- Beside cutting labor costs, Levi says that it can get its products into stores more quickly from contractors than from its own plants.

Economic Analysis

■ Figure 1 shows how Levi Strauss's market share has shrunk from 48 percent to 25 percent, squeezed by designer brands (such as Calvin Klein, Tommy Hilfiger, Mossimo, Ralph Lauren, and Donna Karan) and other brands (such as Lee, Wrangler, and The Gap) and store brands (such as J.C. Penney and Sears).

■ The predicament faced by Levi Strauss illustrates all the aspects of the firm and its economic problem as described in this chapter.

■ Levi Strauss and Company is in business to maximize profit. The firm might engage in philanthropic acts, but to do so, it must first maximize profit.

■ During the 1990s, the market for jeans became more competitive and the company's profit was squeezed.

■ Most large suppliers of jeans are publicly owned companies with many stockholders. Levi Strauss is a privately owned company that remains under the control of the descendants of Levi Strauss, who created the firm more than 100 years ago.

■ Jeans can be supplied to the consumer at the lowest possible cost if some firms specialize in *designing* jeans, some in *manufacturing* jeans, some in *marketing,* and some in *information* services.

■ The technology for *designing* and *marketing* jeans is sophisticated and uses the latest information systems. Firms link computers to retailers to manage inventories and use the Internet to obtain customers' measurements.

■ The technology for *manufacturing* jeans involves a small number of operations and basic parts. It uses simple machines and relatively low-skilled labor.

■ Because of the technology for manufacturing jeans, they can be made at least cost in countries that have low labor costs and by achieving economies from long production runs of one particular type of jeans.

■ By closing some of its factories in North America and buying jeans from specialist manufacturers, Levi Strauss is capturing these cost savings and economies.

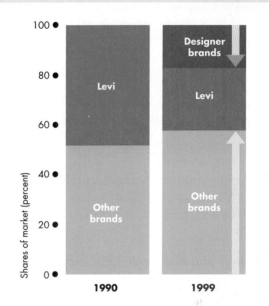

Figure 1 Levi Strauss's share shrinks

SUMMARY

KEY POINTS

The Firm and Its Economic Problem (pp. 198–200)

- Firms hire and organize resources to produce and sell goods and services.
- Firms seek to maximize economic profit, which is total revenue minus opportunity cost.
- Technology, information, and markets limit a firm's profit.

Technology and Economic Efficiency (pp. 201–202)

- A method of production is technologically efficient when it is not possible to increase output without using more inputs.
- A method of production is economically efficient when the cost of producing a given output is as low as possible.

Information and Organization (pp. 203–206)

- Firms use a combination of command systems and incentive systems to organize production.
- Faced with incomplete information and uncertainty, firms induce managers and workers to perform in ways consistent with the firm's goals.
- Proprietorships, partnerships, and corporations use ownership, incentives, and long-term contracts to cope with the principal-agent problem.

Markets and the Competitive Environment (pp. 207–211)

- Perfect competition occurs when there are many buyers and sellers of an identical product and when new firms can easily enter a market.
- Monopolistic competition occurs when a large number of firms compete with each other by making slightly different products.
- Oligopoly is a situation in which a small number of firms compete with each other.
- Monopoly is a firm that produces a good or service for which there are no close substitutes and that is protected by a barrier that prevents the entry of competitors.

Firms and Markets (pp. 212–213)

- Firms coordinate economic activities when they can perform a task more efficiently—at lower cost—than markets can.
- Firms economize on transactions costs and achieve the benefits of economies of scale, economies of scope, and economies of team production.

KEY FIGURE AND TABLES ◆

KEY TERMS

PROBLEMS

*1. One year ago, Jack and Jill set up a vinegar bottling firm (called JJVB). Use the following information to calculate JJVB's explicit costs and implicit costs during its first year of operation:
   a. Jack and Jill put $50,000 of their own money into the firm.
   b. They bought equipment for $30,000.
   c. They hired one employee to help them for an annual wage of $20,000.
   d. Jack gave up his previous job, at which he earned $30,000, and spent all his time working for JJVB.
   e. Jill kept her old job, which paid $30 an hour, but gave up 10 hours of leisure each week (for 50 weeks) to work for JJVB.
   f. JJVB bought $10,000 of goods and services from other firms.
   g. The market value of the equipment at the end of the year was $28,000.

2. One year ago, Ms Moffat and Mr. Spieder opened a cheese firm (called MSCF). Use the following information to calculate MSCF's explicit costs and implicit costs during its first year of operation:
   a. Moffat and Spieder put $70,000 of their own money into the firm.
   b. They bought equipment for $40,000.
   c. They hired one employee to help them for an annual wage of $18,000.
   d. Moffat gave up her previous job, at which she earned $22,000, and spent all her time working for MSCF.
   e. Spieder kept his old job, which paid $20 an hour, but gave up 20 hours of leisure each week (for 50 weeks) to work for MSCF.
   f. MSCF bought $5,000 of goods from other firms.
   g. The market value of the equipment at the end of the year was $37,000.

*3. Four methods for doing a tax return are: personal computer, pocket calculator, pocket calculator with pencil and paper, pencil and paper. With a PC, the job takes an hour; with a pocket calculator, it takes 12 hours; with a pocket calculator and pencil and paper, it takes 12 hours; and with a pencil and paper, it takes 16 hours. The PC and its software cost $1,000, the pocket calculator costs $10, and the pencil and paper cost $1.
   a. Which, if any, of the methods is technologically efficient?
   b. Which method is economically efficient if the wage rate is
      (i) $5 an hour?
      (ii) $50 an hour?
      (iiii) $500 an hour?

4. Sue can do her accounting assignment by using: a personal computer; a pocket calculator; a pocket calculator and a pencil and paper; or a pencil and paper. With a PC, Sue completes the job in half an hour; with a pocket calculator, it takes 4 hours; with a pocket calculator and with a pencil and paper, it takes 5 hours; and with a pencil and paper, it takes 14 hours. The PC and its software cost $2,000, the pocket calculator costs $15, and the pencil and paper cost $3.
   a. Which, if any, of the methods is technologically efficient?
   b. Which method is economically efficient if Sue's wage rate is
      (i) $10 an hour?
      (ii) $20 an hour?
      (iii) $50 an hour?

*5. Alternative ways of laundering 100 shirts are:

Method	Labor (hours)	Capital (machines)
a	1	10
b	5	8
c	20	4
d	50	1

   a. Which methods are technologically efficient?
   b. Which method is economically efficient if:
      (i)   The wage rate is $1 an hour and the rental cost of a machine is $100 an hour?
      (ii) The wage rate is $5 an hour and the rental cost of a machine is $50 an hour?
      (iii) The wage rate is $50 an hour and the rental cost of a machine is $5 an hour?

6. Alternative ways of making 100 shirts a day are:

Method	Labor (hours)	Capital (machines)
a	10	50
b	20	40
c	50	20
d	100	10

a. Which methods are technologically efficient?
b. Which method is economically efficient if the hourly wage rate and rental rate are:
  (i) Wage rate $1, rental rate $100
  (ii) Wage rate $5, rental rate $50
  (iii) Wage rate $50, rental rate $5

*7. Sales of the firms in the tattoo industry are:

Firm	Sales (dollars)
Bright Spots	450
Freckles	325
Love Galore	250
Native Birds	200
Other 15 firms	800

a. Calculate the four firm concentration ratio.
b. What is the structure of the tattoo industry?

8. Sales of the firms in the pet food industry are:

Firm	Sales (thousands of dollars)
Big Collar, Inc.	50
Shiny Coat, Inc.	75
Friendly Pet, Inc.	60
Nature's Way, Inc.	65
Other 8 firms	400

a. Calculate the four firm concentration ratio.
b. What is the structure of the industry?

*9. Market shares of chocolate makers are:

Firm	Market share (percent)
Mayfair, Inc.	15
Bond, Inc.	10
Magic, Inc.	20
All Natural, Inc.	15
Truffles, Inc.	25
Gold, Inc.	15

a. Calculate the Herfindahl-Hirschman Index.
b. What is the structure of the industry?

10. Market shares of mat makers are:

Firm	Market share (percent)
Made-to-Last, Inc.	20
Big Wheel, Inc.	17
Magic Carpet, Inc.	22
Supreme, Inc.	17
Copra, Inc.	24

a. Calculate the Herfindahl-Hirschman Index.
b. What is the structure of the industry?

CRITICAL THINKING

 1. Study the news article about Levi Strauss and Company in *Reading Between the Lines* on pp. 214–215 and then:
a. Describe the economic problem that the firm faced in 1998.
b. Use the links on the Parkin Web site to find information about some of Levi Strauss's main competitors. What do you think the economic problems of these competitors are?
c. Do you think the market for blue jeans is an example of monopoly, oligopoly, monopolistic competition, or perfect competition? Explain your answer.
d. Use the links on the Parkin Web site to find information about *where* Levi Strauss and Company is closing factories. For the factory nearest to you, what special problems do you think will arise?
e. Compare and contrast how Levi Strauss achieves technological efficiency and economic efficiency.
f. If more and more manufacturing leaves the United States and goes to other countries, what do you think the effect will be on the U.S. economy? (Hint: Think about the *PPF* and efficiency.)

2. Use the links on the Parkin Web site to obtain information about the auto industry.
a. What are the main economic problems faced by auto producers?
b. Why are auto producers merging?

3. Use the links on the Parkin Web site to obtain information about the steel industry. Then describe the main economic problems faced by steel producers and explain why they are seeking protection from international competition.

Chapter 11

Output and Costs

Survival of the Fittest

Size does not guarantee survival in business. Of the 100 largest companies in the United States in 1917, only 22 still remained in that league in 1997. But remaining small does not guarantee survival either. Every year, millions of small businesses close down. Call a random selection of restaurants and fashion boutiques from *last* year's yellow pages and see how many have vanished. What does a firm have to do to be one of the survivors? ◆ Firms differ in lots of ways—from Mom and Pop's convenience store to multinational giants producing hi-tech goods. But regardless of their size or what they produce, all firms must decide how much to produce and how to produce it. How do firms make these decisions? ◆ Most car makers in the United States can produce more cars than they can sell. Why do car makers have expensive equipment lying around that isn't fully used? Many electric utilities in the United States don't have enough production equipment on hand to meet demand on the coldest and hottest days and must buy power from other producers. Why don't these firms install more equipment so that they can supply the market themselves?

◆ In this chapter we are going to answer these questions. To do so, we will study the economic decisions of a small, imaginary firm— Sidney's Sweaters, Inc., a producer of knitted sweaters. The firm is owned and operated by Sidney. By studying the economic problems of Sidney's Sweaters and the way in which Sidney copes with them, we will get a clear view of the problems that face *all* firms—small ones like Sidney's Sweaters as well as the giants. We're going to begin by setting the scene and describing the time frames in which Sidney makes his business decisions.

After studying this chapter, you will be able to:

- Distinguish between the short run and the long run
- Explain the relationship between a firm's output and labor employed in the short run
- Explain the relationship between a firm's output and costs in the short run
- Derive and explain a firm's short-run cost curves
- Explain the relationship between a firm's output and costs in the long run
- Derive and explain a firm's long-run average cost curve

Decision Time Frames

PEOPLE WHO OPERATE FIRMS MAKE MANY DECI-sions. All of the decisions are aimed at one overriding objective: maximum attainable profit. But the decisions are not all equally critical. Some of the decisions are big ones. Once made, they are costly (or impossible) to reverse. If such a decision turns out to be incorrect, it might lead to the failure of the firm. Some of the decisions are small ones. They are easily changed. If one of these decisions turns out to be incorrect, the firm can change its actions and survive.

The biggest decision that any firm makes is what industry to enter. For most entrepreneurs, their background knowledge and interests drive this decision. But the decision also depends on profit prospects. No one sets up a firm without believing that it will be profitable. And profit depends on total revenue and opportunity cost (see Chapter 10, pp. 198–199).

The firm that we study has already chosen the industry in which to operate. It has also chosen its most effective method of organization. But it has not decided the quantity to produce, the quantities of resources to hire, or the price at which to sell its output.

Decisions about the quantity to produce and the price to charge depend on the type of market in which the firm operates. Perfect competition, monopolistic competition, oligopoly, and monopoly all confront the firm with their own special problems.

But decisions about how to produce a given output do not depend on the type of market in which the firm operates. These decisions are similar for *all* types of firms in *all* types of markets.

The actions that a firm can take to influence the relationship between output and cost depend on how soon the firm wants to act. A firm that plans to change its output rate tomorrow has fewer options than one that plans to change its output rate six months from now.

To study the relationship between a firm's output decision and its costs, we distinguish two decision time frames:

- The short run
- The long run

The Short Run

The **short run** is a time frame in which the quantities of some resources are fixed. For most firms, the fixed resources are the firm's buildings and capital. The management organization and the technology it uses are also fixed in the short run. We call the collection of fixed resources the firm's *plant*. So in the short run, a firm's plant is fixed.

For Sidney's Sweaters, the fixed plant is its factory building and its knitting machines. For an electric power utility, the fixed plant is its buildings, generators, computers, and control systems. For an airport, the fixed plant is the runways, terminal buildings, and traffic control facilities.

To increase output in the short run, a firm must increase the quantity of variable inputs it uses. Labor is usually the variable input. So to produce more output, Sidney's Sweaters must hire more labor and operate its knitting machines for more hours per day. Similarly, an electric power utility must hire more labor and operate its generators for more hours per day. And an airport must hire more labor and operate its runways, terminals, and traffic control facilities for more hours per day.

Short-run decisions are easily reversed. The firm can increase or decrease output in the short run by increasing or decreasing the labor hours it hires.

The Long Run

The **long run** is a time frame in which the quantities of *all* resources can be varied. That is, the long run is a period in which the firm can change its *plant*.

To increase output in the long run, a firm is able to choose whether to change its plant as well as whether to increase the quantity of labor it hires. Sidney's Sweaters can decide whether to install some additional knitting machines, use a new type of machine, reorganize its management, or hire more labor. An electric power utility can decide whether to to install more generators. And an airport can decide whether to build more runways, terminals, and traffic control facilities.

Long-run decisions are *not* easily reversed. Once a plant decision is made, the firm must live with it for some time. To emphasize this fact, we call the *past* cost of buying a new plant a **sunk cost**. A sunk cost is irrelevant to the firm's decisions. The only costs that influence its decisions are the short-run cost of changing its labor inputs and the long-run cost of changing its plant in the future.

We're going to study costs in the short run and the long run. We begin with the short run and describe the technology constraint the firm faces.

Short-Run Technology Constraint

TO INCREASE OUTPUT IN THE SHORT RUN, A FIRM must increase the quantity of labor employed. We describe the relationship between output and the quantity of labor employed by using three related concepts:

- Total product
- Marginal product
- Average product

These product concepts can be illustrated either by product schedules or product curves. Let's look first at the product schedules.

TABLE 11.1
Total Product, Marginal Product, and Average Product

	Labor (workers per day)	Total product (sweaters per day)	Marginal product (sweaters per additional worker)	Average product (sweaters per worker)
a	0	0		
			4	
b	1	4		4.00
			6	
c	2	10		5.00
			3	
d	3	13		4.33
			2	
e	4	15		3.75
			1	
f	5	16		3.20

Total product is the total amount produced. Marginal product is the change in total product that results from a one-unit increase in labor. For example, when labor increases from 2 to 3 workers a day (row c to row d), total product increases from 10 to 13 sweaters. (Marginal product is shown between the rows to emphasize that it is the result of changing labor.) The marginal product of going from 2 to 3 workers is 3 sweaters. Average product is total product divided by the quantity of labor employed. For example, the average product of 3 workers is 4.33 sweaters per worker (13 sweaters a day divided by 3 workers).

Product Schedules

Table 11.1 shows some data that describe Sidney's Sweaters' total product, marginal product, and average product. The numbers tell us how Sidney's Sweaters' production increases as more workers are employed. They also tell us about the productivity of Sidney's Sweaters' labor force.

Focus first on the columns headed "Labor" and "Total product." **Total product** is the total quantity Sidney produced. You can see from the numbers in these columns that as Sidney employs more labor, total product increases. For example, when Sidney employs 1 worker, total product is 4 sweaters a day and when it employs 2 workers, total product is 10 sweaters a day. Each increase in the workers employed brings an increase in total product.

Marginal product tells us by how much total product increases when employment increases. The **marginal product** of labor is the increase in total product that results from a one-unit increase in the quantity of labor employed. For example, in Table 11.1, when Sidney increases employment from 2 to 3 workers, marginal product is 3 sweaters—total product goes from 10 to 13 sweaters.

Average product tells how productive workers are on the average. The **average product** of labor is equal to total product divided by the quantity of labor employed. For example, in Table 11.1, the average product of 3 workers is 4.33 sweaters per worker—13 sweaters a day divided by 3 workers.

If you look closely at the numbers in Table 11.1, you can see some patterns. For example, as labor increases, marginal product at first increases and then begins to decrease. For example, marginal product increases from 4 sweaters to 6 sweaters a day when the second worker is hired and then decreases to 3 sweaters a day when the third worker is hired. Average product also at first increases and then decreases. The relationships between employment and the three product concepts can be seen more clearly by looking at the product curves.

Product Curves

The product curves are graphs of the relationships between employment and the three product concepts you've just studied. They show how total product, marginal product, and average product change as employment changes. They also show the relationships among the three concepts. Let's look at the product curves.

Total Product Curve

Figure 11.1 shows Sidney's Sweaters' total product curve, *TP*. As employment increases, so does the number of sweaters knitted. Points *a* through *f* on the curve correspond to the same rows in Table 11.1.

The total product curve is similar to the *production possibility frontier* (explained in Chapter 3). It separates the attainable output levels from those that are unattainable. All the points that lie above the curve are unattainable. Points that lie below the curve, in the orange area, are attainable. But they are inefficient—they use more labor than is necessary to produce a given output. Only the points *on* the total product curve are technologically efficient.

Notice especially the shape of the total product curve. As employment increases from zero to 1 worker per day, the curve becomes steeper. Then, as employment continues to increase to 3, 4, and 5 workers a day, the curve becomes less steep. The steeper the slope of the total product curve, the greater is marginal product, as you are about to see.

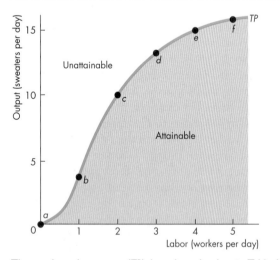

FIGURE 11.1

Total Product Curve

The total product curve (*TP*), based on the data in Table 11.1, shows how the quantity of sweaters produced changes as the quantity of labor employed changes. For example, 2 workers can produce 10 sweaters a day (point *c*). Points *a* through *f* on the curve correspond to the rows of Table 11.1. The total product curve separates attainable outputs from unattainable outputs. Points below the *TP* curve are inefficient.

Marginal Product Curve

Figure 11.2 shows Sidney's Sweaters' marginal product of labor. Part (a) reproduces the total product curve, which is the same as the total product curve in Fig. 11.1. Part (b) shows the marginal product curve, *MP*.

In part (a), the orange bars illustrate the marginal product of labor. The height of each bar measures marginal product. Marginal product is also measured by the slope of the total product curve. Recall that the slope of a curve is the change in the value of the variable measured on the *y*-axis—output—divided by the change in the variable measured on the *x*-axis—labor input—as we move along the curve. A one-unit increase in labor input, from 2 to 3 workers, increases output from 10 to 13 sweaters, so the slope from point *c* to point *d* is 3, the same as the marginal product that we've just calculated.

We've calculated the marginal product of labor for a series of unit increases in the quantity of labor. But labor is divisible into smaller units than one person. It is divisible into hours and even minutes. By varying the amount of labor in the smallest imaginable units, we can draw the marginal product curve shown in Fig. 11.2(b). The *height* of this curve measures the *slope* of the total curve at a point. Part (a) shows that an increase in employment from 2 to 3 workers increases output from 10 to 13 sweaters (an increase of 3). The increase in output of 3 sweaters appears on the vertical axis of part (b) as the marginal product of going from 2 to 3 workers. We plot that marginal product at the midpoint between 2 and 3 workers. Notice that marginal product shown in Fig. 11.2(b) reaches a peak at 1.5 units of labor, and at that point, marginal product is 6 sweaters. The peak occurs at 1.5 units of labor because the total product curve is steepest when employment increases from 1 to 2 workers.

The total product and marginal product curves are different for different firms and different types of goods. Ford Motor Company's product curves are different from those of Jim's Burger Stand, which in turn are different from those of Sidney's sweater factory. But the shapes of the product curves are similar, because almost every production process has two features:

■ Increasing marginal returns initially
■ Diminishing marginal returns eventually

Increasing Marginal Returns Increasing marginal returns occur when the marginal product of an additional worker exceeds the marginal product of the

FIGURE 11.2
Marginal Product

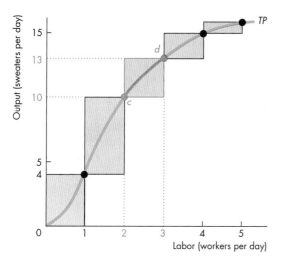

(a) Total product

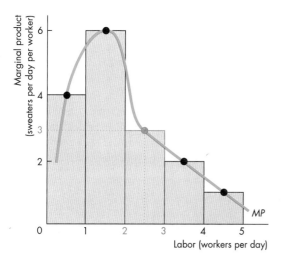

(b) Marginal product

Marginal product is illustrated by the orange bars. For example, when labor increases from 2 to 3, marginal product is the orange bar whose height is 3 sweaters. (Marginal product is shown midway between the labor inputs to emphasize that it is the result of *changing* inputs.) The steeper the slope of the total product curve (*TP*) in part (a), the larger is marginal product (*MP*) in part (b). Marginal product increases to a maximum (in this example, when the second worker is employed) and then declines—diminishing marginal returns.

previous worker. Increasing marginal returns arise from increased specialization and division of labor in the production process.

For example, if Sidney employs just one worker, that person must learn all the aspects of sweater production: running the knitting machines, fixing breakdowns, packaging and mailing sweaters, buying and checking the type and color of the wool. All these tasks must be performed by that one person.

If Sidney hires a second person, the two workers can specialize in different parts of the production process. As a result, two workers produce more than twice as much as one. The marginal product of the second worker is greater than the marginal product of the first worker. Marginal returns are increasing.

Diminishing Marginal Returns Most production processes experience increasing marginal returns initially. But all production processes eventually reach a point of *diminishing* marginal returns. **Diminishing marginal returns** occur when the marginal product of an additional worker is less than the marginal product of the previous worker.

Diminishing marginal returns arise from the fact that more and more workers are using the same capital and working in the same space. As more workers are added, there is less and less for the additional workers to do that is productive. For example, if Sidney hires a third worker, output increases but not by as much as it did when he hired the second worker. In this case, after two workers are hired, all gains from specialization and the division of labor have been exhausted. By hiring a third worker, the factory produces more sweaters but the equipment is being operated closer to its limits. There are even times when the third worker has nothing to do because the machines are running without the need for further attention. Adding yet more and more workers continues to increase output but by successively smaller amounts. Marginal returns are diminishing. This phenomenon is such a pervasive one that it is called a "law"—"the law of diminishing returns." The **law of diminishing returns** states that

As a firm uses more of a variable input, with a given quantity of fixed inputs, the marginal product of the variable input eventually diminishes.

We are going to return to the law of diminishing returns when we study a firm's costs. But before we do that, let's look at the average product of labor and the average product curve.

Average Product Curve

Figure 11.3 illustrates Sidney's Sweaters' average product of labor, *AP*. It also shows the relationship between average product and marginal product. Points *b* through *f* on the average product curve correspond to those same rows in Table 11.1. Average product increases from 1 to 2 workers (its maximum value at point *c*) but then decreases as yet more workers are employed. Notice also that average product is largest when average product and marginal product are equal. That is, the marginal product curve cuts the average product curve at the point of maximum average product. For employment levels at which marginal product exceeds average product, average product is increasing. For employment levels at which marginal product is less than average product, average product is decreasing.

The relationship between the average and marginal product curves is a general feature of the relationship between the average and marginal values of any variable. Let's look at a familiar example.

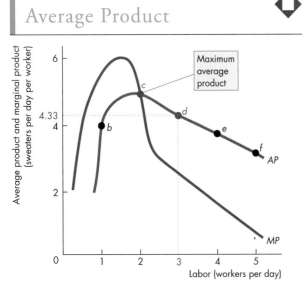

FIGURE 11.3

Average Product

The figure shows the average product and the connection between the average product and marginal product. With 1 worker, marginal product exceeds average product, so average product is increasing. With 2 workers, marginal product equals average product, so average product is at its maximum. With more than 2 workers, marginal product is less than average product, so average product is decreasing.

Marginal Grade and Grade Point Average

To see the relationship between average product and marginal product, think about the similar relationship between Sidney's average grade and marginal grade over five semesters. (Suppose that Sidney is a part-time student who takes just one course each semester.) In the first semester, Sidney takes calculus and his grade is a 2. This grade is his marginal grade. It is also his average grade—his GPA. In the next semester, Sidney takes French and gets a 3. French is Sidney's marginal course, and his marginal grade is 3. His GPA rises to 2.5. Because his marginal grade exceeds his average grade, it pulls his average up. In the third semester, Sidney takes economics and gets a 4—his new marginal grade. Because his marginal grade exceeds his GPA, it again pulls his average up. Sidney's GPA is now 3, the average of 2, 3, and 4. The fourth semester, he takes history and gets a 3. Because his marginal grade is equal to his average, his GPA does not change. In the fifth semester, Sidney takes English and gets a 2. Because his marginal grade, a 2, is below his GPA of 3, his GPA falls.

This everyday relationship between marginal and average values agrees with that between marginal and average product. Sidney's GPA increases when his marginal grade exceeds his GPA. His GPA falls when his marginal grade is below his GPA. And his GPA is constant when his marginal grade equals his GPA. The relationship between marginal product and average product is exactly the same as that between Sidney's marginal and average grades.

REVIEW QUIZ

- Explain how the marginal product of labor and the average product of labor change as the quantity of labor employed increases (a) initially and (b) eventually.
- What is the law of diminishing returns? Why does marginal product eventually diminish?
- Explain the relationship between marginal product and average product. How does average product change when marginal product exceeds average product? How does average product change when average product exceeds marginal product? Why?

Sidney cares about his product curves because they influence his costs. Let's look at Sidney's costs.

Short-Run Cost

To PRODUCE MORE OUTPUT IN THE SHORT RUN, a firm must employ more labor, which means it must increase its costs. We describe the relationship between output and cost by using three cost concepts:

- Total cost
- Marginal cost
- Average cost

Total Cost

A firm's **total cost** (*TC*) is the cost of all the productive resources it uses. Total cost includes the cost of land, capital, and labor. It also includes the cost of entrepreneurship, which is *normal profit* (see Chapter 10, p. 199). We divide total cost into total fixed cost and total variable cost.

Total fixed cost (*TFC*) is the cost of all the firm's fixed inputs. Because the quantity of a fixed input does not change as output changes, fixed cost does not change as output changes.

Total variable cost (*TVC*) is the cost of all the firm's variable inputs. Because a firm must change the quantity of variable inputs to change its output, total variable cost changes as output changes.

Total cost is the sum of total fixed cost and total variable cost. That is,

$$TC = TFC + TVC.$$

The table in Fig. 11.4 shows Sidney's total costs. With one knitting machine that costs $25 a day, *TFC* is $25. To produce more sweaters, Sidney hires more labor, which costs $25 a day. *TVC*, which increases as output increases, is the number of workers multiplied by $25. For example, to produce 13 sweaters a day, Sidney hires 3 workers and *TVC* is $75. *TC* is the sum of *TFC* and *TVC*, so to produce 13 sweaters a day, Sidney's total cost, *TC*, is $100. Check the calculation in each row of the table.

Figure 11.4 graphs Sidney's total cost curves. These curves graph total cost against output. The green total fixed cost curve (*TFC*) is horizontal because total fixed cost does not change when output changes. It is a constant at $25. The purple total variable cost curve (*TVC*) and the blue total cost curve (*TC*) both increase with output. The vertical distance between the *TVC* and *TC* curve is total fixed cost as shown by the arrows.

Let's now look at Sidney's Sweaters' marginal cost.

FIGURE 11.4

Total Cost Curves

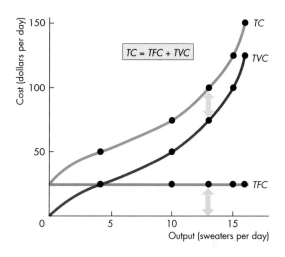

	Labor (workers per day)	Output (sweaters per day)	Total fixed cost (*TFC*)	Total variable cost (*TVC*)	Total cost (*TC*)
			(dollars per day)		
a	0	0	25	0	25
b	1	4	25	25	50
c	2	10	25	50	75
d	3	13	25	75	100
e	4	15	25	100	125
f	5	16	25	125	150

Sidney rents a knitting machine for $25 a day. This amount is Sidney's Sweaters' total fixed cost. Sidney hires workers at a wage rate of $25 a day, and this cost is Sidney's Sweaters' total variable cost. For example, if Sidney employs 3 workers, total variable cost is (3 × $25), which equals $75. Total cost is the sum of total fixed cost and total variable cost. For example, when Sidney employs 3 workers, total cost is $100—total fixed cost of $25 plus total variable cost of $75. The graph shows Sidney's Sweaters' total cost curves. Total fixed cost (*TFC*) is constant—it graphs as a horizontal line—and total variable cost (*TVC*) increases as output increases. Total cost (*TC*) also increases as output increases. The vertical distance between the total cost curve and the total variable cost curve is total fixed cost, as illustrated by the two arrows.

Marginal Cost

In Fig. 11.4, total variable cost and total cost increase at a decreasing rate at small levels of output and then begin to increase at an increasing rate as output increases. To understand these patterns in the changes in total cost, we need to use the concept of *marginal cost*.

A firm's **marginal cost** is the increase in total cost that results from a one-unit increase in output. We calculate marginal cost as the increase in total cost divided by the increase in output. The table in Fig. 11.5 shows this calculation. When, for example, output increases from 10 sweaters to 13 sweaters, total cost increases from $75 to $100. The change in output is 3 sweaters, and the change in total cost is $25. The marginal cost of one of those 3 sweaters is ($25 ÷ 3), which equals $8.33.

Figure 11.5 graphs the marginal cost data in the table as the red marginal cost curve, *MC*. This curve is U-shaped because, when Sidney hires a second worker, marginal cost decreases, but when he hires a third, a fourth, and a fifth worker, marginal cost successively increases.

Marginal cost decreases at small outputs because of economies from greater specialization. It eventually increases because of *the law of diminishing returns*. The law of diminishing returns means that each additional worker produces a successively smaller addition to output. So to get an additional unit of output, ever more workers are required. Because more workers are required to produce one additional unit of output, the cost of the additional output—marginal cost—must eventually increase.

Marginal cost tells us how total cost changes as output changes. The final cost concept tells us what it costs, on the average, to produce a unit of output. Let's now look at Sidney's Sweaters' average costs.

Average Cost

There are three average costs:

1. Average fixed cost
2. Average variable cost
3. Average total cost

Average fixed cost (*AFC*) is total fixed cost per unit of output. **Average variable cost** (*AVC*) is total variable cost per unit of output. **Average**

total cost (*ATC*) is total cost per unit output. The average cost concepts are calculated from the total cost concepts as follows:

$$TC = TFC + TVC.$$

Divide each total cost term by the quantity produced, *Q*, to give

$$\frac{TC}{Q} = \frac{TFC}{Q} + \frac{TVC}{Q}$$

or

$$ATC = AFC + AVC.$$

The table in Fig. 11.5 shows the calculation of average total cost. For example, when output is 10 sweaters, average fixed cost is ($25 ÷ 10), which equals $2.50, average variable cost is ($50 ÷ 10), which equals $5.00, and average total cost is ($75 ÷ 10), which equals $7.50. Note that average total cost is equal to average fixed cost ($2.50) plus average variable cost ($5.00).

Figure 11.5 shows the average cost curves. The green average fixed cost curve (*AFC*) slopes downward. As output increases, the same constant fixed cost is spread over a larger output. The blue average total cost curve (*ATC*) and the purple average variable cost curve (*AVC*) are U-shaped. The vertical distance between the average total cost and average variable cost curves is equal to average fixed cost—as indicated by the two arrows. That distance shrinks as output increases because average fixed cost declines with increasing output.

The marginal cost curve intersects the average variable cost curve and the average total cost curve at their minimum points. That is, when marginal cost is less than average cost, average cost is decreasing, and when marginal cost exceeds average cost, average cost is increasing. This relationship holds for both the *ATC* curve and the *AVC* curve and is another example of the relationship you saw in Figure 11.3 for average product and marginal product and in Sidney's course grades.

Why the Average Total Cost Curve Is U-Shaped

Average total cost, *ATC*, is the sum of average fixed cost, *AFC*, and average variable cost, *AVC*. So the shape of the *ATC* curve combines the shapes of the *AFC* and *AVC* curves. The U-shape of the average

FIGURE 11.5

Marginal Cost and Average Costs

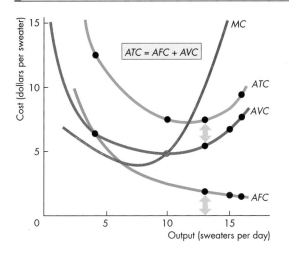

Marginal cost is calculated as the change in total cost divided by the change in output. When output increases from 4 to 10 sweaters, an increase of 6, total cost increases by $25 and marginal cost is $25 ÷ 6, which equals $4.17. Each average cost concept is calculated by dividing the related total cost by output. When 10 sweaters are produced, AFC is $2.50 ($25 ÷ 10), AVC is $5 ($50 ÷ 10), and ATC is $7.50 ($75 ÷ 10).

The figure shows the marginal cost curve and the average cost curves. The marginal cost curve (MC) is U-shaped and intersects the average variable cost curve and the average total cost curve at their minimum points. Average fixed cost (AFC) decreases as output increases. The average total cost curve (ATC) and average variable cost curve (AVC) are U-shaped. The vertical distance between these two curves is equal to average fixed cost, as illustrated by the two arrows.

	Labor (workers per day)	Output (sweaters per day)	Total fixed cost (TFC)	Total variable cost (TVC)	Total cost (TC)	Marginal cost (MC) (dollars per additional sweater)	Average fixed cost (AFC)	Average variable cost (AVC)	Average total cost (ATC)
				(dollars per day)				(dollars per sweater)	
a	0	0	25	0	25		—	—	—
						.... 6.25			
b	1	4	25	25	50		6.25	6.25	12.50
						.... 4.17			
c	2	10	25	50	75		2.50	5.00	7.50
						.... 8.33			
d	3	13	25	75	100		1.92	5.77	7.69
						.... 12.50			
e	4	15	25	100	125		1.67	6.67	8.33
						.... 25.00			
f	5	16	25	125	150		1.56	7.81	9.38

total cost curve arises from the influence of two opposing forces:

- Spreading fixed cost over a larger output
- Eventually diminishing returns

When output increases, the firm spreads its fixed costs over a larger output and its average fixed cost decreases—its average fixed cost curve slopes downward.

Diminishing returns means that as output increases, ever-larger amounts of labor are needed to produce an additional unit of output. So average

variable cost eventually increases, and the AVC curve eventually slopes upward.

The shape of the average total cost curve combines these two effects. Initially, as output increases, both average fixed cost and average variable cost decrease, so average total cost decreases and the ATC curve slopes downward. But as output increases further and diminishing returns set in, average variable cost begins to increase. Eventually, average variable cost increases more quickly than average fixed cost decreases, so average total cost increases and the ATC curve slopes upward.

Cost Curves and Product Curves

The technology that a firm uses determines its costs. Figure 11.6 shows the links between the firm's technology constraint (its product curves) and its cost curves. The upper part of the figure shows the average product curve and the marginal product curve—like those in Fig. 11.3. The lower part of the figure shows the average variable cost curve and the marginal cost curve—like those in Fig. 11.5.

The figure highlights the links between technology and costs. As labor increases initially, marginal product and average product rise and marginal cost and average variable cost fall. Then, at the point of maximum marginal product, marginal cost is a minimum. As labor increases further, marginal product diminishes and marginal cost increases. But average product continues to rise and average variable cost continues to fall. Then, at the point of maximum average product, average variable cost is a minimum. As labor increases further, average product diminishes and average variable cost increases.

Shifts in the Cost Curves

The position of a firm's short-run cost curves depends on two factors:

■ Technology
■ Prices of productive resources

Technology A technological change that increases productivity shifts the total product curve upward. It also shifts the marginal product curve and the average product curve upward. Because with a better technology, the same inputs can produce more output, technological change lowers costs and shifts the cost curves downward.

For example, advances in robot production techniques have increased productivity in the car industry. As a result, the product curves of Chrysler, Ford, and GM have shifted upward, and their cost curves have shifted downward. But the relationships between their product curves and cost curves have not changed. The curves are still linked in the way shown in Fig. 11.6.

Often, when technology advances, a firm uses more capital (a fixed input) and less labor (a variable input). For example, today telephone companies use computers to connect long-distance calls in place of

FIGURE 11.6
Product Curves and Cost Curves

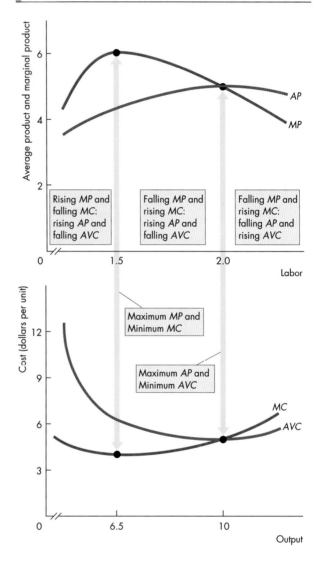

A firm's marginal product curve is linked to its marginal cost curve. If marginal product rises, marginal cost falls. If marginal product is a maximum, marginal cost is a minimum. If marginal product diminishes, marginal cost rises. A firm's average product curve is linked to its average variable cost curve. If average product rises, average variable cost falls. If average product is a maximum, average variable cost is a minimum. If average product diminishes, average variable cost rises.

TABLE 11.2

A Compact Glossary of Costs

Term	Symbol	Definition	Equation
Fixed cost		Cost that is independent of the output level; cost of a fixed input	
Variable cost		Cost that varies with the output level; cost of a variable input	
Total fixed cost	TFC	Cost of the fixed inputs	
Total variable cost	TVC	Cost of the variable inputs	
Total cost	TC	Cost of all inputs	$TC = TFC + TVC$
Total product	TP	Total quantity produced (output Q)	
Marginal cost	MC	Change in total cost resulting from a one-unit increase in output	$MC = \Delta TC \div \Delta Q$
Average fixed cost	AFC	Total fixed cost per unit of output	$AFC = TFC \div Q$
Average variable cost	AVC	Total variable cost per unit of output	$AVC = TVC \div Q$
Average total cost	ATC	Total cost per unit of output	$ATC = AFC + AVC$

the human operators they employed in the 1980s. When such a technological change occurs, fixed costs increase and variable costs decrease. This change in the mix of fixed cost and variable cost means that at small output levels, average total cost might increase, while at large output levels, average total cost decreases.

Prices of Resources An increase in the price of a productive resource increases costs and shifts the cost curves. But how the curves shift depends on which resource price changes. An increase in rent or some other component of *fixed* cost shifts the fixed cost curves (*TFC* and *AFC*) upward and shifts the total cost curve (*TC*) upward but leaves the variable cost curves (*AVC* and *TVC*) and the marginal cost curve (*MC*) unchanged. An increase in the wage rate or some other component of *variable* cost shifts the variable curves (*TVC* and *AVC*) upward and shifts the (*MC*) upward but leaves the fixed cost curves (*AFC* and *TFC*) unchanged. So, for example, if truck drivers' wage rate increases, the variable cost and marginal cost of transportation services increase. If the

interest expense paid by a trucking company increases, the fixed cost of transportation services increases.

You've now completed your study of short-run costs. All the concepts that you've met are summarized in a compact glossary in Table 11.2.

REVIEW QUIZ

- What relationships do a firm's short-run cost curves show?
- How does marginal cost change as output increases (a) initially and (b) eventually?
- What does the law of *diminishing returns* imply for the shape of the marginal cost curve?
- What is the shape of the average fixed cost curve and why?
- What are the shapes of the average variable cost curve and the average total cost curve and why?

Long-Run Cost

IN THE SHORT RUN, A FIRM CAN VARY THE QUANtity of labor but the quantity of capital is fixed. In the long run, a firm can vary both the quantity of labor and the quantity of capital. We are now going to see how costs vary when the quantities of labor and capital vary. That is, we are going to study a firm's long-run costs. *Long-run cost* is the cost of production when a firm uses the economically efficient quantities of labor and capital. There are no *fixed* costs in the long run.

The behavior of long-run cost depends on the firm's *production function*, which is the relationship between the maximum output attainable and the quantities of both labor and capital.

The Production Function

Table 11.3 shows Sidney's Sweaters' production function. The table lists total product schedules for four different quantities of capital. We identify the quantity of capital by the plant size. The numbers for Plant 1 are for a factory with one knitting machine—the case we've just studied. The other three plants have 2, 3, and 4 machines. If Sidney's Sweaters doubles its capital to 2 knitting machines, the various amounts of labor can produce the outputs shown in the second column of the table. The last two columns show the outputs of yet larger quantities of capital.

Diminishing Returns Diminishing returns occur at all four quantities of capital as the quantity of labor increases. You can check that fact by calculating the marginal product of labor in plants with 2, 3, and 4 machines. At each plant size, as the quantity of labor increases, its marginal product (eventually) diminishes.

Diminishing Marginal Product of Capital Diminishing returns also occur as the quantity of capital increases. You can check that fact by calculating the marginal product of capital at a given quantity of labor. The *marginal product of capital* is the change in total product divided by the change in capital when the quantity of labor is constant—equivalently, the change in output resulting from a one-unit increase in the quantity of capital. For example, if Sidney's Sweaters has 3 workers and increases its capital from 1 machine to 2 machines, output increases from 13 to 18 sweaters a day. The marginal product of capital is 5 sweaters per day. If Sidney's Sweaters increases the

TABLE 11.3

The Production Function

Labor (workers per day)	Output (sweaters per day)			
	Plant 1	Plant 2	Plant 3	Plant 4
1	4	10	13	15
2	10	15	18	21
3	13	18	22	24
4	15	20	24	26
5	16	21	25	27
Knitting machines (number)	1	2	3	4

The table shows the total product data for four quantities of capital. The greater the plant size, the larger is the total product for any given quantity of labor. But for a given plant size, the marginal product of labor diminishes. And for a given quantity of labor, the marginal product of capital diminishes.

number of machines from 2 to 3, output increases from 18 to 22 sweaters per day. The marginal product of capital is 4 sweaters per day, down from 5 sweaters per day when 2 machines were used.

Let's now see what the production function implies for long-run costs.

Short-Run Cost and Long-Run Cost

Continue to assume that labor costs $25 per worker per day and capital costs $25 per machine per day. Using these input prices and the data in Table 11.3, we can calculate and graph the average total cost curves for factories with 1, 2, 3, and 4 knitting machines. We've already studied the costs of a factory with 1 machine in Figs. 11.4 and 11.5. In Fig. 11.7, the average total cost curve for that case is ATC_1. Figure 11.7 also shows the average total cost curve for a factory with 2 machines, ATC_2, with 3 machines, ATC_3, and with 4 machines, ATC_4.

You can see, in Fig. 11.7, that plant size has a big effect on the firm's average total cost. Two things stand out:

FIGURE 11.7
Short-Run Costs of Four Different Plants

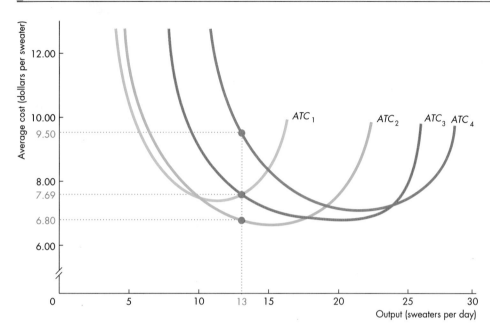

The figure shows short-run average total cost curves for four different quantities of capital. Sidney's Sweaters can produce 13 sweaters a day with 1 machine on ATC_1 or with 3 machines on ATC_3 for an average cost of $7.69 per sweater. Sidney's Sweaters can also produce 13 sweaters by using 2 knitting machines on ATC_2 for $6.80 per sweater or 4 machines on ATC_4 for $9.50 per sweater. If Sidney's Sweaters produces 13 sweaters a day, the least-cost method of production—the long-run method—is with 2 machines on ATC_2.

■ Each short-run average total cost curve is U-shaped.
■ For each short-run average total cost curve, the larger the plant, the greater is the output at which average total cost is a minimum.

Each short-run average total cost curve is U-shaped because, as the quantity of labor increases, its marginal product at first increases and then diminishes. And these patterns in the marginal product of labor, which we examined in some detail for the plant with 1 knitting machine on pp. 222–223, occur at all plant sizes.

The minimum average total cost for a larger plant occurs at a greater output than it does for a smaller plant because the larger plant has a higher fixed cost and therefore, for any given output level, a higher average fixed cost.

Which one of the short-run average cost curves Sidney's Sweaters operates on depends on its plant size. But in the long run, Sidney chooses the plant size. And which plant size he chooses depends on the output he plans to produce. The reason is that the average total cost of producing a given output depends on the plant size.

To see why, suppose that Sidney plans to produce 13 sweaters a day. With 1 machine, the average total cost curve is ATC_1 (in Fig. 11.7) and the average total cost of 13 sweaters a day is $7.69 per sweater. With 2 machines, on ATC_2, average total cost is $6.80 per sweater. With 3 machines on ATC_3, average total cost is $7.69 per sweater, the same as with 1 machine. Finally, with 4 machines, on ATC_4, average total cost is $9.50 per sweater.

The economically efficient plant size for producing a given output is the one that has the lowest average total cost. For Sidney, the economically efficient plant to use to produce 13 sweaters a day is the one with 2 machines.

In the long run, Sidney chooses the plant size that minimizes average total cost. When a firm is producing a given output at the least possible cost, it is operating on its *long-run average cost curve*.

The **long-run average cost curve** is the relationship between the lowest attainable average total cost and output when both the plant size and labor are varied. The long-run average cost curve is a planning curve. It tells the firm the plant size and the quantity of labor to use at each output to minimize cost. Once the plant size is chosen, the firm operates on the short-run cost curves that apply to that plant size.

The Long-Run Average Cost Curve

Figure 11.8 shows Sidney's Sweaters' long-run average cost curve *LRAC*. This long-run average cost curve is derived from the short-run average total cost curves in Fig. 11.7. For output rates up to 10 sweaters a day, average total cost is the lowest on ATC_1. For output rates between 10 and 18 sweaters a day, average total cost is the lowest on ATC_2. For output rates between 18 and 24 sweaters a day, average total cost is the lowest on ATC_3. And for output rates in excess of 24 sweaters a day, average total cost is the lowest on ATC_4. The segment of each of the four average total cost curves along which the average total cost is lowest is highlighted in dark blue in Fig. 11.8. The scallop-shaped curve made up of these four segments is the long-run average cost curve.

Economies and Diseconomies of Scale

Economies of scale are features of a firm's technology that lead to falling long-run average cost as output increases. When economies of scale are present, the *LRAC* curve slopes downward. The *LRAC* curve in Fig. 11.8 shows that Sidney's Sweaters experiences economies of scale for outputs up to 15 sweaters a day.

With given input prices, economies of scale occur if the percentage increase in output exceeds the percentage increase in all inputs. For example, if, when a firm increases its labor and capital by 10 percent, output increases by more than 10 percent, its average total cost falls. Economies of scale are present.

The main source of economies of scale is greater specialization of both labor and capital. For example, if GM produces 100 cars a week, each worker must perform many different tasks and the capital must be general-purpose machines and tools. But if GM produces 10,000 cars a week, each worker specializes and becomes highly proficient in a small number of tasks. Also, the capital is specialized and productive.

Diseconomies of scale are features of a firm's technology that lead to rising long-run average cost as output increases. When diseconomies of scale are present, the *LRAC* curve slopes upward. In Fig. 11.8, Sidney's Sweaters experiences diseconomies of scale at outputs greater than 15 sweaters a day.

With given input prices, diseconomies of scale occur if the percentage increase in output is less than

---

FIGURE 11.8

Long-Run Average Cost Curve

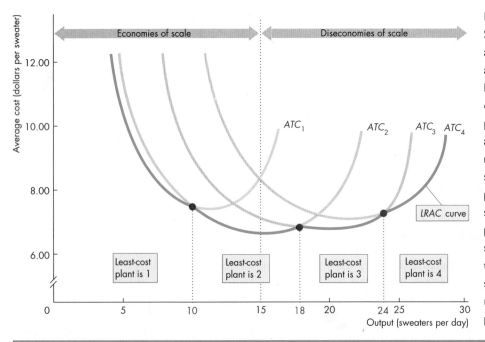

In the long run, Sidney's Sweaters can vary both capital and labor inputs. The long-run average cost curve traces the lowest attainable average total cost of production. Sidney's produces on its long-run average cost curve, if it uses 1 machine to produce up to 10 sweaters a day, 2 machines to produce between 10 and 18 sweaters a day, 3 machines to produce between 18 and 24 sweaters a day, and 4 machines to produce more than 24 sweaters a day. Within each range, Sidney's varies its output by varying the labor input.

the percentage increase in inputs. For example, if, when a firm increases its labor and capital by 10 percent, output increases by less than 10 percent, its average total cost rises. Diseconomies of scale are present.

The main source of diseconomies of scale is the difficulty of managing a very large enterprise. The larger the firm, the greater is the challenge of organizing it and the greater is the cost of communicating both up and down the management hierarchy and among managers. Eventually, management complexity brings rising average cost. Diseconomies of scale occur in all production processes but perhaps only at a very large output rate.

Constant returns to scale are features of a firm's technology that lead to constant long-run average cost as output increases. When constant returns to scale are present, the *LRAC* curve is horizontal.

With given input prices, constant returns to scale occur if the percentage increase in output equals the percentage increase in inputs. For example, if, when a firm increases its labor and capital by 10 percent, output increases by 10 percent, its average total cost is constant. Constant returns to scale are present.

For example, General Motors can double its production of Chevy Cavaliers by doubling its production facility for those cars. It can build an identical production line and hire an identical number of workers. With the two identical production lines, GM produces exactly twice as many cars.

Minimum Efficient Scale A firm experiences economies of scale up to some output level. Beyond that level, it moves into constant returns to scale or diseconomies of scale. A firm's **minimum efficient scale** is the smallest quantity of output at which long-run average cost reaches its lowest level.

The minimum efficient scale plays a role in determining market structure, as you will learn in the next three chapters. The minimum efficient scale also helps to answer some questions about real businesses.

Economies of Scale at Sidney's Sweaters Sidney's production function, shown in Table 11.3, illustrates economies of scale and diseconomies of scale. If Sidney's inputs increase from 1 machine and 1 worker to 2 of each, a 100 percent increase in all inputs, output increases by more than 100 percent, from 4 sweaters to 15 sweaters a day. Sidney's experiences economies of scale, and its long-run average cost decreases. But if Sidney's inputs increase to 3 machines and 3 workers, a 50 percent increase, output increases by less than 50 percent, from 15

sweaters to 22 sweaters a day. Now Sidney's experiences diseconomies of scale, and its long-run average cost increases. Sidney's minimum efficient scale is at 15 sweaters a day.

Producing Cars and Generating Electric Power At the beginning of this chapter, we posed the question: Why do car makers have expensive equipment lying around that isn't fully used? You can now answer this question. A car maker uses the plant that minimizes the average total cost of producing the output that it can sell. But it operates below the efficient minimum scale. Its short-run average total cost curve looks like ATC_1. If it could sell more cars, it would produce more cars and its average total cost would fall.

We also noted that many electric utilities don't have enough production equipment to meet demand on the coldest and hottest days and have to buy power from other producers. You can now see why. A power producer uses the plant size that minimizes the average total cost of producing the output that it can sell on a normal day. But it produces above the minimum efficient scale and experiences diseconomies of scale. Its short-run average total cost curve looks like ATC_3. With a larger plant size, its average total costs of producing its normal output would be higher.

R E V I E W   Q U I Z

- What does a firm's production function show and how is it related to a total product curve?
- Does the law of diminishing returns apply to capital as well as labor? Explain why.
- What does a firm's long-run average cost curve show? How is it related to the firm's short-run average cost curves?
- What are economies of scale and diseconomies of scale? How do they arise? And what do they imply for the shape of the long-run average cost curve?
- How is a firm's minimum efficient scale determined?

◆ *Reading Between the Lines* on pp. 234–235 applies what you've learned about a firm's product curves and cost curves. It looks at the total product curves and cost curves of Exxon and Mobil before and after a proposed merger of these two oil producing giants.

Lowering the Cost of Oil

THE NEW YORK TIMES, DECEMBER 2, 1998

Exxon and Mobil Announce $80 Billion Deal to Create World's Largest Company

BY ALLEN R. MYERSON AND AGIS SALPUKAS

Exxon, the United States' largest oil company, formally agreed on Tuesday to buy Mobil, the next-largest, for $80 billion in stock, to form the world's biggest corporation. ...

The agreement would reunite the two largest pieces of John D. Rockefeller's Standard Oil Trust, which was broken up in 1911 in the nation's most celebrated antitrust case.

The companies contended Tuesday that they now confront global competitors and plunging energy prices, making their recombination and the resulting savings a necessity. But while the companies said they could save $2.8 billion annually, the greatest costs would be paid by employees. The companies said 9,000 workers out of 123,000 worldwide were likely to find themselves without jobs.

Lee Raymond, the chairman and chief executive of Exxon, who would add the title of president in the combined company, said repeatedly that further efficiency, not brute size, was his goal. "This is the case of the whole being greater than the sum of the parts," he said at a news conference, later adding: "I have always had the view that the objective is to be best. If in being best you also have to be biggest, that's fine."

© 1998 *The New York Times*. Reprinted with permission.
Further reproduction prohibited.

Essence of the Story

■ Exxon and Mobil plan to merge.

■ The goal of the merger is to achieve cost savings, and the companies say that with the merger, costs can be cut by $2.8 billion a year.

■ The labor force of the merged company would be 9,000 workers fewer than the existing combined labor forces of the two companies.

■ Exxon and Mobil are huge firms that:
- Explore to find new oil and natural gas deposits
- Extract raw materials
- Transport raw materials to refineries
- Refine and process raw materials
- Transport and sell refined products

■ These firms are large because there are economies of scale in many of their production activities and especially in exploration.

■ Figure 1 shows the technology these firms face in the form of a total product curve. Exxon and Mobil operate on total product curve TP_0. Mobil employs 43,000 people and produces 1.46 billion barrels of oil a year, and Exxon employs 80,000 people and produces 3 billion barrels of oil a year.*

■ If Exxon and Mobil merge into a single very large firm, they will be able to operate on a new total product curve. The new curve is TP_1 in Fig. 1.

*The numbers of employees are data from Exxon and Mobil. The numbers of barrels produced are the author's calculation of the barrels of oil equivalent of Exxon's and Mobil's total sales. The firms actually sell several different products.

■ You can interpret Lee Raymond's statement, "This is the case of the whole being greater than the sum of the parts," as meaning that the combined firm does not move along the existing total product curve TP_0 but jumps to a new, higher total product curve TP_1 and increases productivity.

■ Figure 2 shows the effect of the merger on average total cost.

■ The average total cost curve on which the two firms operate before the merger is ATC_0. Both firms have a similar level of average total cost, but given the assumed total product curve in Fig. 1, Mobil operates in the region of falling average total cost and Exxon operates in the region of rising average total cost.

■ After the merger, the average total cost curve shifts to ATC_1. The bigger merged firm has greater fixed costs than the two separate firms, so at small output rates, average total cost is higher in the new firm than in the existing firms.

■ But at the large output rate at which the combined firm will operate, average total cost is lower for the merged firm.

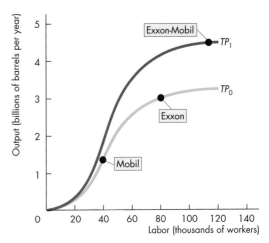

Figure 1 Total product

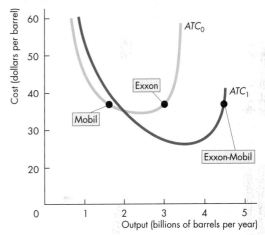

Figure 2 Average total cost

■ Notice that the new combined firm might operate on the upward-sloping portion of its new ATC curve, as in this example, even though it has benefited from economies of scale.

SUMMARY

KEY POINTS

Decision Time Frames (p. 220)

- In the short run, the quantity of one resource is fixed, and the quantities of the other resources can be varied.
- In the long run, the quantities of all resources can be varied.

Short-Run Technology Constraint (pp. 221–224)

- A total product curve shows the quantity a firm can produce with a given quantity of capital and different quantities of labor.
- Initially, the marginal product of labor increases as the quantity of labor increases but eventually, marginal product diminishes—the law of diminishing returns.
- Average product also increases initially and eventually diminishes.

Short-Run Cost (pp. 225–229)

- As output increases, total fixed cost is constant and total variable cost and total cost increase.
- As output increases, average fixed cost decreases; average variable cost, average total cost, and marginal cost decrease at small outputs and increase at large outputs. These cost curves are U-shaped.

Long-Run Cost (pp. 230–233)

- Long-run cost is the cost of production when all inputs—labor and capital—have been adjusted to their economically efficient levels.
- There is a set of short-run cost curves for each different plant size. There is one least-cost plant size for each output. The larger the output, the larger is the plant size that will minimize average total cost.
- The long-run average cost curve traces out the lowest attainable average total cost at each output when both capital and labor inputs can be varied.
- With economies of scale, the long-run average cost curve slopes downward. With diseconomies of scale, the long-run average cost curve slopes upward.

KEY FIGURES AND TABLE ◆

KEY TERMS

PROBLEMS

*1. Rubber Duckies total product schedule is:

Labor (workers per week)	Output (boats per week)
1	1
2	3
3	6
4	10
5	15
6	21
7	26
8	30
9	33
10	35

a. Draw the total product curve.
b. Calculate the average product of labor and draw the average product curve.
c. Calculate the marginal product of labor and draw the marginal product curve.
d. What is the relationship between average product and marginal product when Rubber Duckies produces (i) fewer than 30 boats a week and (ii) more than 30 boats a week?

2. Charlie's Chocolates' total product schedule is:

Labor (workers per day)	Output (boxes per day)
1	12
2	24
3	48
4	84
5	132
6	192
7	240
8	276
9	300
10	312

a. Draw the total product curve.
b. Calculate the average product of labor and draw the average product curve.
c. Calculate the marginal product of labor and draw the marginal product curve.
d. What is the relationship between the average product and marginal product when Charlie's Chocolates produces (i) fewer than 276 boxes a day and (ii) more than 276 boxes a day?

*3. In problem 1, suppose that the price of labor is $400 a week and total fixed cost is $1,000 a week.
a. Calculate total cost, total variable cost, and total fixed cost for each output and draw the short-run total cost curves.
b. Calculate average total cost, average fixed cost, average variable cost, and marginal cost at each output and draw the short-run average and marginal cost curves.

4. In problem 2, the price of labor is $50 per day and total fixed costs are $50 per day.
a. Calculate total cost, total variable cost, and total fixed costs for each level of output and draw the short-run total cost curves.
b. Calculate average total cost, average fixed cost, average variable cost, and marginal cost at each level of output and draw the short-run average and marginal cost curves.

*5. In problem 3, suppose that Rubber Duckies' total fixed cost increases to $1,100 a week. Explain what changes occur to the short-run average and marginal cost curves.

6. In problem 4, suppose that the price of labor increases to $70 per day. Explain what changes occur to the short-run average and marginal cost curves.

*7. In problem 3, Rubber Duckies buys a second plant and now the total product of each quantity of labor doubles. The total fixed cost of operating each plant is $1,000 a week. The wage rate is $400 a week.
a. Set out the average total cost schedule when Rubber Duckies operates two plants.
b. Draw the long-run average cost curve.
c. Over what output range is it efficient to operate one plant and two plants?

8. In problem 4, Charlie's Chocolates buys a second plant and now the total product of each quantity of labor doubles. The total fixed cost of operating each plant is $50 a day. The wage rate is $50 a day.
a. Set out the average total cost curve when Charlie's operates two plants.
b. Draw the long-run average cost curve.
c. Over what output range is it efficient to operate one plant and two plants?

*9. The table shows the production function of Bonnie's Balloon Rides:

Labor (workers per day)	Output (rides per day)			
	Plant 1	Plant 2	Plant 3	Plant 4
1	4	10	13	15
2	10	15	18	21
3	13	18	22	24
4	15	20	24	26
5	16	21	25	27
Balloons (number)	1	2	3	4

Bonnie must pay $500 a day for each balloon she rents and $250 a day for each balloon operator she hires.
a. Find and graph the average total cost curve for each plant size.
b. Draw Bonnie's long-run average cost curve.
c. What is Bonnie's minimum efficient scale?
d. Explain how Bonnie uses her long-run average cost curve to decide how many balloons to rent.

10. The table shows the production function of Mario's Pizza-to-Go.

Labor (workers per day)	Output (pizzas per day)			
	Plant 1	Plant 2	Plant 3	Plant 4
1	4	8	11	13
2	8	12	15	17
3	11	15	18	20
4	13	17	20	22
Ovens (number)	1	2	3	4

Mario must pay $100 a day for each oven he rents and $75 a day for each kitchen hand he hires.
a. Find and graph the average total cost curve for each plant size.
b. Draw Mario's long-run average cost curve.
c. Over what output range does Mario experience economies of scale?
d. Explain how Mario uses his long-run average cost curve to decide how many ovens to rent.

CRITICAL THINKING

1. Study *Reading Between the Lines* on pp. 234–235 and then:
    a. Sketch the average product curve and the marginal product curve that correspond to the total product curve TP_0.
    b. Sketch the average product curve and the marginal product curve that correspond to the total product curve TP_1.
    c. Why does Fig. 2 show Mobil operating on the downward-sloping portion of the ATC curve and Exxon operating on the upward-sloping portion?
    d. Use the links on the Parkin Web site to obtain information about the labor force, revenue, and cost of other big oil companies.
    e. Using the size of the labor force and total cost data, how does the merged Exxon-Mobil compare with the other big oil companies?
    f. Which of the big oil companies do you think is the most efficient and why?

2. A telecommunication company is considering replacing human telephone operators with computers. This change will increase total fixed cost and decrease total variable cost. Either use the spreadsheet on the Parkin Web site or create your own example and sketch:
    a. The total cost curves for the original technology that uses human operators.
    b. The average cost curves for the original technology that uses human operators.
    c. The marginal cost curves for the original technology that uses human operators.
    d. The total cost curves for the new technology that uses computers.
    e. The average cost curves for the new technology that uses computers.
    f. The marginal cost curves for the new technology that uses computers.

3. A spreadsheet on the Parkin Web site provides information about the cost of operating an ATM. Use the data to work out the average cost curves for an ATM. Under what conditions might a bank *not* install an ATM but use a human teller instead?

Perfect Competition

In 1998, Americans spent more than $10 billion on ice cream. Competition in ice cream is fierce. National names such as Baskin-Robbins, Häagen-Dazs, and Ben and Jerry's compete with Bart's, Annabel's, and hundreds of private label store brands for a place in a crowded market. New firms enter and try their luck while other firms are squeezed out of the business. How does competition affect prices and profits? What causes some firms to enter an industry and others to leave it? What are the effects on profits and prices of new firms entering and old firms leaving an industry? ◆ On a typical day in 1998, a million people were unemployed because they had been laid off by employers seeking to trim their costs and avoid bankruptcy. Ice cream producers, computer makers, and firms in almost every sector of the economy laid off workers in 1995, even though the economy was expanding and the total number of jobs was growing. Why do firms lay off workers? When will a firm temporarily shut down, laying off its workers? ◆ Over the past few years, there has been a dramatic fall in the prices of personal computers. For example, a slow computer cost almost $4,000 a few years ago, and a fast one costs only $1,000 today. What goes on in an industry when the price of its output falls sharply? What happens to the profits of the firms producing such goods?

Hot Rivalry in Ice Cream

◆ Ice cream, computers, and most other goods are produced by more than one firm, and these firms compete with each other for sales. To study competitive markets, we are going to build a model of a market in which competition is as fierce and extreme as possible— more extreme than in the examples we've just considered. We call this situation "perfect competition."

After studying this chapter, you will be able to:

■ Define perfect competition

■ Explain how price and output are determined in a competitive industry

■ Explain why firms sometimes shut down temporarily and lay off workers

■ Explain why firms enter and leave an industry

■ Predict the effects of a change in demand and of a technological advance

■ Explain why perfect competition is efficient

Competition

THE FIRMS THAT YOU STUDY IN THIS CHAPTER face the force of raw competition. We call this extreme form of competition perfect competition. **Perfect competition** is an industry in which

- Many firms sell identical products to many buyers.
- There are no restrictions on entry into the industry.
- Established firms have no advantage over new ones.
- Sellers and buyers are well informed about prices.

Farming, fishing, wood pulping and paper milling, the manufacture of paper cups and plastic shopping bags, grocery retailing, photo finishing, lawn service, plumbing, painting, dry cleaning, and the provision of laundry services are all examples of highly competitive industries.

How Perfect Competition Arises

Perfect competition arises if the minimum efficient scale of a single producer is small relative to the demand for the good or service (see Chapter 11, pp. 233). A firm's **minimum efficient scale** is the smallest quantity of output at which long-run average cost reaches its lowest level. Where the minimum efficient scale of a firm is small relative to the demand, there is room for many firms in an industry.

Second, perfect competition arises if each firm is perceived to produce a good or service that has no unique characteristics so that consumers don't care which firm they buy from.

Price Takers

Firms in perfect competition must make many decisions. But one thing they do *not* decide is the price at which to sell their output. Firms in perfect competition are said to be price takers. A **price taker** is a firm that cannot influence the price of a good or service.

The key reason why a perfectly competitive firm is a price taker is that it produces a tiny proportion of the total output of a particular good and buyers are well informed about the prices of other firms.

Imagine that you are a wheat farmer in Kansas. You have a thousand acres under cultivation—which sounds like a lot. But then you go on a drive through

Colorado, Oklahoma, Texas, and back up to Nebraska and the Dakotas. You find unbroken stretches of wheat covering millions of acres. And you know there are similar vistas in Canada, Argentina, Australia, and Ukraine. Your thousand acres is a drop in the ocean. Nothing makes your wheat any better than any other farmer's, and all the buyers of wheat know the price at which they can do business.

If everybody else sells their wheat for $4 a bushel and you want $4.10, why would people buy from you? They can simply go to the next farmer, and the one after that, and the next and buy all they need for $4. This price is determined in the market for wheat, and you are a *price taker*.

The *market* demand for wheat is not perfectly elastic. The market demand curve is downward sloping, and its elasticity depends on the substitutability of other grains such as barley, rye, corn, and rice for wheat. But the demand for wheat from farm *A* is perfectly elastic because wheat from farm *B* is a *perfect substitute* for wheat from farm *A*. A price taker faces a perfectly elastic demand curve.

Economic Profit and Revenue

A firm's goal is to maximize **economic profit**, which is equal to total revenue minus total cost. Total cost is the *opportunity cost* of production, which includes the firm's **normal profit**, the return that the firm's entrepreneur can obtain in the best alternative business.

A firm's **total revenue** equals the price of its output multiplied by the number of units of output sold (price × quantity). **Marginal revenue** is the change in total revenue that results from a one-unit increase in the quantity sold. Marginal revenue is calculated by dividing the change in total revenue by the change in the quantity sold.

Figure 12.1 illustrates these revenue concepts. Sidney's Sweaters is one of a thousand similar small firms. In Fig. 12.1(a), demand and supply in the sweater market determine the price, which is $25 a sweater. Sidney must take this price. He cannot influence it by changing the quantity of sweaters he produces.

The table shows three different quantities of sweaters produced. As the quantity varies, the price remains constant—in this example at $25 a sweater. Total revenue is equal to the price multiplied by the quantity sold. For example, if Sidney sells 8 sweaters, his total revenue is 8 × $25, which equals $200.

FIGURE 12.1
Demand, Price, and Revenue in Perfect Competition

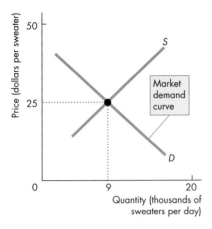

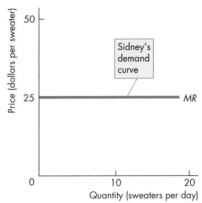

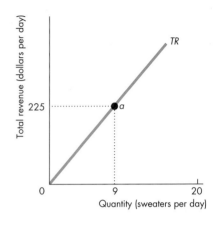

(a) Sweater market

(b) Sidney's demand and marginal revenue

(c) Sidney's total revenue

Quantity sold (Q) (sweaters per day)	Price (P) (dollars per sweater)	Total revenue (TR = P × Q) (dollars)	Marginal revenue (MR = ΔTR/ΔQ) (dollars per additional sweater)
8	25	200	
			25
9	25	225	
			25
10	25	250	

Market demand and supply determine the market price. In part (a), the market price is $25 a sweater and 9,000 sweaters are bought and sold. Sidney faces a perfectly elastic demand at the market price of $25 a sweater, part (b). The table calculates Sidney's total revenue and marginal revenue. Part (b) of the figure shows Sidney's demand curve, which is also its marginal revenue curve (MR). Part (c) shows Sidney's total revenue curve (TR). Point a corresponds to the second row of the table.

Marginal revenue is the change in total revenue that results from a one-unit change in quantity. For example, when the quantity sold increases from 8 to 9, total revenue increases from $200 to $225, so marginal revenue is $25 a sweater. (Notice that in the table, marginal revenue appears *between* the lines for the quantities sold to remind you that marginal revenue results from the *change* in the quantity sold.)

Because the price remains constant when the quantity sold changes, the change in total revenue that results from a one-unit increase in the quantity sold equals price. Therefore in perfect competition, marginal revenue equals price.

Figure 12.1(b) shows Sidney's marginal revenue curve (MR). This curve tells us the change in total revenue that results from selling one more sweater. This curve is also the firm's demand curve. The firm, being a price taker, can sell any quantity it chooses at this price. The firm faces a perfectly elastic demand for its output.

The total revenue curve (TR) in part (c) shows the total revenue at each quantity sold. For example, if Sidney sells 9 sweaters, total revenue is $225 (point a). Because each additional sweater sold brings in a constant amount—$25—the total revenue curve is an upward-sloping straight line.

R E V I E W   Q U I Z

- Explain why a firm in perfect competition is a price taker.
- In perfect competition, what is the relationship between a firm's demand curve and the market demand curve?
- In perfect competition, why is a firm's demand curve also its marginal revenue curve?
- In perfect competition, why is the total revenue curve an upward-sloping straight line?

The Firm's Decisions in Perfect Competition

FIRMS IN A PERFECTLY COMPETITIVE INDUSTRY face a given market price and have the revenue curves that you've studied. These revenue curves summarize the market constraint faced by a perfectly competitive firm.

Firms also have a technology constraint, which is described by the product curves (total product, average product, and marginal product) that you studied in Chapter 11. The technology available to the firm determines its costs, which are described by the cost curves (total cost, average cost, and marginal cost) that you also studied in Chapter 11.

The task of the competitive firm is to make the maximum economic profit possible, given the constraints it faces. To achieve this objective, a firm must make four key decisions: two in the short run and two in the long run.

Short-Run Decisions   The short run is a time frame in which each firm has a given plant and the number of firms in the industry is fixed. But many things can change in the short run, and the firm must react to these changes. For example, the price for which the firm can sell its output might have a seasonal fluctuation, or it might fluctuate with general business fluctuations. The firm must react to such short-run price fluctuations and decide:

1. Whether to produce or to shut down
2. If the decision is to produce, what quantity to produce

Long-Run Decisions   The long run is a time frame in which each firm can change the size of its plant and decide whether to leave the industry. Other firms can decide to enter the industry. So in the long run, both the plant size of each firm and the number of firms in the industry can change. Also in the long run, the constraints facing firms can change. For example, the demand for the good can permanently fall, or technological advance can change the industry's costs. The firm must react to such long-run changes and decide:

1. Whether to increase or decrease its plant size
2. Whether to stay in the industry or leave it

The Firm and the Industry in the Short Run and the Long Run   To study a competitive industry, we begin by looking at an individual firm's short-run decisions. We then see how the short-run decisions of all firms in a competitive industry combine to determine the industry price, output, and economic profit. Then we turn to the long run and study the effects of long-run decisions on the industry price, output, and economic profit. All the decisions we study are driven by a single objective: to maximize economic profit.

Profit-Maximizing Output

A perfectly competitive firm maximizes economic profit by choosing its output level. One way of finding the profit-maximizing output is to study a firm's total revenue and total cost and to find the output level at which total revenue exceeds total cost by the largest amount. Figure 12.2 shows how to do this for Sidney's Sweaters. The table lists Sidney's total revenue and total cost at different outputs, and part (a) of the figure shows Sidney's total revenue and total cost curves. These curves are graphs of the numbers shown in the first three columns of the table. The total revenue curve (*TR*) is the same as that in Fig. 12.1(c). The total cost curve (*TC*) is similar to the one that you met in Chapter 11. As output increases, so does total cost.

Economic profit equals total revenue minus total cost. The fourth column of the table in Fig. 12.2 shows Sidney's economic profit, and part (b) of the figure illustrates these numbers as Sidney's profit curve. This curve shows that Sidney makes an economic profit at outputs between 4 and 12 sweaters a day. At outputs less than 4 sweaters a day, Sidney incurs an economic loss. Sidney also incurs an economic loss if output exceeds 12 sweaters a day. At outputs of 4 sweaters and 12 sweaters a day, total cost equals total revenue and Sidney's economic profit is zero. An output at which total cost equals total revenue is called a *break-even point*. The firm's economic profit is zero but because normal profit is part of total cost, the firm makes normal profit at a break-even point. That is, at the break-even point, the entrepreneur makes an income equal to the best alternative return forgone.

Notice the relationship between the total revenue, total cost, and profit curves. Economic profit is measured by the vertical distance between the total revenue and total cost curves. When the total revenue

FIGURE 12.2

Total Revenue, Total Cost, and Economic Profit

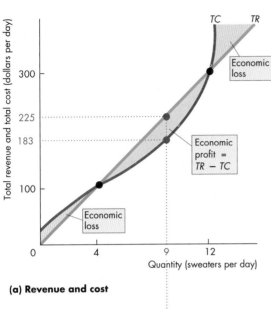

(a) Revenue and cost

(b) Economic profit and loss

Quantity (Q) (sweaters per day)	Total revenue (TR) (dollars)	Total cost (TC) (dollars)	Economic profit (TR – TC) (dollars)
0	0	22	–22
1	25	45	–20
2	50	66	–16
3	75	85	–10
4	100	100	0
5	125	114	11
6	150	126	24
7	175	141	34
8	200	160	40
9	225	183	42
10	250	210	40
11	275	245	30
12	300	300	0
13	325	360	–35

The table lists Sidney's total revenue, total cost, and economic profit. Part (a) graphs the total revenue and total cost curves. Economic profit, in part (a), is the height of the blue area between the total cost and total revenue curves. Sidney's makes maximum economic profit, $42 a day ($225 – $183), when it produces 9 sweaters—the output at which the vertical distance between the total revenue and total cost curves is at its largest. At outputs of 4 sweaters a day and 12 sweaters a day, Sidney's makes zero economic profit—these are break-even points. At outputs less than 4 and greater than 12 sweaters a day, Sidney's incurs an economic loss. Part (b) shows Sidney's profit curve. The profit curve is at its highest when economic profit is at a maximum. The profit curve cuts the horizontal axis at the break-even points.

curve in part (a) is above the total cost curve, between 4 and 12 sweaters, the firm is making an economic profit, and the profit curve in part (b) is above the horizontal axis. At the break-even point, where the total cost and total revenue curves intersect, the profit curve intersects the horizontal axis. The profit curve is at a maximum when TR exceeds TC by the largest amount. In this example, profit maximization occurs at an output of 9 sweaters a day. At this output, Sidney's economic profit is $42 a day.

Marginal Analysis

Another way of finding the profit-maximizing output is to use *marginal analysis* and compare marginal revenue, *MR,* with marginal cost, *MC.* As output increases, marginal revenue remains constant but marginal cost changes. At low output levels, marginal cost decreases, but it eventually increases. So where the marginal cost curve intersects the marginal revenue curve, marginal cost is rising.

If marginal revenue exceeds marginal cost (if *MR > MC*), then the extra revenue from selling one more unit exceeds the extra cost incurred to produce it. The firm makes an economic profit on the marginal unit, so its economic profit increases if output increases.

If marginal revenue is less than marginal cost (if *MR < MC*), then the extra revenue from selling one more unit is less than the extra cost incurred to produce it. The firm incurs an economic loss on the marginal unit, so its economic profit decreases if output increases and its economic profit increases if output *decreases.*

If marginal revenue equals marginal cost (if *MR = MC*), economic profit is maximized. The rule *MR = MC* is a prime example of marginal analysis. Let's check that this rule works to find the profit-maximizing output by returning to Sidney's sweater factory.

Look at Fig. 12.3. The table records Sidney's marginal revenue and marginal cost. Marginal revenue is a constant $25 a sweater. Over the range of outputs shown in the table, marginal cost increases from $19 a sweater to $35 a sweater.

Focus on the highlighted rows of the table. If Sidney increases output from 8 sweaters to 9 sweaters, marginal revenue is $25 and marginal cost is $23. Because marginal revenue exceeds marginal cost, economic profit increases. The last column of the table shows that economic profit increases from $40 to $42, an increase of $2. The blue area in the figure shows this economic profit from the ninth sweater.

If Sidney increases output from 9 sweaters to 10 sweaters, marginal revenue is still $25, but marginal cost is $27. Because marginal revenue is less than marginal cost, economic profit decreases. The last column of the table shows that economic profit decreases from $42 to $40. The red area in the figure shows this loss from the tenth sweater.

Sidney maximizes economic profit by producing 9 sweaters a day, the quantity at which marginal revenue equals marginal cost.

FIGURE 12.3

Profit-Maximizing Output

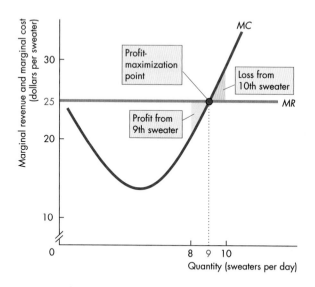

Quantity (Q) (sweaters per day)	Total revenue (TR) (dollars)	Marginal revenue (MR) (dollars per additional sweater)	Total cost (TC) (dollars)	Marginal cost (MC) (dollars per additional sweater)	Economic profit (TR − TC) (dollars)
7	175		141		34
		25		19	
8	200		160		40
		25		23	
9	225		183		42
		25		27	
10	250		210		40
		25		35	
11	275		245		30

Another way of finding the profit-maximizing output is to determine the output at which marginal revenue equals marginal cost. The table shows that if output increases from 8 to 9 sweaters, marginal cost is $23, which is less than the marginal revenue of $25. If output increases from 9 to 10 sweaters, marginal cost is $27, which exceeds the marginal revenue of $25. The figure shows that marginal cost and marginal revenue are equal when Sidney produces 9 sweaters a day. If marginal revenue exceeds marginal cost, an increase in output increases economic profit. If marginal revenue is less than marginal cost, an increase in output decreases economic profit. If marginal revenue equals marginal cost, economic profit is maximized.

The Firm's Short-Run Supply Curve

A perfectly competitive firm's short-run supply curve shows how the firm's profit-maximizing output varies as the market price varies, other things remaining the same. Figure 12.4 shows how to derive Sidney's supply curve. Part (a) shows Sidney's marginal cost and average variable cost curves, and part (b) shows Sidney's supply curve. There is a direct link between the marginal cost and average variable cost curves and the supply curve. Let's see what that link is.

Temporary Plant Shutdown In the short run, a firm cannot avoid incurring its fixed cost. But the firm can avoid variable costs by temporarily laying off its workers and shutting down. If a firm shuts down it produces no output and it incurs a loss equal to total fixed cost. This loss is the largest that a firm need incur. A firm shuts down if the price falls below the minimum of average variable cost. The **shutdown point** is the output and price at which the firm just covers its total variable cost—point s in Fig. 12.4(a). If the price is \$17, the marginal revenue curve is MR_0 and the profit-maximizing output is 7 sweaters a day at point s. But both price and average variable cost equal \$17, so Sidney makes no economic profit on these 7 sweaters. His economic loss equals total fixed cost. At a price below \$17, no matter what quantity Sidney produces, average *variable* cost exceeds price and the economic loss exceeds total fixed cost. At a price below \$17, Sidney shuts down.

The Short-Run Supply Curve If the price is above minimum average variable cost, Sidney maximizes profit by producing the output at which marginal cost equals price. We can determine the quantity produced at each price from the marginal cost curve. At a price of \$25, the marginal revenue curve is MR_1 and Sidney maximizes profit by producing 9 sweaters. At a price of \$31, the marginal revenue curve is MR_2 and Sidney produces 10 sweaters.

   Sidney's short-run supply curve, shown in Fig. 12.4(b), has two separate parts: First, at prices that exceed minimum average variable cost, the supply curve is the same as the marginal cost curve above the shutdown point (s). Second, at prices below minimum average variable cost, Sidney shuts down and produces nothing. Its supply curve runs along the vertical axis. At a price of \$17, Sidney is indifferent between shutting down and producing 7 sweaters a day. Either way, Sidney incurs a loss of \$22 a day.

FIGURE 12.4
A Firm's Supply Curve

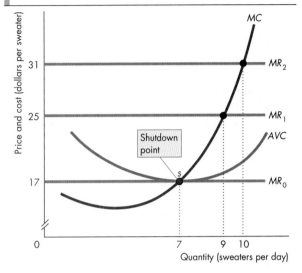

(a) Marginal cost and average variable cost

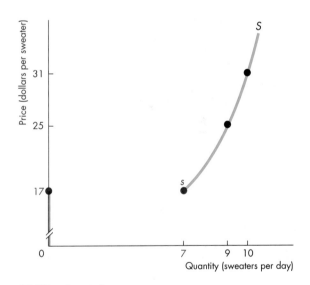

(b) Sidney's supply curve

Part (a) shows Sidney's profit-maximizing output at various market prices. At \$25 a sweater, Sidney produces 9 sweaters. At \$17 a sweater, Sidney produces 7 sweaters. At any price below \$17 a sweater, Sidney produces nothing. Sidney's shutdown point is s. Part (b) shows Sidney's supply curve—the number of sweaters Sidney will produce at each price. It is made up of the marginal cost curve (part a) at all points above the average variable cost curve and the vertical axis at all prices below minimum average variable cost.

Short-Run Industry Supply Curve

The **short-run industry supply curve** shows the quantity supplied by the industry at each price when the plant size of each firm and the number of firms remain constant. The quantity supplied by the industry at a given price is the sum of the quantities supplied by all firms in the industry at that price.

Figure 12.5 shows the supply curve for the competitive sweater industry. In this example, the industry consists of 1,000 firms exactly like Sidney's Sweaters. At each price, the quantity supplied by the industry is 1,000 times the quantity supplied by a single firm.

The table in Fig. 12.5 shows the firm's and the industry's supply schedule and how the industry supply curve is constructed. At prices below $17, every firm in the industry shuts down; the quantity supplied by the industry is zero. At a price of $17, each firm is indifferent between shutting down and producing nothing or operating and producing 7 sweaters a day. Some firms will shut down and others will supply 7 sweaters a day. The quantity supplied by each firm is *either* 0 or 7 sweaters, but the quantity supplied by the industry is *between* 0 (all firms shut down) and 7,000 (all firms produce 7 sweaters a day each).

To construct the industry supply curve, we sum the quantities supplied by the individual firms. Each of the 1,000 firms in the industry has a supply schedule like Sidney's. At prices below $17, the industry supply curve runs along the price axis. At a price of $17, the industry supply curve is horizontal—supply is perfectly elastic. As the price rises above $17, each firm increases its quantity supplied, and the quantity supplied by the industry increases by 1,000 times that of each firm.

R E V I E W   Q U I Z

- Why does a firm in perfect competition produce the quantity at which marginal cost equals price?
- What is the lowest price at which a firm will produce an output? Explain why.
- What is the largest economic loss that a firm incurs in the short run and why?
- What is the relation among a firm's supply curve, its marginal cost curve, and its average variable cost curve?
- How do we derive an industry supply curve?

FIGURE 12.5

Industry Supply Curve

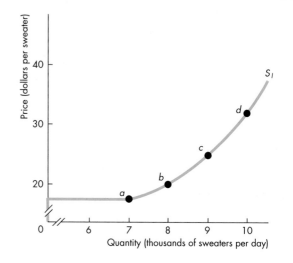

	Price (dollars per sweater)	Quantity supplied by Sidney's Sweaters (sweaters per day)	Quantity supplied by industry (sweaters per day)
a	17	0 or 7	0 to 7,000
b	20	8	8,000
c	25	9	9,000
d	31	10	10,000

The industry supply schedule is the sum of the supply schedules of all individual firms. An industry that consists of 1,000 identical firms has a supply schedule similar to that of the individual firm, but the quantity supplied by the industry is 1,000 times as large as that of the individual firm (see table). The industry supply curve is S_I. Points a, b, c, and d correspond to the rows of the table. At the shutdown price of $17, each firm produces either 0 or 7 sweaters per day, so the industry supply curve is perfectly elastic at the shutdown price.

So far, we have studied a single firm in isolation. We have seen that the firm's profit-maximizing actions depend on the market price, which the firm takes as given. But how is the market price determined? Let's find out.

Output, Price, and Profit in Perfect Competition

To DETERMINE THE MARKET PRICE AND THE quantity bought and sold in a perfectly competitive market, we need to study how market demand and market supply interact. We begin this process by studying a perfectly competitive market in the short run when the number of firms is fixed and each firm has a given plant size.

Short-Run Equilibrium

Industry demand and industry supply determine the market price and industry output. Figure 12.6(a) shows a short-run equilibrium. The supply curve S is the same as S_I in Fig. 12.5.

If demand is at the level shown by the demand curve D_1, the equilibrium price is $20. Although industry demand and supply determine this price, each firm takes the price as given and produces its profit-maximizing output, which is 8 sweaters a day. Because the industry has 1,000 firms, industry output is 8,000 sweaters a day.

A Change in Demand

Changes in demand bring changes to short-run industry equilibrium. Figure 12.6(b) shows these changes.

If demand increases, the demand curve shifts rightward to D_2. The price rises to $25. At this price, each firm maximizes profit by increasing its output. The new output level is 9 sweaters a day for each firm and 9,000 sweaters a day for the industry.

If demand decreases, the demand curve shifts leftward to D_3. The price now falls to $17. At this price, each firm maximizes profit by decreasing its output. The new output level is 7 sweaters a day for each firm and 7,000 sweaters a day for the industry.

If the demand curve shifts farther leftward than D_3, the price remains constant at $17 because the industry supply curve is horizontal at that price. Some firms continue to produce 7 sweaters a day,

---

FIGURE 12.6
Short-Run Equilibrium

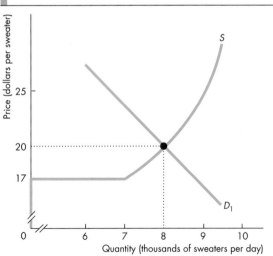

(a) Equilibrium

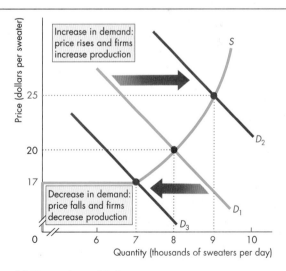

(b) Change in equilibrium

In part (a), the industry's supply curve is S. Demand is D_1, and the price is $20. At this price, each firm produces 8 sweaters a day and the industry produces 8,000 sweaters a day. In part (b), when demand increases to D_2, the price rises to $25 and each firm increases its output to 9 sweaters a day. Industry output is 9,000 sweaters a day. When demand decreases to D_3, the price falls to $17 and each firm decreases its output to 7 sweaters a day. Industry output is 7,000 sweaters a day.

and others temporarily shut down. Firms are indifferent between these two activities, and whichever they choose, they incur an economic loss equal to total fixed cost. The number of firms that continue to produce is just enough to satisfy the market demand at a price of $17.

Let's now look at the profits that firms make and the losses they can incur in a short-run equilibrium.

Profits and Losses in the Short Run

In short-run equilibrium, although the firm produces the profit-maximizing output, it does not necessarily end up making an economic profit. It might do so, but it might alternatively break even (makes a normal profit) or incur an economic loss. To determine which of these outcomes occurs, we compare the firm's total revenue and total cost, or equivalently, we compare price with average total cost. If price equals average total cost, a firm breaks even—makes normal profit. If price exceeds average total cost, a firm makes an economic profit. If price is less than average total cost, a firm incurs an economic loss. Figure 12.7 shows these three possible short-run profit outcomes.

Three Possible Profit Outcomes In part (a), the price of a sweater is $20. Sidney produces 8 sweaters a day. Average total cost is also $20 a sweater, so Sidney makes normal profit and zero economic profit.

In part (b), the price of a sweater is $25. Profit is maximized when output is 9 sweaters a day. Here, price exceeds average total cost (*ATC*), so Sidney makes an economic profit. This economic profit is $42 a day. It is made up of $4.67 per sweater ($25.00 − $20.33) multiplied by the number of sweaters ($4.67 × 9 = $42). The blue rectangle shows this economic profit. The height of that rectangle is profit per sweater, $4.67, and the length is the quantity of sweaters produced, 9 a day, so the area of the rectangle measures Sidney's economic profit of $42 a day.

In part (c), the price of a sweater is $17. Here, price is less than average total cost and Sidney incurs an economic loss. Price and marginal revenue are $17 a sweater, and the profit-maximizing (in this case, loss-minimizing) output is 7 sweaters a day. Sidney's total revenue is $119 a day (7 × $17). Average total cost is $20.14 a sweater, so the economic loss is $3.14 per sweater ($20.14 − $17.00). This loss per sweater multiplied by the number of sweaters is $22 ($3.14 × 7 = $22). The red rectangle shows this

FIGURE 12.7
Three Possible Profit Outcomes in the Short Run

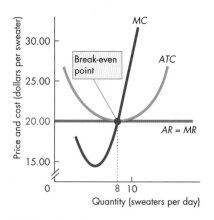
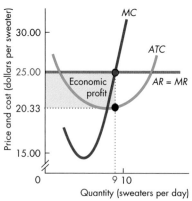
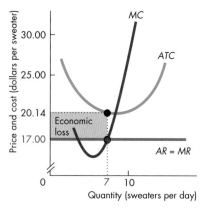

(a) Normal profit (b) Economic profit (c) Economic loss

In the short run, firms might break even (making a normal profit), make an economic profit, or incur an economic loss. If the price equals minimum average total cost, the firm breaks even and makes a normal profit (part a). If the price exceeds the average total cost of producing the profit-maximizing output, the firm makes an economic profit (the blue rectangle in part b). If the price is below minimum average total cost, the firm incurs an economic loss (the red rectangle in part c).

economic loss. The height of that rectangle is economic loss per sweater, $3.14, and the length is the quantity of sweaters produced, 7 a day, so the area of the rectangle measures Sidney's economic loss of $22 a day.

Long-Run Adjustments

In short-run equilibrium, a firm might make an economic profit, incur an economic loss, or break even (make normal profit). Although each of these three situations is a short-run equilibrium, only one of them is a long-run equilibrium. To see why, we need to examine the forces at work in a competitive industry in the long run.

In the long run, an industry adjusts in two ways:

- Entry and exit
- Changes in plant size

Let's look first at entry and exit.

Entry and Exit

In the long run, firms respond to economic profit and economic loss by either entering or exiting an industry. Firms enter an industry in which firms are making an economic profit, and they exit an industry in which firms are incurring an economic loss. Temporary economic profit or temporary economic loss, like the win or loss at a casino, do not trigger entry or exit. But the prospect of persistent economic profit or loss does.

Entry and exit influence price, the quantity produced, and economic profit. The immediate effect of these decisions is to shift the industry supply curve. If more firms enter an industry, supply increases and the industry supply curve shifts rightward. If firms exit an industry, supply decreases and the industry supply curve shifts leftward.

Let's see what happens when new firms enter an industry.

The Effects of Entry Figure 12.8 shows the effects of entry. Suppose that all the firms in the sweater industry have cost curves like Sidney's in Fig. 12.7. At any price greater than $20, firms make an economic profit. At any price less than $20, firms incur an economic loss. And at a price of $20, firms make zero economic profit. Also suppose that the demand curve for sweaters is D. If the industry supply curve is S_1, sweaters sell for $23 and 7,000 sweaters a day are produced. Firms in the industry

make an economic profit. This economic profit is a signal for new firms to enter the industry. As these events unfold, supply increases and the industry supply curve shifts rightward to S_0. With the greater supply and unchanged demand, the market price falls from $23 to $20 a sweater and the quantity produced by the industry increases from 7,000 to 8,000 sweaters a day.

Industry output increases, but Sidney's Sweaters and the other firms in the industry *decrease* output! As the price falls, each firm moves down along its supply curve and produces less. But because the number of firms in the industry increases, the industry as a whole produces more.

Because the price falls, each firm's economic profit decreases. When the price falls to $20, economic profit disappears and each firm makes a normal profit.

You have just discovered a key proposition:

As new firms enter an industry, the price falls and the economic profit of each existing firm decreases.

FIGURE 12.8

Entry and Exit

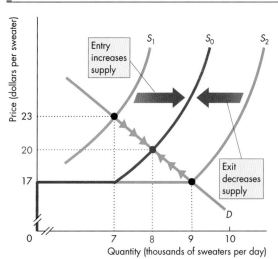

When new firms enter the sweater industry, the industry supply curve shifts rightward, from S_1 to S_0. The equilibrium price falls from $23 to $20, and the quantity produced increases from 7,000 to 8,000 sweaters. When firms exit the sweater industry, the industry supply curve shifts leftward, from S_2 to S_0. The equilibrium price rises from $17 to $20, and the quantity produced decreases from 9,000 to 8,000 sweaters.

An example of this process occurred during the 1980s in the personal computer industry. When IBM introduced its first PC, there was little competition and the price of a PC gave IBM a big profit. But new firms such as Compaq, NEC, Dell, and a host of others entered the industry with machines that were technologically identical to IBM's. In fact, they were so similar that they came to be called "clones." The massive wave of entry into the personal computer industry shifted the supply curve rightward and lowered the price and the economic profit for all firms.

Let's now look at the effects of exit.

The Effects of Exit Figure 12.8 shows the effects of exit. Suppose that firms' costs and market demand are the same as before. But now suppose the supply curve is S_2. The market price is $17, and 9,000 sweaters a day are produced. Firms now incur an economic loss. This economic loss is a signal for some firms to exit the industry. As firms exit, the supply curve shifts leftward to S_0. With the decrease in supply, industry output decreases from 9,000 to 8,000 sweaters and the price rises from $17 to $20.

As the price rises, Sidney's Sweaters, like each other firm in the industry, moves up along its supply curve and increases output. That is, for each firm that remains in the industry, the profit-maximizing output increases. Because the price rises and each firm sells more, economic loss decreases. When the price rises to $20, each firm makes normal profit.

You have just discovered a second key proposition:

As firms leave an industry, the price rises and the economic loss of each remaining firm decreases.

An example of a firm leaving an industry is International Harvester, a manufacturer of farm equipment. For decades, people associated the name "International Harvester" with tractors, combines, and other farm machines. But International Harvester wasn't the only maker of farm equipment. The industry became intensely competitive, and the firm began losing money.

International Harvester exited because it was incurring an economic loss. Its exit decreased supply and made it possible for the remaining firms in the industry to break even.

You've now seen how economic profits induce entry, which in turn lowers profits, and you've seen how economic losses induce exit, which in turn eliminates losses. Let's now look at changes in plant size.

Changes in Plant Size

A firm changes its plant size if, by doing so, it can lower its costs and increase its economic profit. You can probably think of lots of examples of firms changing their plant size.

One example that has almost certainly happened near your campus in recent years is a change in the plant size of Kinko's or similar copy shops. Another is the number of FedEx vans that you see on the streets and highways. Another is the number of square feet of retail space devoted to selling computers and video games. These are examples of firms increasing their plant size to seek larger profits.

There are also many examples of firms decreasing their plant size to avoid economic losses. One of these is Schwinn, the Chicago-based maker of bicycles. As competition from Asian bicycle makers became tougher, Schwinn cut back. Many firms have scaled back their operations—a process called *downsizing*—in recent years.

Figure 12.9 shows a situation in which Sidney can increase his profit by increasing the plant size. With its current plant, Sidney's marginal cost curve is MC_0 and its short-run average total cost curve is $SRAC_0$. The market price is $25 a sweater, so Sidney's marginal revenue curve is MR_0 and Sidney maximizes profit by producing 6 sweaters a day.

Sidney's Sweaters' long-run average cost curve is $LRAC$. By increasing its plant size—installing more knitting machines—it can move along its long-run average cost curve. As Sidney increases the plant size, the short-run marginal cost curve shifts rightward.

Recall that a firm's short-run supply curve is linked to its marginal cost curve. As Sidney's marginal cost curve shifts rightward, so does its supply curve. If Sidney's Sweaters and the other firms in the industry increase their plants, the short-run industry supply curve shifts rightward and the market price falls. The fall in the market price limits the extent to which Sidney can profit from increasing the plant size.

Figure 12.9 also shows Sidney's Sweaters in a long-run competitive equilibrium. This situation arises when the market price has fallen to $20 a sweater. Marginal revenue is MR_1, and Sidney maximizes profit by producing 8 sweaters a day. In this situation, Sidney cannot increase his profit by changing the plant size. Sidney is producing at minimum long-run average cost (point m on $LRAC$).

Because Sidney is producing at minimum long-run average cost, it has no incentive to change the plant size.

FIGURE 12.9

Plant Size and Long-Run Equilibrium

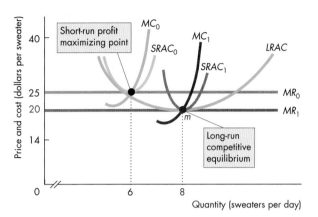

Initially, Sidney's plant has marginal cost curve MC_0 and short-run average total cost curve $SRAC_0$. The market price is $25 a sweater, and Sidney's marginal revenue is MR_0. The short-run profit-maximizing quantity is 6 sweaters a day. Sidney can increase his profit by increasing the plant size. If all firms in the sweater industry increase their plant sizes, the short-run industry supply increases and the market price falls. In long-run equilibrium, a firm operates with the plant size that minimizes its average cost. Here, Sidney operates the plant with short-run marginal cost MC_1 and short-run average cost $SRAC_1$. Sidney is also on the long-run average cost curve $LRAC$ and produces at point m. Output is 8 sweaters a day, and average total cost equals the price of a sweater—$20.

Either a bigger plant or a smaller plant has a higher long-run average cost. If Fig. 12.9 describes the situation of all firms in the sweater industry, the industry is in long-run equilibrium. No firm has an incentive to change its plant size. Also, because each firm is making zero economic profit (normal profit), no firm has an incentive to enter the industry or to leave it.

Long-Run Equilibrium

Long-run equilibrium occurs in a competitive industry when economic profit is zero (when firms earn normal profit). If the firms in a competitive industry are making economic profit, new firms enter the industry. If firms can lower their costs by increasing

their plant size, they expand. Each of these actions increases industry supply, shifts the industry supply curve rightward, lowers the price, and decreases economic profit.

Firms continue to enter and economic profit continues to decrease as long as firms in the industry are earning positive economic profits. When economic profit has been eliminated, firms stop entering the industry. And when firms are operating with the least-cost plant size, they stop expanding.

If the firms in a competitive industry are incurring an economic loss, some firms exit the industry. If firms can lower their costs by decreasing their plant size, they downsize. Each of these actions decreases industry supply, shifts the industry supply curve leftward, raises the price, and increases economic profit (shrinks economic loss).

Firms continue to exit and economic loss continues to shrink as long as firms in the industry are incurring economic losses. When economic loss has been eliminated, firms stop exiting the industry. And when firms are operating with the least-cost plant size, they stop downsizing.

So in long-run equilibrium in a competitive industry, firms neither enter nor exit the industry and neither expand nor downsize. Each firm earns normal profit.

R E V I E W Q U I Z

- When a firm in perfect competition produces the quantity that maximizes profit, what is the relationship among the firm's marginal cost, marginal revenue, and price?
- If firms in a competitive industry make economic profits, what happens to supply, price, output, and economic profit?
- If firms in a competitive industry incur economic losses, what happens to supply, price, output, and economic profit?

You've seen how a competitive industry adjusts toward its long-run equilibrium. But a competitive industry is rarely *in* a state of long-run equilibrium. It is constantly and restlessly evolving toward such an equilibrium. The constraints that firms face are constantly changing. The two most persistent sources of change are in tastes and technology. Let's see how a competitive industry reacts to such changes.

Changing Tastes and Advancing Technology

INCREASED AWARENESS OF THE HEALTH HAZARDS of smoking has caused a decrease in the demand for tobacco and cigarettes. The development of inexpensive car and air transportation has caused a huge decrease in the demand for long-distance trains and buses. Solid-state electronics have caused a large decrease in the demand for TV and radio repair. The development of good-quality inexpensive clothing has decreased the demand for sewing machines. What happens in a competitive industry when there is a permanent decrease in the demand for its products?

The development of the microwave oven has produced an enormous increase in demand for paper, glass, and plastic cooking utensils and for plastic wrap. The widespread use of the personal computer has brought a huge increase in the demand for floppy disks. What happens in a competitive industry when the demand for its product increases?

Advances in technology are constantly lowering the costs of production. New biotechnologies have dramatically lowered the costs of producing many food and pharmaceutical products. New electronic technologies have lowered the cost of producing just about every good and service. What happens in a competitive industry when technological change lowers its production costs?

Let's use the theory of perfect competition to answer these questions.

A Permanent Change in Demand

Figure 12.10(a) shows a competitive industry that initially is in long-run equilibrium. The demand curve is D_0, the supply curve is S_0, the market price is P_0, and industry output is Q_0. Figure 12.10(b) shows a single firm in this initial long-run equilibrium. The firm produces q_0 and makes a normal profit and zero economic profit.

Now suppose that demand decreases and the demand curve shifts leftward to D_1, as shown in part (a). The price falls to P_1, and the quantity supplied by the industry decreases from Q_0 to Q_1 as the industry slides down its short-run supply curve S_0. Part (b) shows the situation facing a firm. Price is now below the firm's minimum average total cost, so the firm incurs an economic loss. But to keep its loss to a

minimum, the firm adjusts its output to keep marginal cost equal to price. At a price of P_1, each firm produces an output of q_1.

The industry is now in short-run equilibrium but not long-run equilibrium. It is in short-run equilibrium because each firm is maximizing profit. But it is not in long-run equilibrium because each firm is incurring an economic loss—its average total cost exceeds the price.

The economic loss is a signal for some firms to leave the industry. As they do so, short-run industry supply gradually decreases and the supply curve gradually shifts leftward. As industry supply decreases, the price rises. At each higher price, a firm's profit-maximizing output is greater, so the firms remaining in the industry increase their output as the price rises. Each firm slides up its marginal cost or supply curve (part b). That is, as firms exit the industry, industry output decreases but the output of the firms that remain in the industry increases. Eventually, enough firms leave the industry for the industry supply curve to have shifted to S_1 (part a). At this time, the price has returned to its original level, P_0. At this price, the firms remaining in the industry produce q_0, the same quantity that they produced before the decrease in demand. Because firms are now making normal profits and zero economic profit, no firm wants to enter or exit the industry. The industry supply curve remains at S_1, and industry output is Q_2. The industry is again in long-run equilibrium.

The difference between the initial long-run equilibrium and the final long-run equilibrium is the number of firms in the industry. A permanent decrease in demand has decreased the number of firms. Each remaining firm produces the same output in the new long-run equilibrium as it did initially and earns a normal profit. In the process of moving from the initial equilibrium to the new one, firms incur economic losses.

We've just worked out how a competitive industry responds to a permanent *decrease* in demand. A permanent increase in demand triggers a similar response, except in the opposite direction. The increase in demand brings a higher price, economic profit, and entry. Entry increases industry supply and eventually lowers the price to its original level.

The demand for airline travel in the United States has increased permanently in recent years, and the deregulation of the airlines has freed up firms to seek profit opportunities in this industry. The result has been a massive rate of entry of new airlines. The

FIGURE 12.10

A Decrease in Demand

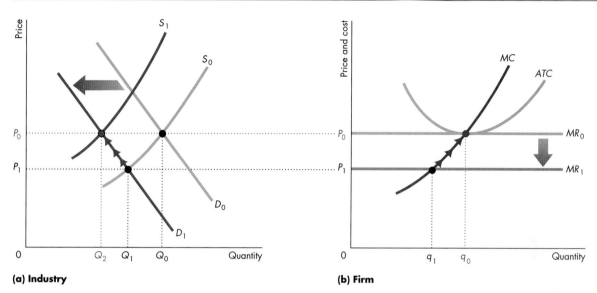

(a) Industry

(b) Firm

An industry starts out in long-run competitive equilibrium. Part (a) shows the industry demand curve D_0, the industry supply curve S_0, the equilibrium quantity Q_0, and the market price P_0. Each firm sells its output at price P_0, so its marginal revenue curve is MR_0 in part (b). Each firm produces q_0 and makes a normal profit. Demand decreases permanently from D_0 to D_1 (part a). The equilibrium price falls to P_1, each firm decreases its output to q_1 (part b), and industry output decreases to Q_1 (part a).

In this new situation, firms incur economic losses and some firms leave the industry. As they do so, the industry supply curve gradually shifts leftward, from S_0 to S_1. This shift gradually raises the market price from P_1 back to P_0. While the price is below P_0, firms incur economic losses and some firms leave the industry. Once the price has returned to P_0, each firm makes a normal profit. Firms have no further incentive to leave the industry. Each firm produces q_0, and industry output is Q_2.

---

process of competition and change in the airline industry is similar to what we have just studied (but with an increase in demand rather than a decrease in demand).

We've now studied the effects of a permanent change in demand for a good. To study these effects, we began and ended in a long-run equilibrium and examined the process that takes a market from one equilibrium to another. It is this process, not the equilibrium points, that describes the real world.

One feature of the predictions that we have just generated seems odd: In the long run, regardless of whether demand increases or decreases, the price returns to its original level. Is this outcome inevitable? In fact, it is not. It is possible for the long-run equilibrium price to remain the same, rise, or fall.

External Economies and Diseconomies

The change in the long-run equilibrium price depends on external economies and external diseconomies. **External economies** are factors beyond the control of an individual firm that lower its costs as the *industry* output increases. **External diseconomies** are factors outside the control of a firm that raise the firm's costs as industry output increases. With no external economies or external diseconomies, a firm's costs remain constant as the industry output changes.

Figure 12.11 illustrates these three cases and introduces a new supply concept: the long-run industry supply curve.

A **long-run industry supply curve** shows how the quantity supplied by an industry varies as the market price varies after all the possible adjustments have been made, including changes in plant size and the number of firms in the industry.

Part (a) shows the case we have just studied—no external economies or diseconomies. The long-run industry supply curve (LS_A) is perfectly elastic. In this case, a permanent increase in demand from D_0 to D_1 has no effect on the price in the long run. The increase in demand brings a temporary increase in price to P_S and a short-run quantity increase from Q_0 to Q_S. Entry increases short-run supply from S_0 to S_1, which lowers the price to its original level, P_0, and increases the quantity to Q_1.

Part (b) shows the case of external diseconomies. The long-run supply industry curve (LS_B) slopes upward. A permanent increase in demand from D_0 to D_1 increases the price in both the short run and the long run. As in the previous case, the increase in demand brings a temporary increase in price to P_S and a short-run quantity increase from Q_0 to Q_S. Entry increases short-run supply from S_0 to S_2, which lowers the price to P_2 and increases the quantity to Q_2.

One source of external diseconomies is congestion. The airline industry provides a good example. With bigger airline industry output, there is more congestion of airports and airspace, which results in longer delays and extra waiting time for passengers and airplanes. These external diseconomies mean that as the output of air transportation services increases (in the absence of technological advances), average cost increases. As a result, the long-run supply curve is upward sloping. So a permanent increase in demand brings an increase in quantity and a rise in the price. (Industries with external diseconomies might nonetheless have a falling price because technological advances shift the long-run supply curve downward.)

Part (c) shows the case of external economies. In this case, the long-run industry supply curve (LS_C) slopes downward. A permanent increase in demand from D_0 to D_1 increases the price in the short run and lowers it in the long run. Again, the increase in demand brings a temporary increase in price to P_S and a short-run quantity increase from Q_0 to Q_S. Entry increases short-run supply from S_0 to S_3, which lowers the price to P_3 and increases the quantity to Q_3.

FIGURE 12.11

Long-Run Changes in Price and Quantity

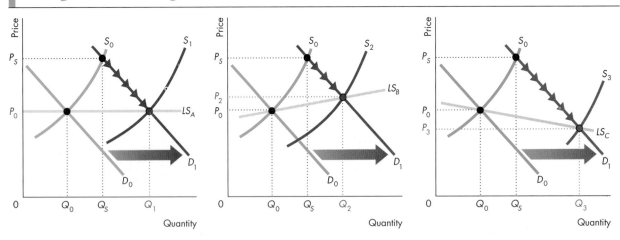

(a) Constant-cost industry   **(b) Increasing-cost industry**   **(c) Decreasing-cost industry**

Three possible changes in price and quantity occur in the long run. When demand increases from D_0 to D_1, entry occurs and the industry supply curve shifts from S_0 to S_1. In part (a), the long-run supply curve, LS_A, is horizontal. The quantity increases from Q_0 to Q_1, and the price remains constant at P_0. In part (b), the long-run supply curve is LS_B; the price rises to P_2, and the quantity increases to Q_2. This case occurs in industries with external diseconomies. In part (c), the long-run supply curve is LS_C; the price falls to P_3, and the quantity increases to Q_3. This case occurs in an industry with external economies.

One of the best examples of external economies is the growth of specialist support services for an industry as it expands. As farm output increased in the nineteenth and early twentieth centuries, the services available to farmers expanded and average farm costs fell. For example, new firms specialized in the development and marketing of farm machinery and fertilizers. As a result, average farm costs decreased. Farms enjoyed the benefits of external economies. As a consequence, as the demand for farm products increased, the output increased but the price fell.

Over the long term, the prices of many goods and services have fallen, not because of external economies but because of technological change. Let's now study this influence on a competitive market.

Technological Change

Industries are constantly discovering lower-cost techniques of production. Most cost-saving production techniques cannot be implemented, however, without investing in new plant and equipment. As a consequence, it takes time for a technological advance to spread through an industry. Some firms whose plants are on the verge of being replaced will be quick to adopt the new technology, while other firms whose plants have recently been replaced will continue to operate with an old technology until they can no longer cover their average variable cost. Once average variable cost cannot be covered, a firm will scrap even a relatively new plant (embodying an old technology) in favor of a plant with a new technology.

New technology allows firms to produce at a lower cost. As a result, as firms adopt a new technology, their cost curves shift downward. With lower costs, firms are willing to supply a given quantity at a lower price, or, equivalently, they are willing to supply a larger quantity at a given price. In other words, industry supply increases, and the industry supply curve shifts rightward. With a given demand, the quantity produced increases and the price falls.

Two forces are at work in an industry undergoing technological change. Firms that adopt the new technology make an economic profit. So there is entry by new-technology firms. Firms that stick with the old technology incur economic losses. They either exit the industry or switch to the new technology.

As old-technology firms disappear and new-technology firms enter, the price falls and the quantity produced increases. Eventually, the industry arrives at a long-run equilibrium in which all the firms use the new technology and make a zero economic profit (a normal profit). Because in the long run competition eliminates economic profit, technological change brings only temporary gains to producers. But the lower prices and better products that technological advances bring are permanent gains for consumers.

The process that we've just described is one in which some firms experience economic profits and others experience economic losses. It is a period of dynamic change for an industry. Some firms do well, and others do badly. Often, the process has a geographical dimension—the expanding new-technology firms bring prosperity to what was once the boondocks, and traditional industrial regions decline. Sometimes, the new-technology firms are in a foreign country, while the old-technology firms are in the domestic economy. The information revolution of the 1990s has produced many examples of changes like these. Commercial banking, traditionally concentrated in New York, San Francisco, and other large cities, now flourishes in Charlotte, North Carolina, which has become the nation's number three commercial banking city. Television shows and movies, traditionally made in Los Angeles and New York, are now made in large numbers in Orlando, Florida. Technological advances are not confined to the information and entertainment industry. Even milk production is undergoing a major technological change because of genetic engineering.

REVIEW QUIZ

- Describe the course of events in a competitive industry that follow a decrease in demand. What happens to output, price, and economic profit in the short run and in the long run?
- Describe the course of events in a competitive industry that follow an increase in demand. What happens to output, price, and economic profit in the short run and in the long run?
- Describe the course of events in a competitive industry that follow the adoption of a new technology. What happens to output, price, and economic profit in the short run and in the long run?

Competition and Efficiency

A COMPETITIVE INDUSTRY CAN ACHIEVE AN EFFI-
cient use of resources. You studied efficiency in
Chapter 6 using only the concepts of demand, supply, consumer surplus and producer surplus. But now
that you have learned what lies behind the demand
and supply curves of a competitive market, you can
gain a deeper understanding of how the competitive
market achieves efficiency.

Efficient Use of Resources

Recall that resource use is efficient when we produce
the goods and services that people value most highly
(see Chapter 6, pp. 108–109). If someone can become
better off without anyone else becoming worse off,
resources are not being used efficiently. For example,
suppose we produce a computer that no one uses and
that no one will ever use. Suppose also that some people are clamoring for more video games. If we produce one less computer and reallocate the unused
resources to produce more video games, some people
will become better off and no one will be worse off.

In the more technical language that you have
learned, resource use is efficient when marginal benefit equals marginal cost. In the computer and video
games example, the marginal benefit of video games
exceeds the marginal cost. And the marginal cost of a
computer exceeds its marginal benefit. So by producing fewer computers and more video games, we move
resources toward a higher-value use.

Choices, Equilibrium, and Efficiency

We can use what you have learned about the decisions
made by consumers and competitive firms and market
equilibrium to describe an efficient use of resources.

Choices Consumers allocate their budgets to get the
most value possible out of them. And we derive a
consumer's demand curve by finding how the best
budget allocation changes as the price of a good
changes. So consumers get the most value out of their
resources at all points along their demand curves,
which are also their marginal benefit curves.

Competitive firms produce the quantity that
maximizes profit. And we derive the firm's supply
curve by finding the profit-maximizing quantity at
each price. So firms get the most value out of their
resources at all points along their supply curves, which
are also their marginal cost curves. (On their supply
curves, firms are *technologically efficient*—they get the
maximum possible output from given inputs—and
economically efficient—they combine resources to minimize cost. See Chapter 10, pp. 201–202.)

Equilibrium In competitive equilibrium, the quantity
demanded equals the quantity supplied. So the price
equals the consumers' marginal benefit and the producers' marginal cost. In this situation, the gains
from trade between consumers and producers are
maximized. These gains from trade are the consumer
surplus plus the producer surplus.

The gains from trade for consumers are measured
by *consumer surplus*, which is the area between the
demand curve and the price paid. (See Chapter 6,
p. 111.) The gains from trade for producers are measured by *producer surplus*, which is the area between
the marginal cost curve and the price received. The
total gains from trade are the sum of consumer surplus and producer surplus.

Efficiency If the people who consume and produce a
good or service are the only ones affected by it, and if
the market for it is in equilibrium, then resources are
being used efficiently. They cannot be reallocated to
increase their value.

In such a situation, there are no *external benefits*
or *external costs*. **External benefits** are benefits that
accrue to people other than the buyer of a good. For
example, you might get a benefit from your neighbor's expenditure on her garden. Your neighbor buys
the quantities of garden plants that make her as well
off as possible, not her plus you.

In the absence of external benefits, the market
demand curve measures marginal *social* benefit—the
value that *everyone* places on one more unit of a good
or service.

External costs are costs not borne by the producer of a good or service but by someone else. For
example, a firm might lower its costs by polluting.
The cost of pollution is an external cost. Firms produce the output level that maximizes their own profit
and they do not count the cost of pollution as a
charge against their profit.

In the absence of external costs, the market supply curve measures marginal *social* cost—the entire
marginal cost that *anyone* bears to produce one more
unit of a good or service.

An Efficient Allocation Figure 12.12 shows an efficient allocation. Consumers are efficient at all points on the demand curve, D (which is also the marginal benefit curve MB). Producers are efficient at all points on the supply curve, S (which is also the marginal cost curve MC). Resources are used efficiently at the quantity Q^* and price P^*. Marginal benefit equals marginal cost, and the sum of producer surplus (blue area) and consumer surplus (green area) is maximized.

If output is Q_0, marginal cost is C_0 and marginal benefit is B_0. Producers can supply more of the good for a cost lower than the price consumers are willing to pay and everyone gains by increasing the quantity produced. If output is greater than Q^*, marginal cost exceeds marginal benefit. It costs producers more to supply the good than the price consumers are willing to pay and everyone gains by decreasing the quantity produced.

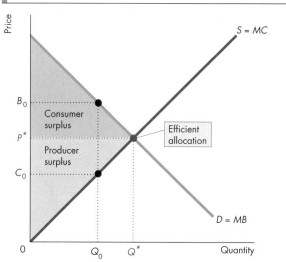

FIGURE 12.12

Efficiency of Competition

The efficient use of resources requires: consumers to be efficient, which occurs when they are on their demand curves; firms to be efficient, which occurs when they are on their supply curves; and the market to be in equilibrium with no external benefits or external costs. Resources are used efficiently at the quantity Q^* and the price P^*. With no external benefits or external costs, perfect competition achieves an efficient use of resources. If output is Q_0, the cost of producing one more unit, C_0, is less than its marginal benefit, B_0, and resources are not used efficiently.

Efficiency of Perfect Competition

Perfect competition achieves efficiency if there are no external benefits and external costs. In such a case, the benefits accrue to the buyers of the good and the costs are borne by its producer. In Fig. 12.12, the equilibrium quantity Q^* at the price P^* is efficient.

There are three main obstacles to efficiency:

1. Monopoly
2. Public goods
3. External costs and external benefits

Monopoly Monopoly (Chapter 13) restricts output below its competitive level to raise price and increase profit. Government policies (Chapter 19) arise to limit such use of monopoly power.

Public goods Goods such as national defense, the enforcement of law and order, the provision of clean drinking water, and the disposal of sewage and garbage are examples of public goods. Left to competitive markets, too small a quantity of them would be produced. Government institutions and policies (Chapter 18) help to overcome the problem of providing an efficient quantity of public goods.

External Costs and External Benefits The production of steel and chemicals can generate air and water pollution and perfect competition might produce too large a quantity of these goods. Government policies (Chapter 20) attempt to cope with external costs and benefits.

◆ You've now completed your study of perfect competition. And *Reading Between the Lines* on pp. 258–259 gives you an opportunity to use what you have learned to understand recent events in the highly competitive market for personal computers.

Although many markets approximate the model of perfect competition, many do not. Your next task is to study markets at the opposite extreme of market power—monopoly. Then, in Chapter 14, we'll study markets that lie between perfect competition and monopoly—monopolistic competition (competition with monopoly elements) and oligopoly (competition among a few producers). When you have completed this study, you'll have a toolkit that enables you to understand the variety of real-world markets.

Competition in the PC Industry

THE NEW YORK TIMES, NOVEMBER 13, 1998

Dell Reports Record Earnings and Revenues in 3rd Quarter

BY LAWRENCE M. FISHER

Dell Computer Corp. reported record third-quarter revenue and earnings Thursday as it continued to grow at several times the rate of the personal computer industry as a whole.

As always, Dell officials credited the strength of their direct sales model, in which the company bypasses distributors and dealers and builds each computer to order. Because the company holds very little inventory, it takes advantage of lower component costs, and is always selling a fresher product, which can command a higher profit margin. Dell said sales from its World Wide Web site exceeded $10 million a day for the first time during the quarter, three times the level in the quarter a year earlier.

Competitors have attempted to emulate the Dell model but with modest success so far. ...

For the quarter ended Nov. 1, Dell reported earnings of $384 million, ... up 55 percent from $248 million, in the [same] period a year earlier. Sales rose 51 percent, to $4.82 billion from $3.19 billion. ...

Dell has been gaining market share both internationally and in high-growth sectors like servers and laptop computers. ...

... while Compaq, IBM and Hewlett-Packard have all announced plans to emulate portions of Dell's business model, with various build-to-order plans, all have had difficulty in making the transition. Most are moving to a target inventory level of four weeks, while Dell maintains just eight days of inventory, allowing it to turn over inventory 46 times a year.

© 1998 The New York Times. Reprinted with permission. Further reproduction prohibited.

Essence of the Story

■ Dell Computer Corporation is an efficient, low-cost, and profitable maker of PCs and servers.

■ Dell sells directly to the customer and builds each computer to order. The firm maintains 8 days of inventory. An increasing volume of Dell's business is done on the Internet.

■ Attempts to copy Dell's business model by Compaq, IBM, and Hewlett-Packard have been only modestly successful. These firms hold more than 4 weeks of inventories.

■ The PC industry is highly competitive. We'll assume that it is perfectly competitive because one supplier's PC is a very close substitute for another supplier's PC.

■ The industry is in short-run equilibrium but not in long-run equilibrium. Many firms are earning economic profit. And economic profit is encouraging the entry of new firms and the expansion of existing firms.

■ Figure 1 shows the market for PCs 5 years ago and the effects of entry on the price and quantity of PCs.

■ The industry demand curve is D. Five years ago, the industry supply curve was S_0. The price was $5,000 per PC (think of this as an average PC), and the quantity produced by the industry was 25 million a year.

■ Supply then increases because of entry. The supply curve shifts rightward to S_1. (We'll assume that demand didn't change. In fact, demand did increase but by much less than the increase in supply.)

■ The price fell to $3,000 per PC, and the quantity produced by the industry increased to 35 million a year.

■ Figure 2 shows the situation facing one PC producer that has not adopted the latest and least-cost technology for making PCs.

■ The marginal cost curve is MC_0, and the average total cost curve is ATC_0. At $5,000 per PC, the marginal revenue curve is MR_0. The firm maximizes profit by producing 1 million PCs a year. Economic profit is $500 million a year.

■ When the price falls to $3,000 per PC, the marginal revenue curve is MR_1. If the firm sticks with its existing technology, it incurs an economic loss.

■ Figure 3 shows how the successful firm adopts a new technology to cut costs. Dell's build-to-order technology is an example because it lowers the cost of holding inventory.

■ When costs fall, the average total cost curve shifts downward to ATC_1 and the marginal cost curve shifts downward to MC_1. The firm expands output—in this example, to 3 million PCs a year. Economic profit is restored and, in this example, increases to $1.5 billion a year.

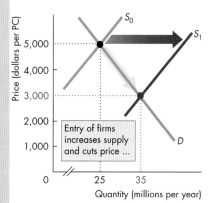

Figure 1 PC industry

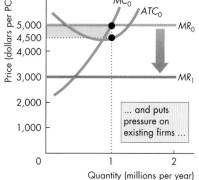

Figure 2 One PC firm

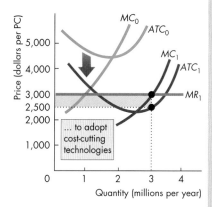

Figure 3 Cost-cutting technology

259

SUMMARY

KEY POINTS

Competition (pp. 240–241)

- Perfect competition arises when demand is large relative to the minimum efficient scale of production and when firms produce identical products.
- A perfectly competitive firm is a price taker.

The Firm's Decisions in Perfect Competition (pp. 242–246)

- The firm produces the output at which marginal revenue (price) equals marginal cost.
- If price is less than minimum average variable cost, the firm temporarily shuts down.
- A firm's supply curve is the upward-sloping part of its marginal cost curve above minimum average variable cost.
- An industry supply curve shows the sum of the quantities supplied by each firm at each price.

Output, Price, and Profit in Perfect Competition (pp. 247–251)

- Market demand and supply determine price.
- The firm produces the output at which price equals marginal cost.
- In the short run, a firm can make an economic profit, incur an economic loss, or break even.
- Economic profit induces entry. Economic loss induces exit.
- Entry and plant expansion increase supply and lower price and profit. Exit and plant contraction decrease supply and raise price and profit.
- In long-run equilibrium, economic profit is zero. There is no entry, exit, or change in plant size.

Changing Tastes and Advancing Technology (pp. 252–255)

- A permanent decrease in demand leads to a smaller industry output and a smaller number of firms.
- A permanent increase in demand leads to a larger industry output and a larger number of firms.

- The long-run effect of a change in demand on price depends on whether there are external economies (price falls) or external diseconomies (price rises) or neither (price remains constant).
- New technologies increase supply and in the long run lower the price and increase the quantity.

Competition and Efficiency (pp. 256–257)

- Resources are used efficiently when we produce goods and services in the quantities that people value most highly.
- When there are no external benefits and external costs, perfect competition achieves an efficient allocation. Marginal benefit equals marginal cost and the sum of consumer surplus and producer surplus is maximized.
- The existence of monopoly, public goods, and external costs and external benefits are obstacles to efficiency.

KEY FIGURES ◆

KEY TERMS

PROBLEMS

*1. Quick Copy is one of the many copy shops near the campus. The figure shows Quick Copy's cost curves.

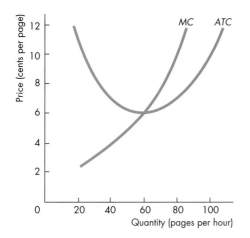

a. If the market price of copying one page is 10 cents, what is Quick Copy's profit-maximizing output?
b. Calculate Quick Copy's profit.
c. With no change in demand or technology, how will the price change in the long run?

2. Bob's is one of many burger stands along the beach. The figure shows Bob's cost curves.

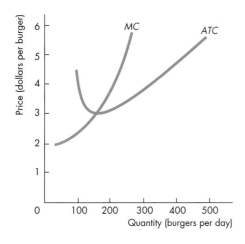

a. If the market price of a burger is $4, what is Bob's profit-maximizing output?
b. Calculate the profit that Bob's makes.
c. With no change in demand or technology, how will the price change in the long run?

*3. Pat's Pizza Kitchen is a price taker. Pat's cost of producing pizzas is:

Output (pizzas per hour)	Total cost (dollars per hour)
0	10
1	21
2	30
3	41
4	54
5	69

a. If a pizza sells for $14, what is Pat's profit-maximizing output per hour? How much economic profit does Pat make?
b. What is Pat's shutdown point?
c. Derive Pat's supply curve.
d. Over what price range will Pat leave the pizza industry?
e. Over what price range will other firms with costs identical to Pat's enter the industry?
f. What is the price of a pizza in the long run?

4. Lucy's Lasagna is a price taker. Lucy's cost of producing lasagna is:

Output (plates per hour)	Total cost (dollars per hour)
0	5
1	20
2	26
3	35
4	46
5	59

a. If lasagna sells for $7.50 a plate, what is Lucy's profit-maximizing output?
b. What is Lucy's shutdown point?
c. Over what price range will Lucy leave the lasagna industry?
d. Over what price range will other firms with costs identical to Lucy's enter the industry?
e. What is the price of lasagna in the long run?

*5. The market demand schedule for cassettes is:

Price (dollars per cassettes)	Quantity demanded (thousands of cassettes per week)
3.65	500
5.20	450
6.80	400
8.40	350
10.00	300
11.60	250
13.20	200
14.80	150

The market is perfectly competitive, and each firm has the following cost structure:

Output (cassettes per week)	Marginal cost (dollars per additional cassette)	Average variable cost (dollars per cassette)	Average total cost (dollars per cassette)
150	6.00	8.80	15.47
200	6.40	7.80	12.80
250	7.00	7.00	11.00
300	7.65	7.10	10.43
350	8.40	7.20	10.06
400	10.00	7.50	10.00
450	12.40	8.00	10.22
500	12.70	9.00	11.00

There are 1,000 firms in the industry.
a. What is the market price?
b. What is the industry's output?
c. What is the output produced by each firm?
d. What is the economic profit made by each firm?
e. Do firms enter or exit the industry?
f. What is the number of firms in the long run?

6. The same demand conditions as those in problem 5 prevail, and there are 1,000 firms in the industry, but total fixed costs increase by $980. What now are your answers to the questions in problem 5?

*7. In problem 5, a fall in the price of a compact disc decreases the demand for cassettes and the demand schedule becomes:

Price (dollars per cassette)	Quantity demanded (thousands of cassettes per week)
2.95	500
4.13	450
5.30	400
6.48	350
7.65	300
8.83	250
10.00	200
11.18	150

What now are your answers to the questions in problem 5?

8. In problem 6, a fall in the price of a compact disc decreases the demand for cassettes and the demand schedule becomes that given in problem 7. What now are your answers to the questions in problem 6?

CRITICAL THINKING

1. After you have studied Reading Between the Lines on pp. 258–259, answer the following questions.
   a. What is the main difference between the technology used by Dell Computer Corporation and that used by other PC makers?
   b. How does Dell get information about what its customers want to buy? (Hint: Visit http://www.dell.com)
   c. How do other firms get information about what their customers want to buy? (Hint: To whom do the other producers sell?)
   d. Why do you think Dell has a smaller inventory than most other PC producers?
   e. Is it always better to have a small inventory? If it is, why doesn't Dell cut its inventory to 2 days or 1 day?
   f. Suppose that PC technology stops advancing and the industry settles down into a long-run equilibrium. Describe that equilibrium and illustrate it in a graph.
   g. Suppose that PC technology does not stop advancing. Describe the evolution of the industry.

2. Why have the prices of pocket calculators and VCRs fallen? What do you expect has happened to the costs and economic profits of the firms that make these products? Explain your answer.

3. What has been the effect of an increase in world population on the wheat market and the individual wheat farmer? Explain your answer.

4. Visit the Parkin Web site and study the Web Reading Between the Lines, "Dumping Steel." Then answer the following questions:
   a. What is the argument in the news article about limiting steel imports?
   b. Do you agree with the argument? Why or why not?
   c. Why does the United States claim that foreign steel is being dumped here? (Use the links in the Web Reading Between the Lines to answer this question.)

Monopoly

You have been reading a lot in this book about firms that want to maximize profit. But perhaps you've been looking around at some of the places where you do business and wondering whether they are really so intent on profit. After all, don't you get a student's discount when you get a haircut? Don't museums and movie theaters give discounts to students, too? And what about the airline that gives a discount for buying a ticket in advance? Are your barber and movie theater owner, as well as the museum and airline operators, simply generous folks to whom the model of profit-maximizing firms does not apply? Aren't they simply throwing profit away by cutting ticket prices and offering discounts? ◆ When you buy electric power, you don't shop around. You buy from your electric power utility, which is your only available supplier. If you live in New York City and want cable TV service, you have only one option: buy from Manhattan Cable. These are examples of a single producer of a good or service controlling its supply. Such firms are obviously not like firms in perfectly competitive industries. They don't face a market-determined price. They can choose their own price. How do such firms behave? How do they choose the quantity to produce and the price at which to sell it? How does their behavior compare with firms in perfectly competitive industries? Do such firms charge prices that are too high and that damage the interests of consumers? Do such firms bring any benefits?

◆ In this chapter, we study markets in which an individual firm can influence the quantity of goods supplied and exert an influence on price. We also compare the performance of a firm in such markets with that of a competitive market and examine whether monopoly is as efficient as competition.

The Profits of Generosity

After studying this chapter, you will be able to:

- ■ Explain how monopoly arises and distinguish between single-price monopoly and price-discriminating monopoly

- ■ Explain how a single-price monopoly determines its output and price

- ■ Compare the performance and efficiency of single-price monopoly and competition

- ■ Define rent seeking and explain why it arises

- ■ Explain how price discrimination increases profit

- ■ Explain how monopoly regulation influences output, price, economic profit, and efficiency

Market Power

MARKET POWER AND COMPETITION ARE THE TWO forces that operate in most markets. **Market power** is the ability to influence the market, and in particular the market price, by influencing the total quantity offered for sale.

The firms in perfect competition that you studied in Chapter 12 have no market power. They face the force of raw competition and are price takers. The firms that we study in this chapter operate at the opposite extreme. They face no competition and exercise raw market power. We call this extreme *monopoly*. A **monopoly** is an industry that produces a good or service for which no close substitute exists and in which there is one supplier that is protected from competition by a barrier preventing the entry of new firms.

Examples of monopoly include your local phone, gas, electricity, and water suppliers as well as DeBeers, the South African diamond producer, and Microsoft Corporation, the software developer that created your computer's operating system.

How Monopoly Arises

Monopoly has two key features:

■ No close substitute
■ Barriers to entry

No Close Substitute   Even if only one firm produces a good that has a close substitute, that firm effectively faces competition from the producers of the substitute. Water supplied by a local public utility is an example of a good that does not have close substitutes. While it does have a close substitute for drinking—bottled spring water—it has no effective substitutes for showering or washing a car.

Monopolies are constantly under attack from new products and ideas that substitute for products produced by monopolies. For example, Federal Express, UPS, the fax machine, and e-mail have weakened the monopoly of the U.S. Postal Service. Similarly, the satellite dish has weakened the monopoly of cable television companies.

But new products also are constantly creating monopolies. An example is Microsoft's monopoly in DOS during the 1980s and in the Windows operating system today.

Barriers to Entry   Legal or natural constraints that protect a firm from potential competitors are **barriers to entry**. A firm can sometimes create its own barrier to entry by acquiring a significant portion of a key resource. DeBeers, for example, controls more than 80 percent of the world's supply of natural diamonds. But most monopolies arise from two other types of barrier: legal barriers and natural barriers.

Legal Barriers to Entry   Legal barriers to entry create legal monopoly. A **legal monopoly** is a market in which competition and entry are restricted by the granting of a public franchise, government license, patent, or copyright,

A *public franchise* is an exclusive right granted to a firm to supply a good or service. An example is the U.S. Postal Service, which has the exclusive right to carry first-class mail. A *government license* controls entry into particular occupations, professions, and industries. Examples of this type of barrier to entry are medicine, law, dentistry, schoolteaching, architecture, and many other professional services. Licensing does not always create monopoly, but it does restrict competition.

A *patent* is an exclusive right granted to the inventor of a product or service. A *copyright* is an exclusive right granted to the author or composer of a literary, musical, dramatic, or artistic work. Patents and copyrights are valid for a limited time period that varies from country to country. In the United States, a patent is valid for 20 years. Patents encourage the *invention* of new products and production methods. They also stimulate *innovation*—the use of new inventions—by encouraging inventors to publicize their discoveries and offer them for use under license. Patents have stimulated innovations in areas as diverse as soybean seeds, pharmaceuticals, memory chips, and video games.

Natural Barriers to Entry   Natural barriers to entry create a **natural monopoly**, which is an industry in which one firm can supply the entire market at a lower price than two or more firms can.

Figure 13.1 shows a natural monopoly in the distribution of electric power. Here, the demand curve for electric power is *D* and the average total cost curve is *ATC*. Because average total cost decreases as output increases, economies of scale prevail over the entire length of the *ATC* curve. One firm can produce 4 million kilowatt-hours at 5 cents a kilowatt-hour. At this price, the quantity demanded is 4 million kilowatt-hours. So if the price were 5 cents, one firm could supply the entire market. If two firms shared the market, it would cost each of them 10 cents a kilowatt-hour to produce a total of 4 million kilowatt-hours. If four firms shared the market, it would cost each of them 15 cents a kilowatt-hour to produce a total of 4 million kilowatt-hours. So in conditions like those shown in Fig. 13.1, one firm can supply the entire market at a lower cost than two or more firms can. The distribution of electric power is an example of natural monopoly. So is the distribution of water and gas.

Most monopolies are regulated in some way by government agencies. We will study such regulation at the end of this chapter. But for two reasons, we'll first study unregulated monopoly. First, we can better understand why governments regulate monopolies and the effects of regulation if we also know how an unregulated monopoly behaves. Second, even in industries with more than one producer, firms often

have a degree of monopoly power, and the theory of monopoly sheds light on the behavior of such firms and industries.

A major difference between monopoly and competition is that a monopoly sets its own price. But in doing so, it faces a market constraint. Let's see how the market limits a monopoly's pricing choices.

Monopoly Price-Setting Strategies

All monopolies face a tradeoff between price and the quantity sold. To sell a larger quantity, the monopolist must charge a lower price. But there are two broad monopoly situations that create different tradeoffs. They are:

■ Price discrimination
■ Single price

Price Discrimination Many firms price discriminate, and most are *not* monopolies. Airlines offer a dizzying array of different prices for the same trip. Pizza producers charge one price for a single pizza and almost give away a second pizza. These are examples of *price discrimination*. **Price discrimination** is the practice of selling different units of a good or service for different prices. Different customers might pay different prices (like airline passengers), or one customer might pay different prices for different quantities bought (like the bargain price for a second pizza).

When a firm price discriminates, it looks as if it is doing its customers a favor. In fact, it is charging the highest possible price for each unit sold and making the largest possible profit.

Not all monopolies can price discriminate. The main obstacle to price discrimination is resale by customers who buy for a low price. Because of resale possibilities, price discrimination is limited to monopolies that sell services that cannot be resold.

Single Price DeBeers sells diamonds (of a given size and quality) for the same price to all its customers. If it tried to sell at a low price to some customers and at a higher price to others, only the low-price customers would buy from DeBeers. Others would buy from DeBeers' low-price customers.

DeBeers is a *single-price* monopoly. A **single-price monopoly** is a firm that must sell each unit of its output for the same price to all its customers.

We'll look first at single-price monopoly.

FIGURE 13.1
Natural Monopoly

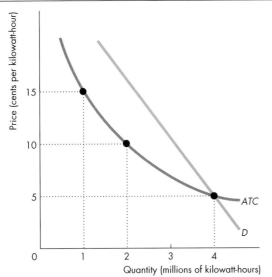

The demand curve for electric power is D, and the average total cost curve is ATC. Economies of scale exist over the entire ATC curve. One firm can distribute 4 million kilowatt-hours at a cost of 5 cents a kilowatt-hour. This same total output costs 10 cents a kilowatt-hour with two firms and 15 cents a kilowatt-hour with four firms. So one firm can meet the market demand at a lower cost than two or more firms can, and the market is a natural monopoly.

A Single-Price Monopoly's Output and Price Decision

To UNDERSTAND HOW A SINGLE-PRICE MONOPOLY makes its output and price decision, we must first study the link between price and marginal revenue.

Price and Marginal Revenue

Because in a monopoly there is only one firm, the firm's demand curve is the market demand curve. Let's look at Bobbie's Barbershop, the sole supplier of haircuts in Cairo, Nebraska. The table in Fig. 13.2 shows Bobbie's demand schedule. At a price of $20, she sells no haircuts. The lower the price, the more haircuts per hour Bobbie can sell. For example, at $12, consumers demand 4 haircuts per hour (row *e*).

Total revenue (*TR*) is the price (*P*) multiplied by the quantity sold (*Q*). For example, in row *d*, Bobbie sells 3 haircuts at $14 each, so total revenue is $42. *Marginal revenue* (*MR*) is the change in total revenue (ΔTR) resulting from a one-unit increase in the quantity sold. For example, if the price falls from $16 (row *c*) to $14 (row *d*), the quantity sold increases from 2 to 3 haircuts. Total revenue rises from $32 to $42, so the change in total revenue is $10. Because the quantity sold increases by 1 haircut, marginal revenue equals the change in total revenue and is $10. Marginal revenue is placed between the two rows to emphasize that marginal revenue relates to the *change* in the quantity sold.

Figure 13.2 shows Bobbie's demand curve (*D*) and marginal revenue curve (*MR*) and also illustrates the calculation we've just made. Notice that at each level of output, marginal revenue is less than price—the marginal revenue curve lies below the demand curve. Why is marginal revenue less than price? The reason is that when the price is lowered to sell one more unit, two opposing forces affect total revenue. The lower price results in a revenue loss, and the increased quantity sold results in a revenue gain. For example, at a price of $16, Bobbie sells 2 haircuts (point *c*). If she lowers the price to $14, she sells 3 haircuts and has a revenue gain of $14 on the third haircut. But she now receives only $14 on the first two—$2 less than before. As a result, she loses $4 of revenue on the first 2 haircuts. To calculate marginal revenue, she must deduct this amount from the revenue gain of $14. So her marginal revenue is $10, which is less than the price.

FIGURE 13.2

Demand and Marginal Revenue

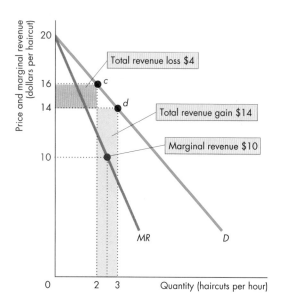

	Price (P) (dollars per haircut)	Quantity demanded (Q) (haircuts per hour)	Total revenue (TR = P × Q) (dollars)	Marginal revenue (MR = ΔTR/ΔQ) (dollars per additional haircut)
a	20	0	0	
				18
b	18	1	18	
				14
c	16	2	32	
				10
d	14	3	42	
				6
e	12	4	48	
				2
f	10	5	50	

The table shows Bobbie's demand schedule. Total revenue (TR) is price multiplied by quantity sold. For example, in row c the price is $16 a haircut, 2 haircuts are sold, and total revenue is $32. Marginal revenue (MR) is the change in total revenue that results from a one-unit increase in the quantity sold. For example, when the price falls from $16 to $14 a haircut, the quantity sold increases by 1 haircut and total revenue increases by $10. Marginal revenue is $10. The demand curve, D, and the marginal revenue curve, MR, are based on the numbers in the table and illustrate the calculation of marginal revenue when the price falls from $16 to $14.

Marginal Revenue and Elasticity

A single-price monopoly's marginal revenue is related to the *elasticity of demand* for its good. The demand for a good can be *elastic* (the elasticity of demand is greater than 1), *inelastic* (the elasticity of demand is less than 1), or *unit elastic* (the elasticity of demand is equal to 1). Demand is *elastic* if a 1 percent fall in price brings a greater than 1 percent increase in the quantity demanded. Demand is *inelastic* if a 1 percent fall in price brings a less than 1 percent increase in the quantity demanded. And demand is *unit elastic* if a 1 percent fall in price brings a 1 percent increase in the quantity demanded.

If demand is elastic, a fall in price brings an increase in total revenue—the increase in revenue from the increase in quantity sold outweighs the decrease in revenue from the lower price—and marginal revenue is positive. If demand is inelastic, a fall in price brings a decrease in total revenue—the increase in revenue from the increase in quantity sold is outweighed by the decrease in revenue from the lower price—and marginal revenue is negative. If demand is unit elastic, total revenue does not change—the increase in revenue from the increase in quantity sold offsets the decrease in revenue from the lower price—and marginal revenue is zero. (Chapter 5, pp. 92–93, explains the relationship between total revenue and elasticity more fully.)

Figure 13.3 illustrates the relationship between marginal revenue, total revenue, and elasticity. As the price of a haircut gradually falls from $20 to $10, the quantity of haircuts demanded increases from 0 to 5 an hour. Over this output range, marginal revenue is positive (part a), total revenue increases (part b), and the demand for haircuts is elastic. As the price falls from $10 to $0 a haircut, the quantity of haircuts demanded increases from 5 to 10 an hour. Over this output range, marginal revenue is negative (part a), total revenue decreases (part b), and the demand for haircuts is inelastic. When the price is $10 a haircut, marginal revenue is zero, total revenue is a maximum, and the demand for haircuts is unit elastic.

Monopoly Demand Is Always Elastic The relationship between marginal revenue and elasticity that you've just discovered implies that a profit-maximizing monopoly never produces an output in the inelastic range of its demand curve. If it did so, it could charge a higher price, produce a smaller quantity, and increase its profit. Let's now look more closely at a monopoly's price and output decision.

FIGURE 13.3

Marginal Revenue and Elasticity

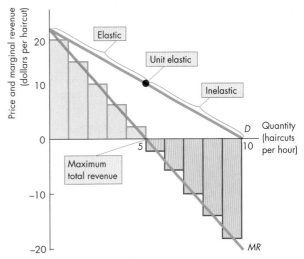

(a) Demand and marginal revenue curves

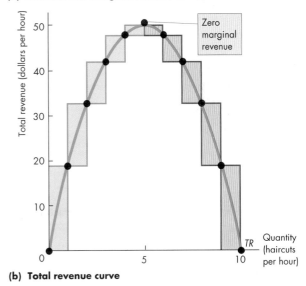

(b) Total revenue curve

Bobbie's demand curve (*D*) and marginal revenue curve (*MR*) are shown in part (a), and total revenue curve (*TR*) is shown in part (b). Over the range from 0 to 5 haircuts an hour, a price cut increases total revenue, so marginal revenue is positive, as shown by the blue bars. Demand is elastic. Over the range 5 to 10 haircuts an hour, a price cut decreases total revenue, so marginal revenue is negative, as shown by the red bars. Demand is inelastic. At 5 haircuts an hour, total revenue is maximized, and marginal revenue is zero. Demand is unit elastic.

Output and Price Decision

To determine the output level and price that maximize a monopoly's profit, we need to study the behavior of both revenue and costs as output varies. A monopoly and a competitive firm face the same types of technology and cost constraints. But they face different market constraints. The competitive firm is a price taker, whereas the monopoly's production decision influences the price it receives. Let's see how.

Bobbie's revenue, which we studied in Fig. 13.2, is shown again in Table 13.1. The table also contains information on Bobbie's costs and economic profit. Total cost (*TC*) rises as output increases, and so does total revenue (*TR*). Economic profit equals total revenue minus total cost. As you can see in the table, the maximum profit ($12) occurs when Bobbie sells 3 haircuts for $14 each. If she sells 2 haircuts for $16 each or 4 haircuts for $12 each, her economic profit will be only $8.

You can see why 3 haircuts is Bobbie's profit-maximizing output by looking at the marginal revenue and marginal cost columns. When Bobbie increases output from 2 to 3 haircuts, her marginal revenue is $10 and her marginal cost is $6. Profit increases by the difference—$4 an hour. If Bobbie

increases output yet further, from 3 to 4 haircuts, her marginal revenue is $6 and her marginal cost is $10. In this case, marginal cost exceeds marginal revenue by $4, so profit decreases by $4 an hour. When marginal revenue exceeds marginal cost, profit increases if output increases. When marginal cost exceeds marginal revenue, profit increases if output decreases. When marginal cost and marginal revenue are equal, profit is maximized.

The information set out in Table 13.1 is shown graphically in Fig. 13.4. Part (a) shows Bobbie's total revenue curve (*TR*) and total cost curve (*TC*). Economic profit is the vertical distance between *TR* and *TC*. Bobbie maximizes her profit at 3 haircuts an hour—economic profit is $42 minus $30, or $12.

A monopoly, like a competitive firm, maximizes profit by producing the output at which marginal cost equals marginal revenue. Figure 13.4(b) shows Bobbie's demand curve (*D*) and marginal revenue curve (*MR*) along with her marginal cost curve (*MC*) and average total cost curve (*ATC*). Bobbie maximizes her profit by doing 3 haircuts an hour. But what price does she charge for a haircut? To set the price, the monopolist uses the demand curve and finds the highest price at which it can sell the profit-maximizing output. In Bobbie's case, the highest price at which she can sell 3 haircuts an hour is $14.

TABLE 13.1

A Monopoly's Output and Price Decision

Price (P) (dollars per haircut)	Quantity demanded (Q) (haircuts per hour)	Total revenue (TR = P × Q) (dollars)	Marginal revenue (MR = ΔTR/ΔQ) (dollars per additional haircut)	Total cost (TC) (dollars)	Marginal cost (MC = ΔTC/ΔQ) (dollars per additional haircut)	Profit (TR − TC) (dollars)
20	0	0		20		−20
			18		1	
18	1	18		21		−3
			14		3	
16	2	32		24		+8
			10		6	
14	3	42		30		+12
			6		10	
12	4	48		40		+8
			2		15	
10	5	50		55		−5

This table gives the information needed to find the profit-maximizing output and price. Total revenue (*TR*) equals price multiplied by the quantity sold. Profit equals total revenue minus total cost (*TC*). Profit is maximized when the price is $14 and 3 haircuts are sold. Total revenue is $42, total cost is $30, and economic profit is $12 ($42 − $30).

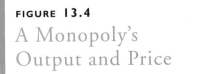

FIGURE 13.4

A Monopoly's Output and Price

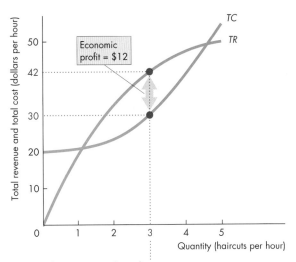

(a) Total revenue and total cost curves

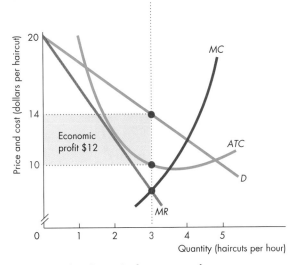

(b) Demand and marginal revenue and cost curves

In part (a), economic profit equals total revenue (*TR*) minus total cost (*TC*) and is maximized at 3 haircuts an hour. In part (b), economic profit is maximized when marginal cost (*MC*) equals marginal revenue (*MR*). The price is determined by the demand curve (*D*) and is $14. Economic profit, the blue rectangle, is $12—the profit per haircut ($4) multiplied by 3 haircuts.

All firms maximize profit by producing the output at which marginal revenue equals marginal cost. For a competitive firm, price equals marginal revenue, so price also equals marginal cost. For a monopoly, price exceeds marginal revenue, so price also exceeds marginal cost.

A monopoly charges a price that exceeds marginal cost, but does it always make an economic profit? In Bobbie's case, when she produces 3 haircuts an hour, her average total cost is $10 (read from the *ATC* curve) and her price is $14 (read from the *D* curve). Her profit per haircut is $4 ($14 minus $10). Bobbie's economic profit is shown by the blue rectangle, which equals the profit per haircut ($4) multiplied by the number of haircuts (3), for a total of $12.

If firms in a perfectly competitive industry make a positive economic profit, new firms enter. That does not happen in a monopolistic industry. Barriers to entry prevent new firms from entering. So in a monopolistic industry, a firm can make a positive economic profit and continue to do so indefinitely. Sometimes that profit is large, as in the international diamond business.

Bobbie makes a positive economic profit. But suppose that the owner of the shop that Bobbie rents increases Bobbie's rent. If Bobbie pays an additional $12 an hour, her fixed cost increases by $12 an hour. Her marginal cost and marginal revenue don't change, so her profit-maximizing output remains at 3 haircuts an hour. Her profit decreases by $12 an hour to zero. If Bobbie pays more than an additional $12 an hour for her shop rent, she incurs an economic loss. If this situation were permanent, Bobbie would go out of business. But entrepreneurs are a hardy lot, and Bobbie might find another shop where the rent is less.

R E V I E W   Q U I Z

- What is the relationship between marginal cost and marginal revenue when a single-price monopoly maximizes profit?
- How does a single-price monopoly determine the price it will charge its customers?
- What is the relationship among price, marginal revenue, and marginal cost when a single-price monopoly is maximizing profit?
- Why can a monopoly make a positive economic profit even in the long run?

Single-Price Monopoly and Competition Compared

IMAGINE AN INDUSTRY THAT IS MADE UP OF MANY small firms operating in perfect competition. Then imagine that a single firm buys out all these small firms and creates a monopoly.

What will happen in this industry? Will the price rise or fall? Will the quantity produced increase or decrease? Will economic profit increase or decrease? Will either the original competitive situation or the new monopoly situation be efficient?

These are the questions we're now going to answer. First, we look at the effects of monopoly on the price and quantity produced. Then we turn to the questions about efficiency.

Comparing Output and Price

Figure 13.5 shows the market we'll study. The market demand curve is D. The demand curve is the same, regardless of how the industry is organized. But the supply side and the equilibrium are different in monopoly and competition. First, let's look at the case of perfect competition.

Perfect Competition Initially, with many small perfectly competitive firms in the market, the market supply curve is S. This supply curve is obtained by summing the supply curves of all the individual firms in the market.

In perfect competition, equilibrium occurs where the supply curve and the demand curve intersect. The quantity produced by the industry is Q_C, and the price is P_C. Each firm takes the price P_C and maximizes its profit by producing the output at which its own marginal cost equals the price. Because each firm is a small part of the total industry, there is no incentive for any firm to try to manipulate the price by varying its output.

Monopoly Now suppose that this industry is taken over by a single firm. Consumers do not change, so the demand curve remains the same as in the case of perfect competition. But now the monopoly recognizes this demand curve as a constraint on its sales. And the monopoly is confronted with the marginal revenue curve, MR.

The monopoly maximizes profit by producing the quantity at which marginal revenue equals marginal

cost. To find the monopoly's marginal cost curve, first recall that in perfect competition, the industry supply curve is the sum of the supply curves of the firms in the industry. Also recall that each firm's supply curve is its marginal cost curve (see Chapter 12, p. 245). So when the industry is taken over by a single firm, competitive industry's supply curve becomes the monopoly's marginal cost curve. To remind you of this fact, the supply curve is also labeled MC.

The output at which marginal revenue equals marginal cost is Q_M. This output is smaller than the competitive output Q_C. And the monopoly charges the price P_M, which is higher than P_C. We have established that:

Compared to a perfectly competitive industry, a single-price monopoly restricts its output and charges a higher price.

We've seen how the output and price of a monopoly compare with those in a competitive industry. Let's now compare the efficiency of the two types of market.

FIGURE 13.5

Monopoly's Smaller Output and Higher Price

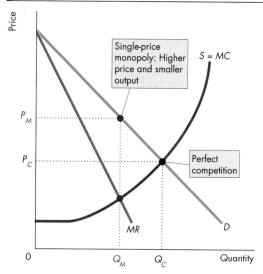

A competitive industry produces the quantity Q_C at price P_C. A single-price monopoly produces the quantity Q_M at which marginal revenue equals marginal cost and sells that quantity for the price P_M. Compared to perfect competition, a single-price monopoly restricts output and raises the price.

Efficiency Comparison

When we studied efficiency in perfect competition, (see Chapter 12, pp. 256-257), we discovered that if there are no external costs and benefits, perfect competition results in an efficient use of resources. Along the demand curve, consumers are efficient. Along the supply curve, producers are efficient. And where the curves intersect—the competitive equilibrium—both consumers and producers are efficient. Price equals marginal cost, and the sum of consumer surplus and producer surplus is maximized.

Monopoly restricts output below the competitive level and is inefficient. If a monopoly increases its output by one unit, marginal benefit exceeds marginal cost and resources are used more efficiently.

Figure 13.6 illustrates the inefficiency of monopoly and shows the loss of consumer and producer surpluses in a monopoly. In perfect competition (part a), consumers pay P_C for each unit. The marginal benefit to consumers is shown by the demand curve ($D = MB$). This price measures the value of the good to the consumer. Value minus price equals *consumer surplus* (see Chapter 6, p. 111). In Fig. 13.6(a), consumer surplus is shown by the green triangle.

The marginal cost of production (opportunity cost) in perfect competition is shown by the supply curve ($S = MC$). The amount received by the producer in excess of this marginal cost is *producer surplus.* In Fig. 13.6(a), the blue area shows producer surplus.

At the competitive equilibrium, marginal benefit equals marginal cost and the sum of consumer surplus and producer surplus is maximized. Resource use is efficient.

A monopoly (part b) restricts output to Q_M and sells that output for P_M. Consumer surplus decreases to the smaller green triangle. Consumers lose partly by having to pay more for the good and partly by getting less of it. Part of the original producer surplus is also lost. The total loss resulting from the smaller monopoly output (Q_M) is the gray triangle in Fig. 13.6(b). The part of the gray triangle above P_C is the loss of consumer surplus, and the part of the triangle below P_C is a loss of producer surplus. The entire gray triangle measures the loss of consumer surplus plus producer surplus. This loss is called the *deadweight loss.* The smaller output and higher price drive a wedge between marginal benefit and marginal cost and eliminates the producer surplus and the consumer surplus on the output that a competitive industry would have produced but that the monopoly does not.

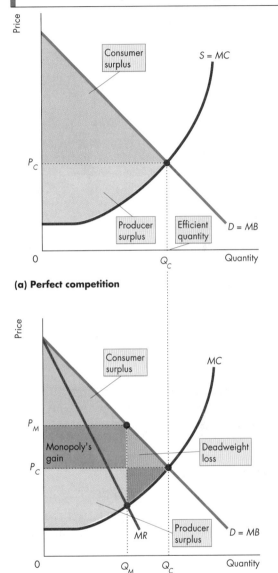

(a) Perfect competition

(b) Monopoly

In perfect competition (part a), the quantity Q_C is sold at the price P_C. Consumer surplus is shown by the green triangle. In long-run equilibrium, firms' economic profits are zero and consumer surplus is maximized. A single-price monopoly (part b) restricts output to Q_M and increases the price to P_M. Consumer surplus is the smaller green triangle. The monopoly takes the blue rectangle and creates a deadweight loss (the gray triangle).

Redistribution of Surpluses

You've seen that monopoly is inefficient. The sum of consumer surplus and producer surplus is smaller with monopoly than with competition. There is a social loss. But monopoly also brings a *redistribution* of surpluses.

Some of the loss in consumer surplus goes to the monopoly. In Fig. 13.6, the monopoly gets the difference between the higher price, P_M, and the competitive price, P_C, on the quantity sold, Q_M. So the monopoly takes the part of the consumer surplus shown by the blue rectangle. This portion of the loss of consumer surplus is not a loss to society. It is redistribution from consumers to the monopoly.

Rent Seeking

You've seen that monopoly creates a deadweight loss and so is inefficient. But the social cost of monopoly exceeds the deadweight loss because of an activity called rent seeking. **Rent seeking** is the attempt to capture a consumer surplus, a producer surplus, or an economic profit. The activity is not confined to monopoly. But attempting to capture the economic profit of a monopoly is a major form of rent seeking.

You've seen that a monopoly makes its economic profit by diverting part of consumer surplus to itself. Thus the pursuit of an economic profit by a monopoly is rent seeking. It is the attempt to capture consumer surplus.

Rent seekers pursue their goals in two main ways. They might

- Buy a monopoly
- Create a monopoly

Buy a Monopoly To rent seek by buying a monopoly, a person searches for a monopoly that is for sale at a lower price than the monopoly's economic profit. Trading taxicab licenses is an example of this type of rent seeking. In some cities, taxicabs are regulated. The city restricts both the fares and the number of taxis that can operate, so operating a taxi results in economic profit or rent. A person who wants to operate a taxi must buy a license from someone who already has one. This type of rent seeking transfers rents from the buyer to the seller of the monopoly. The only person who ends up with rent is the one who created the monopoly in the first place. Even so, people rationally devote their time and effort to seeking out profitable

monopoly businesses to buy. In the process, they use up scarce resources that could otherwise have been employed in producing goods and services.

Create a Monopoly Rent seeking by creating monopoly is mainly a political activity. It takes the form of lobbying and trying to influence the political process. Such influence might be sought by making campaign contributions in exchange for legislative support or by indirectly seeking to influence political outcomes through publicity in the media or more direct contacts with politicians and bureaucrats. An example of a monopoly right that was created in this way is the government-imposed restrictions on the quantities of textiles that may be imported into the United States. Another is a regulation that limits the number of oranges that may be sold in the United States. These are regulations that restrict output and increase price.

This type of rent seeking is a costly activity that uses up scarce resources. Taken together, firms spend billions of dollars lobbying Congress, state legislators, and local officials in the pursuit of licenses and laws that create barriers to entry and establish a monopoly right. Everyone has an incentive to rent seek, and because there are no barriers to entry into the rent-seeking activity, there is a great deal of competition for new monopoly rights.

Rent-Seeking Equilibrium

Barriers to entry create monopoly. But there is no barrier to entry into rent seeking. Rent seeking is like perfect competition. If an economic profit is available, a new rent seeker will try to get some of it. And competition among rent seekers pushes up the price that must be paid for a monopoly right to the point at which only a normal profit can be made by operating the monopoly. For example, competition for the right to operate a taxi in New York City leads to a price of more than $100,000 for a taxi license, which is sufficiently high to eliminate economic profit for taxi operators and leave them with normal profit.

Figure 13.7 shows a rent-seeking equilibrium. The cost of rent seeking is a fixed cost that must be added to a monopoly's other costs. Rent seeking and rent-seeking costs increase to the point at which no economic profit is made. The average total cost curve, which includes the fixed cost of rent seeking, shifts upward until it just touches the demand curve. Economic profit is zero. It has been lost in rent

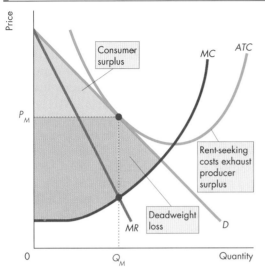

FIGURE 13.7

Rent-Seeking Equilibrium

With competitive rent seeking, a monopoly uses all its economic profit to prevent another firm from taking its economic rent. The firm's rent-seeking costs are fixed costs. They add to total fixed cost and to average total cost. The *ATC* curve shifts upward until, at the profit-maximizing price, the firm breaks even.

seeking. Consumer surplus is unaffected. But the deadweight loss of monopoly now includes the original deadweight loss triangle plus the lost economic profit, shown by the enlarged gray area in the figure.

R E V I E W   Q U I Z

- Why does a single-price monopoly produce a smaller output and charge a higher price than what would prevail if the industry were perfectly competitive?
- Why is a single-price monopoly inefficient?
- What is rent seeking and how does it influence the inefficiency of monopoly?

So far, we've considered only a single-price monopoly. But many monopolies do not operate with a single price. Instead, they price discriminate. Let's now see how price-discriminating monopoly works.

Price Discrimination

PRICE DISCRIMINATION—SELLING A GOOD OR service at a number of different prices—is widespread. You encounter it when you travel, go to the movies, get your hair cut, buy pizza, or visit an art museum. Most price discriminators are *not* monopolies, but monopolies price discriminate when they can do so.

To be able to price discriminate, a monopoly must:

1. Identify and separate different buyer types
2. Sell a product that cannot be resold

Price discrimination is charging different prices for a single good or service because of differences in buyers' willingness to pay and not because of differences in production costs. So not all price *differences* are price *discrimination.* Some goods that are similar but not identical have different prices because they have different production costs. For example, the cost of producing electricity depends on time of day. If an electric power company charges a higher price for consumption between 7:00 and 9:00 in the morning and between 4:00 and 7:00 in the evening than it does at other times of the day, it is not price discriminating.

At first sight, it appears that price discrimination contradicts the assumption of profit maximization. Why would a movie operator allow children to see movies at half price? Why would a hairdresser charge students and senior citizens less? Aren't these firms losing profit by being nice to their customers?

Deeper investigation shows that far from losing profit, price discriminators make a bigger profit than they would otherwise. So a monopoly has an incentive to find ways of discriminating and charging each buyer the highest possible price. Some people pay less with price discrimination, but others pay more.

Price Discrimination and Consumer Surplus

The key idea behind price discrimination is to convert consumer surplus into economic profit. Demand curves slope downward because the value that people place on any good decreases as the quantity consumed of that good increases. When all the units consumed are sold for a single price, consumers benefit. The benefit is the value the consumers get from each unit of the good minus the price actually paid for it. We call this benefit *consumer surplus*. (If you need to refresh your understanding of consumer surplus, flip back to Chapter 6, page 111.) Price discrimination is an attempt by a monopoly to capture as much of the consumer surplus as possible for itself.

To extract every dollar of consumer surplus from every buyer, the monopoly would have to offer each individual customer a separate price schedule based on that customer's own willingness to pay. Clearly, such price discrimination cannot be carried out in practice because a firm does not have enough information about each consumer's demand curve.

But firms try to extract as much consumer surplus as possible, and to do so, they discriminate in two broad ways:

■ Among units of a good
■ Among groups of buyers

Discriminating Among Units of a Good One method of price discrimination charges each buyer a different price on each unit of a good bought. A discount for bulk buying is an example of this type of discrimination. The larger the order, the larger is the discount—and the lower is the price. (Note that some discounts for bulk arise from lower costs of production for greater bulk. In these cases, such discounts are not price discrimination.)

Discriminating Among Groups of Buyers Price discrimination often takes the form of discriminating between different groups of consumers on the basis of age, employment status, or some other easily distinguished characteristic. This type of price discrimination works when each group has a different average willingness to pay for the good or service.

For example, a face-to-face sales meeting with a customer might bring a large and profitable order. For salespeople and other business travelers, the marginal benefit from a trip is large and the price that such a traveler will pay for a trip is high. In contrast, for a vacation traveler, any of several different trips or even no vacation trip are options. So for vacation travelers, the marginal benefit of a trip is small and the price that such a traveler will pay for a trip is low. Because business travelers are willing to pay more than vacation travelers are, it is possible for an airline to profit by price discriminating between these two groups. Similarly, because students have a lower willingness to pay for a haircut than a working person does, it is possible for a hairdresser to profit by price discriminating between these two groups.

Let's see how an airline exploits the differences in demand by business and vacation travelers and increases its profit by price discriminating.

Profiting by Price Discriminating

Global Air has a monopoly on an exotic route. Figure 13.8 shows the demand curve (*D*) and the marginal revenue curve (*MR*) for travel on this route. It also shows Global Air's marginal cost curve (*MC*) and average total cost curve (*ATC*).

Initially, Global is a single-price monopoly and maximizes its profit by producing 8,000 trips a year (the quantity at which *MR* equals *MC*). The price is $1,200 per trip. The average total cost of a trip is $600, so economic profit is $600 a trip. On 8,000 trips, Global's economic profit is $4.8 million a year, shown by the blue rectangle. Global's customers enjoy a consumer surplus shown by the green triangle.

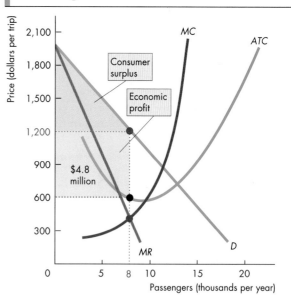

FIGURE 13.8

A Single Price of Air Travel

Global Airlines has a monopoly on an air route. The firm faces demand curve (*D*) and marginal revenue curve (*MR*). It has marginal cost curve (*MC*) and average total cost curve (*ATC*). As a single-price monopoly, Global maximizes profit by selling 8,000 trips a year at $1,200 a trip. Its profit is $4.8 million a year, which is shown by the blue rectangle. Global's customers enjoy a consumer surplus shown by the green triangle.

Global is struck by the fact that many of its customers are business travelers, and Global suspects that they are willing to pay more than $1,200 a trip. So Global does some market research, which tells Global that some business travelers are willing to pay as much as $1,800 a trip. Also, these customers almost always change their travel plans at the last moment. Another group of business travelers is willing to pay $1,600. These customers know a week ahead when they will travel, and they never want to stay over a weekend. Yet another group would pay up to $1,400, and these travelers know two weeks ahead when they will travel and they don't want to stay away over a weekend.

So Global announces a new fare schedule. No restrictions, $1,800; 7-days advance purchase, no cancellation, $1,600; 14-days advance purchase, no cancellation, $1,400; 14-days advance purchase, must stay over weekend, $1,200.

Figure 13.9 shows the outcome with this new fare structure and also shows why Global is pleased

with its new fares. It sells 2,000 seats at each of its four prices. Global's economic profit increases by the blue steps in Fig. 13.9. Its economic profit is now its original $4.8 million a year plus an additional $2.4 million from its new higher fares. Consumer surplus has shrunk to the smaller green area.

Perfect Price Discrimination

But Global reckons it can do even better. It plans to achieve **perfect price discrimination,** which is price discrimination that extracts the entire consumer surplus. To do so, Global must get creative and come up with a host of additional business fares ranging between $2,000 and $1,200, each of which appeals to a small segment of the business market and that together they extract the entire consumer surplus from the business travelers.

Once Global is discriminating finely between different customers and getting from each the maximum they are willing to pay, something special happens to marginal revenue. Recall that for the single-price monopoly, marginal revenue is less than price. The reason is that when the price is cut to sell a larger quantity, the price is lower on all units sold. But with perfect price discrimination, Global sells only the marginal seat at the lower price. All the other customers continue to buy for the highest price they are willing to pay. So for the perfect price discriminator, marginal revenue equals price and the demand curve becomes the marginal revenue curve.

With marginal revenue equal to price, Global can obtain yet greater profit by increasing output up to the point at which price (and marginal revenue) is equal to marginal cost.

So Global now seeks additional travelers who will not pay as much as $1,200 a trip but who will pay more than marginal cost. More creative pricing comes up with vacation specials and other fares that have combinations of advance reservation, minimum-stay, and other restrictions that make these fares unattractive to its existing customers but attractive to a further group of travelers. With all these fares and specials, Global increases sales, extracts the entire consumer surplus, and maximizes economic profit.

Figure 13.10 shows the outcome with perfect price discrimination. The dozens of fares paid by the original travelers who are willing to pay between $1,200 and $2,000 has extracted the entire consumer surplus from this group and converted it into economic profit for Global.

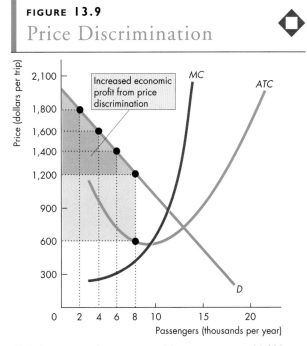

FIGURE 13.9
Price Discrimination

Global revises its fare structure. No restrictions at $1,800; 7-day advance purchase at $1,600; 14-day advance purchase at $1,400; and must stay over weekend at $1,200. Global sells 2,000 units at each of its four new fares. Its economic profit increases by $2.4 million a year to $7.2 million a year, which is shown by the original blue rectangle plus the blue steps. Global's customers' consumer surplus shrinks.

FIGURE 13.10

Perfect Price Discrimination

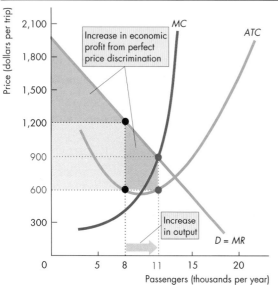

Dozens of fares discriminate among many different types of business traveler, and many new low fares with restrictions appeal to vacation travelers. With perfect price discrimination, Global's demand curve becomes its marginal revenue curve. Economic profit is maximized when the lowest price equals marginal cost. Global sells 11,000 tickets at between $2,000 and $900 each and makes an economic profit of $9.35 million a year.

The new fares between $900 and $1,200 have attracted 3,000 additional travelers, but Global has taken their entire consumer surplus also. Global is earning an economic profit of more than $9 million.

Real-world airlines are just as creative as Global, as you can see in the cartoon!

Would it bother you to hear how little I paid for this flight?

From William Hamilton, "Voodoo Economics," ©1992 by
The Chronicle Publishing Company, p.3.
Reprinted with permission of Chronicle Books.

Efficiency and Rent Seeking with Price Discrimination

With perfect price discrimination, output increases to the point at which price equals marginal cost—where the marginal cost curve intersects the demand curve. This output is identical to that of perfect competition. Perfect price discrimination pushes consumer surplus to zero but increases producer surplus to equal the sum of consumer surplus and producer surplus in perfect competition. Deadweight loss with perfect price discrimination is zero. So perfect price discrimination achieves efficiency.

The more perfectly the monopoly can price discriminate, the closer its output gets to the competitive output and the more efficient is the outcome.

But there are two differences between perfect competition and perfect price discrimination. First, the distribution of the surplus is different. It is shared by consumers and producers in perfect competition while the producer gets it all with perfect price discrimination. Second, because the producer grabs the surplus, rent seeking becomes profitable.

People use resources in pursuit of rents, and the bigger the rents, the more resources get used in pursuing them. With free entry into rent seeking, the long-run equilibrium outcome is that rent seekers use up the entire producer surplus.

REVIEW QUIZ

- What is price discrimination and how is it used to increase a monopoly's profit?
- What happens to consumer surplus when a monopoly price discriminates?
- What happens to consumer surplus, economic profit, and output if a monopoly perfectly price discriminates?
- What are some of the ways that real-world airlines use to price discriminate?

You've seen that monopoly is profitable for the monopolist but costly for other people. It results in inefficiency. Because of these features of monopoly, it is subject to policy debate and regulation. We'll now study the key monopoly policy issues.

Monopoly Policy Issues

THE COMPARISON OF MONOPOLY AND COMPETI-
tion makes monopoly look bad. Monopoly is inefficient, and it captures consumer surplus and converts
it into producer surplus or pure waste in the form of
rent-seeking costs. If monopoly is so bad, why do we
put up with it? Why don't we have laws that crack
down on monopoly so hard that it never rears its
head? We do indeed have laws that limit monopoly
power and regulate the prices that monopolies are
permitted to charge. But monopoly also brings some
benefits. We begin this review of monopoly policy
issues by looking at the benefits of monopoly. We
then look at monopoly regulation.

Gains from Monopoly

The main reasons why monopoly exists is that it has
potential advantages over a competitive alternative.
These advantages arise from:

■ Incentives to innovation
■ Economies of scale and economies of scope

Incentives to Innovation Invention leads to a wave of
innovation as new knowledge is applied to the production process. Innovation may take the form of
developing a new product or a lower-cost way of
making an existing product. Controversy has raged
over whether large firms with monopoly power or
small competitive firms lacking such monopoly
power are the most innovative. It is clear that some
temporary monopoly power arises from innovation.
A firm that develops a new product or process and
patents it obtains an exclusive right to that product
or process for the term of the patent.

But does the granting of a monopoly, even a
temporary one, to an innovator increase the pace of
innovation? One line of reasoning suggests that it
does. Without protection, an innovator is not able to
enjoy the profits from innovation for very long. Thus
the incentive to innovate is weakened. A contrary
argument is that monopolies can afford to be lazy
while competitive firms cannot. Competitive firms
must strive to innovate and cut costs even though
they know that they cannot hang on to the benefits
of their innovation for long. But that knowledge
spurs them on to greater and faster innovation.

The evidence on whether monopoly leads to
greater innovation than competition is mixed. Large
firms do more research and development than do
small firms. But measuring research and development
is measuring the volume of inputs into the process of
innovation. What matters is not input but output.
Two measures of the output of research and development are the number of patents and the rate of productivity growth. On these measures, there is no clear
evidence that big is better. But there is a clear pattern
in the process of diffusion of technological knowledge. After innovation, a new process or product
spreads gradually through the industry, with large
firms jumping on the bandwagon more quickly than
the remaining small firms. Thus large firms speed the
process of diffusion of technological advances.

Economies of Scale and Scope Economies of scale
and scope can lead to natural monopoly. And as you
saw at the beginning of this chapter, in a *natural
monopoly*, a single firm can produce at a lower average cost than a larger number of smaller firms can.

A firm experiences *economies of scale* when an
increase in its output of a good or service brings a
decrease in the average total cost of producing it—see
Chapter 11, pp. 232. A firm experiences *economies of
scope* when an increase in the *range of goods produced*
brings a decrease in average total cost—see Chapter 10,
p. 213. Economies of scope occur when different goods
can share specialized (and usually costly) capital
resources. For example, McDonald's can produce both
hamburgers and french fries at a lower average total cost
than can two separate firms—a burger firm and a
french fries firm—because at McDonald's hamburgers
and french fries share the use of specialized food storage
and preparation facilities. A firm that produces a wide
range of products can hire specialist computer programmers, designers, and marketing experts whose
skills can be used across the product range, thereby
spreading their costs and lowering the average total cost
of production of each of the goods.

There are many examples in which a combination
of economies of scale and economies of scope arise,
but not all of them lead to monopoly. Some examples
are the brewing of beer, the manufacture of refrigerators and other household appliances, the manufacture
of pharmaceuticals, and the refining of petroleum.

Examples of industries in which economies of
scale are so significant that they lead to a natural
monopoly are becoming more rare. Public utilities
such as gas, electric power, local telephone service,
and garbage collection once were natural monopolies.

But technological advances now enable us to separate the *production* of electric power or natural gas from its *distribution*. The provision of water, though, remains a natural monopoly.

Large-scale firms that have control over supply and can influence price—and that therefore behave like the monopoly firm that you've studied in this chapter—can reap economies of scale and scope. Small, competitive firms cannot. Consequently, there are situations in which the comparison of monopoly and competition that we made earlier in this chapter is not valid. Recall that we imagined the takeover of a large number of competitive firms by a monopoly firm. But we also assumed that the monopoly would use exactly the same technology as the small firms and have the same costs. If one large firm can reap economies of scale and scope, its marginal cost curve will lie below the supply curve of a competitive industry made up of many small firms. It is possible for such economies of scale and scope to be so large as to result in a larger output and lower price under monopoly than a competitive industry would achieve.

Where significant economies of scale and scope exist, it is usually worth putting up with monopoly and regulating its prices.

Regulating Natural Monopoly

Where demand and cost conditions create a natural monopoly, a federal, state, or local government agency usually steps in to regulate the prices of the monopoly. By regulating a monopoly, some of the worst aspects of monopoly can be avoided or at least made more moderate. Let's look at monopoly price regulation.

Figure 13.11 shows the demand curve *D*, the marginal revenue curve, *MR*, the average total cost curve *ATC*, and the marginal cost curve *MC* for a gas distribution company that is a natural monopoly.

The firm's marginal cost is constant at 10 cents per cubic foot. But average total cost decreases as output increases. The reason is that the natural gas company has a large investment in pipelines and so has high fixed costs. These fixed costs are part of the company's average total cost and so appear in the *ATC* curve. The average total cost curve slopes downward because as the number of cubic feet sold increases, the fixed cost is spread over a larger number units. (If you need to refresh your memory on how the average total cost curve is calculated, take a quick look back at Chapter 11, pp. 226–227.)

This one firm can supply the entire market at a lower cost than two firms can because average total cost is falling even when the entire market is supplied. (Refer back to pp. 264–265 if you need a quick refresher on natural monopoly.)

Profit Maximization First, suppose the natural gas company is not regulated and instead maximizes profit. Figure 13.11 shows the outcome in this case. The company produces 2 million cubic feet a day, the quantity at which marginal cost equals marginal revenue. It prices this gas at 20 cents a cubic foot and makes an economic profit of 2 cents a cubic foot, or $40,000 a day.

This outcome is fine for the gas company, but it is inefficient. Price or marginal benefit is 20 cents a cubic foot when marginal cost is only 10 cents a cubic foot. Also, the gas company is making a big profit. What can regulation do to improve this outcome?

The Efficient Regulation If the monopoly regulator wants to achieve an efficient use of resources, it must require the gas monopoly to produce the quantity of gas that brings marginal benefit into equality with marginal cost. Marginal benefit is what the consumer is willing to pay and is shown by the demand curve. Marginal cost is shown by the firm's marginal cost curve. You can see in Fig. 13.11 that this outcome occurs if the price is regulated at 10 cents per cubic foot and if 4 million cubic feet per day are produced. The regulation that produces this outcome is called a marginal cost pricing rule. A **marginal cost pricing rule** sets price equal to marginal cost. It maximizes total surplus in the regulated industry. In this example, that surplus is all consumer surplus and it equals the area of the triangle beneath the demand curve and above the marginal cost curve.

The marginal cost pricing rule is efficient. But it leaves the natural monopoly incurring an economic loss. Because average total cost falls as output increases, marginal cost is below average total cost. And because price equals marginal cost, price is below average total cost. Average total cost minus price is the loss per unit produced. It's pretty obvious that a natural gas company that is required to use a marginal cost pricing rule will not stay in business for long. How can a company cover its costs and, at the same time, obey a marginal cost pricing rule?

One possibility is price discrimination. The company might charge a higher price to some customers but marginal cost to the customers who pay least.

FIGURE 13.11

Regulating a Natural Monopoly

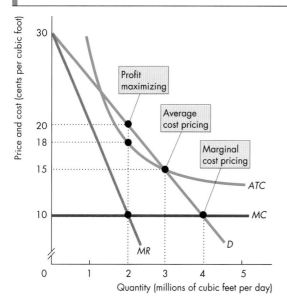

A natural monopoly is an industry in which average total cost is falling even when the entire market demand is satisfied. A natural gas producer faces the demand curve D. The firm's marginal cost is constant at 10 cents per cubic foot, as shown by the curve labeled MC. Fixed costs are large, and the average total cost curve, which includes average fixed cost, is shown as ATC. A marginal cost pricing rule sets the price at 10 cents per cubic foot and produces 4 million cubic feet per day. The firm incurs an economic loss. An average cost pricing rule sets the price at 15 cents per cubic foot and produces 3 million cubic feet per day. The firm makes a normal profit.

Another possibility is to use a two-part price (called a two-part tariff). For example, the gas company might charge a monthly fixed fee that covers its fixed cost and then charge for gas consumed at marginal cost.

But a natural monopoly cannot always cover its costs in these ways. If a natural monopoly cannot cover its total cost from its customers, and if the government wants it to follow a marginal cost pricing rule, the government must give the firm a subsidy. In such a case, the government raises the revenue for the subsidy by taxing some other activity. But as we saw in Chapter 7, taxes themselves generate deadweight loss. Thus the deadweight loss resulting from additional taxes must be subtracted from the efficiency

gained by forcing the natural monopoly to adopt a marginal cost pricing rule.

Average Cost Pricing   Regulators almost never impose efficient pricing because of its consequences for the firm's profit. Instead, they compromise by permitting the firm to cover all its costs and to earn a normal profit. Normal profit, recall, is a cost of production and we include it along with the firm's other fixed costs in the average total cost curve. So pricing to cover cost and normal profit means setting price equal to average total cost—called an **average cost pricing rule**.

Figure 13.11 shows the average cost pricing outcome. The natural gas company charges 15 cents a cubic foot and sells 3 million cubic feet per day. This outcome is better for consumers than the unregulated profit-maximizing outcome. The price is 5 cents a cubic foot lower, and the quantity consumed is 1 million cubic feet per day more. And the outcome is better for the producer than the marginal cost pricing rule outcome. The firm earns normal profit. The outcome is inefficient, but less so than the unregulated profit-maximizing outcome.

REVIEW QUIZ

- What are the two main reasons why monopoly is worth tolerating?
- Can you provide some examples of economies of scale and economies of scope?
- Why might the incentive to innovate be greater for a monopoly than for a small competitive firm?
- What is the price that achieves an efficient outcome for a regulated monopoly? And what is the problem with this price?
- Compare the consumer surplus, producer surplus, and deadweight loss that arises from average cost pricing with those of profit-maximization pricing and marginal cost pricing.

◆ You've now studied perfect competition and monopoly, and you've seen how price discrimination can increase a firm's profit. *Reading Between the Lines* on pp. 280–281 looks at price discrimination in action in the airline industry. In the next chapter, we study markets that lie between the extremes of competition and monopoly and that blend elements of the two.

Price Discrimination in Action

USA TODAY, FEBRUARY 23, 1999

Flights at a Premium

BY GARY STOLLER, USA TODAY

The cost of flying at the last minute has outraged large corporations, become a small-business owner's nightmare, and discouraged other spur-of-the-moment weekday travelers.

But are the complaints legitimate and the prices really restrictive if you need to get up and go immediately? USA TODAY analyzed roundtrip fares on nine randomly selected routes and found that on most routes the ticket price for a next-day flight was at least double the cheapest fare, which often required an advance purchase and a Saturday-night stay. And on some routes, the next-day fare was more than six times greater.

On the New York–San Francisco route, American and United telephone reservations agents quoted a $1,902 coach price, and a TWA agent provided a $1,909 fare. That's about $1,600 more than each airline's cheapest advance-purchase tickets. ...

Of the nine routes USA TODAY

analyzed, American's next-day $1,220 Dallas-Denver ticket cost more per mile—94 cents—than any other last-minute coach fare. The same coach seat on American could be had for $194, or 15 cents a mile with a ticket bought at least 21 days out. ...

"Unquestionably, the last-minute traveler pays a heavy penalty," says Norman Sherlock, executive director of the 2,000-member National Business Travel Association, which consists primarily of corporate travel managers. Airline pricing strategies "are designed to take advantage of that fact of life."

High last-minute prices are simply "the way airline pricing works," says David Fuscus, a spokesman for the Air Transport Association, which represents the airlines. "If a traveler books in advance, we know we're getting an economic benefit. But we also hold open seats for the last-minute traveler and take a chance that we're going to lose that economic benefit. So a person booking at the last minute pays a premium."

1999 USA TODAY. Reprinted with permission.
Further reproduction prohibited.

Essence of the Story

■ The cheapest airfares require a 21-day advance purchase and a Saturday-night stay.

■ The price for a next-day flight is more than double the cheapest fare, and on some routes it is more than six times greater.

■ On the New York–San Francisco route, American, United, and TWA charge about $1,900 for a next-day ticket and about $300 for the cheapest advance-purchase ticket.

■ Norman Sherlock, who represents business travelers, says, "the last-minute traveler pays a heavy penalty."

■ David Fuscus, who represents the airlines, says that the last-minute traveler pays a premium because the airlines hold seats open and run the risk of not filling them.

- The willingness to pay for a flight by someone who must travel to close a business deal is usually greater than the willingness to pay by someone who plans to travel to enjoy a relaxing weekend.

- Figure 1 shows the willingness to pay of 260 people who might take one American Airlines flight between New York and San Francisco.

- At one extreme are 20 people who are willing to pay $1,900 or even more for a seat. At the other extreme are 20 people who are willing to pay only $125 or less.

- Assume that American Airlines flies an airplane with 240 seats.

- Suppose that the airline offers all the seats for $269. Smart "seat traders" know that many people, especially last-minute travelers, are willing to pay much more than the $269 at which the airline is selling tickets. So they buy all the seats and resell them just before the flight.

- Envision the scene at the airport. Seat traders auction tickets, getting the highest prices possible from anxious travelers.

- Travelers pay the amount they are willing to pay. Seat traders capture the consumer surplus, and the airline scrapes by with a normal profit.

- We don't observe the scene just described. Instead, the airline sets prices to capture as much consumer surplus as possible by offering seats based on conditions such as Saturday-night stays and a 21-day advance purchase.

- Figure 2 shows the outcome when the airline offers six different fares ranging from $1,900 to $269. The consumer retains a small amount of consumer surplus (the green triangles), but the airline grabs most of it and converts it into producer surplus (the blue area).

- Norman Sherlock is not correct. Business travelers do not pay a penalty. They pay what they are willing to pay.

- David Fuscus is not correct. The airlines don't hold seats open and run the risk of not filling them. They sell each seat for the most the consumer is willing to pay for it.

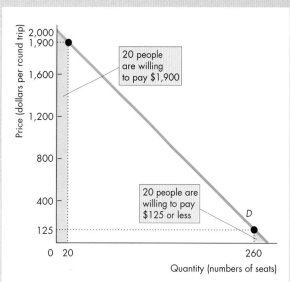

Figure 1 Willingness to pay

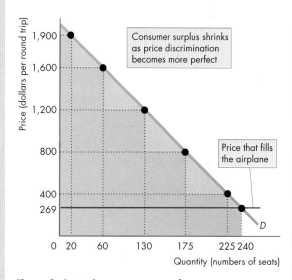

Figure 2 Capturing consumer surplus

You're The Voter

- Does airline price discrimination need government attention? Why or why not?

- Can the free market be relied upon to deliver the efficient quantity of air travel? Why or why not?

- How would you vote on a bill that requires the airlines to sell every seat for the same price? Why?

SUMMARY

KEY POINTS

Market Power (pp. 264–265)

- A monopoly is an industry with a single supplier of a good or service that has no close substitutes and in which barriers to entry prevent competition.
- Barriers to entry may be legal (public franchise, license, patent, copyright, firm owns control of a resource) or natural (created by economies of scale).
- A monopoly might be able to price discriminate when there is no resale possibility.
- Where resale is possible, a firm charges one price.

A Single-Price Monopoly's Output and Price Decision (pp. 266–269)

- A monopoly's demand curve is the market demand curve, and a single-price monopoly's marginal revenue is less than price.
- A monopoly maximizes profit by producing the output at which marginal revenue equals marginal cost and by charging the maximum price that consumers are willing to pay for that output.

Single-Price Monopoly and Competition Compared (pp. 270–273)

- A single-price monopoly charges a higher price and produces a smaller quantity than a perfectly competitive industry.
- A single-price monopoly restricts output and creates a deadweight loss.
- Monopoly imposes costs that equal its deadweight loss plus the cost of the resources devoted to rent seeking.

Price Discrimination (pp. 273–276)

- Price discrimination is an attempt by the monopoly to convert consumer surplus into economic profit.
- Perfect price discrimination extracts all the consumer surplus. Such a monopoly charges a different price for each unit sold and obtains the maximum price that each consumer is willing to pay for each unit bought.

- With perfect price discrimination, the monopoly produces the same output as would a perfectly competitive industry.
- Rent seeking with perfect price discrimination might eliminate the entire consumer surplus and producer surplus.

Monopoly Policy Issues (pp. 277–279)

- Monopolies with large economies of scale and scope can produce a larger quantity at a lower price than a competitive industry can achieve, and monopoly might be more innovative than competition.
- Efficient regulation requires a monopoly to charge a price equal to marginal cost, but for a natural monopoly, such a price is less than average total cost.
- Average cost pricing is a compromise pricing rule that covers a firm's costs and provides a normal profit but is not efficient. It is more efficient than unregulated profit maximization.

KEY FIGURES AND TABLE

KEY TERMS

PROBLEMS

💻 *1. Minnie's Mineral Springs, a single-price monopoly, faces the demand schedule:

Price (dollars per bottle)	Quantity demanded (bottles)
10	0
8	1
6	2
4	3
2	4
0	5

a. Calculate Minnie's total revenue schedule.
b. Calculate its marginal revenue schedule.

2 Dolly's Diamond Mines, a single-price monopoly, faces the demand schedule:

Price (dollars per pound)	Quantity demanded (pounds per day)
2,200	5
2,000	6
1,800	7
1,600	8
1,400	9
1,200	10

a. Calculate Dolly's total revenue schedule.
b. Calculate its marginal revenue schedule.

💻 *3. Minnie's Mineral Springs in problem 1 has the following total cost:

Quantity produced (bottles)	Total cost (dollars)
0	1
1	3
2	7
3	13
4	21
5	31

Calculate the profit-maximizing levels of
a. Output
b. Price
c. Marginal cost
d. Marginal revenue
e. Economic profit
f. Does Minnie's use resources efficiently? Explain your answer.

4. Dolly's Diamond Mines in problem 2 has the following total cost:

Quantity produced (pounds per day)	Total cost (dollars)
5	8,000
6	9,000
7	10,200
8	11,600
9	13,200
10	15,000

Calculate the profit-maximizing levels of
a. Output
b. Price
c. Marginal cost
d. Marginal revenue
e. Economic profit
f. Does Dolly's Mines use resources efficiently? Explain your answer.

*5. The figure illustrates the situation facing the publisher of the only newspaper containing local news in an isolated community.

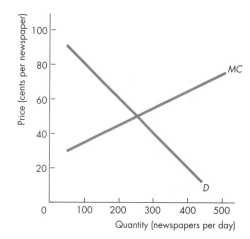

a. What quantity of newspapers will maximize the publisher's profit?
b. What price will the publisher charge?
c. What is the publisher's daily total revenue?
d. At the price charged for a newspaper, is the demand elastic or inelastic? Why?

6. In problem 5, the publisher installs a new printing press that makes the marginal cost constant at 20 cents per copy.
a. What quantity of newspapers will maximize the publisher's profit?

b. What price will the publisher charge?

c. What is the publisher's daily total revenue?

d. At the price charged, is the demand for newspapers elastic or inelastic? Why?

*7. In problem 5, what is:

a. The efficient quantity of newspapers to print each day? Explain your answer.

b. The consumer surplus?

c. The deadweight loss created by the monopoly newspaper publisher?

8. In problem 6, what is:

a. The efficient quantity of newspapers to print each day? Explain your answer.

b. The consumer surplus?

c. The deadweight loss created by the monopoly newspaper publisher?

*9. What is the maximum value of resources that will be used in rent seeking to acquire Minnie's monopoly? Considering this loss, what is the total social cost of Minnie's monopoly?

10. What is the maximum value of resources that will be used in rent seeking to acquire Dolly's monopoly? Considering this loss, what is the total social cost of Dolly's monopoly?

*11. The figure shows the situation facing a natural monopoly.

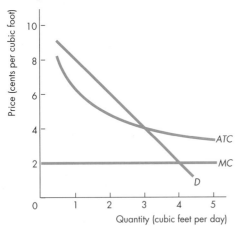

What quantity will be produced and what will be the deadweight loss if the firm is:

a. An unregulated profit maximizer?

b. Regulated to earn only normal profit?

c. Regulated to be efficient?

12. If in problem 11 marginal cost falls by 50 percent, what are the answers to the three questions posed in problem 11?

CRITICAL THINKING

 1. Study *Reading Between the Lines* on pp. 280–281 and then answer the following questions:

a. Why can airlines price discriminate?

b. Who benefits from and who pays for price discrimination?

c. If price discrimination by the airlines were illegal, how would last-minute travelers get the seats they are willing to pay for?

d. Does the ability to price discriminate guarantee the airlines a profitable business? Why or why not? Explain your answer.

e. Why do you think the cost per mile between Dallas and Denver is higher than the cost per mile on other routes in the United States? (Hint: Think about competition on that route.)

f. Use the links on the Parkin Web site and make some phone calls to obtain the alternative fares being offered today on an air route that appeals to you. Examine the criteria for the different fares and explain how the different fares capture consumer surplus.

 2. Use the links on the Parkin Web site to study the market for computer chips.

a. Is it correct to call Intel a monopoly? Why or why not?

b. How does Intel try to raise barriers to entry in this market?

 3. Use the links on the Parkin Web site to obtain information about Microsoft. Then answer the following questions.

a. Is it correct to call Microsoft a monopoly? Why or why not?

b. How do you think that Microsoft sets the price of Windows 98 and decides how many copies of the program to sell?

c. How would the arrival of a viable alternative operating system to Windows affect Microsoft?

d. How would you regulate the software industry to ensure that resources are used efficiently?

e. "Anyone is free to buy stock in Microsoft, so everyone is free to share in Microsoft's economic profit, and the bigger that economic profit, the better for all." Evaluate this statement.

Monopolistic Competition and Oligopoly

Every week, we receive a newspaper stuffed with supermarket fliers describing this week's "specials," providing coupons and other enticements, all designed to grab our attention and persuade us that A&P, Kroger, Safeway, Alpha Beta, Winn Dixie, Stop & Shop, Shop 'n' Save, and H.E.B.'s have the best deals in town. One claims the lowest price, another the best brands, yet another the best value for money even if its prices are not the lowest. How do firms locked in fierce competition with other firms set their prices, pick their products, and choose the quantities to produce? How are the profits of such firms affected by the actions of other firms? ◆ Before 1994, only one firm made the chips that drive IBM and compatible PCs: Intel Corporation. During 1994, the prices of powerful personal computers based on Intel's fast Pentium chips collapsed. The reason: Intel suddenly faced competition from new chip producers such as Advanced Micro Devices Inc. and Cyrix Corp. The price of Intel's Pentium processor, set at more than $1,000 when it was launched in 1993, fell to less than $200 by spring 1996, and today you can buy a Pentium-class computer for less than $600. How did competition among a small number of chip makers bring such rapid falls in the prices of chips and computers?

Fliers and War Games

◆ The theories of monopoly and perfect competition do not predict the kind of behavior that we've just described. There are no fliers and coupons, best brands, or price wars in perfect competition because each firm produces an identical product and is a price taker. And there are none in monopoly because each monopoly firm has the entire market to itself. To understand coupons, fliers, and price wars, we need the richer models explained in this chapter.

After studying this chapter, you will be able to:

- Explain how price and output are determined in a monopolistically competitive industry
- Explain why advertising costs are high in a monopolistically competitive industry
- Explain why the price might be sticky in an oligopoly industry
- Explain how price and output are determined when an industry has one dominant firm and several small firms
- Use game theory to make predictions about price wars and competition among a small number of firms

Monopolistic Competition

YOU HAVE STUDIED TWO TYPES OF MARKET STRUCTURE: perfect competition and monopoly. In perfect competition, a large number of firms produce identical goods, there are no barriers to entry, and each firm is a price taker. In the long run, there is no economic profit. In monopoly, a single firm is protected from competition by barriers to entry and can make an economic profit, even in the long run.

Many real-world markets are competitive, but not as fiercely so as perfect competition. Firms in these markets possess some power to set their prices as monopolies do. We call this type of market *monopolistic competition.*

Monopolistic competition is a market structure in which:

- A large number of firms compete
- Each firm produces a differentiated product
- Firms compete on product quality, price, and marketing
- Firms are free to enter and exit.

Large Number of Firms

In monopolistic competition, as in perfect competition, the industry consists of a large number of firms. The presence of a large number of firms has three implications for the firms in the industry.

Small Market Share In monopolistic competition, each firm supplies a small part of the total industry output. Consequently, each firm has only limited power to influence the price of its product. Each firm's price can deviate from the average price of other firms by a relatively small amount.

Ignore Other Firms A firm in monopolistic competition must be sensitive to the average market price of the product. But it does not pay attention to any one individual competitor. Because all the firms are relatively small, no one firm can dictate market conditions, so no one firm's actions directly affect the actions of the other firms.

Collusion Impossible Firms in monopolistic competition would like to make agreements with each other to fix a higher price—called collusion. But because there are many firms, collusion is not possible.

Product Differentiation

A firm practices **product differentiation** if it makes a product that is slightly different from the products of competing firms. A differentiated product is one that is a close substitute but not a perfect substitute for the products of the other firms. Some people will pay more for one variety of the product, so when its price rises, the quantity demanded falls but it does not (necessarily) fall to zero. For example, Adidas, Asics, Diadora, Etonic, Fila, New Balance, Nike, Puma, and Reebok all make differentiated running shoes. Other things remaining the same, if the price of Adidas running shoes rises and the prices of the other shoes remain constant, Adidas sells fewer shoes and the other producers sell more. But Adidas shoes don't disappear unless the price rises by a large enough amount.

Competing on Quality, Price, and Marketing

Product differentiation enables a firm to compete with other firms in three areas: product quality, price, and marketing.

Quality The quality of a product is the physical attributes that make it different from the products of other firms. Quality includes design, reliability, the service provided to the buyer, and the buyer's ease of access to the product. Quality lies on a spectrum that runs from high to low. Some firms—Dell Computers is an example—offer high-quality products. They are well designed and reliable, and the customer receives quick and efficient service. Other firms offer lower-quality products. They are less well designed, might not work perfectly, or the buyer must travel some distance to obtain them.

Price Because of product differentiation, a firm in monopolistic competition faces a downward-sloping demand curve. So, like a monopoly, the firm can set both its price and its output. But there is a tradeoff between the product's quality and price. A firm that makes a high-quality product can charge a higher price than a firm that makes a low-quality product.

Marketing Because of product differentiation, a firm in monopolistic competition must market its product. Marketing takes two main forms: advertising and packaging. A firm that produces a high-quality product wants to sell it for a suitably high price. To be able to do so, the firm must advertise and package its product in a way that convinces buyers that they are getting the higher quality for which they are paying a higher price. For example, drug companies advertise and package their brand-name drugs to persuade buyers that these items are superior to the lower-priced generic alternatives. Similarly, a low-quality producer uses advertising and packaging to persuade buyers that although the quality is low, the low price more than compensates for this fact.

Entry and Exit

In monopolistic competition, there is free entry and free exit. Consequently, a firm cannot make an economic profit in the long run. When firms make an economic profit, new firms enter the industry. This entry lowers prices and eventually eliminates economic profit. When economic losses are incurred, some firms leave the industry. This exit increases prices and profits and eventually eliminates the economic loss. In long-run equilibrium, firms neither enter nor leave the industry and the firms in the industry make zero economic profit.

Examples of Monopolistic Competition

Figure 14.1 shows ten industries that are good examples of monopolistic competition. These industries have a large number of firms (shown in parentheses after the name of the industry). In the most concentrated of these industries, canned foods, the largest four firms produce only 25 percent of total sales and the largest twenty firms produce only 60 percent of total sales. Gas stations, food stores, dry cleaners, and haircutters also all operate in monopolistic competition.

REVIEW QUIZ

- What are the distinguishing characteristics of monopolistic competition?
- How do firms in monopolistic competition compete?
- In addition to the examples shown in Fig. 14.1, provide some examples of industries around your school that operate in monopolistic competition.

FIGURE 14.1
Examples of Monopolistic Competition

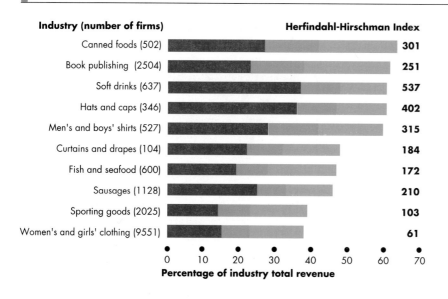

These industries operate in monopolistic competition. The number of firms in the industry is shown after the name of the industry. The red bars show the percentage of industry sales by the largest 4 firms. The green bars show the percentage of industry sales by the next 4 largest firms, and the blue bars show the percentage of industry sales by the next 12 largest firms. So the entire bar shows the percentage of industry sales by the largest 20 firms. The Herfindahl-Hirschman Index is shown on the right.

Output and Price in Monopolistic Competition

WE ARE NOW GOING TO LEARN HOW OUTPUT and price are determined in monopolistic competition. First, we will suppose that the firm has already decided on the quality of its product and on its marketing program. For a given product and a given amount of marketing activity, the firm faces given costs and market conditions.

Figure 14.2 shows how a firm in monopolistic competition determines its price and output. Part (a) deals with the short run, and part (b) deals with the long run. We'll concentrate first on the short run.

Short Run: Economic Profit

The demand curve D shows the demand for the firm's product. It is the demand curve for Nautica jackets, not jackets in general. The curve labeled MR is the marginal revenue curve associated with the demand curve. It is derived just like the marginal revenue curve of a single-price monopoly that you studied in Chapter 13, p. 266. The figure also shows the firm's average total cost (ATC) and marginal cost (MC). These curves are similar to the cost curves that you first encountered in Chapter 11.

Nautica maximizes profit by producing the output at which marginal revenue equals marginal cost. In Fig. 14.2, this output is 150 jackets a day. Nautica charges the maximum price that buyers are willing to pay for this quantity, which is determined by the demand curve. This price is $190 a jacket. When Nautica produces 150 jackets a day, its average total cost is $140 a jacket, so it makes a short-run economic profit of $7,500 a day ($50 a jacket multiplied by 150 jackets a day). The blue rectangle shows this economic profit.

So far, the firm in monopolistic competition looks just like a single-price monopoly. It produces

---

FIGURE 14.2

Output and Price in Monopolistic Competition

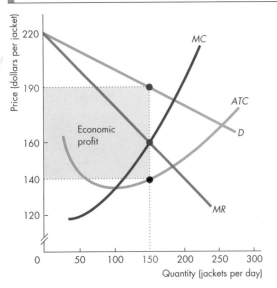

(a) Short run

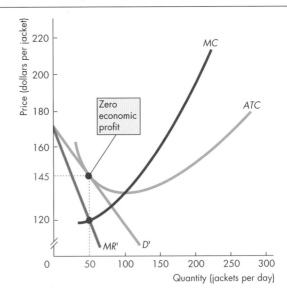

(b) Long run

Part (a) shows the short-run outcome. Profit is maximized by producing 150 jackets per day and selling them for $190 per jacket. Average total cost is $140 per jacket, and the firm makes an economic profit (the blue rectangle) of $7,500 a day.

Economic profit encourages new entrants in the long run, and part (b) shows the long-run outcome. The entry of new firms

decreases each firm's demand and shifts the demand curve and marginal revenue curve leftward. When the demand curve has shifted to D', the marginal revenue curve is MR' and the firm is in long-run equilibrium. The output that maximizes profit is 50 jackets a day, and the price is $145 per jacket. Average total cost is also $145 per jacket, so economic profit is zero.

the quantity at which marginal revenue equals marginal cost and then charges the highest price that buyers are willing to pay for that quantity, determined by the demand curve. The key difference between monopoly and monopolistic competition lies in what happens next.

Long Run: Zero Economic Profit

There is no restriction on entry in monopolistic competition, so economic profit attracts new entrants. As new firms enter the industry, the firm's demand curve and marginal revenue curve start to shift leftward. At each point in time, the firm maximizes its short-run profit by producing the quantity at which marginal revenue equals marginal cost and by charging the highest price that buyers are willing to pay for this quantity. But as the demand curve shifts leftward, the profit-maximizing quantity and price fall.

Figure 14.2(b) shows the long-run equilibrium. Nautica's demand curve has shifted leftward to D', and its marginal revenue curve has shifted leftward to MR'. Nautica produces 50 jackets a day and sells them at a price of $145 each. At this output level, average total cost is also $145 a jacket, so Nautica is making zero economic profit.

When all the firms are making zero economic profit, there is no incentive for new firms to enter the industry.

If demand is so low relative to costs that firms are incurring economic losses, exit will occur. As firms leave an industry, the demand facing the remaining firms increases and their demand curves shift rightward. The exit process ends when all firms in the industry are making zero economic profit.

Monopolistic Competition and Efficiency

When we studied a perfectly competitive industry, we discovered that in some circumstances, such an industry allocates resources efficiently. A key feature of efficiency is that marginal benefit equals marginal cost. Price measures marginal benefit, so efficiency requires price to equal marginal cost. When we studied monopoly, we discovered that such a firm creates an inefficient use of resources because it restricts output to a level at which price exceeds marginal cost. In such a situation, the marginal benefit exceeds marginal cost and production is less than its efficient level.

Monopolistic competition shares this feature of monopoly. Even though firms make zero economic profit in long-run equilibrium, the monopolistically competitive industry produces an output at which price equals average total cost but exceeds marginal cost. This outcome means that firms in monopolistic competition always have excess capacity in long-run equilibrium.

Excess Capacity   A firm's **capacity output** is the output at which average total cost is a minimum—the output at the bottom of the U-shaped *ATC* curve. This output is 100 jackets a day in Fig. 14.3. Firms in monopolistic competition always have *excess capacity* in the long run. In Fig. 14.3, the firm produces 50 jackets a day and has excess capacity of 50 jackets a day. That is, the firm produces a smaller output than that which minimizes average total cost. Consequently, the consumer pays a price that exceeds

FIGURE 14.3
Excess Capacity

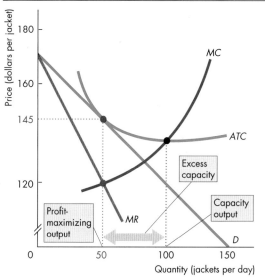

In the long run, entry decreases demand to the point at which the firm makes zero economic profit. Here, the firm produces 50 jackets a day. The firm's capacity output is the output at which average total cost is a minimum. Here, capacity output is 100 jackets a day. Because the demand curve in monopolistic competition slopes downward, the output that maximizes profit is always less than capacity output in long-run equilibrium. The firm operates with excess capacity in long-run equilibrium.

minimum average total cost. This result arises from the fact that the firm faces a downward-sloping demand curve. The demand curve slopes down because of product differentiation, so product differentiation creates excess capacity.

You can see the excess capacity in monopolistic competition all around you. Family restaurants (except for the truly outstanding ones) almost always have some empty tables. You can always get a pizza delivered in less than 30 minutes. It is rare that every pump at a gas station is in use with customers waiting in line. There is always an abundance of realtors ready to help find or sell a home.

These industries are all examples of monopolistic competition. The firms have excess capacity. They could sell more by cutting their prices. But they would then incur losses.

Because in monopolistic competition, price exceeds marginal cost, this market structure, like monopoly, is inefficient. The marginal cost of producing one more unit of output is less than the marginal benefit to the consumer, determined by the price the consumer is willing to pay. But the inefficiency of monopolistic competition arises from product differentiation—from product variety. Consumers value variety, but it is achievable only if firms make differentiated products. So the loss in efficiency that occurs in monopolistic competition must be weighed against the gain of greater product variety.

REVIEW QUIZ

- How does a firm in monopolistic competition decide how much to produce and at what price to offer its product for sale?
- Why can a firm in monopolistic competition earn an economic profit only in the short run?
- Is monopolistic competition efficient?
- Why do firms in monopolistic competition operate with excess capacity?

You've seen how the firm in monopolistic competition determines its output and price in the short run and the long run when it produces a given product and undertakes a *given* marketing effort. But how does the firm choose its product quality and marketing effort? We'll now study these decisions.

Product Development and Marketing

WHEN WE STUDIED A FIRM'S OUTPUT AND PRICE decision, we supposed that it had already made its product and marketing decisions. We're now going to study these decisions and their impact on the firm's output, price, and economic profit.

Innovation and Product Development

To enjoy economic profits, firms in monopolistic competition must be in a state of continuous product development. The reason is that wherever economic profits are earned, imitators emerge and set up business. So to maintain its economic profit, a firm must seek out new products that will provide it with a competitive edge, even if only temporarily. A firm that manages to introduce a new and differentiated variety will temporarily increase the demand for its product and will be able to temporarily increase its price. It will make an economic profit. Eventually, new firms that make close substitutes for the new product will enter and compete away the economic profit arising from this initial advantage. So to restore economic profit, the firm must again innovate.

The decision to innovate is based on the same type of profit-maximizing calculation that you've already studied. Innovation and product development are costly activities, but they also bring in additional revenues. The firm must balance the cost and benefit at the margin. At a low level of product development, the marginal revenue from a better product exceeds the marginal cost. When the marginal dollar spent on product development brings in a dollar of revenue, the firm is spending the profit-maximizing amount on product development.

For example, when Eidos Interactive released Tomb Raider III, it was probably not the best game that Eidos could have created. Rather, it was the game that balanced the marginal benefit and willingness of the consumer to pay for further game enhancements against the marginal cost of these enhancements.

Efficiency and Product Innovation Is product innovation an efficient activity? Does it benefit the consumer? There are two views about these questions. One view is that monopolistic competition brings to market many improved products that bring great benefits to the consumer. Clothing, kitchen and other household appliances, computers, computer programs, cars, and many other products keep getting better every year, and the consumer benefits from these improved products.

But many so-called improvements amount to little more than changing the appearance of a product. And sometimes, the improvement is restricted to a different look in the packaging. In these cases, there is little objective benefit to the consumer.

But regardless of whether a product improvement is real or imagined, its value to the consumer is its marginal benefit, which equals the amount the consumer is willing to pay. In other words, the value of a product improvement is the increase in price that the consumer is willing to pay. The marginal benefit to the producer is marginal revenue, which equals marginal cost. Because price exceeds marginal cost in monopolistic competition, product development is not pushed to its efficient level.

Marketing

Some product differentiation is achieved by designing and developing products that are actually different from those of the other firms. But firms also attempt to create a consumer perception of product differentiation even when actual differences are small. Advertising and packaging are the principal means that firms use to achieve this end. An American Express card is a different product from a Visa card. But the actual differences are not the main ones that American Express emphasizes in its marketing. The deeper message is that if you use an American Express card, you can be like Tiger Woods (or some other high-profile successful person).

Marketing Expenditures Firms in monopolistic competition incur huge costs to persuade buyers to appreciate and value the differences between their own products and those of their competitors. So a large proportion of the prices that we pay cover the cost of selling a good. And this proportion is increasing. Advertising in newspapers and magazines and on radio and television is the main selling cost. But it is not the only one. Selling costs include the cost of shopping malls that look like movie sets; glossy catalogs and brochures; and the salaries, airfares, and hotel bills of salespeople.

The total scale of selling costs is hard to estimate, but some components can be measured. A survey

conducted by a commercial agency suggests that for cleaning supplies and toys, around 15 percent of the price of an item is spent on advertising. Figure 14.4 shows some estimates for other industries.

For the U.S. economy as a whole, there are some 20,000 advertising agencies that employ more than 200,000 people and have total revenue of $45 billion. But these numbers are only part of the total cost of advertising because firms have their own internal advertising departments, the cost of which can only be guessed.

Advertising expenditures and other selling costs affect the profits of firms in two ways. They increase costs, and they change demand. Let's look at these effects.

Selling Costs and Total Costs Selling costs such as advertising expenditures increase the costs of a monopolistically competitive firm above those of a competitive firm or a monopoly. Advertising costs and other selling costs are fixed costs. They do not vary as total output varies. So, just like fixed production

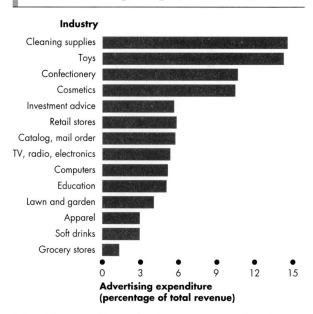

FIGURE 14.4
Advertising Expenditures

Industry

Advertising expenditure (percentage of total revenue): 0, 3, 6, 9, 12, 15

- Cleaning supplies
- Toys
- Confectionery
- Cosmetics
- Investment advice
- Retail stores
- Catalog, mail order
- TV, radio, electronics
- Computers
- Education
- Lawn and garden
- Apparel
- Soft drinks
- Grocery stores

Advertising expenditures are a large percentage of total revenue for producers of cleaning supplies, toys, confectionery, and cosmetics.

Source: Schoenfeld & Associates, Lincolnwood, Illinois, reported at http://www.toolkit.cch.com/text/p03_7006.stm

costs, advertising costs per unit decrease as production increases.

Figure 14.5 shows how selling costs and advertising expenditures change a firm's average total cost. The blue curve shows the average total cost of production. The red curve shows the firm's average total cost of production plus advertising. The height of the red area between the two curves shows the average fixed cost of advertising. The *total* cost of advertising is fixed. But the *average* cost of advertising decreases as output increases.

The figure shows that if advertising increases the quantity sold by a large enough amount, it can lower average total cost. For example, if the quantity sold increases from 25 jackets a day with no advertising to 130 jackets a day with advertising, average total cost falls from $170 a jacket to $160 a jacket. The reason is that although the *total* fixed cost has increased, the greater fixed cost is spread over a greater output, so average total cost decreases.

FIGURE 14.5

Selling Costs and
Total Cost

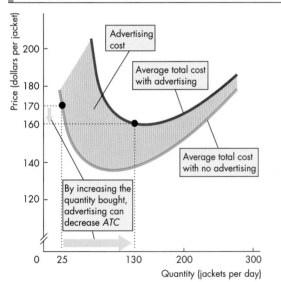

Selling costs such as the cost of advertising are fixed costs. When added to the average total cost of production, these costs increase average total cost (ATC) by a greater amount at small outputs than at large outputs. If advertising enables the quantity sold to increase from 25 jackets to 130 jackets a day, it *lowers* average total cost from $170 to $160 a jacket.

Selling Costs and Demand Advertising and other selling efforts change the demand for a firm's products. But how? Does demand increase or does it decrease? The most natural answer is that advertising increases demand. By informing people about the quality of its products or by persuading people to switch from the products of other firms, a firm might expect to increase the demand for its own products.

But all firms in monopolistic competition advertise. And all seek to persuade customers that they have the best deal around. If advertising enables a firm to survive, it might increase the number of firms. And to the extent that it increases the number of firms, it *decreases* the demand faced by any one firm.

Efficiency: The Bottom Line To the extent that selling costs provide consumers with services that they value and with information about the precise nature of the differentiation of products, they serve a useful purpose to the consumer and enable a better product choice to be made. But the opportunity cost of the additional service and information must be weighed against the gain to the consumer.

The bottom line on the question of efficiency of monopolistic competition is ambiguous. In some cases, the gains from extra product variety unquestionably offset the selling costs and the extra cost arising from excess capacity. The tremendous varieties of books and magazines, clothing, food, and drinks are examples of such gains. It is less easy to see the gains from being able to buy brand-name drugs that have a chemical composition identical to that of a generic alternative. But some people do willingly pay more for the brand-name alternative.

REVIEW QUIZ

- What are the two main ways other than by adjusting price in which a firm in monopolistic competition competes with other firms?
- Why might product innovation and development be efficient and why might it be inefficient?
- How do advertising expenditures influence a firm's cost curves? Do they increase or decrease average total cost?
- How do advertising expenditures influence a firm's demand curve? Do they increase or decrease demand?
- Why is it difficult to determine whether monopolistic competition is efficient or inefficient? What is your opinion about the bottom line and why?

Oligopoly

ANOTHER TYPE OF MARKET THAT STANDS BETWEEN the extremes of perfect competition and monopoly is oligopoly. **Oligopoly** is a market structure in which a small number of firms compete.

In oligopoly, the quantity sold by any one firm depends on that firm's price *and* on the other firms' prices and quantities sold. To see why, suppose you run one of the three gas stations in a small town. If you cut your price and your two competitors don't cut theirs, your sales increase and the sales of the other two firms decrease. With lower sales, the other firms most likely cut their prices too. If they do cut their prices, your sales and profits take a tumble. So before deciding to cut your price, you must predict how the other firms will react and attempt to calculate the effects of those reactions on your own profit.

Several models have been developed to explain the prices and quantities in oligopoly markets. But no one theory has been found that can explain all the different types of behavior that we observe in such markets. The models fall into two broad groups: traditional models and game theory models. We'll look at examples of both types, starting with two traditional models.

The Kinked Demand Curve Model

The kinked demand curve model of oligopoly is based on the assumption that each firm believes that:

1. If it raises its price, others will not follow.
2. If it cuts its price, so will the other firms.

Figure 14.6 shows the demand curve (D) that a firm believes it faces. The demand curve has a kink at the current price, P, and quantity, Q. A small price rise above P brings a big decrease in the quantity sold. The other firms hold their current price and the firm has the highest price for the good, so it loses its market share. Even a large price cut below P brings only a small increase in the quantity demanded. In this case, other firms match the price cut, so the firm gets no price advantage over its competitors.

The kink in the demand curve creates a break in the marginal revenue curve (MR). To maximize profit, the firm produces the quantity at which marginal cost equals marginal revenue. That quantity, Q, is where the marginal cost curve passes through the gap ab in the marginal revenue curve. If marginal cost fluctuates

FIGURE 14.6

The Kinked Demand Curve Model

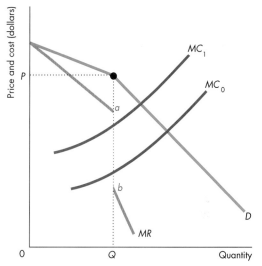

The price in an oligopoly market is P. Each firm believes it faces the demand curve D. A small price rise above P brings a big decrease in the quantity sold because other firms do not raise their prices. Even a big price cut below P brings only a small increase in the quantity sold because other firms also cut their prices. Because the demand curve is kinked, the marginal revenue curve, MR, has a break ab. Profit is maximized by producing Q. The marginal cost curve passes through the break in the marginal revenue curve. Marginal cost changes inside the range ab leave the price and quantity unchanged.

between a and b, like the marginal cost curves MC_0 and MC_1, the firm does not change its price or its output. Only if marginal cost fluctuates outside the range ab does the firm change its price and output. So the kinked demand curve model predicts that price and quantity are insensitive to small cost changes.

A problem with the kinked demand curve model is that the firms' beliefs about the demand curve are not always correct and firms can figure out that they are not correct. If marginal cost increases by enough to cause the firm to increase its price and if all firms experience the same increase in marginal cost, they all increase their prices together. The firm's belief that others will not join it in a price rise is incorrect. A firm that bases its actions on beliefs that are wrong does not maximize profit and might even end up incurring an economic loss.

Dominant Firm Oligopoly

A second traditional model explains a dominant firm oligopoly, which arises when one firm—the dominant firm—has a big cost advantage over the other firms and produces a large part of the industry output. The dominant firm sets the market price, and the other firms are price takers. Examples of dominant firm oligopoly are a large gasoline retailer or a big video rental store that dominates its local market.

To see how a dominant firm oligopoly works, suppose that 11 firms operate gas stations in a city. Big-G is the dominant firm. Figure 14.7 shows the market for gas in this city. In part (a), the demand curve D tells us the total quantity of gas demanded in the city at each price. The supply curve S_{10} is the supply curve of the 10 small suppliers.

Part (b) shows the situation facing Big-G. Its marginal cost curve is MC. Big-G's demand curve is XD, and its marginal revenue curve is MR. Big-G's demand curve shows the excess demand not met by the 10 small firms. For example, at a price of $1 a gallon, the quantity demanded is 20,000 gallons, the quantity supplied by the 10 small firms is 10,000 gallons, and the excess quantity demanded is 10,000, measured by the distance ab in both parts of the figure.

To maximize profit, Big-G operates like a monopoly. It sells 10,000 gallons a week for a price of $1 a gallon. The 10 small firms take the price of $1 a gallon. They behave just like firms in perfect competition. The quantity of gas demanded in the entire city at $1 a gallon is 20,000 gallons, as shown in part (a). Of this amount, Big-G sells 10,000 gallons and the 10 small firms each sell 1,000 gallons.

The traditional theories of oligopoly do not enable us to understand all oligopoly markets, and in recent years, economists have developed new models based on game theory. Let's now learn about game theory.

FIGURE 14.7

A Dominant Firm Oligopoly

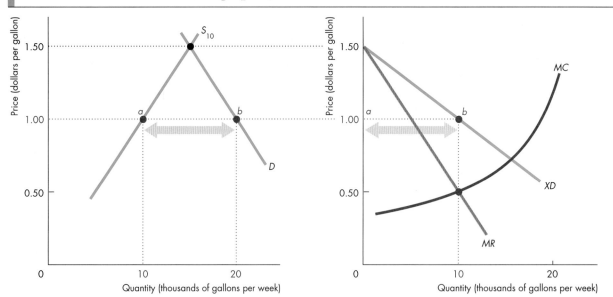

(a) Ten small firms and market demand

(b) Big-G's price and output decision

The demand curve for gas in a city is D in part (a). There are 10 small competitive firms that together have a supply curve of S_{10}. In addition, there is 1 large firm, Big-G, shown in part (b). Big-G faces the demand curve XD, determined as market demand D minus the supply of the other 10 firms S_{10}—the demand that is not satisfied by the small firms. Big-G's mar-

ginal revenue is MR, and its marginal cost is MC. Big-G sets its output to maximize profit by equating marginal cost, MC, and marginal revenue, MR. This output is 10,000 gallons per week. The price at which Big-G can sell this quantity is $1 a gallon. The other 10 firms take this price, and each firm sells 1,000 gallons per week.

Game Theory

THE MAIN TOOL THAT ECONOMISTS USE TO analyze *strategic behavior*—behavior that takes into account the expected behavior of others and the mutual recognition of interdependence—is called **game theory**. Game theory was invented by John von Neumann in 1937 and extended by von Neumann and Oskar Morgenstern in 1944. Today, it is one of the major research fields in economics.

Game theory seeks to understand oligopoly as well as other forms of economic, political, social, and even biological rivalries by using a method of analysis specifically designed to understand games of all types, including the familiar games of everyday life. We will begin our study of game theory, and its application to the behavior of firms, by thinking about familiar games.

What Is a Game?

What is a game? At first thought, the question seems silly. After all, there are many different games. There are ball games and parlor games, games of chance and games of skill. But what is it about all these different activities that make them games? What do all these games have in common? All games share three features:

- Rules
- Strategies
- Payoffs

Let's see how these common features of games apply to a game called "the prisoners' dilemma." This game, it turns out, captures some of the essential features of oligopoly, and it gives a good illustration of how game theory works and how it generates predictions.

The Prisoners' Dilemma

Art and Bob have been caught red-handed, stealing a car. Facing airtight cases, each will receive a sentence of 2 years for the crime. During his interviews with the two prisoners, the district attorney begins to suspect that he has stumbled on the two people who were responsible for a multimillion-dollar bank robbery some months earlier. But this is just a suspicion. The district attorney has no evidence on which he can convict them of the greater crime unless he can get them to confess. The district attorney decides to make the prisoners play a game with the following rules.

Rules   Each prisoner (player) is placed in a separate room and cannot communicate with the other player. Each is told that he is suspected of having carried out the bank robbery and that:

If both of them confess to the larger crime, each will receive a sentence of 3 years for both crimes.

If he alone confesses and his accomplice does not, he will receive an even shorter sentence of 1 year while his accomplice will receive a 10-year sentence.

Strategies   In game theory, **strategies** are all the possible actions of each player. Art and Bob each have two possible actions:

- Confess to the bank robbery
- Deny having committed the bank robbery

Payoffs   Because there are two players, each with two strategies, there are four possible outcomes:

1. Both confess.
2. Both deny.
3. Art confesses and Bob denies.
4. Bob confesses and Art denies.

Each prisoner can work out exactly what happens to him—his *payoff*—in each of these four situations. We can tabulate the four possible payoffs for each of the prisoners in what is called a payoff matrix for the game. A **payoff matrix** is a table that shows the payoffs for every possible action by each player for every possible action by each other player.

Table 14.1 shows a payoff matrix for Art and Bob. The squares show the payoffs for each prisoner—the red triangle in each square shows Art's, and the blue triangle shows Bob's. If both prisoners confess (top left), each gets a prison term of 3 years. If Bob confesses but Art denies (top right), Art gets a 10-year sentence and Bob gets a 1-year sentence. If Art confesses and Bob denies (bottom left), Art gets a 1-year sentence and Bob gets a 10-year sentence. Finally, if both of them deny (bottom right), neither can be convicted of the bank robbery charge, but both are sentenced for the car theft—a 2-year sentence.

Equilibrium   The equilibrium of a game occurs when player *A* takes the best possible action given the action of player *B* and player *B* takes the best possible action given the action of player *A*. In the case of the prisoners' dilemma, the equilibrium occurs when Art makes his best choice given Bob's choice and when Bob makes his best choice given Art's choice. Let's find the equilibrium of the prisoners' dilemma game.

First, look at the situation from Art's point of view. If Bob confesses, it pays Art to confess because in that case, he is sentenced to 3 years rather than 10 years. If Bob does not confess, it still pays Art to confess because in that case he receives 1 year rather than 2 years. So Art's best action is to confess.

Second, look at the situation from Bob's point of view. If Art confesses, it pays Bob to confess because in that case, he is sentenced to 3 years rather than 10 years. If Art does not confess, it still pays Bob to confess because in that case, he receives 1 year rather than 2 years. So Bob's best action is to confess.

Because each player's best action is to confess, each does confess, each gets a 3-year prison term, and the district attorney has solved the bank robbery. This is the equilibrium of the game.

Nash Equilibrium The equilibrium concept that we have used is called a **Nash equilibrium**; it is so named because it was first proposed by John Nash of Princeton University, who received the Nobel Prize for Economic Science in 1994.

The prisoners' dilemma has a special kind of Nash equilibrium called a dominant strategy equilibrium. A *dominant strategy* is a strategy that is the same regardless of the action taken by the other player. In other words, each player has a unique best action regardless of what the other player does. A **dominant strategy equilibrium** occurs when there is a dominant strategy for each player.

The Dilemma Now that you have found the solution to the prisoners' dilemma, you can better see the dilemma. The dilemma arises as each prisoner contemplates the consequences of denying. Each prisoner knows that if both of them deny, they will receive only a 2-year sentence for stealing the car. But neither has any way of knowing that his accomplice will deny. Each poses the following questions: Should I deny and rely on my accomplice to deny so that we will both get only 2 years? Or should I confess in the hope of getting just 1 year (provided that my accomplice denies), knowing that if my accomplice does confess, we will both get 3 years in prison? The dilemma is resolved by finding the equilibrium of the game.

TABLE 14.1

Prisoners' Dilemma Payoff Matrix

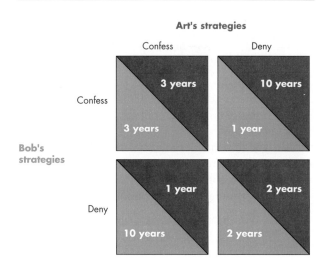

Art's strategies

	Confess	Deny
Confess	3 years / 3 years	10 years / 1 year
Deny	1 year / 10 years	2 years / 2 years

Bob's strategies

Each square shows the payoffs for the two players, Art and Bob, for each possible pair of actions. In each square, the red triangle shows Art's payoff and the blue triangle shows Bob's. For example, if both confess, the payoffs are in the top left square. The equilibrium of the game is for both players to confess, and each gets a 3-year sentence.

A Bad Outcome For the prisoners, the equilibrium of the game, with each confessing, is not the best outcome. If neither of them confesses, each gets only 2 years for the lesser crime. Isn't there some way in which this better outcome can be achieved? It seems that there is not, because the players cannot communicate with each other. Each player can put himself in the other player's place, and so each player can figure out that there is a dominant strategy for each of them. The prisoners are indeed in a dilemma. Each knows that he can serve 2 years only if he can trust the other to deny. But each prisoner also knows that it is not in the other's best interest to deny. So each prisoner knows that he must confess, thereby delivering a bad outcome for both.

Let's now see how we can use the ideas we've just developed to understand a host of economic situations such as price fixing, price wars, and other aspects of the behavior of firms in oligopoly.

An Oligopoly Price-Fixing Game

To UNDERSTAND HOW OLIGOPOLIES FIX PRICES, we're going to study a special case of oligopoly called duopoly. **Duopoly** is a market structure in which two producers compete with each other. You can probably find some examples of duopoly in your city. Many cities have only two suppliers of milk, two local newspapers, two taxi companies, two car rental firms, two copy centers, or two college bookstores. But the main reason for studying duopoly is not its realism. It is because it captures the essence of oligopoly and yet is more revealing.

Our goal is to predict the prices charged and the quantities produced by the two firms. To pursue that goal, we're going to study the duopoly game.

Suppose that two firms, Trick and Gear, enter into a collusive agreement. A **collusive agreement** is an agreement between two (or more) producers to restrict output in order to raise prices and profits. Such an agreement is illegal in the United States and is undertaken in secret. A group of firms that has entered into a collusive agreement to restrict output and increase prices and profits is called a **cartel**. The strategies that firms in a cartel can pursue are to:

- Comply
- Cheat

Complying simply means sticking to the agreement. Cheating means breaking the agreement in a manner designed to benefit the cheating firm.

Because each firm has two strategies, there are four possible combinations of actions for the two firms:

- Both firms comply.
- Both firms cheat.
- Trick complies and Gear cheats.
- Gear complies and Trick cheats.

We'll begin by describing the cost and demand conditions in a duopoly industry.

Cost and Demand Conditions

Trick and Gear face identical costs, and Fig. 14.8(a) shows their average total cost curve (*ATC*) and marginal cost curve (*MC*). Figure 14.8(b) shows the market demand curve for switchgears (*D*). Each firm produces an identical switchgear product, so one firm's switchgear is a perfect substitute for the other's. The price of each firm's product, therefore, is identical. And the higher the price, the smaller is the quantity demanded.

This industry is a natural duopoly. Two firms can produce this good at a lower cost than either one firm or three firms can. For each firm, average total cost is at its minimum when production is 3,000 units a week. And when price equals minimum average total cost, the total quantity demanded is 6,000 units a week. So two firms can just supply that quantity.

FIGURE 14.8

Costs and Demand

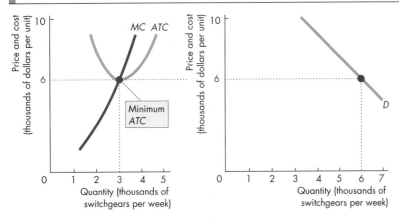

(a) Individual firm

(b) Industry

The average total cost curve for each firm is *ATC*, and the marginal cost curve is *MC* (part a). Minimum average total cost is at $6,000 a unit, and it occurs at an output of 3,000 units a week. Part (b) shows the industry demand curve. At a price of $6,000, the quantity demanded is 6,000 units per week. The two firms can produce this output at the lowest possible average cost. If the market had one firm, it would be profitable for another to enter. If the market had three firms, one would exit. There is room for just two firms in this industry. It is a natural duopoly.

Colluding to Maximize Profits

Let's begin by working out the payoffs to the two firms if they collude to make the maximum industry profit by acting like a monopoly. The calculations that the two firms will perform are exactly the same calculations that a monopoly performs. (You can refresh your memory of these calculations by looking at Chapter 13, pp. 268–269.) The only thing that the duopolists must do that is additional to what a monopolist must do is to agree on how much of the total output each of them will produce.

Figure 14.9 shows the price and quantity that maximize industry profit for the duopolists. Part (a) shows the situation for each firm, and part (b) shows the situation for the industry as a whole. The curve labeled MR is the industry marginal revenue curve. This marginal revenue curve is exactly like that of a single-price monopoly. The curve labeled MC_I is the industry marginal cost curve if each firm produces the same output. That curve is constructed by adding together the outputs of the two firms at each level of marginal cost. That is, at each level of marginal cost, industry output is twice as much as the output of each firm. Thus the curve MC_I in part (b) is twice as far to the right as the curve MC in part (a).

To maximize industry profit, the duopolists agree to restrict output to the rate that makes the industry marginal cost and marginal revenue equal. That output rate, as shown in part (b), is 4,000 switchgears a week.

The highest price for which the 4,000 switchgears can be sold is $9,000 each. This is the price that Trick and Gear agree to charge.

To hold the price at $9,000 a unit, production must not exceed 4,000 units a week. So Trick and Gear must agree on production levels for each of them that totals 4,000 units a week. Let's suppose that they agree to split the market equally so that each firm produces 2,000 switchgears a week. Because the firms are identical, this division is the most likely.

The average total cost (ATC) of producing 2,000 switchgears a week is $8,000, so the profit per unit is $1,000 and economic profit is $2 million (2,000 units × $1,000 per unit). The economic profit of each firm is represented by the blue rectangle in Fig. 14.9(a).

We have just described one possible outcome for a duopoly game: The two firms collude to produce the monopoly profit-maximizing output and divide that output equally between themselves. From the industry point of view, this solution is identical to a monopoly. A duopoly that operates in this way is indistinguishable from a monopoly. The economic profit that is made by a monopoly is the maximum total profit that can be made by colluding duopolists.

But with price greater than marginal cost, either firm might think of trying to increase profit by cheating on the agreement and producing more than the agreed amount. Let's see what happens if one of the firms does cheat in this way.

FIGURE 14.9

Colluding to Make Monopoly Profits

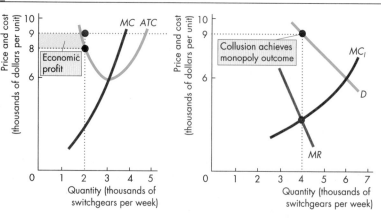

(a) Individual firm   (b) Industry

The industry marginal cost curve, MC_I (part b) is the horizontal sum of the two firms' marginal cost curves, MC (part a). The industry marginal revenue curve is MR. To maximize profit, the firms produce 4,000 units a week (the quantity at which marginal revenue equals marginal cost). They sell that output for $9,000 a unit. Each firm produces 2,000 units a week. Average total cost is $8,000 a unit, so each firm makes an economic profit of $2 million (blue rectangle)—2,000 units multiplied by $1,000 profit a unit.

One Firm Cheats on a Collusive Agreement

To set the stage for cheating on their agreement, Trick convinces Gear that demand has decreased and that it cannot sell 2,000 units a week. Trick tells Gear that it plans to cut its price in order to sell the agreed 2,000 units each week. Because the two firms produce an identical product, Gear matches Trick's price cut but still produces only 2,000 units a week.

In fact, there has been no decrease in demand. Trick plans to increase output, which it knows will lower the price, and Trick wants to ensure that Gear's output remains at the agreed level.

Figure 14.10 illustrates the consequences of Trick cheating. Suppose that Trick (the cheat) increases output to 3,000 units a week (part b). If Gear (the complier) sticks to the agreement to produce only 2,000 units a week (part a), total output is 5,000 a week, and given market demand in part (c), the price falls to $7,500 a unit.

Gear continues to produce 2,000 units a week at a cost of $8,000 a unit and incurs a loss of $500 a unit, or $1 million a week. This economic loss is the red rectangle in part (a). Trick produces 3,000 units a

week at an average total cost of $6,000. With a price of $7,500, Trick makes a profit of $1,500 a unit and therefore an economic profit of $4.5 million. This economic profit is the blue rectangle in part (b).

We've now described a second possible outcome for the duopoly game: One of the firms cheats on the collusive agreement. In this case, the industry output is larger than the monopoly output and the industry price is lower than the monopoly price. The total economic profit made by the industry is smaller than the monopoly economic profit. Trick (the cheat) makes an economic profit of $4.5 million, and Gear (the complier) incurs an economic loss of $1 million. The industry makes an economic profit of $3.5 million, which is $0.5 million less than the economic profit a monopoly would make. But the profit is distributed unevenly. Trick makes a bigger economic profit while Gear incurs an economic loss.

A similar outcome would arise if Gear cheated and Trick complied with the agreement. The industry profit and price would be the same, but in this case Gear (the cheat) would make an economic profit of $4.5 million and Trick (the complier) would incur an economic loss of $1 million.

Let's next see what happens if both firms cheat.

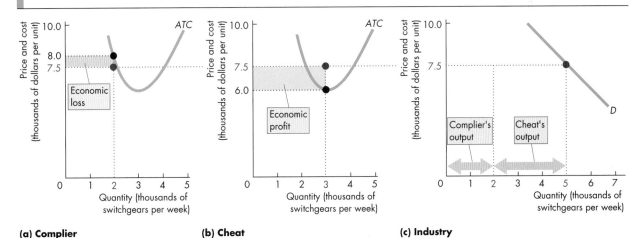

FIGURE 14.10

One Firm Cheats

(a) Complier　　　　**(b) Cheat**　　　　**(c) Industry**

One firm, shown in part (a), complies with the agreement and produces 2,000 units. The other firm, shown in part (b), cheats on the agreement and increases its output to 3,000 units. Given the market demand curve, shown in part (c), and with a total production of 5,000 units a week, the price falls to

$7,500. At this price, the complier in part (a) incurs an economic loss of $1 million ($500 per unit × 2,000 units), shown by the red rectangle. In part (b), the cheat makes an economic profit of $4.5 million ($1,500 per unit × 3,000 units), shown as the blue rectangle.

Both Firms Cheat

Suppose that instead of just one firm cheating on the collusive agreement, both firms cheat. In particular, suppose that each firm behaves in exactly the same way as the cheating firm that we have just analyzed. Each tells the other that it is unable to sell its output at the going price and that it plans to cut its price. But because both firms cheat, each will propose a successively lower price. As long as price exceeds marginal cost, each firm has an incentive to increase its production—to cheat. Only when price equals marginal cost is there no further incentive to cheat. This situation arises when the price has reached $6,000. At this price, marginal cost equals price. Also, price equals minimum average total cost. At a price less than $6,000, each firm incurs an economic loss. At a price of $6,000, each firm covers all its costs and makes zero economic profit (makes normal profit). Also, at a price of $6,000, each firm wants to produce 3,000 units a week, so the industry output is 6,000 units a week. Given the demand conditions, 6,000 units can be sold at a price of $6,000 each.

Figure 14.11 illustrates the situation just described. Each firm, shown in part (a), produces 3,000 units a week, and at this output level, average total cost is a minimum ($6,000 per unit). The market as a whole, shown in part (b), operates at the point at which the demand curve (D) intersects the industry marginal cost curve. This marginal cost curve is constructed as the horizontal sum of the marginal

cost curves of the two firms. Each firm has lowered its price and increased its output to try to gain an advantage over the other firm. Each has pushed this process as far as it can without incurring an economic loss.

We have now described a third possible outcome of this duopoly game: Both firms cheat. If both firms cheat on the collusive agreement, the output of each firm is 3,000 units a week and the price is $6,000. Each firm makes zero economic profit.

The Payoff Matrix

Now that we have described the strategies and payoffs in the duopoly game, let's summarize the strategies and the payoffs in the form of the game's payoff matrix and then calculate the equilibrium.

Table 14.2 sets out the payoff matrix for this game. It is constructed in exactly the same way as the payoff matrix for the prisoners' dilemma in Table 14.1. The squares show the payoffs for the two firms—Gear and Trick. In this case, the payoffs are profits. (In the case of the prisoners' dilemma, the payoffs were losses.)

The table shows that if both firms cheat (top left), they achieve the perfectly competitive outcome—each firm makes zero economic profit. If both firms comply (bottom right), the industry makes the monopoly profit and each firm earns an economic profit of $2 million. The top right and bottom left squares show what happens if one firm

---

FIGURE 14.11

Both Firms Cheat

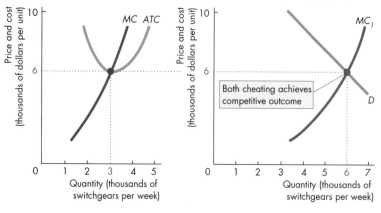

(a) Individual firm   **(b) Industry**

If both firms cheat by increasing production, the collusive agreement collapses. The limit to the collapse is the competitive equilibrium. Neither firm will cut price below $6,000 (minimum average total cost), for to do so results in economic losses. In part (a), both firms produce 3,000 units a week at an average total cost of $6,000 a unit. In part (b), with a total production of 6,000 units, the price falls to $6,000. Each firm now makes zero economic profit because price equals average total cost. The output and price are the ones that would prevail in a competitive industry.

TABLE 14.2

Duopoly Payoff Matrix

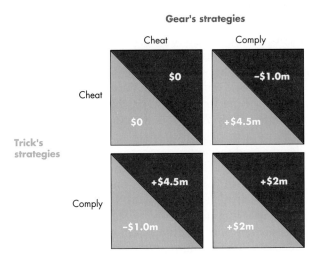

Each square shows the payoffs from a pair of actions. For example, if both firms comply with the collusive agreement, the payoffs are recorded in the bottom right square. The red triangle shows Gear's payoff, and the blue triangle shows Trick's. The equilibrium is a Nash equilibrium in which both firms cheat.

cheats while the other complies. The firm that cheats collects an economic profit of $4.5 million, and the one that complies incurs a loss of $1 million.

This duopoly game is like the prisoners' dilemma that we examined earlier in this chapter; it is a duopolists' dilemma.

Equilibrium of the Duopolists' Dilemma

What do the firms do? Do they comply or cheat? To answer these questions, we must find the equilibrium of the duopoly dilemma.

Look at things from Gear's point of view. Gear reasons as follows: Suppose that Trick cheats. If I comply, I will incur an economic loss of $1 million. If I also cheat, I will make zero economic profit. Zero is better than *minus* $1 million, so I'm better off if I cheat. Now suppose Trick complies. If I cheat, I will make an economic profit of $4.5 million; and if I comply, I will make an economic profit of $2 million. A $4.5 million profit is better than a $2 million

profit, so I'm better off if I cheat. So regardless of whether Trick cheats or complies, it pays Gear to cheat. Cheating is Gear's dominant strategy.

Trick comes to the same conclusion as Gear because the two firms face an identical situation. So both firms cheat. The equilibrium of the duopoly game is that both firms cheat. And although the industry has only two firms, the price and quantity are the same as in a competitive industry and each firm makes zero economic profit.

Although we have done this analysis for only two firms, it would not make any difference (other than to increase the amount of arithmetic) if we were to play the game with three, four, or more firms. In other words, although we have analyzed duopoly, the game theory approach can also be used to analyze oligopoly. The analysis of oligopoly is much harder, but the essential ideas that we have learned also apply to oligopoly.

Repeated Games

The games we've studied are played just once. In contrast, most real-world games get played repeatedly. This fact suggests that real-world duopolists might find some way of learning to cooperate so that their efforts to collude are more effective.

If a game is played repeatedly, one player has the opportunity to penalize the other player for previous "bad" behavior. If Gear cheats this week, perhaps Trick will cheat next week. Before Gear cheats this week, won't it take account of the possibility of Trick cheating next week? What is the equilibrium of this more complicated prisoners' dilemma game when it is repeated indefinitely?

Actually, there is more than one possible equilibrium. One is the Nash equilibrium that we have just analyzed. Both players cheat, and each makes zero economic profit forever. In such a situation, it will never pay one of the players to start complying unilaterally; because to do so would result in a loss for that player and a profit for the other. The price and quantity remain at the competitive levels forever. But another equilibrium, called a cooperative equilibrium, is possible. A **cooperative equilibrium** is an equilibrium in which the players make and share the monopoly profit.

A cooperative equilibrium may occur if each player knows that the other player will punish cheating. There are two extremes of punishment. The smallest penalty that one player can impose on the other is what is called "tit for tat." A *tit-for-tat strategy* is one in which a player cooperates in the current period if the other player cooperated in the previous period but cheats in the current period if the other player cheated in the previous period. The most severe form of punishment that one player can impose on the other arises in what is called a trigger strategy. A *trigger strategy* is one in which a player cooperates if the other player cooperates but plays the Nash equilibrium strategy forever thereafter if the other player cheats.

In the duopoly game between Gear and Trick, a tit-for-tat strategy keeps both players cooperating and earning monopoly profits. Let's see why.

If both firms stick to the collusive agreement in period 1, each makes an economic profit of $2 million. Suppose that Trick contemplates cheating in period 2. The cheating produces a quick $4.5 million economic profit and inflicts a $1 million economic loss on Gear. Adding up the profits over two periods of play, Trick comes out ahead by cheating ($6.5 million compared with $4 million if it did not cheat). The next period, Gear punishes Trick with its tit-for-tat response and cheats. But Trick must cooperate to induce Gear to cooperate again in period 4. Gear now makes an economic profit of $4.5 million, and Trick incurs an economic loss of $1 million. Adding up the profits over three periods of play, Trick would have made more profit by cooperating. In that case, its economic profit would have been $6 million compared with $5.5 million from cheating and generating Gear's tit-for-tat response.

What is true for Trick is also true for Gear. Because each firm makes a larger profit by sticking with the collusive agreement, both firms do so and the monopoly price, quantity, and profit prevail.

In reality, whether a cartel works like a one-play game or a repeated game depends primarily on the number of players and the ease of detecting and punishing cheating. The larger the number of players, the harder it is to maintain a cartel.

Games and Price Wars

The theory of price and output determination under duopoly can help us understand real-world behavior and, in particular, price wars. Some price wars can be interpreted as the implementation of a tit-for-tat strategy. We've seen that with a tit-for-tat strategy in place, firms have an incentive to stick to the monopoly price. But fluctuations in demand lead to fluctuations

in the monopoly price, and sometimes, when the price changes, it might seem to one of the firms that the price has fallen because the other has cheated. In this case, a price war will break out. The price war will end only when each firm has satisfied itself that the other is ready to cooperate again. There will be cycles of price wars and the restoration of collusive agreements. Fluctuations in the world price of oil can be interpreted in this way.

Some price wars arise from the entry of a small number of firms into an industry that had previously been a monopoly. Although the industry has a small number of firms, the firms are in a prisoners' dilemma, and they cannot impose effective penalties for price cutting. The behavior of prices and outputs in the computer chip industry during 1995 and 1996 can be explained in this way. Until 1995, the market for Pentium chips for IBM-compatible computers was dominated by one firm, Intel Corporation, which was able to make maximum economic profit by producing the quantity of chips at which marginal cost equaled marginal revenue. The price of Intel's chips was set to ensure that the quantity demanded equaled the quantity produced. Then in 1995 and 1996, with the entry of a small number of new firms, the industry became an oligopoly. If the firms had maintained Intel's price and shared the market, together they could have made economic profits equal to Intel's profit. But the firms were in a prisoners' dilemma. So prices tumbled closer to competitive levels.

REVIEW QUIZ

- Why does a collusive agreement to restrict output and raise price create a game like the prisoners' dilemma?
- What creates an incentive for firms in a collusive agreement to cheat and increase production?
- What is the equilibrium strategy for each firm in a prisoners' dilemma and why do the firms not collude?
- If a prisoners' dilemma game is played repeatedly, what punishment strategies might the players employ and how does playing the game repeatedly change the equilibrium?

The game theory approach can be extended to deal with a much wider range of choices that firms face. Let's look at some other oligopoly games.

Other Oligopoly Games

FIRMS MUST DECIDE WHETHER TO MOUNT expensive advertising campaigns; whether to modify their product; whether to make their product more reliable (the more reliable a product, usually, the more expensive it is to produce but the more people are willing to pay for it); whether to price discriminate and, if so, among which groups of customers and to what degree; whether to undertake a large research and development (R&D) effort aimed at lowering production costs; or whether to enter or leave an industry. All of these choices can be analyzed by using game theory. The basic method that you have studied can be applied to these problems by working out the payoff for each of the alternative strategies and then finding the equilibrium of the game.

We'll look at two examples: first an R&D game and second an entry-deterrence game.

An R&D Game

Disposable diapers were first marketed in 1966. The two market leaders from the start of this industry have been Procter & Gamble (makers of Pampers) and Kimberly-Clark (makers of Huggies). Procter & Gamble has about 40 percent of the total market, and Kimberly-Clark has about 33 percent. When the disposable diaper was first introduced in 1966, it had to be cost-effective in competition with reusable, laundered diapers. A costly research and development effort resulted in the development of machines that could make disposable diapers at a low enough cost to achieve that initial competitive edge. But as the industry has matured, a large number of firms have tried to get into the business and take market share away from the two industry leaders, and the industry leaders themselves have battled each other to maintain or increase their own market share.

During the early 1990s, Kimberly-Clark was the first to introduce Velcro closures. And in 1996, Procter & Gamble was the first to introduce "breathable" diapers into the U.S. market. The key to success in this industry (or any industry) is designing products that people value highly relative to the cost of producing them. The firm that develops the most highly valued product and also develops the least-cost technology for producing it gains a competitive edge, undercutting the rest of the market, increasing its market share, and

increasing its profit. But the research and development effort that must be undertaken to achieve product improvements and cost reductions is itself costly. This cost of research and development must be deducted from the profit resulting from the increased market share that lower costs achieve. If no firm does R&D, every firm can be better off, but if one firm initiates the R&D activity, all must follow.

Each firm is in a research and development dilemma situation that is similar to the game played by Art and Bob. Although the two firms play an ongoing game against each other, it has more in common with the one-play game than with a repeated game. The reason is that research and development is a long-term process. Effort is repeated, but payoffs occur only infrequently and with uncertainty.

Table 14.3 illustrates the dilemma (with hypothetical numbers) for the R&D game that Kimberly-Clark and Procter & Gamble are playing. Each firm

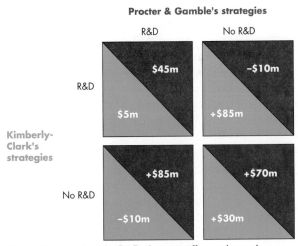

TABLE 14.3

Pampers Versus Huggies: An R&D Game

If both firms undertake R&D, their payoffs are those shown in the top left square. If neither firm undertakes R&D, their payoffs are in the bottom right square. When one firm undertakes R&D and the other one does not, their payoffs are in the top right and bottom left squares. The red triangle shows Procter & Gamble's payoff, and the blue triangle shows Kimberly-Clark's. The dominant strategy equilibrium for this game is for both firms to undertake R&D. The structure of this game is the same as that of the prisoners' dilemma.

has two strategies: to spend $25 million a year on R&D or to spend nothing on R&D. If neither firm spends on R&D, they make a joint profit of $100 million: $30 million for Kimberly-Clark and $70 million for Procter & Gamble (bottom right square of the payoff matrix). If each firm conducts R&D, market shares are maintained but each firm's profit is lower by the amount spent on R&D (top left square of the payoff matrix). If Kimberly-Clark pays for R&D but Procter & Gamble does not, Kimberly-Clark gains a large part of Procter & Gamble's market. Kimberly-Clark profits, and Procter & Gamble loses (top right square of the payoff matrix). Finally, if Procter & Gamble conducts R&D and Kimberly-Clark does not, Procter & Gamble gains market share from Kimberly-Clark, increasing its profit, while Kimberly-Clark incurs a loss (bottom left square).

Confronted with the payoff matrix in Table 14.3, the two firms calculate their best strategies. Kimberly-Clark reasons as follows: If Procter & Gamble does not undertake R&D, we will make $85 million if we do and $30 million if we do not; so it pays us to do R&D. If Procter & Gamble conducts R&D, we will lose $10 million if we don't and make $5 million if we do. Again, R&D pays off. Thus conducting R&D is a dominant strategy for Kimberly-Clark. It pays, regardless of Procter & Gamble's decision.

Procter & Gamble reasons similarly: If Kimberly-Clark does not undertake R&D, we will make $70 million if we follow suit and $85 million if we conduct R&D. It therefore pays to conduct R&D. If Kimberly-Clark does undertake R&D, we will make $45 million by doing the same and lose $10 million by not doing R&D. Again, it pays us to conduct R&D. So for Procter & Gamble, R&D is also a dominant strategy.

Because R&D is a dominant strategy for both players, it is the Nash equilibrium. The outcome of this game is that both firms conduct R&D. They make less profit than they would if they could collude to achieve the cooperative outcome of no R&D.

The real-world situation has more players than Kimberly-Clark and Procter & Gamble. A large number of other firms share a small portion of the market, all of them ready to eat into the market share of Procter & Gamble and Kimberly-Clark. So the R&D effort by these two firms not only serves the purpose of maintaining shares in their own battle, but also helps to keep barriers to entry high enough to preserve their joint market share.

Let's now study an entry-deterrence game in which a firm tries to prevent other firms from entering an industry. Such a game is played in a type of market called a contestable market.

Contestable Markets

A **contestable market** is a market in which one firm (or a small number of firms) operates but in which both entry and exit are free, so the firm (or firms) in the market faces competition from *potential* entrants. Examples of contestable markets are routes served by airlines and by barge companies that operate on the major waterways. These markets are contestable because even though only one or a few firms actually operate on a particular air route or river, other firms could enter those markets if an opportunity for economic profit arose and could exit those markets if the opportunity for economic profit disappeared. The potential entrance prevents the firm (or few firms) from making an economic profit.

If the HHI is used to determine the degree of competition, a contestable market appears to be uncompetitive. But a contestable market behaves as if it were perfectly competitive. You can see why by thinking about a game that we'll call an entry-deterrence game.

Entry-Deterrence Game

In the entry-deterrence game we'll study, there are two players. One player is Agile Air, the only firm operating on a particular route. The other player is Wanabe Inc., a potential entrant that is making a normal profit in its current business. The strategies for Agile Air are to set its price at the monopoly profit-maximizing level or at the competitive (zero economic profit) level. The strategies for Wanabe are to enter and set a price just below that of Agile or to not enter.

Table 14.4 shows the payoffs for the two firms. If Wanabe does not enter, Agile earns a normal profit by setting a competitive price or earns maximum monopoly profit (a positive economic profit) by setting the monopoly price. If Wanabe does enter and undercuts Agile's price, Agile incurs an economic loss regardless of whether it sets its price at the competitive or monopoly level. The reason is that Wanabe takes the market with the lower price, so Agile incurs a cost but has zero revenue. If Agile sets a competitive price, Wanabe earns a normal profit if it does not enter or incurs an economic loss if it enters and

TABLE 14.4

Agile Versus Wanabe: An Entry-Deterrence Game

Agile's strategies

	Monopoly price	Competitive price
Enter and set price below Agile's price	Economic loss / Economic profit	Economic loss / Economic loss
Not enter	Monopoly profit / Normal profit	Normal profit / Normal profit

Wanabe's strategies

Agile is the only firm in a contestable market. If Agile sets the monopoly price, Wanabe earns an economic profit by entering and undercutting Agile's price or a normal profit by not entering. So if Agile sets the price at the monopoly level, Wanabe will enter. If Agile sets the competitive price, Wanabe earns a normal profit if it does not enter or incurs an economic loss if it does enter. So if Agile sets the price at the competitive level, Wanabe will not enter. With entry, Agile incurs an economic loss regardless of the price it sets. The Nash equilibrium of this game is for Agile to set the competitive price, for Wanabe not to enter, and for both firms to make normal profit.

undercuts Agile by setting a price that is less than average total cost. If Agile sets the monopoly price, Wanabe earns a positive economic profit by entering or a normal profit by not entering.

The Nash equilibrium for this game is a competitive price at which Agile Air earns a normal profit and Wanabe does not enter. If Agile sets the monopoly price, Wanabe would enter and, by undercutting Agile's price, would take all the business, leaving Agile with an economic loss equal to total cost. Agile avoids this outcome by sticking with the competitive price and deterring Wanabe from entering.

Limit Pricing   **Limit pricing** is the practice of charging a price below the monopoly profit-maximizing price and producing a quantity greater than that

at which marginal revenue equals marginal cost in order to deter entry. The game that we've just studied is an example of limit pricing, but the practice is more general. For example, a firm can use limit pricing to try to convince potential entrants that its own costs are so low that new entrants will incur an economic loss if they enter the industry. To see how this works, let's go back to Agile and Wanabe.

Wanabe knows the current market price but does not know Agile's costs and profit. It can infer those costs, though. Suppose Wanabe believes that marginal revenue is 50 percent of price. If the price is $100, then Wanabe estimates that marginal revenue is $50. Wanabe might assume that Agile is maximizing profit by setting marginal revenue equal to marginal cost. Given this assumption, Wanabe estimates Agile's marginal cost to be $50. If Wanabe's marginal cost is greater than $50, it can't compete with Agile, so it will drop the idea of entering this industry. But if its marginal cost is less than $50, it might be able to enter the industry and also drive Agile out.

Recognizing that Wanabe reasons in this way, Agile might decide to use limit pricing to send a false but possibly believable signal to Wanabe. Agile might cut its price to (say) $80 to make Wanabe believe that its marginal cost is only $40 (50 percent of $80). The lower Wanabe believes Agile's marginal cost to be, the less likely is Wanabe to enter. The strategic use of limit pricing makes it possible, in some situations, for a firm (or group of firms) to maintain a monopoly or collusive oligopoly and limit entry.

◆ The two market structures you've studied in this chapter—monopolistic competition and oligopoly—are the most common ones you encounter in real-world markets. *Reading Between the Lines* on pages 306–307 shows you monopolistic competition in action and the excess capacity it creates for airlines.

A key element in our study of markets for goods and services is the behavior of firms' costs. Costs are determined by technology and by the prices of productive resources. We have treated resource prices as given. We are now going to see how resource prices are themselves determined. Resource prices interact with the goods market that we have just studied in two ways. First, they determine the firm's production costs. Second, they determine household incomes and therefore influence the demand for goods and services. Resource prices also affect the distribution of income. We study each of these interactions in the next three chapters.

Monopolistic Competition in the Air

THE DALLAS MORNING NEWS, JANUARY 2, 1999

Capacity Growth to Benefit Air Travelers

BY TERRY MAXON /
THE DALLAS MORNING NEWS

The prosperity of the late 1990s may have clouded some airline executives' short-term memory.

Hundreds of airplanes ordered during the recent profitable years soon will roll off the assembly line, adding thousands of potential seats to airlines' schedules. At the same time, demand from passengers probably won't grow as fast, analysts say.

Airlines will be left to fly with more empty seats or cut fares. Either way, airline profits get squeezed, but travelers win.

"This is something we've seen coming from years away, quite literally," said airline analyst Sam Buttrick, of Paine Webber Inc. "With too much capacity sloshing around, ... it's going to put a damper" on earnings.

Or as American Airlines Inc. chairman Donald J. Carty joked last week: "It's the capacity, stupid." ...

But what's bad for airline profits can be good for consumers.

In the early 1990s, airlines offered frequent fare sales with deep cuts to lure people onto airplanes. That could happen again, analysts said.

© 1999 *The Dallas Morning News.* Reprinted with permission.
Further reproduction prohibited.

Essence of the Story

■ A few years ago, when profits were high, the airlines ordered hundreds of new airplanes.

■ Many of these planes will be delivered during 1999.

■ The demand for air travel is predicted to increase by less than the increase in airline capacity.

■ Airlines will have more excess capacity or will cut fares.

■ Airline profits will fall.

■ Consumers will get lower prices and more empty seats.

■ The market for air travel is an example of monopolistic competition.

■ Figure 1 shows the situation facing an airline before the delivery of new airplanes described in the news article. The average total cost curve is ATC_0, the marginal cost curve is MC_0, the demand curve is D, and the marginal revenue curve is MR.

■ To maximize profit, the airline operates at the intersection of the marginal revenue and marginal cost curves. It sells 10 million travel miles a year for a price of 20 cents per mile.

■ The airline earns an economic profit shown by the blue rectangle.

■ Capacity output occurs where ATC_0 is minimized. So the airline operates with excess capacity.

■ Despite having some excess capacity, faced with an economic profit and anticipating further increases in demand, the airline ordered some new planes to be delivered a few years in the future.

■ But when the new planes were delivered, demand had not increased as anticipated.

■ Figure 2 shows the effect of the new planes with (an assumed) no change in demand.

■ The new planes increase the airline's capacity and put the airline on a new average total cost curve and marginal cost curve. These new curves are ATC_1 and MC_1, respectively, in Fig. 2.

■ At the higher output levels that the airline anticipated when it ordered the new planes, average total cost is lower on ATC_1 than it is on ATC_0. (See pp. 230–231 for an explanation of the cost curves for different plant sizes.)

■ But at the low output levels at which the airline must operate, average total cost is higher on ATC_1 than it is on ATC_0.

■ To maximize profit (at the intersection of the marginal revenue and marginal cost curves), the airline increases output to 12 million travel miles a year and cuts the price to 18 cents per mile.

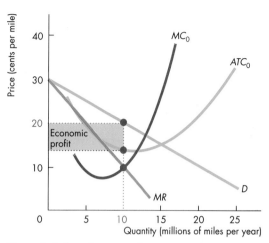

Figure 1 Before the expansion

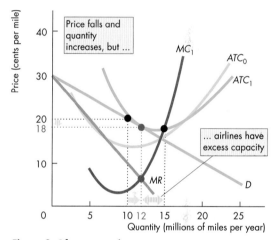

Figure 2 After expansion

■ The airline now earns zero economic profit (an assumption).

■ Capacity output occurs where ATC_1 is minimized, at 15 million miles a year. So the airline operates with even more excess capacity than before.

■ Eventually, when demand increases, the airline might again make a positive economic profit. But more entry and expansion will keep competing that economic profit away.

SUMMARY

KEY POINTS

Monopolistic Competition (pp. 286–287)

- Monopolistic competition occurs when a large number of firms compete with each other on product quality, price, and marketing.

Output and Price in Monopolistic Competition (pp. 288–290)

- Firms in monopolistic competition face downward-sloping demand curves and produce the quantity at which marginal revenue equals marginal cost.
- Entry and exit result in zero economic profit and excess capacity in long-run equilibrium.

Product Development and Marketing (pp. 290–292)

- Firms in monopolistic competition innovate and develop new products to maintain economic profit.
- Advertising expenditures increase total cost, but they might lower average total cost if they increase the quantity sold by enough.
- Advertising expenditures might increase demand, but they might also decrease the demand facing a firm by increasing competition.
- Whether monopolistic competition is inefficient depends on the value we place on product variety.

Oligopoly (pp. 293–294)

- If rivals match price cuts but do not match price hikes, they face a kinked demand curve and change prices only when large cost changes occur.
- If one firm dominates a market, it acts like a monopoly and the small firms take its price as given and act like perfectly competitive firms.

Game Theory (pp. 295–296)

- Game theory is a method of analyzing strategic behavior.
- In a prisoners' dilemma, two prisoners acting in their own interest harm their joint interest.

An Oligopoly Price-Fixing Game (pp. 297–302)

- An oligopoly (duopoly) price-fixing game is a prisoners' dilemma.
- The firms might collude, one firm might cheat, or both firms might cheat.
- In a one-play game, both firms cheat and output and price are the same as in perfect competition.
- In a repeated game, a punishment strategy can produce a cooperative equilibrium in which price and output are the same as in a monopoly.

Other Oligopoly Games (pp. 303–305)

- A firm's decisions about whether to enter or leave an industry, how much to spend selling the product, whether to modify its product, and whether to undertake research and development can be studied by using game theory.

KEY FIGURES AND TABLE ◆

KEY TERMS

PROBLEMS

*1. The figure shows the situation facing Lite and Kool Inc., a producer of running shoes.

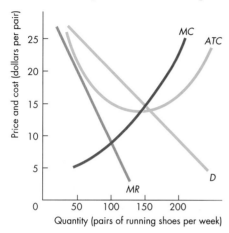

a. What quantity does Lite and Kool produce?
b. What does it charge?
c. How much profit does Lite and Kool make?

2. The figure shows the situation facing Well Done Inc., a producer of steak sauce.

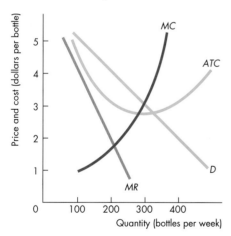

a. What quantity does Well Done produce?
b. What does it charge?
c. How much profit does Well Done make?

*3. A firm in monopolistic competition produces running shoes. If it spends nothing on advertising, it can sell no shoes at $100 a pair, and for each $10 cut in price, the quantity of shoes it can sell increases by 25 pairs a day so at $20 a

pair, it can sell 200 pairs a day. The firm's total fixed cost is $4,000 a day. Its average variable cost and marginal cost are a constant $20 per pair. If the firm spends $3,000 a day on advertising, it can double the quantity of shoes sold at each price.

a. If the firm doesn't advertise, what is the quantity of shoes produced and what is the price per pair?
b. What is the firm's economic profit or economic loss?
c. If the firm does advertise, what is the quantity of shoes produced and what is the price per pair?
d. What is the firm's economic profit or economic loss?
e. Will the firm advertise or not? Why?

4. The firm in problem 3 has the same demand and costs as before if it does not advertise. But it hires a new advertising agency. If the firm spends $3,000 a day on advertising with the new agency, it can double the amount that consumers are willing to pay at each quantity demanded.

a. If the firm hires the new agency, what is the quantity of shoes produced and what is the price per pair?
b. What is the firm's economic profit or economic loss?
c. Will the firm advertise or not? Why?
d. What is the firm's economic profit in the long run?

*5. A firm with a kinked demand curve experiences an increase in its fixed costs. Explain the effects on the firm's price, output, and economic profit/loss.

6. A firm with a kinked demand curve experiences an increase in its variable cost. Explain the effects on the firm's price, output, and economic profit/loss.

*7. An industry with one very large firm and 100 very small firms experiences an increase in the demand for its product. Use the dominant firm model to explain the effects on the price, output, and economic profit of

a. The large firm
b. A typical small firm

8. An industry with one very large firm and 100 very small firms experiences an increase in total variable cost. Use the dominant firm model to

explain the effects on the price, output, and economic profit of

a. The large firm

b. A typical small firm

*9. Consider the following game: The game has two players, and each player is asked a question. The players can answer the question honestly, or they can lie. If both answer honestly, each receives a payoff of $100. If one answers honestly and the other lies, the liar gains at the expense of the honest player. In that event, the liar receives a payoff of $500 and the honest player gets nothing. If both lie, then each receives a payoff of $50.

a. Describe this game in terms of its players, strategies, and payoffs.

b. Construct the payoff matrix.

c. What is the equilibrium for this game?

10. Describe the game known as the prisoners' dilemma. In describing the game:

a. Make up a story that motivates the game.

b. Work out a payoff matrix.

c. Describe how the equilibrium of the game is arrived at.

*11. Two firms, Soapy and Sudsies, are the only producers of soap powder. They collude and agree to share the market equally. If neither firm cheats on the agreement, each makes $1 million economic profit. If either firm cheats, the cheater increases its economic profit to $1.5 million while the firm that abides by the agreement incurs an economic loss of $0.5 million. Neither firm can police the other's actions.

a. What is the economic profit for each firm if both cheat?

b. Construct the payoff matrix of a game that is played just once.

c. Describe the best strategy for each firm in a game that is played once.

d. What is the equilibrium if the game is played once?

e. If this duopoly game can be played many times, describe some of the strategies that each firm might adopt.

12. Two firms, Faster and Quicker, are the only two producers of sports cars on an island that has no contact with the outside world. The firms collude and agree to share the market equally. If neither firm cheats on the agreement, each firm makes $3 million economic profit. If either

firm cheats, the cheater can increase its economic profit to $4.5 million, while the firm that abides by the agreement incurs an economic loss of $1 million. Neither firm has any way of policing the actions of the other.

a. What is the economic profit for each firm if they both cheat?

b. What is the payoff matrix of a game that is played just once?

c. Describe the best strategy for each firm in a game that is played once.

d. What is the equilibrium if the game is played once?

e. If this game can be played many times, what are two strategies that could be adopted?

CRITICAL THINKING

1. Study *Reading Between the Lines* on pp. 306–307 and then answer the following questions:

a. Why are the airlines an example of monopolistic competition?

b. How does an airline determine the price per mile and the number of travel miles to sell?

c. Can the airlines earn economic profits in the long run? Why or why not?

d. In addition to cutting prices, what other actions might the airlines take when faced with an increase in capacity? (Hint: Think about advertising and other selling efforts.)

e. Could the airlines collude to increase their profits? Explain the difficulties they face, the benefits they would receive, and the costs to the consumer from such an action.

2. Suppose that Netscape and Microsoft each develop their own versions of an amazing new Web browser that allows advertisers to target consumers with great precision. Also, the new browser is easier and more fun to use than existing browsers. Each firm is trying to decide whether to sell the browser or to give it away free. What are the likely benefits from each action and which is likely to occur? Explain.

3. Why do Coca-Cola Company and PepsiCo spend huge amounts on advertising? Do they benefit? Does the consumer benefit? Explain your answer.

Understanding Firms and Markets

Managing Change

Our economy is constantly changing. Every year, new goods appear and old ones disappear. New firms are born and old ones die. This process of change is initiated and managed by firms operating in markets. When a new product is invented, just one or two firms sell it initially. For example, when the personal computer first became available, there was an Apple or an IBM. The IBM-PC had just one operating system, DOS, made by Microsoft. One firm, Intel, made the chip that ran the IBM-PC. These are examples of industries in which the producer has market power to determine the price of the product and the quantity produced. The extreme case of a single producer that cannot be challenged by new competitors is *monopoly*, which Chapter 13 explained. ◆ But not all industries with just one producer are monopolies. In many cases, the firm that is first to produce a new good faces severe competition from new rivals. One firm facing potential competition is the case of a *contestable market*. If demand increases and makes space for more than one firm, an industry becomes increasingly competitive. Even with just two rivals, the industry changes its face in a dramatic way. *Duopoly*—the case of just two producers—illustrates this dramatic change. The two firms must pay close attention to each other's production and prices and must predict the effects of their own actions on the actions of the other firm. We call this situation one of *strategic interdependence*. As the number of rivals grows, the industry becomes an *oligopoly*, a market in which a small number of firms devise strategies and pay close attention to the strategies of their competitors. ◆ With the continued arrival of new firms in an industry, the market eventually becomes competitive. Competition might be limited because each firm produces its own special version or brand of a good. This case is called *monopolistic competition* because it has elements of both monopoly and competition. Chapter 14 explored the behavior of firms in all of these types of markets that lie between monopoly at the one extreme and perfect competition at the other. ◆ When competition is extreme—the case that we call *perfect competition*—the market changes again in a dramatic way. Now the firm is unable to influence price. Chapter 12 explained this case. ◆ Often, an industry that is competitive becomes less so as the bigger and more successful firms in the industry begin to swallow up the smaller firms, either by driving them out of business or by acquiring their assets. Through this process, an industry might return to oligopoly or even monopoly. You can see such a movement in the auto and banking industries today. ◆ By studying firms and markets, we gain a deeper understanding of the forces that allocate scarce resources and begin to see the anatomy of the invisible hand. ◆ Many economists have advanced our understanding of these forces and we'll now meet two of them. John von Neumann pioneered the idea of game theory. And Avinash Dixit is one of today's leading students of strategic behavior.

The Economist

John von Neumann *was one of the great minds of the twentieth century. Born in Budapest, Hungary, in 1903, Johnny, as he was known, showed early mathematical brilliance. His first mathematical publication was an article that grew out of a lesson with his tutor, which he wrote at the age of 18! But it was at the age of 25, in 1928, that von Neumann published the article that began a flood of research on game theory—a flood that has still not subsided today. In that article, he proved that in a zero-sum game (like sharing a pie), there exists a best strategy for each player.*

Von Neumann invented the computer and built the first modern practical computer, and he worked on the "Manhattan Project," which developed the atomic bomb at Los Alamos, New Mexico, during World War II.

Von Neumann believed that the social sciences would progress only if they used mathematical tools. But he believed that they needed different tools from those developed from the physical sciences.

"Real life consists of bluffing, of little tactics of deception, of asking yourself what is the other man going to think I mean to do."

JOHN VON NEUMANN,
*told to Jacob Bronowski
(in a London taxi) and
reported in*
The Ascent of Man

The Issues

It is not surprising that firms with market power will charge higher prices than those charged by competitive firms. But how much higher?

This question has puzzled generations of economists. Adam Smith said, "The price of a monopoly is upon every occasion the highest which can be got."

But he was wrong. Antoine-Augustin Cournot (see p. 150) first worked out the price a monopoly will charge. It is not the "highest which can be got" but the price that maximizes profit. Cournot's work was not appreciated until almost a century later when Joan Robinson explained how a monopoly sets its price.

Questions about monopoly became urgent and practical during the 1870s, a time when rapid technological change and falling transportation costs enabled huge monopolies to emerge in the United States. Monopolies dominated oil, steel, railroads, tobacco, and even sugar. Industrial empires grew ever larger.

The success of the nineteenth century monopolies led to the creation of our antitrust laws—laws that limit the use of monopoly power. Those laws have been used to prevent monopolies from being set up and to break up existing monopolies. They were used during the 1960s to end a conspiracy between General Electric, Westinghouse, and other firms when they colluded to fix their prices instead of competing with each other. The laws were used during the 1980s to bring greater competition to long-distance telecommunication. But in spite of antitrust laws, near monopolies still exist. Among the most prominent today are those in computer chips and operating systems. Like their forerunners, today's near monopolies make huge profits. But unlike the situation in the nineteenth century, the technological change taking place today is strengthening the forces of competition. Today's information technologies are creating substitutes for services that previously had none. Direct satellite TV is competing with cable, and new phone companies are competing with the traditional phone monopolies.

Then

Ruthless greed, exploitation of both workers and customers—these are the traditional images of monopolies and the effects of their power. These images appeared to be an accurate description during the 1880s, when monopolies stood at their peak of power and influence. One monopolist, John D. Rockefeller, Sr., built his giant Standard Oil Company, which by 1879 was refining 90 percent of the nation's oil and controlling its entire pipeline capacity.

Now

Despite antitrust laws that regulate monopolies, they still exist. One is the monopoly in cable television. In many cities, one firm decides which channels viewers will receive and the price they will pay. During the 1980s, with the advent of satellite technology and specialist cable program producers such as CNN and HBO, the cable companies expanded their offerings. At the same time, they steadily increased prices and their businesses became very profitable. But the very technologies that made cable television profitable are now challenging its market power. Direct satellite TV services are eroding cable's monopoly and bringing greater competition to this market.

Today, many economists who work on microeconomics use the ideas that John von Neumann pioneered. Game theory is the tool of choice. One economist who has made good use of this tool (and many other tools) is Avinash Dixit of Princeton University, whom you can meet on the following pages.

Avinash K. Dixit

is the Sherrerd University Professor of Economics at Princeton University. Born in 1944 in Bombay, India, he was an undergraduate at the University of Cambridge, England, and a graduate student at MIT.

Professor Dixit has worked on a wide range of economic problems but his most widely known work is his 1991 book Thinking Strategically (with Barry J. Nalebuff), which became an international best seller. This book explains how to use game theory in business, politics, and even in social and family situations. Professor Dixit has also

Avinash Dixit

explained how a firm establishes and maintains a dominant market position. He has revolutionized the way we think about irreversible decisions—decisions on which we can't go back (or can only reverse at great cost). Michael Parkin talked with Professor Dixit about these issues.

Professor Dixit, what is game theory and how do economists use it?

Game theory is a framework for thinking about decisions when your best choice depends on what someone else is choosing and vice versa. Such interdependence is called strategic interaction. For example, a chess player making an opening move with the white pieces must calculate how the opponent with the black pieces will respond, knowing in turn that black is taking into account how white will respond at the next move, and so on. The outcome for each player depends on the actions of the other player, and each player makes his or her actions based on awareness of this interdependence.

Strategic interactions occur for either of two reasons. The first arises in small groups of people, firms, or nations where the choices of each have a significant impact on the others. The classic example in economics is an industry with a small number of firms, such as the U.S. auto industry. Before the 1970s, three major auto firms existed in the United States: General Motors, Ford, and Chrysler. Each firm had to decide which vehicles to produce, how to price them, and how many people to employ. While making these decisions, the firm also had to take into account the likely responses to these decisions by the other two firms. In international relations, war or peace among major powers hinges upon similar calculations by each nation's leaders of the interests and responses of others.

The second reason strategic interactions occur is if the market for a product or service extends over time or is of uncertain quality. Consider, for example, that someone is interested in having a home built and needs a contractor. He or she can choose from among many contractors, and a contractor can similarly choose from among numerous potential clients. But once a choice is made, the contractor and client become linked in a bilateral relationship. The builder might procrastinate or do a poor quality job, and the client might be slow with future payments. In anticipation of these problems, a contract is negotiated, monitored, and enforced.

> We frequently play games in which the opponent is not another person but ourselves or, more accurately, our future self. Your future self is going to give in to temptations of the moment and do things you know would be really bad for you—eat more, exercise less, or study less diligently.

Can you give some everyday examples of how game theory helps a person to think strategically and make a better decision?
We frequently play games in which the opponent is not another person but ourselves or, more accurately, our future self. Your future self is going to give in to temptations of the moment and do things you know would be really bad for you—eat more, exercise less, or study less diligently. You can defeat this "opponent" by taking actions right now that diminish your future self's freedom of action. For example, you could join a group where other members will pressure you into keeping your current good resolutions to diet and exercise and study. In game theory, such actions are called "commitments." Finding good devices of commitment is a very important kind of strategy we all have to practice in our daily lives.

Another very important class of games is that of "no-win" interactions, which are best avoided altogether or resolved by prior negotiation. In game theory, these interactions are typically "prisoners' dilemma" or "chicken" games, in which each person's pursuit of private advantage can lead to mutual harm. The nuclear arms race between the United States and the Soviet Union was the most dramatic example. Each country thought that a hundred more missiles would give it a decisive edge. The result of this thinking was very costly escalation of weapons with no net advantage to either country.

How do firms such as Microsoft and Intel use strategic thinking to dominate their markets?
Firms can become dominant or powerful in their markets for many reasons. First, a firm can be much better than others, producing a higher-quality product and selling it at a lower price. Second, a firm can take predatory strategic actions that increase and sustain its own dominance. For example, it can preemptively install capacity that exceeds what its current production would justify. This acts as a credible demonstration of its willingness to produce more and fight a price war and thereby deters other firms from entering or growing. And third, a product might have such strong economies of scale that the market is most efficiently served by just one firm, but which one emerges in this position can be a matter of historical accident. In practice, all three factors may be present—a firm may get an initial stroke of good luck, then use superior technology or management to lever it into a dominant position, and finally use predatory practices to preserve such a position.

All three factors operated in the computer industry. Both processor chips and operating systems have very large initial design costs but low costs of production or duplication of each copy thereafter. Thus we have good reasons to expect the markets to be dominated by one or a few firms. Which ones?

In the case of Microsoft and Intel, the fact that IBM chose them for its first PC clearly launched them into a favorable position. In the summer of 1980, IBM needed an operating system for their original personal computer. The obvious choice was CP-M, developed by Digital Research in California. The IBM team flew out to see Digital's chief, Gary Kildall. But he forgot the appointment and went flying in his small plane. In his absence, his wife wouldn't sign IBM's nondisclosure agreement. The IBM team left and then went on to Seattle to see Bill Gates, whose Basic language program they also wanted. Hearing that IBM needed an operating system, Gates bought one called QDOS—Quick and Dirty Operating System—from another local company, turned it into MS-DOS, and sold it to IBM as PC-DOS. The rest is history. This was a historical accident par excellence.

Microsoft and Intel made the most of the advantage they got from dealing with IBM. But the reason for their near-total dominance of the industry is a matter of controversy. The Microsoft-lovers argue that for the majority of business and home PC users, the company has delivered a good product at a good price. Microsoft-haters allege predation. They say

Microsoft has used unfair strategies to make it impossible for others to compete. For example, Microsoft insists on contracts with suppliers of DOS-Windows PCs whereby the suppliers have to pay Microsoft a royalty for each unit they ship, whether or not it has a Microsoft operating system. I suspect there is some truth on both sides.

Can you explain your key insight about irreversible investment decisions?

If an action cannot be reversed, or can be reversed only at a great cost, you are more cautious about taking it. Two conditions create this scenario. The first is uncertainty. You can never be entirely sure what the future will bring, but the passage of time and active searching reveals further information. The second is a window of opportunity. Most decisions can be postponed.

Waiting gives you an "option" that is very similar to a financial option—the right but not the obligation to do something in the future if conditions are right then. You can either buy or sell stock at various times. If the future brings new information that shows the action be to undesirable, then the waiting has enabled you to avoid a mistake. If the new information reaffirms the desirability of the action, then you can go ahead, having lost only the benefit that would have flowed from the action for the few weeks' or months' delay.

Your choice of a major or of an area of specialization in graduate school is a good application of this principle. Nuclear physics may appear to be an attractive career at one point in time and finance or law at another, but conditions change. There is much to be said for acquiring a broad set of flexible skills of wide applicability while learning more about your own interests and the prospects of particular career paths and delaying irreversible specialization.

Who are the giant economists of the past whose ideas have been most fruitful in your work?

I have drawn inspiration and knowledge from the work of so many great economists that it is very difficult to pick one or two. But if forced, I would choose Paul Samuelson and Thomas Schelling. Samuelson's *Foundations of Economic Analysis* and *Economics* were the first two books I read on the subject, Samuelson was one of my teachers in graduate school, and almost all my research has been influenced by the fundamental principles and techniques of optimization and equilibrium that I learned from him.

Thomas Schelling's books, most particularly *The Strategy of Conflict* and *Micromotives and Macrobehavior*, have been immensely influential for my thinking. You can learn about the formalism of game theory from dry mathematical articles and books, but to appreciate the importance of game theory for almost all aspects of life—interactions in the family, social

groups, business, and international relations—you have to read Schelling.

> Economics teaches us the fundamentals of decision making—to be clear about objectives, recognize constraints and thereby opportunity costs, handle uncertainty, and know how to update information in the light of new observations.

What is the case for majoring in economics today? What are the profits from an economics degree?

In very practical terms, an economics major is a good background for professional graduate training in law and business. But perhaps more important, economics is among the "broad set of flexible skills of wide applicability" that I recommended earlier. Economics teaches us the fundamentals of decision making—to be clear about objectives, recognize constraints and thereby opportunity costs, handle uncertainty, and know how to update information in the light of new observations. The techniques that are used in such analysis—mathematics, probability, and statistics—are also useful for many other applications. Studying economics is buying an option that can be exercised later in many kinds of careers and many walks of life.

It might not be your birthday, and even if it is, chances are you are spending most of it working. But at the end of the week or month (or, if you're devoting all your time to college, when you graduate), you will receive the *returns* from your labor. Those returns vary a lot. Pedro Lopez, who spends his chilly winter days in a small container suspended from the top of Chicago's John Hancock Tower cleaning windows, makes a happy return of $12 an hour. Katie Couric, who hosts a 2-hour morning show each weekday, makes a very happy return of $7 million a year. Students working at what have been called "McJobs"—serving fast food or laboring in the fields of southern California—earn just a few dollars an hour. Why aren't *all* jobs well paid? ◆ Most of us have little trouble spending our pay. But most of us do manage to save some of what we earn. What determines the amount of saving that people do and the returns they make on that saving? How do the returns on saving influence the allocation of savings across the many industries and activities that use our capital resources? ◆ Some people receive income from supplying land, but the amount earned varies enormously with the land's location and quality. For example, an acre of farmland in Iowa rents for about $1,000 a year, while a block on Chicago's "Magnificent Mile" rents for several million dollars a year. What determines the rent that people are willing to pay for different blocks of land? Why are rents so enormously high in big cities and so relatively low in the great farming regions of the nation?

◆ In this chapter we study the markets for productive resources—labor, capital, land, and entrepreneurship—and learn how their prices and people's incomes are determined.

Many Happy Returns

After studying this chapter, you will be able to:

■ Explain how firms choose the quantities of labor, capital, and natural resources to employ

■ Explain how people choose the quantities of labor, capital, and natural resources to supply

■ Explain how wages, interest, and natural resource prices are determined in competitive resource markets

■ Explain the concept of economic rent and distinguish between economic rent and opportunity cost

Resource Prices and Incomes

GOODS AND SERVICES ARE PRODUCED BY USING the four economic resources: *labor, capital, land,* and *entrepreneurship.* (These resources are defined in Chapter 3, p. 36.) Incomes are determined by *resource prices*—the *wage* rate for labor, the *interest* rate for capital, the *rental* rate for land, and the rate of *normal profit* for entrepreneurship—and the quantities of resources used.

In addition to the four resource incomes, a residual income, *economic profit* (or *economic loss*) is paid to (or borne by) firms' owners. For a small firm, the owner is usually the entrepreneur. For a large corporation, the owners are the stockholders, who supply capital.

An Overview of a Competitive Resource Market

We're going to learn how competitive resource markets determine the prices, quantities used, and incomes of productive resources. The tool that we use is the demand and supply model. The quantity demanded of a resource depends on its price, and the law of demand applies to resources just as it does to goods and services. The lower the price of a resource, other things remaining the same, the greater is the quantity demanded. Figure 15.1 shows the demand curve for a resource as the curve labeled *D*.

The quantity supplied of a resource also depends on its price. With a possible exception that we'll identify later in this chapter, the law of supply applies to resources. The higher the price of a resource, other things remaining the same, the greater is the quantity supplied of the resource. Figure 15.1 shows the supply curve of a resource as the curve labeled *S*.

The equilibrium resource price is determined at the point of intersection of the demand and supply curves. In Fig. 15.1, the price is *PR* and the quantity used is *QR*.

The income earned by the resource is its price multiplied by the quantity used. In Fig. 15.1, the resource income equals the area of the blue rectangle. This income is the total income received by the factor. Each person who supplies the factor receives the factor price multiplied by the quantity supplied by that person. Changes in demand and supply change the equilibrium price and quantity and change income.

An increase in demand shifts the demand curve rightward and increases price, quantity, and income. An increase in supply shifts the supply curve rightward and decreases price. The quantity used increases, and the income of the resource can increase, decrease, or remain constant. The change in income that results from a change in supply depends on the elasticity of demand for the resource. If demand is elastic, income rises; if demand is inelastic, income falls; and if demand is unit elastic, income remains constant (see Chapter 5, pp. 92–93).

The rest of this chapter explores the influences on the demand for and supply of productive resources. It also studies the influences on the elasticities of supply and demand for resources. These elasticities have major effects on resource prices, quantities used, and incomes.

We begin with the market for labor. But most of what we learn about the labor market also applies to the other resource markets that we study later in the chapter.

FIGURE 15.1

Demand and Supply in a Resource Market

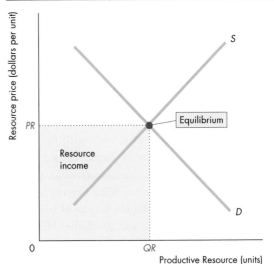

The demand curve for a productive resource (D) slopes downward, and the supply curve (S) slopes upward. Where the demand and supply curves intersect, the resource price (PR) and the quantity of a resource used (QR) are determined. The resource income is the product of the resource price and the quantity of the resource, as represented by the blue rectangle.

Labor Markets

FOR MOST OF US, THE LABOR MARKET IS OUR ONLY source of income. And in recent years, many people have had a tough time. But over the years, both wages and the quantity of labor have moved steadily upward. Figure 15.2(a) shows the record since 1960. Using 1992 dollars to remove the effects of inflation, total compensation per hour of work increased by 90 percent from $10 in 1960 to more than $19 in 1998. Over the same period, the quantity of labor employed increased by 79 percent from 127 billion hours in 1960 to 227 billion hours in 1998.

Figure 15.2(b) shows why wages and employment increased. The demand for labor increased from LD_{60} to LD_{98} and this increase was much larger than the increase in supply from LS_{60} to LS_{98}.

A lot of diversity lies behind the average wage rate and the aggregate quantity of labor. During the 1980s and 1990s, some wages grew much more rapidly than the average and others fell. To understand changes in the labor market, we must probe the forces that influence the demand for labor and the supply of labor. This chapter studies these forces (and Chapter 16 takes a deeper look at them). We begin on the demand side of the labor market.

The Demand for Labor

The demand for labor is a derived demand. A **derived demand** is a demand for a productive resource, which is *derived* from the demand for the goods and services produced by the resource. The derived demand for labor (and the other resources demanded by firms) is driven by the firm's objective, which is to maximize profit.

You learned in Chapters 12, 13, and 14 that a profit-maximizing firm produces the output at which marginal cost equals marginal revenue. This principle holds true for all firms, regardless of whether they operate in perfect competition, monopolistic competition, oligopoly, or monopoly.

A firm that maximizes profit hires the quantity of labor that can produce the profit-maximizing output. What is that quantity of labor? And how does it change as the wage rate changes? We can answer these questions by comparing the *marginal* revenue earned by hiring one more worker with the *marginal* cost of that worker. Let's look first at the marginal revenue side of this comparison.

FIGURE 15.2

Labor Market Trends in the United States

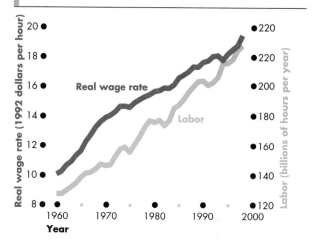

(a) Labor and wage rate

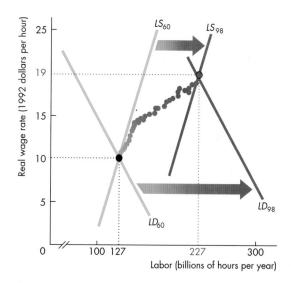

(b) Changes in demand and supply in the labor market

Between 1960 and 1998, the real wage rate increased by 90 percent and the quantity of labor employed increased by 79 percent. Part (a) shows these increases. Part (b) shows the changes in demand and supply that have generated the trends. The demand for labor increased from LD_{60} to LD_{98}, and the supply of labor increased from LS_{60} to LS_{98}. Demand increased by more than supply, so both the real wage rate and the quantity of labor employed increased.

Source: Economic Report of the President, 1998 and author's assumptions.

Marginal Revenue Product

The change in total revenue that results from employing one more unit of labor is called the **marginal revenue product** of labor. Table 15.1 shows you how to calculate marginal revenue product for a perfectly competitive firm.

The first two columns show the total product schedule for Max's Wash 'n' Wax car wash service. The numbers tell us how the number of car washes per hour varies as the quantity of labor varies. The third column shows the *marginal product of labor*—the change in total product that results from a one-unit increase in the quantity of labor employed. (Look back at p. 221 for a quick refresher on these concepts.)

The car wash market in which Max operates is perfectly competitive, and he can sell as many washes as he chooses at $4 a wash, the (assumed) market price. So Max's *marginal revenue* is $4 a wash.

Given this information, we can now calculate *marginal revenue product* (fourth column). It equals marginal product multiplied by marginal revenue. For example, the marginal product of hiring a second worker is 4 car washes an hour, and because marginal revenue is $4 a wash, the marginal revenue product of the second worker is $16 (4 washes at $4 each).

The last two columns of Table 15.1 show an alternative way to calculate the marginal revenue product of labor. Total revenue is equal to total product multiplied by price. For example, two workers produce 9 washes per hour and generate a total revenue of $36 (9 washes at $4 each). One worker produces 5 washes per hour and generates a total revenue of $20 (5 washes at $4 each). Marginal revenue product, in the sixth column, is the change in total revenue from hiring one more worker. When the second worker is hired, total revenue increases from $20 to $36, an increase of $16. So the marginal revenue product of the second worker is $16, which agrees with our previous calculation.

Diminishing Marginal Revenue Product As the quantity of labor increases, marginal revenue product diminishes. For a firm in perfect competition, marginal revenue product diminishes because marginal product diminishes. For a monopoly (or in monopolistic competition or oligopoly), marginal revenue product diminishes for a second reason. When more labor is hired and total product increases, the firm must cut its price to sell the extra product. So marginal product *and* marginal revenue decrease, both of which bring decreasing marginal revenue product.

TABLE 15.1
Marginal Revenue Product at Max's Wash 'n' Wax

	Quantity of labor (L) (workers)	Total product (TP) (car washes per hour)	Marginal product (MP = $\Delta TP/\Delta L$) (washes per additional worker)	Marginal revenue product (MRP = MR × MP) (dollars per additional worker)	Total revenue (TR = P × TP) (dollars)	Marginal revenue product (MRP = $\Delta TR/\Delta L$) (dollars per additional worker)
a	0	0		20	0	
			5			20
b	1	5		16	20	
			4			16
c	2	9		12	36	
			3			12
d	3	12		8	48	
			2			8
e	4	14		4	56	
			1			4
f	5	15			60	

The car wash market is perfectly competitive and the price is $4 a wash. Marginal revenue is also $4 a wash. Marginal revenue product equals marginal product (column 3) multiplied by marginal revenue. For example, the marginal product of the second worker is 4 washes and marginal revenue is $4 a wash. So the marginal revenue product of the second worker (in column 4) is $16. Alternatively, if Max hires 1 worker (row b), total product is 5 washes an hour and total revenue is $20 (column 5). If he hires 2 workers (row c), total product is 9 washes an hour and total revenue is $36. By hiring the second worker, total revenue rises by $16—the marginal revenue product of labor is $16.

The Labor Demand Curve

Figure 15.3 shows how the labor demand curve is derived from the marginal revenue product curve. The *marginal revenue product curve* graphs the marginal revenue product of a resource at each quantity of the resource hired. Figure 15.3(a) illustrates the marginal revenue product curve for workers employed by Max. The horizontal axis measures the number of workers that Max hires, and the vertical axis measures the marginal revenue product of labor. The blue bars show the marginal revenue product of labor as Max employs more workers. These bars correspond to the numbers in Table 15.1. The curve labeled *MRP* is Max's marginal revenue product curve.

A firm's marginal revenue product curve is also its demand for labor curve. Figure 15.3(b) shows Max's demand for labor curve (*D*). The horizontal axis measures the number of workers hired—the same as in part (a). The vertical axis measures the wage rate in dollars per hour. In Fig. 15.3(a), when Max increases the quantity of labor employed from 2 workers an hour to 3 workers an hour, his marginal revenue product is $12 an hour. In Fig. 15.3(b), at a wage rate of $12 an hour, Max hires 3 workers an hour.

The marginal revenue product curve is also the demand for labor curve because the firm hires the profit-maximizing quantity of labor. If the wage rate is less than marginal revenue product, the firm can increase its profit by employing one more worker. Conversely, if the wage rate is greater than marginal revenue product, the firm can increase its profit by employing one fewer worker. But if the wage rate equals marginal revenue product, then the firm cannot increase its profit by changing the number of workers it employs. The firm is making the maximum possible profit. Thus the quantity of labor demanded by the firm is such that the wage rate equals the marginal revenue product of labor.

Because the marginal revenue product curve is also the demand curve, and because marginal revenue product diminishes as the quantity of labor employed increases, the demand for labor curve slopes downward. The lower the wage rate, other things remaining the same, the more workers a firm hires.

When we studied a firm's output decision, we discovered that a condition for maximum profit is that marginal revenue equals marginal cost. We've now discovered another condition for maximum profit: Marginal revenue product of a resource equals the resource's price. Let's study the connection between these two conditions.

FIGURE 15.3

The Demand for Labor at Max's Wash 'n' Wax

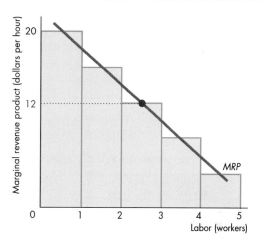

(a) Marginal revenue product

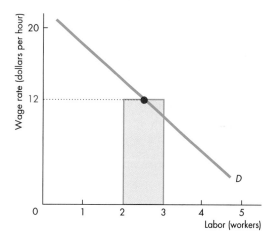

(b) Demand for labor

Max's Wash 'n' Wax operates in a perfectly competitive car wash market and can sell any quantity of washes at $4 a wash. The blue bars in part (a) represent the firm's marginal revenue product of labor. They are based on the numbers in Table 15.1. The orange line is the firm's marginal revenue product of labor curve. Part (b) shows Max's demand for labor curve. This curve is identical to Max's marginal revenue product curve. Max demands the quantity of labor that makes the wage rate equal to the marginal revenue product of labor. The demand for labor curve slopes downward because marginal revenue product diminishes as the quantity of labor employed increases.

Equivalence of Two Conditions for Profit Maximization

Profit is maximized when at the quantity of labor hired, *marginal revenue product* equals the wage rate and when at the output produced, *marginal revenue* equals *marginal cost*.

These two conditions for maximum profit are equivalent. The quantity of labor that maximizes profit produces the output that maximizes profit.

To see the equivalence of the two conditions for maximum profit, first recall that

Marginal revenue product = Marginal revenue × Marginal product.

If we call marginal revenue product *MRP*, marginal revenue *MR*, and marginal product *MP*,

$$MRP = MR \times MP.$$

If we call the wage rate *W*, the first condition for maximum profit is

$$MRP = W.$$

But $MRP = MR \times MP$, so

$$MR \times MP = W.$$

This equation tells us that when profit is maximized, marginal revenue multiplied by marginal product equals the wage rate.

Divide the last equation by marginal product, *MP*, to obtain

$$MR = W \div MP.$$

This equation states that when profit is maximized, marginal revenue equals the wage rate divided by the marginal product of labor.

The wage rate divided by the marginal product of labor equals marginal cost. It costs the firm *W* to hire one more hour of labor. But the labor produces *MP* units of output. So the cost of producing one of those units of output, which is marginal cost, is *W* divided by *MP*.

If we call marginal cost *MC*, then

$$MR = MC,$$

which is the second condition for maximum profit.

Because the first condition for maximum profit implies the second condition, these two conditions are equivalent.

Table 15.2 summarizes the reasoning and calculations that show the equivalence between the two conditions for maximum profit.

TABLE 15.2

Two Conditions for Maximum Profit

Symbols

Marginal product	**MP**
Marginal revenue	**MR**
Marginal cost	**MC**
Marginal revenue product	**MRP**
Resource price	**PR**

Two Conditions for Maximum Profit

1.	**MR = MC**		2.	**MRP = PR**

Equivalence of Conditions

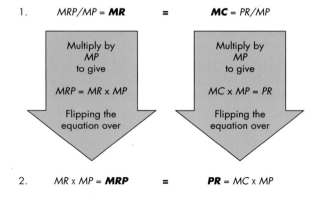

1. $MRP/MP = $ **MR** $=$ **MC**$ = PR/MP$

> Multiply by MP to give
> $MRP = MR \times MP$
> Flipping the equation over

> Multiply by MP to give
> $MC \times MP = PR$
> Flipping the equation over

2. $MR \times MP = $ **MRP** $=$ **PR**$ = MC \times MP$

The two conditions for maximum profit are that marginal revenue (*MR*) equals marginal cost (*MC*) and marginal revenue product (*MRP*) equals the price of the resource (*PR*). These two conditions are equivalent because marginal revenue product (*MRP*) equals marginal revenue (*MR*) multiplied by marginal product (*MP*) and the resource price (*PR*) equals marginal cost (*MC*) multiplied by marginal product (*MP*).

Max's Numbers Check the numbers for Max's Wash 'n' Wax and confirm that the conditions you've just examined work. Max's profit-maximizing labor decision is to hire 3 workers if the wage rate is $12 an hour. When Max hires 3 hours of labor, marginal product is 3 washes per hour. Max sells the 3 washes an hour for a marginal revenue of $4 a wash. So marginal revenue product is 3 washes multiplied by $4 a wash, which equals $12 per hour. At a wage rate of $12 an hour, Max is maximizing profit.

Equivalently, Max's marginal cost is $12 an hour divided by 3 washes per hour, which equals $4 per wash. At a marginal revenue of $4 a wash, Max is maximizing profit.

You've discovered that the law of demand applies for labor just as it does for goods and services. Other things remaining the same, the lower the wage rate (the price of labor), the greater is the quantity of labor demanded.

Let's now study the influences that change the demand for labor and shift the demand for labor curve.

Changes in the Demand for Labor

The demand for labor depends on three factors:

1. The price of the firm's output
2. The prices of other productive resources
3. Technology

The higher the price of a firm's output, the greater is its demand for labor. The price of output affects the demand for labor through its influence on marginal revenue product. A higher price for the firm's output increases marginal revenue, which, in turn, increases the marginal revenue product of labor. A change in the price of a firm's output leads to a shift in the firm's demand for labor curve. If the price of the firm's output increases, the demand for labor increases, and the demand for labor curve shifts rightward.

The other two influences affect the *long-run demand for labor*, which is the relationship between the wage rate and the quantity of labor demanded when all resources can be varied. In contrast, the *short-run demand for labor* is the relationship between the wage rate and the quantity of labor demanded when the quantities of the other resources are fixed and labor is the only variable resource. In the long run, a change in the relative price of productive resources—such as the relative price of labor and capital—leads to a substitution away from the resource whose relative price has increased and toward the resource whose relative price has decreased. So if the price of capital

decreases relative to that of labor, the firm substitutes capital for labor and increases the quantity of capital demanded.

But the demand for labor might increase or decrease. If the lower price of capital increases the scale of production by enough, the demand for labor increases. Otherwise, the demand for labor decreases.

Finally, a new technology that changes the marginal product of labor changes the demand for labor. For example, the electronic telephone exchange has decreased the demand for telephone operators. This same new technology has increased the demand for telephone engineers. Again, these effects are felt in the long run when the firm adjusts all its resources and incorporates new technologies into its production process. Table 15.3 summarizes the influences on a firm's demand for labor.

We saw in Fig. 15.3 that the demand for labor has increased over time and the demand curve has shifted rightward. We can now give some of the reasons for this increase in demand. Advances in technology and investment in new capital increase the marginal product of labor and increase the demand for labor.

TABLE 15.3

A Firm's Demand for Labor

The Law of Demand

(Movements along the demand curve for labor)

The quantity of labor demanded by a firm

Decreases if:	Increases if:
■ The wage rate increases	■ The wage rate decreases

Changes in Demand

(Shifts in the demand curve for labor)

A firm's demand for labor

Decreases if:	Increases if:
■ The firm's output price decreases	■ The firm's output price increases
■ A new technology decreases the marginal product of labor	■ A new technology increases the marginal product of labor

(Changes in the prices of other resources have an ambiguous effect on the demand for labor.)

Market Demand

So far, we've studied the demand for labor by an individual firm. The market demand for labor is the total demand by all firms. The market demand for labor curve is derived (similarly to the market demand curve for any good or service) by adding together the quantities demanded by all firms at each wage rate. Because a firm's demand for labor curve slopes downward, so does the market demand curve.

Elasticity of Demand for Labor

The elasticity of demand for labor measures the responsiveness of the quantity of labor demanded to the wage rate. This elasticity is important because it tells us how labor income changes when the supply of labor changes. An increase in supply (other things remaining the same) brings a lower wage rate. If demand is inelastic, an increase in supply decreases labor income. But if demand is elastic, an increase in supply brings a lower wage rate and increases labor income. And if the demand for labor is unit elastic, a change in supply leaves labor income unchanged.

The demand for labor is less elastic in the short run, when only labor can be varied, than in the long run, when labor and other resources can be varied. The elasticity of demand for labor depends on:

- The labor intensity of the production process
- The elasticity of demand for the product
- The substitutability of capital for labor

Labor Intensity   A labor-intensive production process is one that uses a lot of labor and little capital. Home building is an example. The greater the degree of labor intensity, the more elastic is the demand for labor. To see why, first suppose that wages are 90 percent of total cost. A 10 percent increase in the wage rate increases total cost by 9 percent. Firms will be sensitive to such a large change in total cost, so if wages increase, firms will decrease the quantity of labor demanded by a relatively large amount. But if wages are 10 percent of total cost, a 10 percent increase in the wage rate increases total cost by only 1 percent. Firms will be less sensitive to this increase in cost, so if wages increase in this case, firms will decrease the quantity of labor demanded by a relatively small amount.

The Elasticity of Demand for the Product   The greater the elasticity of demand for the good, the larger is the elasticity of demand for the labor used to produce it. An increase in the wage rate increases marginal cost and decreases the supply of the good. The decrease in the supply of the good increases the price of the good and decreases the quantity demanded of the good and the quantities of the resources used to produce it. The greater the elasticity of demand for the good, the larger is the decrease in the quantity demanded of the good, and so the larger is the decrease in the quantities of the productive resources used to produce it.

The Substitutability of Capital for Labor   The more easily capital can be used instead of labor in production, the more elastic is the long-run demand for labor. For example, it is easy to use robots rather than assembly line workers in car factories and to use grape-picking machines for labor in vineyards. So the long-run demand for these types of labor is more elastic. At the other extreme, it is difficult (but possible) to substitute computers for newspaper reporters, bank loan officers, and teachers. So the long-run demand for these types of labor is less elastic.

Let's now turn from the demand side of the labor market to the supply side and examine the decisions that people make about how to allocate time between working and other activities.

The Supply of Labor

People can allocate their time to two broad activities: labor supply and leisure. (Leisure is a catchall. It includes all activities other than supplying labor.) For most people, leisure is more enjoyable than supplying labor. We'll look at Jill's labor supply decision. Like most people, Jill enjoys her leisure time, and she would be pleased if she didn't have to spend her weekends working a supermarket checkout line.

But Jill has chosen to work weekends. The reason is that she is offered a wage rate that exceeds her *reservation wage*. Jill's reservation wage is the lowest wage at which she is willing to supply labor. If the wage rate exceeds her reservation wage, she supplies some labor. But how much labor does she supply? The quantity of labor that Jill supplies depends on the wage rate.

Substitution Effect   Other things remaining the same, the higher the wage rate she is offered, at least over a range, the greater is the quantity of labor that Jill supplies. The reason is that Jill's wage rate is her *opportunity cost of leisure.* If she quits work an hour early to catch a movie, the cost of that extra hour of leisure is the wage rate that Jill forgoes. The higher the wage rate, the less willing Jill is to forgo the income and take the extra leisure time. This tendency for a higher wage rate to induce Jill to work longer hours is a *substitution effect.*

But there is also an *income effect* that works in the opposite direction to the substitution effect.

Income Effect The higher Jill's wage rate, the larger is her income. A larger income, other things remaining the same, induces Jill to increase her demand for most goods. Leisure is one of those goods. Because an increase in income creates an increase in the demand for leisure, it also creates a decrease in the quantity of labor supplied.

Backward-Bending Supply of Labor Curve As the wage rate rises, the substitution effect brings an increase in the quantity of labor supplied while the income effect brings a decrease in the quantity of labor supplied. At low wage rates, the substitution effect is larger than the income effect, so as the wage

rate rises, people supply more labor. But as the wage rate continues to rise, the income effect eventually becomes larger than the substitution effect and the quantity of labor supplied decreases. The labor supply curve is *backward bending.*

Figure 15.4(a) shows the labor supply curves for Jill, Jack, and Kelly. Each labor supply curve is backward bending but the three people have different reservation wage rates.

Market Supply The market supply of labor curve is the sum of the individual supply curves. Figure 15.4(b) shows the market supply curve (S_M) derived from the supply curves of Jill, Jack, and Kelly (S_A, S_B, S_C) in Fig. 15.4(a). At wage rates of less than $1 an hour, no one supplies any labor. At a wage rate of $1 an hour, Jill works but Jack and Kelly don't. As the wage rate increases and reaches $7 an hour, all three of them work. The market supply curve S_M eventually bends backward, but it has a long upward-sloping section.

Changes in the Supply of Labor The supply of labor changes when influences other than the wage rate change. The key factors that change the supply of labor and that have increased it over the years are:

FIGURE 15.4

The Supply of Labor

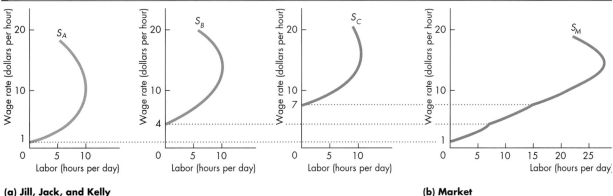

(a) Jill, Jack, and Kelly

(b) Market

Part (a) shows the labor supply curves of Jill (S_A), Jack (S_B), and Kelly (S_C). Each person has a reservation wage below which he or she will supply no labor. As the wage rises, the quantity of labor supplied increases to a maximum. If the wage continues to rise, the quantity of labor supplied begins to decrease. Each

person's supply curve eventually bends backward. Part (b) shows how, by adding the quantities of labor supplied by each person at each wage rate, we derive the market supply curve of labor (S_M). The market supply curve has a long upward-sloping region before it bends backward.

- Adult population
- Technological change and capital accumulation in home production

An increase in the adult population increases the supply of labor. Also, an increase in capital in home production (of meals, laundry services, and cleaning services) increases the supply of labor. These factors that have increased the supply of labor have shifted the labor supply curve rightward.

Let's now build on what we've learned about the demand for labor and the supply of labor and study labor market equilibrium and the trends in wage rates and employment.

Labor Market Equilibrium

Wages and employment are determined by equilibrium in the labor market. You saw in Fig. 15.2 that the wage rate and employment have both increased over the years. You can now explain why.

Trends in the Demand for Labor The demand for labor has *increased* because of technological change and the accumulation of capital, and the demand for labor curve has shifted steadily rightward.

Many people are surprised that technological change and capital accumulation *increase* the demand for labor. They see new technologies *destroying jobs*, not creating them. Downsizing became a catchword of the 1990s as the computer and information age took hold and eliminated millions of "good" jobs, even of managers. So how can it be that technological change *creates* jobs and increases the demand for labor?

Technological change destroys some jobs and creates others. But it creates more jobs than it destroys, and *on the average* the new jobs pay more than the old ones did. But to benefit from the advances in technology, people must acquire new skills and change their jobs. For example, during the past 15 years, the demand for typists has fallen almost to zero. But the demand for people who can type (on a computer rather than a typewriter) and do other things as well has increased. And the output of these people is worth more than that of a typist. So the demand for people with typing (and other) skills has increased.

Trends in the Supply of Labor The supply of labor has increased because of population growth and technological change and capital accumulation in the home. The mechanization of home production of fast-food preparation services (the freezer and the microwave oven) and laundry services (the automatic washer and dryer and drip dry clothing) has decreased the time spent on activities that once were full-time jobs inside the home and has led to a large increase in the supply of labor. As a result, the supply of labor has steadily increased, but at a slower pace than the demand for labor.

Trends in Equilibrium Because technological advances and capital accumulation have increased demand by more than population growth and technological change in home production has increased supply, both wages and employment have increased. But not everyone has shared in the advancing prosperity that comes from higher wage rates. Some groups have been left behind, and some have even seen their wage rates fall. Why?

Two key reasons can be identified. First, technological change affects the marginal productivity of different groups in different ways. High-skilled computer-literate workers have benefited from the information revolution while low-skilled workers have suffered. The demand for the services of the first group has increased, and the demand for the services of the second group has decreased. (Draw a supply and demand figure, and you will see that these changes widen the wage difference between the two groups.) Second, international competition has lowered the marginal revenue product of low-skilled workers and so decreased the demand for their labor. We look further at skill differences in Chapter 16 and at trends in the distribution of income in Chapter 17.

REVIEW QUIZ

- Why do we call the demand for labor a *derived demand*? From what is it derived?
- What is the distinction between marginal revenue product and marginal revenue? Provide an example that illustrates the distinction.
- When a firm's marginal revenue product equals the wage rate, marginal revenue also equals marginal cost. Why? Provide a numerical example different from that in the text.
- What determines the amount of labor that households plan to supply?
- Describe and explain the trends in wage rates and employment.

Capital Markets

CAPITAL MARKETS ARE THE CHANNELS THROUGH which firms obtain *financial* resources to buy *physical* capital resources. These financial resources come from saving. The *price of capital*, which adjusts to make the quantity of capital supplied equal to the quantity demanded, is the interest rate.

For most of us, capital markets are where we make our biggest ticket transactions. We borrow in a capital market to buy a home. And we lend in capital markets to build up a fund on which to live when we retire. Do the rates of return in capital markets increase as wage rates do? Figure 15.5(a) answers this question by showing the record since 1960. Measuring interest rates as *real* interest rates, which means that we subtract the loss in the value of money from inflation, the rate of return has fluctuated. It averaged around 3 percent a year in the 1960s, became negative in the 1970s, climbed to almost 9 percent in 1984, and steadied at around 5 percent in the 1990s. Over the same period, the quantity of capital employed increased steadily. In 1998, it stood at around $22 trillion (1992 dollars), up by 175 percent from its 1960 level.

Figure 15.5(b) shows why these changes in the capital market occurred. Demand increased from KD_{60} to KD_{98}, and this increase was similar to the increase in supply from KS_{60} to KS_{98}. To understand changes in the capital market, we must again probe the forces of demand and supply. Many of the ideas that you've already met in your study of demand and supply in the labor market apply to the capital market as well. But there are some special features of capital. Its main special feature is that in the capital market, people must compare *present* costs with *future* benefits. Let's discover how these comparisons are made by studying the demand for capital.

The Demand for Capital

A firm's demand for *financial* capital stems from its demand for *physical* capital, and the amount that a firm plans to borrow in a given time period is determined by its planned investment—purchases of new capital. This decision is driven by its attempt to maximize profit. As a firm increases the quantity of capital employed, other things remaining the same, the marginal revenue product of capital eventually diminishes. To maximize profit, a firm increases its

FIGURE 15.5

Capital Market Trends in the United States

(a) Capital stock and interest rate

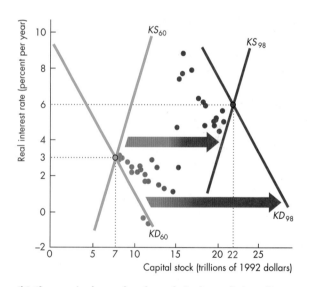

(b) Changes in demand and supply in the capital market

The real interest rate (the interest rate adjusted for inflation) fluctuated between a negative return in 1974 and 1975 and a high of almost 9 percent in 1984. It was steady at 3 percent in the 1960s and 5 percent in the 1990s. During the same period, the quantity of capital employed increased by 175 percent. Part (a) shows this record. Part (b) shows the changes in demand and supply that have generated the changes in the capital market. The demand for capital increased from KD_{60} to KD_{98} and the supply of capital increased from KS_{60} to KS_{98}.

plant size and uses more capital if the marginal revenue product of capital exceeds the cost of capital. But the marginal revenue product comes in the future, and capital must be paid for in the present. So the firm must convert *future* marginal revenue products into a *present value* so that it can be compared with the price of a new piece of capital equipment.

To make this conversion, we use the technique of discounting.

Discounting and Present Value

Discounting is converting a future amount of money to a present value. And the **present value** of a future amount of money is the amount that, if invested today, will grow to be as large as that future amount when the interest that it will earn is taken into account.

The easiest way to understand discounting and present value is to begin with the relationship between an amount invested today, the interest that it earns, and the amount that it will grow to in the future. The future amount is equal to the present amount (present value) plus the interest it will accumulate in the future. That is,

Future amount = Present value + Interest income.

The interest income is equal to the present value multiplied by the interest rate, r, so

Future amount = Present value + ($r \times$ Present value)

or

Future amount = Present value $\times$ (1 + r).

If you have $100 today and the interest rate is 10 percent a year ($r = 0.1$), one year from today you will have $110—the original $100 plus $10 interest. Check that the above formula delivers that answer: $100 \times 1.1 = \$110$.

The formula that we have just used calculates a future amount one year from today from the present value and an interest rate. To calculate the present value, we just work backward. Instead of multiplying the present value by (1 + r), we divide the future amount by (1 + r). That is,

$$\text{Present value} = \frac{\text{Future amount}}{(1 + r)}.$$

You can use this formula to calculate present value. This calculation of present value is called discounting. Let's check that we can use the present value formula by calculating the present value of $110 one year from now when the interest rate is 10 percent a

year. You'll be able to guess that the answer is $100 because we just calculated that $100 invested today at 10 percent a year becomes $110 in one year. Thus it follows immediately that the present value of $110 in one year's time is $100. But let's use the formula. Putting the numbers into the above formula, we have

$$\text{Present value} = \frac{\$110}{(1 + 0.1)}$$

$$= \frac{\$110}{1.1} = \$100.$$

Calculating the present value of an amount of money one year from now is the easiest case. But we can also calculate the present value of an amount any number of years in the future. As an example, let's see how we calculate the present value of an amount of money that will be available two years from now.

Suppose that you invest $100 today for two years at an interest rate of 10 percent a year. The money will earn $10 in the first year, which means that by the end of the first year, you will have $110. If the interest of $10 is invested, then the interest earned in the second year will be a further $10 on the original $100 plus $1 on the $10 interest. Thus the total interest earned in the second year will be $11. The total interest earned overall will be $21 ($10 in the first year and $11 in the second year). After two years, you will have $121. From the definition of present value, you can see that the present value of $121 two years hence is $100. That is, $100 is the present amount that, if invested at an interest rate of 10 percent a year, will grow to $121 two years from now.

To calculate the present value of an amount of money two years in the future, we use the formula

$$\text{Present value} = \frac{\begin{array}{c}\text{Amount of money}\\ \text{two years in future}\end{array}}{(1 + r)^2}.$$

Use this formula to calculate the present value of $121 two years from now at an interest rate of 10 percent a year. With these numbers, the formula gives

$$\text{Present value} = \frac{\$121}{(1 + 0.1)^2}$$

$$= \frac{\$121}{(1.1)^2}$$

$$= \frac{\$121}{1.21}$$

$$= \$100.$$

We can calculate the present value of an amount of money any number of years in the future by using a formula based on the two that we've already used. The general formula is

$$\text{Present value} = \frac{\text{Amount of money } n \text{ years in future}}{(1+r)^n}.$$

For example, if the interest rate is 10 percent a year, $100 to be received 10 years from now has a present value of $38.55. That is, if $38.55 is invested today at an interest rate of 10 percent, it will accumulate to $100 in 10 years. (You might check that calculation on your pocket calculator.)

You've seen how to calculate the present value of an amount of money one year in the future, two years in the future, and n years in the future. Most practical applications of present value calculate the present value of a sequence of future amounts of money that spread over several years. To calculate the present value of a sequence of amounts over several years, we use the formula you have learned and apply it to each year. We then sum the present values for each year to find the present value of the sequence of amounts.

For example, suppose that a firm expects to receive $100 a year for each of the next five years. And suppose that the interest rate is 10 percent per year (0.1 per year). The present value (PV) of these five payments of $100 each is calculated by using the following formula:

$$PV = \frac{\$100}{1.1} + \frac{\$100}{1.1^2} + \frac{\$100}{1.1^3} + \frac{\$100}{1.1^4} + \frac{\$100}{1.1^5},$$

which equals

$$PV = \$100.00 + \$90.91 + \$82.64 + \$75.13 + \$68.30$$

$$= \$416.98.$$

You can see that the firm receives $500 over five years. But because the money arrives in the future, it is not worth $500 today. Its present value is only $416.98. And the farther in the future it arrives, the smaller is its present value. The $100 received one year in the future is worth $90.91 today. And the $100 received five years in the future is worth only $68.30 today.

Let's now see how a firm uses the concept of present value to achieve an efficient use of capital.

The Present Value of a Computer We'll see how a firm decides how much capital to buy by calculating the present value of a new computer.

Tina runs Taxfile, Inc., a firm that sells advice to taxpayers. Tina is considering buying a new computer that costs $10,000. The computer has a life of two years, after which it will be worthless. If Tina buys the computer, she will pay $10,000 now and she expects to generate business that will bring in an additional $5,900 at the end of each of the next two years.

To calculate the present value, PV, of the marginal revenue product of a new computer, Tina calculates

$$PV = \frac{MRP_1}{(1+r)} + \frac{MRP_2}{(1+r)^2}.$$

Here, MRP_1 is the marginal revenue product received by Tina at the end of the first year. It is converted to a present value by dividing it by $(1+r)$, where r is the interest rate (expressed as a proportion). The term MRP_2 is the marginal revenue product received at the end of the second year. It is converted to a present value by dividing it by $(1+r)^2$.

If Tina can borrow or lend at an interest rate of 4 percent a year, the present value of her marginal revenue product is given by

$$PV = \frac{\$5,900}{(1+0.04)} + \frac{\$5,900}{(1+0.04)^2}$$

$$PV = \$5,673 + \$5,455$$

$$PV = \$11,128.$$

The present value (PV) of $5,900 one year in the future is $5,900 divided by 1.04 (4 percent as a proportion is 0.04). The present value of $5,900 two years in the future is $5,900 divided by $(1.04)^2$. Tina works out those two present values and then adds them to get the present value of the future flow of marginal revenue product, which is $11,128.

Table 15.4, parts (a) and (b), summarizes the data and the calculations we've just made. Review these calculations and make sure you understand them.

Tina's Decision to Buy Tina decides whether to buy the computer by comparing the present value of its future flow of marginal revenue product with its purchase price. She makes this comparison by calculating the net present value (NPV) of the computer. **Net present value** is the present value of the future flow of marginal revenue product generated by the capital minus the cost of the capital. If net present value is positive, the firm buys additional capital. If the net present value is negative, the firm does not buy additional capital. Table 15.4(c) shows the

TABLE 15.4

Net Present Value of an Investment—Taxfile, Inc.

(a) Data

Price of computer	$10,000
Life of computer	2 years
Marginal revenue product	$5,900 at end of each year
Interest rate	4% a year

(b) Present value of the flow of marginal revenue product

$$PV = \frac{MRP_1}{(1 + r)} + \frac{MRP_2}{(1 + r)^2}$$

$$= \frac{\$5,900}{1.04} + \frac{\$5,900}{(1.04)^2}$$

$$= \$5,673 + \$5,455$$

$$= \$11,128.$$

(c) Net present value of investment

NPV = PV of marginal revenue product – Cost of computer

$$= \$11,128 - \$10,000$$

$$= \$1,128.$$

calculation of Tina's net present value of a computer. The net present value is $1,128—greater than zero—so Tina buys the computer.

Tina can buy any number of computers that cost $10,000 and have a life of two years. But like all other factors of production, capital is subject to diminishing marginal returns. The greater the amount of capital employed, the smaller is its marginal revenue product. So if Tina buys a second computer or a third one, she gets successively smaller marginal revenue products from the additional machines.

Table 15.5(a) sets out Tina's marginal revenue products for one, two, and three computers. The marginal revenue product of one computer (the case just reviewed) is $5,900 a year. The marginal revenue product of a second computer is $5,600 a year, and the marginal revenue product of a third computer is

$5,300 a year. Table 15.5(b) shows the calculations of the present values of the marginal revenue products of the first, second, and third computers.

You've seen that with an interest rate of 4 percent a year, the net present value of one computer is positive. At an interest rate of 4 percent a year, the present value of the marginal revenue product of a second computer is $10,562, which exceeds its price by $562. So Tina buys a second computer. But at an interest rate of 4 percent a year, the present value of the marginal revenue product of a third computer is $9,996, which is $4 less than the price of the computer. So Tina does not buy a third computer.

A Change in the Interest Rate We've seen that at an interest rate of 4 percent a year, Tina buys two computers but not three. Suppose that the interest rate is 8 percent a year. In this case, the present value of the first computer is $10,521 (see Table 15.5b), so Tina still buys one computer because it has a positive net present value. At an interest rate of 8 percent a year, the net present value of the second computer is $9,986, which is less than $10,000, the price of the computer. So at an interest rate of 8 percent a year, Tina buys only one computer.

Suppose that the interest rate is even higher, at 12 percent a year. In this case, the present value of the marginal revenue product of one computer is $9,971 (see Table 15.5b). At this interest rate, Tina buys no computers.

These calculations trace Taxfile's demand schedule for capital, which shows the value of computers demanded by Taxfile at each interest rate. Other things remaining the same, as the interest rate rises, the quantity of capital demanded decreases. The higher the interest rate, the smaller is the quantity of *physical* capital demanded. But to finance the purchase of *physical* capital, firms demand *financial* capital. So the higher the interest rate, the smaller is the quantity of *financial* capital demanded.

Demand Curve for Capital

The quantity of capital demanded by a firm depends on the marginal revenue product of capital and the interest rate. A firm's demand curve for capital shows the relationship between the quantity of capital demanded by the firm and the interest rate, other things remaining the same. The market demand

---

TABLE 15.5

Taxfile's Investment Decision

(a) Data

Price of computer	$10,000
Life of computer	2 years
Marginal revenue product:	
Using 1 computer	$5,900 a year
Using 2 computers	$5,600 a year
Using 3 computers	$5,300 a year

(b) Present value of the flow of marginal revenue product

If r = 0.04 (4% a year):

Using 1 computer: $PV = \dfrac{\$5,900}{1.04} + \dfrac{\$5,900}{(1.04)^2} = \$11,128.$

Using 2 computers: $PV = \dfrac{\$5,600}{1.04} + \dfrac{\$5,600}{(1.04)^2} = \$10,562.$

Using 3 computers: $PV = \dfrac{\$5,300}{1.04} + \dfrac{\$5,300}{(1.04)^2} = \$9,996.$

If r = 0.08 (8% a year):

Using 1 computer: $PV = \dfrac{\$5,900}{1.08} + \dfrac{\$5,900}{(1.08)^2} = \$10,521$

Using 2 computers: $PV = \dfrac{\$5,600}{1.08} + \dfrac{\$5,600}{(1.08)^2} = \$9,986.$

If r = 0.12 (12% a year):

Using 1 computer: $PV = \dfrac{\$5,900}{1.12} + \dfrac{\$5,900}{(1.12)^2} = \$9,971.$

---

curve (as in Fig. 15.5b) shows the relationship between the total quantity of capital demanded and the interest rate, other things remaining the same.

Changes in the Demand for Capital Figure 15.5(b) shows that the demand for capital has increased steadily over the years. The demand for capital changes when expectations about the future marginal revenue product of capital change. An increase in the expected marginal revenue product of capital increases the demand of capital. Two main factors that change the marginal revenue product of capital and bring changes in the demand for capital are:

1. Population growth
2. Technological change

An increase in the population increases the demand for all goods and services and so increases the demand for the capital that produces them. Advances in technology increase the demand for some types of capital and decrease the demand for other types. For example, the development of diesel engines for railroad transportation decreased the demand for steam engines and increased the demand for diesel engines. In this case, the railroad industry's overall demand for capital did not change much. In contrast, the development of desktop computers increased the demand for office computing equipment, decreased the demand for electric typewriters, and increased the overall demand for capital in the office.

Let's now turn to the supply side of the capital market.

The Supply of Capital

The quantity of capital supplied results from people's saving decisions. The main factors that determine saving are:

■ Income
■ Expected future income
■ Interest rate

Income Saving is the act of converting *current* income into *future* consumption. Usually, the higher a person's income, the more he or she plans to consume both in the present and in the future. But to increase *future* consumption, the person must save. So, other things remaining the same, the higher a person's income, the more he or she saves. The relationship between saving and income is remarkably stable. Most people save a constant proportion of their income.

Expected Future Income Because a major reason for saving is to increase future consumption, the amount that a person saves depends not only on its current income but also on his or her *expected future income*. If a person's current income is high and expected future income is low, he or she will have a high level of saving. But if the person's current income is low and expected future income is high, he or she will have a low (perhaps even negative) level of saving.

Young people (especially students) usually have low current incomes compared with their expected future income. To smooth out consumption over their lifetime, young people consume more than they earn and incur debts. Such people have a negative amount of saving. In middle age, most people's incomes reach their peak. At this stage in life, saving is at its maximum. After retirement, people spend part of the wealth they have accumulated during their working lives.

Interest Rate A dollar saved today grows into a dollar plus interest tomorrow. The higher the interest rate, the greater is the amount that a dollar saved today becomes in the future. Thus the higher the interest rate, the greater is the opportunity cost of current consumption. With a higher opportunity cost of current consumption, people cut their consumption and increase their saving.

Supply Curve of Capital

The supply curve of capital (like that in Fig. 15.5b) shows the relationship between the quantity of capital supplied and the interest rate, other things remaining the same. An increase in the interest rate brings an increase in the quantity of capital supplied and a movement along the supply curve. The supply of capital is inelastic in the short run but probably quite elastic in the long run. The reason is that in any given year, the total amount of saving is small relative to the stock of capital in existence. So even a large change in the amount of saving brings only a small change in the quantity of capital supplied.

Changes in the Supply of Capital The main influences on the supply of capital are the size and age distribution of the population and the level of income.

Other things remaining the same, an increase in the population or an increase in income brings an increase in the supply of capital. Also, other things remaining the same, the larger the proportion of middle-aged people, the higher is the amount of saving. The reason is that middle-aged people do most of the saving as they build up a pension fund to provide a retirement income. Any one of the factors that

increases the supply of capital shifts the supply curve of capital rightward.

Let's now use what we've learned about the demand for and supply of capital and see how the interest rate is determined.

The Interest Rate

Saving plans and investment plans are coordinated through capital markets, and the real interest rate adjusts to make these plans compatible.

Figure 15.6 shows the capital market. Initially, the demand for capital is KD_0, and the supply of capital is KS_0. The equilibrium real interest rate is 6 percent a year, and the quantity of capital is $10 trillion. If the interest rate exceeds 6 percent a year, the quantity of capital supplied exceeds the quantity of capital demanded and the interest rate falls. And if the interest rate is less than 6 percent a year, the quantity of

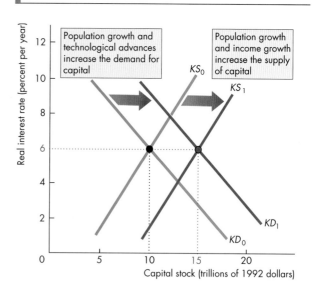

FIGURE 15.6

Capital Market Equilibrium

Initially, the demand for capital is KD_0, and the supply of capital is KS_0. The equilibrium interest rate is 6 percent a year, and the capital stock is $10 trillion. Over time, both demand and supply increase to KD_1 and KS_1 respectively. The capital stock increases, but the real interest rate is constant. Demand and supply increase because they are influenced by common factors.

capital demanded exceeds the quantity of capital supplied and the interest rate rises.

Over time, both the demand for capital and the supply of capital increase. The demand curve shifts rightward to KD_1, and the supply curve also shifts rightward, to KS_1. Both curves shift because the same forces influence both. Population growth increases both demand and supply. Technological advances increase demand and bring higher incomes, which in turn increase supply. Because both demand and supply increase over time, the quantity of capital trends upward and the real interest rate has no trend.

Although the real interest rate does not follow a rising or falling trend, it does fluctuate, as you can see in Fig. 15.5(a). The reason is that the demand for capital and the supply of capital do not change in lockstep. Sometimes, rapid technological change brings an increase in the demand for capital *before* it brings rising incomes that increase the supply of capital. When this sequence of events occurs, the real interest rate rises. The 1990s appeared to be such a time, as you can see in Fig. 15.5(a).

At other times, the demand for capital grows slowly or even decreases temporarily. In this situation, supply outgrows demand and the real interest rate falls. Figure 15.5(a) shows that 1975 was one of these times.

R E V I E W   Q U I Z

- What is discounting and how is it used to calculate a present value? When might you want to calculate a present value to make a decision?
- How does a firm compare the future marginal revenue product of capital with the current cost of capital?
- What are the main influences on a firm's demand for capital?
- What are the main influences on the supply of capital?
- What have been the main trends in the quantity of capital and interest rates? How can we explain these trends by using the demand for capital and the supply of capital?

The lessons that we've just learned about capital markets can be used to understand the prices of exhaustible natural resource prices. Let's see how.

Land and Exhaustible Natural Resource Markets

LAND IS THE QUANTITY OF NATURAL RESOURCES. All natural resources are called *land,* and they fall into two categories:

- Nonexhaustible
- Exhaustible

Nonexhaustible natural resources are natural resources that can be used repeatedly. Examples are land (in its everyday sense), rivers, lakes, and rain.

Exhaustible natural resources are natural resources that can be used only once and that cannot be replaced once they have been used. Examples are coal, natural gas, and oil—the hydrocarbon fuels.

The demand for a natural resource as an input into production is based on the same principle of marginal revenue product as the demand for labor (and the demand for capital). But the supply of a natural resource is special. Let's look first at the supply of a nonexhaustible natural resource.

The Supply of Land (Nonexhaustible Natural Resource)

The quantity of land and other nonexhaustible natural resources available is fixed. The quantity supplied cannot be changed by individual decisions. People can vary the amount of land they own. But when one person buys some land, another person sells it. The aggregate quantity of land supplied of any particular type and in any particular location is fixed, regardless of the decisions of any individual. This fact means that the supply of each particular piece of land is perfectly inelastic. Figure 15.7 illustrates such a supply. Regardless of the rent available, the quantity of land supplied on Chicago's "Magnificent Mile" is a fixed number of square feet.

Because the supply of land is fixed regardless of its price, price is determined by demand. The greater the demand for a specific piece of land, the higher is its price.

Expensive land can be, and is, used more intensively than inexpensive land. For example, high-rise buildings enable land to be used more intensively. However, to use land more intensively, it has to be combined with another productive resource—capital. Increasing the amount of capital per block of land does not change the supply of land itself.

FIGURE 15.7

The Supply of Land

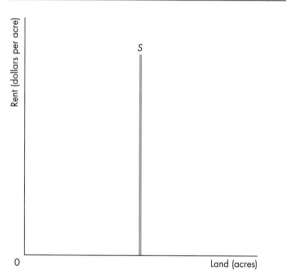

The supply of a given piece of land is perfectly inelastic. No matter what the rent, no more land than the quantity that exists can be supplied.

Although the supply of each type of land is fixed and its supply is perfectly inelastic, each individual firm, operating in competitive land markets, faces an elastic supply of land. For example, Fifth Avenue in New York City has a fixed amount of land, but Doubleday, the bookstore, could rent some space from Saks, the department store. Each firm can rent the quantity of land that it demands at the going rent, as determined in the marketplace. Thus provided that land markets are competitive, firms are price takers in these markets, just as they are in the markets for other productive resources.

The Supply of an Exhaustible Natural Resource

The *stock* of a natural resource is the quantity in existence at a given time. This quantity is fixed and is independent of the price of the resource. The *known* stock of a natural resource is the quantity that has been discovered. This quantity increases over time because advances in technology enable ever less accessible sources to be discovered. Both of these *stock* concepts influence the price of a natural resource.

But the influence is indirect. The direct influence on price is the rate at which the resource is supplied for use in production—called the *flow* supply.

The flow supply of an exhaustible natural resource is *perfectly elastic* at a price that equals the present value of the expected price next period.

To see why, think about the economic choices of Saudi Arabia, a country that possesses a large inventory of oil. Saudi Arabia can sell an additional billion barrels of oil right now and use the income it receives to buy U.S. bonds. Or it can keep the billion barrels in the ground and sell them next year. If it sells the oil and buys U.S. bonds, it earns the interest rate on the bonds. If it keeps the oil and sells it next year, it earns the price increase or loses the price decrease between now and next year.

If Saudi Arabia expects the price to rise next year by a percentage that equals the current interest rate, the price that it expects next year equals $(1 + r)$ multiplied by this year's price. For example, if this year's price is $12 a barrel and the interest rate is 5 percent ($r = 0.5$), then next year's expected price is 1.05 × $12, which equals $12.60 a barrel.

With the price expected to rise to $12.60 next year, Saudi Arabia is indifferent between selling now for $12 and not selling now but waiting until next year and selling for $12.60. It expects to make the same return either way. So, at $12 a barrel, Saudi Arabia will sell whatever quantity is demanded.

But if Saudi Arabia expects the price to rise next year by a percentage that exceeds the current interest rate, it expects to make a bigger return by hanging on to the oil than it can make from selling the oil and buying bonds. So it keeps the oil and sells none. And if it expects the price to rise next year by a percentage that is less than the current interest rate, the bond gives a bigger return than the oil so it sells as much oil as it can.

Recall the idea of discounting and present value. The minimum price at which Saudi Arabia is willing to sell oil is the present value of the expected future price. At this price, it will sell as much oil as buyers demand. So its supply is perfectly elastic.

Price and the Hotelling Principle

Figure 15.8 shows the equilibrium in a natural resource market. Because supply is perfectly elastic at the present value of next period's expected price, the actual price of the natural resource equals the present value of next period's expected price. Also, because the current price is the present value of the expected

FIGURE 15.8

An Exhaustible Natural Resource Market

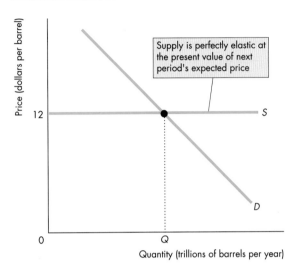

The supply of an exhaustible natural resource is perfectly elastic at the *present value* of next period's expected price. The demand for an exhaustible natural resource is determined by its marginal revenue product. The price is determined by supply and equals the *present value* of next period's expected price.

FIGURE 15.9

Falling Resource Prices

The prices of metals (here an average of the prices of aluminum, copper, iron ore, lead, manganese, nickel, silver, tin, and zinc) have tended to fall over time, not rise as predicted by the Hotelling Principle. The reason is that unanticipated advances in technology have decreased the cost of extracting metals and greatly increased the exploitable known reserves.

Source: International Financial Statistics, International Monetary Fund, Washington, D.C. (various issues).

future price, the price of the resource is expected to rise at a rate equal to the interest rate.

The proposition that the price of a resource is expected to rise at a rate equal to the interest rate is called the *Hotelling Principle*. It was first realized by Harold Hotelling, a mathematician and economist at Columbia University. But as Fig. 15.9 shows, *actual* prices do not follow the path of *expected* prices predicted by the Hotelling Principle. Why do natural resource prices sometimes fall rather than follow their expected path and increase over time?

The key reason is that the future is unpredictable. Expected technological change is reflected in the price of a natural resource. But a previously unexpected new technology that leads to the discovery or the more efficient use of an exhaustible natural resource causes its price to fall. Over the years, as technology has advanced, we have become more efficient in our use of exhaustible resources. And we haven't just become more efficient. We've become more efficient than we expected to.

REVIEW QUIZ

- Why is the supply of a *nonexhaustible* natural resource such as land perfectly inelastic?
- At what price is the flow supply of an exhaustible natural resource perfectly elastic and why?
- Why is the price of an exhaustible natural resource expected to rise at a rate equal to the interest rate?
- Why do the prices of exhaustible resources not follow the path predicted by the Hotelling Principle?

People supply resources to earn an income. But some people earn enormous incomes. Are such incomes necessary to induce people to work and supply other resources? Let's now answer this question.

Income, Economic Rent, and Opportunity Cost

YOU'VE NOW SEEN HOW RESOURCE PRICES ARE determined by the interaction of demand and supply. And you've seen that demand is determined by marginal productivity and supply is determined by the resources available and by people's choices about their use. The interaction of demand and supply in resource markets determines who receives a large income and who receives a small income.

Large and Small Incomes

A national morning show host earns a large income because she has a high marginal revenue product—reflected in the demand for her services—and few people have the combination of talents needed for this kind of job —reflected in the supply. Equilibrium occurs at a high wage rate and a small quantity employed.

People who work at McJobs earn a low wage rate because they have a low marginal revenue product—reflected in the demand—and many people are able and willing to supply their labor for these jobs. Equilibrium occurs at a low wage rate and a large quantity employed.

If the demand for morning show hosts increases, their incomes increase by a large amount and the number of morning show hosts barely changes. If the demand for workers in McJobs increases, the number of people doing these jobs increases by a large amount and the wage rate barely changes.

Another difference between a morning show host and a fast-food cook is that if the morning show host is hit with a pay cut, she will probably still supply her services, but if a fast-food cook is hit with a pay cut, he will probably quit. This difference arises from the interesting distinction between economic rent and opportunity cost.

Economic Rent and Opportunity Cost

The total income of a productive resource is made up of its economic rent and its opportunity cost. **Economic rent** is the income received by the owner of a resource over and above the amount required to induce that owner to offer the resource for use. Any productive resource can receive an economic rent. The income that is required to induce the supply of a productive resource is the opportunity cost of using a productive resource—the value of the resource in its next best use.

Figure 15.10(a) illustrates the way in which a resource income has an economic rent and opportunity cost component. The figure shows the market for a productive resource. It could be *any* productive resource—labor, capital, or land—but we'll suppose that it is labor. The demand curve is *D*, and its supply curve is *S*. The wage rate is *W*, and the quantity employed is *C*. The income earned is the sum of the yellow and green areas. The yellow area below the supply curve measures opportunity cost, and the green area above the supply curve but below the resource price measures economic rent.

To see why the area below the supply curve measures opportunity cost, recall that a supply curve can be interpreted in two different ways. It shows the quantity supplied at a given price, and it shows the minimum price at which a given quantity is willingly supplied. If suppliers receive only the minimum amount required to induce them to supply each unit of the productive resource, they will be paid a different price for each unit. The prices will trace the supply curve, and the income received is entirely opportunity cost—the yellow area in Fig. 15.10(a).

The concept of economic rent is similar to the concept of consumer surplus that you met in Chapter 6 (p. 111). Recall that consumer surplus is the maximum price someone is willing to pay, as indicated by the demand curve, minus the price paid. In a parallel sense, economic rent is the price a person receives for the use of a resource minus the minimum price at which a given quantity of the resource is willingly supplied.

Economic rent is not the same thing as the "rent" that a farmer pays for the use of some land or the "rent" that you pay for your apartment. Everyday "rent" is a price paid for the services of land or a building. *Economic rent* is a component of the income received by any productive resource.

The portion of the income of a productive resource that consists of economic rent depends on the elasticity of the supply of the productive resource. When the supply of a productive resource is perfectly inelastic, its entire income is economic rent. Most of the income of Garth Brooks and Pearl Jam is economic rent. Also, a large part of the income of a major league baseball player is economic rent. When the supply of a productive resource is perfectly elastic, none of its income is economic rent.

FIGURE 15.10

Economic Rent and Opportunity Cost

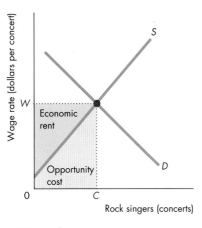

(a) General case

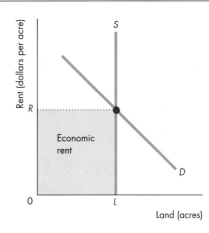

(b) All economic rent

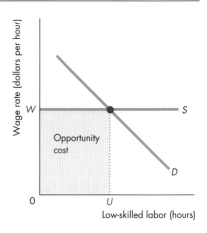

(c) All opportunity cost

When a resource supply curve slopes upward—the general case—as in part (a), part of the resource income is economic rent (green) and part is opportunity cost (yellow). When the supply of a productive resource is perfectly inelastic (the supply curve is vertical), as in part (b), the entire resource income is economic rent. When the supply of the productive resource is perfectly elastic, as in part (c), the resource's entire income is opportunity cost.

Most of the income of a baby-sitter is opportunity cost. In general, when the supply curve is neither perfectly elastic nor perfectly inelastic, like that illustrated in Fig. 15.10(a), some part of the resource income is economic rent and the other part is opportunity cost.

Figure 15.10, parts (b) and (c), shows the other two possibilities. Part (b) shows the market for a particular parcel of land in New York City. The quantity of land is fixed in size at *L* acres. Therefore the supply curve of the land is vertical—perfectly inelastic. Suppose that the demand curve in Fig. 15.10(b) shows the marginal revenue product of this block of land. Then it commands a rent of *R*. The entire income accruing to the owner of the land is the green area in the figure. This income is *economic rent*.

Figure 15.10(c) shows the market for a productive resource that is in perfectly elastic supply. An example of such a market might be that for low-skilled labor in a poor country such as India or China. In those countries, large amounts of labor flock to the cities and are available for work at the going wage rate (in this case, *W*). Thus in these situations, the supply of labor is almost perfectly elastic. The entire income earned by this labor is the yellow area. This income is *opportunity cost*. They receive no economic rent.

R E V I E W   Q U I Z

- Why does Katie Couric earn a larger income than does a baby sitter?
- What is the distinction between an economic rent and an opportunity cost?
- Was the income that the Chicago Bulls paid to Michael Jordan an economic rent or compensation for his opportunity cost?
- Is a Big Mac more expensive in Manhattan than in Little Rock because rents are higher in Manhattan or are rents higher in Manhattan because people are willing to pay more there for a Big Mac?

Reading Between the Lines on pp. 338–339 looks at the market for basketball players. The next chapter studies labor markets more closely and explains differences in wage rates among high-skilled and low-skilled workers, males and females, and racial and ethnic minorities. Chapter 17 looks at how the market economy distributes income and at efforts by governments to redistribute income and modify the market outcome.

Reading Between the Lines

The Market for Basketball Players

THE NEW YORK TIMES, JANUARY 7, 1999

With Little Time on Clock, NBA and Players Settle

BY MIKE WISE

NEW YORK—National Basketball Association players and owners brought an end to the most calamitous and costly labor dispute in league history Wednesday, agreeing to an 11th-hour deal that saved the season only a day before the owners were to vote on canceling it. ...

The crux of the disagreement for the past six months has been how to divide the $2 billion in annual revenue that the league generates. Although both sides made some concessions at the end, the league achieved its main goal of containing the contracts of high-salaried players, and received some unprecedented concessions from the union.

It insisted on and received a maximum salary provision, and no other professional sport has a limit on individual salaries. It also eliminated some of the crippling loopholes to its salary cap that had sent salaries skyrocketing in the last five years, and it refused to yield to the union's request for a greater percentage of revenue.

In the end, the union was left to try to hold onto some of the terms that had provided its players the highest average salary in pro sports, $2.6 million. It also achieved its stated priority of significantly bettering the economic position of its middle-class players, those making around the median salary of $1.3 million.

> **THE DEAL**
>
> MAXIMUM SALARY
>
> Ranging from $9 million for players with 1 to 6 years' experience to $14 million for veterans with 10 years of experience. No other sport has a cap on individual salaries.
>
> PERCENTAGE OF REVENUE
>
> The players will receive 55 percent of revenues toward their salaries in years 4, 5, and 6 of the contract. There is no fixed percentage for years 1 through 3.
>
> SALARY INCREASES
>
> The maximum salary increase will be 10 percent. Free agents who re-sign with their own team can receive up to 12 percent.

The union will receive 55 percent of total revenue toward salaries in the last three years of the deal. That was less than the players had hoped for, and the feeling among many of them was that they had given in to many of the league's demands at the last moment. Still, it was better than the prospect of no season and many more millions of dollars in lost paychecks. ...

© 1999 *The New York Times*. Reprinted with permission. Further reproduction prohibited.

Essence of the Story

■ The National Basketball Association players and owners agreed to a new contract in January 1999 and ended a six-month dispute.

■ The disagreement was over how to divide the $2 billion in annual revenue that the league generates.

■ The players will receive 55 percent of revenues toward their salaries in years 4, 5, and 6 of the contract. There is no fixed percentage for years 1 through 3.

■ The maximum salary will range from $9 million for players with 1 to 6 years of experience to $14 million for players with 10 years of experience.

■ The maximum salary increase will be 10 percent except for free agents who re-sign with their own team; they can receive up to 12 percent.

■ Basketball players are a special productive resource. The supply of top players' services is limited because they are extraordinarily talented and other people cannot replicate the special things that they do.

■ Figure 1 shows the marginal revenue product of players. The best players have a marginal revenue product that exceeds $20 million a year. The marginal revenue product of several players exceeds $10 million a year.

■ The marginal revenue product of players is the demand for players in a competitive labor market.

■ Figure 2 shows how the market for basketball players would work if it were competitive. The demand curve, D, is derived from the marginal revenue product curve in Fig. 1.

■ The supply is S. Supply is (assumed to be) elastic at a low salary rate up to 420 players and perfectly inelastic at 420 players.

■ This supply curve reflects two facts. First, the opportunity cost of playing basketball for most players is low—probably less than $100,000 a year. Second, the number of people who can play the game at the skill level that generates these high marginal revenue products is limited to a few hundred. (There are around 420 players in the 29 NBA teams.)

■ A competitive market might deliver a salary of $1 million a year. In this case, the total salary bill would be $420 million a year.

■ The total revenue of the NBA is $2 billion a year, so the competitive salary (on the assumptions just made) would be 21 percent of total revenue. Most of the players' income is economic rent.

■ Figure 3 shows how the players do better than the competitive market outcome and capture more economic rent by negotiating an agreement with the owners.

■ In Figure 3, the players take 55 percent of the total revenue and the highest-paid player earns a salary of $14 million a year. The green steps show other salary levels.

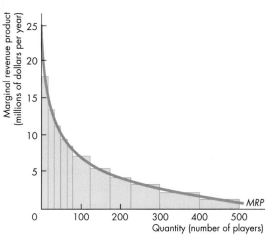

Figure 1 **The marginal revenue product of basketball players**

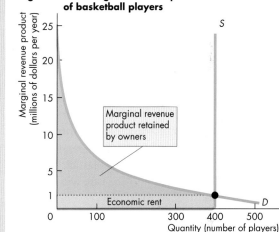

Figure 2 **A competitive market for basketball players**

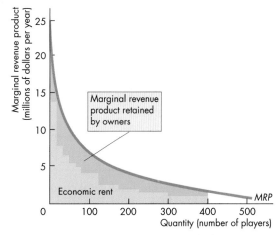

Figure 3 **A rent-sharing contract**

SUMMARY

KEY POINTS

Resource Prices and Incomes (p. 318)

- An increase in the demand for a productive resource increases its price and total income; a decrease in the demand for a productive resource decreases its price and total income.
- An increase in the supply of a productive resource increases the quantity used but decreases price and might increase or decrease its total income depending on whether demand is elastic or inelastic.

Labor Markets (pp. 319–326)

- The demand for labor is determined by the marginal revenue product of labor.
- The demand for labor increases if the price of the firm's output rises or if technological change and capital accumulation increase marginal product.
- The elasticity of demand for labor depends on the labor intensity of production, the elasticity of demand for the product, and the ease with which labor can be substituted for capital.
- The quantity of labor supplied increases as the real wage rate increases but at high wage rates, the supply curve eventually bends backward.
- The supply of labor increases with population growth and with technological change and capital accumulation in home production.
- Real wages and employment increase because demand increases by more than supply.

Capital Markets (pp. 327–333)

- To make an investment decision, a firm compares the *present value* of the marginal revenue product of capital with the price of capital.
- Population growth and technological change increase the demand for capital.
- The higher the interest rate, the greater are the level of saving and quantity of capital supplied.
- The supply of capital increases as incomes increase.
- Capital market equilibrium determines interest rates.

Land and Exhaustible Natural Resource Markets (pp. 333–335)

- The demand for a natural resource is determined by its marginal revenue product.
- The supply of land is inelastic.
- The supply of an exhaustible natural resource is perfectly elastic at a price equal to the present value of the expected future price.
- The price of an exhaustible natural resource is expected to rise at a rate equal to the interest rate but fluctuates and sometimes falls.

Incomes, Economic Rent, and Opportunity cost (pp. 336–337)

- Economic rent is the income received by a resource owner over and above the amount needed to induce the owner to supply the productive resource for use.
- The rest of a resource's income is opportunity cost.
- When the supply of a resource is perfectly inelastic, its entire income is economic rent; when supply is perfectly elastic, the entire income is opportunity cost.

KEY FIGURES AND TABLES ◆

KEY TERMS

PROBLEMS

*1. The figure illustrates the market for blueberry pickers:

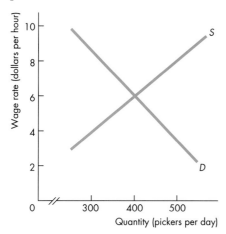

a. What is the wage rate paid to blueberry pickers?
b. How many blueberry pickers get hired?
c. What is the income received by blueberry pickers?

2. In problem 1, if the demand for blueberry pickers increases by 100 a day,
a. What is the new wage rate paid to the pickers?
b. How many additional pickers get hired?
c. What is the total income paid to pickers?

*3. Wanda owns a fish shop. She employs students to sort and pack the fish. Students can pack the following amounts of fish in an hour:

Number of students	Quantity of fish (pounds)
1	20
2	50
3	90
4	120
5	145
6	165
7	180
8	190

Wanda can sell her fish for 50¢ a pound, and the wage rate of packers is $7.50 an hour.
a. Calculate the marginal product of the students and draw the marginal product curve.

b. Calculate the marginal revenue product of the students and draw the marginal revenue product curve.
c. Find Wanda's demand for labor curve.
d. How many students does Wanda employ?

4. Barry makes party ice. He employs workers to bag the ice who can produce the following quantities in an hour:

Number of workers	Quantity of ice (bags)
1	40
2	100
3	180
4	240
5	290
6	330
7	360
8	380

Barry can sell ice for 25¢ a bag, and the wage rate of baggers is $5.00 an hour.
a. Calculate the marginal product of the workers and draw the marginal product curve.
b. Calculate the marginal revenue product of the workers and draw the marginal revenue product curve.
c. Find Barry's demand for labor curve.
d. How much ice does Barry sell?

*5. Back at Wanda's fish shop described in problem 3, the price of fish falls to 33.33¢ a pound but fish packers' wages remain at $7.50 an hour.
a. What happens to Wanda's marginal product?
b. What happens to her marginal revenue product?
c. What happens to her demand for labor curve?
d. What happens to the number of students that she employs?

6. Back at Barry's party ice shop described in problem 4, the price of party ice falls to 10¢ a bag but baggers' wages remain at $5.00 an hour.
a. What happens to Barry's marginal product?
b. What happens to his marginal revenue product?
c. What happens to his demand for labor curve?
d. What happens to the number of students that he employs?

*7. Back at Wanda's fish shop described in problem 3, packers' wages increase to $10 an hour but the price of fish remains at 50¢ a pound.
   a. What happens to marginal revenue product?
   b. What happens to Wanda's demand for labor curve?
   c. How many students does Wanda employ?

8. Back at Barry's party ice shop described in problem 4, baggers' wages increase to $10 an hour but the price of ice remains at 25¢ a bag.
   a. What happens to marginal revenue product?
   b. What happens to Barry's demand for labor curve?
   c. How many baggers does Barry employ?

*9. Use the information in problem 3 to calculate Wanda's marginal revenue, marginal cost, and marginal revenue product. Show that when Wanda is making maximum profit, marginal cost equals marginal revenue and marginal revenue product equals the wage rate.

10. Use the information in problem 4 to calculate Barry's marginal revenue, marginal cost, and marginal revenue product. Show that when Barry is making maximum profit, marginal cost equals marginal revenue and marginal revenue product equals the wage rate.

*11. Venus makes Firecrackers, which she sells in December each year for New Year's celebrations. She must decide how many firecracker production lines to install. Each production line costs $1 million and operates for only two years after which it must be replaced. With one production line, Venus expects to sell $590,000 worth of firecrackers a year. With two production lines, she expects to sell $1,150,000 worth of firecrackers each year. And with three production lines, she expects to sell $1,680,000 worth of firecrackers a year. The interest rate is 5 percent a year. How many production lines does Venus install? Explain your answer.

12. Vulcan Balloon Rides must decide how many balloons to operate. Each balloon costs $10,000 and must be replaced after three years of service. With one balloon, Vulcan expects to sell $5,900 worth of rides a year. With two balloons, it expects to sell $11,500 worth of rides each year. And with three balloons, it expects to sell $16,800 worth of rides a year. The interest

rate is 8 percent a year. How many balloons does Vulcan operate? Explain your answer.

*13. Greg has found an oil well in his back yard. A geologist estimates that a total of 10 million barrels can be pumped for a pumping cost of a dollar a barrel. The price of oil is $20 a barrel. How much oil does Greg sell each year? If you can't predict how much he will sell, what extra information would you need to be able to do so?

14. Orley has a wine cellar in which he keeps choice wines from around the world. What does Orley expect to happen to the prices of the wines he keeps in his cellar? Explain your answer. How does Orley decide which wine to drink and when to drink it?

*15. In problem 1, show on the figure the blueberry pickers'
   a. Economic rent.
   b. Opportunity cost.

16. In problem 2, draw a figure to show the blueberry pickers'
   a. Economic rent.
   b. Opportunity cost.

CRITICAL THINKING

1. 1. Study *Reading Between the Lines* on pp. 338–339 and answer the following questions:
   a. Why did the basketball players strike?
   b. Why don't the players sign a deal that gives them their entire marginal revenue product?
   c. Why do you think Michael Jordan retired? What does his retirement tell you about his opportunity cost of playing?
   d. Why didn't the Bulls offer Michael Jordan a deal that he couldn't refuse?

2. "We are running out of natural resources and must take urgent action to conserve our precious reserves." "There is no shortage of resources that the market cannot cope with." Debate these two views. List the pros and cons for each.

3. Why do we keep finding new reserves of oil? Why don't we do once-and-for-all a big survey that catalogs the earth's entire inventory of natural resources?

Chapter 16

Labor Markets

As you well know, college is not just a party. Those exams and problem sets require a lot of time and effort. Are they worth the sweat that goes into them? What is the payoff? Is it sufficient to make up for the years of tuition, room and board, and lost wages? (You could, after all, be working for pay now instead of slogging through this economics course.) ◆ Many workers belong to labor unions. Usually, union workers earn a higher wage than nonunion workers in comparable jobs. Why? How are unions able to get higher wages for their members than the wages that nonunion workers are paid? ◆ Among the most visible and persistent differences in earnings are those between men and women and between whites and minorities. White men, on the average, earn incomes that are one third higher than the incomes earned by black men and white women. Black men and white women earn more,

The Sweat of Our Brows

in descending order, than Hispanic men, black women, and Hispanic women, who earn only 58 cents for each dollar earned by the average white man. Certainly, a lot of individuals defy the averages. But why do minorities and women so consistently earn less than white men? Is it because of discrimination and exploitation? Or is it because of economic factors? Or is it a combination of the two? ◆ Equal pay legislation has resulted in comparable-worth programs that try to ensure that jobs of equivalent value receive the same pay regardless of the pay set by the market. Can comparable-worth programs bring economic help to women and minorities? ◆ We hear a lot these days about immigration. How does immigration affect the economic well-being of both immigrants and native Americans?

◆ In this chapter, we answer questions such as these by continuing our study of labor markets. We study the effects of education and training, labor unions, gender and race, comparable-worth laws, and immigration.

After studying this chapter, you will be able to:

■ Explain why college graduates earn more, on the average, than high school graduates

■ Explain why union workers earn higher wages than nonunion workers

■ Explain why, on the average, men earn more than women and whites earn more than minorities

■ Predict the effects of a comparable-worth program

■ Explain the effects of immigration on the wages of immigrants and native Americans

Skill Differentials

EVERYONE IS SKILLED, BUT THE VALUE THE market places on different types of skills varies a great deal. So differences in skills lead to large differences in earnings. For example, a clerk in a law firm earns less than a tenth of the earnings of the attorney he assists. An operating room assistant earns less than a tenth of the earnings of the surgeon she works with. Differences in skills arise partly from differences in education and partly from differences in on-the-job training. Differences in earnings between workers with varying levels of education and training can be explained by using a model of competitive labor markets. In the real world, there are many different levels and varieties of education and training. To keep our analysis as clear as possible, we'll study a model economy with two different skill levels and two types of labor: high-skilled labor and low-skilled labor. We'll study the demand for and supply of these two types of labor and see why there is a difference in their wages and what determines that difference. Let's begin by looking at the demand for the two types of labor.

The Demand for High-Skilled and Low-Skilled Labor

High-skilled workers can perform a variety of tasks that low-skilled workers would perform badly or perhaps could not even perform at all. Imagine an untrained, inexperienced person performing surgery or piloting an airplane. High-skilled workers have a higher marginal revenue product than low-skilled workers. As we learned in Chapter 15, a firm's demand for labor curve is the same as the marginal revenue product of labor curve.

Figure 16.1(a) shows the demand curves for high-skilled (D_H) and low-skilled labor (D_L). At any given level of employment, firms are willing to pay a higher wage rate to a high-skilled worker than to a low-skilled worker. The gap between the two wage rates measures the marginal revenue product of skill—for example, at an employment level of 2,000 hours, firms are willing to pay $12.50 for a high-skilled worker and only $5 for an low-skilled worker, a difference of $7.50 an hour. Thus the marginal revenue product of skill is $7.50 an hour.

The Supply of High-Skilled and Low-Skilled Labor

Skills are costly to acquire. Furthermore, a worker usually pays the cost of acquiring a skill before benefiting from a higher wage. For example, attending college usually leads to a higher income, but the higher income is not earned until after graduation. These facts imply that the acquisition of a skill is an investment. To emphasize the investment nature of acquiring a skill, we call that activity an investment in human capital. **Human capital** is the accumulated skill and knowledge of human beings.

The opportunity cost of acquiring a skill includes actual expenditures on such things as tuition and room and board and also a cost in the form of lost or reduced earnings while the skill is being acquired. When a person goes to school full time, that cost is the total earnings forgone. However, some people acquire skills on the job. Such skill acquisition is called on-the-job training. Usually, a worker undergoing on-the-job training is paid a lower wage than one doing a comparable job but not undergoing training. In such a case, the cost of acquiring the skill is the difference between the wage paid to a person not being trained and that paid to a person being trained.

Supply Curves of High-Skilled and Low-Skilled Labor

The position of the supply curve of high-skilled workers reflects the cost of acquiring the skill. Figure 16.1(b) shows two supply curves: one for high-skilled workers and the other for low-skilled workers. The supply curve for high-skilled workers is S_H, and that for low-skilled workers is S_L.

The high-skilled workers' supply curve lies above the low-skilled workers' supply curve. The vertical distance between the two supply curves is the compensation that high-skilled workers require for the cost of acquiring the skill. For example, suppose that the quantity of low-skilled labor supplied is 2,000 hours at a wage rate of $5 an hour. This wage rate compensates the low-skilled workers mainly for their time on the job. Consider next the supply of high-skilled workers. To induce 2,000 hours of high-skilled labor to be supplied, firms must pay a wage rate of $8.50 an hour. This wage rate for high-skilled labor is higher than that for low-skilled labor because high-skilled labor must be compensated not only for the time on the job but also for the time and other costs of acquiring the skill.

FIGURE 16.1

Skill Differentials

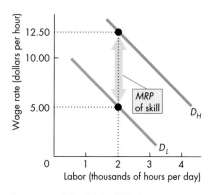

(a) Demand for high-skilled and low-skilled labor

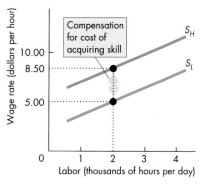

(b) Supply of high-skilled and low-skilled labor

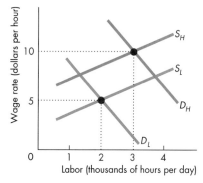

(c) Markets for high-skilled and low-skilled labor

Part (a) illustrates the marginal revenue product of skill. Low-skilled workers have a marginal revenue product that gives rise to the demand curve marked D_L. High-skilled workers have a higher marginal revenue product than low-skilled workers. Therefore the demand curve for high-skilled workers, D_H, lies to the right of D_L. The vertical distance between these two curves is the marginal revenue product of the skill.

Part (b) shows the effects of the cost of acquiring skills on the supply curves of labor. The supply curve for low-skilled

workers is S_L. The supply curve for high-skilled workers is S_H. The vertical distance between these two curves is the required compensation for the cost of acquiring a skill.

Part (c) shows the equilibrium employment and the wage differential. Low-skilled workers earn a wage rate of $5 an hour, and 2,000 hours of low-skilled labor are employed. High-skilled workers earn a wage rate of $10, and 3,000 hours of high-skilled labor are employed. The wage rate for high-skilled workers always exceeds that for low-skilled workers.

Wage Rates of High-Skilled and Low-Skilled Labor

To work out the wage rates of high-skilled and low-skilled labor, we have to bring together the effects of skill on the demand and supply of labor.

Figure 16.1(c) shows the demand curves and the supply curves for high-skilled and low-skilled labor. These curves are exactly the same as those plotted in parts (a) and (b). Equilibrium occurs in the market for low-skilled labor where the supply and demand curves for low-skilled labor intersect. The equilibrium wage rate is $5 an hour, and the quantity of low-skilled labor employed is 2,000 hours. Equilibrium in the market for high-skilled workers occurs where the supply and demand curves for high-skilled workers intersect. The equilibrium wage rate is $10 an hour, and the quantity of high-skilled labor employed is 3,000 hours.

As you can see in part (c), the equilibrium wage rate of high-skilled labor is higher than that of low-skilled labor. This outcome occurs for two reasons: First, high-skilled labor has a higher marginal revenue product than low-skilled labor, so at a given wage rate, the quantity of high-skilled labor demanded exceeds that of low-skilled labor. Second, skills are costly to acquire, so at a given wage rate, the quantity of high-skilled labor supplied is less than that of low-skilled labor. The wage differential (in this case, $5 an hour) depends on both the marginal revenue product of the skill and the cost of acquiring it. The higher the marginal revenue product of the skill, the larger is the vertical distance between the demand curves. The more costly it is to acquire a skill, the larger is the vertical distance between the supply curves. The higher the marginal revenue product of the skill and the more costly it is to acquire, the larger is the wage differential between high-skilled and low-skilled workers.

Do Education and Training Pay?

Figure 16.2 shows that there are large and persistent differences in earnings based on the degree of education and training. This figure also highlights the second main source of earnings differences: age. Age is strongly correlated with experience and the degree of on-the-job training a person has had. So as a person gets older, up to middle age, earnings increase.

Rates of return on high school and college education have been estimated to be in the range of 5 to 10 percent a year after allowing for inflation, which suggest that a college degree is a better investment than almost any other that a person can undertake.

Education is an important source of earnings differences. But there are others, and one of them is labor unions. Let's see how unions affect wages and why union wages tend to exceed nonunion wages.

FIGURE 16.2

Education and Earnings

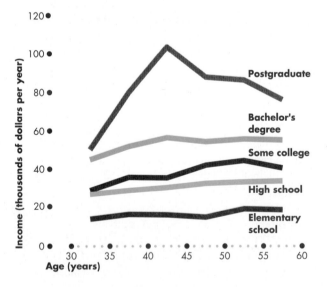

Earnings of male employees at various ages and with varying school levels are shown. Earnings increase with length of education. For postgraduates, earnings peak in the middle forties. For other groups, earnings peak in the middle fifties. These differences show the importance of experience and education in influencing skill differentials.

Source: U.S. Bureau of the Census, *Money Income in the United States 1995* and *Current Population Reports Consumer Income*, Series P-60, (1996).

Union-Nonunion Wage Differentials

WAGE DIFFERENTIALS CAN ARISE FROM MONOPOLY power in the labor market. Just as monopoly producers can restrict output and raise price, so a monopoly owner of a resource can restrict supply and raise the price of the resource.

The main source of monopoly power in the labor market is the labor union. A **labor union** is an organized group of workers whose purpose it is to increase wages and influence other job conditions for its members. The union seeks to restrict competition and, as a result, increases the price at which labor is traded.

There are two main types of union: craft unions and industrial unions. A **craft union** is a group of workers who have a similar range of skills but work for many different firms in many different industries and regions. Examples are the carpenters' union and the electrical workers union (IBEW). An **industrial union** is a group of workers who have a variety of skills and job types but work for the same industry. The United Auto Workers (UAW) and the United Steelworkers of America (USWA) are industrial unions.

Most unions are members of the AFL-CIO. The AFL-CIO was created in 1955 when two labor organizations combined: the American Federation of Labor (AFL), which was founded in 1886 to organize craft unions, and the Congress of Industrial Organizations (CIO), founded in 1938 to organize industrial unions. The AFL-CIO provides many services to member unions, such as training union organizers and acting as a national voice in the media and in the political arena.

Unions vary enormously in size. Craft unions are the smallest, and industrial unions are the biggest. Figure 16.3 shows the 12 largest unions in the United States—measured by number of members. Union strength peaked in the 1950s, when 35 percent of the nonagricultural work force belonged to unions. That percentage has declined steadily since 1955 and is now only 12 percent. Changes in union membership, however, have been uneven. Some unions have declined dramatically, while others, especially those in the government sector such as the American Federation of State, County and Municipal Employees, have increased in strength.

Union organization is based on a subdivision known as the local. The *local* is a subunit of a union

FIGURE 16.3

Unions with the
Largest Membership

Teamsters

State, County, and Municipal Employees

Service Employees (SEIU)

Food and Commercial Workers (UFCW)

Auto Workers (UAW)

Electrical Workers (IBEW)

Teachers (AFT)

Communication Workers (CWA)

Machinists and Aerospace (IAM)

Steelworkers (USWA)

Carpenters

Laborers

Unions

0   300   600   900   1,200   1,500

Number of members (thousands)

Each of the 12 largest labor unions in the United States, shown here, has more than 350,000 members.

Source: U.S. Bureau of the Census, *Statistical Abstract of the United States: 1996,* 116th edition, p. 436, Table 682.

that organizes the individual workers. In craft unions, the local is based on a geographical area; in industrial unions, the local is based on a plant or an individual firm.

There are three possible forms of organization for a local: an open shop, a closed shop, or a union shop. An *open shop* is an arrangement in which workers can be employed without joining the union—there is no union restriction on who can work in the "shop." A *closed shop* is an arrangement in which only union members can be employed by a firm. Closed shops have been illegal since the passage of the Taft-Hartley Act in 1947. A *union shop* is an arrangement in which a firm can hire nonunion workers, but in order for such workers to remain employed, they must join the union within a brief period specified by the union.

Union shops are illegal in the 20 states that have passed right-to-work laws. A *right-to-work law* allows an individual to work at any firm without joining a union.

Unions negotiate with employers or their representatives in a process called **collective bargaining**. The main weapons available to the union and the employer in collective bargaining are the strike, the lockout, and the use of replacement workers. A *strike* is a group decision to refuse to work under prevailing conditions. A *lockout* is a firm's refusal to operate its plant and employ its workers. Each party uses the threat of a strike, lockout, or the use of replacement workers to try to get an agreement in its own favor. Sometimes, when the two parties in the collective bargaining process cannot agree on the wage rate or other conditions of employment, they agree to submit their disagreement to binding arbitration. *Binding arbitration* is a process in which a third party—an arbitrator—determines wages and other employment conditions on behalf of the negotiating parties.

Although they are not labor unions in a legal sense, professional associations act similarly to labor unions. A *professional association* is an organized group of professional workers such as lawyers, dentists, or physicians (an example of which is the American Medical Association—AMA). Professional associations control entry into the professions and license practitioners, ensuring the adherence to minimum standards of competence. But they also influence the compensation and other labor market conditions of their members.

Union's Objectives and Constraints

A union has three broad objectives that it strives to achieve for its members:

1. To increase compensation
2. To improve working conditions
3. To expand job opportunities

Each of these objectives contains a series of more detailed goals. For example, in seeking to increase members' compensation, a union operates on a variety of fronts: wage rates, fringe benefits, retirement pay, and such things as vacation allowances. In seeking to improve working conditions, a union is concerned with occupational health and safety as well as the environmental quality of the workplace. In seeking to expand job opportunities, a union tries to get greater job security for existing union members and to find ways of creating additional jobs for them.

A union's ability to pursue its objectives is restricted by two sets of constraints—one on the supply side of the labor market and the other on the demand side. On the supply side, the union's activities are limited by how well it can restrict nonunion workers from offering their labor in the same market as union labor. The larger the fraction of the work force controlled by the union, the more effective the union can be in this regard. It is difficult for unions to operate in markets where there is an abundant supply of willing nonunion labor. For example, the market for farm labor in southern California is very tough for a union to organize because of the ready flow of nonunion, often illegal, labor from Mexico. At the other extreme, unions in the construction industry can better pursue their goals because they can influence the number of people who can obtain skills as electricians, plasterers, and carpenters. The professional associations of dentists and physicians are best able to restrict the supply of dentists and physicians. These groups control the number of qualified workers by controlling either the examinations that new entrants must pass or entrance into professional degree programs.

On the demand side of the labor market, the union faces a tradeoff that arises from firms' profit-maximizing decisions. Because labor demand curves slope downward, anything a union does that increases the wage rate or other employment costs decreases the quantity of labor demanded.

Despite the difficulties they face, unions do operate in competitive labor markets. Let's see how they do so.

Unions in a Competitive Labor Market

When a union operates in an otherwise competitive labor market, it seeks to increase wages and other compensation and to limit employment reductions by increasing demand for the labor of its members. That is, the union tries to take actions that shift the demand curve for its members' labor rightward.

Figure 16.4 illustrates a competitive labor market that a union enters. The demand curve is D_C, and the supply curve is S_C. Before the union enters the market, the wage rate is $7 an hour and 100 hours of labor are employed.

Now suppose that a union is formed to organize the workers in this market. The union can attempt to increase wages in this market in two ways. It can

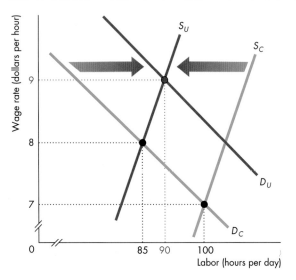

FIGURE 16.4

A Union in a Competitive Labor Market

In a competitive labor market, the demand curve is D_C and the supply curve is S_C. Competitive equilibrium occurs at a wage rate of $7 an hour with 100 hours employed. By restricting employment below the competitive level, the union shifts the supply of labor to S_U. If the union can do no more than that, the wage rate will increase to $8 an hour, but employment will fall to 85 hours. If the union can increase the demand for labor (by increasing the demand for the good produced by union members or by raising the price of substitute labor) and shift the demand curve to D_U, then it can increase the wage rate still higher, to $9 an hour, and achieve employment of 90 hours.

try to restrict the supply of labor, or it can try to stimulate the demand for labor. First, look at what happens if the union has sufficient control over the supply of labor to be able to artificially restrict that supply below its competitive level—to S_U. If that is all the union is able to do, employment falls to 85 hours of labor and the wage rate rises to $8 an hour. The union simply picks its preferred position along the demand curve that defines the tradeoff it faces between employment and wages.

You can see that if the union can only restrict the supply of labor, it raises the wage rate but decreases the number of jobs available. Because of this outcome unions try to increase the demand for labor and shift the demand curve rightward. Let's see what they might do to achieve this outcome.

How Unions Try to Change the Demand for Labor

Unless a union can take actions that change the demand for the labor that it represents, it has to accept the fact that a higher wage rate can be obtained only at the price of lower employment.

The union tries to operate on the demand for labor in two ways. First, it tries to make the demand for union labor less elastic. Second, it tries to increase the demand for union labor. Making the demand for labor less elastic does not eliminate the tradeoff between employment and wages, but it does make the tradeoff less unfavorable. If a union can make the demand for labor less elastic, it can increase the wage rate at a lower cost in terms of lost employment opportunities. But if the union can increase the demand for labor, it might even be able to increase both the wage rate and the employment opportunities of its members.

Some of the methods used by a union to increase the demand for the labor of its members are to:

■ Increase the marginal product of union members

■ Encourage import restrictions

■ Support minimum wage laws

■ Support immigration restrictions

■ Increase demand for the good produced

Unions try to increase the marginal product of their members, which in turn increases the demand for their labor, by organizing and sponsoring training schemes, by encouraging apprenticeship and other on-the-job training activities, and by professional certification.

One of the best examples of import restrictions is the support by the United Auto Workers union (UAW) for import restrictions on foreign cars.

Unions support minimum wage laws to increase the cost of employing low-skilled labor. An increase in the wage rate of low-skilled labor leads to a decrease in the quantity demanded of low-skilled labor and to an increase in demand for high-skilled union labor, a substitute for low-skilled labor.

Restrictive immigration laws decrease the supply and increase the wage rate of low-skilled workers. As a result, the demand for high-skilled union labor increases.

Because the demand for labor is a derived demand, an increase in the demand for the good produced increases the demand for union labor. The best examples of attempts by unions in this activity are in the textile and auto industries. The garment workers' union urges us to buy union-made clothes, and the UAW asks us to buy only American cars made by union workers.

Figure 16.4 illustrates the effects of an increase in the demand for the labor of a union's members. If the union can also take steps that increase the demand for labor to D_U, it can achieve an even bigger increase in the wage rate with a smaller fall in employment. By maintaining the restricted labor supply at S_U, the union increases the wage rate to $9 an hour and achieves an employment level of 90 hours of labor.

Because a union restricts the supply of labor in the market in which it operates, its actions increase the supply of labor in nonunion markets. Workers who can't get union jobs must look elsewhere for work. This increase in supply in nonunion markets lowers the wage rate in those markets and further widens the union-nonunion wage differential.

The Scale of Union-Nonunion Wage Differentials

We have seen that unions can influence the wage rate by restricting the supply of labor and increasing the demand for labor. How much of a difference to wage rates do unions make in practice?

Union wage rates are, on the average, 30 percent higher than nonunion wage rates. In mining and financial services, union and nonunion wages are similar. In services, manufacturing, and transportation, the differential is between 11 and 19 percent. In wholesale and retail trades, the differential is 28 percent, and in construction, it is 65 percent.

But these union-nonunion wage differentials don't give a true measure of the effects of unions. In some industries, union wages are higher than nonunion wages because union members do jobs that involve greater skill. Even without a union, those workers receive a higher wage. To calculate the effects of unions, we have to examine the wages of unionized and nonunionized workers who do nearly identical work. The evidence suggests that after allowing for skill differentials, the union-nonunion wage differential lies between 10 percent and 25 percent. For example, airline pilots who belong to the Air Line

Pilots' Association earn about 25 percent more than nonunion pilots with the same level of skill.

Let's now turn our attention to the case in which employers have considerable influence in the labor market.

Monopsony

A **monopsony** is a market in which there is a single buyer. This market type is unusual but it does exist. With the growth of large-scale production over the last century, large manufacturing plants such as coal mines, steel and textile mills, and car manufacturers became the major employer in some regions, and in some places a single firm employed almost all the labor. Today, in some parts of the country, managed health-care organizations are the major employer of health-care professionals. These firms have monopsony power.

In monopsony, the employer determines the wage rate and pays the lowest wage at which it can attract the labor it plans to hire. A monopsony makes a bigger profit than a group of firms that compete with each other for their labor. Let's find out how they achieve this outcome.

Like all firms, a monopsony has a downward-sloping marginal revenue product curve, which is *MRP* in Fig. 16.5. This curve tells us the extra revenue the monopsony receives by selling the output produced by an extra hour of labor. The supply of labor curve is *S*. This curve tells us how many hours are supplied at each wage rate. It also tells us the minimum wage for which a given quantity of labor is willing to work.

A monopsony recognizes that to hire more labor, it must pay a higher wage; equivalently, by hiring less labor, it can pay a lower wage. Because a monopsony controls the wage rate, the marginal cost of labor exceeds the wage rate. The marginal cost of labor is shown by the curve *MCL*. The relationship between the marginal cost of labor curve and the supply curve is similar to the relationship between the marginal cost and average cost curves that you studied in Chapter 11. The supply curve is like the average cost of labor curve. In Fig. 16.5, the firm can hire 49 hours of labor for a wage rate of just below $4.90 an hour. The firm's total labor cost is $240. But suppose that the firm hires 50 hours of labor. It can hire the 50 hours of labor for $5 an hour. The total cost of labor is now $250 an hour. So, hiring the 50th hour of labor increases the cost of labor from $240 to $250, which

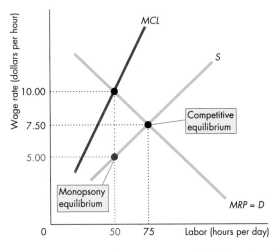

FIGURE 16.5

A Monopsony Labor Market

A monopsony is a market structure in which there is a single buyer. A monopsony in the labor market has marginal revenue product curve *MRP* and faces a labor curve *S*. The marginal cost of labor curve is *MCL*. Making the marginal cost of labor equal to marginal revenue product maximizes profit. The monopsony hires 50 hours of labor and pays the lowest wage for which that labor will work, which is $5 an hour.

is a $10 increase. The marginal cost of labor is $10 an hour. The curve *MCL* shows the $10 marginal cost of hiring the 50th hour of labor.

To calculate the profit-maximizing quantity of labor to hire, the firm sets the marginal cost of labor equal to the marginal revenue product of labor. That is, the firm wants the cost of the last worker hired to equal the extra total revenue brought in. In Fig. 16.5, this outcome occurs when the monopsony employs 50 hours of labor. What is the wage rate that the monopsony pays? To hire 50 hours of labor, the firm must pay $5 an hour, as shown by the supply of labor curve. So each worker is paid $5 an hour. But the marginal revenue product of labor is $10 an hour, which means that the firm makes an economic profit of $5 on the last hour of labor that it hires. Compare this outcome with that in a competitive labor market. If the labor market shown in Fig. 16.5 were competitive, equilibrium would occur at the point of intersection of the demand curve and the supply curve. The wage rate would be $7.50 an hour, and 75 hours of labor a day would be employed. So, compared with a competitive labor market, a monopsony decreases both the wage rate and the level of employment.

The ability of a monopsony to lower the wage rate and employment level and make an economic profit depends on the elasticity of the labor supply. The more elastic the supply of labor, the less opportunity a monopsony has to cut wages and employment and make an economic profit.

Monopsony Tendencies   Today, monopsony is rare. Workers can commute long distances to a job, so most people have more than one potential employer. But firms that are dominant employers in isolated communities do face an upward-sloping supply of labor curve and so have a marginal cost of labor that exceeds the wage rate. But in such situations, there is also, usually, a union. Let's see how unions and monopsonies interact.

Monopsony and Unions   When we studied monopoly in Chapter 13, we discovered that a single seller in a market is able to determine the price in that market. We have just studied monopsony—a market with a single buyer—and discovered that in such a market, the buyer is able to determine the price. Suppose that a union starts to operate in a monopsony labor market. A union is like a monopoly. It controls the supply of labor and acts like a single seller of labor. If the union (monopoly seller) faces a monopsony buyer, the situation is one of **bilateral monopoly**. In bilateral monopoly, the wage rate is determined by bargaining between the two sides. Let's study the bargaining process.

In Fig. 16.5, if the monopsony is free to determine the wage rate and the level of employment, it hires 50 hours of labor for a wage rate of $5 an hour. But suppose that a union represents the workers and can, if necessary, call a strike. Also suppose that the union agrees to maintain employment at 50 hours but seeks the highest wage rate the employer can be forced to pay. That wage rate is $10 an hour. That is, the wage rate equals the marginal revenue product of labor. It is unlikely that the union will get the wage rate up to $10 an hour. But it is also unlikely that the firm will keep the wage rate down to $5 an hour. The monopsony firm and the union bargain over the wage rate, and the result is an outcome between $10 an hour (the maximum that the union can achieve) and $5 an hour (the minimum that the firm can achieve).

The actual outcome of the bargaining depends on the costs that each party can inflict on the other as a result of a failure to agree on the wage rate. The firm can lock out its workers and threaten to use replacement workers, and the workers can shut the plant by striking. Each party knows the other's strength and knows what it will lose if it does not agree to the other's demands. If the two parties are equally strong and they realize it, they will split the difference and agree to a wage rate of $7.50 an hour. If one party is stronger than the other—and both parties know that—the agreed wage will favor the stronger party. Usually, an agreement is reached without a strike or a lockout. The threat—knowledge that such an event can occur—is usually enough to bring the bargaining parties to an agreement. But when a strike or lockout does occur, it is often because one party has misjudged the costs each party can inflict on the other.

Minimum wage laws have interesting effects in monopsony labor markets. Let's study these effects.

Monopsony and the Minimum Wage

In a competitive labor market, a minimum wage that exceeds the equilibrium wage decreases employment (see Chapter 7, pp. 133–134). In a monopsony labor market, a minimum wage can *increase* both the wage rate and employment. Let's see how.

Figure 16.6 shows a monopsony labor market in which the wage rate is $5 an hour and 50 hours of labor are employed. A minimum wage law is passed that requires employers to pay at least $7.50 an hour. The monopsony in Fig. 16.6 now faces a perfectly elastic supply of labor at $7.50 an hour up to 75 hours. Above 75 hours, a higher wage than $7.50 an hour must be paid to hire additional hours of labor. Because the wage rate is a fixed $7.50 an hour up to 75 hours, the marginal cost of labor is also constant at $7.50 up to 75 hours. Beyond 75 hours, the marginal cost of labor rises above $7.50 an hour. To maximize profit, the monopsony sets the marginal cost of labor equal to its marginal revenue product. That is, the monopsony hires 75 hours of labor at $7.50 an hour. The minimum wage law has made the supply of labor perfectly elastic and made the marginal cost of labor the same as the wage rate up to 75 hours. The law has not affected the supply of labor curve or the marginal cost of labor at employment levels above 75 hours. The minimum wage law has succeeded in raising the wage rate by $2.50 an hour and increasing the amount of labor employed by 25 hours a day.

FIGURE 16.6
Minimum Wage in Monopsony

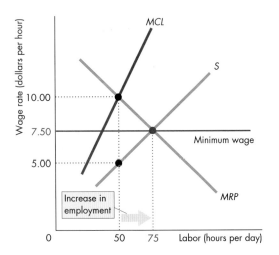

In a monopsony labor market, the wage rate is $5 an hour and 50 hours are hired. If a minimum wage law increases the wage rate to $7.50 an hour, employment increases to 75 hours.

REVIEW QUIZ

- Why are the wage rates of high-skilled workers greater than those of low-skilled workers?
- What are the main methods that labor unions use to increase the wage rates of their members above the levels of nonunion wages rates?
- What is a monopsony and why is a monopsony able to pay a lower wage rate than a competitive firm?
- What is the effect of a minimum wage in a monopsony? What is the effect of a minimum wage in a competitive labor market? Why are the two effects different?

You now understand two sources of wage differentials: skill differentials and the actions of labor unions. These two sources of wage differences are easy to see and to analyze. The third source of wage differentials, sex and race, is harder to explain but it is the most sensitive of the sources of income differentials.

Wage Differentials Between Sexes and Races

THE OBJECTIVE OF THIS SECTION IS TO SHOW you how to use economic analysis to address a controversial and emotionally charged issue. Figure 16.7 gives a quick view of the earnings differences that exist between the sexes and the races and also shows how those differences have evolved since 1955. The wages of each race and sex group are expressed as a percentage of the wages of white men. In 1997, the most recent year for which we have data, these percentages ranged from 75 for white women to 53 for women of Hispanic origin.

Why do the differentials shown in Fig. 16.7 exist? Do they arise because there is discrimination against women and members of minority races, or is there some other explanation? These controversial questions generate an enormous amount of passion. It is not my

FIGURE 16.7
Sex and Race Differentials

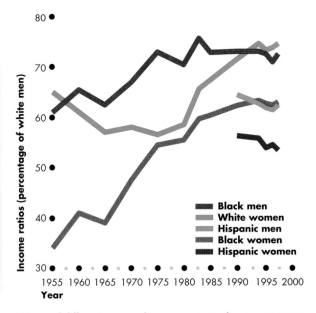

Wages of different race and sex groups are shown as percentages of white male wages. These differentials have persisted over many years, but their magnitudes have changed.

Source: U.S. Bureau of the Census, Statistical Abstract of the United States: 1998, 118th edition.

intention to make you angry, but that might happen as an unintended consequence of this discussion.

We are going to examine four possible explanations for earnings differences:

- Job types
- Discrimination
- Differences in human capital
- Differences in the degree of specialization

Job Types

Some of the sex differences in wages arise because men and women do different jobs and the jobs that men do are better paid. But today, greater numbers of women are entering jobs such as those of bus driver, police officer, and construction worker, traditionally done by men. The trend is strongest in professions such as architecture, medicine, law, and accounting. The percentage of enrollments in university courses in these subjects for women has increased from less than 20 percent in 1970 to as high as 50 percent today.

But many women and minorities earn less than white men even when they do the same job. One possible reason is discrimination. Let's see how discrimination might affect wage rates.

Discrimination

Suppose that black females and white males have identical abilities as investment advisors. Figure 16.8 shows the supply curves of black females, S_{BF} (in part a), and of white males, S_{WM} (in part b). The marginal revenue product of investment advisors, as shown by the two curves labeled *MRP* in parts (a) and (b), is the same for both groups.

If everyone is free of prejudice about race and sex, the market determines a wage rate of $40,000 a year for both groups of investment advisors. But if the customers of investment houses are prejudiced against women and minorities, this prejudice is reflected in wages and employment.

Suppose that the marginal revenue product of the black females, when discriminated against, is MRP_{DA}, where *DA* stands for "discriminated against." Suppose that the marginal revenue product for white males, the group discriminated in favor of, is MRP_{DF}, where *DF* stands for "discriminated in favor of." With these marginal revenue product curves, black females earn $20,000 a year, and only 1,000 will work as investment advisors. White males earn $60,000 a year, and 3,000 of them will work as investment advisors.

FIGURE 16.8
Discrimination

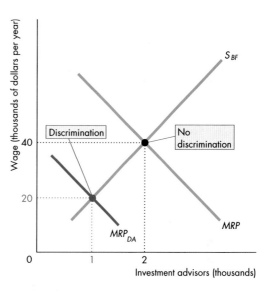

(a) Black females

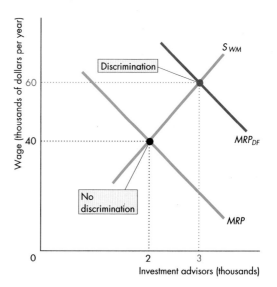

(b) White males

With no discrimination, the wage rate is $40,000 a year and 2,000 of each group are hired. With discrimination against blacks and women, the marginal revenue product curve in part (a) is MRP_{DA} and in part (b) it is MRP_{DF}. The wage rate for black women falls to $20,000 a year, and only 1,000 are employed. The wage rate for white men rises to $60,000 a year, and 3,000 are employed.

Economists disagree about whether prejudice actually causes wage differentials, and one line of reasoning suggests that it does not. In the example you've just studied, customers who buy from white men pay a higher service charge for investment advice than do the customers who buy from black women. This price difference acts as an incentive to encourage people who are prejudiced to buy from the people against whom they are prejudiced. This force could be so strong as to eliminate the effects of discrimination altogether. Suppose, as is true in manufacturing, that a firm's customers never meet its workers. If such a firm discriminates against women or minorities, it cannot compete with firms that hire these groups because its costs are higher than those of the nonprejudiced firms. So only those firms that do not discriminate survive in a competitive industry.

Let's now turn to the third source of wage differences: differences in human capital.

Differences in Human Capital

The more human capital a person possesses, the more that person earns, other things being equal. We measure human capital by using three indicators, which are:

1. Years of schooling
2. Years of work experience
3. Number of job interruptions

A larger proportion of men (25 percent) than women (20 percent) have completed 4 years of college. And a larger proportion of whites (24 percent) than blacks (13 percent) have completed a BA degree or higher. These differences in education levels among the sexes and the races are becoming smaller. But they have not yet been eliminated.

The more years of work and the fewer job interruptions a person has had, the higher is the person's wage, other things being equal. Interruptions to a career reduce the effectiveness of job experience and bring lower incomes. Historically, job interruptions are more serious for women than for men because women's careers have been interrupted for bearing and rearing children. This factor is a possible source of lower wages, on the average, for women. But maternity leave and day-care facilities are making career interruptions for women less common.

A final source of earnings differences, the relative degree of specialization of women and men, affects women's incomes adversely.

Differences in the Degree of Specialization

Couples must choose how to allocate their time between working for a wage and doing jobs in the home such as cooking, cleaning, shopping, organizing vacations and, most important, bearing and rearing children. Let's look at the choices of Bob and Sue.

Bob might specialize in earning an income and Sue in taking care of the home. Or Sue might specialize in earning an income and Bob in taking care of the home. Or both of them might earn an income and share home production jobs.

The allocation they choose depends on their preferences and on the earning potential of each of them. The choice of an increasing number of households is for each person to diversify between earning an income and doing some home chores. But in most households, Bob will specialize in earning an income and Sue will both earn an income and take care of the home. It seems likely that with this allocation, Bob will earn more than Sue. If Sue devotes time and effort to ensuring Bob's mental and physical well-being, the quality of Bob's market labor will be higher than if he were diversified. If the roles were reversed, Sue would be able to supply market labor that earns more than Bob.

To test whether the degree of specialization accounts for earnings differentials between the sexes, economists have studied two groups: "never married" men and "never married" women. The available evidence suggests that, on the average, when they have the same amount of human capital—measured by years of schooling, work experience, and career interruptions—the wages of these two groups are not significantly different.

R E V I E W   Q U I Z

- What are the possible reasons for wage rate differences between the sexes and the races?
- How might differences in the degree of specialization result in the wage rates earned by men being higher than those earned by women?

Because labor markets bring unequal incomes, governments intervene in these markets to modify the wages and employment levels that they determine. One potentially far-reaching intervention is comparable-worth laws. Let's see how these laws work.

Comparable-Worth Laws

CONGRESS PASSED THE EQUAL PAY ACT IN 1963 and the Civil Rights Act in 1964. These acts require equal pay for equal work. They are attempts to remove the most blatant forms of discrimination between men and women and between whites and minorities. But many people believe that these acts do not go far enough. In their view, getting paid the *same* wage for doing the *same* job is just the first step that has to be taken. What's important is that jobs that are *comparable*—require the same levels of skills and responsibilities—receive the *same* wages, regardless of whether the jobs are done by men or women or by blacks or whites. Paying the same wage for different jobs that are judged to be comparable is called *comparable worth.*

Figure 16.9 shows how comparable-worth laws work. Part (a) shows the market for oil rig operators, and part (b) shows the market for school teachers. The marginal revenue product curves (MRP_R and

MRP_T) and the supply curves (S_R and S_T) are shown for each type of labor. Competition generates a wage rate W_R for oil rig operators and W_T for teachers.

Suppose it is decided that these two jobs are of comparable worth and that the courts enforce a wage rate of W_C for both groups. What happens? First, there is a shortage of oil rig operators. Oil rig companies are able to hire only S_R workers at the wage rate W_C. They cut back their production or build more expensive labor-saving oil rigs. Also the number of teachers employed decreases. But this decrease occurs because school boards demand fewer teachers. At the higher wage W_C, school boards demand only D_T teachers. The quantity of teachers supplied is S_T, and the difference between S_T and D_T is the number of unemployed teachers looking for jobs. These teachers eventually accept nonteaching jobs (which they don't like as much as teaching jobs), quite likely at a lower rate of pay than that of teachers.

Although comparable-worth laws can eliminate wage differences, they can do so only by incurring costly unintended consequences. They limit job

FIGURE 16.9
The Problem with Comparable Worth

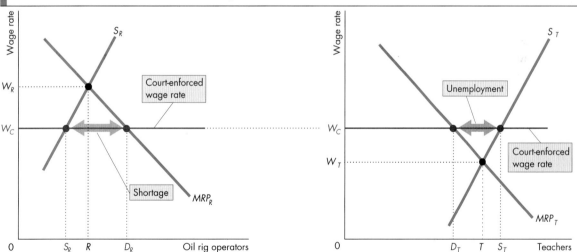

(a) Market for oil rig operators

Part (a) shows the demand for and supply of oil rig operators, MRP_R and S_R, and part (b) shows the demand for and supply of school teachers, MRP_T and S_T. The competitive equilibrium wage rate for oil rig operators is W_R, and that for teachers is W_T. If an evaluation of the two jobs finds that they have comparable worth and rules that the wage rate W_C be paid to

(b) Market for teachers

both types of workers, such a wage creates a shortage of oil rig operators and a surplus of teachers. Oil producers search for labor-saving ways of producing oil (that are more expensive), and teachers search for other jobs (that are less desirable to them and probably are less well paid).

opportunities and create unemployment among workers whose wages they raise. And they make it hard for employers to hire workers whose wages are held down. Only in the rare case of a monopsonistic labor market does equalizing wage rates not create permanent surpluses and shortages of skills. In this situation, a comparable-worth law works in a similar way to a minimum wage law.

Effective Wage Policies

We have now surveyed the major sources of wage differentials, and one stands out: the level of education. People with postgraduate degrees earn much more than college graduates, who in turn earn much more than high school graduates, who in turn carn morc than people who have not completed high school. This source of differences in earnings is the main one on which an effective policy can operate.

By pursuing the most effective education available in grade school, high school, and college and university, people can equip themselves with human capital that brings significantly higher earnings. But in today's rapidly changing world, education and human capital accumulation must be an ongoing enterprise. The most successful workers are those who are able to repeatedly retool and actively embrace each new technological advance. The least successful are those who get locked into a particular technology and are unable or unwilling to adapt when that technology becomes redundant.

So an effective wage policy is one that emphasizes the importance of ongoing education and training.

R E V I E W Q U I Z

- What is a comparable-worth law and what does it seek to achieve?
- Do comparable-worth laws eliminate wage differences? What other effects do comparable-worth laws have that benefit or harm lower-paid workers?
- What is the most effective policy that can eliminate wage differentials between men and women and between whites and minorities?

We're now going to turn to the final topic of this chapter: immigration.

Immigration

SIXTY MILLION PEOPLE, OR 1.2 PERCENT OF THE world's current population, have migrated from the country in which they were born. And close to one third of these immigrants live in the United States.[1] We'll study four questions about U.S. immigration:

- How many people immigrate into the United States, where do they come from, and what skills do they bring?
- How does immigration affect employment and wage rates of native-born Americans?
- How do new immigrants perform in the United States?
- What are the effects of immigrants on the government budget?

Scale, Origin, and Skills of U.S. Immigrants

Almost 800,000 legal immigrants have arrived in the United States during each of the last few years. More than a quarter of these new immigrants, plus a further 200,000 to 300,000 a year, have come from Mexico.

The scale and pattern of immigration have changed over the years. Figure 16.10(a) shows that immigration was huge during the late nineteenth century and the first 30 years of the twentieth century. It fell during the 1930s and 1940s but built up again after World War II. By the 1980s, a new large wave of immigration was under way.

Figure 16.10(b) shows that before World War II, most immigration was either directly from Europe or indirectly from Europe via Canada. But gradually, over the decades, Asia, Mexico, and other American countries replaced Europe and Canada as the places of origin of new immigrants.

The skills that immigrants bring with them vary enormously. But the averages are interesting and important. We can measure skills of immigrants in two ways, by earnings and education levels. Based on earnings, newly arrived immigrants are less productive, on the average, than native Americans. And over the years, they have been getting less skilled relative

---

[1]This section on immigration draws extensively on George J. Borjas, "The Economics of Immigration," *Journal of Economic Literature*, Vol. XXXII (December 1994). pp. 1667–1717.

FIGURE 16.10

The Scale and Sources of U.S. Immigration

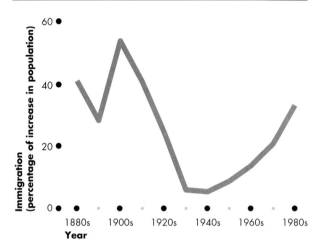

(a) Amount of immigration

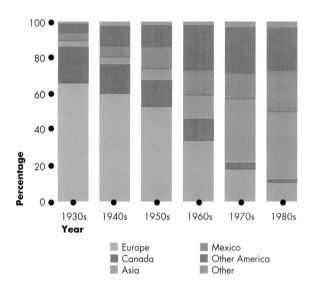

(b) Region of origin of immigrants

Part (a) shows the scale of immigration into the United States, decade by decade, since the 1880s. After a big wave during the 50 years to 1930, immigration decreased. A new wave began after World War II, which continued to rise through the 1980s. Before 1930, almost all the immigrants came from Europe. But over the years, Asia and other American countries have replaced Europe as the main source of new immigrants.

to native Americans. New immigrants who arrived during the 1960s earned 17 percent less than comparable Americans. Those who arrived during the 1970s earned 28 percent less than native Americans. And those who arrived during the 1980s earned 32 percent less than native Americans. Based on education levels, immigrants are also becoming less skilled, relative to native Americans. The percentage of immigrants who have not completed high school has decreased, but only slightly, and stands at almost 40 percent. In contrast, the high school dropout rate for native Americans has decreased from 40 percent in 1970 to less than 15 percent today.

At the other end of the education spectrum, the percentage of immigrants who are college graduates has increased somewhat, but the percentage of native American college graduates has increased faster.

To summarize the anatomy of U.S. immigrants: They are increasingly from Asia and Latin America, and their skill level is lower than that of native Americans and has been getting relatively lower.

Immigrants and the Labor Market

Immigration increases the supply of labor. By so doing, it lowers the wage rates of existing workers. At the same time, it decreases the supply of labor and raises wage rates in the country the immigrants are leaving. Figure 16.11 shows these effects in the labor markets of the United States (part a) and Mexico (part b). The demand for labor in the United States is LD_{US}, and in Mexico, it is LD_M. Before immigration takes place, 125 million workers in the United States earn $15 an hour and 50 million workers in Mexico earn $1 an hour. (The numbers are hypothetical.)

With free movement, Mexicans enter the United States as long as, by doing so, they can increase their incomes. In this example, the labor force of the United States increases to 150 million and the wage rate falls to $8 an hour. In Mexico, the labor force decreases to 25 million and the wage rate rises to $8 an hour. When the wage rates are the same, there is no incentive for anyone to migrate between the two countries.

The outcome shown in Fig. 16.11 would be unlikely to occur because people would not vote for an open border immigration law. Instead, we vote for immigration laws that prevent the free movement of people and so prevent the outcome shown in Fig. 16.11.

But does immigration move wage rates in the directions shown in the figure? Does it lower the wages of existing workers? The answer is ambiguous.

FIGURE 16.11

Immigration and the Labor Market

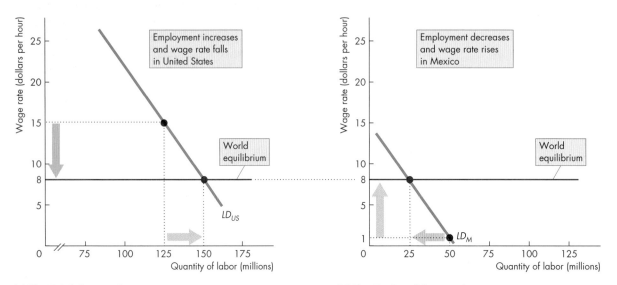

(a) The U.S. labor market

(b) The Mexican labor market

Part (a) shows the labor market in the United States. The demand for labor is LD_{US}, and with 125 million workers, the wage rate is $15 an hour. Part (b) shows the labor market in Mexico. The demand for labor is LD_M, and with 50 million workers, the wage rate is $1 an hour. With free movement of people between the two countries, people leave Mexico and migrate to the United States. Employment increases and the wage rate falls in the United States, and employment decreases and the wage rate rises in Mexico. The world equilibrium occurs when the wage rate is equal in the two countries, at $8 an hour.

It might lower wages. But it might raise them. Either way, the effect is probably small.

According to George Borjas, a leading authority on this topic, immigration might be partly responsible for the fall in the earnings of low-skilled Americans during the 1980s.

There are several reasons why immigration does not have the dramatic effect on domestic wages that Fig. 16.11 shows. First, immigrants bring not only a supply of labor but also a demand for goods and services. Consequently, firms expand and the demand for labor increases. This increase in the demand for labor limits the extent to which the wage rate falls. Second, some immigrants bring capital with them. This additional capital is invested in businesses and brings an increase in the demand for labor. Third, immigrants are not necessarily *substitutes* for domestic labor. They might be *complements* with it. For example, a shortage of low-skilled labor might cause a firm to close down and lay off its high-skilled workers.

Immigration might restore the ability of the firm to operate profitably and enable it to hire again.

For these three reasons, the effect of immigration on wage rates is smaller than the direct effect shown in Fig. 16.11.

Let's next look at the economic fortunes of the immigrants themselves.

How Do New Immigrants Perform in the United States?

We've seen that when a new immigrant arrives in the United States, he or she earns less, on the average, than similarly qualified native Americans. We've also seen that this earnings gap has been widening and is today close to one third. But what happens to immigrants in the years that follow their arrival?

The answer depends on when the immigrant arrived, the number of years elapsed since arriving, the ethnicity, and the language skills of the immigrant.

As a rule, immigrants' earnings grow more rapidly than the earnings of native Americans. That is, there is a tendency for immigrants' earnings to converge on and even to surpass the earnings of similar native Americans. But this tendency was stronger in the past than it is today. By 1990, immigrants who had arrived in the United States before 1970 had, on the average, reached income levels equal to those of native Americans. Those who had arrived before 1950 had income levels that averaged 26 percent *more* than the incomes of native Americans.

For more recent immigrant groups, there is still a tendency for incomes to grow faster than those of non-immigrants. But the starting gap is now so wide and the speed of convergence so slow that many new immigrants will never earn as much as their native equivalents.

This tendency for the immigrant to perform less well than a native American is more pronounced among Hispanic immigrants than among other ethnic groups. But it is also present among Asian immigrants.

Because the immigrant groups that perform least well are from countries in which English is not a major language, language skills might be playing a role. Studies of the influence of language on earnings agree with this suspicion. It has been estimated that immigrants who are proficient in the English language earn 17 percent more, on the average, than immigrants who are not proficient in English. This estimate, combined with the fact that an increasing percentage of immigrants have no English, explains some of the tendency for the most recent wave of immigrants to converge to non-immigrant earnings levels at a slower speed than that of earlier waves.

If the current group of immigrants might not catch up with the earnings of native Americans, what are the prospects for their children? Will they complete the convergence process? We do not know enough to be able to answer this question. But we do know that there is a strong correlation between the earnings of new immigrant families and the earnings of their children. Because of this correlation, there is a possiblity that convergence will continue to be slow.

Immigrants and the Government Budget

Since the mid-1960s, the United States has created a huge social welfare safety net. Do immigrants benefit more from our social programs than they contribute to them?

Immigrants have qualified for welfare assistance in increasing numbers over the past 20 years. In 1970, 6 percent of all native households and 5.9 percent of all immigrant households received some form of welfare. By 1990, these percentages were 7.4 for native households and 9.1 for immigrant households. Partly as a reaction to this trend, Congress passed legislation making it more difficult for immigrants to qualify for welfare and this new law might change the trend.

But there are huge differences in the extent to which different groups of immigrants use welfare. Those who rely most heavily on it are new immigrants from Cambodia, Laos, the Dominican Republic, and Vietnam.

But immigrants pay taxes. And their total tax payments are much greater than their welfare receipts. Data from the 1990 Census tell us that immigrants pay $85 billion in taxes and receive $24 billion in welfare benefits. Immigrants also impose other hard-to-quantify costs on the government, so we cannot say for sure what the net cost or benefit of immigration is for the government's budget.

R E V I E W Q U I Z

- Where do most of the immigrants to the United States come from? Has the number of immigrants increased or decreased in recent years?
- How does immigration influence wage rates? Is the effect small or large?
- How do the wage rates and skills of new immigrants compare with those of people who have been in the United States for some time?
- Do recent immigrants rely more on welfare than earlier waves of immigrants did? Why might this be so?

◆ *Reading Between the Lines* on pages 360–361 returns to the U.S. labor markets and looks at Navy's problem in enlisting the number of sailors that it demands. It examines different ways in which a labor market can cope with a shortage and achieve equilibrium.

In the next chapter, we're going to examine the distributions of income and wealth that result from the operation of labor markets and the markets for other productive resources.

A Labor Market in Action

THE NEW YORK TIMES, JANUARY 16, 1999

Enlistments Falling, Navy Lowers Education Standard

Facing a shortage of sailors at sea, the Navy announced today that it would have to lower educational standards for new recruits as part of a series of initiatives to increase enlistments. Since the end of the cold war, the Navy has required that 95 percent of new recruits have a high school diploma, but for the first time in a decade, it will require no more than 90 percent. ...

The difficulty in recruiting—which has also hit the Army and, to a lesser extent, the Air Force and the Marine Corps—has forced the Navy to send ships to sea with less than full crews. In recent weeks, the Navy disclosed today, it has had as many as 22,000 empty positions—or bunks—in its 327-ship fleet. ...

The services attribute the shortages in new recruits to a variety of factors, from a booming economy and low unemployment rate to the fact that 70 percent of young people go straight to college after finishing high school, compared with less than half a decade ago.

But the Navy's response is certain to provoke criticism that the service is lowering the standards of its enlisted sailors. The Army faced sharp attacks from Congress when it announced a similar change two years ago. The Marine Corps continues to require at least 95 percent of enlistees to have diplomas. The Air Force also has a minimum standard of 90 percent but for the last 15 years has never fallen below 99 percent. ...

The Navy, with 372,000 officers and enlisted personnel, needs 160,000 sailors to fill its ships at sea. The shortages have left some ships, including aircraft carriers and submarines, at less than 90 percent strength.

© 1999 *The New York Times*. Reprinted with permission. Further reproduction prohibited.

Essence of the Story

■ The Navy needs 160,000 sailors to fill its ships at sea but is unable to recruit this number and is 22,000 short.

■ Faced with this shortage, the Navy announced plans to lower educational standards for new recruits.

■ In the future, only 90 percent of new recruits will be required to have a high school diploma, down from the previous requirement of 95 percent of recruits.

■ The Navy says that the shortage of new recruits arises because the unemployment rate is low and 70 percent of young people go straight to college after finishing high school, more than double the rate of a decade ago.

■ But the Navy's decision is expected to provoke criticism of the falling standards.

Economic Analysis

- Figure 1 shows the current predicament of the Navy in the market for sailors.

- The Navy's demand for sailors is determined by their marginal revenue product and is shown by the demand curve *D*.

- The supply of sailors is determined by the decisions of high school students and high school graduates and is shown by the supply curve *S*.

- The current wage rate of new recruits averages $11,000 a year. (This information is not provided in the news article.)

- At the current wage rate, the quantity of labor demanded is 160,000 sailors, which is the quantity reported in the news article. The news article also reports a shortage of 22,000 sailors. So we can infer that the quantity of labor supplied at the current wage rate is 138,000 sailors.

- The Navy raises the wage rate or lowers the recruiting standards.

- Figure 2 shows what happens if the Navy raises the wage rate. The wage rises to the equilibrium level, which is $12,000 (an assumption). The quantity demanded decreases, and the quantity supplied increases.

- Figure 3 shows what happens if the Navy lowers the recruiting standards. Supply increases, and the supply curve shifts rightward. A lower educational standard decreases marginal product. The Navy reorganizes some tasks, the demand for sailors decreases, and the demand curve shifts leftward. The equilibrium quantity decreases to 150,000 sailors.

You're The Voter

- Would you vote for the lowering of recruiting standards in the Navy? Why or why not?

- Would you vote for an increase in funding for the Navy to enable it to offer a higher wage rate? Explain.

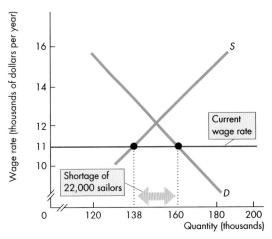

Figure 1 The Navy's predicament

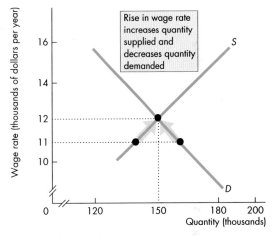

Figure 2 Solution 1: Raise the wage rate

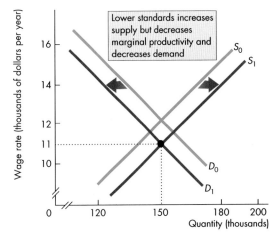

Figure 3 Solution 2: Lower the standards required

361

SUMMARY

KEY POINTS

Skill Differentials (pp. 344–346)

- Skill differentials arise from differences in marginal revenue products and because skills are costly to acquire.
- Wage rates of high-skilled and low-skilled labor are determined by demand and supply in the two labor markets.

Union-Nonunion Wage Differentials (pp. 346–352)

- Labor unions influence wages by controlling the supply of labor.
- In competitive labor markets, unions obtain higher wages only at the expense of lower employment, but they try to influence the demand for labor.
- In a monopsony a union can increase the wage rate without sacrificing employment.
- Bilateral monopoly occurs when a union confronts a single buyer of labor. The wage rate is determined by bargaining between the two parties.
- Union workers earn 10 to 25 percent more than comparable nonunion workers.

Wage Differentials Between Sexes and Races (pp. 352–354)

- Earnings differentials between men and women and between whites and minorities arise from differences in types of jobs, discrimination, differences in human capital, and differences in degree of specialization.
- Well-paid jobs are more likely to be held by white men than by women and minorities. But discrimination is hard to measure objectively.
- Historically, white males have had more human capital than other groups. Human capital differences arising from schooling differences have been falling but they have not been eliminated.
- Differentials based on work experience have kept women's pay below that for men because women's careers have traditionally been interrupted more frequently than those of men. This difference is smaller today than in the past.

- Differentials arising from different degrees of specialization are probably important and might persist. Men have traditionally been more specialized in market activity, on the average, than women.

Comparable-Worth Laws (pp. 355–356)

- Comparable-worth laws determine wages by using objective characteristics rather than what the market will pay to assess the value of different types of jobs.
- Determining wages through comparable worth will result in a decrease in the number of people employed in jobs on which the market places a lower value and shortages of workers that the market values more highly.

Immigration (pp. 356–359)

- U.S. immigration has followed waves. A big increase occurred during the 1970s and 1980s. The origin of immigrants has shifted from Europe to Asia and Latin America. Immigrants have become less skilled than in the past.
- Immigration lowers wage rates but only slightly.
- Immigrants enter with low earnings but in the past their earnings have converged on those of native Americans. This convergence has slowed. Immigrants now use welfare more than in the past.

KEY FIGURES

KEY TERMS

PROBLEMS

*1. The demand for and supply of low-skilled labor are given by the following figure:

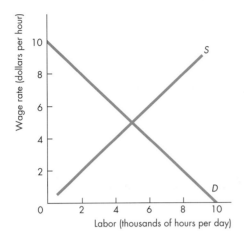

Workers can be trained—can obtain a skill—and their marginal productivity doubles. (The marginal product at each employment level is twice the marginal product of a low-skilled worker.) But the cost of acquiring the skill adds $2 an hour to the wage that must be offered to attract high-skilled labor. What is:
a. The wage rate of low-skilled labor?
b. The quantity of low-skilled labor employed?
c. The wage rate of high-skilled labor?
d. The quantity of high-skilled labor employed?

2. The demand for and supply of low-skilled labor are given by the following figure:

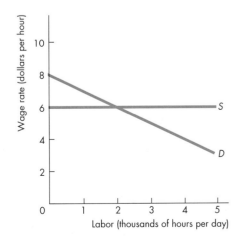

Workers can be trained—can obtain a skill—and their marginal productivity increases by $5 an hour. (The marginal product at each employment level is $5 greater than that of a low-skilled worker.) The cost of acquiring the skill adds $3 an hour to the wage that must be offered to attract high-skilled labor. What is:
a. The wage rate of low-skilled labor?
b. The quantity of low-skilled labor employed?
c. The wage rate of high-skilled labor?
d. The quantity of high-skilled labor employed?
e. Why does the wage rate increase by exactly the cost of acquiring the skill?

*3. Suppose in problem 1 that high-skilled workers become unionized and the union restricts the amount of high-skilled labor to 5,000 hours. What is:
a. The wage rate of high-skilled workers?
b. The wage differential between low- and high-skilled workers?

4. Suppose in problem 2 that high-skilled workers become unionized and the union restricts the amount of high-skilled labor to 2,000 hours. What is:
a. The wage rate of high-skilled workers?
b. The wage differential between low- and high-skilled workers?

*5. If in problem 1, the government introduces a minimum wage rate of $6 an hour for low-skilled workers
a. What is the wage rate paid to low-skilled workers?
b. How many hours of low-skilled labor gets hired each day?

6. If in problem 2, the government introduces a minimum wage rate of $8 an hour for low-skilled workers
a. What is the wage rate paid to low-skilled workers?
b. How many hours of low-skilled labor gets hired each day?

*7. A monopsony gold-mining firm operates in an isolated part of the Amazon basin. The table shows the firm's labor supply schedule (columns 1 and 2) and total product schedule (columns 2 and 3). The price of gold is $1.40 per grain.

Wage rate (dollars per day)	Workers (number per day)	Quantity of gold produced (grains per day)
5	0	0
6	1	10
7	2	25
8	3	45
9	4	60
10	5	70
11	6	75

a. What wage rate does the company pay?
b. How many workers does the gold mine hire?
c. What is the marginal revenue product at the quantity of labor employed?

8. A monopsony logging firm operates in an isolated part of the Alaska. The table shows the firm's labor supply schedule (columns 1 and 2) and total product schedule (columns 2 and 3). The price of logs is $1.50 per ton.

Wage rate (dollars per day)	Workers (number per day)	Quantity of logs produced (tons per day)
2.50	0	0
3.00	1	7
3.50	2	13
4.00	3	18
4.50	4	22
5.00	5	25
5.50	6	27

a. What wage rate does the company pay?
b. How many workers does the logging firm hire?
c. What is the marginal revenue product at the quantity of labor employed?

*9. In problem 7, explain the effects of a court-enforced wage rate above the equilibrium wage rate on employment and unemployment.

10. In problem 8, explain the effects of the arrival of new immigrants on the demand for labor, the supply of labor, and the wage rate.

CRITICAL THINKING

1. Study the *Reading Between the Lines* on pp. 360–361 and then answer the following questions:
   a. What problem did the Navy face in the labor market at the time the news article was written?
   b. What was the Navy's proposed solution?
   c. Explain the predicted effects of the Navy's proposed solution.
   d. Describe the changes that might occur on a Navy ship after the adoption of lower recruiting standards. (Hint: Be imaginative. Think about the types of jobs that a person who has not graduated from high school might not be able to do well that a high school graduate can handle.)
   e. Explain the market solution to the Navy's problem.
   f. Describe the changes that might occur on a Navy ship if the wage rises to the equilibrium level with no change in recruiting standards. (Hint: Think about how a ship might cope with fewer sailors.)

2. Use the link on the Parkin Web site to visit the AFL-CIO and look at the "Don't Buy List." Choose an item on this list that interests you and explain why the AFL-CIO recommends a boycott of this item. Explain how not buying this item increases either the wage rate or employment level of union members.

3. Use the link on the Parkin Web site to visit the Bureau of Labor Statistics (BLS) and obtain data for the past three months on usual weekly earnings and the level of employment.
   a. What has happened to earnings and employment during the past three months?
   b. Try to explain the changes by using the tools of demand and supply.

4. "Wages should be determined on the basis of what is fair." Debate this proposition. Set out the cases for and against. Then determine and explain your verdict.

5. Suppose that all nations permitted free migration. Which nations would be the biggest suppliers of immigrants and why? Which nations would attract most immigrants and why? Describe the world economy 10 years after the start of this process.

Chapter 17

Inequality, Redistribution, and Health Care

Fifty-three stories above Manhattan is a penthouse with unobstructed views of Central Park, the Hudson River, and the city skyline. Its price? $4 million. "Now, you can be one of the enviable few to fly Around the World by Supersonic Concorde ... for just $32,000 per person," trumpets an advertisement in *The New Yorker*. Not quite within view of the $4 million penthouse, but not far from it, is Fort Washington Armory in Upper Manhattan. What was opened as a temporary shelter in 1981 permanently houses close to 1,000 men who sleep in one football-field-sized room. These men live on the edge of despair and in fear of AIDS and other life-threatening diseases. ◆ Why are some people exceedingly rich while others are very poor and own almost nothing? Are the rich getting richer and the poor getting poorer? Does the information we have about the inequality of income and wealth in the United States paint an accurate picture or a misleading one? How do taxes and social security, welfare, and health-care programs influence economic inequality?

Riches and Rags

◆ In this chapter, we study economic inequality—its extent, its sources, and its potential remedies. We look at taxes and government programs that redistribute incomes and study their effects on economic inequality in the United States. We also study the different ways in which health care can be delivered and their effects on economic efficiency and equality. Let's begin by looking at some facts about economic inequality.

After studying this chapter, you will be able to:

- Describe the inequality in income and wealth in the United States

- Explain why wealth inequality is greater than income inequality

- Explain how economic inequality arises

- Explain the effects of taxes and social security and welfare programs on economic inequality

- Explain the effects of health-care reform on economic inequality

Economic Inequality in the United States

WE STUDY INEQUALITY BY LOOKING AT THE distribution of income and the distribution of wealth. A household's income is the amount that it receives in a given period. A household's wealth is the value of the things it owns at a point in time. We measure income inequality by looking at the percentage of total income received by a given percentage of households. And we can measure wealth inequality by looking at the percentage of total wealth owned by a given percentage of households.

In 1997, the average U.S. household income, before tax and not counting government transfers, was close to $50,000. But there was considerable inequality around that number. The poorest 20 percent of households received 3.6 percent of total income while the richest 20 percent received 49.4 percent of total income.

The wealth distribution is even more unequal. Average household wealth in 1992 was $193,000. But the poorest 90 percent of households owned about one third of total wealth. The next 9 percent owned another third of total wealth. And the wealthiest 1 percent of households owned the remaining one third of total wealth.

Lorenz Curves

Figure 17.1 shows the distributions of income and wealth. The table divides households into five groups, called *quintiles*, that range from the lowest income (row *a*) to highest income (row *e*). It shows the percentages of income of each of these groups. For example, row *a* tells us that the lowest quintile of households receives 3.6 percent of total income. The table also shows the *cumulative* percentages of households and income. For example, row *b* tells us that the lowest two quintiles (lowest 40 percent) of households receive 12.5 percent of total income (3.6 percent for the lowest quintile and 8.9 percent for the next lowest). The data on cumulative income shares are illustrated by a Lorenz curve. A **Lorenz curve** graphs the cumulative percentage of income against the cumulative percentage of households.

If income were distributed equally to every household, the cumulative percentages of income received by the cumulative percentages of households

FIGURE 17.1

Lorenz Curves for Income and Wealth

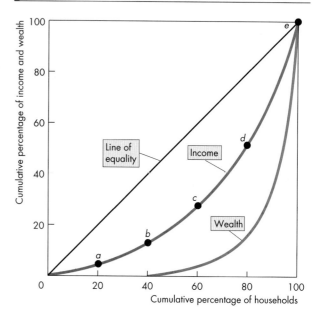

Households		Income		Wealth	
Percentage	Cumulative percentage	Percentage	Cumulative percentage	Percentage	Cumulative percentage
a Lowest 20	20	3.6	3.6	0	0
b Second 20	40	8.9	12.5	0	0
c Third 20	60	15.0	27.5	4	4
d Fourth 20	80	23.2	50.7	11	15
e Highest 20	100	49.4	100.0	85	100

The cumulative percentages of income and wealth are graphed against the cumulative percentage of households. If income and wealth were distributed equally, each 20 percent of households would have 20 percent of the income and wealth—the line of equality. Points *a* through *e* on the Lorenz curve for income correspond to the rows of the table. The Lorenz curves show that income and wealth are unequally distributed and wealth more unequally distributed than income. (Note there is a rounding approximation in the data.)

Sources: U.S. Bureau of the Census, Current Population Reports, P-60-200, *Money Income in the United States (With Separate Data on Valuation of Noncash Benefits),* U.S. Government Printing Office, Washington, D.C. 1998, and Robert D. Avery and Arthur B. Kennickell, "Measurement of Household Saving Obtained from First Differencing Wealth Estimates" (Washington, D.C.: Federal Reserve Board, February 1990).

would fall along the straight line labeled "Line of equality." The actual distribution of income is shown by the Lorenz curve labeled "Income." The closer the Lorenz curve is to the line of equality, the more equal is the distribution.

Figure 17.1 also shows a Lorenz curve for wealth. This curve is based on the distribution described in the table. Total wealth is divided approximately equally between the wealthiest 1 percent, the next 9 percent, and the other 90 percent of households.

You can see from the two Lorenz curves in Fig. 17.1 that the Lorenz curve for wealth is much farther away from the line of equality than the Lorenz curve for income is, so the distribution of wealth is much more unequal than the distribution of income.

Inequality over Time

Figure 17.2 shows how the distribution of income has changed since 1970.

- The share of income received by the richest 20 percent of households has increased.
- The share of income received by all four other groups of households has decreased.

The higher-income groups have gained because rapid technological change has increased the return to education. The lower-income groups have suffered for a variety of reasons; one of them is increased international mobility and competition that are keeping down the wages of the low skilled. The trends that are visible in Fig. 17.2 are real, but they are exaggerated after 1989 and more so after 1994 by a change in the method of measuring large incomes.

Who Are the Rich and the Poor?

The lowest-income household in the United States today is likely to be a black woman over 65 years of age who lives alone somewhere in the South and has fewer than eight years of elementary school education. The highest-income household in the United States today is likely to be a college-educated white married couple between 45 and 54 years of age living together with two children somewhere in the West.

These snapshot profiles are the extremes in Fig. 17.3. That figure illustrates the importance of education, size of household, marital status, age of householder, race, and region of residence in influencing the size of a household's income. The range of variation

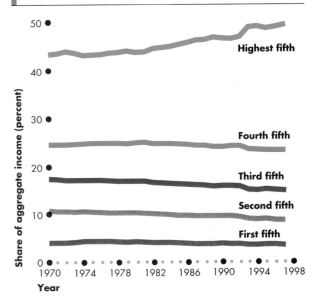

FIGURE 17.2

Trends in the Distribution of Income: 1950–1997

The distribution of income in the United States became more unequal between 1970 and 1997. The percentage of income earned by the highest fifth increased steadily through the 1970s and 1980s and sharply during the 1990s.

Source: U.S. Bureau of the Census, Current Population Reports, P-60-200, *Money Income in the United States (With Separate Data on Valuation of Noncash Benefits),* and Current Population Reports, *Consumer Income,* P-60-168 U.S. Government Printing Office, Washington, D.C. 1990 and 1998.

associated with education is the largest. On the average, people who have not completed grade 9 earn $15,400 a year, while people with a bachelor's degree or more earn an average of $60,000 a year. Four-person households have incomes that average more than $51,000 while one-person households have an average income of about $18,000. Single females, on the average, have incomes of $16,400 a year, while married couples earn an average joint income of $50,000 a year. The oldest and youngest households have lower incomes than middle-aged households. Black households have an average income of $23,500, while white households have an average income of just over $38,000. Finally, incomes are lowest in the South and highest in the Northeast. But incomes in the West and the Midwest are close to those in the Northeast and much higher than incomes in the South.

FIGURE 17.3

The Distribution of Income by Selected Household Characteristics in 1997

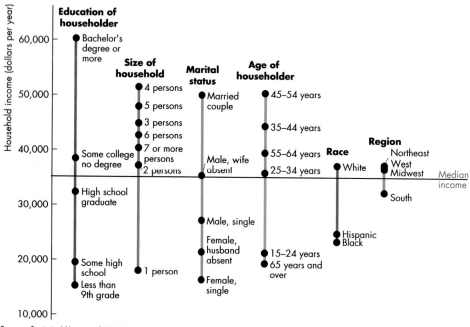

Education is the single biggest factor affecting household income distribution, but size of household, marital status, and age of householder are also important. Race and region of residence also play a role.

Sources: *Statistical Abstract of the United States: 1998*, 118th edition Table 740.

Poverty

Households at the low end of the income distribution are so poor that they are considered to be living in poverty. **Poverty** is a state in which a household's income is too low to be able to buy the quantities of food, shelter, and clothing that are deemed necessary. Poverty is a relative concept. Millions of people living in Africa and Asia survive on incomes of less than $400 a year. In the United States, the poverty level is calculated each year by the Social Security Administration. In 1997, the poverty level for a four-person household was an income of $16,813. In that year, 35.6 million Americans lived in households that had incomes below the poverty level. Many of these households benefited from Medicare and Medicaid, two government programs that benefit the poorest households and lift some of them above the poverty level.

The distribution of poverty by race is unequal: 11 percent of white households, 27.1 percent of Hispanic origin households, and 26.5 percent of black households are below the poverty level. Poverty is also influenced by household status. Almost 32 percent of households in which the householder is a female and no husband is present are below the poverty level, while fewer than 12 percent of other households are.

Poverty rates in the United States are falling, and especially for black families.

REVIEW QUIZ

- Which is distributed more unequally: income or wealth?
- Has the distribution of income become more equal or more unequal?
- Which group of households has experienced the largest increase in income share during the past 20 years?
- The influences on a household's income are age of householder, education of members, household size, marital status, race, and region of residence. Rank the items in decreasing order of importance.

Comparing Like with Like

To DETERMINE THE DEGREE OF INEQUALITY, we compare one person's economic situation with another person's. But what is the correct measure of a person's economic situation? Is it income or is it wealth? And is it *annual* income, the measure we've used so far in this chapter, or income over a longer time period—for example, over a family's lifetime?

Wealth Versus Income

Wealth is a stock of assets, and income is the flow of earnings that results from the stock of wealth. Suppose that a person owns assets worth $1 million—has a wealth of $1 million. If the rate of return on assets is 5 percent a year, then this person receives an income of $50,000 a year from those assets. We can describe this person's economic condition by using either the wealth of $1 million or the income of $50,000. When the rate of return is 5 percent a year, $1 million of wealth equals $50,000 of income in perpetuity. Wealth and income are simply different ways of looking at the same thing.

But in Fig. 17.1, the distribution of wealth is much more unequal than the distribution of income. Why? It is because the wealth data measure tangible assets and exclude the value of human capital while the income data measure income from both tangible assets and human capital.

Table 17.1 illustrates the consequence of omitting human capital from the wealth data. Lee has twice the wealth and twice the income of Peter. But Lee's human capital is less than Peter's—$200,000 compared with $499,000. And Lee's income from human capital of $10,000 is less than Peter's income from human capital of $24,950. Lee's nonhuman capital is larger than Peter's—$800,000 compared with $1,000. And Lee's income from nonhuman capital of $40,000 is larger than Peter's income from nonhuman capital of $50.

The national wealth and income surveys record their incomes of $50,000 and $25,000, respectively, which indicate that Lee is twice as well off as Peter. And they record their tangible assets of $800,000 and $1,000, respectively, which indicate that Lee is 800 times as wealthy as Peter. Because the national survey of wealth excludes human capital, the income distribution is a more accurate measure of economic inequality than the wealth distribution.

TABLE 17.1

Capital, Wealth, and Income

	Lee		Peter	
	Wealth	**Income**	**Wealth**	**Income**
Human capital	200,000	10,000	499,000	24,950
Nonhuman capital	800,000	40,000	1,000	50
Total	$1,000,000	$50,000	$500,000	$25,000

When wealth is measured to include the value of human capital as well as nonhuman capital, the distribution of income and the distribution of wealth display the same degree of inequality.

Annual or Lifetime Income and Wealth?

A typical family's income changes over time. It starts out low, grows to a peak when the family's workers reach retirement age, and then falls after retirement. Also, a typical family's wealth changes over time. Like income, it starts out low, grows to a peak at the point of retirement, and falls after retirement.

Suppose we look at three families that have identical lifetime incomes. One family is young, one is middle aged, and one is retired. The middle-aged family has the highest income and wealth, the retired family has the lowest, and the young family falls in the middle. The distributions of annual income and wealth in a given year are unequal, but the distributions of lifetime income and wealth are equal. So some of the measured inequality arises from the fact that different families are at different stages in the life cycle. Inequality of annual incomes overstates the degree of lifetime inequality.

R E V I E W   Q U I Z

- Is the distribution of income or the distribution of wealth the more accurate indicator of the degree of inequality? Why is one of these a better measure than the other?
- Is the distribution of lifetime income or the distribution of annual income the more accurate indicator of the degree of inequality? Why is one of these a better measure than the other?

Let's look at the sources of economic inequality.

Resource Prices, Endowments, and Choices

A FAMILY'S INCOME DEPENDS ON THREE THINGS:

- Resource prices
- Resource endowments
- Choices

The distribution of income depends on the distribution of these three things across the population. The first two are outside our individual control and are determined by market forces and by history. From the viewpoint of each one of us, they appear to be determined by luck. The last item is under individual control. We make choices that influence our incomes. Let's look at the three factors that influence incomes.

Resource Prices

Everyone faces the same interest rates in capital markets, but people face differing wage rates in the labor market. And the labor market is the biggest single source of income for most people. To what extent do variations in wage rates account for the unequal distribution of income? The answer is that they do to some extent, but wage differences cannot account for all the inequality. High-skilled workers earn about 3.5 times as much as low-skilled workers. Highly paid professionals earn about 3 times as much as high-skilled workers. So the highest-paid professionals earn around 10 times what the least skilled are paid.

Differences in resource endowments are another.

Resource Endowments

There is a large amount of variety in a family's endowments of capital and of human abilities. Differences in capital make a big contribution to differences in incomes. But so do differences in ability.

Physical and mental abilities (some inherited, some learned) have a normal, or bell-shaped, distribution—like the distribution of heights. The distribution of ability across individuals is a major source of inequality in income and wealth. But it is not the only source. If it were, the distributions of income and wealth would look like the bell-shaped curve that describes the distribution of heights. In fact, these distributions are skewed toward high incomes and look like the curve in Fig. 17.4. This figure shows income on the horizontal axis and the percentage of households receiving each income on the vertical axis. In 1997, the median household income—the income that separates households into two groups of equal size—was $37,000. The most common income—called the mode income—is less than the median income. The mean income—also called the average income—is greater than the median income and in 1997 was $50,000. A skewed distribution like the one shown in Fig. 17.4 is one in which many more families have incomes below the average than above it, a large number of families have low incomes, and a small number of families have high incomes. The distribution of (nonhuman) wealth has a shape similar to that of the distribution of income but is even more skewed.

The skewed distribution of income cannot be explained by the bell-shaped distribution of individual abilities. It results from the choices that people make.

FIGURE 17.4

The Distribution of Income

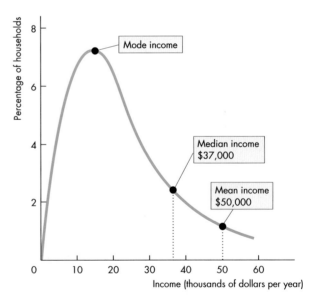

The distribution of income is unequal and is not symmetric around the mean income. There are many more households with incomes below the mean income than above it. Also, the distribution has a long, thin upper tail representing a small number of households that earn very large incomes.

Choices

While many poor families feel trapped and do not have many options open to them, a family's income and wealth depend partly on the choices that its members make. You are going to discover that the choices people make exaggerate the differences among them and make the distribution of income more unequal than the distribution of abilities, as well as making the distribution of income skewed.

Wages and the Supply of Labor   Other things remaining the same, the quantity of labor that a person supplies usually increases as that person's wage rate increases. A person who has a low wage rate chooses to work fewer hours than a person who has a high wage rate.

Because the quantity of labor supplied increases as the wage rate increases, the distribution of income is more unequal than the distribution of hourly wages and skewed, like the one shown in Fig. 17.4. People whose wage rates are below the average tend to work fewer hours than the average, and their incomes bunch together below the average. People whose wage rates are above the average tend to work more hours than the average, and their incomes stretch out above the average.

Saving and Bequests   Another choice that results in unequal distributions in income and wealth is the decision to save and make bequests. A *bequest* is a gift from one generation to the next. The higher a family's income, the more that family tends to save and accumulate wealth across generations.

Saving and bequests are not inevitably a source of increased inequality. If a family saves to redistribute an uneven income over the life cycle and enable consumption to be constant, the act of saving decreases the degree of inequality. If a lucky generation that has a high income saves a large amount and makes a bequest to a generation that is unlucky, this act of saving also decreases the degree of inequality. But two features of bequests make intergenerational transfers of wealth a source of increased inequality:

■ Debts cannot be bequeathed
■ Mating is assortative

Debts Cannot Be Bequeathed   Although a person may die with debts that exceed assets—with negative wealth—debts cannot be forced onto other family members. Because a zero inheritance is the smallest inheritance that anyone can receive, bequests can only add to future generations' wealth and income potential.

Most people inherit nothing or a very small amount. A few people inherit enormous fortunes. As a result, bequests make the distribution of income persistently more unequal than the distribution of ability and job skills. A family that is poor in one generation is more likely to be poor in the next. A family that is wealthy in one generation is likely to be wealthy in the next. But there is a tendency for income and wealth to converge, across generations, to the average. Although there can be long runs of good luck or bad luck, or good judgment or bad judgment, such long runs are uncommon across generations. But a feature of human behavior slows the convergence of wealth to the average and makes inequalities persist—assortative mating.

Assortative Mating   *Assortative mating* is the tendency for people to marry within their own socioeconomic class. In the vernacular, "like attracts like." Although there is a good deal of folklore that "opposites attract," perhaps such Cinderella tales appeal to us because they are so rare in reality. Marriage partners tend to have similar socioeconomic characteristics. Wealthy individuals seek wealthy partners. The consequence of assortative mating is that inherited wealth becomes more unequally distributed.

R E V I E W   Q U I Z

■ What role do wage rates, endowments, and choices play in creating income inequality?

■ What is the main reason that wage rates are unequal?

■ If the distribution of endowments is bell shaped, what makes the distribution of income skewed?

■ Which choices that people make generate the skew in the distribution of income?

■ How do bequests and assortative mating make the distribution of wealth more unequal and skewed?

We've now examined why inequality exists. Next, we're going to see how taxes and government programs redistribute income and wealth.

Income Redistribution

THE THREE MAIN WAYS THAT GOVERNMENTS IN the United States redistribute income are:

▪ Income taxes
▪ Income maintenance programs
▪ Subsidized services

Income Taxes

Income taxes may be progressive, regressive, or proportional. A **progressive income tax** is one that taxes income at a marginal rate that increases with the level of income. The term "marginal," applied to income tax rates, refers to the fraction of the last dollar earned that is paid in taxes. A **regressive income tax** is one that taxes income at a marginal rate that decreases with the level of income. A **proportional income tax** (also called a *flat-rate income tax*) is one that taxes income at a constant rate, regardless of the level of income.

The tax rates that apply in the United States are composed of two parts: federal and state taxes. Some cities, such as New York City, also have an income tax. There is variety in the detailed tax arrangements in the individual states, but the tax system, at both the federal and state levels, is progressive. The poorest working households receive money from the government through an earned income tax credit. The middle-income households pay 15 percent of each additional dollar they earn, and successively richer households pay 28 percent and 31 percent of each additional dollar earned.

Income Maintenance Programs

Three main types of programs redistribute income by making direct payments (in cash, services, or vouchers) to people in the lower part of the income distribution. They are:

■ Social security programs
■ Unemployment compensation
■ Welfare programs

Social Security The main social security program is OASDHI—Old Age, Survivors, Disability, and Health Insurance. Monthly cash payments to retired or disabled workers or their surviving spouses and children are paid for by compulsory payroll taxes on both employers and employees. In 1998, total social security expenditure was more than $350 billion, and 41 million people received an average monthly social security check of $721.

The other component of social security is Medicare, which provides hospital and health insurance for the elderly and disabled.

Unemployment Compensation To provide an income to unemployed workers, every state has established an unemployment compensation program. Under these programs, a tax is paid based on the income of each covered worker and such a worker receives a benefit when he or she becomes unemployed. The details of the benefits vary from state to state.

Welfare Programs The purpose of welfare is to provide incomes for people who do not qualify for social security or unemployment compensation. They are

1. Supplementary Security Income (SSI) program, designed to help the neediest elderly, disabled, and blind people
2. Temporary Assistance for Needy Households (TANF) program, designed to help households who have inadequate financial resources
3. Food Stamp program, designed to help the poorest households obtain a basic diet
4. Medicaid, designed to cover the costs of medical care for households receiving help under the SSI and TANF programs

Subsidized Services

A great deal of redistribution takes place in the United States through the provision of subsidized services—services provided by the government at prices far below the cost of production. The taxpayers who consume these goods and services receive a transfer in kind from the taxpayers who do not consume them. The two most important areas in which this form of redistribution takes place are education—both kindergarten through grade 12 and college and university—and health care.

In 1998–99, students enrolled in the University of California system paid annual tuition fees of $3,766. The cost of providing a year's education at the

University of California at Berkeley or San Diego in 1998–99 was $15,000. So households with a member enrolled in these institutions received a benefit from the government of more than $11,000 a year.

Government provision of health-care services has grown to equal the scale of private provision. Programs such as Medicaid and Medicare bring high-quality and high-cost health care to millions of people who earn too little to buy such services themselves.

The Scale of Income Redistribution

A household's income in the absence of government redistribution is called *market income*. We can measure the scale of income redistribution by calculating the percentage of market income paid in taxes and the percentage received in benefits at each income level. The data available include redistribution through taxes and cash and noncash benefits to welfare recipients. They do not include the value of subsidized services such as college, which might decrease the total amount of redistribution from the rich to the poor.

Figure. 17.5 shows the scale of redistribution. The blue Lorenz curve describes the market distribution of income. It is the same as that in Fig. 17.1. The red Lorenz curve shows the distribution of income after all taxes and benefits including Medicaid and Medicare benefits. The distribution after taxes and benefits is much less unequal than the market distribution. The lowest 20 percent of households receive only 3.6 percent of market income but 13 percent of income after taxes and benefits. The highest 20 percent of households receive 49.4 percent of market income but only 31 percent of income after taxes. Redistribution increases the share of total income received by the lowest 60 percent of households. It decreases the share of total income received by the highest 40 percent of households.

Another measure of the scale of redistribution is provided by the sources of income at different points of the income distribution. The poorest 20 percent of households receive more than 70 percent of their income from the government. The second 20 percent receive 43 percent of their income from the government. In contrast, the richest 20 percent receive almost nothing from the government but receive a third of their income from capital—interest and dividends from financial assets. The proportion of income from capital for the other 80 percent of households is remarkably constant at about 8 percent.

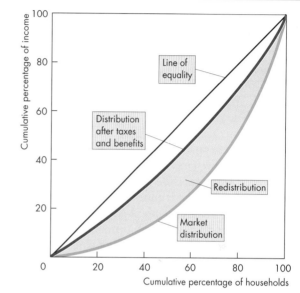

FIGURE 17.5
Income Redistribution

Taxes and income maintenance programs reduce the degree of inequality that the market generates. In 1997, the 20 percent of households with the lowest incomes received net benefits that increased their share of total income from 3.6 percent to 13 percent. The 20 percent of households with the highest incomes paid taxes that decreased their share of total income from 49.4 percent to 31 percent of total income.

Sources: U.S. Bureau of the Census, Current Population Reports, P–60–193, *Money Income in the United States (With Separate Data on Valuation of Noncash Benefits),* U.S. Government Printing Office, Washington, D.C, 1998, and the author's calculations.

The Big Tradeoff

The redistribution of income creates what has been called the **big tradeoff**, a tradeoff between equity and efficiency. The big tradeoff arises because redistribution uses scarce resources and weakens incentives.

A dollar collected from a rich person does not translate into a dollar received by a poor person. Some of it gets used up in the process of redistribution. Tax-collecting agencies such as the Internal Revenue Service and welfare-administering agencies (as well as tax accountants and lawyers) use skilled labor, computers, and other scarce resources to do their work. The bigger the scale of redistribution, the greater is the opportunity cost of administering it.

But the cost of collecting taxes and making welfare payments is a small part of the total cost of redistribution. A bigger cost arises from the inefficiency—deadweight loss—of taxes and benefits. Greater equality can be achieved only by taxing productive activities such as work and saving. Taxing people's income from their work and saving lowers the after-tax income they receive. This lower income makes them work and save less, which in turn result in smaller output and less consumption not only for the rich who pay the taxes but also for the poor who receive the benefits.

It is not only taxpayers who face weaker incentives to work. Benefit recipients also face weaker incentives. In fact, under the welfare arrangements that prevailed before the 1996 reforms, the weakest incentives to work were those faced by families that benefited from welfare. When a welfare recipient got a job, benefits were withdrawn and eligibility for programs like Medicaid ended, so the family in effect paid a tax of more than 100 percent on its earnings. This arrangement locked poor families in a welfare trap.

So the scale and methods of income redistribution must pay close attention to the incentive effects of taxes and benefits. Let's look at the way lawmakers are tackling the big tradeoff today.

A Major Welfare Challenge

The poorest people in the United States (see pp. 367–368) are young women who have not completed high school, have a child (or children), live without a partner, and are more likely black or Hispanic than white. These young women and their children present a major welfare challenge.

First, their numbers are large. In 1992 (the most recent year for which census data are available), there were 10 million single-mother families. This number is almost 30 percent of families with never-married children under 21. In 1991 (again the most recent year with census data), these families were owed $18 billion in child support. Of this amount, $6 billion was not paid and a quarter of the women received no support from their absent partners.

The long-term solution to the poverty problem that these people face is education and job training—acquiring human capital. The short-term solution is welfare. But welfare must be designed to minimize the disincentive to pursue the long-term goal. This is what the current welfare program in the United States tries to do.

Passed in 1996, *The Personal Responsibility and Work Opportunities Reconciliation Act* created the Temporary Assistance for Needy Families (TANF) program. TANF is a block grant paid to the states to administer payments to individuals. It is not an open-ended entitlement program. An adult member of a family receiving assistance must either work or perform community service. And there is a five-year limit for assistance.

These measures go a long way toward removing some serious poverty problems while being sensitive to the potential inefficiency of welfare. But they don't go as far as some economists want to go. Let's look at a more radical reform of welfare: the negative income tax.

Negative Income Tax

A negative income tax is *not* on the political agenda. But it is popular among economists, and it is the subject of several real-world experiments.

A **negative income tax** gives every family a *guaranteed minimum annual income* and taxes *all* income above the guaranteed minimum at a fixed *marginal tax rate*. Suppose the guaranteed minimum annual income is $10,000 and the marginal tax rate is 25 percent. A family with no market income receives the $10,000 guaranteed minimum income from the government. This family "pays" income tax of *minus* $10,000, hence the name *negative* income tax. A family with a market income of $40,000 also receives the $10,000 guaranteed minimum income from the government. But it also pays $10,000—25 percent of its market income—to the government. So this family pays no income tax. It has the break-even income. Families with a market income of between zero and $40,000 "pay" a negative income tax. They receive more from the government than they pay. A family with a market income of $60,000 receives the $10,000 guaranteed minimum income from the government, but it pays $15,000—25 percent of its market income—to the government. So this family pays income tax of $5,000. All families with incomes greater than $40,000 pay income tax to the government.

Figure 17.6 illustrates a negative income tax and compares it with our pre-1996 arrangements. In both parts of the figure, the horizontal axis measures *market income* and the vertical axis measures income *after* taxes are paid and benefits are received. The 45° line shows the hypothetical case of "no redistribution."

FIGURE 17.6

Comparing Traditional Programs and a Negative Income Tax

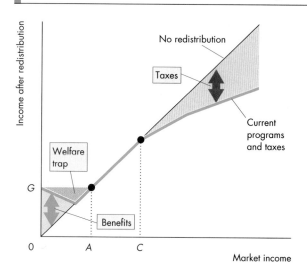

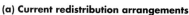

(a) Current redistribution arrangements

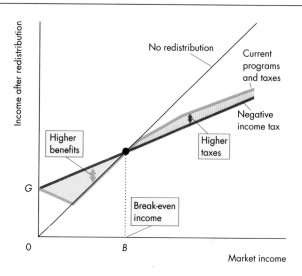

(b) A negative income tax

Part (a) shows traditional redistribution arrangements—the blue curve. Benefits of G are paid to those with no income. As incomes increase from zero to A, benefits are withdrawn, *lowering* income after redistribution below G and creating a welfare trap—the gray triangle. As incomes increase from A to C, there is no redistribution. As incomes increase above C, income taxes are paid at successively higher rates.

In part (b), a negative income tax gives a guaranteed annual income of G and decreases benefits at the same rate as the tax rate on incomes. The red line shows how market incomes translate into income after redistribution. Families with market incomes below B, the break-even income, receive net benefits. Those with market incomes above B pay net taxes.

Part (a) shows traditional redistribution arrangements—the blue curve. Benefits of *G* are paid to those with no income. As incomes increase from zero to *A*, benefits are withdrawn. This arrangement creates a *welfare trap*, shown as the gray triangle. It does not pay a person to work if the income he or she can earn is less than *A*. Over the income range *A* to *C*, each additional dollar of market income increases income after redistribution by a dollar. At incomes greater than *C*, income taxes are paid and at successively higher rates, so income after redistribution is smaller than market income.

Part (b) shows the negative income tax. The guaranteed annual income is *G,* and the break-even income is *B*. Families with market incomes below *B* receive an additional net benefit (blue area), and those with incomes above *B* pay additional taxes (red area). A negative income tax removes the welfare trap and gives greater encouragement to low-income families to seek more employment, even at a low

wage. It also overcomes many of the other problems arising from existing income maintenance programs.

R E V I E W   Q U I Z

- What are the four methods that governments in the United States use to redistribute income?
- How large is the scale of redistribution in the United States?
- What is the major welfare challenge and how is it being tackled in the United States today?
- What problem is a negative income tax designed to solve? Why don't we have a negative income tax?

Health and the cost of health care are major sources of inequality, and we now study the economics of health care and health-care reform.

Health-Care Reform

EXPENDITURE PER PERSON ON HEALTH CARE IS greater in the United States than in any other country. Also, the percentage of total income spent on health care in the United States exceeds that of any other country. An American who has a good job and the comprehensive health insurance that goes with it enjoys a high degree of security and receives the highest-quality health care. Let's look at the scale of spending on health care and at who does the spending.

Total spending on health care in the United States was 14 percent of total income in 1998 and, at its current trend, would reach 20 percent of total income by the early 2000s. The government meets 47 percent of the total health-care cost, and this share has increased from 25 percent in 1965, as Fig. 17.7

shows. The government's share of the cost is made up of its expenditures on Medicare and Medicaid ($356 billion in 1996) and the premiums it pays to private health-care insurance companies for government employees. The other 53 percent of the cost of health care is met by private health-care insurance (up from 25 percent of total payments in 1965 to 37 percent in 1991) and by direct payments by patients (*down* from 42 percent of total payments in 1965 to 17 percent in 1996).

Despite our large commitment of resources and our high quality of care, many people perceive health care in the United States to be in crisis. Why? There are two main problem areas:

1. Health-care costs appear to be out of control.
2. Private health-care insurance does not cover everyone.

Let's take a closer look at these problems.

Problem of Health-Care Costs

Health-care costs have increased more rapidly than consumer prices, on the average, as Fig. 17.8 shows. Two separate factors create the gap between the rate of increase in health-care costs and average price increases: the health-care cost gap.

First, health care is a labor-intensive personal service with limited scope for labor-saving technological change. Health-care labor costs—wage rates of medical workers from surgeons to janitors—generally increase at a faster rate than do average prices, and because there is limited scope for labor-saving changes in health-care technology, these higher labor costs are reflected in higher costs for the final health-care product.

Second, the main effect of the technological change that does take place in health care is to improve the quality of the product. For example, the applications of computer technology and advances in drugs have broadened the range of conditions that can be treated. But the cost of using new technologies to treat previously untreatable conditions steadily rises. Both sources of the health-care cost gap can be expected to persist.

Figure 17.9 shows the market for health care. Initially (say in 1980), the demand curve was D_0, the supply curve was S_0, the quantity was Q_0, and the price was P_0. Increasing incomes, longer life spans, and advances in the medical conditions that can be treated increase the demand for health-care

FIGURE 17.7

Who Pays for Health Care?

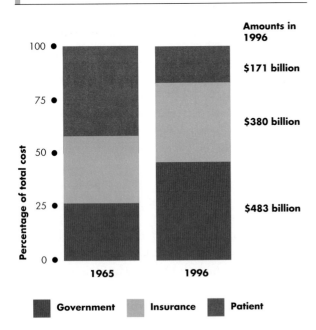

Government pays 47 percent of the total cost of health care, up from 26 percent in 1965. The direct payments by patients declined from 42 percent of the total in 1965 to 17 percent in 1996.

Source: U.S. Bureau of the Census, *Statistical Abstract of the United States: 1998,* 118th edition, Table 164.

FIGURE 17.8
The Rising Cost of Health Care

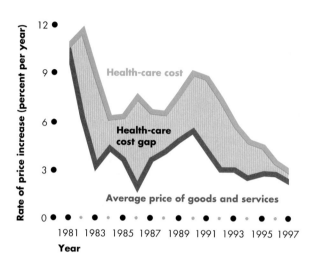

The cost of health care has increased much faster than the average price of other goods and services. The reasons are that health care is a labor-intensive industry—a personal service industry—so labor costs increase and quality improvements have changed the nature of the product and increased its cost.

Source: Statistical Abstract of the United States: 1998, 118th edition Table 179.

FIGURE 17.9
The Market for Health Care

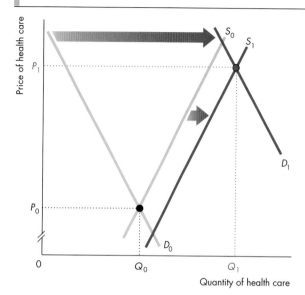

Initially (say in 1980), demand was D_0, supply was S_0, the quantity was Q_0, and the price was P_0. Increasing incomes and technological advances that expand the range of conditions that can be treated increase demand and shift the demand curve rightward to D_1. Advancing technology also increases supply, but increasing wages and more costly equipment and drugs counteract this increase in supply. The net result is that the supply curve shifts rightward to S_1. The quantity increases by a moderate amount, to Q_1, and the price increases steeply, to P_1.

services, and the demand curve shifts rightward from D_0 to D_1. Technological advances in health care have increased supply of health-care services. But the increase in supply is smaller than the increase in demand because some factors have worked to decrease supply. One of these factors is the increasing wage rates of health-care workers; another is the increasing cost of ever more sophisticated health-care technologies. The net effect of the positive and negative influences on supply is a rightward shift in the supply curve to S_1. The quantity of health care has increased to Q_1—and the price has risen to P_1—a relatively large increase.

The forces at work that produce the changes shown in Fig. 17.9 do not appear to be temporary, and they may be expected to bring similar changes in the future.

Health-Care Insurance

More than 50 percent of the health-care dollar is spent on less than 10 percent of the population. Another 30 percent is spent on 20 percent of the population. Health-care spending on the healthiest 70 percent of people is less than 20 percent of total health-care cost.

Because the costs are high and the frequency of use is low, most people choose to finance their health care by insurance. But health-care insurance, like all types of insurance, faces two problems: *moral hazard* and *adverse selection.*[1] Moral hazard in health insurance is the tendency for people who are covered by

---

[1]These problems and other aspects of insurance are explained more fully in Chapter 21, pp. 453–454.

insurance to use more health services or to be less careful about avoiding health risks than they otherwise would. Adverse selection in health insurance is the tendency for people who know they have a greater chance than the average of falling ill to be the ones most likely to buy health insurance.

For example, a person might buy insurance only a few days before going on a ski trip to Colorado (adverse selection). Covered by insurance, this person makes a faster run down the ski slope, knowing that the cost of fixing a broken ankle will be borne, in part, by the insurance company (moral hazard).

But the main adverse selection and moral hazard problems do not arise from reckless young skiers. They arise from the decisions of cautious physicians who elect to perform tests and procedures that are demanded by equally cautious patients only because someone else is paying for them.

Insurance companies set their premium levels sufficiently high to cover claims arising from people who have been adversely selected and who face moral hazard. But to attract profitable business from low-risk customers, insurance companies give preference to the healthy and employed. They also limit the coverage of preexisting conditions and claims arising from major illness. The result is that many people are uninsured or are insured for minor problems but not for catastrophic illness.

Reform Proposals

Health-care reform is a major political issue. Almost always, when some feature of the economy is not working the way people want it to, some people reach the conclusion that the government must step in to deal with the problem and others reach the opposite conclusion and identify existing government intervention as the source of the problem. So it is with health care. We'll end our brief study of the economics of health care by examining a range of alternative proposals for improving the performance of the health-care sector.

A Bigger Role for Government?   The world is rich in examples of health-care systems in which government plays a major role. The most complete such example is next door, in Canada.

Each province of Canada (a province is a bit like a state) administers a comprehensive health insurance program. The resources that the health-care sector uses are paid for by taxes. Some of these taxes are called Health Insurance Contributions, but funds from the general income tax are also used to pay the health-care bill.

The government is the sole provider of health-care services. It runs the hospitals, pays the doctors and other health-care professionals, and buys drugs for people with low incomes. People choose their family doctor, but the family doctor assigns people to specialists and hospitals.

Private health care is illegal in Canada. No one is permitted to offer services outside the government program, and no health-care provider is permitted to charge a fee greater than the one prescribed by the government. Doctors ration procedures for which there is an excess demand by lengthening waiting lines.

The wealthiest Canadians bypass the government system by purchasing health-care services in the United States (and occasionally Europe). Other Canadians complain but put up with services that are becoming more inadequate.

Britain and Australia are two other countries that are famed for their government-operated health care systems. In each of these countries, the government provides tax-funded health care at a zero price (or very low price) to anyone who demands it. At the same time, private insurers, doctors, and hospitals compete with the government sector. In Australia, people are provided with a tax incentive to buy private insurance and, in effect, opt out of the state scheme.

If health care is operated as a branch of government and financed with taxes, tax rates must continually rise to pay for the health care that people demand. There are two reasons why taxes must keep rising. First, as our incomes increase, we choose to spend a larger proportion of income on health. (Health care has a high *income elasticity* of demand.) Second, advances in health-care technology keep expanding the range of feasible treatments. But the cost of new technologies does not fall as quickly as our demand to use them rises. The combination of these factors means that if the government is to be the sole provider of health-care services, taxes must forever keep rising.

Make the Private Health-Care Market Work Better?
Many Republicans want to scale back the federal government's funding of health-care services. Proposals have been made to cut the projected increase by $270 billion from Medicare over a seven-year period. People who can afford to buy their own health care would no longer be eligible for Medicare, and people

would be given incentives to switch from high-cost fee-for-service providers to lower-cost managed-care providers.

The hope is that by cutting the scale of public expenditure, health-care costs would rise less quickly. There is evidence that this is a realistic hope. Removing the effects of inflation, the cost of Medicaid and Medicare has increased more than fourfold since 1970, while the cost of private health care has less than doubled.

By providing tax incentives that encourage employers to buy medical insurance, the government has made the private part of health care less efficient. Although *employers* buy medical insurance, it is the *employees* who pay for it. The compensation package, which consists of wages plus medical insurance, is determined by the forces of demand and supply. The amount that employers spend buying medical insurance is subtracted from the total compensation to determine the amount to be paid as wages.

But the income tax laws interact with employer-provided medical insurance to create a big problem. Employees pay income tax on their wages but not on the value of their medical insurance. So suppose a firm and its workers are negotiating a new compensation package. Will wages rise by $100 per employee, or will medical insurance premiums rise by $100 per employee to improve the quality of medical insurance? (Improved medical insurance might take the form of a lower deductible or a wider coverage.)

If a firm's labor cost is going to increase by $100 per employee, the firm doesn't care whether it pays the $100 in higher wages or in improved health insurance. But the employees care. Because wages are taxed, an extra $100 in wages translates into around $60 in disposable income. So employees must compare the value of improved health insurance that costs $100 with an additional $60 of disposable income. If the value employees place on improved medical insurance that costs $100 exceeds $60, they will opt for the insurance rather than the higher wages. If employers were not permitted to shelter the benefits from income tax in this way, wages would be higher and people would decide for themselves how much medical insurance coverage to buy.

There would be a strengthened incentive to buy insurance at a lower cost with a larger deductible and smaller range of coverage. With a larger deductible, people would have a stronger incentive to economize on medical treatments and the moral hazard and adverse selection problems would be lessened.

But the fundamental problem is that rising health-care costs stem from forces that are going to persist. Advances in health-care technology can be expected to keep the demand for health care increasing briskly. And the increasing cost of applying new medical technologies and steadily rising wage rates for skilled health-care workers can be expected to keep supply growing more slowly than demand. The result: The price that balances the quantities demanded and supplied will continue to increase faster than the average rise in prices.

REVIEW QUIZ

- What are the main problems with health care in the United States?
- Why do health-care costs increase more quickly than average prices?
- What are the *moral hazard* and *adverse selection* problems faced by providers of health insurance? Provide some examples of each.
- How do some other countries deal with health care? Do they offer any lessons to the United States?
- How might the market for health care be made to work better in the United States?

We've examined economic inequality in the United States, and we've seen that there is a large amount of inequality across families and individuals. Some of that inequality arises from comparing families at different stages in the life cycle. But even if we take a lifetime view, inequality remains. Some of that inequality arises from differences in wage rates. And economic choices accentuate those differences.

We've also seen that inequality has been increasing. *Reading Between the Lines* on pages 380–381 looks at the widening gap between the rich and the poor in the United States today.

We've seen that actions in the political marketplace redistribute income to alleviate the worst aspects of poverty. Our next task is to look more fully at the ways in which government actions modify the outcome of the market economy. We look at sources of market failure and the ways in which government actions aim to overcome it. We also look at what is called the political marketplace and the potential for it to fail too.

The Changing Income Distribution

THE NEW YORK TIMES, JANUARY 4, 1999

... *Problems Tarnishing a Robust Economy*

BY MICHAEL M. WEINSTEIN

It might seem churlish to find fault with a best-in-a-generation economy. Unemployment and inflation rates are at record lows, and low-paid workers are, for the first time in decades, receiving wage increases that outpace price increases. But despite the benefits of a temporarily buoyant economy, deep-seated problems remain.

Frank Levy, an economist at the Massachusetts Institute of Technology, notes that the best time to tackle problems is when the economy is flush. He points to increasing inequality at a time of stagnating wages in his new book, "The New Dollars and Dreams" (Russell Sage Foundation, 1998). Borrowing a phrase from Sen. Daniel Patrick Moynihan, D-N.Y., Levy warns against "defining deviancy down—accepting economic outcomes as normal today that would have been seen as pathological 10 or 20 years ago." ...

A study by Sheldon Danziger of the University of Michigan shows that from 1969 to 1997, when the earnings of college graduates rose briskly, the inflation-adjusted median earnings of white male high-school graduates 25 to 34 fell nearly 30 percent. An economy that was supposed to lift everyone to new highs of income and consumption instead pushed the least skilled workers down.

Danziger points to a stunning statistic: the earnings of these less skilled white workers fell so far that they earned less in 1997 than their black counterparts, a notoriously underpaid group, had earned almost 30 years earlier. And those black male high-school graduates fared almost as badly. From 1969 to 1997, their inflation-adjusted earnings fell 25 percent.

Levy's data show that the richest one-half of 1 percent of American taxpayers account for about 11 percent of aggregate income, and about 5 percent of households take home 20 percent of total income. The share of income captured by the bottom 60 percent of households is falling. Only college graduates, about a quarter of the work force, are racking up significant wage gains.

There is substantial evidence that the nature of technology in an information-intensive era is stacked in favor of workers with college-level verbal and math skills. That leaves at least half of the work force behind.

© 1999 *The New York Times*. Reprinted with permission.
Further reproduction prohibited.

Essence of the Story

■ Sheldon Danziger of the University of Michigan says that from 1969 to 1997, the earnings of college graduates rose quickly but the inflation-adjusted earnings of white male high-school graduates were less in 1997 than the earnings of black male high-school graduates in 1969.

■ Frank Levy of MIT says that the richest ½ percent of American taxpayers earn 11 percent of total income, 5 percent of households earn 20 percent of total income, and the income share of the bottom 60 percent of households is falling.

■ Only people with college degrees are experiencing significant wage increases.

■ Technology in the information-intensive age favors workers with college-level verbal and math skills.

Economic Analysis

■ Figure 1 shows the Lorenz curve suggested by the news article (and other data in Fig. 17.1 on p. 366). The curve shows great inequality, even among the rich.

■ Figure 2 shows why the incomes of high school graduates have fallen. In 1969, the supply curve was S_{69} and the demand curve was D_{69}. The market was in equilibrium at quantity Q_0 and annual wages of $10,000.

■ Between 1969 and 1997, an increase in the population increased the supply of high school graduate labor. The supply curve shifted rightward to S_{97}.

■ The demand for high school graduate labor also increased but by a small amount. The increase in demand was small because advances in technology displaced high school graduate labor with machines. The demand curve shifted rightward to D_{97}.

■ In 1997, the market for high school graduate labor was in equilibrium at a wage of $7,000 a year (adjusted for inflation).

■ Figure 3 shows why the incomes of college graduates increased during recent years.

■ The technological advances that have decreased the demand for high school graduate labor have increased the demand for college graduates. The demand curve shifted rightward from D_{69} to D_{97}.

■ The increase in population and the increase in the number of people completing college have increased the supply of college graduates. But the increase in supply was smaller than the increase in demand. The supply curve shifted rightward from S_{69} to S_{97}.

■ The equilibrium wage rate of college graduates increased from $50,000 to $70,000 a year (adjusted for inflation).

■ The wage gap between the two groups will begin to narrow if high school graduates acquire more skills and if further technological change increases the demand for high school graduates.

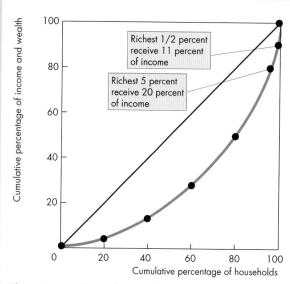

Figure 1 Great inequality, even among the rich

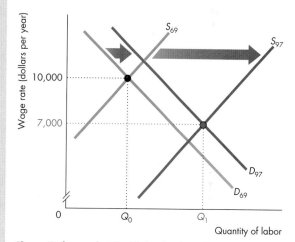

Figure 2 The market for high school graduates

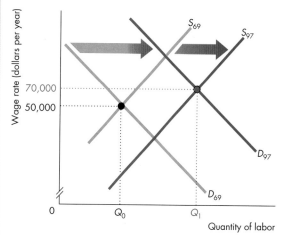

Figure 3 The market for college graduates

381

SUMMARY

KEY POINTS

Economic Inequality in the United States (pp. 366–368)

■ The richest 1 percent of Americans own almost one third of the total wealth in the country.

■ Income is distributed less unevenly than wealth. Throughout the 1970s, 1980s, and 1990s, inequality increased.

■ The poorest people in the United States are single black women over 65 years of age with less than eight years of schooling who live in the South. The richest people live in the West and are college-educated, middle-aged, white families in which husband and wife live together.

Comparing Like with Like (p. 369)

■ The distribution of wealth exaggerates the degree of inequality because it excludes human capital.

■ The distributions of annual income and wealth exaggerate lifetime inequality because they do not take the life cycle into account.

Resource Prices, Endowments, and Choices (pp. 370–371)

■ Differences in income and wealth arise from differences in resource prices, endowments, and choices.

■ People who face high wage rates generally work longer than those who face low wage rates, so the distribution of income becomes more unequal and more skewed than the distribution of wage rates.

Income Redistribution (pp. 372–375)

■ Governments redistribute income through income taxes, income maintenance programs, and provision of subsidized services.

■ Income taxes are progressive.

■ Redistribution creates a "big tradeoff" between equity and efficiency, which arises because the process of redistribution uses resources and weakens incentives to work and save.

■ Traditional income maintenance programs create a welfare trap that discourages work, so poverty is persistent. Reforms seek to lessen the severity of the welfare trap. A more radical negative income tax reform would encourage people on welfare to find work.

Health-Care Reform (pp. 376–379)

■ Total spending on health care in the United States is 14 percent of total income (45 percent met by the government, 35 percent by private insurance payments, and 20 percent by direct payments by patients.)

■ Health-care costs have increased more rapidly than consumer prices.

■ Health-care insurance faces moral hazard—the tendency for people who are insured to take greater risks—and adverse selection—the tendency for people with the greatest chance of making an insurance claim to be the ones who buy insurance.

■ Some people suggest that health-care reform requires greater government intervention, as in Canada, Britain, and Australia; others say that market forces need strengthening.

KEY FIGURES

KEY TERMS

PROBLEMS

*1. You are provided with the following information about income shares in an economy:

Percentage of households	Income shares (percent)
Lowest 20%	5
Second 20%	11
Third 20%	17
Fourth 20%	24
Highest 20%	43

a. Draw the Lorenz curve for income in this economy.
b. Compare the distribution of income in this economy with that in the United States. Is U.S. income distributed more equally or less equally than that in the economy described in the table?

2. You are provided with the following information about wealth shares in an economy:

Percentage of households	Wealth shares (percent)
Lowest 20%	0
Second 20%	1
Third 20%	3
Fourth 20%	11
Highest 20%	85

a. Draw the Lorenz curve for wealth in this economy.
b. Compare the distribution of wealth in this economy with that in the United States. Is U.S. wealth distributed more equally or less equally than that in the economy described in the table?
c. Explain which of the two variables—income in problem 1 or wealth in problem 2—is more unequally distributed.

*3. Imagine an economy with five people who are identical in all respects. Each lives for 70 years. For the first 14 of those years, they earn no income. For the next 35 years, they work and earn $30,000 a year from their work. For their remaining years, they are retired and have no income from labor. To make the arithmetic easy, let's suppose that the interest rate in this economy is zero; the individuals consume all their income during their lifetime and at a constant annual rate. What are the distributions of income and wealth in this economy if the individuals have the following ages:
a. All are 45
b. 25, 35, 45, 55, 65
Does case (a) have greater inequality than case (b)?

4. In the economy described in problem 3, there is a "baby boom." Two people who were born in the same year are now 25. One person is 35, one is 45, one is 55, and no one is 65. What are the distributions of income and wealth:
a. This year?
b. 10 years in the future?
c. 20 years in the future?
d. 30 years in the future?
e. 40 years in the future?
f. Comment on and explain the changes in the distributions of income and wealth in this economy.

*5. An economy consists of 10 people, each of whom has the following labor supply schedule:

Wage rate (dollars per hour)	Hours worked per day
1	1
2	2
3	4
4	6
5	8

The people differ in ability and earn different wage rates. The distribution of *wage rates* is as follows:

Wage rate (dollars per hour)	Number of people
1	1
2	2
3	4
4	2
5	1

a. Calculate the average wage rate.
b. Calculate the ratio of the highest to the lowest wage rate.
c. Calculate the average daily income.
d. Calculate the ratio of the highest to the lowest daily income.
e. Sketch the distribution of hourly wage rates.
f. Sketch the distribution of daily incomes.

g. What important lesson is illustrated by this problem?

6. In the economy described in problem 5, the productivity of low-skilled labor falls and that of high-skilled labor rises. Consequently, the distribution of *wage rates* changes to the following:

Wage rate (dollars per hour)	Number of people
0	1
1	2
3	4
5	2
6	1

The labor supply schedule is the same as in problem 5. For this changed situation:

a. Calculate the average wage rate.
b. Calculate the ratio of the highest to the lowest wage rate.
c. Calculate the average daily income.
d. Calculate the ratio of the highest to the lowest daily income.
e. Sketch the distribution of hourly wage rates.
f. Sketch the distribution of daily incomes.
g. What important lesson is illustrated by comparing the economy in this problem with the one in problem 5?

*7. The table shows the distribution of market income in an economy.

Percentage of households	Income (millions of dollars)
Lowest 20%	5
Second 20%	10
Third 20%	18
Fourth 20%	28
Highest 20%	39

The government redistributes income by collecting income taxes and paying benefits shown in the following table:

Percentage of households	Income taxes (percent of income)	Benefits (millions of dollars)
Lowest 20%	0	10
Second 20%	10	8
Third 20%	15	3
Fourth 20%	20	0
Highest 20%	30	0

a. Draw the Lorenz curve for this economy after taxes and benefits.
b. Is the scale of redistribution of income in this economy greater or smaller than in the United States?

8. In the economy described in problem 7, the government replaces its existing taxes and benefits with a negative income tax. What changes do you expect to occur in the economy?

CRITICAL THINKING

 1. Study *Reading Between the Lines* on pp. 380-381, and then:
a. Describe the main facts about the distribution of income reported in the news article.
b. Explain how you think the tax system and the welfare system change the situation described in the news article?
c. Use the link on the Parkin Web site to visit the Employment Policy Foundation and read the article on "tracking 'same families' over time." How does what you learn here change your interpretation of the news article?

 2. Use the link on the Parkin Web site to visit the U.S. Census Bureau. Obtain data on poverty and income distribution for your own state (or county if the data are available). Then:
a. Describe the main facts about poverty and the distribution of income in your state (county).
b. Compare the situation in your state (county) with that in the rest of the country.
c. Explain why you think your state (county) is performing better/worse than the nation as a whole?

3. Use the link on the Parkin Web site to visit the National Governors' Association. Obtain information on *The Personal Responsibility and Work Opportunity Reconciliation Act* of 1996. Then describe and evaluate the Act. In what ways do you think the 1996 law improves on the programs that it replaces?

Understanding Resource Markets

During the past 35 years, the rich have been getting richer and the poor poorer. This trend is new. From the end of World War II until 1965, the poor got richer at a faster pace than the rich and the gap between rich and poor narrowed a bit. What are the forces that generate these trends? The answer to this question is the forces of demand and supply in resource markets. These forces determine wages, interest rates, and the prices of land and natural resources. These forces also determine people's incomes. ◆ The three categories of resources are human, capital, and natural. Human resources include labor, human capital, and entrepreneurship. The income of labor and human capital depends on wage rates and employment levels, which are determined in labor markets. The income from capital depends on interest rates and the amount of capital, which are determined in capital markets. The income from natural resources depends on prices and quantities that are determined in natural resource markets. Only the return to entrepreneurship is not determined directly in a market. That return is normal profit plus economic profit, and it depends on how successful each entrepreneur is in the business that he or she runs. ◆ The chapters in this part study the forces at play in resource markets and explain how those forces have led to changes in the distribution of income. ◆ The overview of all the resource markets in Chapter 15 explained

For Whom?

how the demand for resources results from the profit-maximizing decisions of firms. You studied these decisions from a different angle in Chapters 10–14, where you learned how firms choose their profit-maximizing output and price. Chapter 15 explained how a firm's profit-maximizing decisions determine its demand for productive resources. It also explained how resource supply decisions are made and how equilibrium in resource markets determines resource prices and the incomes of resource owners. ◆ Some of the biggest incomes earned by superstars are a surplus that we call *economic rent.* ◆ Chapter 15 used labor resources and the labor market as its main example. But it also looked at some special features of capital markets and natural resource markets. ◆ Chapter 16 looked more closely at the labor market and studied the main sources of differences among people's wages. ◆ Chapter 17 studied the distribution of income. This chapter took you right back to the fundamentals of economics and answered one of the big economic questions: Who gets to consume the goods and services that are produced? ◆ Many outstanding economists have advanced our understanding of resource markets and the role they play in helping to resolve the conflict between the demands of humans and the resources available. One of them is Thomas Robert Malthus, whom you can meet on the following page. You can also enjoy the insights of Claudia Goldin, a professor of economics at Harvard University and a prominent contemporary labor economist.

The Economist

Thomas Robert Malthus

(1766–1834), an English clergyman and economist, was an extremely influential social scientist. In his best-selling Essay on the Principle of Population, *published in 1798, he predicted that population growth would outstrip food production and said that wars, famine, and disease were inevitable unless population growth was held in check by what he called "moral restraint." By "moral restraint," he meant marrying at a late age and living a celibate life. He married at the age of 38 a wife of 27, marriage ages that he recommended for others. Malthus's ideas were regarded as too radical in their day. And they led Thomas Carlyle, a contemporary thinker, to dub economics the "dismal science." But the ideas of Malthus had a profound influence on Charles Darwin, who got the key idea that led him to the theory of natural selection from reading the* Essay on the Principle of Population. *And David Ricardo and the classical economists were strongly influenced by Malthus's ideas.*

"The passion between the sexes has appeared in every age to be so nearly the same, that it may always be considered, in algebraic language as a given quantity."

THOMAS ROBERT MALTHUS
An Essay on the Principle of Population

The Issues

Is there a limit to economic growth, or can we expand production and population without effective limit? Thomas Malthus gave one of the most influential answers to these questions in 1798. He reasoned that population, unchecked, would grow at a geometric rate—1, 2, 4, 8, 16 … —while the food supply would grow at an arithmetic rate—1, 2, 3, 4, 5 … . To prevent the population from outstripping the available food supply, there would be periodic wars, famines, and plagues. In Malthus's view, only what he called moral restraint could prevent such periodic disasters.

As industrialization proceeded through the nineteenth century, Malthus's idea came to be applied to all natural resources, especially those that are exhaustible.

Modern-day Malthusians believe that his basic idea is correct and that it applies not only to food but also to every natural resource. In time, these prophets of doom believe, we will be reduced to the subsistence level that Malthus predicted. He was a few centuries out in his predictions but not dead wrong.

One modern-day Malthusian is ecologist Paul Ehrlich, who believes that we are sitting on a "population bomb." Governments must, says Ehrlich, limit both population growth and the resources that may be used each year.

In 1931, Harold Hotelling developed a theory of natural resources with different predictions from those of Malthus. The Hotelling Principle is that the relative price of an exhaustible natural resources will steadily rise, bringing a decline in the quantity used and an increase in the use of substitute resources.

Julian Simon (who died in 1998) challenged both the Malthusian gloom and the Hotelling Principle. He believed that people are the "ultimate resource" and predicted that a rising population lessens the pressure on natural resources. A bigger population provides a larger number of resourceful people who can work out more efficient ways of using scarce resources. As these solutions are found, the prices of exhaustible resources actually fall. To demonstrate his point, in 1980, Simon bet Ehrlich that the prices of five metals—copper, chrome, nickel, tin, and tungsten—would fall during the 1980s. Simon won the bet!

Then

No matter whether it is agricultural land, an exhaustible natural resource, or the space in the center of Chicago, and no matter whether it is 1998 or, as shown here, 1892, there is a limit to what is available, and we persistently push against that limit. Economists see urban congestion as a consequence of the value of doing business in the city center relative to the cost. They see the price mechanism, bringing ever-higher rents and prices of raw materials, as the means of allocating and rationing scarce natural resources. Malthusians, in contrast, explain congestion as the consequence of population pressure, and they see population control as the solution.

Now

In Tokyo, the pressure on space is so great that in some residential neighborhoods, a parking space costs $1,700 a month. To economize on this expensive space—and to lower the cost of car ownership and hence boost the sale of new cars—Honda, Nissan, and Toyota, three of Japan's big car producers, have developed a parking machine that enables two cars to occupy the space of one. The most basic of these machines costs a mere $10,000—less than 6 months' parking fees.

Malthus developed his ideas about population growth in a world in which women played a limited role in the economy. Malthus did not consider the opportunity cost of women's time a factor to be considered in predicting trends in the birth rate and population growth. But today, the opportunity cost of women's time is a crucial factor because women play an expanded role in the labor force. One woman who has made significant contributions to our knowledge of labor markets and the role of women in those markets is Claudia Goldin. You can meet Professor Goldin on the following pages.

387

Claudia Goldin

Claudia Goldin, *born in New York City, was an undergraduate at Cornell University and a graduate student at the University of Chicago, where she obtained her Ph.D. in 1972. Now Professor of Economics at Harvard University and Program Director at the National Bureau of Economic Research, Dr. Goldin is one of the world's foremost scholars. Her work combines economic history and labor economics and has investigated a wide range of important problems such as slavery in the American South, strategic factors in American economic development during the nineteenth century, and the evolution of labor markets during the twentieth century. She has studied the effects of technological change and the role of women in the labor market. Not only a brilliant research economist, Professor Goldin has received honors for her undergraduate teaching.*

Michael Parkin talked with Professor Goldin about her research and about trends in the U.S. labor markets.

Professor Goldin, why and how did you get into economics?
I entered Cornell University from the Bronx High School of Science intending to be a microbiologist, but I first wanted to acquire a strong liberal arts education. Economics appealed to me because of its rigor, its internal consistency, and, most of all, its relevance. But only after I took economics from Fred Kahn (who later, as head of the Civil Aeronautics Board, deregulated the airline industry) did I decide to major in the subject. I traded the laboratory of the scientist for that of the social scientist. Ours, I should add, is more challenging because we have to devise controlled experiments from already existing data.

In 1896, 18 percent of women were in the labor force; in 1996, 58 percent were in the labor force. What have been the driving forces behind this substantial change?
In 1896, most of the 18 percent were young, single, foreign-born, and black. Women generally worked for pay only before they married, although black women and poor women worked regardless of their marital status and age. In 1896, fewer than 5 percent of all married women were in the paid labor force. Therefore the question is why have married and adult women entered the labor force in such large numbers in the past 100 years. Contrary to popular opinion, the first large increase in married women's employment did not occur during the resurgence of feminism in the late 1960s, nor did it occur among the younger age groups. The large initial movement into the labor force occurred during the 1940s and 1950s among women older than 40 years. A host of long-run factors had been operating to reduce the time demands of women in their homes. These include the markedly reduced birth rate and the appearance of market goods substituting for those produced within the home, such as factory-made bread and clothing.

"I traded the laboratory of the scientist for that of the social scientist."

How do you explain the timing and the extent of the explosion in women's employment?

It was rooted in two changes earlier in the century. Between 1915 and 1930, the proportion of all Americans graduating from high school vastly increased, and at the same time, there was a surge in the demand for educated labor in the burgeoning clerical and sales sectors. Young women entered these jobs in droves in the 1920s but generally exited when they married. After World War II, rising wages and an increased demand

"...the first large increase in married women's employment did not occur during the resurgence of feminism in the late 1960s..."

for labor drew these women back into the labor force. Younger married women were raising the baby boom of the 1950s and were less willing to trade the household for the marketplace. The shift of employment from manufacturing to office and sales work from 1920 to 1950 was an important factor in enabling adult and married women to work for pay. And the generation of older women in the 1950s, who had the requisite education for these jobs, was ripe for this monumental change in employment. They, not the young

women of their era, were the real pioneers in women's employment. But the trailblazers did not view these changes as part of a larger social movement.

In the 1970s and 1980s, younger women greatly increased their participation in the labor force, and in the 1980s, even women with infants expanded their employment. In short, rising real wages, falling relative prices of market substitutes for home-produced goods, a declining demand for goods within the home, and a shift of jobs from blue collar to white collar led women to enter the labor force. But the timing of the changes suggests that various norms and institutional rigidities had to be broken down for the long-run forces to operate. These were accomplished first during the 1940s and 1950s.

What have we learned from your work and the work of other labor economists about the sources of persistent wage differences between men and women?

From the mid-1950s to 1980, the ratio of female to male full-time, weekly (median) earnings was constant at about 0.60. Women as a group made little if any noticeable progress relative to men. But from 1981 to the present, the ratio increased by approximately 16 percentage points to 0.76. The analysis of the period of stability and the subsequent period of a narrowing gap reveals much about the sources of gender differences in earnings. The factors that economists group under the heading of "human capital" are most relevant. When working women's job expe-

rience and education advanced on those of men, their relative earnings increased, and when these factors remained constant compared with those of men, women's relative earnings were stable. The aspirations and expectations of teenaged girls are another factor. These young women formed far more realistic expectations in the 1970s than in the 1960s, when they severely underestimated their future participation in the labor force. Young women today are in a much better position to prepare themselves for a lifetime of labor market work than were their elders. We also know that in the 1980s, the returns to education and job experience increased for women relative to men. We aren't certain why this has been the case. Some of the increase could be due to better education or women's greater willingness to undertake more demanding jobs. But we cannot dismiss the notion that the labor market became more gender-neutral in the 1980s, and we also cannot dismiss the role of policy interventions in making it so.

What trend do we observe in the wage differences between blacks and whites?

Similar forces have operated over the long run to narrow differences in earnings between white and black males and between white and black females. In 1940, the ratio of the earnings of black men to white men was astoundingly low—0.43—but by 1980, it was 0.73. Among college graduate men about 35 years old, the increase was even greater—from 0.45 in 1940 to 0.81 in 1980. On the average, black women have made greater progress relative to white women than have black men relative to white men.

What caused these extraordinary changes?

There were two compelling factors—educational changes, including advances in the quality of the education of black Americans, and the movement of blacks from the low-wage South to the higher-wage North. But there were critical junctures in this history. Two occurred during World Wars I and II and led to the greater integration of blacks into the white-dominated manufacturing sector and to an enormous migration to the North. The third occurred during the mid-1960s, when the Civil Rights Act led to further inroads by blacks into the higher-wage manufacturing sector. Unfortunately, some of the gains made since World War I were reversed in the 1980s. I don't mean that we have turned the clock back with regard to education and prejudice. The 1980s were a period of widening inequality in which the lower-educated and the manufacturing sector in particular lost a tremendous amount of ground, and black Americans are still disproportionately represented in these two groups.

What have been the main effects of affirmative action programs? Have they helped or hindered the progress of women and minorities?

Affirmative action is a complex doctrine under which federal contractors, that is, firms that sell goods or services to the federal government, have target levels for the hiring and promotion of women and minorities. There are direct effects from affirmative

action programs and, possibly, indirect effects. Most scholarly work has been focused on the direct effects and finds that affirmative action programs have increased the employment and earnings of minorities. There is little evidence, however, that the programs have served to increase the employment and earnings of women. The indirect effects are more difficult to quantify.

Let's look at the economics profession, for example. Far fewer women than men major in economics, so it isn't surprising that women are vastly underrepresented as teachers and researchers in the field. If we want to know whether having more women economics professors would encourage more female undergraduates to major in economics—that is, if there is a "role model effect"—we could test whether female enrollments increase when women teach the basic economics courses, such as principles. If so, we can make a case for affirmative action as a means of increasing the pool of candidates for a field and thus increasing the future employment of the group even in the absence of further affirmative action. Another possible indirect effect has been the subject of considerable controversy and forms the basis of the conservative attack on the programs. It is that women and minorities get hired or promoted under affirmative action when they should not have been. Such actions will then reinforce discriminatory views of women and minorities as being incompetent at particular jobs and can, in addition, make both groups more complacent and less competitive. I know of no hard evidence to substantiate such claims.

What are the most important labor market problems that we don't understand and that the next generation of economists will work on and possibly solve?

A pressing problem today is why the wage structure and distribution of earnings widened so substantially during the past 10 or 15 years. We need to know more about the interaction among education, inherent ability, and new technologies, such as the computer revolution. What makes some individuals more able to adapt while others are left behind? What types of educational and training interventions will help workers make the transition?

> The labor market isn't yet structured or ready for the egalitarian family.

Returning to gender differences in the workplace, I wonder whether the gap in earnings can ever be eliminated, given the structure of jobs and the division of labor in the home. If women are still expected to raise children and do a disproportionate share of household work, they will not advance with men in the labor market. Even if individual husbands and wives would like to create the egalitarian home, the husband is likely to confront considerable problems if he asks his employer for family leave, shorter hours, or a flexible schedule, even at greatly reduced pay. The labor market isn't yet structured or ready for the egalitarian family. I see this restructuring of the workplace as a major issue facing the next generation of labor economists.

Chapter 18

Market Failure and Public Choice

In 1996, the federal, state, and local governments in the United States employed more than 19 million people and spent $2.4 trillion. Independent government agencies employed yet another million people. Do we need this much government? Is government, as conservatives sometimes suggest, too big? Is government "the problem"? Or, despite its enormous size, is government too small to do all the things it must attend to? Is government, as liberals sometimes suggest, not contributing enough to economic life? ◆ Government touches many aspects of our lives. It is present at our birth, supporting the hospitals in which we are born and helping to train the doctors and nurses who deliver us. It is present throughout our education, support-ing schools and colleges and helping to train our teachers. It is present throughout our working lives, taxing our incomes, regulating our work environment, and paying us bene-fits when we are unemployed. It is present throughout our retirement, paying us a small income and, when we die, taxing our bequests. And government provides services such as the enforcement of law and order and the provision of national defense. But the government does not make all our choices. We decide what work to do, how much to save, and what to spend our income on. Why does the government participate in some aspects of our lives but not others? ◆ Almost everyone, from the poor single mother to the wealthy taxpayer, grumbles about govern-ment services. Why is the bureaucracy so unpopular? And what deter-mines the scale on which public services are provided?

Government— the Solution or the Problem?

◆ We begin our study of governments and markets by describing the government sector and explaining how, in the absence of a govern-ment, the market economy fails to achieve an efficient allocation of resources. We also explain how the scale of government is determined.

After studying this chapter, you will be able to:

- Explain how the eco-nomic role for govern-ment arises from market failure and inequality

- Distinguish between public goods and private goods and explain the free-rider problem

- Explain how the quan-tity of public goods is determined

- Explain why most of the government's revenue comes from income taxes and why income taxes are progressive

- Explain why some goods are taxed at a much higher rate than others

The Economic Theory of Government

THE ECONOMIC THEORY OF GOVERNMENT SEEKS to predict the economic actions that governments take and the consequences of those actions. Governments exist to help people cope with scarcity and provide a nonmarket mechanism for allocating scarce resources. Four economic problems that governments help people to cope with are:

- Public goods
- Monopoly
- Externalities
- Economic inequality

Public Goods

Some goods and services are consumed either by everyone or by no one. Examples are national defense, law and order, and sewage and waste disposal services. National defense systems cannot isolate individuals and refuse to protect them. Airborne diseases from untreated sewage do not favor some people and hit others. A good or service that is consumed either by everyone or by no one is called a **public good**.

The market economy fails to deliver the efficient quantity of public goods because of a free-rider problem. Everyone tries to free ride on everyone else because the good is available to all whether they pay for it or not. We'll study public goods and the free-rider problem later in this chapter.

Monopoly

Monopoly and *rent seeking* prevent the allocation of resources from being efficient. Every business tries to maximize profit, and when a monopoly exists, it can increase profit by restricting output and increasing price. Until fairly recently, for example, AT&T had a monopoly on long-distance telephone services, and the quantity of long-distance services was much smaller and the price much higher than they are today. Since the breakup of AT&T, the quantity of long-distance calls has exploded.

Some monopolies arise from *legal barriers to entry*—barriers to entry created by governments— but a major activity of government is to regulate monopoly and to enforce laws that prevent cartels and other restrictions on competition. We study these regulations and laws in Chapter 19.

Externalities

An **externality** is a cost or benefit that arises from an economic transaction and that falls on people who do not participate in that transaction. For example, when a chemical factory (legally) dumps its waste into a river and kills the fish, it imposes an external cost on the members of a fishing club who fish downstream. External costs and benefits are not usually taken into account by the people whose actions create them. For example, when the chemical factory decides whether to dump waste into the river, it does not take the fishing club's views into account. When a homeowner fills her garden with spring bulbs, she generates an external benefit for all the passersby. In deciding how much to spend on this lavish display, she takes into account only the benefits accruing to herself. We study externalities in Chapter 20.

These three problems from which government economic activity arises create an *inefficient* use of resources, a situation called **market failure.** When market failure occurs, the market produces too many of some goods and services and too few of some others. In these cases, the cost of producing a good does not equal the value people place on it. By reallocating resources, it is possible to make some people better off while making no one worse off. So some government activity is an attempt to modify the market outcome so as to moderate the effects of market failure.

Economic Inequality

Government economic activity also arises because an unregulated market economy delivers what most people regard as an unfair distribution of income. To lessen the degree of inequality, governments tax some people and pay benefits to others. You studied inequality and redistribution in Chapter 17. In this chapter, we look further at taxes and try to explain why the income tax is progressive and why some goods are taxed at extremely high rates.

Before we begin to study each of these problems from which government activity arises, let's look at the arena in which governments operate—the "political marketplace."

Public Choice and the Political Marketplace

Government is a complex organization made up of millions of individuals, each with his or her *own* economic objective. Government policy is the outcome of the choices made by these individuals. To analyze these choices, economists have developed a *public choice theory* of the political marketplace. The actors in the political marketplace are:

- Voters
- Politicians
- Bureaucrats

Figure 18.1 illustrates the choices and interactions of these actors. Let's look at each in turn.

Voters   Voters are the consumers in the political marketplace. In markets for goods and services, people express their preferences by their willingness to pay. In the political marketplace, they express their preferences by their votes, campaign contributions, and lobbying activity. Public choice theory assumes that people support the policies they believe will make them better off and oppose the policies they believe will make them worse off. It is voters' *perceptions* rather than reality that guide their choices.

Politicians   Politicians are the entrepreneurs of the political marketplace. Public choice theory assumes that the objective of a politician is to get elected and to remain in office. Votes to a politician are like economic profit to a firm. To get enough votes, politicians propose policies that they expect will appeal to a majority of voters.

Bureaucrats   Bureaucrats are the hired officials in government departments. They are the producers or firms in the political marketplace. Public choice theory assumes that bureaucrats aim to maximize their own utility and that to achieve this objective, they try to maximize the budget of their department.

The bigger the budget of a department, the greater is the prestige of its chief and the larger is the opportunity for promotion for people farther down the bureaucratic ladder. So all the members of a department have an interest in maximizing the department's budget. To maximize their budgets, bureaucrats devise programs that they expect will appeal to politicians and they help politicians to explain their programs to voters.

FIGURE 18.1

The Political Marketplace

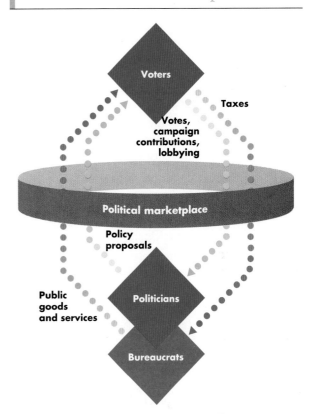

Voters express their demands for policies by voting, making campaign contributions, and lobbying. Politicians propose policies to appeal to a majority of voters. Bureaucrats try to maximize the budgets of their departments. A political equilibrium emerges in which no group can improve its position by making a different choice.

Political Equilibrium

Voters, politicians, and bureaucrats make choices to best further their own objectives. But each group is constrained by the preferences of the other groups and by what is technologically feasible. The outcome that results from the choices of voters, politicians, and bureaucrats is a **political equilibrium**, which is a situation in which all their choices are compatible and in which no group can improve its position by making a different choice. Let's see how voters, politicians, and bureaucrats interact to determine the quantity of public goods.

Public Goods and the Free-Rider Problem

WHY DOES THE GOVERNMENT PROVIDE GOODS and services such as national defense and public health? Why don't we buy our national defense from North Pole Protection, Inc., a private firm that competes for our dollars in the marketplace in the same way that McDonald's and Coca-Cola do? The answer to these questions lies in the free-rider problem created by public goods. Let's explore this problem. We begin by looking at the nature of a public good.

Public Goods

A *public good* is a good or service that can be consumed simultaneously by everyone and from which no one can be excluded. The first feature of a public good is called nonrivalry. A good is *nonrival* if the consumption by one person does not decrease the consumption by another person. An example is watching a television show. The opposite of nonrival is rival. A good is *rival* if the consumption by one person decreases the consumption by another person. An example is eating a hotdog.

The second feature of a public good is that it is nonexcludable. A good is *nonexcludable* if it is impossible, or extremely costly, to prevent someone from benefiting from a good. An example is national defense. It would be difficult to exclude someone from being defended. The opposite of nonexcludable is excludable. A good is *excludable* if it is possible to prevent a person from enjoying the benefits of a good. An example is cable television. Cable companies can ensure that only those people who have paid the fee receive programs.

Figure 18.2 classifies goods according to these two criteria and gives examples of goods in each category. National defense is a *pure* public good. One person's consumption of the security provided by our national defense system does not decrease the security of someone else—defense is nonrival. And the military cannot select those whom it will protect and those whom it will leave exposed to threats—defense is nonexcludable.

Many goods have a public element but are not pure public goods. An example is a highway. A highway is nonrival until it becomes congested. One more car on a highway with plenty of space does not

FIGURE 18.2
Public Goods and Private Goods

	Rival	**Nonrival**
Excludable	**Pure private goods** Food Car House	**Excludable and nonrival** Cable television Bridge Highway
Non-excludable	**Nonexcludable and rival** Fish in the ocean Air	**Pure public goods** Lighthouse National defense

A pure public good (bottom right) is one for which consumption is nonrival and from which it is impossible to exclude a consumer. Pure public goods pose a free-rider problem. A pure private good (top left) is one for which consumption is rival and from which consumers can be excluded. Some goods are nonexcludable but are rival (bottom left), and some goods are nonrival but are excludable (top right).

Source: Adapted from and inspired by E. S. Savas, *Privatizing the Public Sector*, Chatham House Publishers, Inc., Chatham, NJ, 1982, p. 34.

reduce anyone else's consumption of transportation services. But once the highway becomes congested, one extra vehicle lowers the quality of the service available to everyone else—it becomes rival like a private good. Also, users can be excluded from a highway by tollgates. Another example is fish in the ocean. Ocean fish are rival because a fish taken by one person is not available for anyone else. Ocean fish are also nonexcludable because it is difficult to prevent people from catching them.

The Free-Rider Problem

Public goods create a free-rider problem. A **free rider** is a person who consumes a good without paying for it. Public goods create a *free-rider problem* because the quantity of the good that a person is able to consume is not influenced by the amount the person pays for the good. So no one has an incentive to pay for a public good. Let's look more closely at the free-rider problem by studying an example.

The Benefit of a Public Good

Suppose that for its defense, a country must launch some surveillance satellites. The benefit provided by a satellite is the *value* of its services. The value of a *private* good is the maximum amount that a *person* is willing to pay for one more unit, which is shown by the person's demand curve. The value of a *public* good is the maximum amount that all the *people* are willing to pay for one more unit of it.

To calculate the value placed on a public good, we use the concepts of total benefit and marginal benefit. *Total benefit* is the dollar value that a person places on a given level of provision of a public good. The greater the quantity of a public good, the larger is a person's total benefit. *Marginal benefit* is the increase in total benefit that results from a one-unit increase in the quantity of a public good.

Figure 18.3 shows the marginal benefit that arises from defense satellites for a society with just two members, Lisa and Max. Lisa's and Max's marginal benefits are graphed as MB_L and MB_M, respectively, in parts (a) and (b) of the figure. The marginal benefit from a public good is similar to the marginal benefit from a private good—its magnitude diminishes as the quantity of the good increases. For Lisa, the marginal benefit from the first satellite is $80, and from the second it is $60. By the time 4 satellites are deployed, Lisa's marginal benefit is zero. For Max, the marginal benefit from the first satellite is $50, and from the second it is $40. By the time 4 satellites are deployed, Max perceives only $10 worth of marginal benefit.

Part (c) shows the economy's marginal benefit curve, *MB*. An individual's marginal benefit curve for a public good is similar to the individual's demand curve for a private good. But the economy's marginal benefit curve for a public good is different from the market demand curve for a private good. To obtain the market demand curve for a private good, we sum the quantities demanded by all individuals at each price—we sum the individual demand curves horizontally (see Chapter 8, p. 165). But to find the economy's marginal benefit curve of a public good, we sum the marginal benefits of each individual at each quantity—we sum the individual marginal benefit curves *vertically*. The resulting marginal benefit for the economy made up of Lisa and Max is the economy's marginal benefit curve graphed in part (c)—the curve *MB*. Lisa's marginal benefit from the first satellite gets added to Max's marginal benefit from the first satellite because they *both* enjoy security from the first satellite.

FIGURE 18.3
Benefits of a Public Good

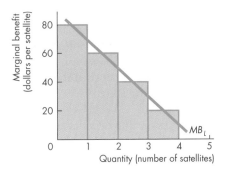

(a) Lisa's marginal benefit

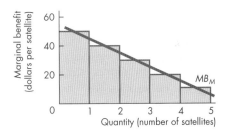

(b) Max's marginal benefit

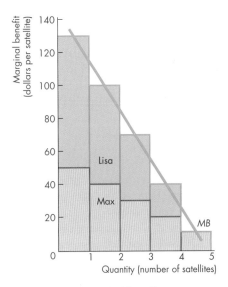

(c) Economy's marginal benefit

The marginal benefit to the economy at each quantity of the public good is the sum of the marginal benefits of all individuals. The marginal benefit curves are MB_L for Lisa, MB_M for Max, and *MB* for the economy.

The Efficient Quantity of a Public Good

An economy with two people would not buy any satellites—because the total benefit falls far short of the cost. But an economy with 250 million people might. To determine the efficient quantity, we need to take the cost as well as the benefit into account.

The cost of a satellite is based on technology and the prices of the resources used to produce it (just like the cost of producing sweaters, which you studied in Chapter 11).

Figure 18.4 sets out the benefits and costs. The second and third columns of the table show the total and marginal benefits. The next two columns show the total and marginal cost of producing satellites. The final column shows net benefit. Total benefit, *TB*, and total cost, *TC*, are graphed in part (a) of the figure.

The efficient quantity is the one that maximizes *net benefit*—total benefit minus total cost—and occurs when 2 satellites are provided.

The fundamental principles of marginal analysis that you have used to explain how consumers maximize utility and how firms maximize profit can also be used to calculate the efficient scale of provision of a public good. Figure 18.4(b) shows this alternative approach. The marginal benefit curve is *MB*, and the marginal cost curve is *MC*. When marginal benefit exceeds marginal cost, net benefit increases if the quantity produced increases. When marginal cost exceeds marginal benefit, net benefit increases if the quantity produced decreases. Marginal benefit equals marginal cost with 2 satellites. So making marginal cost equal to marginal benefit maximizes net benefit and uses resources efficiently.

Private Provision

We have now worked out the quantity of satellites that maximizes net benefit. Would a private firm— North Pole Protection, Inc.—deliver that quantity? It would not. To do so, it would have to collect $15 billion to cover its costs—or $60 from each of the 250 million people in the economy. But no one would have an incentive to buy his or her share of the satellite system. Everyone would reason as follows: The number of satellites provided by North Pole Protection, Inc., is not affected by my $60. But my own private consumption is greater if I free ride and do not pay my share of the cost of the satellite system. If I do not pay, I enjoy the same level of security and I can buy more private goods. Therefore I will spend my $60 on other goods and free ride on the public good. This is the free-rider problem.

If everyone reasons the same way, North Pole Protection has zero revenue and so provides no satellites. Because two satellites is the efficient level, private provision is inefficient.

Public Provision

Suppose there are two political parties, the Hawks and the Doves, that agree with each other on all issues except for the quantity of satellites. The Hawks would like to provide 4 satellites at a cost of $50 billion, with benefits of $50 billion and a net benefit of zero, as shown in Fig. 18.4. The Doves would like to provide 1 satellite at a cost of $5 billion, a benefit of $20 billion, and a net benefit of $15 billion—see Fig. 18.4.

Before deciding on their policy proposals, the two political parties do a "what-if" analysis. Each party reasons as follows. If each party offers the satellite program it wants—Hawks 4 satellites and Doves 1 satellite—the voters will see that they will get a net benefit of $15 billion from the Doves and zero net benefit from the Hawks, and the Doves will win the election.

Contemplating this outcome, the Hawks realize that their party is too hawkish to get elected. They figure that they must scale back their proposal to 2 satellites. At this level of provision, total cost is $15 billion, total benefit is $35 billion, and net benefit is $20 billion. If the Doves stick with 1 satellite, the Hawks will win the election.

But contemplating this outcome, the Doves realize that they must match the Hawks. They too propose to provide 2 satellites on exactly the same terms as the Hawks. If the two parties offer the same number of satellites, the voters are indifferent between the parties. They flip coins to decide their votes, and each party receives around 50 percent of the vote.

The result of the politicians' "what-if" analysis is that each party offers 2 satellites, so regardless of who wins the election, this is the quantity of satellites installed. And this quantity is efficient. It maximizes the perceived net benefit of the voters. Thus in this example, competition in the political marketplace results in the efficient provision of a public good. But for this outcome to occur, voters must be well informed and evaluate the alternatives. But as you will see below, they do not always have an incentive to achieve this outcome.

FIGURE 18.4

The Efficient Quantity of a Public Good

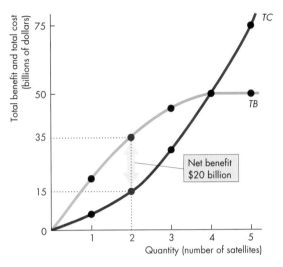

(a) Total benefit and total cost

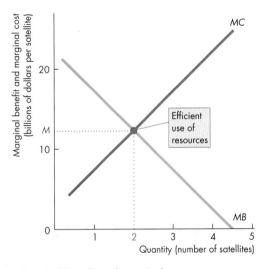

(b) Marginal benefit and marginal cost

Quantity (number of satellites)	Total benefit (billions of dollars)	Marginal benefit (billions of dollars per satellite)	Total cost (billions of dollars)	Marginal cost (billions of dollars per satellite)	Net benefit (billions of dollars)
0	0		0		0
		20		5	
1	20		5		15
		15		10	
2	35		15		20
		10		15	
3	45		30		15
		5		20	
4	50		50		0
		0		25	
5	50		75		−25

Net benefit—the vertical distance between total benefit, *TB*, and total cost, *TC*—is maximized when 2 satellites are installed (part a) and where marginal benefit, *MB*, equals marginal cost, *MC* (part b). The Doves would like to provide 1 satellite, and the Hawks would like to provide 4. But each party recognizes that its only hope of being elected is to provide 2 satellites—the quantity that maximizes net benefit and so leaves no room for the other party to improve on.

The Principle of Minimum Differentiation In the example we've just studied, both parties propose identical policies. This tendency toward identical policies is an example of the **principle of minimum differentiation**, which is the tendency for competitors to make themselves identical to appeal to the maximum number of clients or voters. This principle not only describes the behavior of political parties but also explains why fast food restaurants cluster in the same block and even why new auto models share similar features. If McDonald's opens a restaurant in a new location, it is likely that Burger King will open next door to McDonald's rather than a mile down the road. If Chrysler designs a new van with a sliding door on the driver's side, most likely Ford will too.

The Role of Bureaucrats

We have analyzed the behavior of politicians but not that of the bureaucrats who translate the choices of the politicians into programs and who control the day-to-day activities that deliver public goods. Let's now see how the economic choices of bureaucrats influence the political equilibrium.

To do so, we'll stick with the previous example. We've seen that competition between two political parties delivers the efficient quantity of satellites. But will the Defense Department—the Pentagon—cooperate and accept this outcome?

Suppose the objective of the Pentagon is to maximize the defense budget. With 2 satellites being provided at minimum cost, the defense budget is $15 billion (see Fig. 18.4). To increase its budget, the Pentagon might do two things. First, it might try to persuade the politicians that 2 satellites cost more than $15 billion. As Fig. 18.5 shows, if possible, the Pentagon would like to convince Congress that 2 satellites cost $35 billion—the entire benefit. Second, and pressing its position even more strongly, the Pentagon might argue for more satellites. It might press for 4 satellites and a budget of $50 billion. In this situation, total benefit and total cost are equal and net benefit is zero.

The Pentagon wants to maximize its budget, but won't the politicians prevent it from doing so because the Pentagon's preferred outcome costs votes? They will if voters are well informed and know what is best for them. But voters might be rationally ignorant. In this case, well-informed interest groups might enable the Pentagon to achieve its objective.

Rational Ignorance

A principle of public choice theory is that it is rational for a voter to be ignorant about an issue unless that issue has a perceptible effect on the voter's income. **Rational ignorance** is the decision *not* to acquire information because the cost of doing so exceeds the expected benefit. For example, each voter knows that he or she can make virtually no difference to the defense policy of the U.S. government. Each voter also knows that it would take an enormous amount of time and effort to become even moderately well informed about alternative defense technologies. So voters remain relatively uninformed about the technicalities of defense issues. (Though we are using

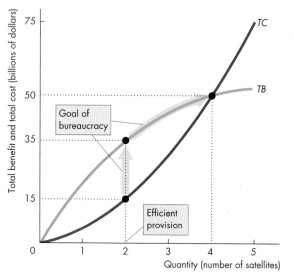

FIGURE 18.5
Bureaucratic Overprovision

The goal of a bureaucracy is to maximize its budget. A bureaucracy that maximizes its budget will seek to increase its budget so that its total cost equals total benefit and then to use its budget to expand output and expenditure. Here, the Pentagon tries to get $35 billion to provide 2 satellites. It would like to increase the quantity of satellites to 4 with a budget of $50 billion.

defense policy as an example, the same applies to all aspects of government economic activity.)

All voters are consumers of national defense. But not all voters are producers of national defense. Only a small number are in this latter category. Voters who own or work for firms that produce satellites have a direct personal interest in defense because it affects their incomes. These voters have an incentive to become well informed about defense issues and to operate a political lobby aimed at furthering their own interests. In collaboration with the defense bureaucracy, these voters exert a larger influence than do the relatively uninformed voters who only consume this public good.

When the rationality of the uninformed voter and special interest groups are taken into account, the political equilibrium provides public goods in excess of the efficient quantity. So in the satellite example, 3 or 4 satellites might be installed rather than the efficient quantity, which is 2 satellites.

Two Types of Political Equilibrium

We've seen that two types of political equilibrium are possible: efficient and inefficient. These two types of political equilibrium correspond to two theories of government:

■ Public interest theory
■ Public choice theory

Public Interest Theory   Public interest theory predicts that governments make choices that achieve efficiency. This outcome occurs in a perfect political system in which voters are fully informed about the effects of policies and refuse to vote for outcomes that can be improved upon.

Public Choice Theory   Public choice theory predicts that governments make choices that result in inefficiency. This outcome occurs in political markets in which voters are rationally ignorant and base their votes only on issues that they know affect their own net benefit. Voters pay more attention to their interests as producers than their interests as consumers, and public officials also act in their own best interest. The result is *government failure* that parallels market failure.

Why Government Is Large and Grows

Now that we know how the quantity of public goods is determined, we can explain part of the reason for the growth of government. Government grows, in part, because the demand for some public goods increases at a faster rate than the demand for private goods. There are two possible reasons for this growth:

■ Voter preferences
■ Inefficient overprovision

Voter Preferences   The growth of government can be explained by voter preferences in the following way. As voters' incomes increase (as they usually do in most years), the demand for many public goods increases more quickly than income. (Technically, the *income elasticity of demand* for many public goods is greater than 1—see Chapter 5, pp. 96–97.) Many (and the most expensive) public goods are in this category. They include transportation systems such as highways, airports, and air-traffic control systems; public health; education; and national defense. If

politicians did not support increases in expenditures on these items, they would not get elected.

Inefficient Overprovision   Inefficient overprovision might explain the *size* of government but not its *growth rate*. It (possibly) explains why government is *larger* than its efficient scale, but it does not explain why governments use an increasing proportion of total resources.

Voters Strike Back

If government grows too large, relative to what voters are willing to accept, there might be a voter backlash against government programs and a large bureaucracy. Electoral success during the 1990s at the state and federal level required politicians of all parties to embrace smaller, leaner, and more efficient government as part of their platform.

Another way in which voters—and politicians—can try to counter the tendency of bureaucrats to expand their budgets is to privatize the *production* of public goods. Government *provision* of a public good does not automatically imply that a government-operated bureau must *produce* the good. Garbage collection (public good) is often done by a private firm, and experiments are being conducted with private fire departments and even private prisons.

REVIEW QUIZ

■ What is the free-rider problem and why does it make the private provision of a public good inefficient?
■ Under what conditions will competition among politicians for votes result in an efficient quantity of a public good?
■ How do rationally ignorant voters and budget-maximizing bureaucrats prevent competition in the political marketplace from producing the efficient quantity of a public good? Do they result in too much or too little public provision of public goods?

We've now seen how voters, politicians, and bureaucrats interact to determine the quantity of a public good. But public goods are paid for with taxes. Taxes also redistribute income. How does the political marketplace determine the scale and variety of taxes that we pay?

Taxes

TAXES GENERATE THE FINANCIAL RESOURCES that governments use to provide voters with public goods and other benefits. Five types of taxes are used:

- Income taxes
- Social Security taxes
- Sales taxes
- Property taxes
- Excise taxes

Figure 18.6 shows the relative amounts raised by these five types of tax in 1998. Income taxes are the biggest tax source and raised 52 percent of tax revenues in 1998. Social Security taxes are the next biggest revenue source, and they raised 24 percent of total taxes in 1998. State sales taxes and local government property taxes each raise about 10 percent of total taxes. Finally, excise taxes raise a small amount of government revenue. Although they raise a small amount of revenue, excise taxes have a big impact on some markets, as you'll discover later in this chapter. Let's take a closer look at each type of tax.

FIGURE 18.6

Government Tax Revenues

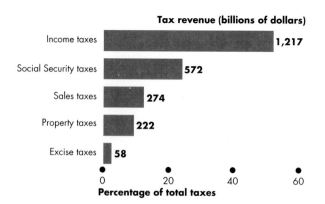

Almost a half of government revenues comes from income taxes. Almost a third comes from Social Security taxes. Excise taxes bring in a small amount of revenue, but these taxes have big effects on a small number of markets.

Source: Federal Budget Historical Table 2.1 and *Economic Report of the President,* 1999.

Income Taxes

Income taxes are paid on personal incomes and corporate profits. In 1998, the personal income tax raised $829 billion for the federal government and another $160 billion for state and local governments. Corporate profits taxes raised $190 billion for the federal government and $30 billion for the state governments. We'll look first at the effects of personal income taxes and then at corporate profits taxes.

Personal Income Tax The amount of income tax that a person pays depends on her or his *taxable income,* which equals total income minus a *personal exemption* and a *standard deduction* or other allowable deductions. In 1998, the personal exemption was $2,700 and the standard deduction was $4,250 for a single person. So for such a person, taxable income equals total income minus $6,950.

The *tax rate* (percent) depends on the income level and for a single person increases according to the scale:

$0 to $25,350	15 percent
$25,351 to $61,400	28 percent
$61,401 to $128,100	31 percent
$128,101 to $278,450	36 percent
Over $278,450	39.6 percent

The percentages in this list are marginal tax rates. A **marginal tax rate** is the percentage of an additional dollar of income that is paid in tax. For example if taxable income increases from $25,000 to $25,001, the additional tax paid is 15 cents and the marginal tax rate is 15 percent. If income increases from $278,450 to $278,451, the additional tax paid is 39.6 cents and the marginal tax rate is 39.6 percent.

The **average tax rate** is the percentage of income that is paid in tax. The average tax rate is less than the marginal tax rate. For example, suppose a single person earns $50,000 in a year. Tax paid is zero on the first $6,950 plus $3,803 (15 percent) on the next $25,350, plus $4,956 (28 percent) on the remaining $17,700. Total taxes equal $8,759, which is 17.5 percent of $50,000. The average tax rate is 17.5 percent.

If the average tax rate increases as income increases, the tax is a *progressive tax.* The personal income tax is a progressive tax. To see this feature of the income tax, calculate another average tax rate for someone whose income is $100,000 a year. Tax paid is zero on the first $6,950 plus $3,803 (15 percent) on the next $25,350, plus $10,094 (28 percent) on the next $36,050, plus $9,182 on the remaining $31,650.

Total taxes equal $23,708, which is 23.7 percent of $100,000. The average tax rate is 23.7 percent.

A progressive tax contrasts with a *proportional tax*, which has the same average tax rate at all income levels, and a *regressive tax*, which has a decreasing average tax rate as income increases.

The Effect of Income Taxes   Figure 18.7 shows how the income tax affects labor markets. Part (a) shows the market for low-wage workers and part (b) shows the market for high-wage workers. These labor markets are competitive, and with no income taxes, they work just like all the other competitive markets you have studied. The demand curves are *LD*, and the supply curves are *LS* (in both parts of the figure). Both groups work 40 hours a week. Low-wage workers earn $9.50 an hour, and high-wage workers earn $175 an hour. What happens when an income tax is introduced?

If low-wage workers are willing to supply 40 hours a week for $9.50 an hour when there is no tax, then

they are willing to supply that same quantity in the face of a 15 percent tax only if the wage rises to $11.18 an hour. That is, they want to get the $9.50 an hour they received before plus the 15 percent tax that they now must pay to the government. So the supply of labor decreases because the amount received from work is lowered by the amount of income tax paid. The acceptable wage rate at each level of employment rises by the amount of the tax that must be paid. For low-wage workers who face a tax rate of 15 percent, the supply curve shifts to *LS + tax*. The equilibrium wage rate rises to $10 an hour, but the after-tax wage rate falls to $8.50 an hour. Employment falls to 36 hours a week.

For high-wage workers who face a tax rate of 39.6 percent, the supply curve shifts to *LS + tax*. The equilibrium wage rate rises to $200 an hour, and the after-tax wage rate falls to $121 an hour. Employment falls to 32 hours a week. The decrease in employment of high-wage workers is larger than that of low-wage workers because of the differences in the marginal tax rates they each face.

FIGURE 18.7

The Effects of Income Taxes

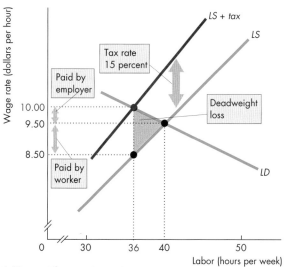

(a) Lowest income tax rate

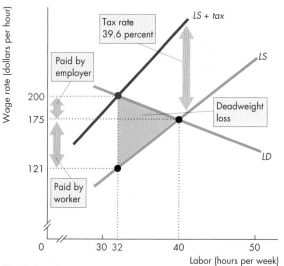

(b) Highest income tax rate

The demand for labor is *LD*, and with no income taxes, the supply of labor is *LS* (both parts). In part (a), low-wage workers earn $9.50 an hour and each works 40 hours a week. In part (b), high-wage workers earn $175 an hour and each works 40 hours a week. An income tax decreases the supply of labor and the labor supply curve shifts leftward. For low-wage workers in part (a), whose marginal tax rate is 15 per-

cent, supply decreases to *LS + tax*. Employment falls to 36 hours a week. For high-wage workers in part (b), whose marginal tax rate is 39.6 percent, supply decreases to *LS + tax*. Employment falls to 32 hours a week. The deadweight loss from the high marginal tax rate on high-wage workers is much larger than that from the low marginal tax rate on low-wage workers.

Notice that the income tax is paid by both the employer and the worker. In the case of low-wage workers, the employer pays an extra 50 cents an hour and the worker pays $1 an hour. In the case of high-wage workers, employers pay an extra $25 an hour and workers pay $54 an hour. The exact split depends on the elasticities of demand and supply.

Notice also the difference in the *deadweight loss* for the two groups. (Check Chapter 6, pp. 116–117, if you need a refresher on the concept of deadweight loss.) The deadweight loss is much larger for the high-wage workers than for the low-wage workers.

Why Do We Have a Progressive Income Tax?   We have a progressive income tax because it is part of the political equilibrium. A majority of voters support it, so politicians who also support it get elected.

The economic model that predicts progressive income taxes is called the *median voter* model. The core idea of the median voter model is that political parties pursue policies that are most likely to attract the support of the median voter. The median voter is the one in the middle—one half of the population lies on one side and one half on the other. So a political party must win the support of the median voter if it is to win an election. Let's see how the median voter model predicts a progressive income tax.

Imagine that government programs benefit everyone equally and are paid for by a proportional income tax. Everyone pays the same percentage of their income. In this situation, there is a redistribution from high-income voters to low-income voters. Everyone benefits equally, but because high-income voters have larger incomes, they pay larger taxes.

Is this situation the best one possible for the median voter? It is not. Suppose that instead of using a proportional tax, the marginal tax rate is lowered for low-income voters and increased for high-income voters—a progressive tax. Low-income voters are now better off, and high-income voters are worse off. Low-income voters will support this change, and high-income voters will oppose it. But there are many more low-income voters than high-income voters, so the low-income voters win.

The median voter is a low-income voter. In fact, because the distribution of income is skewed, the median voter has a smaller income than the average income (see Fig. 17.4 on pp. 370). This fact raises an interesting question: Why doesn't the median voter support taxes that skim off all income above the average and redistribute it to everyone with a below-average income. This tax would be so progressive that

it would result in equal incomes after taxes and transfers were paid.

The answer is that such high taxes would discourage effort and saving to the point that the median voter would be worse off with such a radical redistribution than under the arrangements that prevail today.

Let's now look at corporate profits taxes.

Corporate Profits Tax   In popular discussions of taxes, corporate profits taxes are seen as a free source of revenue for the government. Taxing people is bad, but taxing corporations is just fine.

It turns out that taxing corporations is very inefficient. We use an inefficient tax because it redistributes income in favor of the median voter, just like the income tax. Let's see why taxing corporate profits is inefficient.

First, the tax is misnamed. It is only partly a tax on economic profit. It is mainly a tax on the income from capital. Taxing the income from capital works like taxing the income from labor except for two critical differences: The supply of capital is highly (perhaps perfectly) elastic, and the quantity of capital influences the productivity of labor and wage income. Because the supply of capital is highly elastic, the tax is fully borne by firms and the quantity of capital decreases. With a smaller capital stock than we would otherwise have, the productivity of labor and incomes are lower than they would otherwise be.

Social Security Taxes

Social Security taxes are the contributions paid by employers and employees to provide social security benefits, unemployment compensation, and health and disability benefits to workers (see Chapter 17, p. 372).

Unions lobby to get employers to pay a bigger share of these taxes, and employers' organizations lobby to get workers to pay a bigger share of them. But this lobbying effort is not worth much because who *really* pays these taxes depends in no way on who writes the checks. It depends on the elasticities of demand and supply for labor.

Figure 18.8 shows you why. In both parts of the figure, the demand curve LD and the supply curve LS are identical. With no Social Security tax, the quantity of labor employed is QL^* and the wage rate is W^*.

A Social Security tax is now introduced. In Fig. 18.8(a), the employee pays the tax; in Fig. 18.8(b), the employer pays. When the employee pays, supply decreases and the supply of labor curve shifts leftward to $LS + tax$. The vertical distance between the supply curve LS and the new supply curve $LS + tax$ is the amount of the tax. The wage rate rises to WC, the after-tax wage rate falls to WT, and employment decreases to QL_0.

When the employer pays (in Fig. 18.8b), demand decreases and the demand for labor curve shifts leftward to $LD - tax$. The vertical distance between the demand curve LD and the new demand curve $LD - tax$ is the amount of the tax. The wage rate falls to WT, but the cost of labor rises to WC and employment decreases to QL_0.

So regardless of which side of the market is taxed, the outcome is identical. If the demand for labor is perfectly inelastic or if the supply of labor is perfectly elastic, the employer pays the entire tax. And if the demand for labor is perfectly elastic or if the supply of labor is perfectly inelastic, the employee pays the entire tax. These cases are exactly like those for the sales tax that you studied in Chapter 7 on pp. 135–138.

Sales Taxes

Sales taxes are the taxes levied by state governments on a wide range of goods and services. We studied the effects of these taxes in Chapter 7. There is one feature of these taxes, though, that we need to note. They are *regressive*. The reason they are regressive is that saving increases with income and sales taxes are paid only on the part of income that is spent.

Suppose, for example, that the sales tax is 8 percent. A family with an income of $20,000 that spends all its income pays $1,600 in sales tax. Its average tax rate is 8 percent. A family with an income of $100,000 that spends $60,000 and saves $40,000 pays sales taxes of $4,800 (8 percent of $60,000). So this family's average tax rate is 4.8 percent.

If the sales tax is regressive, why is it supported by the median voter? It is the entire tax code that matters, not an individual tax. So a regressive sales tax is voted for only as part of an overall tax regime that is progressive.

Property Taxes

Property taxes are collected by local governments and are used to provide local public goods. A **local public good** is a public good that is consumed by all the people who live in a particular area. Examples of local public goods are parks, museums, and safe neighborhoods.

FIGURE 18.8

Social Security Taxes

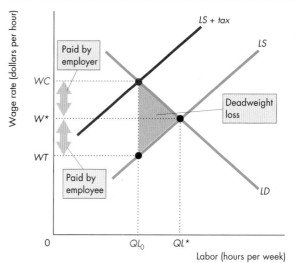

(a) Tax on employees

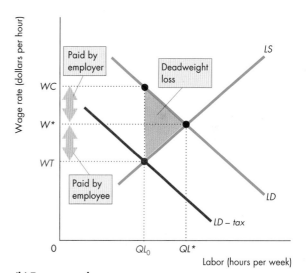

(b) Tax on employers

The labor demand curve is LD, and the supply curve is LS. With no Social Security taxes, the quantity of labor employed is QL^* and the wage rate is W^* (in both parts). In part (a), employees pay the Social Security tax. Supply decreases, and the supply of labor curve shifts leftward to $LS + tax$. The wage rate rises to WC, the after-tax wage rate falls to WT, and employment decreases to QL_0. In part (b), employers pay the Social Security tax. Demand decreases, and the demand for labor curve shifts leftward to $LD - tax$. The wage rate falls to WT, but the cost of labor rises to WC and employment decreases to QL_0. The outcome is identical in both cases.

There is a much closer connection between property taxes paid and benefits received than in the case of federal and state taxes. This close connection makes property taxes similar to a price for local services. Because of this connection, property taxes change both the demand for and supply of property in a neighborhood. A higher property tax lowers supply, but improved local public goods increase demand. So some neighborhoods have high taxes and high-quality local government services, and other neighborhoods have low taxes and low-quality services. Both can exist in the political equilibrium.

Excise Taxes

An **excise tax** is a tax on the sale of a particular commodity. The total amount raised by these taxes is small, but they have a big impact on some markets. Let's study the effects of an excise tax by considering the tax on gasoline shown in Fig. 18.9. The demand curve for gasoline is *D*, and the supply curve is *S*. If there is no tax on gasoline, its price is 60¢ a gallon and 400 million gallons of gasoline a day are bought and sold.

Now suppose that a tax is imposed on gasoline at the rate of 60¢ a gallon. As a result of the tax, the supply of gasoline decreases and the supply curve shifts leftward. The magnitude of the shift is such that the vertical distance between the original and the new supply curve is the amount of the tax. The new supply curve is the red curve, *S + tax*. The new supply curve intersects the demand curve at 300 million gallons a day and $1.10 a gallon. This situation is the new equilibrium after the imposition of the tax.

The excise tax creates a deadweight loss made up of the loss of consumer surplus and the loss of producer surplus. The dollar value of that loss is $30 million a day. Because 300 million gallons of gasoline are sold each day and the tax is 60¢ a gallon, total revenue from the gasoline tax is $180 million a day (300 million gallons multiplied by 60¢ a gallon). So to raise tax revenue of $180 million dollars a day by using the gasoline tax, a deadweight loss of $30 million a day—one sixth of the tax revenue—is incurred.

One of the main influences on the deadweight loss arising from an excise tax is the elasticity of demand for the commodity. The demand for gasoline is fairly inelastic. As a consequence, when a tax is imposed, the quantity demanded falls by a smaller percentage than the percentage rise in price.

FIGURE 18.9

An Excise Tax

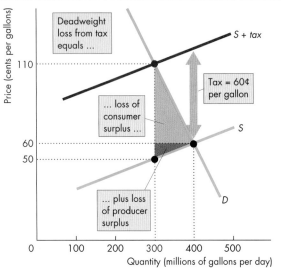

The demand curve for gasoline is *D*, and the supply curve is *S*. In the absence of any taxes, gasoline will sell for 60¢ a gallon and 400 million gallons a day will be bought and sold. When a tax of 60¢ a gallon is imposed, the supply curve shifts leftward to become the curve *S + tax*. The new equilibrium price is $1.10 a gallon, and 300 million gallons a day are bought and sold. The excise tax creates a deadweight loss represented by the gray triangle. The tax revenue collected is 60¢ a gallon on 300 million gallons, which is $180 million a day. The deadweight loss from the tax is $30 million a day. That is, to raise tax revenue of $180 million a day, a deadweight loss of $30 million a day is incurred.

To see the importance of the elasticity of demand, let's consider a different commodity—orange juice. So that we can make a quick and direct comparison, let's assume that the orange juice market is exactly as big as the market for gasoline. Figure 18.10 illustrates this market. The demand curve for orange juice is *D*, and the supply curve is *S*. Orange juice is not taxed, and so the price of orange juice is 60¢ a gallon—where the supply curve and the demand curve intersect—and the quantity of orange juice is 400 million gallons a day.

Now suppose that the government contemplates abolishing the gasoline tax and taxing orange juice instead. The demand for orange juice is more elastic than the demand for gasoline. It has many good substitutes in the form of other fruit juices. The government wants to raise $180 million a day so that its

FIGURE 18.10

Why We Don't Tax Orange Juice

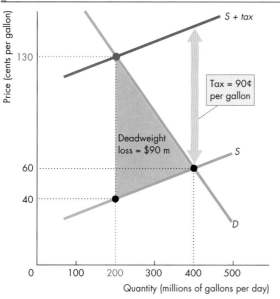

The demand curve for orange juice is D, and the supply curve is S. The equilibrium price is 60¢ a gallon, and 400 million gallons of juice a day are traded. To raise $180 million of tax revenue, a tax of 90¢ a gallon will have to be imposed. The introduction of this tax shifts the supply curve to S + tax. The price rises to $1.30 a gallon, and the quantity bought and sold falls to 200 million gallons a day. The deadweight loss is represented by the gray triangle and equals $90 million a day. The deadweight loss from taxing orange juice is much larger than that from taxing gasoline (Fig. 18.9) because the demand for orange juice is much more elastic than the demand for gasoline. Items that have a low elasticity of demand are taxed more heavily than items that have a high elasticity of demand.

total revenue is not affected by this tax change. The government's economists, armed with their statistical estimates of the demand and supply curves for orange juice that appear in Fig. 18.10, work out that a tax of 90¢ a gallon will do the job. With such a tax, the supply curve shifts leftward to become the curve labeled S + tax. This new supply curve intersects the demand curve at a price of $1.30 a gallon and at a quantity of 200 million gallons a day. The price at which suppliers are willing to produce 200 million gallons a day is 40¢ a gallon. The government collects a tax of 90¢ a gallon on 200 million gallons a day, so

it collects a total revenue of $180 million a day—exactly the amount that it requires.

But what is the deadweight loss in this case? The answer can be seen by looking at the gray triangle in Fig. 18.10. The magnitude of that deadweight loss is $90 million. Notice how much bigger the deadweight loss is from taxing orange juice than from taxing gasoline. In the case of orange juice, the deadweight loss is one half the revenue raised, while in the case of gasoline, it is only one sixth. What accounts for this difference? The supply curves are identical in each case, and the examples were also set up to ensure that the initial no-tax prices and quantities were identical. The difference between the two cases is the elasticity of demand: In the case of gasoline, the quantity demanded falls by only 25 percent when the price almost doubles. In the case of orange juice, the quantity demanded falls by 50 percent when the price only slightly more than doubles.

You can see why taxing orange juice is not on the political agenda of any of the major parties. Vote-seeking politicians seek out taxes that benefit the median voter. Other things being equal, this means that they try to minimize the deadweight loss of raising a given amount of revenue. Equivalently, they tax items with poor substitutes more heavily than items with close substitutes.

REVIEW QUIZ

■ How do income taxes influence employment and efficiency? Why are income taxes progressive?

■ Can Congress make employers pay a larger share of the Social Security tax?

■ Why do some neighborhoods have high taxes and high-quality services and others have low taxes and low-quality services?

■ Why does the government impose excise taxes at high rates on goods that have a low elasticity of demand?

◆ *Reading Between the Lines* on pages 406–407 looks at the politically sensitive market for day-care services. It shows how this market can be influenced by subsidies (that work like taxes but bring lower prices). And it asks whether increasing the quantity of day-care services is efficient. In the next two chapters, we are going to look at government economic actions in the face of monopolies and externalities.

The Politics and Economics of Day Care

THE WALL STREET JOURNAL, MARCH 30, 1999

Bills to Improve Day Care Gain In Augusta

BY CAROL GENTRY

AUGUSTA, Maine—A raft of new child-care measures, including tax breaks, low-interest loans and scholarships, have won near-unanimous support in committees and are speeding toward passage in the Legislature.

The nine bills sponsored by Sen. Susan Longley, a Democrat from rural Liberty, are the private-sector component of a massive child-care initiative called Start ME Right that aims to expand the overwhelmed system and improve its quality. Start ME Right calls for $26 million in public-sector spending over two years, a significant commitment in a state where child-care issues have long been relegated to the back burner in favor of business development and job growth. That means it's likely to face a bruising fight in the Appropriations Committee next month.

But most of Sen. Longley's bills call for little or no new state spending. Instead they invite business interests to join children's advocates in pushing for child-care solutions and tinker with tax breaks to spur improvements in child-care services. And by framing child care as a central economic development issue, Sen. Longley has gotten the attention of conservative lawmakers and built a broad coalition in support of her bills.

"Child care is the third-largest industry in our state, and we haven't been treating it like a business," she says. "It's hugely important, both for the child and family and for the development of the state."

...

As things stand now, Maine puts a smaller percentage of its tax dollars into child care than any other New England state, says Lee Parker, director of Bath-Brunswick Child Care Services, a child-care agency.

...

Children's advocates are hoping that Sen. Longley's emphasis on the economic development angle will resonate with Gov. King, who has been focusing heavily on business-recruiting efforts during his five years in office.

Says Ms. Parker: "If we're going to attract business here, we have to be able to say it's a crackerjack place to raise your kids."

Copyright © 1999 Dow Jones & Company, Inc. Reprinted with permission. Further reproduction prohibited.

Essence of the Story

- Start ME Right, Maine's child-care program, seeks $26 million in public spending. This spending increase does not have unanimous support.

- But almost all of the legislators (liberal Democrats, conservative Republicans, and independents) support nine bills sponsored by Senator Susan Longley.

- Senator Longley's bills call for little new state spending but seek to expand and improve the quality of child care by the use of tax breaks, low-interest loans, and scholarships.

- Senator Longley says that child care is the third largest industry in Maine, and it is important for both the child and family and for the economic development of the state.

■ Day-care service is a *private* good, not a *public* good. But it is a politically sensitive good because it influences the work choices and incomes of parents.

■ Figure 1 shows the labor market problem confronting two people who are identical in all ways except that one has a young child and the other does not. The supply curve of labor for the person with no child is S_N. The supply curve of labor for the parent is S_C.

■ The parent's labor supply curve requires a higher wage at each quantity supplied to meet the cost of child care (assumed to be $4 an hour).

■ If the market wage faced by these two people is $8 an hour, the parent stays at home and the nonparent works a 30-hour week and earns $240 a week.

■ If child-care services are subsidized, more parents will decide to work.

■ Figure 2 shows how a subsidy influences the market for child-care services. The demand curve is D, and the supply curve is S. With no subsidy, the price of child care is $5 an hour and 4 million places are available.

■ If child-care service providers receive a subsidy of $2 an hour, the supply curve shifts downward by the amount of the subsidy. The price falls to $4 an hour, and the number of places available increases to 6 million.

■ Figure 3 emphasizes that the provision of more child-care services is not a free lunch. The opportunity cost is the other goods and services forgone—here the move from *a* to *b* costs 6 units of other goods and services.

■ The economic marketplace would deliver outcome *a*. The political marketplace might deliver outcome *b*.

■ Should governments provide free day care on demand? Why or why not?

■ Should the cost of day care be fully tax deductible? Why or why not?

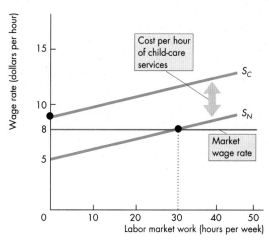

Figure 1 Parent's work decision

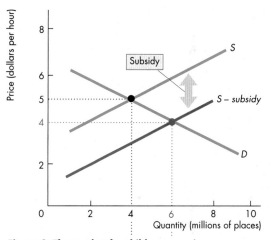

Figure 2 The market for child-care services

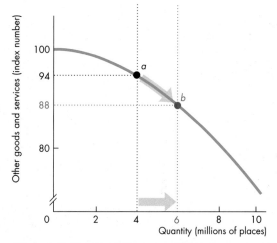

Figure 3 No free lunch but more efficient?

SUMMARY

KEY POINTS

The Economic Theory of Government
(pp. 392–393)

- Government exists to provide public goods, regulate monopoly, cope with externalities, and reduce economic inequality.
- Public choice theory explains how voters, politicians, and bureaucrats interact in a political marketplace.

Public Goods and the Free-Rider Problem
(pp. 394–399)

- A public good is a good or service that is consumed by everyone and that is *nonrival* and *nonexcludable*.
- A public good creates a *free-rider* problem—no one has an incentive to pay their share of the cost of providing a public good.
- The efficient level of provision of a public good is that at which net benefit is maximized. Equivalently, it is the level at which marginal benefit equals marginal cost.
- Competition between political parties, each of which tries to appeal to the maximum number of voters, can lead to the efficient scale of provision of a public good and to both parties proposing the same policies—the principle of minimum differentiation.
- Bureaucrats try to maximize their budgets, and if voters are rationally ignorant, producer interests may result in voting to support taxes that provide public goods in quantities that exceed those that maximize net benefit.

Taxes (pp. 400–405)

- Government revenue comes from income taxes, Social Security taxes, sales taxes, property taxes, and excise taxes.
- Income taxes decrease the level of employment and create a deadweight loss.

- Taxes can be progressive (the average tax rate rises with income), proportional (the average tax rate is constant), or regressive (the average tax rate falls with income).
- Income taxes are progressive because this arrangement is in the interest of the median voter.
- Social Security taxes are paid by the employer and the employee (and sales taxes are paid by the buyer and the seller) in amounts that depend on the elasticities of demand and supply.
- Property taxes change both demand and supply and can result in neighborhoods with high taxes and high-quality services and with low taxes and low-quality services.
- Excise taxes at high rates on commodities such as gasoline create a smaller deadweight loss than would taxes on commodities with more elastic demands.

KEY FIGURES

KEY TERMS

PROBLEMS

*1. You are provided with the following information about a sewage disposal system that a city of 1 million people is considering installing:

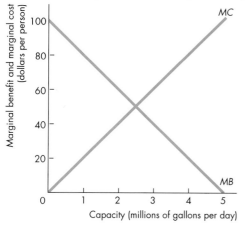

a. What is the capacity that achieves maximum net benefit?
b. How much will each person have to pay in taxes to pay for the efficient capacity level?
c. What is the political equilibrium if voters are well informed?
d. What is the political equilibrium if voters are rationally ignorant and bureaucrats achieve the highest attainable budget?

2. You are provided with the following information about a mosquito control program:

Quantity (square miles sprayed per day)	Marginal cost (dollars per day)	Marginal benefit (dollars per day)
0	0	0
1	1,000	5,000
2	2,000	4,000
3	3,000	3,000
4	4,000	2,000
5	5,000	1,000

a. What is the quantity of spraying that achieves maximum net benefit?
b. What is the total tax revenue needed to pay for the efficient quantity of spraying?
c. What is the political equilibrium if voters are well informed?
d. What is the political equilibrium if voters are rationally ignorant and bureaucrats achieve the highest attainable budget?

*3. An economy has two groups of people, A and B. The population consists of 80 percent A-types and 20 percent B-types. A-types have a perfectly elastic supply of labor at a wage rate of $10 an hour. B-types have a perfectly inelastic supply of labor, and their equilibrium wage rate is $100 an hour.
a. What kinds of tax arrangements do you predict this economy will adopt?
b. Analyze the labor market in this economy and explain what will happen to the wage rates and employment levels of the two groups when the taxes you predict in your answer to part (a) are introduced.

4. Suppose that in the economy described in problem 3, the proportion of A-types is 20 percent and the proportion of B-types is 80. Everything else remains the same.
a. Now what kinds of tax arrangements do you predict the economy will adopt?
b. Analyze the labor market in this economy and explain what will happen to the wage rates and employment levels of the two groups when the taxes you predict in your answer to part (a) are introduced.
c. Compare the economy in problem 3 with the economy in this problem. Which economy more closely resembles our actual economy?

*5. An economy has a competitive labor market, which is described by the following demand schedule and supply schedule:

Wage Rate (dollars per hour)	Quantity demanded (hours per week)	Quantity supplied (hours per week)
20	0	50
16	15	40
12	30	30
8	45	20
4	60	10
0	75	0

a. What are the equilibrium wage rate and hours of work done?
b. If a $4 an hour Social Security tax is imposed on employers:
(i) What is the new wage rate?
(ii) What is the new number of hours worked?

     (iii) What is the after-tax wage rate?
     (iv) What is the tax revenue?
     (v) What is the deadweight loss?

6. In the economy described in problem 5, the Social Security tax on employers is eliminated and a new Social Security tax of $4 is imposed on employees.
   a. What is the new wage rate?
   b. What is the new number of hours worked?
   c. What is the after-tax wage rate?
   d. What is the tax revenue?
   e. What is the deadweight loss?
   f. Compare the situation in problem 5 with that in this problem and explain the similarities and differences in the two situations.

*7. In a competitive market for cookies:

Price (dollars per pound)	Quantity demanded (pounds per month)	Quantity supplied (pounds per month)
10	0	28
8	4	24
6	8	20
4	12	16
2	16	12

   a. Find the equilibrium price and quantity.
   b. If cookies are taxed $2 a pound:
     (i) What is the new price of cookies?
     (ii) What is the new quantity bought?
     (iii) What is the tax revenue?
     (iv) What is the deadweight loss?

8. In the competitive market for cookies in problem 7, the government wants to change the tax to the one that brings in the greatest possible amount of revenue.
   a. What is that tax rate?
   b. What is the new price of cookies?
   c. What is the new quantity bought?
   d. What is the tax revenue?
   e. What is the deadweight loss?

CRITICAL THINKING

1. Study *Reading Between the Lines* on pp. 406–407, and then:
   a. Describe the measures that Senator Longley proposes and predict their effects on child-care services and labor markets in Maine.
   b. Why do people generally agree that increasing the quantity of child-care services above the quantity that the marketplace would deliver is a good thing? (Hint: Think about who benefits from child-care services other than the parent and child.)
   c. Do you think it is efficient to increase the quantity of child-care services above the quantity that the market would deliver?

2. Use the links on the Parkin Web site to obtain information about child-care services.
   a. How has the quantity of child-care services changed in recent years?
   b. How much does the average family spend on child care?
   c. What percentage of family income is spent on child care by a family with a monthly income of (i) $4,500 or more, (ii) $3,000 to $4,499, (iii) $1,200 to $2,999, and (iv) less than $1,200.

3. Your local city council believes that by installing computers to control the traffic signals, it can improve the speed of traffic flow. The bigger the computer the council buys, the better job it can do. The officials who are working on the proposal want to determine the scale of the system that will win them the most votes. The city bureaucrats want to maximize the budget. Suppose that you are an economist who is observing this public choice. Your job is to calculate the quantity of this public good that uses resources efficiently.
   a. What data would you need to reach your own conclusions?
   b. What does the public choice theory predict will be the quantity chosen?
   c. How could you, as an informed voter, attempt to influence the choice?
   d. What does the public interest theory predict will be the quantity chosen?

19

Regulation and Antitrust Law

When you consume water or local telephone service you usually buy from a regulated monopoly. Why are the industries that produce these items regulated? How are they regulated? Do the regulations work in the public interest—the interest of all consumers and producers—or do they serve special interests—the interests of particular groups of consumers or producers? ◆ Cable TV has been on a regulatory roller coaster. It was initially regulated, but in 1984 it was deregulated. After deregulation, the profits of cable TV firms soared and in 1992, Congress re-regulated the industry only to deregulate it yet again in 1996. Why has cable TV been deregulated, re-regulated, and then deregulated again? ◆ Some years ago, PepsiCo and 7-Up wanted to merge. Coca-Cola and Dr Pepper also wanted to merge. But the government blocked these mergers with its antitrust laws. It used these same laws to break up the American Telephone and Telegraph Company (AT&T). This action brought competition into the market for long-distance telephone service and permitted previously struggling firms such as MCI and Sprint to expand and flourish. The government has also used its

Public Interest or Special Interests?

antitrust laws to punish Archer Daniel Midland for price fixing, to permit Boeing and McDonnell Douglas to merge their aircraft building businesses, and to permit mergers of big banks. These same laws will determine whether Microsoft has monopolized the markets for computer operating systems and Web browsers. What are antitrust laws? How have they evolved over the years? How are they used today? Do they serve the public interest or the special interests of producers?

◆ This chapter studies government regulation. It draws on your earlier study of how markets work and on your knowledge of consumer surplus and producer surplus. It shows how consumers and producers can redistribute the gains from trade in the political marketplace, and it identifies who stands to win and who stands to lose from government regulation.

After studying this chapter, you will be able to:

■ Define regulation and antitrust law

■ Distinguish between the public interest and capture theories of regulation

■ Explain how regulation affects prices, outputs, profits, and the distribution of the gains from trade between consumers and producers

■ Explain how antitrust law has been applied in a number of landmark cases

■ Explain how antitrust law is used today

Market Intervention

THE GOVERNMENT INTERVENES IN MONOPOLISTIC and oligopolistic markets to influence prices, quantities produced, and the distribution of the gains from economic activity. It intervenes in two main ways:

- Regulation
- Antitrust law

Regulation

Regulation consists of rules administered by a government agency to influence economic activity by determining prices, product standards and types, and the conditions under which new firms may enter an industry. To implement its regulations, the government establishes agencies to oversee the regulations and ensure their enforcement. The first national regulatory agency to be set up in the United States was the Interstate Commerce Commission (ICC), established in 1887. Over the years since then, up to the late 1970s, regulation of the economy grew until, at its peak, almost a quarter of the nation's output was produced by regulated industries. Regulation applied to banking and financial services, telecommunications, gas and electric utilities, railroads, trucking, airlines and buses, many agricultural products, and even haircutting and braiding. Since the late 1970s, there has been a tendency to deregulate the U.S. economy.

Deregulation is the process of removing restrictions on prices, product standards and types, and entry conditions. In recent years, deregulation has occurred in domestic air transportation, telephone service, interstate trucking, and banking and financial services. Cable TV was deregulated in 1984, re-regulated in 1992, and deregulated again in 1996.

Antitrust Law

An **antitrust law** is a law that regulates and prohibits certain kinds of market behavior, such as price fixing, monopoly, and monopolistic practices. Antitrust law is enacted by Congress and enforced through the judicial system. Lawsuits under the antitrust laws may be initiated either by government agencies or by injured private parties.

The main thrust of antitrust law is the prohibition of monopoly practices of restricting output to achieve higher prices and profits. The first antitrust law—the Sherman Act—was passed in 1890. Successive acts and amendments have strengthened and refined the body of antitrust law. Antitrust law (like all law) depends as much on the decisions of the courts and of the Supreme Court as on the statutes passed by Congress. Over the 100 years since the passage of the Sherman Act, there have been some interesting changes in the court's interpretation of the law and in how vigorously the law has been enforced. We'll study these later in this chapter.

To understand why the government intervenes in the markets for goods and services and to work out the effects of its interventions, we need to identify the gains and losses that government actions can create. These gains and losses are the consumer surpluses and producer surpluses associated with different output levels and prices. We first study the economics of regulation.

Economic Theory of Regulation

THE ECONOMIC THEORY OF REGULATION IS part of the broader theory of public choice that is explained in Chapter 18. Here, we apply public choice theory to regulation. We'll examine the demand for government actions, the supply of those actions, and the political equilibrium that emerges.

Demand for Regulation

People and firms demand regulation that makes them better off. They express this demand through political activity—voting, lobbying, and making campaign contributions. But engaging in political activity is costly, so people demand political action only if the benefit that they individually receive from such action exceeds their individual costs in obtaining it. The four main factors that affect the demand for regulation are:

1. Consumer surplus per buyer
2. Number of buyers
3. Producer surplus per firm
4. Number of firms

The larger the consumer surplus per buyer that results from regulation, the greater is the demand for regulation by buyers. Also, as the number of buyers increases, so does the demand for regulation. But numbers alone do not necessarily translate into an effective political force. The larger the number of buyers, the greater is the cost of organizing them, so the demand for regulation does not increase proportionately with the number of buyers.

The larger the producer surplus per firm that arises from a particular regulation, the larger is the demand for that regulation by firms. Also, as the number of firms that might benefit from some regulation increases, so does the demand for that regulation. But again, large numbers do not necessarily mean an effective political force. The larger the number of firms, the greater is the cost of organizing them.

For a given consumer or producer surplus, the smaller the number of households or firms that share the surplus, the larger is the demand for the regulation that creates the surplus.

Supply of Regulation

Politicians and bureaucrats supply regulation. According to public choice theory, politicians choose policies that appeal to a majority of voters, thereby enabling themselves to achieve and maintain office. Bureaucrats support policies that maximize their budgets (see Chapter 18, p. 398). Given these objectives of politicians and bureaucrats, the supply of regulation depends on the following three factors:

1. Consumer surplus generated per buyer
2. Producer surplus generated per firm
3. The number of voters benefited

The larger the consumer surplus per buyer or producer surplus per firm generated and the larger the number of people affected by a regulation, the greater is the tendency for politicians to supply that regulation. If regulation benefits a large number of people by enough for it to be noticed and if the recipients know the source of the benefits, that regulation appeals to politicians and is supplied. If regulation benefits a *small* number of people by a large amount per person, that regulation also appeals to politicians, provided that its costs are spread widely and are not easily identified. If regulation benefits a large number of people but by too small an amount

per person to be noticed, that regulation does not appeal to politicians and is not supplied.

Political Equilibrium

In equilibrium, the regulation that exists is such that no interest group finds it worthwhile to use additional resources to press for changes and no group of politicians finds it worthwhile to offer different regulations. Being in a political equilibrium is not the same thing as everyone being in agreement. Lobby groups will devote resources to trying to change regulations that are already in place. Others will devote resources to maintaining the existing regulations. But no one will find it worthwhile to *increase* the resources they are devoting to such activities. Also, political parties might not agree with each other. Some support the existing regulations, and others propose different regulations. In equilibrium, no one wants to change the proposals that they are making.

What will a political equilibrium look like? The answer depends on whether the regulation serves the public interest or the interest of the producer. Let's look at these two possibilities.

Public Interest Theory   The **public interest theory** is that regulations are supplied to satisfy the demand of consumers and producers to maximize total surplus—that is, to attain allocative efficiency. The public interest theory implies that the political process relentlessly seeks out deadweight loss and introduces regulations that eliminate it. For example, where monopoly practices exist, the political process will introduce price regulations to ensure that outputs increase and prices fall to their competitive levels.

Capture Theory   The **capture theory** is that the regulations are supplied to satisfy the demand of producers to maximize producer surplus—that is, to maximize economic profit. The key idea of the capture theory is that the cost of regulation is high and only those regulations that increase the surplus of small, easily identified groups and that have low organization costs are supplied by the political process. Such regulations are supplied even if they impose costs on others, provided that those costs are spread thinly and widely enough that they do not decrease votes.

The predictions of the capture theory are less clear-cut than those of the public interest theory. The capture theory predicts that regulations give large and visible benefits to cohesive interest groups and impose small costs on everyone else. Those costs per person are so small that no one finds it worthwhile to incur the cost of organizing an interest group to avoid them.

Whichever theory of regulation is correct, according to public choice theory, the political system delivers the amounts and types of regulations that best further the electoral success of politicians. Because producer-oriented and consumer-oriented regulation are in conflict with each other, the political process can't satisfy both groups in any particular industry. Only one group can win. This makes the regulatory actions of government a bit like a unique product—for example, a painting by Leonardo da Vinci. There is only one original, and it will be sold to just one buyer. Normally, a unique commodity is sold at auction; the highest bidder takes the prize. Equilibrium in the regulatory process is similar: The suppliers satisfy the demands of the highest bidder. If the producer demand offers a bigger return to the politicians, either directly through votes or indirectly through campaign contributions, then the producers' interests will be served. If the consumer demand translates into a larger number of votes, then the consumers' interests will be served by regulation.

R E V I E W Q U I Z

- How do consumers and producers express their demand for regulation? What are their objectives? What are the costs of expressing a demand for regulation?
- When politicians and bureaucrats supply regulation, what are they trying to achieve? Do politicians and bureaucrats have the same objectives?
- What is a political equilibrium? When does the political equilibrium achieve economy efficiency? When does the political equilibrium serve the interests of producers?

We have now completed our study of the *theory* of regulation in the marketplace. Let's turn our attention to the regulations that exist in our economy today. Which theory of regulation best explains these real-world regulations? Which regulations are in the public interest and which are in the interest of producers?

Regulation and Deregulation

THE PAST 20 YEARS HAVE SEEN DRAMATIC changes in the way in which the U.S. economy is regulated by government. We're going to examine some of these changes. To begin, we'll look at what is regulated and also at the scope of regulation. Then we'll turn to the regulatory process and examine how regulators control prices and other aspects of market behavior. Finally, we'll tackle the more difficult and controversial questions: Why do we regulate some things but not others? Who benefits from the regulations that we have—consumers or producers?

The Scope of Regulation

The first federal regulatory agency, the Interstate Commerce Commission (ICC), was set up in 1887 to control prices, routes, and the quality of service of interstate railroads. Its scope later covered trucking lines, bus lines, water carriers, and, in more recent years, oil pipelines. Following the establishment of the ICC, the federal regulatory environment remained static until the years of the Great Depression. Then, in the 1930s, more agencies were established—the Federal Power Commission, the Federal Communications Commission, the Securities and Exchange Commission, the Federal Maritime Commission, the Federal Deposit Insurance Corporation, and, in 1938, the Civil Aeronautical Agency, which was replaced in 1940 by the Civil Aeronautics Board. There was a further lull until the establishment during the 1970s of the Copyright Royalty Tribunal and the Federal Energy Regulatory Commission. In addition to these, there are many state and local regulatory commissions.

In the mid-1970s, almost one quarter of the economy was subject to some form of regulation. Heavily regulated industries—those subject both to price regulation and to regulation of entry of new firms—were electricity, natural gas, telephones, airlines, highway freight services, and railroads.

During the 1980s and 1990s, a deregulation process stimulated competition in broadcasting, telecommunications, banking and finance, and all forms of transportation (air, rail, and road, passengers, and freight.)

What exactly do regulatory agencies do? How do they regulate?

The Regulatory Process

Though regulatory agencies vary in size and scope and in the detailed aspects of economic life that they control, all agencies have features in common.

First, the bureaucrats who are the key decision makers in a regulatory agency are appointed by the administration or Congress in the case of federal agencies and by state and local governments. In addition, all agencies have a permanent bureaucracy made up of experts in the industry being regulated and often recruited from the regulated firms. Agencies have financial resources, voted by Congress or state or local legislatures, to cover the costs of their operations.

Second, each agency adopts a set of practices or operating rules for controlling prices and other aspects of economic performance. These rules and practices are based on well-defined physical and financial accounting procedures, but they are extremely complicated in practice and hard to administer.

In a regulated industry, individual firms are usually free to determine the technology that they will use in production. But they are not free to determine the prices at which they will sell their output, the quantities that they will sell, or the markets that they will serve. The regulatory agency grants certification to a company to serve a particular market and with a particular line of products, and it determines the level and structure of prices that will be charged. In some cases, the agency also determines the quantity that firms may produce.

To analyze the way in which regulation works, it is convenient to distinguish between the regulation of natural monopoly and the regulation of cartels. Let's begin with the regulation of natural monopoly.

Natural Monopoly

Natural monopoly was defined in Chapter 13 (p. 264) as an industry in which one firm can supply the entire market at a lower cost than two or more firms can. Examples of natural monopolies include local distribution of cable television signals, electricity and gas, and urban rail services. For these activities, most of the costs are fixed and the larger the output, the lower its average total cost. It is much more expensive to have two or more competing sets of wires, pipes,

and train lines serving every neighborhood than it is to have a single set. (Whether an industry is a natural monopoly changes over time as technology changes. With the introduction of fiber-optic cables, telephone companies and cable television companies can compete with each other in both markets, so what was once a natural monopoly is gradually becoming a more competitive industry. Direct satellite TV is also beginning to break the cable monopoly.)

Let's consider the example of cable TV, which is shown in Fig. 19.1. The demand curve for cable TV is *D*. The cable TV company's marginal cost curve is *MC*. That marginal cost curve is (assumed to be) horizontal at $10 per household per month—that is, the cost of providing each additional household with a month of cable programming is $10. The cable company has a heavy investment in satellite receiving dishes, cables, and control equipment and so has high fixed costs. These fixed costs are part of the company's average total cost curve, shown as *ATC*. The average total cost curve slopes downward because as the number of households served increases, the fixed cost is spread over a larger number of households. (To refresh your memory on the average total cost curve, take a quick look at Chapter 11, p. 226.)

Regulation in the Public Interest How will cable TV be regulated, according to the public interest theory? In the public interest theory, regulation maximizes total surplus, which occurs if marginal cost equals price. As you can see in Fig. 19.1, that outcome occurs if the price is regulated at $10 per household per month and if 8 million households are served. Such a regulation is called a marginal cost pricing rule. A **marginal cost pricing rule** sets price equal to marginal cost. It maximizes total surplus in the regulated industry.

A natural monopoly that is regulated to set price equal to marginal cost incurs an economic loss. Because its average total cost curve is falling, marginal cost is below average total cost. Because price equals marginal cost, price is below average total cost. Average total cost minus price is the loss per unit produced. It's pretty obvious that a cable TV company that is required to use a marginal cost pricing rule will not stay in business for long. How can a company cover its costs and, at the same time, obey a marginal cost pricing rule?

One possibility is price discrimination (see Chapter 13, pp. 273–276). Another possibility is to use a two-part price (called a *two-part tariff*). For example, local telephone companies can charge consumers a monthly fee for being connected to the telephone system and then charge a price equal to marginal cost for each local call. A cable TV operator can charge a one-time connection fee that covers its fixed cost and then charge a monthly fee equal to marginal cost.

If a natural monopoly cannot cover its total cost from its customers and if the government wants it to follow a marginal cost pricing rule, the government must give the firm a subsidy. In this case, the government raises the revenue for the subsidy by taxing some other activity. But as we saw in Chapter 18, taxes themselves generate deadweight loss. Thus the deadweight

loss resulting from additional taxes must be subtracted from the efficiency gained by forcing the natural monopoly to adopt a marginal cost pricing rule.

It is possible that deadweight loss will be minimized by permitting the natural monopoly to charge a higher price than marginal cost rather than by taxing some other sector of the economy to subsidize the natural monopoly. Such a pricing arrangement is called an average cost pricing rule. An **average cost pricing rule** sets price equal to average total cost. Figure 19.2 shows the average cost pricing solution. The cable TV operator charges $15 a month and serves 6 million households. A deadweight loss arises, which is shown by the gray triangle in the figure.

Capturing the Regulator What does the capture theory predict about the regulation of this industry? According to the capture theory, regulation serves the interests of the producer, which means getting the regulator to set the price equal to the monopoly's

FIGURE 19.1
Natural Monopoly: Marginal Cost Pricing

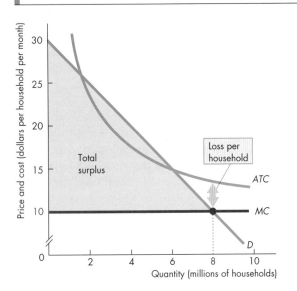

A natural monopoly is a firm that can supply the entire market at a lower price than two or more firms can. A cable TV operator faces the demand curve D. The firm's marginal cost is constant at $10 per household per month, as shown by the curve labeled MC. Fixed costs are large, and the average total cost curve, which includes average fixed cost, is shown as ATC. A marginal cost pricing rule that maximizes total surplus sets the price at $10 a month, with 8 million households being served. The resulting consumer surplus is shown as the green area. The firm incurs a loss on each household, indicated by the red arrow. To remain in business, the firm must price discriminate, use a two-part tariff, or receive a subsidy.

FIGURE 19.2
Natural Monopoly: Average Cost Pricing

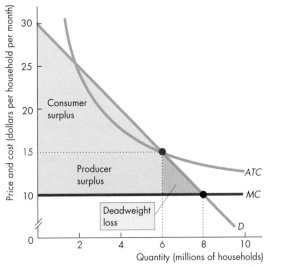

Average cost pricing sets price equal to average total cost. The cable TV operator charges $15 a month and serves 6 million households. In this situation, the firm breaks even—average total cost equals price. Deadweight loss, shown by the gray triangle, is generated. Consumer surplus is reduced to the green area.

unregulated price. To work out the price that achieves this goal, we need to look at the relationship between marginal revenue and marginal cost. A monopoly maximizes profit by producing the output at which marginal revenue equals marginal cost. The monopoly's marginal revenue curve in Fig. 19.3 is the curve *MR*. Marginal revenue equals marginal cost when output is 4 million households. The monopoly charges a price of $20 a month and makes the profit shown by the blue area. Thus a regulation that best serves the interest of the producer will set the price at this level.

But how can a producer go about obtaining regulation that results in this monopoly profit-maximizing outcome? To answer this question, we need to look at the way in which agencies determine a regulated price. A key method used is called rate of return regulation.

FIGURE 19.3

Natural Monopoly: Profit Maximization

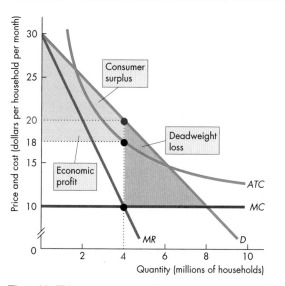

The cable TV operator would like to maximize profit. To do so, marginal revenue (*MR*) is made equal to marginal cost. At a price of $20 a month, 4 million households buy cable service. Consumer surplus is reduced to the green triangle. The deadweight loss increases to the gray triangle. The monopoly makes the profit shown by the blue rectangle. If the producer can capture the regulator, the outcome will be the situation shown here.

Rate of Return Regulation **Rate of return regulation** determines a regulated price by setting the price at a level that enables the regulated firm to earn a specified target percent return on its capital. The target rate of return is determined with reference to what is normal in competitive industries. This rate of return is part of the opportunity cost of the natural monopolist and is included in the firm's average total cost. By examining the firm's total cost, including the normal rate of return on capital, the regulator attempts to determine the price at which average total cost is covered. Thus rate of return regulation is equivalent to average cost pricing.

In Fig. 19.2, average cost pricing results in a regulated price of $15 a month with 6 million households being served. Thus rate of return regulation, based on a correct assessment of the producer's average total cost curve, results in a price that favors the consumer and does not enable the producer to maximize monopoly profit. The special interest group will have failed to capture the regulator, and the outcome will be closer to that predicted by the public interest theory of regulation.

But there is a feature of many real-world situations that the above analysis does not take into account: the ability of the monopoly firm to mislead the regulator about its true costs.

Inflating Costs The managers of a firm might be able to inflate the firm's costs by spending part of the firm's revenue on inputs that are not strictly required for the production of the good. By this device, the firm's apparent costs exceed the true costs. On-the-job luxury in the form of sumptuous office suites, limousines, free baseball tickets (disguised as public relations expenses), company jets, lavish international travel, and entertainment are all ways in which managers can inflate costs.

If the cable TV operator manages to inflate its costs and persuade the regulator that its true average total cost curve is that shown as *ATC (inflated)* in Fig. 19.4, then the regulator, applying the normal rate of return principle, will regulate the price at $20 a month. In this example, the price and quantity will be the same as those under unregulated monopoly. It might be impossible for firms to inflate their costs by as much as the amount shown in the figure. But to the extent that costs can be inflated, the apparent average total cost curve lies somewhere between the true *ATC* curve and *ATC (inflated)*. The greater the ability of the firm to pad its costs in this way, the

FIGURE 19.4
Natural Monopoly: Inflating Costs

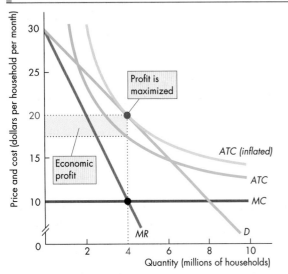

If the cable TV operator is able to inflate its costs to *ATC (inflated)* and persuade the regulator that these are genuine minimum costs of production, rate of return regulation results in a price of $20 a month—the profit-maximizing price. To the extent that the producer can inflate costs above average total cost, the price rises, output falls, and deadweight loss increases. The profit is captured by the managers, not the shareholders (owners) of the firm.

more closely its profit (measured in economic terms) approaches the maximum possible. The shareholders of this firm don't receive this economic profit because it gets used up in baseball tickets, luxury offices, and the other actions taken by the firm's managers to inflate the company's costs.

Incentive Regulation and Deregulation Partly for the reasons we've just examined, rate of return regulation is increasingly being replaced by incentive regulation schemes. An **incentive regulation scheme** is a type of regulation that gives a firm an incentive to operate efficiently and keep costs under control. Today, a majority of states have adopted incentive regulation schemes for telecommunications rather than traditional rate of return regulation. These new schemes take two main forms: price caps (adopted in California, New Jersey, Oregon, and Rhode Island) and earnings sharing plans (adopted in Colorado,

Connecticut, Florida, Georgia, Kentucky, Tennessee, and Texas). Under a price cap regulation, the regulators set the maximum price that may be charged and hold that cap (adjusted for inflation) for several years. If profits are considered too high, the price cap will be lowered. Under earnings-sharing regulation, if profits rise above a certain level, they must be shared with the firm's customers. There is some evidence that under these types of regulations, local telephone companies are attempting to cut costs.

Sometimes, technological change occurs that destroys a natural monopoly. When this happens, deregulation and the introduction competition are possible. Technologies that permit many gas and electricity producers to share a common distribution network is an example.

Public Interest or Capture?

It is not clear whether actual regulation produces prices and quantities that more closely correspond with the predictions of capture theory or with public interest theory. One thing is clear, however. Price regulation does not require natural monopolies to use the marginal cost pricing rule. If it did, most natural monopolies would make losses and receive hefty government subsidies to enable them to remain in business. But there are even exceptions to this conclusion. For example, many local telephone companies do appear to use marginal cost pricing for local telephone calls. They cover their total cost by charging a flat fee each month for being connected to their telephone system but then permitting each call to be made at its marginal cost—zero or something very close to it.

A test of whether natural monopoly regulation is in the public interest or the interest of the producer is to examine the rates of return earned by regulated natural monopolies. If those rates of return are significantly higher than those in the rest of the economy, then, to some degree, the regulator might have been captured by the producer. If the rates of return in the regulated monopoly industries are similar to those in the rest of the economy, then we cannot tell for sure whether the regulator has been captured or not, for we cannot know the extent to which costs have been inflated by the managers of the regulated firms.

Table 19.1 shows rates of return in regulated natural monopolies as well as the economy's average rate of return. In the 1960s, rates of return in regulated natural monopolies were somewhat below the economy

TABLE 19.1

Rates of Return in Regulated Monopolies

Industry	Years 1962–69	Years 1970–77
Electricity	3.2	6.1
Gas	3.3	8.2
Railroad	5.1	7.2
Average of above	3.9	7.2
Economy average	6.6	5.1

Source: Paul W. MacAvoy, *The Regulated Industries and the Economy* (New York: W.W. Norton, 1979), 49–60.

average; in the 1970s, those returns exceeded the economy average. Overall, the rates of return achieved by regulated natural monopolies were not very different from those in the rest of the economy. We can conclude from these data either that natural monopoly regulation does, to some degree, serve the public interest or that natural monopoly managers inflate their costs by amounts sufficiently large to disguise the fact that they have captured the regulator and that the public interest is not being served.

A final test of whether regulation of natural monopoly is in the public interest or the producers' interest is

TABLE 19.2

Gains from Deregulating Natural Monopolies

Industry	Consumer surplus	Producer surplus	Total surplus
	(billions of 1990 dollars)		
Railroads	8.5	3.2	11.7
Telecommunications	1.2	0.0	1.2
Cable television	0.8	0.0	0.8
Total	10.5	3.2	13.7

Source: Clifford Winston, "Economic Deregulation: Days of Reckoning for Microeconomists," *Journal of Economic Literature*, XXXI, September 1993, pp. 1263–1289, and the author's calculations.

to study the changes in consumer surplus and producer surplus following deregulation. Microeconomists have researched this issue, and Table 19.2 summarizes their conclusions. In the case of railroad deregulation, which occurred during the 1980s, both consumers and producers gained, and by large amounts. The gains from deregulation of telecommunications and cable television were smaller and accrued only to consumers. These findings suggest that railroad regulation hurt everyone, while regulation of telecommunications and cable television hurt only consumers.

We've now examined the regulation of natural monopoly. Let's next turn to regulation in oligopolistic industries—the regulation of cartels.

Cartel Regulation

A *cartel* is a collusive agreement among a number of firms that is designed to restrict output and achieve a higher profit for the cartel's members. Cartels are illegal in the United States and in most other countries. But international cartels can sometimes operate legally, such as the international cartel of oil producers known as OPEC (the Organization of Petroleum Exporting Countries).

Illegal cartels can arise in oligopolistic industries. An oligopoly is a market structure in which a small number of firms compete with each other. We studied oligopoly (and duopoly—two firms competing for a market) in Chapter 14. There we saw that if firms manage to collude and behave like a monopoly, they can set the same price and sell the same total quantity as a monopoly firm would. But we also discovered that in such a situation, each firm will be tempted to cheat, increasing its own output and profit at the expense of the other firms. A possible result of such cheating on the collusive agreement is the unraveling of the monopoly equilibrium and the emergence of a competitive outcome with zero economic profit for producers. Such an outcome benefits consumers at the expense of producers.

How is oligopoly regulated? Does regulation prevent monopoly practices or does it encourage those practices?

According to the public interest theory, oligopoly is regulated to ensure a competitive outcome. Consider, for example, the market for trucking tomatoes from the San Joaquin Valley to Los Angeles, illustrated in Fig. 19.5. The market demand curve for trips is D. The industry marginal cost curve—and the competitive supply curve—is *MC*. Public interest regulation will regulate the price of a trip at $20, and there will be 300 trips a week.

How would this industry be regulated according to the capture theory? Regulation that is in the producer interest will maximize profit. To find the outcome in this case, we need to determine the price and quantity when marginal cost equals marginal revenue. The marginal revenue curve is *MR*. So marginal cost equals marginal revenue at 200 trips a week. The price of a trip is $30.

One way of achieving this outcome is to place an output limit on each firm in the industry. If there are 10 trucking companies, an output limit of 20 trips per company ensures that the total number of trips in a week is 200. Penalties can be imposed to ensure that no single producer exceeds its output limit.

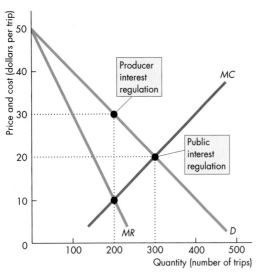

FIGURE 19.5
Collusive Oligopoly

Ten trucking firms transport tomatoes from the San Joaquin Valley to Los Angeles. The demand curve is *D*, and the industry marginal cost curve is *MC*. Under competition, the *MC* curve is the industry supply curve. If the industry is competitive, the price of a trip will be $20 and 300 trips will be made each week. Producers will demand regulation that restricts entry and limits output to 200 trips a week, where industry marginal revenue (*MR*) is equal to industry marginal cost (*MC*). This regulation raises the price to $30 a trip and results in each producer making maximum profit—as if it is a monopoly.

All the firms in the industry would support this type of regulation because it helps to prevent cheating and to maintain a monopoly outcome. Each firm knows that without effectively enforced production quotas, every firm has an incentive to increase output. (For each firm, price exceeds marginal cost, so a greater output brings a larger profit.) So each firm wants a method of preventing output from increasing above the industry profit-maximizing level, and the quotas enforced by regulation achieve this end. With this type of cartel regulation, the regulator enables a cartel to operate legally and in its own best interest.

What does cartel regulation do in practice? Some regulation has benefited the producer. When the Interstate Commerce Commission regulated trucking, producers persistently earned economic profits. Also, by forming a strong labor union, truck drivers captured a large part of the producer surplus.

Some regulation has benefited both the producer and the consumer. When the Civil Aeronautics Board regulated the airlines, they earned economic profits, but they competed by offering high-cost services that benefited consumers and eventually eroded profits.

Table 19.3 provides some evidence in support of the conclusion that regulation increased profits in trucking and airlines. If regulation ensured a competitive outcome, rates of return in regulated oligopolies would be no higher than those in the economy as a whole. As the numbers in Table 19.3 show, rates of return in airlines and trucking were close to twice the economy average rate of return in the 1960s. In the 1970s, the rate of return in trucking remained higher than the economy average (although by a smaller

TABLE 19.3
Rates of Return in
Regulated Oligopolies

| Industry | Years | |
	1962–69	1970–77
Airlines	12.8	3.0
Trucking	13.6	8.1
Economy average	6.6	5.1

Source: Paul W. MacAvoy, *The Regulated Industries and the Economy* (New York: W.W. Norton, 1979), 49–60.

margin than had prevailed in the 1960s). Airline rates of return in the 1970s fell to below the economy average. The overall picture that emerges from examining data on rates of return is mixed. The regulation of oligopoly does not always result in higher profit, but there are many situations in which it does.

Further evidence on oligopoly regulation can be obtained from the performance of prices and profit following deregulation. If, following deregulation, prices and profit fall, then, to some degree, the regulation must have been serving the interest of the producer.

In contrast, if, following deregulation, prices and profits remain constant or increase, then the regulation may be presumed to have been serving the public interest. Because there has been a substantial amount of deregulation in recent years, we can use this test of oligopoly regulation to see which of the two theories better fits the facts.

The evidence is mixed, but in the cases of the airlines and trucking, the two main oligopolies that have been deregulated, prices fell and there was a large increase in the volume of business. Table 19.4 summarizes the estimated effects of deregulation of airlines and trucking on consumer surplus, producer surplus, and total surplus. Most of the gains were in consumer surplus. In the case of the airlines, there was a gain in producer surplus as well.

But the table shows that in the trucking industry, producer surplus decreased by almost $5 billion a year. This outcome implies that the regulation benefited the producer by restricting competition and enabling prices to exceed their competitive levels.

Making Predictions

Most industries have a few producers and many consumers. In this situation, public choice theory predicts that regulation protects producer interests and that politicians are rewarded with campaign contributions rather than votes. But there are situations in which the consumer interest has prevailed. There are also cases in which the balance has switched from producer to consumer, as seen in the deregulation process that began in the late 1970s.

Deregulation has occurred for three main reasons. First, economists have become more confident and vocal in predicting gains from deregulation. Second, a large increase in energy prices in the 1970s increased the cost of regulation borne by consumers. These price hikes made route regulation in the transportation sector extremely costly and changed the balance in favor of consumers in the political equilibrium. Third, technological change ended some natural monopolies. New technologies enable small producers to offer low-cost long-distance telephone services. These producers want a share of the business—and profit—of AT&T. Furthermore, as communication technology improve, the cost of communication falls and the cost of organizing larger groups of consumers also falls.

If this line of reasoning is correct, there will be more public interest regulation and deregulation in the future.

TABLE 19.4

Gains from Deregulating Oligopolies

Industry	Consumer surplus	Producer surplus	Total surplus
	(billions of 1990 dollars)		
Airlines	11.8	4.9	16.7
Trucking	15.4	−4.8	10.6
Total	27.2	0.1	27.3

Source: Clifford Winston, "Economic Deregulation: Days of Reckoning for Microeconomists," *Journal of Economic Literature*, XXXI, September 1993, pp. 1263–1289, and the author's calculations.

REVIEW QUIZ

- When did regulation begin in the United States, what was regulated, and when did regulation reach its peak?
- Why does natural monopoly need to be regulated?
- What pricing rule enables a natural monopoly to operate in the public interest and why is that rule difficult to implement?
- What pricing rule is typically used to regulate a natural monopoly and what problems does it create?
- What is incentive regulation and how does it work?
- How might cartels be regulated in the public interest?

Let's now leave regulation and turn to the other method of intervention in markets: antitrust law.

Antitrust Law

ANTITRUST LAW PROVIDES AN ALTERNATIVE WAY in which the government may influence the marketplace. As in the case of regulation, antitrust law can be formulated in the public interest, to maximize total surplus, or in private interests, to maximize the surpluses of particular special interest groups such as producers.

The Antitrust Laws

The antitrust laws are easily summarized. The first antitrust law, the Sherman Act, was passed in 1890 in an atmosphere of outrage and disgust at the actions and practices of J.P. Morgan, John D. Rockefeller, and W.H. Vanderbilt—the so-called robber barons. Ironically, the most lurid stories of the actions of these great American capitalists are not of their monopolization and exploitation of consumers but of their sharp practices against each other. Nevertheless, monopolies did emerge—for example, the spectacular control of the oil industry by John D. Rockefeller.

A wave of mergers at the turn of the century produced stronger antitrust laws. The Clayton Act of 1914 supplemented the Sherman Act, and the Federal Trade Commission, an agency charged with enforcing the antitrust laws, was created.

Table 19.5 summarizes the two main provisions of the Sherman Act. Section 1 of the Act is precise.

TABLE 19.5

The Sherman Act of 1890

Section 1:

Every contract, combination in the form of trust or otherwise, or conspiracy, in restraint of trade or commerce among the several States, or with foreign nations, is hereby declared to be illegal.

Section 2.

Every person who shall monopolize, or attempt to monopolize, or combine or conspire with any other person or persons, to monopolize any part of the trade or commerce among the several States, or with foreign nations, shall be deemed guilty of a felony

---

TABLE 19.6

The Clayton Act and Its Amendments

Clayton Act	1914
Robinson-Patman Act	1936
Celler-Kefauver Act	1950

These Acts prohibit the following practices *only* if they substantially lessen competition or create monopoly:

1. Price discrimination

2. Contracts that require other goods to be bought from the same firm (called tying arrangements)

3. Contracts that require a firm to buy all its requirements of a particular item from a single firm (called requirements contracts)

4. Contracts that prevent a firm from selling competing items (called exclusive dealing)

5. Contracts that prevent a buyer from reselling a product outside a specified area (called territorial confinement)

6. Acquiring a competitor's shares or assets

7. Becoming a director of a competing firm

Conspiring with others to restrict competition is illegal. But section 2 is general and imprecise. Just what is an "attempt to monopolize"? The Clayton Act and its two amendments, the Robinson-Patman Act of 1936 and Celler-Kefauver of 1950, which outlaw specific practices, provided greater precision. Table 19.6 describes these practices and summarizes the main provisions of these three Acts.

Landmark Antitrust Cases

The real force of any law arises from its interpretation. The interpretation of the antitrust laws has been clear on price fixing (section 1 of the Sherman Act) but less clear on attempts to monopolize (section 2 of the Sherman Act and the Clayton Act) and rulings have fluctuated between favoring producers and consumers. Table 19.7 summarizes the landmark cases.

Price Fixing Court decisions have made *any* price fixing deal a violation of Section 1 of the Sherman Act. Taking someone's life is a serious offense. But it is not always a violation of the murder law. In contrast, price fixing is always a violation of the antitrust law. Accidents and other involuntary causes of death are recognized as reasons not to convict someone of murder. But if the Justice Department can prove the existence of price fixing, a defendant can offer no acceptable excuse.

A 1927 case against *Trenton Potteries Company* and others first established this hard line, which is known as the *per se* interpretation of the law. The court ruled that an agreement between Trenton Potteries and others to fix the prices of sanitary pottery violated the Sherman Act even if the prices themselves were reasonable. Price fixing *per se* (in and of itself) is a violation of the law.

In 1961, General Electric, Westinghouse, and other electrical component manufacturers were found guilty of a price-fixing conspiracy. This case was the first one in which the executives (rather than the company itself) were fined and jailed.

A recent costly example that illustrates this strict interpretation of the law is that of Archer Daniels Midland. In 1996, this firm, which is a major producer of agricultural products, was fined $100 million for conspiring with foreign producers to fix the prices of lysine and citric acid, two additives that are used in various food products.

Attempts to Monopolize The most important early antitrust cases were those involving the American Tobacco Company and Standard Oil Company, which were decided in 1911. These two companies were found guilty of violations under the Sherman Act and ordered to divest themselves of large holdings in other companies. The breakup of John D. Rockefeller's Standard Oil Company resulted in the creation of the oil companies that today are household names, such as Amoco, Chevron, Exxon, and Sohio.

In finding these companies to be in violation of the provisions of the Sherman Act, the Supreme Court enunciated the "rule of reason." The rule of reason states that monopoly arising from mergers and agreements among firms is not necessarily illegal. Only if there is an unreasonable restraint of trade does the arrangement violate the provisions of the Sherman Act.

TABLE 19.7
Landmark Antitrust Cases

Case	Year	Verdict and consequence
1. Price Fixing		
Trenton Potteries Company	1927	*Guilty*: Agreement to fix prices was *per se* a violation of the Sherman Act, regardless of whether the prices themselves are "reasonable."
General Electric, Westinghouse, and others	1961	*Guilty*: Price-fixing conspiracy; executives fined and jailed.
Archer Daniels Midland	1996	*Guilty*: Price-fixing conspiracy; fined $100 million.
2. Attempts to Monopolize?		
American Tobacco Co. and *Standard Oil Co.*	1911	*Guilty*: Ordered to divest themselves of large holdings in other companies; "rule of reason" enunciated—only *unreasonable* combinations guilty under Sherman Act.
U.S. Steel Co.	1920	*Not guilty*: Although U.S. Steel had a very large market share (near monopoly), mere "size alone is not an offense"; application of the "rule of reason."
Alcoa	1945	*Guilty*: Too big—had too large a share of the market.
Aspen Skiing	1985	*Guilty*: Owner of three of the four downhill ski facilities refused to offer an all-Aspen ticket and share revenues on a use-basis with the owner of the other facility.
Spectrum Sports	1993	*Not guilty*: Although Spectrum Sports was the national distributor of sorbothane (used in athletic products), no evidence was present that the company had attempted to monopolize the relevant market.

The rule of reason was widely regarded as removing the force of the Sherman Act itself. This view was reinforced in 1920 when U.S. Steel Company was acquitted of violations under the act even though it had a very large (more than 50 percent) share of the U.S. steel market. Applying the "rule of reason," the court declared that "size alone is not an offense."

In a case that some people interpreted as challenging the "rule of reason," the *Alcoa* case, decided in 1945, Alcoa was judged to be in violation of the antitrust law because it was too big. It had too large a share of the aluminum market. This relatively tough interpretation of the law continued through the late 1960s.

Of the many other cases concerning the attempt to monopolize, we look at two interesting and relatively recent ones. During the 1970s, the Aspen Skiing Company, which owned three of the four downhill ski facilities in Aspen, offered an all-Aspen ticket and shared the revenues with Aspen Highlands Skiing Corp. that owned the fourth facility. Revenues were split based on a survey of users. In 1977, Aspen Skiing refused to offer the all-Aspen ticket unless Aspen Highland agreed to accept a low fixed share of the revenue. The all-Aspen ticket was not offered, and Aspen Highland lost business. The court held that the Aspen Skiing Company was attempting to monopolize.

When Spectrum Sports became the national distributor of sorbothane athletic products, (sorbothane is a shock-absorber), some injured companies alleged that Spectrum had attempted to monopolize. The court held that Spectrum could not be held to have attempted to monopolize absent evidence that it had engaged in monopoly practices.

Today's Showcase: The United States Versus Microsoft

Microsoft has been charged with specific violations of the antitrust laws, and in 1998 a trial of these charges began.

The Case Against Microsoft   The claims against Microsoft are that the firm:

1. Possesses monopoly power in the market for PC operating systems.
2. Uses below-cost pricing (called predatory pricing) and tying arrangements to achieve a monopoly in the market for Web browsers.
3. Uses other anticompetitive practices to strengthen its monopoly in these two markets.

Microsoft, it is claimed, operates behind barriers to entry that arise from economies of scale and network economies. Microsoft's average total cost falls as production increases (economies of scale) because the costs of developing software are large but are a fixed cost while the marginal cost of one copy of Windows is small. The benefit to Windows users increases as the number of users increases (network economies) because with more users, the range of Windows applications expands.

When Microsoft entered the Internet browser market with Internet Explorer (IE), it offered it for a zero price. This is viewed as predatory pricing—an attempt to drive out the competition and monopolize a market. Microsoft now has integrated IE with Windows 98, which means that no one using this operating system needs a separate browser such as Netscape Communicator. Microsoft's critics claim that this practice is illegal product tying.

Microsoft's Response   Microsoft challenges all these claims. It says that although Windows dominates today, it is vulnerable to new operating systems. It also claims that integrating Internet Explorer with Windows 98 provides a product of greater consumer value. It is not tying. It is one product.

Microsoft will be the subject of ongoing investigation, and you should try to keep track of developments.

Merger Rules

The Federal Trade Commission (FTC) uses guidelines to determine which mergers it will examine and possibly block based on the Herfindahl-Hirschman index (HHI), which is explained in Chapter 10 (p. 208). A market in which the HHI is less than 1,000 is regarded as competitive. An index between 1,000 and 1,800 indicates a moderately concentrated market, and a merger in this market that would increase the index by 100 points is examined by the FTC. An index above 1,800 indicates a concentrated market, and a merger in this market that would increase the index by 50 points is examined. Figure 19.6(a) summarizes these guidelines.

The FTC used these guidelines to analyze two recently proposed mergers in the market for soft drinks. In 1986, PepsiCo announced its intention to buy 7-Up for $380 million. A month later, Coca-Cola said it would buy Dr Pepper for $470 million.

FIGURE 19.6

The HHI Merger Guidelines

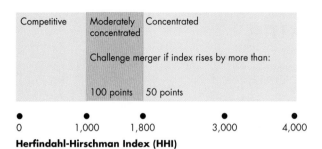

(a) The merger guidelines

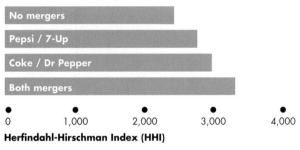

(b) Product mergers in soft drinks

The FTC scrutinizes proposed mergers if the HHI exceeds 1,000. Proposed mergers between producers of carbonated soft drinks were blocked in 1986 by application of these guidelines.

Whether this market is concentrated depends on how it is defined. The market for *all* soft drinks, which includes *carbonated* drinks marketed by these four companies plus *fruit juices* and *bottled water*, has an HHI of 120, so it is highly competitive. But the market for *carbonated* soft drinks is highly concentrated. Coca-Cola has a 39 percent share, PepsiCo has 28 percent, Dr Pepper is next with 7 percent, then comes 7-Up with 6 percent. One other producer, RJR, has a 5 percent market share. So the five largest firms in this market have an 85 percent market share. If we assume that the other 15 percent of the market consists of 15 firms, each with a 1 percent market share, the Herfindahl-Hirschman index is

$$HHI = 39^2 + 28^2 + 7^2 + 6^2 + 5^2 + 15 = 2,430.$$

With an HHI of this magnitude, a merger that increases the index by 50 points is examined by the FTC. Figure 19.6(b) shows how the HHI would have changed with the mergers. The PepsiCo and 7-Up merger would have increased the index by more than 300 points, the Coca-Cola and Dr Pepper merger would have increased it by more than 500 points, and both mergers together would have increased the index by almost 800 points. The FTC decided to define the market narrowly and, with increases of these magnitudes, blocked the mergers.

Public or Special Interest?

It is clear from the historical contexts in which antitrust law has evolved that its intent has been to protect and pursue the public interest and restrain the profit-seeking and anticompetitive actions of producers. But it is also clear from the above brief history of antitrust legislation and cases that, from time to time, the interest of the producer has had an influence on the way in which the law has been interpreted and applied. Nevertheless, the overall thrust of antitrust law appears to have been directed toward achieving efficiency and therefore to serving the public interest.

R E V I E W   Q U I Z

- What are the four Acts of Congress that make up our antitrust laws? When were these laws enacted?
- When is price fixing not a violation of the antitrust laws?
- What is an attempt to monopolize an industry?
- Name three antitrust cases that involve price fixing. What did the court decide?

We've reviewed the public interest and capture theories of government intervention. And we've seen that regulators do sometimes get captured by the regulated and work against the interest of consumers. But this outcome does not always occur.

In *Reading Between the Lines*, on pages 426–427, you can see a recent example of antitrust law being used to penalize fixing in an attempt to protect the public interest.

Price Fixing

THE NEW YORK TIMES, OCTOBER 15, 1996

Archer Daniels Agrees to Big Fine for Price Fixing

BY KURT EICHENWALD

The Archer Daniels Midland Company, long one of the country's most powerful corporations, agreed to plead guilty to conspiring with competitors to fix the prices of two agricultural products and pay $100 million in fines, the company announced yesterday.

The fine is by far the largest ever obtained by the Justice Department in a criminal price-fixing case, eclipsing the next highest by almost seven times. ...

In the plea, Archer Daniels—a food processing giant that advertises itself as the "Supermarket to the World"—will admit that it fixed prices of lysine, a feed additive, and citric acid, an organic acid used in various foods and beverages.

Under the deal, Archer Daniels will pay $70 million in fines for fixing lysine prices and $30 million for the citric acid case. ...

"The $100 million fine is shareholder assets that are being squandered to pay for criminal activity that never should have occurred," said James E. Burton, chief executive of the California Public Employees Retirement System, one of the nation's largest pension funds and an investor in Archer Daniels. ...

The company's financial power means that Archer Daniels will be able to pay its $100 million in fines—as well as another $90 million it has agreed to pay to settle class action suits relating to the investigation—without feeling much pain. The company has more than $1.3 billion in cash and liquid securities on hand; its profits last year approached $700 million and its businesses continue to boom. ...

Copyright ©1996 The New York Times Company.
Reprinted with permission.

Essence of the Story

■ Archer Daniels Midland (ADM) paid fines totaling $100 million for fixing the prices of lysine and citric acid.

■ The fine is seven times larger than the previous largest.

■ One large investor in ADM complained that the fine was squandering shareholder assets.

■ With $1.3 billion in cash and liquid assets and a profit of close to $700 million a year, ADM was easily able to pay the fine.

Economic Analysis

■ Here, we'll focus on fixing the price of lysine, for which ADM paid a $70 million fine.

■ First, a few technical facts. Lysine is an amino acid that is essential in the diets of most animals.

■ Animal food such as soybeanmeal contain lysine, but corn is deficient in lysine. So animals can be fed soybeanmeal or corn supplemented with lysine.

■ Now to the economics. Cost-conscious farmers use the least-cost diet. They buy lysine only if corn plus lysine costs less than soybeanmeal. So the price of lysine cannot rise much above the gap between the price of soybeanmeal and the price of corn.

■ The figure shows the (worldwide) market for lysine. The demand curve, D, is highly elastic because lysine competes with soybeanmeal.

■ The marginal cost of lysine is MC. In a competitive market, the marginal cost curve is the supply curve, S.

■ Equilibrium in a competitive market occurs at the quantity Q_C and the price P_C.

■ If the producers of lysine collude to fix the price, and if they act like a monopoly, their marginal revenue curve is MR in the figure.

■ To maximize economic profit, the firms fix the price at P_M, the highest price at which they can sell Q_M, the quantity at which marginal revenue equals marginal cost. The firms allocate the total output Q_M among themselves.

■ This action brings gains to producers—their economic profit increases by the blue area in the figure.

■ This action imposes costs on consumers because it decreases consumer surplus and also creates deadweight loss, the gray area in the figure.

■ The fine imposed on ADM decreases its profit and returns some of the loss to the taxpayers (consumers).

■ Some ADM stockholders say that their assets are being used to pay the fine. This claim is not exactly correct. The illegal price fixing increased ADM's profit, which boosted its share price and benefited its stockholders. The fine corrects this situation.

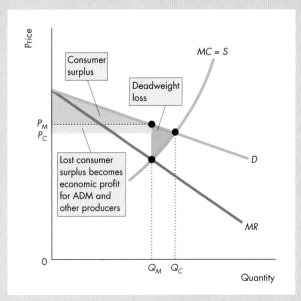

■ It is not known if the fine is large enough to wipe out the gains from price fixing or to leave ADM and its stockholders with a net gain from illegal actions.

■ But what is known is that the deadweight loss from price fixing is lost forever. No fine can restore this loss.

You're The Voter

■ The largest fine for price fixing before the ADM fine was $15 million, imposed on Dyno Nobel for price fixing. Is the ADM fine is too large, too small, or about right? Explain.

■ Price fixing is punishable by fines or by possibly jailing the people found responsible. This news article reports only the fine on ADM. But in January 1997, a Chicago federal grand jury indicted three former top executives of ADM, along with a Japanese executive, for conspiring to fix prices and allocate sales in the worldwide market for lysine. How would you use economic reasoning to decide which penalty is likely to be more effective (a) to deter price fixing and (b) to compensate those who lose from it?

427

SUMMARY

KEY POINTS

Market Intervention (p. 412)

- Governments intervene in monopoly and oligopoly markets with regulation and antitrust law.

Economic Theory of Regulation (pp. 412–414)

- Consumers and producers express their demand for the regulation by voting, lobbying, and making campaign contributions.
- The larger the surplus per person generated by a regulation, the greater the number of gainers, and the smaller the number of losers, the larger is the demand for the regulation.
- Regulation is supplied by politicians, who pursue votes and bureaucrats who pursue large budgets.
- The larger the surplus per person generated and the larger the number of people affected by it, the larger is the supply of regulation.
- Public interest theory predicts that regulation maximizes total surplus. Capture theory predicts that regulation maximizes producer surplus.

Regulation and Deregulation (pp. 414–421)

- Federal regulation began in 1887 (with the Interstate Commerce Commission) and expanded until the mid-1970s, since when much deregulation has occurred.
- Regulation is conducted by agencies that are controlled by politically appointed bureaucrats and staffed by a permanent bureaucracy of experts.
- Regulation has often had little effect on profits, and deregulation has often brought gains for consumers and producers.

Antitrust Law (pp. 422–425)

- Antitrust law is an alternative way in which the government can control monopoly and monopolistic practices.
- The first antitrust law, the Sherman Act, was passed in 1890, and the law was strengthened in 1914 when the Clayton Act was passed and the Federal Trade Commission was created.

- All price-fixing agreements are violations of the Sherman Act, and no acceptable excuse exists.
- The first landmark cases (against the American Tobacco Company and Standard Oil Company) established the "rule of reason," which held that an attempt to monopolize is illegal; monopoly itself is not illegal.
- The Federal Trade Commission uses guidelines to determine which mergers to examine and possibly block based on the Herfindahl-Hirschman Index.
- The intent of antitrust law is to protect the public interest. This intent has been served most of the time. But sometimes the interest of the producer has influenced the way in which the law has been interpreted and applied.

KEY FIGURES AND TABLES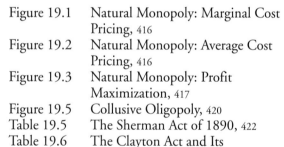

KEY TERMS

PROBLEMS

*1. Elixir Springs, Inc., is an unregulated natural monopoly that bottles Elixir, a unique health product with no substitutes. The total fixed cost incurred by Elixir Springs is $150,000, and its marginal cost is 10¢ a bottle. The figure illustrates the demand for Elixir.

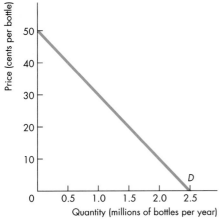

a. What is the price of a bottle of Elixir?
b. How many bottles does Elixir Springs sell?
c. Does Elixir Springs maximize total surplus or producer surplus?

2. Cascade Springs, Inc., is a natural monopoly that bottles water from a spring high in the Rocky Mountains. The total fixed cost that it incurs is $120,000, and its marginal cost is 20 cents a bottle. The figure illustrates the demand for Cascade Springs bottled water.

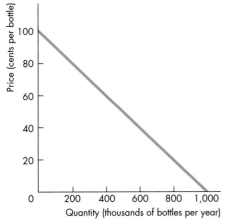

a. What is the price of Cascade Springs water?
b. How many bottles does Cascade Springs sell?
c. Does Cascade Springs maximize total surplus or producer surplus?

*3. The government regulates Elixir Springs in problem 1 by imposing a marginal cost pricing rule.
a. What is the price of a bottle of Elixir?
b. How many bottles does Elixir Springs sell?
c. What is Elixir Springs' economic profit?
d. What is the consumer surplus?
e. Is the regulation in the public interest? Explain.

4. The government regulates Cascade Springs in problem 2 by imposing a marginal cost pricing rule.
a. What is the price of Cascade Springs water?
b. How many bottles does Cascade Springs sell?
c. What is the economic profit?
d. What is the consumer surplus?
e. Is the regulation in the public interest? Explain.

*5. The government regulates Elixir Springs in problem 1 by imposing an average cost pricing rule.
a. What is the price of a bottle of Elixir?
b. How many bottles does Elixir Springs sell?
c. What is Elixir Springs' economic profit?
d. What is the consumer surplus?
e. Is the regulation in the public interest? Explain.

6. The government regulates Cascade Springs in problem 2 by imposing an average cost pricing rule.
a. What is the price of Cascade Springs water?
b. How many bottles does Cascade Springs sell?
c. What is the economic profit?
d. What is the consumer surplus?
e. Is the regulation in the public interest? Explain.

*7. Two airlines share an international route.

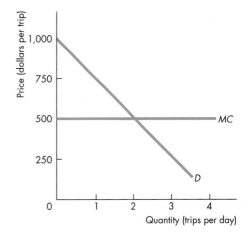

The figure shows the market demand curve for trips on this route and the marginal cost curve that each firm faces. This air route is regulated.

a. What is the price of a trip and what is the number of trips per day if the regulation is in the public interest?

b. What is the price of a trip and what is the number of trips per day if the airlines capture the regulator?

c. What is the deadweight loss in part (b)?

d. What do you need to know to predict whether the regulation is in the public interest or the producer interest?

8. Two phone companies offer local calls in an area. The figure shows the market demand curve for calls and the marginal costs curves of each firm. These firms are regulated.

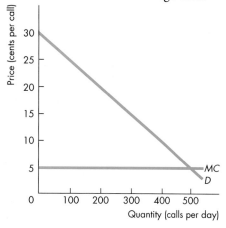

a. What is the price of a call and what is the number of calls per day if the regulation is in the public interest?

b. What is the price of a call and what is the number of calls per day if the phone companies capture the regulator?

c. What is the deadweight loss in part (b)?

d. What do you need to know to predict whether the regulation is in the public interest or the producer interest?

*9. Explain the difference between regulation and antitrust law. What types of situations do each apply to? Give an example of the use of each.

10. Describe the difference between the way in which the two parts of the Sherman Act have been applied. Why do you think one part has been interpreted more strictly than the other?

CRITICAL THINKING

1. Study *Reading Between the Lines* on pp. 426–427, and then answer the following questions:

a. To what charges did Archer Daniels Midland plead guilty?

b. Why is price fixing a problem? Who gains and who loses?

c. Why is it likely that the demand for lysine is highly elastic? What effect does the elasticity of demand have on a firm's ability to increase price in a price-fixing agreement?

d. What is citric acid used for? Is it likely that the demand for citric acid is highly elastic?

e. Critically evaluate the claim of James E. Burton.

f. Try to think of some different ways in which price fixing can be prevented. Use economic reasoning to explain why each method you have thought of will work.

2. Why is the Department of Justice concerned about the practices of Microsoft? What provision of the antitrust laws is Microsoft alleged to have violated? What is Microsoft's response?

3. What regulatory problems if any, are created by new technologies that enable people to connect to the Internet using a cable modem (and cable television lines) and make long-distance calls over the Internet?

4. Use the link on the Parkin Web site to visit the Federal Trade Commission, where you can obtain information about Intel, the computer chip maker.

a. What was the FTC's problem with Intel?

b. What did Intel agree to do?

c. Explain how Intel's agreement will influence the price, quantity, and consumer and producer surplus in the market for computer chips.

5. Use the link on the Parkin Web site to visit the Department of Justice on the World Wide Web and go to the page on press releases for 1997. Read the press release on price fixing by California crab catchers.

a. Explain how the price of crabs was fixed.

b. Explain what the Department of Justice did about the problem.

Chapter 20

Externalities, the Environment, and Knowledge

We burn huge quantities of fossil fuels—coal, natural gas, and oil—that cause acid rain and possibly global warming. The persistent and large-scale use of chlorofluorocarbons (CFCs) may have caused irreparable damage to the earth's ozone layer, thereby exposing us to additional ultraviolet rays, which increase the incidence of skin cancer. We dump toxic waste into rivers, lakes, and oceans. These environmental issues are simultaneously everybody's problem and nobody's problem. What, if anything, can government do to protect our environment? How can government action help us to take account of the damage that we cause others every time we turn on our heating or air conditioning systems? ◆ Almost every day, we hear about a new discovery—in medicine, engineering, chemistry, physics, or even economics. The advance of knowledge seems boundless. And more and more people are learning more and more of what is already known. The stock of knowledge—what is known and how many people know it—is increasing, apparently without bound. We are getting smarter. But is our stock of knowledge advancing fast enough? Are we spending enough on research and development? Do we spend enough on education? Do enough people remain in school for long enough? Would we be better off if we spent more on research and education?

Greener and Smarter

◆ In this chapter, we study the problems that arise because many of our actions create externalities. They affect other people, for ill or good, in ways that we do not usually take into account when we make our own economic choices. We study two big areas—the environment and the accumulation of knowledge—in which these problems are especially important. Externalities are a major source of *market failure*. When market failure occurs, we must either live with the inefficiency it creates or try to achieve greater efficiency by making some *public choices*. This chapter studies these choices. It begins by looking at external costs that affect the environment.

After studying this chapter, you will be able to:

- Explain how property rights can sometimes overcome externalities

- Explain how emission charges, marketable permits, and taxes can be used to achieve efficiency in the face of external costs

- Explain how subsidies can be used to achieve efficiency in the face of external benefits

- Explain how scholarships, below-cost tuition, and research grants make the quantity of education and invention more efficient

- Explain how patents increase efficiency

Economics of the Environment

ENVIRONMENTAL PROBLEMS ARE NOT NEW, AND they are not restricted to rich industrial countries. Preindustrial towns and cities in Europe had severe sewage disposal problems that created cholera epidemics and plagues that killed tens of millions of people. Nor is the desire to find solutions to environmental problems new. The development in the fourteenth century of pure water supplies and of garbage and sewage disposal are examples of early contributions to improving the quality of the environment.

Popular discussions of the environment usually pay little attention to economics. They focus on physical aspects of the environment, not costs and benefits. A common assumption is that if people's actions cause *any* environmental degradation, those actions must cease. In contrast, an economic study of the environment emphasizes costs and benefits. An economist talks about the efficient amount of pollution or environmental damage. This emphasis on costs and benefits does not mean that economists, as citizens, do not share the same goals as others and value a healthy environment. Nor does it mean that economists have the right answers and everyone else has the wrong ones (or vice versa). Economics provides a set of tools and principles that clarify the issues. It does not provide an agreed list of solutions. The starting point for an economic analysis of the environment is the demand for a healthy environment.

The Demand for Environmental Quality

The demand for a clean and healthy environment is greater today than it has ever been. We express our demand for a better environment in several ways. We join organizations that lobby for environmental regulations and policies. We vote for politicians who support the environmental policies that we want to see implemented. (All politicians at least pay lip service to the environment today.) We buy "green" products and avoid hazardous products, even if we pay a bit more to do so. And we pay higher housing costs and commuting costs to live in pleasant neighborhoods.

The demand for a cleaner environment has grown for two main reasons. First, as our incomes increase, we demand a larger range of goods and services, and one of these "goods" is a high-quality environment. We value clean air, unspoiled natural scenery, and wildlife, and we are willing and able to pay for them.

Second, as our knowledge of the effects of our actions on the environment grows, we are able to take measures that improve the environment. For example, now that we know how sulfur dioxide causes acid rain and how clearing rain forests destroys natural stores of carbon dioxide, we are able, in principle, to design measures that limit these problems.

Let's look at the range of environmental problems that have been identified and the actions that create those problems.

The Sources of Environmental Problems

Environmental problems arise from pollution of the air, water, and land, and these individual sources of pollution interact through the *ecosystem*.

Air Pollution Figure 20.1(a) shows the five economic activities that create most of our air pollution. It also shows the relative contributions of each activity. More than two thirds of air pollution comes from road transportation and industrial processes. Only one sixth arises from electric power generation.

A common belief is that air pollution is getting worse. On many fronts, as we will see later in this chapter, *global* air pollution *is* getting worse. But air pollution in the United States is getting less severe for most substances. Figure 20.1(b) shows the trends in the concentrations of six air pollutants. While lead has been almost eliminated from our air and sulfur dioxide, carbon monoxide, and suspended particulates have been reduced substantially, levels of other pollutants have remained more stable.

While the facts about the sources and trends in air pollution are not in doubt, there is considerable disagreement among scientists about the *effects* of air pollution. The least controversial problem is *acid rain*, which is caused by sulfur dioxide and nitrogen oxide emissions from coal- and oil-fired generators of electric utilities. Acid rain begins with air pollution, leads to water pollution, and damages vegetation.

More controversial are airborne substances (suspended particulates) such as lead from leaded gasoline. Some scientists believe that in sufficiently large concentrations, these substances (189 of which have currently been identified) cause cancer and other life-threatening conditions.

FIGURE 20.1

Air Pollution

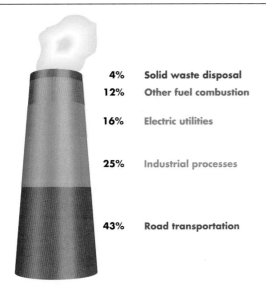

4%	Solid waste disposal
12%	Other fuel combustion
16%	Electric utilities
25%	Industrial processes
43%	Road transportation

(a) Sources of emission

Part (a) shows that road transportation is the largest source of air pollution, followed by industrial processes and electric utilities. Part (b) shows that lead has almost been eliminated from our air and concentrations of carbon monoxide, sulfur dioxide, and suspended particulates have decreased. But

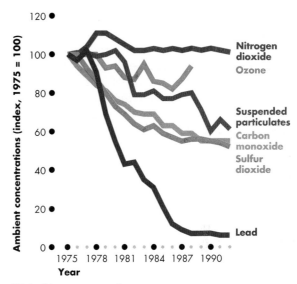

(b) Ambient concentrations

nitrogen dioxide and ozone levels have persisted at close to their 1975 levels.

Source: U.S. Environmental Protection Agency, *National Air Quality and Emissions Trends Report,* 1996.

Even more controversial is *global warming,* which some scientists believe results from the carbon dioxide emissions of road transportation and electric utilities, methane created by cows and other livestock, and nitrous oxide emissions of electric utilities and from fertilizers. The earth's average temperature has increased over the past 100 years, but most of the increase occurred *before* 1940. Determining what causes changes in the earth's temperature and separating out the effect of carbon dioxide and other factors are proving to be very difficult.

Equally controversial is the problem of *ozone layer depletion,* which some scientists believe results from chlorofluorocarbons (CFCs) from refrigeration equipment and (in the past) aerosols. There is no doubt that a hole in the ozone layer exists over Antarctica and that the ozone layer protects us from cancer-causing ultraviolet rays from the sun. But how our industrial activity influences the ozone layer is simply not understood at this time.

One air pollution problem has almost been eliminated: lead from gasoline. In part, this happened because the cost of living without leaded gasoline, it turns out, is not high. But sulfur dioxide and the so-called greenhouse gases are a much tougher problem to tackle. Their alternatives are costly or have environmental problems of their own. The major sources of these pollutants are road vehicles and electric utilities. Road vehicles can be made "greener" in a variety of ways. One is with new fuels—some alternatives that are being investigated are alcohol, natural gas, propane and butane, and hydrogen. Another way of making cars and trucks "greener" is to change the chemistry of gasoline. Refiners are working on reformulations of gasoline that cut tailpipe emissions. Similarly, electric power can be generated in cleaner ways by harnessing solar power, tidal power, or geothermal power. Technically possible, these methods are more costly than conventional carbon-fueled generators. Another alternative is nuclear power. This method is good for air pollution but bad for land and water pollution because there is no known safe method of disposing of spent nuclear fuel.

Water Pollution   The largest sources of water pollution are the dumping of industrial waste and treated sewage in lakes and rivers and the runoff from fertilizers. A more dramatic source is the accidental spilling of crude oil into the oceans such as the *Exxon Valdez* spill in Alaska in 1989 and an even larger spill in the Russian Arctic in 1994. The most frightening is the dumping of nuclear waste into the ocean by the former Soviet Union.

There are two main alternatives to polluting the waterways and oceans. One is the chemical processing of waste to render it inert or biodegradable. The other, in wide use for nuclear waste, is to use land sites for storage in secure containers.

Land Pollution   Land pollution arises from dumping toxic waste products. Ordinary household garbage does not pose a pollution problem unless dumped garbage seeps into the water supply. This possibility increases as less-suitable landfill sites are used. It is estimated that 80 percent of existing landfills will be full by 2010. Some regions (New York, New Jersey, and other East Coast states) and some countries (Japan and the Netherlands) are seeking less costly alternatives to landfill, such as recycling and incineration. Recycling is an apparently attractive alternative, but it requires an investment in new technologies to be effective. Incineration is a high-cost alternative to landfill, and it produces air pollution. These alternatives are not free, and they become efficient only when the cost of using landfill is high.

We've seen that the demand for a high-quality environment has grown, and we've described the range of environmental problems. Let's now look at the ways in which these problems can be handled. We'll begin by looking at property rights and how they relate to environmental externalities.

Absence of Property Rights and Environmental Externalities

Externalities arise because of an *absence* of property rights. **Property rights** are social arrangements that govern the ownership, use, and disposal of resources, goods, and services. In modern societies, a property right is a legally established title that is enforceable in the courts.

Property rights are absent when externalities arise. No one owns the air, the rivers, and the oceans. So it is no one's private business to ensure that these resources are used in an efficient way. In fact, there is an incentive to use them more than if there were property rights.

Figure 20.2 shows an environmental externality in the absence of property rights. A chemical factory upstream from a fishing club must decide how to dispose of its waste.

The factory's marginal benefit curve, *MB*, tells us the benefit to the factory of an additional ton of waste dumped into the river. The *MB* curve is also the firm's demand curve for the use of the river, which is a productive resource. The demand for a resource slopes downward because of the law of diminishing returns (see Chapter 15, pp. 320–321).

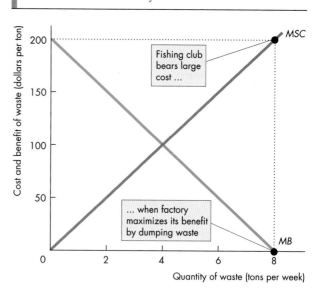

FIGURE 20.2

An Externality

A chemical factory's marginal benefit from dumping its waste into a river is *MB*, and a fishing club's marginal cost of having waste dumped is *MSC*. With no property rights, the factory maximizes total benefit by dumping 8 tons a week, the quantity at which the marginal benefit of dumping equals the marginal cost (zero). With this quantity of waste, the fishing club bears a marginal cost of $200 per ton. This outcome is inefficient because marginal social cost exceeds marginal benefit.

Marginal social cost is the marginal cost incurred by the producer of a good—marginal private cost—plus the marginal cost imposed on others—the external cost. The factory bears no cost of dumping. All the costs are borne by the fishing club. The marginal social cost curve, *MSC*, tells us the cost borne by the club when one additional ton of waste is dumped into the river. Marginal cost increases as the quantity dumped increases.

If no one owns the river, the factory dumps the amount of waste that maximizes *its own* total benefit. Its marginal cost is zero (along the *x*-axis), so it dumps 8 tons a week, the quantity that makes marginal benefit zero. The marginal social cost of the waste, which is borne by the fishing club, is $200 a ton. Marginal cost exceeds marginal benefit, so the outcome is inefficient.

Property Rights and the Coase Theorem

Sometimes it is possible to correct an externality by establishing a property right where one does not currently exist. For example, suppose that the chemical factory owns the river. The fishing club must pay the factory for the right to fish in the river. But the price that the club is willing to pay depends on the number and quality of fish, which in turn depend on how much waste the factory dumps in the river. The greater the amount of pollution, the smaller is the amount the fishing club is willing to pay for the right to fish. The chemical factory is now confronted with the cost of its pollution decision. It might still decide to pollute, but if it does, it faces the opportunity cost of its actions—forgone revenue from the fishing club.

Alternatively, suppose that the fishing club owns the river. Now the factory must pay a fee to the fishing club for the right to dump its waste. The more waste it dumps (equivalently, the more fish it kills), the more it must pay. Again, the factory faces an opportunity cost for the pollution it creates.

Does it matter how property rights are assigned? Does it matter whether the polluter or the victim of the pollution owns the resource that might be polluted? At first thought, ownership seems crucial. And until 1960, that is what everyone thought—including economists who had thought about the problem for longer than a few minutes. But in 1960, Ronald Coase had a remarkable insight, now called the Coase theorem. The **Coase theorem** is the proposition

that if property rights exist and transactions costs are low, private transactions are efficient. Equivalently, with property rights and low transactions costs, there are no externalities. All the costs and benefits are taken into account by the transacting parties. So it doesn't matter how the property rights are assigned.

Figure 20.3 illustrates the Coase theorem. As before, the demand curve for dumping waste is the factory's marginal benefit curve, *MB*. This curve tells us what the factory is willing to pay to dump. With property rights in place, the *MSC* curve is the fishing club's supply curve of river use to the firm. It tells us what the club's members must be paid if they are to put up with inferior fishing and supply the firm with a permit to dump.

The efficient level of waste is 4 tons a week. At this level, the club bears a cost of $100 for the last

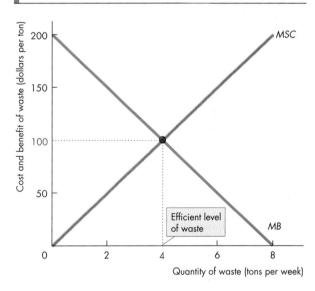

Pollution of a river imposes a marginal social cost, *MSC*, on the victim and provides a marginal benefit, *MB*, to the polluter. The efficient amount of pollution is the quantity that makes marginal benefit equal to marginal social cost—in this example, 4 tons per week. If the polluter owns the river, the victim will pay $400 a week ($100 a ton × 4 tons a week) to the polluter for the assurance that pollution will not exceed 4 tons a week. If the victim owns the river, the polluter will pay $400 for pollution rights to dump 4 tons a week.

ton dumped into the river, and the factory gets a benefit of that amount. If waste disposal is restricted below 4 tons a week, an increase in waste disposal benefits the factory more than it costs the club. The factory can pay the club to put up with more waste disposal, and both the club and the factory can gain. If waste disposal exceeds 4 tons a week, an increase in waste disposal costs the club more than it benefits the factory. The club can now pay the factory to cut its waste disposal, and again, both the club and the factory can gain. Only when the level of waste disposal is 4 tons a week can neither party do any better. This is the efficient level of waste disposal.

The amount of waste disposal is the same regardless of who owns the river. If the factory owns it, the club pays $400 for fishing rights and for an agreement that waste disposal will not exceed 4 tons a week. If the club owns the river, the factory pays $400 for the right to dump 4 tons of waste a week. In both cases, the amount of waste disposal is the efficient amount.

Property rights work if transactions costs are low. The factory and the fishing club can negotiate the deal that produces the efficient outcome. But in many situations, transactions costs are high and property rights cannot be enforced. Imagine the transactions costs if the 50 million people who live in the northeastern part of the United States and Canada tried to negotiate an agreement with the 20,000 factories that emit sulfur dioxide and cause acid rain! In this type of case, governments use alternative methods of coping with externalities. They use:

1. Emission charges
2. Marketable permits
3. Taxes

In the United States, the federal government has established an agency, the Environmental Protection Agency (EPA), to coordinate and administer the nation's environment policies. Let's look at the tools available to the EPA and see how they work.

Emission Charges

Emission charges are a method of using the market to achieve efficiency, even in the face of externalities. The government (or the regulatory agency established by the government) sets the emission charges, which are, in effect, a price per unit of pollution. The more pollution a firm creates, the more it pays in emission charges. This method of dealing with environmental externalities has been used only modestly in the United States, but it is common in Europe. For example, in France, Germany, and the Netherlands, water polluters pay a waste disposal charge.

To work out the emission charge that achieves efficiency, the regulator must determine the marginal social cost and marginal *social* benefit of pollution. **Marginal social benefit** is the marginal benefit received by the buyer of a good—marginal private benefit—plus the marginal benefit to others—the external benefit. To achieve efficiency, the price per unit of pollution must be set to make the marginal social cost of the pollution equal to its marginal social benefit.

Figure 20.4 illustrates an efficient emissions charge. The marginal benefit of pollution is *MB* and accrues to the polluters—there is no *external* benefit. The marginal social cost of pollution is *MSC* and is

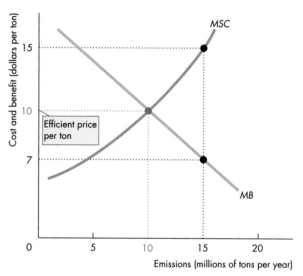

Electric utilities obtain marginal benefits from sulfur dioxide emissions of *MB*, and everyone else bears a marginal social cost of *MSC*. The efficient level of pollution—10 million tons a year in this example—is achieved by imposing an emission charge on the utilities of $10 a ton. If the emission charge is set too low, at $7 a ton, the resulting amount of pollution is greater than the efficient amount—at 15 million tons a year in this example. In this case, the marginal social cost is $15 a ton and it exceeds the marginal benefit of $7 a ton.

entirely an external cost. The efficient level of sulfur dioxide emissions is 10 million tons a year, which is achieved with an emission charge of $10 per ton. At this price, polluters do not find it worthwhile to buy the permission to pollute in excess of 10 million tons a year.

In practice, it is hard to determine the marginal benefit of pollution. And the people who are best informed about the marginal benefit, the polluters, have an incentive to mislead the regulators about the benefit. As a result, if a pollution charge is used, the most likely outcome is for the price to be set too low. For example, in Fig. 20.4, the price might be set at $7 per ton. At this price, polluters find it worthwhile to pay for 15 million tons a year. At this level of pollution, the marginal social cost is $15 a ton, and the amount of pollution exceeds the efficient level.

One way of overcoming excess pollution is to impose a quantitative limit. The most sophisticated way of doing this is with quantitative limits that firms can buy and sell—with marketable permits. Let's look at this alternative.

Marketable Permits

Instead of imposing emission charges on polluters, each potential polluter might be given a pollution limit. To achieve efficiency, marginal benefit and marginal cost must be assessed just as in the case of emission charges. Provided that these benefit-cost calculations are correct, the same efficient outcome can be achieved with quantitative limits as with emission charges. But in the case of quantitative limits, a cap must be set for each polluter. To set these caps at their efficient levels, the marginal benefit of *each* producer must be assessed. If firm H has a higher marginal benefit than firm L, an efficiency gain can be achieved by decreasing the cap of firm L and increasing that of firm H. It is virtually impossible to determine the marginal benefits of each firm, so in practice, quantitative restrictions cannot be allocated to each producer in an efficient way.

Marketable permits are a clever way of overcoming the need for the regulator to know every firm's marginal benefit schedule. Each firm can be allocated a permit to emit a certain amount of pollution, and firms may buy and sell such permits. Firms that have low marginal benefits from sulfur dioxide emissions will be willing to sell their permits to other firms that have a high marginal benefit. If the market in permits is competitive, the price at which firms trade permits makes the marginal benefit of pollution equal for all firms. And if the correct number of permits has been allotted, the outcome can be efficient.

The Market for Emissions in the United States

Markets for emission permits have operated in the United States since the Environmental Protection Agency first implemented air quality programs following the passage of the Clean Air Act in 1970.

Trading in lead pollution permits became common during the 1980s, and this marketable permit program has been rated a success. It enabled lead to be virtually eliminated from the atmosphere of the United States (see Figure 20.1b). But this success might not easily translate to other situations because lead pollution has some special features. First, most lead pollution came from a single source, leaded gasoline. Second, lead in gasoline is easily monitored. Third, the objective of the program was clear: eliminate lead in gasoline.

The EPA is now considering using marketable permits to promote efficiency in the control of chlorofluorocarbons, the gases that are believed to damage the ozone layer.

Taxes and External Costs

Taxes can be used to provide incentives for producers or consumers to cut back on an activity that creates external costs. To see how taxes work, consider the market for transportation services.

The costs borne by the producers of transportation services are not the only costs. External costs arise from the airborne particulates and greenhouse gases caused by vehicle emissions. Further, one person's decision to use a highway imposes congestion costs on others. These costs also are external costs. When all the external marginal costs are added to the marginal cost faced by the producer, we obtain the marginal social cost of transportation.

Figure 20.5 shows the market for transportation services. The demand curve, D, is also the marginal benefit curve, MB. This curve tells us how much consumers value each different quantity of transportation services. The curve MC measures the marginal *private* cost of producing transportation services—the costs directly incurred by the producers of these services. The curve MSC measures the marginal *social* cost, which sums the external costs and private costs.

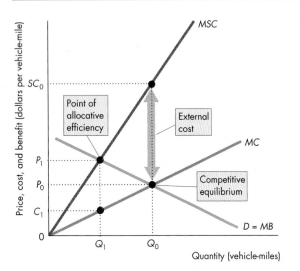

The demand curve for road transportation services is also the marginal benefit curve ($D = MB$). The marginal private cost curve is MC. If the market is unregulated, output is Q_0 vehicle-miles and the price is P_0 per vehicle-mile. Marginal social cost is SC_0 per vehicle-mile. Because of congestion and pollution, the marginal social cost exceeds the marginal private cost. Marginal social cost is shown by curve MSC. If the government imposes a tax so that producers of transportation services must pay the marginal social cost, the MSC curve becomes the relevant marginal cost curve for suppliers' decisions. The price increases to P_1 per vehicle-mile, and the quantity decreases to Q_1 vehicle-miles. Allocative efficiency is achieved.

If the transportation market is competitive and unregulated, the equilibrium will be at the price P_0 and quantity Q_0. Road users will balance their own marginal cost, MC, against their own marginal benefit, MB, and travel Q_0 vehicle-miles at a price (and cost) of P_0 per mile. At this scale of transportation services, the marginal social cost is SC_0. The marginal social cost minus the marginal private cost, $SC_0 - P_0$, is the marginal cost imposed on others—the marginal external cost.

Suppose the government taxes road transportation and that it sets the tax equal to the external marginal cost. By imposing such a tax, the government makes the suppliers of transportation services incur a marginal cost equal to the marginal social cost. That

is, the marginal private cost plus the tax equals the marginal social cost. The market supply curve is now the same as the MSC curve. The price rises to P_1 per vehicle-mile, and at this price, people travel Q_1 vehicle-miles. The marginal cost of the resources used in producing Q_1 vehicle-miles is C_1, and the marginal external cost is P_1 minus C_1. That marginal external cost is paid by the consumer through the tax.

The situation at the price P_1 and the quantity Q_1 is efficient. At a quantity greater than Q_1, marginal social cost exceeds marginal benefit, so net benefit increases by decreasing the quantity of transportation services. At a quantity less than Q_1, marginal benefit exceeds marginal social cost, so net benefit increases by increasing the quantity of transportation services.

A Carbon Fuel Tax? A tax can be imposed on any activity that creates external costs. For example, we could tax *all* air-polluting activities. Because the carbon fuels that we use to power our vehicles and generate our electric power are a major source of pollution, why don't we have a broad-based tax on all activities that burn carbon fuel and set the tax rate high enough to give a large reduction in carbon emissions?

The question becomes even more pressing when we consider not only the current levels of greenhouse gases but also their projected future levels. In 1995, annual carbon emissions worldwide were a staggering 6.8 billion tons. By 2050, with current policies, that annual total is predicted to be 24 billion tons.

Uncertainty About Global Warming Part of the reason we do not have a high, broad-based, carbon fuel tax is that the scientific evidence that carbon emissions produce global warming is not accepted by everyone. Climatologists are uncertain about how carbon emissions translate into atmospheric concentrations—about how the *flow* of emissions translates into a *stock* of pollution. The main uncertainty arises because carbon drains from the atmosphere into the oceans and vegetation at a rate that is not well understood. Climatologists are also uncertain about the connection between carbon concentration and temperature. And economists are uncertain about how a temperature increase translates into economic costs and benefits. Some economists believe that the costs and benefits are almost zero, while others believe that a temperature increase of 5.4 degrees Fahrenheit by 2050 will reduce the total output of goods and services by 20 percent.

Present Cost and Future Benefit   Another factor weighing against a large change in fuel use is that the costs would be borne now, while the benefits, if any, would accrue many years in the future. To compare future benefits with current costs, we must use an interest rate. If the interest rate is 1 percent a year, a dollar today becomes $2.70 in 100 years. If the interest rate is 5 percent a year, a dollar today becomes more than $131.50 in 100 years. So at an interest rate of 1 percent a year, it is worth spending $1 million in 1997 on pollution control to avoid $2.7 million in environmental damage in 2097. At an interest rate of 5 percent a year, it is worth spending $1 million today only if this expenditure avoids $131.5 million in environmental damage in 2097.

Because large uncertain future benefits are needed to justify small current costs, a general tax on carbon fuels is not a high priority on the political agenda.

International Factors   A final factor against a large change in fuel use is the international pattern of the use of carbon fuels. Right now, carbon pollution comes in even doses from the industrial countries and the developing countries. But by 2050, three quarters of the carbon pollution will come from the developing countries (if the trends persist).

One reason for the high pollution rate in some developing countries (notably China, Russia, and other Eastern European countries) is that their governments *subsidize* the use of coal or oil. These subsidies lower producers' marginal costs and encourage the use of fuels. The result is that the quantity of carbon fuels consumed exceeds the efficient quantity—and by a large amount. It is estimated that by 2050, these subsidies will induce annual global carbon emissions of some 10 billion tons—about two fifths of total emissions. If the subsidies were removed, global emissions in 2050 would be 10 billion tons a year less.

A Global Warming Dilemma

With the high output rate of greenhouse gases in the developing world, the United States and the other industrial countries are faced with a global warming dilemma (like the prisoners' dilemma in Chapter 14, pp. 295–296). Decreasing pollution is costly and might bring benefits. But the benefits depend on actions being taken by all countries to limit pollution. If one country acts alone, it bears the cost of limiting pollution and gets almost no benefits. So it

is worthwhile taking steps to limit global pollution only if all nations act together.

Table 20.1 shows the global warming dilemma faced by the United States and the developing countries. The numbers are hypothetical. Each country (we'll call the developing countries a country) has two possible policies: to control carbon emissions or to pollute. If each country pollutes, it receives a zero net return (by assumption), shown in the top left square in the table. If both countries control emissions, each pays the cost and gets the benefit. Its net return is $25 billion, as shown in the bottom right square of the table. If the United States controls emissions but the developing countries do not, the United States alone bears the cost and all countries enjoy a lower level of pollution. In this example, the United States pays $50 billion more than it benefits and the developing countries benefit by $50 billion more than they pay, as shown in the top right corner of the table. Finally, if the developing countries control emissions and the United States does not, the developing countries bear the cost and the United States

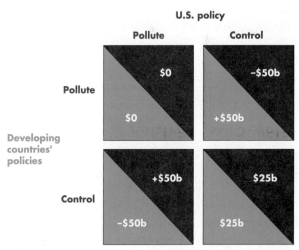

TABLE 20.1

A Global Warming Dilemma

If the United States and developing countries both pollute, the top left square shows their payoffs. If both countries control pollution, the bottom right square shows their payoffs. When one country pollutes and the other one does not, the top right and bottom left squares show their payoffs. The outcome of this game is for both countries to pollute. The structure of this game is the same as that of the prisoners' dilemma.

shares the gains. The developing countries lose $50 billion and the United States gains this amount, as shown in the bottom left corner of the table.

Confronted with these possible payoffs, the United States and the developing countries decide their policies. Each country reasons as follows: If the other country does not control emissions, we break even if we pollute and we lose $50 billion if we control our emissions. Conclusion: Each country is better off individually by polluting. So no one controls emissions, and pollution continues unabated.

Treaties and International Agreements

To break the dilemma, international agreements—treaties—might be negotiated. But such treaties must have incentives for countries to comply with their agreements. Otherwise, even with a treaty, the situation remains as we've just described and illustrated in Table 20.1.

One such international agreement is the *climate convention* that came into effect on March 21, 1994. This convention is an agreement among 60 countries to limit their output of greenhouse gases. But the convention does not have economic teeth. The poorer countries are merely asked to list their sources of greenhouse gases. The rich countries must show how, by 2000, they will return to their 1990 emissions levels.

R E V I E W   Q U I Z

- Why do externalities prevent markets from being efficient?
- How can an externality be eliminated by assigning property rights? How does this method of coping with an externality work?
- How do emission charges and pollution limits work to deal with externalities? Is one preferred over the other?
- How do taxes help us to cope with externalities? At what level must a pollution tax be set if it is to induce firms to produce the efficient quantity of pollution?
- What are the problems that arise when an externality goes beyond the scope of one country?

Economics of Knowledge

KNOWLEDGE, THE THINGS PEOPLE KNOW AND understand, has a profound effect on the economy. The economics of knowledge is an attempt to understand that effect. It is also an attempt to understand the process of knowledge accumulation and the incentives people face to discover, to learn, and to pass on what they know to others. It is an economic analysis of the scientific and engineering processes that lead to the discovery and development of new technologies. And it is a study of the education process of teaching and learning.

You can think of knowledge as being both a consumer good and a productive resource. The demand for knowledge—the willingness to pay to acquire knowledge—depends on the marginal benefit it provides to its possessor. As a consumer good, knowledge provides utility, and this is one source of its marginal benefit. As a productive resource—part of the stock of capital—knowledge increases productivity, and this is another source of its marginal benefit.

Knowledge clearly creates benefits for its possessor. It might also create external benefits. When children learn the basics of reading, writing, and numbers in grade school, they are equipping themselves to be better citizens, better able to communicate and interact with each other. The process continues through high school and college. But when people make decisions about how much schooling to undertake, they undervalue the external benefits that it creates.

External benefits also arise from research and development activities that lead to the creation of new knowledge. Once someone has worked out how to do something, others can copy the basic idea. They do have to work to copy an idea, so they face an opportunity cost. But they do not usually have to pay the person who made the discovery to use it. When Isaac Newton worked out the formulas for calculating the rate of response of one variable to another—calculus—everyone was free to use his method. When a spreadsheet program called VisiCalc was invented, others were free to copy the basic idea. Lotus Corporation developed its 1-2-3 and later Microsoft created Excel, and both became highly successful, but they did not pay for the key idea first used in VisiCalc. When the first shopping mall was built and found to be a successful way of arranging retailing, everyone was free to copy the idea, and malls spread like mushrooms.

When people make decisions about the quantity of education to undertake or the amount of research and development to do, they balance the *private* marginal costs against the private marginal benefits. They undervalue the external benefits. As a result, if we were to leave education and research and development to unregulated market forces, we would get too little of these activities. To deliver them in efficient quantities, we make public choices through governments to modify the market outcome.

Three devices that governments can use to achieve an efficient allocation of resources in the presence of the external benefits from education and research and development are:

- Subsidies
- Below-cost provision
- Patents and copyrights

Subsidies

A **subsidy** is a payment made by the government to producers that depends on the level of output. By subsidizing private activities, government can in principle encourage private decisions to be taken in the public interest. A government subsidy program might alternatively enable private producers to capture resources for themselves. Although subsidies cannot be guaranteed to work successfully, we'll study an example in which they do achieve their desired goal.

Figure 20.6 shows how subsidizing education can increase the amount of education undertaken and achieve an efficient allocation. Suppose that the marginal cost of producing a student-year of college education is a constant $20,000. We'll assume that all these costs are borne by the colleges and that there are no external costs. The marginal social cost is the same as the colleges' marginal cost and is shown by the curve *MC*. The maximum price that students (or parents) are willing to pay for an additional year of college determines the marginal private benefit curve and the demand curve for education. That curve is *D* = *MB*. In this example, a competitive market in private college education results in 20 million students being enrolled in college with tuition at $20,000 a year.

Suppose that the external benefit—the benefit derived by people other than those who receive the education—results in marginal social benefits described by the curve *MSB*. An efficient allocation occurs when marginal social cost equals marginal social benefit. In the example in Fig. 20.6, this equality occurs when 40

million students are enrolled in college. One way of getting 40 million students in college is to subsidize private colleges. In the example, a subsidy of $15,000 per student per year paid to the colleges does the job. With a subsidy of $15,000 and a marginal cost of $20,000, colleges earn an economic profit if the annual tuition exceeds $5,000. Competition among the colleges would drive the tuition down to $5,000, and at this price, 40 million students would enroll in college. So a subsidy can achieve an efficient outcome.

The lessons in this example can be applied to stimulating the rate of increase in the stock of

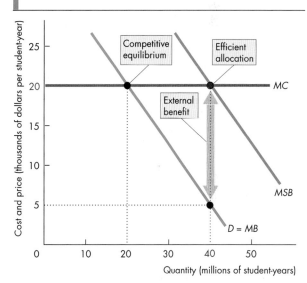

FIGURE 20.6
The Efficient Quantity of Education

The demand curve for education measures the marginal private benefit of education (*D* = *MB*). The curve *MC* shows the marginal cost of education—in this example, $20,000 per student-year. If education is provided in a competitive market, tuition is $20,000 a year and 20 million students enroll. Education produces an external benefit, and adding the external benefit to the marginal private benefit gives marginal social benefit, *MSB*. Education has no external costs, so *MC* is also the marginal social cost of education. An efficient outcome is achieved if the government provides education services to 40 million students a year, which is achieved by either subsidizing private colleges or providing education below cost in public colleges. In this example, students pay an annual tuition of $5,000 and the government pays a subsidy of $15,000.

knowledge—research and development. By subsidizing these activities, the government can move the allocation of resources toward a more efficient outcome. The mechanism that the government uses for this purpose is a research and development grant. In 1997, through the National Science Foundation, the government made research and development grants to universities and federally funded research and development centers of more than $2.5 billion.

Another way to achieve an efficient amount of education or research and development is through public provision below cost.

Below-Cost Provision

Instead of subsidizing private colleges, the government can establish its own colleges (public colleges) that provide schooling below cost. And instead of subsidizing research and development in industry and the universities, the government can establish its own research facilities and make discoveries available to others. Let's see how this approach works by returning to the example in Fig. 20.6.

By establishing public colleges with places for 40 million students, the government can supply the efficient quantity of college education. To ensure that this number of places is taken up, the public colleges would charge a tuition, in this example, of $5,000 a student per year. The government provides this tuition below its marginal cost of $20,000 a student per year. At this price, the number of people who choose to attend college makes the marginal social benefit of education equal to its marginal social cost.

We've now looked at two examples of how government action can help market participants take account of the external benefits deriving from education to achieve an outcome different from that of a private unregulated market. In reality, governments use both methods of encouraging an efficient quantity of education. They subsidize private colleges and universities, and they run their own institutions and sell their services at below cost. But in education, the public sector is by far the larger. In research and development, subsidies to the private sector are far larger than the government direct provision.

Patents and Copyrights

Knowledge may well be the only productive resource that does not display *diminishing marginal productivity*.

More knowledge (about the right things) makes people more productive. And there seems to be no tendency for the additional productivity from additional knowledge to diminish.

For example, in just 15 years, advances in knowledge about microprocessors have given us a sequence of processor chips that has made our personal computers increasingly powerful. Each advance in knowledge about how to design and manufacture a processor chip has brought apparently ever-larger increments in performance and productivity. Similarly, each advance in knowledge about how to design and build an airplane has brought apparently ever larger increments in performance: Orville and Wilbur Wright's "Flyer 1" was a one-seat plane that could hop a farmer's field. The Lockheed Constellation was an airplane that could fly 120 passengers from New York to London, but with two refueling stops in Newfoundland and Ireland. The latest version of the Boeing 747 can carry 400 people nonstop from Los Angeles to Sydney or New York to Tokyo (flights of 7,500 miles that take 13 1/2 hours). Similar examples can be found again and again in fields as diverse as agriculture, biogenetics, communications, engineering, entertainment, medicine, and publishing.

A key reason why the stock of knowledge increases without diminishing returns is the sheer number of different techniques that can in principle be tried. Paul Romer explains this fact with an amazing example. Suppose, says Romer,

> that to make a finished good, 20 different parts have to be attached to a frame, one at a time. A worker could proceed in numerical order, attaching part one first, then part two. ... Or the worker could proceed in some other order, starting with part 10, then adding part seven. ... With 20 parts, a standard (but incredible) calculation shows that there are about 10^{18} different sequences one can use for assembling the final good. This number is larger than the total number of seconds that have elapsed since the big bang created the universe, so we can be confident that in all activities, only a very small fraction of the possible sequences have ever been tried.[1]

---

[1]From Paul Romer, "Ideas and Things," in *The Future Surveyed*, supplement to *The Economist*, 11 September, 1993, pp. 71–72. The "standard calculation" that Romer refers to is the number of ways of selecting and arranging in order 20 objects from 20 objects—also called the number of permutations of 20 objects

Think about all the processes, all the products, and all the different bits and pieces that go into each, and you can see that we have only begun to scratch around the edges of what is possible.

Because knowledge is productive and creates external benefits, it is necessary to use public policies to ensure that those who develop new ideas face incentives that encourage an efficient level of effort. The main way of creating the right incentives is to provide the creators of knowledge with property rights in their discoveries—called **intellectual property rights**. The legal device for creating intellectual property rights is the patent or copyright. A **patent** or **copyright** is a government-sanctioned exclusive right granted to the inventor of a good, service, or productive process to produce, use, and sell the invention for a given number of years. A patent enables the developer of a new idea to prevent, for a limited number of years, others from benefiting freely from an invention. But to obtain the protection of the law, an inventor must make knowledge of the invention public.

Although patents encourage invention and innovation, they do so at an economic cost. While a patent is in place, its holder is a monopolist. And monopoly is another type of market failure. To maximize profit, a monopoly (patent holder) produces the quantity at which marginal cost equals marginal revenue. The monopoly sets the price above marginal cost and equal to the highest price at which the profit-maximizing quantity can be sold. In this situation, consumers value the good more highly (are willing to pay more for one more unit of it) than its marginal cost. So the quantity of the good available is less than the efficient quantity.

But without a patent, the effort to develop new goods, services, or processes is diminished and the flow of new inventions is slowed. So the efficient outcome is a compromise that balances the benefits of more inventions against the cost of temporary monopoly power in newly invented activities.

---

20 at a time. This number is *factorial* 20, or 20! = 20 × 19 × 18 × ... × 2 × 1 = $10^{18.4}$. A standard theory (challenged by observations made by the Hubble Space Telescope in 1994) is that a big bang started the universe 15 billion years, or $10^{17.7}$ seconds, ago. Although $10^{18.4}$ and $10^{17.7}$ look similar, $10^{18.4}$ is *five* times as large as $10^{17.7}$, so if you started trying alternative sequences at the moment of the big bang and took only one second per trial, you would still have tried only one fifth of the possibilities. Amazing?

REVIEW QUIZ

- What is special about knowledge as a consumer good and as a productive resource that creates external benefits?
- What are the external benefits that arise from education and from research and development?
- How might governments use subsidies, below-cost provision, and patents and copyrights to achieve an efficient amount of research and development?
- How might governments use subsidies or below-cost provision to deliver an efficient amount of education?
- Why might knowledge be special in *not* displaying diminishing returns?
- If patents and copyrights can stimulate research, why don't we just award unlimited patents and copyrights to inventors and other creators of new knowledge?

◆ *Reading Between the Lines* on pages 444–445 looks at the challenge to intellectual property rights presented by digital information technologies. As you study this problem, try to reflect on all the topics you've learned about in your study of *microeconomics*. You've learned how all economic problems arise from scarcity, that scarcity forces choices, and that choice implies cost—opportunity cost. Prices (*relative prices*) are opportunity costs and are determined by the interactions of buyers and sellers in markets. People choose what to buy and what resources to sell to maximize utility. Firms choose what to sell and what resources to buy to maximize profit. People and firms interact in markets. But the resulting equilibrium might be inefficient and might be viewed as creating too much inequality. By providing public goods, redistributing income, curbing monopoly power, and coping with externalities, public choice modifies the market outcome.

The next chapter studies some problems for the market economy that arise from uncertainty and incomplete information. But unlike the cases we've studied here, the market does a good job of coping with these problems, as you're about to discover.

Protecting Intellectual Property Rights

THE NEW YORK TIMES, DECEMBER 2, 1996

160 Nations to Weigh Revisions of International Copyright Laws

BY PETER H. LEWIS

Copyright laws are under technological siege. Intended to insure both a financial return to those who create everything from poetry to computer software and reasonable public access to such material, the current laws may be unequal to the task.

Copies of the latest Madonna song, a computer spreadsheet or a telephone directory can all be duplicated and distributed on the Internet at the click of a computer mouse, often with little regard for the legal rights of the owners of their copyrights.

Now, for the first time in the age of the personal computer and the Internet, copyright experts from 160 countries are gathering in Switzerland today to begin to write new international treaties protecting intellectual property in the digital age...

Delegates to the World Intellectual Property Organization diplomatic conference in Geneva,... hope to agree on one or more global pacts to update copyright laws for an era in which anything that can be copyrighted can be digitized, and anything that can be digitized can be distributed almost instantly around the world.

The United States ... delegation, led by Bruce Lehman, the Commissioner of Patents and Trademarks, will offer three proposals to protect literary and artistic works, music recordings and data bases from unauthorized use. ...

Supporters of the American proposals say ... that changes in international copyright law are needed to halt the growing international trend to pirate billions of dollars worth of intellectual property. Without stronger protections, they argue, there will be no incentive to develop new material to sate the appetite of the emerging global information infrastructure. ...

"The central premise of the Administration is that creators of intellectual property will be wary of the electronic marketplace unless the law gives them protection, but I would differ," said Richard B. Hovey, director of the Digital Equipment Corporation's corporate technology and strategy group.

Mr. Hovey said his company and others are already developing hardware and software methods for preventing unauthorized duplication, transmission or playback of copyrighted materials, including not just text and graphics, but also video, audio and multimedia. ...

Copyright ©1996 The New York Times Company.
Reprinted with permission.

Essence of the Story

■ Copyright laws are difficult to enforce in the digital information age when music and other material can be duplicated and distributed on the Internet.

■ Changes in international copyright law are required to stop growing international pirating of intellectual property.

■ Without stronger protection, there will be no incentive to develop new material.

■ Copyright experts are writing new international treaties that protect intellectual property.

■ Digital Equipment Corporation is trying to use the new technologies to prevent unauthorized duplication and protect inventors and authors without a change in the law.

■ A copyright gives the inventor of a good, service, or productive process the exclusive right to produce, use, and sell the invention for a given number of years.

■ During the life of the copyright, the inventor is a monopolist.

■ Figure 1 shows what happens when copyright law is violated. It uses the example of a recording of a Madonna song. The demand for a copy of the song is shown by the demand curve, D.

■ The marginal cost of making one more copy of the Madonna song is constant and is shown by the marginal cost curve, MC.

■ If people freely copy the Madonna song, the marginal cost curve becomes the supply curve in a competitive market.

■ The number of copies made is Q_C, and the price is P_C, which equals marginal cost.

■ This outcome appears to be efficient. Marginal cost equals marginal benefit, and the gains from trade are maximized.

■ But this outcome is not efficient. In fact, it is not even feasible because Madonna has no incentive to record her songs. Without Madonna, there is nothing to copy. The quantity is zero, and the consumer surplus is zero.

■ An enforced copyright law can improve on this situation. Figure 2 shows you how. Again, the demand curve is D, and the marginal cost curve is MC.

■ By being granted a copyright on her song, Madonna becomes a monopolist. Madonna's marginal revenue curve is MR, and she maximizes profit by authorizing Q_{CR} copies to be made, which sell for P_{CR}.

■ The market appears to be inefficient because a deadweight loss, the gray area in Fig. 2, is created.

■ This deadweight loss is unavoidable. But in the long run, it disappears when the life of the copyright ends and the market becomes competitive.

■ The blue area in Fig. 2 shows Madonna's economic profit during the life of her copyright. It is this gain that encourages her to sing and create material that is worth copying.

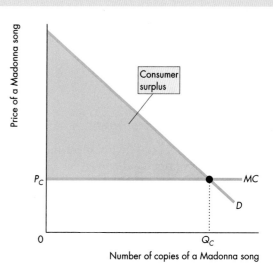

Figure 1 When copyright law is violated

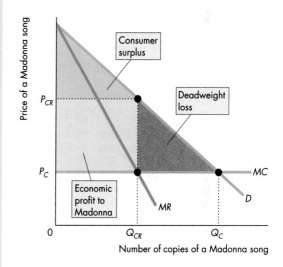

Figure 2 How a copyright works

You're The Voter

■ How would you write the copyright law?

■ How many years' protection would you give the inventor or creator of a new good or service such as a Madonna song?

■ How would you suggest that violators of copyright law be penalized? Use economic reasoning and the concept of efficiency to develop your answers.

SUMMARY

KEY POINTS

Economics of the Environment (pp. 432–440)

- Popular discussion of the environment frames the debate in terms of right and wrong, but economists emphasize costs and benefits and a need to find a way to balance the two.
- The demand for environmental policies has grown because incomes and awareness of the connection between actions and the environment have grown.
- Air pollution arises from road transportation, electric utilities, and industrial processes. In the United States, the trends in most types of air pollution are downward.
- Externalities (environmental and others) arise when property rights are absent. Sometimes it is possible to overcome an externality by assigning a property right.
- The Coase theorem states that if property rights exist and transactions costs are low, private transactions are efficient—there are no externalities. In this case, the same efficient amount of pollution is achieved regardless of *who* has the property right—the polluter or the victim.
- When property rights cannot be assigned, governments might overcome environmental externalities by using emission charges, marketable permits, or taxes.
- Marketable permits were used successfully to virtually eliminate lead from our air.
- Global externalities, such as greenhouse gases and substances that deplete the earth's ozone layer, can be overcome only by international action. Each country acting alone has insufficient incentive to act in the interest of the world as a whole. But there is a great deal of scientific uncertainty and disagreement about the effects of greenhouse gases and ozone depletion, and in the face of this uncertainty, international resolve to act is weak.
- The world is locked in a type of prisoners' dilemma game, in which it is in every country's self-interest to let other countries carry the costs of environmental policies.

Economics of Knowledge (pp. 440–443)

- Knowledge is both a consumer good and a productive resource that creates external benefits.
- External benefits from education—passing on existing knowledge to others—arise because the basic reading, writing, and number skills equip people to interact and communicate more effectively.
- External benefits from research and development—creating and applying new knowledge—arise because once someone has worked out how to do something, others can copy the basic idea.
- To enable the efficient amount of education and innovation to take place, we make public choices through governments to modify the market outcome.
- Three devices are available to governments: subsidies, below-cost provision, and patents and copyrights.
- Subsidies to private schools or the provision of public education below cost can achieve an efficient provision of education.
- Patents and copyrights create intellectual property rights and increase the incentive to innovate. But they do so by creating a temporary monopoly, the cost of which must be balanced against the benefit of more inventive activity.

KEY FIGURES

KEY TERMS

PROBLEMS

*1. A pesticide maker can dump waste into a lake or truck it to a safe storage place. The marginal cost of trucking is a $100 a ton. A trout farm uses the lake, and the table shows how its profit depends on the quantity of waste dumped.

Quantity of waste (tons per week)	Trout farm profit (dollars per week)
0	1,000
1	950
2	875
3	775
4	650
5	500
6	325
7	125

a. What is the efficient amount of waste to be dumped into the lake?
b. If the trout farm owns the lake, how much waste is dumped and how much does the pesticide maker pay to the farmer per ton?
c. If the pesticide maker owns the lake, how much waste is dumped and how much rent does the farmer pay the factory for the use of the lake?

2. A steel smelter is located at the edge of a residential area. The table shows the cost of cutting the pollution of the smelter. It also shows the property taxes that people are willing to pay at different levels of pollution.

Pollution cut (percentage)	Property taxes willingly paid (dollars per day)	Total cost of pollution cut (dollars per day)
0	0	0
10	150	10
20	285	25
30	405	45
40	510	70
50	600	100
60	675	135
70	735	175
80	780	220
90	810	270
100	825	325

Assume that the increase in property taxes that people are willing to pay measures the change in total benefit of cleaner air that results from a change in the percentage decrease in pollution.
a. What is the efficient percentage decrease in pollution?
b. With no regulation of pollution, how much pollution will there be?
c. If the city owns the smelter, how much pollution will there be?
d. If the city is a company town owned by the steel smelter, how much pollution will there be?

*3. Back at the pesticide plant and trout farm described in problem 1, suppose that no one owns the lake and that the government introduces a pollution tax.
a. What is the tax per ton of waste dumped that will achieve an efficient outcome?
b. Explain the connection between the answer to this problem and the answer to problem 1.

4. Back at the steel-smelting city in problem 2, suppose that the city government introduces a pollution tax.
a. What is the tax per percentage of waste dumped that will achieve an efficient outcome?
b. Explain the connection between the answer to this problem and the answer to problem 2.

*5. Using the information provided in problem 1, suppose that no one owns the lake and that the government issues marketable pollution permits to both the farmer and the factory. Each may dump the same amount of waste in the lake, and the total that may be dumped is the efficient amount.
a. What is the quantity that may be dumped into the lake?
b. What is the market price of a permit? Who buys and who sells?
c. What is the connection between the answer to this problem and the answers to problems 1 and 3?

6. Using the information given in problem 2, suppose that the city government issues marketable pollution permits to citizens and the smelter. Each may pollute the air by the same percentage, and the total is the efficient amount.

a. What is the percentage of pollution?
b. What is the market price of a permit? Who buys and who sells?
c. What is the connection between the answer to this problem and the answers to problems 2 and 4?

*7. The marginal cost of educating a student is $4,000 a year and is constant. The figure shows the marginal private benefit curve.

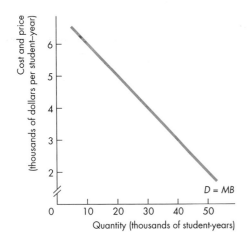

a. With no government involvement and if the schools are competitive, how many students are enrolled and what is the tuition?
b. The external benefit from education is $2,000 per student-year and is constant. If the government provides the efficient amount of education, how many school places does it offer and what is the tuition?

8. A technological advance cuts the marginal cost of educating a student to $2,000 a year and is constant. The marginal private benefit is the same as in problem 7. The external benefit from education increases to $4,000 per student-year and is constant.
a. With no government involvement and if the schools are competitive, how many students are enrolled and what is the tuition?
b. If the government provides the efficient amount of education, how many school places does it offer and what is the tuition?
c. Compare the outcomes in problem 8 with those in problem 7. Explain the differences between the two situations.

CRITICAL THINKING

1. After you have studied *Reading Between the Lines* on pp. 444–445, answer the following questions:
a. Do copyright laws create an efficient or an inefficient outcome?
b. What are the pros and cons of a long copyright period?
c. How could a further technological advance that makes unauthorized copying impossible change copyright law? Who would need protecting from whom in this situation?

2. Use the links on the Parkin Web site to get two viewpoints on global warming. Then answer these questions:
a. What are the benefits and costs of greenhouse gas emissions?
b. Do you think the environmentalists are correct in the view that greenhouse gas emissions must be cut or do you think the costs of reducing greenhouse gas emissions exceed the benefits?
c. If greenhouse gas emissions are to be reduced, should reductions be achieved by assigning quotas or by using the price mechanism?

3. To decrease the amount of overfishing in their territorial waters, the governments of Iceland and New Zealand have introduced private property rights with an allocation of Individual Transferable Quotas (ITQs). To check out the effects of this system, use the link on the Parkin Web site to visit the Fraser Institute in Vancouver. Then answer the following questions:
a. Would the introduction of ITQs in the United States help to replenish U.S. fish stocks?
b. Explain why ITQs give an incentive to not overfish.
c. Who would oppose ITQs and why?

4. Some political leaders want stronger tax incentives to encourage more people to go to college and to remain in college for longer. What are the economic arguments in favor of such a change in incentives? What are the arguments against such a change? Where do you come out on this issue and why?

Uncertainty and Information

Life is like a lottery. You work hard in school, but what will the payoff be? Will you get an interesting, high-paying job or a miserable, low-paying one? You set up a small summer business and work hard at it. But will you make enough income to keep you in school next year or will you get wiped out? How do people make a decision when they don't know its consequences? ◆ As you drive across an intersection on a green light, you see a car on your left that's still moving. Will it stop or will it run the red light? You buy insurance against such a risk, and insurance companies gain from your business. Why are we willing to buy insurance at prices that leave insurance companies with a gain? ◆ Buying a new car—or a used car—is fun, but it's also scary. You could get stuck with a lemon. And cars are not unique. Just about every complicated product you buy could be defective. How do car dealers and retailers induce us to buy what might turn out to be a lemon? ◆ People keep some of their wealth in the bank, some in mutual funds, some in bonds, and some in stocks. Some of these ways of holding wealth have a high return, and some have a low return. Why don't people put all their wealth in the place that has the highest return? Why does it pay to diversify?

◆ In this chapter, we answer questions such as these. We'll begin by explaining how people make decisions when they're uncertain about the consequences. We'll see how it pays to buy insurance, even if its price leaves the insurance company with a profit. We'll explain why we use scarce resources to generate and disseminate information. And we'll look at transactions in a variety of markets in which uncertainty and the cost of acquiring information play important roles. ◆ A recurring theme of economics is that markets help people to use their scarce resources efficiently. Uncertainty and incomplete information are possible reasons why markets might fail to achieve efficiency. But markets do an amazing job of coping with these problems.

Lotteries and Lemons

After studying this chapter, you will be able to:

- Explain how people make decisions when they are uncertain about the consequences

- Explain why people buy insurance and how insurance companies make a profit

- Explain why buyers search and sellers advertise

- Explain how markets cope with private information

- Explain how people use financial markets to lower risk

Uncertainty and Risk

ALTHOUGH WE LIVE IN AN UNCERTAIN WORLD, we rarely ask what uncertainty is. Yet to explain how we make decisions and do business with each other in an uncertain world, we need to think more deeply about uncertainty. What exactly is uncertainty? We also live in a risky world. Is risk the same as uncertainty? Let's begin by defining uncertainty and risk and distinguishing between them.

Uncertainty is a situation in which more than one event may occur but we don't know which one. For example, when farmers plant their crops, they are uncertain about the weather during the growing season.

In ordinary speech, risk is the probability of incurring a loss (or some other misfortune). In economics, **risk** is a situation in which more than one outcome may occur and the *probability* of each possible outcome can be estimated. A *probability* is a number between 0 and 1 that measures the chance of some possible event occurring. A 0 probability means that the event will not happen. A probability of 1 means that the event will occur for sure—with certainty. A probability of 0.5 means that the event is just as likely to occur as not. An example is the probability of a tossed coin falling heads. In a large number of tosses, about half of them will be heads and the other half tails.

Sometimes, probabilities can be measured. For example, the probability that a tossed coin will come down heads is based on the fact that in a large number of tosses, half are heads and half are tails; the probability that an automobile in Chicago in 1998 will be involved in an accident can be estimated by using police and insurance records of previous accidents; the probability that you will win a lottery can be estimated by dividing the number of tickets you have bought by the total number of tickets bought.

Some situations cannot be described by using probabilities based on past observed events. These situations may be unique events, such as the introduction of a new product. How much will sell and at what price? Because the product is new, there is no previous experience on which to base a probability. But the questions can be answered by looking at past experience with *similar* new products, supported by some judgments. Such judgments are called *subjective probabilities*.

Regardless of whether the probability of some event occurring is based on actual data or judgments—or even guesses—we can use probability to study the way in which people make decisions in the face of uncertainty. The first step in doing this is to describe how people assess the cost of risk.

Measuring the Cost of Risk

Some people are more willing to bear risk than others, but almost everyone prefers less risk to more, other things remaining the same. We measure people's attitudes toward risk by using their utility of wealth schedules and curves. The **utility of wealth** is the amount of utility a person attaches to a given amount of wealth. The greater a person's wealth, other things remaining the same, the higher is the person's total utility. Greater wealth brings higher total utility, but as wealth increases, each additional unit of wealth increases total utility by a smaller amount. That is, the *marginal utility of wealth diminishes*.

Figure 21.1 sets out Tania's utility of wealth schedule and curve. Each point *a* through *e* on Tania's utility of wealth curve corresponds to the row of the table identified by the same letter. You can see that as her wealth increases, so does her total utility of wealth. You can also see that her marginal utility of wealth diminishes. When wealth increases from $3,000 to $6,000, total utility increases by 20 units, but when wealth increases by a further $3,000 to $9,000, total utility increases by only 10 units.

We can use Tania's utility of wealth curve to measure her cost of risk. Let's see how Tania evaluates two summer jobs that involve different amounts of risk.

One job, working as a painter, pays enough for her to save $5,000 by the end of the summer. There is no uncertainty about the income from this job and hence no risk. If Tania takes this job, by the end of the summer her wealth will be $5,000. The other job, working as a telemarketer selling subscriptions to a magazine, is risky. If she takes this job, her wealth at the end of the summer depends entirely on her success at selling. She might be a good salesperson or a poor one. A good salesperson makes $9,000 in a summer, and a poor one makes $3,000. Tania has never tried telemarketing, so she doesn't know how successful she'll be. She assumes that she has an equal chance—a probability of 0.5—of making either $3,000 or $9,000. Which outcome does Tania

FIGURE 21.1

The Utility of Wealth

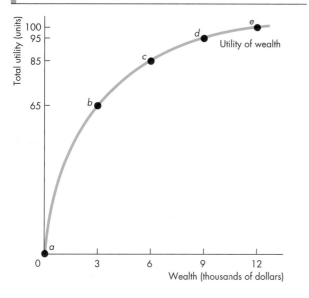

	Wealth (thousands of dollars)	Total utility (units)	Marginal utility (units)
a	0	0	
			65
b	3	65	
			20
c	6	85	
			10
d	9	95	
			5
e	12	100	

The table shows Tania's utility of wealth schedule, and the figure shows her utility of wealth curve. Utility increases as wealth increases, but the marginal utility of wealth diminishes.

prefer: $5,000 for sure from the painting job or a 50 percent chance of either $3,000 or $9,000 from the telemarketing job?

When there is uncertainty, people do not know the *actual* utility they will get from taking a particular action. But it is possible to calculate the utility they *expect* to get. **Expected utility** is the average utility arising from all possible outcomes. So, to choose her summer job, Tania calculates the expected utility from each job. Figure 21.2 shows how she does this.

FIGURE 21.2

Choice Under Uncertainty

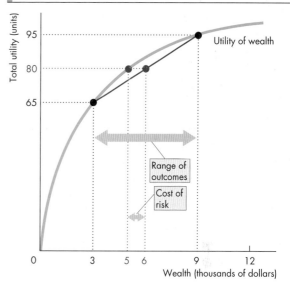

If Tania's wealth is $5,000 and she faces no risk, her utility is 80 units. If she faces an equal probability of having $9,000 with a utility of 95 or $3,000 with a utility of 65, her expected wealth is $6,000. But her expected utility is 80 units—the same as with $5,000 and no uncertainty. Tania is indifferent between these two alternatives. Tania's extra $1,000 of expected wealth is just enough to offset her extra risk.

If Tania takes the painting job, she has $5,000 of wealth and 80 units of utility. There is no uncertainty, so her expected utility equals her actual utility—80 units. But suppose she takes the telemarketing job. If she makes $9,000, her utility is 95 units, and if she makes $3,000, her utility is 65 units. Tania's *expected income* is the average of these two outcomes and is $6,000—($9,000 × 0.5) + ($3,000 × 0.5). This average is called a *weighted average*, the weights being the probabilities of each outcome (both 0.5 in this case). Tania's *expected utility* is the average of these two possible total utilities and is 80 units—(95 × 0.5) + (65 × 0.5).

Tania chooses the job that maximizes her expected utility. In this case, the two alternatives give the same expected utility—80 units—so she is indifferent between them. She is equally likely to take either job. The difference between Tania's expected wealth of $6,000 from the risky job and $5,000 from the no-risk job—$1,000—is just large enough to off-set the additional risk that Tania faces.

The calculations that we've just done enable us to measure Tania's cost of risk. The cost of risk is the amount by which expected wealth must be increased to give the same expected utility as a no-risk situation. In Tania's case, the cost of the risk arising from an uncertain income of $3,000 or $9,000 is $1,000.

If the amount Tania can make from painting remains at $5,000 and the expected income from telemarketing also remains constant while its range of uncertainty increases, Tania will take the painting job. To see this conclusion, suppose that good telemarketers make $12,000 and poor ones make nothing. The average income from telemarketing is unchanged at $6,000, but the range of uncertainty has increased. The table in Fig. 21.1 shows that Tania gets 100 units of utility from a wealth of $12,000 and zero units of utility from a wealth of zero. Thus in this case, Tania's expected utility from telemarketing is 50 units—$(100 \times 0.5) + (0 \times 0.5)$. Because the expected utility from telemarketing is now less than that from painting, she chooses painting.

Risk Aversion and Risk Neutrality

There is a huge difference between Bill Parcells, head coach of the New York Jets, who favors a cautious running game, and Jim Kelly, former quarterback of the Buffalo Bills, who favored a risky passing game. They have different attitudes toward risk. Bill is more *risk averse* than is Jim. Tania is also *risk averse*. The shape of the utility of wealth curve tells us about the attitude toward risk—about the person's degree of *risk aversion*. The more rapidly a person's marginal utility of wealth diminishes, the more risk averse that person is. You can see this fact best by considering the case of *risk neutrality*. A risk-neutral person cares only about *expected wealth* and doesn't mind how much uncertainty there is.

Figure 21.3 shows the utility of wealth curve of a risk-neutral person. It is a straight line, and the marginal utility of wealth is constant. If this person has an expected wealth of $6,000, expected utility is 50 units regardless of the range of uncertainty around that average. An equal probability of having $3,000 or $9,000 gives the same expected utility as a certain $6,000. When Tania's risk increased to this range, she needed an extra $1,000. This person does not. Even if the range of risk becomes $0 to $12,000, the risk-neutral person still gets the same expected utility as a certain $6,000 gives. Most real people are risk averse,

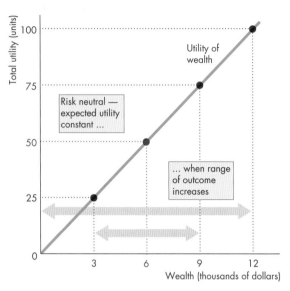

FIGURE 21.3
Risk Neutrality

People's dislike of risk implies a diminishing marginal utility of wealth. A (hypothetical) risk-neutral person has a linear utility of wealth curve and a constant marginal utility of wealth. For a risk-neutral person, expected utility does not depend on the range of uncertainty, and the cost of risk is zero.

and their utility of wealth curves look like Tania's. But the case of risk neutrality illustrates the importance and the consequences of the shape of the utility of wealth curve for a person's degree of risk aversion.

R E V I E W   Q U I Z

- How do people make decisions when they are faced with uncertain outcomes? What do they try to achieve?
- How can we measure the cost of risk?
- What determines the amount that someone would be willing to pay to avoid risk? Is the cost of risk the same for everyone?
- What is a *risk-neutral* person and how much would such a person pay to avoid risk?

Most people are risk averse. Let's now see how insurance enables them to reduce the risk they face.

Insurance

ONE WAY OF REDUCING THE RISK WE FACE IS TO
buy insurance. How does insurance reduce risk? Why
do people buy insurance? And what determines the
amount we spend on insurance? Before we answer
these questions, let's look at the insurance industry in
the United States today.

Insurance Industry in the United States

We spend close to 15 percent of our income, on the
average, on private insurance. That's as much as we
spend on housing and more than we spend on cars
and food. In addition, we buy insurance through our
taxes in the form of social security and unemployment insurance. When we buy private insurance, we
enter into an agreement with an insurance company
to pay an agreed price—called a *premium*—in
exchange for benefits to be paid to us if some specified event occurs. The three main types of insurance
we buy are:

■ Life insurance

■ Health insurance

■ Property and casualty insurance

Life Insurance   Life insurance reduces the risk of
financial loss in the event of death. Almost 80 percent of households in the United States have life
insurance, and the average amount of coverage is
$110,000 per household. More than 2,400 compa-
nies supply life insurance, and the total premiums
paid in a year are more than $450 billion. As you can
see in Fig. 21.4, life insurance has been the greatest
source of private insurance business in recent years.

Health Insurance   Health insurance reduces the risk
of financial loss in the event of illness. It can provide
funds to cover both lost earnings and the cost of
medical care. Private health insurance is growing
rapidly and is profitable. Figure 21.4 shows that it
is almost as large as life insurance.

Property and Casualty Insurance   Property and
casualty insurance reduces the risk of financial loss
in the event of an accident involving damage to persons or property. It includes auto insurance—its
biggest component—workers' compensation; fire,
earthquake, and professional malpractice insurance;

FIGURE 21.4

The Insurance Industry

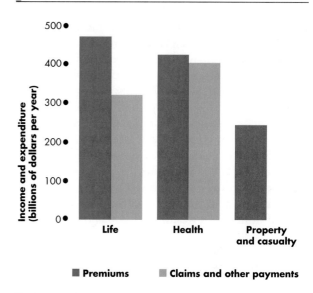

Total expenditure on private insurance is more than a trillion
dollars a year. Most is spent on life insurance and health
insurance.

Source: U.S. Bureau of the Census, *Statistical Abstract of the United States 1995*,
115th edition (Washington, D.C., 1995), Tables 150, 840, 841, and 843–845 and
the author's assumptions and calculations.

and a host of smaller items. Figure 21.4 shows that
we spend almost $250 billion a year on these types
of insurance.

How Insurance Works

Insurance works by pooling risks. It is possible and
profitable because people are risk averse. The probability of any one person having a serious auto accident is small, but the cost of an accident to the person involved is enormous. For a large population,
the probability of one person having an accident is
the proportion of the population that does have an
accident. Because this probability can be estimated,
the total cost of accidents can be predicted. An insurance company can pool the risks of a large population and share the costs. It does so by collecting premiums from everyone and paying out benefits to
those who suffer a loss. If the insurance company
does its calculations correctly, it collects at least as

454

CHAPTER 21 UNCERTAINTY AND INFORMATION

much in premiums as it pays out in benefits and operating costs.

To see why people buy insurance and why it is profitable, let's consider an example. Dan has the utility of wealth curve shown in Fig. 21.5. He owns a car worth $10,000, and that is his only wealth. If there is no risk of his having an accident, his utility will be 100 units. But there is a 10 percent chance (a probability of 0.1) that he will have an accident within a year. Suppose Dan does not buy insurance. If he does have an accident, his car is worthless, and with no insurance, he has no wealth and no utility. Because the probability of an accident is 0.1, the probability of *not* having an accident is 0.9. Dan's expected wealth, therefore, is $9,000 ($10,000 × 0.9 + $0 × 0.1), and his expected utility is 90 units (100 × 0.9 + 0 × 0.1).

Given his utility of wealth curve, Dan has 90 units of utility if his wealth is $7,000 and he faces no uncertainty. That is, Dan's utility of a guaranteed wealth of $7,000 is the same as his utility of a 90 percent chance of having wealth of $10,000 and a 10 percent chance of having nothing. If the cost of an insurance policy that pays out in the event of an accident is less than $3,000 ($10,000 – $7,000), Dan will buy the policy. Thus Dan has a demand for auto insurance at premiums less than $3,000.

Suppose there are lots of people like Dan, each with a $10,000 car and each with a 10 percent chance of having an accident within the year. If an insurance company agrees to pay each person who has an accident $10,000, the company will pay out $10,000 to one tenth of the population, or an average of $1,000 per person. This amount is the insurance company's minimum premium for such insurance. It is less than the value of insurance to Dan because Dan is risk averse. He is willing to pay something to reduce the risk he faces.

Now suppose that the insurance company's operating expenses are a further $1,000 and that it offers insurance for $2,000. The company now covers all its costs—the amounts paid out to policyholders for their losses plus the company's operating expenses. Dan—and all the other people like him—will maximize their utility by buying this insurance.

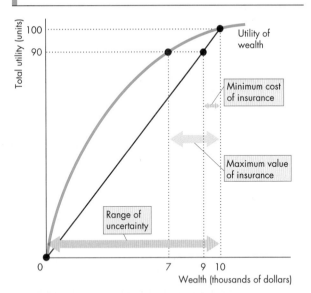

FIGURE 21.5

The Gains from Insurance

Dan has a car valued at $10,000 that gives him a utility of 100 units, but there is a 0.1 probability that he will have an accident, making his car worthless (wealth and utility equal to zero). With no insurance, his expected wealth is $9,000 and his expected utility is 90 units. His guaranteed wealth is $7,000. Dan will pay up to $3,000 for insurance. If an insurance company can offer Dan insurance for $1,000, there is a potential gain from insurance for both Dan and the insurance company.

REVIEW QUIZ

- What types of insurance do we buy and how large a percentage of our incomes do we spend on it (on the average)?
- How does insurance work? How can people avoid unwanted outcomes by insuring against them?
- How can an insurance company offer people a deal worth taking? Why don't the amounts paid in by insurers only just cover the amounts paid out by insurance companies to claimants?

Much of the uncertainty that we face arises from ignorance. We just don't know all the things we could benefit from knowing. But knowledge or information is not free. And government intervention is of little use in dealing with this problem. Governments usually are even less well informed than buyers and sellers. Faced with incomplete information, we must make decisions about how much information to acquire. Let's now study the choices we make about obtaining information and how markets cope with incomplete information.

Information

WE SPEND A HUGE QUANTITY OF OUR SCARCE resources on economic information. **Economic information** includes data on the prices, quantities, and qualities of goods and services and resources.

In the models of perfect competition, monopoly, and monopolistic competition, information is free. Everyone has all the information he or she needs. Households are completely informed about the prices of the goods and services they buy and the factors of production they sell. Similarly, firms are completely informed about consumers' preferences and about the prices and products of other firms.

In contrast, information is scarce in the real world. If it were not, we wouldn't need *The Wall Street Journal* and CNN. And we wouldn't need to shop around for bargains or spend time looking for a job. The opportunity cost of economic information—the cost of acquiring information on prices, quantities, and qualities of goods and services and resources—is called **information cost**.

The fact that many economic models ignore information costs does not make these models useless. They give us insights into the forces generating trends in prices and quantities over periods long enough for information limits not to be important. But to understand how markets work hour by hour and day by day, we must take information problems into account. Let's look at some of the consequences of information cost.

Searching for Price Information

When many firms sell the same good or service, there is a range of prices and buyers want to find the lowest price. But searching takes time and is costly. So buyers must balance the expected gain from further search against the cost of further search. To perform this balancing act, buyers use a decision rule called the *optimal-search rule*—or *optimal-stopping rule*. The optimal-search rule is:

- Search for a lower price until the expected marginal benefit of additional search equals the marginal cost of search.
- When the expected marginal benefit from additional search is less than or equal to the marginal cost, stop searching and buy.

To implement the optimal-search rule, each buyer chooses her or his own reservation price. The buyer's **reservation price** is the highest price that the buyer is willing to pay for a good. The buyer will continue to search for a lower price if the lowest price so far found exceeds the reservation price but will stop searching and buy if the lowest price found is less than or equal to the reservation price. At the buyer's reservation price, the expected marginal benefit of search equals the marginal cost of search.

Figure 21.6 illustrates the optimal-search rule. Suppose you've decided to buy a used Mazda Miata. Your marginal cost of search is $\$C$ per dealer visited and is shown by the horizontal orange line in the figure. This cost includes the value of your time, which is the amount that you could have earned by working instead of cruising around used car lots, and the amount spent on transportation and advice. Your expected marginal benefit of visiting one more dealer

FIGURE 21.6

Optimal-Search Rule

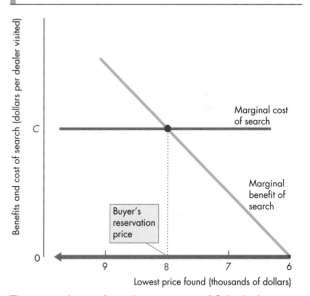

The marginal cost of search is constant at $\$C$. As the lowest price found (measured from right to left on the horizontal axis) declines, the expected marginal benefit of further search diminishes. The lowest price found at which the marginal cost equals the expected marginal benefit is the reservation price. The optimal-search rule is to search until the reservation price is found and then buy at that lowest found price.

depends on the lowest price that you've found. The lower the price you've already found, the lower is your expected marginal benefit of visiting one more dealer, as shown by the blue curve in the figure.

The price at which expected marginal benefit equals marginal cost is your reservation price—$8,000 in the figure. If you find a price equal to or below your reservation price, you stop searching and buy. If you find a price that exceeds your reservation price, you continue to search for a lower price. Individual shoppers differ in their marginal cost of search and so have different reservation prices. As a result, identical items can be found selling for a range of prices.

A Real Car Shopping Trip   Real car shoppers are confronted with a much bigger problem than the one we've just studied. There are many more dimensions of the car they are looking for than its price. They could spend almost forever gathering information about the alternatives. But at some point in their search, they decide they've done enough looking and make a decision to buy. Your imaginary shopping trip to buy a used Mazda Miata rationalizes their decision. Real shoppers think, "The benefits I expect from further search are insufficient to make it worth going on with the process." They don't do the calculations we've just done—at least, not explicitly—but their actions can be explained by those calculations. But buyers are not alone in creating information. Sellers do a lot of it too—in the form of advertising. Let's see what the effects of advertising are.

Advertising

Advertising constantly surrounds us—on television, radio, and billboards and in newspapers and magazines—and costs billions of dollars. How do firms decide how much to spend on advertising? Does advertising create information, or does it just persuade us to buy things we don't really want? What does it do to prices?

Advertising for Profit Maximization   A firm's advertising decision is part of its overall profit-maximization strategy. Firms in perfect competition don't advertise because everyone has all the information there is. But firms selling differentiated products in monopolistic competition and firms locked in the struggle of survival in oligopoly advertise a lot.

The amount of advertising undertaken by firms in monopolistic competition is such that the marginal revenue product of advertising equals its marginal cost. The amount of advertising undertaken by firms in oligopoly is determined by the game they are playing. If that game is a *prisoners' dilemma*, they might spend amounts that lower their combined profits, but they can't avoid advertising without being wiped out by other firms in the industry.

Persuasion or Information   Much advertising is designed to persuade us that the product being advertised is the best in its class. For example, the Pepsi advertisement tells us that Pepsi is really better than Coke. The Coca-Cola advertisement tells us that Coke is really better than Pepsi. But advertising also informs. It provides information about the quality and price of a good or service.

Does advertising mainly persuade or mainly inform? The answer varies for different goods and different types of markets. Goods whose quality can be assessed *before* they are bought are called *search goods*. Typically, the advertising of search goods mainly informs—gives information about price, quality, and location of suppliers. Examples of such goods are gasoline, basic foods, and household goods. Goods whose quality can be assessed only *after* they are bought are called *experience goods*. Typically, the advertising of experience goods mainly persuades—encourages the consumer to buy now and make a judgment later about quality, based on experience with the good. Examples of such goods are cigarettes, alcoholic beverages, and perfume.

Because most advertising involves experience goods, it is likely that advertising is more often persuasive rather than merely informative. But persuasive advertising doesn't necessarily harm the consumer. It might result in lower prices.

Advertising and Prices   Does advertising increase the price of the good advertised? Your immediate response is "Of course it does!" But this conclusion is not always correct. Advertising can lower prices for two different reasons. First, *informative advertising* can lower prices because it increases competition by telling potential buyers about alternative sources of supply. Second, if advertising enables firms to increase their output and reap economies of scale, it is possible that the price of the good will be lower with advertising than without it, provided that there is sufficient competition to prevent firms from restricting output.

R E V I E W   Q U I Z

- What types of economic information do people find useful?
- Why is economic information scarce and how do people economize on its use?
- How do you decide when to stop searching for a lower-priced item to buy?
- What actions do sellers take to increase the information that potential buyers might use and that would encourage them to buy?
- Does advertising always raise costs and raise prices? How might advertising lower costs and prices?

Private Information

So far we have looked at situations in which information is available to everyone and can be obtained with an expenditure of resources. But not all situations are like this. For example, someone might have private information. **Private information** is information that is available to one person but too costly for anyone else to obtain.

Private information affects many economic transactions. One is your knowledge about your driving. You know much more than your auto insurance company does about how carefully and defensively you drive. Another is your knowledge about your work effort. You know far more than your employer about how hard you work. Yet another is your knowledge about the quality of your car. You know whether it's a lemon. But the person to whom you are about to sell it does not and can't find out until after he or she has purchased it from you.

Private information creates two problems:

1. Moral hazard
2. Adverse selection

Moral hazard exists when one of the parties to an agreement has an incentive *after the agreement is made* to act in a manner that brings additional benefits to himself or herself at the expense of the other party. Moral hazard arises because it is too costly for the injured party to monitor the actions of the advantaged party. For example, Jackie hires Mitch as a

salesperson and pays him a fixed wage regardless of his sales. Mitch faces a moral hazard. He has an incentive to put in the least possible effort, benefiting himself and lowering Jackie's profits. For this reason, salespeople are usually paid by a formula that makes their income higher the greater is the volume (or value) of their sales.

Adverse selection is the tendency for people to enter into agreements in which they can use their private information to their own advantage and to the disadvantage of the less informed party. For example, if Jackie offers salespeople a fixed wage, she will attract lazy salespeople. Hardworking salespeople will prefer *not* to work for Jackie because they can earn more by working for someone who pays by results. The fixed-wage contract adversely selects those with private information (knowledge about their work habits) who can use that knowledge to their own advantage and to the disadvantage of the other party.

A variety of devices have evolved that enable markets to function in the face of moral hazard and adverse selection. We've just seen one, the use of incentive payments for salespeople. Let's look at some more and also see how moral hazard and adverse selection influence three real-world markets:

- The market for used cars
- The market for loans
- The market for insurance

The Market for Used Cars

When a person buys a car, it might turn out to be a lemon. If the car is a lemon, it is worth less to the buyer and to everyone else than if it has no defects. Does the used car market have two prices reflecting these two values—a low price for lemons and a higher price for cars without defects? It does not. To see why, let's look at a used car market, first with no dealer warranties and second with warranties.

Used Cars Without Warranties   To make the points as clearly as possible, we'll make some extreme assumptions. There are just two kinds of cars: lemons and those without defects. A lemon is worth $1,000 both to its current owner and to anyone who buys it. A car without defects is worth $5,000 to its current and potential future owners. Whether a car is a lemon is private information that is available only to the current owner. Buyers of used cars can't tell whether they are buying a lemon until *after* they have bought the car and learned as much about it as its current owner knows. There are no dealer warranties.

Because buyers can't tell the difference between a lemon and a good car, they are willing to pay only one price for a used car. What is that price? Are they willing to pay $5,000, the value of a good car? They are not, because there is at least some probability that they are buying a lemon worth only $1,000. If buyers are not willing to pay $5,000 for a used car, are the owners of good cars willing to sell? They are not, because a good car is worth $5,000 to them, so they hang onto their cars. Only the owners of lemons are willing to sell—as long as the price is $1,000 or higher. But, reason the buyers, if only the owners of lemons are selling, all the used cars available are lemons, so the maximum price worth paying is $1,000. Thus the market for used cars is a market for lemons, and the price is $1,000.

Moral hazard exists in the car market because sellers have an incentive to claim that lemons are good cars. But, given the assumptions in the above description of the car market, no one believes such claims. Adverse selection exists, resulting in only lemons actually being traded. The market for used cars is not working well. Good used cars just don't get bought and sold, but people want to be able to buy and sell good used cars. How can they do so? The answer is by introducing warranties into the market.

Used Cars with Warranties   Buyers of used cars can't tell a lemon from a good car, but car dealers sometimes can. For example, they might have regularly serviced the car. They know, therefore, whether they are buying a lemon or a good car and can offer $1,000 for lemons and $5,000 for good cars.[1] But how can they convince buyers that it is worth paying $5,000 for what might be a lemon? The answer is by giving a guarantee in the form of a warranty. The dealer *signals* which cars are good ones and which are lemons. A **signal** is an action taken outside a market that conveys information that can be used by that market. There are many examples of signals, one of which is students' grades. Your grade acts as a *signal* to potential employers.

In the case of the used cars, dealers take actions in the market for car repairs that can be used by the market for cars. For each good car sold, the dealer

gives a warranty. The dealer agrees to pay the costs of repairing the car if it turns out to have a defect. Cars with a warranty are good; cars without a warranty are lemons.

Why do buyers believe the signal? It is because the cost of sending a false signal is high. A dealer who gives a warranty on a lemon ends up paying the high cost of repairs—and risks gaining a bad reputation. A dealer who gives a warranty only on good cars has no repair costs and a reputation that gets better and better. It pays to send an accurate signal. It is rational, therefore, for buyers to believe the signal. Warranties break the lemon problem and enable the used car market to function with two prices, one for lemons and one for good cars.

The Market for Loans

The market for bank loans is one in which private information plays a crucial role. Let's see how.

The quantity of loans demanded by borrowers depends on the interest rate. The lower the interest rate, the greater is the quantity of loans demanded—the demand curve for loans is downward-sloping. The supply of loans by banks and other lenders depends on the cost of lending. This cost has two parts. One is interest, and this interest cost is determined in the market for bank deposits—the market in which the banks borrow the funds that they lend. The other part of the cost of lending is the cost of bad loans—loans that are not repaid—called the default cost. The interest cost of a loan is the same for all borrowers. The default cost of a loan depends on the quality of the borrower.

Suppose that borrowers fall into two classes: low-risk and high-risk. Low-risk borrowers seldom default on their debts and then only for reasons beyond their control. For example, a firm might borrow to finance a project that fails and be unable to repay the bank. High-risk borrowers take high risks with the money they borrow and frequently default on their loans. For example, a firm might borrow to speculate in high-risk mineral prospecting that has a very small chance of paying off.

If banks can separate borrowers into risk categories, they supply loans to low-risk borrowers at one interest rate and to high-risk borrowers at another, higher interest rate. Real banks do this as much as possible. But they cannot always separate their borrowers. They have no sure way of knowing whether they are lending to a low-risk or a high-risk borrower.

---

[1] In this example, to keep the numbers simple, we'll ignore dealers' profit margins and other costs of doing business and suppose that dealers buy cars for the same price as they sell them. The principles are the same with dealers' profit margins.

So the banks charge the same interest rate to both low-risk and high-risk borrowers. If they offered loans to everyone at the low-risk interest rate, borrowers would face moral hazard and the banks would attract a lot of high-risk borrowers—adverse selection. Most borrowers would default, and the banks would incur economic losses. If the banks offered loans to everyone at the high-risk interest rate, most low-risk borrowers, with whom the banks would like to do profitable business, would be unwilling to borrow.

Faced with moral hazard and adverse selection, banks use *signals* to discriminate between borrowers, and they *ration* or limit loans to amounts below the amounts demanded. To restrict the amounts they are willing to lend to borrowers, banks use signals such as length of time in a job, ownership of a home, marital status, age, and business record.

Figure 21.7 shows how the market for loans works in the face of moral hazard and adverse selection. The demand for loans is *D*, and the supply is *S*. The supply curve is horizontal—perfectly elastic supply—because it is assumed that banks have access to a large quantity of funds that have a constant marginal cost of *r*. With no loan limits, the interest rate is *r* and the quantity of loans is *Q*. Because of moral hazard and adverse selection, the banks set loan limits based on signals and restrict the total loans to *L*. At the interest rate *r*, there is an excess demand for loans. A bank cannot increase its profit by making more loans because it can't identify the type of borrower taking the loans. Because the signals used mean that more high-risk borrowers are unsatisfied than low-risk borrowers, it is likely that additional loans will be biased toward high-risk (and high-cost) borrowers.

The Market for Insurance

People who buy insurance face a moral hazard problem, and insurance companies face an adverse selection problem. The moral hazard problem is that a person with insurance coverage for a loss has less incentive than an uninsured person to avoid such a loss. For example, a business with fire insurance has less incentive to take precautions against fire, such as installing a fire alarm or sprinkler system, than a business with no fire insurance does. The adverse selection problem is that people who face greater risks are more likely to buy insurance. For example, a person with a family history of serious illness is more likely to buy health insurance than is a person with a family history of good health.

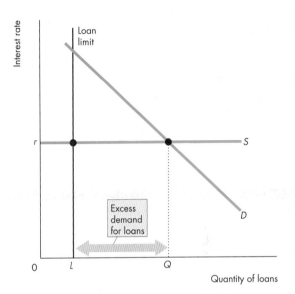

FIGURE 21.7

The Market for Loans

If a bank supplied loans on demand at the going interest rate *r*, the quantity of loans would be *Q*, but most of the loans would be taken by high-risk borrowers. Banks use signals to distinguish between low-risk and high-risk borrowers, and they limit the total loans to *L* and ration them. Banks have no incentive to increase interest rates and increase the quantity of loans because the additional loans would be to high-risk borrowers.

Insurance companies have an incentive to find ways around the moral hazard and adverse selection problems. By doing so, they can lower premiums and increase the amount of business they do. Real-world insurance markets have developed a variety of devices for overcoming or at least moderating these private information problems. Let's see how signals work in markets for insurance by looking at the example of auto insurance.

One of the clearest signals a person can give an auto insurance company is her or his driving record. Suppose that Dan is a good driver and rarely has an accident. If he can demonstrate to the insurance company that his driving record is impeccable over a long enough period, then the insurance company will recognize him as a good driver. Dan will work hard at establishing a reputation as a good driver because he will be able to get his insurance at a lower price.

If all drivers, good and bad alike, can establish good records, then simply having a good record will not convey any information. For the signal to be informative, it must be difficult for bad drivers to fake low risk by having a good record. The signals used in car insurance are the "no-claim" bonuses that drivers accumulate when they do not make an insurance claim.

Another device that insurance companies use is the deductible. A deductible is the amount of a loss that the insured person agrees to bear. For example, most auto insurance policies have the insured person paying the first few hundred dollars worth of damage. The premium varies with the deductible, and the decrease in the premium is more than proportionate to the increase in the deductible. By offering insurance with full coverage—no deductible—on terms that are attractive only to the highest-risk people and by offering coverage with a deductible on more favorable terms that are attractive to other people, insurance companies can do profitable business with everyone. High-risk people choose policies with low deductibles and high premiums; low-risk people choose policies with high deductibles and low premiums.

R E V I E W Q U I Z

- How does private information create moral hazard and adverse selection?
- How do markets for cars use warranties to cope with private information?
- How do markets for insurance use no-claim bonuses to cope with private information?

Managing Risk in Financial Markets

RISK IS A DOMINANT FEATURE OF MARKETS FOR stocks and bonds—indeed for any asset whose price fluctuates. One thing people do to cope with risky asset prices is diversify their asset holdings.

Diversification to Lower Risk

The idea that diversification lowers risk is very natural. It is just an application of not putting all one's eggs into the same basket. How exactly does diversification reduce risk? The best way to answer this question is to consider an example.

Suppose there are two risky projects that you can undertake. Each involves investing $100,000. The two projects are independent of each other, but they both promise the same degree of risk and return.

On each project, you will either make $50,000 or lose $25,000, and the chance that either of these will happen is 50 percent. The expected return on each project is ($50,000 × 0.5) + (–$25,000 × 0.5), which is $12,500. But because the two projects are completely independent, the outcome of one project in no way influences the outcome of the other.

Undiversified Suppose you risk everything, investing the $100,000 in either Project 1 or Project 2. You will either make $50,000 or lose $25,000. Because the probability of each of these outcomes is 50 percent, your expected return is the average of these two outcomes—an expected return of $12,500. But in this case in which only one project is chosen, there is no chance that you will actually make a return of $12,500.

Diversified Suppose instead that you diversify by putting 50 percent of your money into Project 1 and 50 percent into Project 2. (Someone else is putting up the other money in these two projects.) Because the two projects are independent, you now have *four* possible returns:

1. Lose $12,500 on each project, and your return is –$25,000.
2. Make $25,000 on Project 1 and lose $12,500 on Project 2, and your return is $12,500.
3. Lose $12,500 on Project 1 and make $25,000 on Project 2, and your return is $12,500.
4. Make $25,000 on each project, and your return is $50,000.

Each of these four possible outcomes is equally probable—each has a 25 percent chance of occurring. You have lowered the chance that you will earn $50,000, but you have also lowered the chance that you will lose $25,000. And you have increased the chance that you will actually make your expected return of $12,500. By diversifying your portfolio of assets, you have reduced its riskiness while maintaining an expected return of $12,500.

If you are risk averse—if your utility of wealth curve looks like Tania's, which you studied earlier in this chapter—you'll prefer the diversified portfolio to the one that is not diversified. That is, your *expected utility* with a diversified set of assets is greater.

A common way to diversify is to buy stocks in different corporations. Let's look at the market in which these stocks are traded.

The Stock Market

The prices of the stocks are determined by demand and supply. But demand and supply in the stock market is dominated by one thing: the expected future price. If the price of a stock today is higher than the expected price tomorrow, people will sell the stock today. If the price of a stock today is less than its expected price tomorrow, people will buy the stock today. As a result of such trading, today's price equals tomorrow's expected price, and so today's price embodies all the relevant information that is available about the stock. A market in which the actual price embodies all currently available relevant information is called an **efficient market**.

In an efficient market, it is impossible to forecast changes in price. Why? If your forecast is that the price is going to rise tomorrow, you will buy now. Your action of buying today is an increase in demand today and increases *today's* price. It's true that your action—the action of a single trader—is not going to make much difference to a huge market like the New York Stock Exchange. But if traders in general expect a higher price tomorrow and they all act today on the basis of that expectation, then today's price will rise. It will keep on rising until it reaches the expected future price, because only at that price do traders see no profit in buying more stock today.

There is an apparent paradox about efficient markets. Markets are efficient because people try to make a profit. They seek a profit by buying at a low price and selling at a high price. But the very act of buying and selling to make a profit means that the market price moves to equal its expected future value. When it has done that, no one, not even those who are seeking to profit, can *predictably* make a profit. Every profit opportunity seen by traders leads to an action that produces a price change that removes the profit opportunity for others. Even the probability of an intergalactic attack on New York City is taken into account in determining stock market prices—see the cartoon.

"Drat! I suppose the market has already discounted this, too."

Drawing by Lorenz; © 1986 *The New Yorker Magazine, Inc.*

Thus an efficient market has two features:

1. Its price equals the expected future price and embodies all the available information.
2. No forecastable profit opportunities are available.

The key thing to understand about an efficient market such as the stock market is that if something can be anticipated, it will be, and the anticipation of a future event will affect the *current* price of a stock.

Volatility in Stock Prices   If the price of a stock equals its expected future price, why is the stock market so volatile? It is volatile because expectations are volatile. They depend on the information available. As new information becomes available, stock traders form new expectations about the future state of the economy and, in turn, new expectations of future stock prices. New information comes randomly, so prices change randomly.

◆ We've seen how people cope with uncertainty and how markets work when there are information problems. *Reading Between the Lines* on pages 462–463 looks one more time at the problem of picking a portfolio and shows how a person's attitude toward risk influences the type of portfolio selected.

The next part of this book studies *international economics*. It builds on what you learned in Chapter 3 about comparative advantage and shows how countries can gain from specialization and exchange.

A Tradeoff Between Risk and Return

THE NEW YORK TIMES, NOVEMBER 15, 1998

Diversified Pillows for Resting Easy in Storms

BY JONATHAN FUERBRINGER

"We are not trying to hit home runs," said Benjamin Thorndike, lead portfolio manager of the Scudder Pathway Series of funds. "We are trying to do well and sleep well at night."

That's a diversified money manager talking about an investment style that has not always fared well in an era of double-digit annual gains in the Dow Jones industrial average and the Standard & Poor's 500-stock index. ...

The idea is simple. If your investments are spread around—in stocks, in bonds, in foreign stocks, in different kinds of bonds and different kinds of stocks—you have a good chance of getting a cushioning rise in one area while another is plunging. In the third quarter, for example, the return from government and corporate bonds was 4 percent while the Dow, the S&P 500 and the Nasdaq index fell 10 percent or more.

Diversification is not the way to big stock returns because it reduces risk in exchange for lower returns. But it is a way to survive the volatile swings of the stock market, which have become much more common over the last year.

Investors should "find the comfort zone" between return and risk, said Gary Brinson, chief executive of Brinson Partners, which manages a diversified mutual fund. Diversification, he said, means "the path of that return is much less bumpy." ...

But deciding to be diversified is not enough. Investors must decide how much risk to take on, which means looking closely at the mix of investments in their fund or portfolio.

© 1998 The New York Times. Reprinted with permission.
Further reproduction prohibited.

Essence of the Story

■ If investments are spread around in different kinds of bonds and stocks, returns are lower but risk is also lower.

■ Investors need to find the combination of return and risk that makes them comfortable—that enables them to sleep well.

■ Some investors are comfortable taking big risks in exchange for a chance of a big return. Other investors are comfortable only if they invest cautiously.

■ In Fig. 1, a cautious investor sleeps well. This person has wealth of $100,000, and the utility of this wealth is 100 (on the index number scale used in Fig. 1).

■ This person has an opportunity to invest $10,000 in a business venture. There is a 50 percent chance that the business succeeds and pays out $20,000. And there is a 50 percent chance that the business fails and the $10,000 is lost.

■ Expected wealth is $105,000 (0.5 multiplied by $90,000 plus 0.5 multiplied by $120,000). Expected utility is 101 (0.5 multiplied by 91 plus 0.5 multiplied by 111). The investment increases expected utility. So this person sleeps well!

■ In Fig. 2, a cautious investor is beyond the comfort zone. Here the person has $20,000 to invest. There is a 50 percent chance that the business succeeds and pays out $40,000. And there is a 50 percent chance that the business fails and the $20,000 is lost.

■ Expected wealth is $110,000 (0.5 multiplied by $80,000 plus 0.5 multiplied by $140,000). But expected utility is only 98 (0.5 multiplied by 78 plus 0.5 multiplied by 118). Expected wealth increases, but expected utility decreases. The cautious investor is beyond the comfort zone and will not make this investment.

■ Figure 3 shows the case of an investor who is comfortable with a risky investment strategy.

■ This person has $50,000 to invest. There is a 50 percent chance that the business succeeds and pays out $100,000. And there is a 50 percent chance that the business fails and the entire $50,000 is lost. This opportunity is more risky than the one that the cautious investor rejected in Fig. 2.

■ Expected wealth is $125,000 (0.5 multiplied by $50,000 plus 0.5 multiplied by $200,000). Expected utility is 116 (0.5 multiplied by 52 plus 0.5 multiplied by 180). Expected wealth increases and expected utility increases. This person feels better off pursuing this risky opportunity than passing it up.

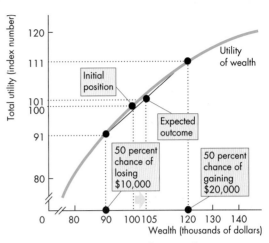

Figure 1 A cautious investor sleeps well

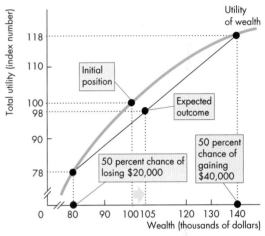

Figure 2 Beyond a cautious investor's comfort zone

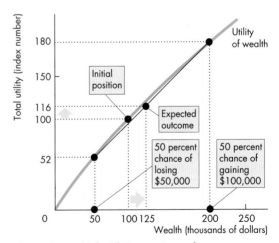

Figure 3 In a high-risk investor's comfort zone

463

SUMMARY

KEY POINTS

Uncertainty and Risk (pp. 450–452)

- Uncertainty is a situation in which more than one event may occur but we don't know which one.
- Risk is uncertainty with probabilities attached to outcomes.
- A person's attitude toward risk, called the degree of risk aversion, is described by a utility of wealth schedule and curve.
- Faced with uncertainty, people choose the action that maximizes expected utility.

Insurance (pp. 453–454)

- We spend 15 percent of our income on insurance to reduce the risk we face.
- The three main types of insurance are life, health, and property and casualty.
- By pooling risks, insurance companies can reduce the risks people face (from insured activities) at a lower cost than the value placed on the lower risk.

Information (pp. 455–457)

- Buyers search for the least-cost source of supply and stop when the expected marginal benefit of search equals the marginal cost of search.
- The price at which the search stops is less than or equal to the buyer's reservation price.
- Advertising provides information, and it might increase prices or decrease them.
- Advertising can lower prices because it increases competition or extends economies of scale.

Private Information (pp. 457–460)

- Private information is one person's knowledge that is too costly for anyone else to discover.
- Private information creates the problems of moral hazard (the use of private information to the advantage of the informed and the disadvantage of the uninformed) and adverse selection (the tendency for people to enter into agreements in which they can use their private information to their own advantage and to the disadvantage of the less informed party).
- Devices that enable markets to function in the face of moral hazard and adverse selection are incentive payments, guarantees such as warranties, rationing, and signals.

Managing Risk in Financial Markets (pp. 460–461)

- Risk can be reduced by diversifying asset holdings, thereby combining the returns on projects that are independent of each other.
- A common way to diversify is to buy stocks in different corporations. Stock prices are determined by the expected future price of the stock.
- Expectations about future stock prices are based on all the information that is available and regarded as relevant.
- A market in which the price equals the expected price is an efficient market.

KEY FIGURES

KEY TERMS

PROBLEMS

*1. The figure shows Lee's utility of wealth curve.

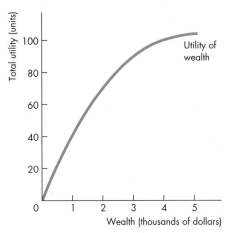

Lee is offered a job as a salesperson in which there is a 50 percent chance that she will make $4,000 a month and a 50 percent chance that she will make nothing.
   a. What is Lee's expected income from taking this job?
   b. What is Lee's expected utility from taking this job?
   c. How much (approximately) would another firm have to offer Lee with certainty to persuade her not to take the risky sales job?

2. The figure shows Colleen's utility of wealth curve.

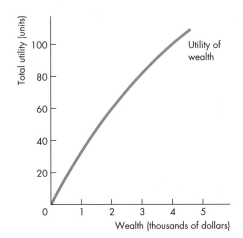

Just like Lee in problem 1, Colleen is offered a job as a salesperson in which there is a 50 percent chance that she will make $4,000 a month and a 50 percent chance that she will make nothing.
   a. What is Colleen's expected income from taking this job?
   b. What is Colleen's expected utility from taking this job?
   c. How much (approximately) would another firm have to offer Colleen with certainty to persuade her not to take the risky sales job?
   d. Explain who is more likely to be willing to take this risky job, Lee or Colleen.

*3. Jimmy and Zenda have the following utility of wealth schedules:

Wealth	Jimmy's utility	Zenda's utility
0	0	0
100	200	512
200	300	640
300	350	672
400	375	678
500	387	681
600	393	683
700	396	684

Who is more risk averse, Jimmy or Zenda?

4. Suppose that Jimmy and Zenda in problem 3 have $400 each and that each sees a business project that involves committing the entire $400 to the project. They reckon that the project could return $600 (a profit of $200) with a probability of 0.85 or $200 (a loss of $200) with a probability of 0.15. Who goes for the project and who hangs onto the initial $400?

*5. Lee in problem 1 has built a small weekend shack on a steep, unstable hillside. She spent all her wealth, which is $5,000, on this project. There is a 75 percent chance that the house will be washed down the hill and be worthless. How much is Lee willing to pay for an insurance policy that pays her $5,000 if the house is washed away?

6. Colleen in problem 2 has built a small weekend shack right next to Lee's (of problem 1). Colleen has spent all her wealth, which is $4,000, on this project. There is a 75 percent chance that the house will be washed down the hill and be worthless. How much is Colleen willing to pay for an insurance policy that pays her $4,000 if the house is washed away?

*7. Lee in problem 1 is shopping for a new car. She plans to borrow the money to pay for the car from the bank. Describe in detail the search problems that Lee faces. What information does she find useful? How does she obtain it? How does she make her decisions?

8. Lee in problem 1 is shopping for a new car. She plans to borrow the money to pay for the car from the bank. Describe in detail the moral hazard and adverse selection problems that Lee faces. What arrangements is she likely to encounter that are designed to cope with these problems?

CRITICAL THINKING

1. Study *Reading Between the Lines* on pp. 462–463 and then answer the following questions:
   a. Why is it rational for some people to take big risks and for other people to be cautious?
   b. Who makes more money on the average: the cautious investor or the one who takes bigger risks? Why?
   c. Why do you think pension funds hold a mixture of stocks and bonds?

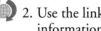 2. Use the links on the Parkin Web site to obtain information on the prices of three stocks that interest you.
   a. Describe the change in the prices of these stocks over the past month.
   b. If you had invested $1,000 in each of these stocks (a total of $3,000) one month ago, how much would your initial investment be worth today?
   c. If you had $3,000 to invest, would you use some of it to buy these stocks? How much would you put in each? How much would you keep in cash?
   d. Form a group with other students and compare your answers to part (c). Which one of you is the most risk averse? Which of you is the least risk averse? Explain your answer.

3. Why do you think it is not possible to buy insurance against having to put up with a low-paying, miserable job? Explain why a market in insurance of this type would not work.

4. Although you can't buy insurance against the risk of being sold a lemon, the market does give you some protection. How? What are the main ways in which markets overcome the lemon problem?

5. Grades send signals to potential employers. Explain why you are better served or worse served by a professor who demands high standards for an A than by one who always ensures that 20 percent of the class gets an A.

6. Merck discovers a new drug that is expected to bring big profits. What happens to the price of Merck's stock? Why wouldn't people put all their wealth into Merck's stock?

We, the People, ...

Thomas Jefferson knew that creating a government of the people, by the people, and for the people was a huge enterprise and one that could easily go wrong. Creating a constitution that made despotic and tyrannical rule impossible was relatively easy. The founding fathers did their best to practice sound economics. They designed a sophisticated system of incentives—of carrots and sticks—to make the government responsive to public opinion and to limit the ability of individual special interests to gain at the expense of the majority. But they were not able to create a constitution that effectively blocks the ability of special interest groups to capture the consumer and producer surpluses that result from specialization and exchange. ◆ We have created a system of government to deal with four economic problems. The market economy would produce too small a quantity of those public goods and services that we must consume together, such as national defense and air-traffic control. It enables monopoly to restrict production and charge too high a price. It produces too large a quantity of some goods and services, the production of which creates pollution. And it generates a distribution of income and wealth that most people believe is too unequal. So we need a government to help cope with these economic problems. But as the founding fathers knew would happen, when governments get involved in the economy, people try to steer the government's actions in directions that bring personal gains at the expense of the general interest. ◆ The four chapters in this part explained the problems with which the market has a hard time coping. Chapter 18 overviewed the entire range of problems and studied one of these problems, public goods, more deeply. Chapter 19 studied antitrust law and the regulation of natural monopoly. And Chapter 20 dealt with externalities. It examined the external costs imposed by pollution and the external benefits that come from education and research. It described some of the ways in which externalities can be dealt with. And it explained that one way of coping with externalities is to strengthen the market and "internalize" the externalities rather than to intervene in the market. Chapter 21 is different from the other three. It looked at the problems of uncertainty and incomplete information and the problems that markets have in the face of these problems. But it also showed you that the market does cope with these problems remarkably well. ◆ Many economists have thought long and hard about the problems discussed in this part. But none has had as profound an effect on our ideas in this area as Ronald Coase, whom you can meet on the following page. You can also meet Walter Williams of George Mason University, another major contributor to our understanding of market failure and government intervention.

The Economist

Ronald Coase *(1910–), was born in England and educated at the London School of Economics, where he was deeply influenced by his teacher, Arnold Plant, and by the issues of his youth: communist central planning versus free markets. Professor Coase has lived in the United States since 1951. He first visited America as a 20-year-old on a traveling scholarship during the depths of the Great Depression. It was on this visit, and before he had completed his bachelor's degree, that he conceived the ideas that 60 years later were to earn him the 1991 Nobel Prize for Economic Science. He discovered and clarified the significance of transaction costs and property rights for the functioning of the economy. Ronald Coase has revolutionized the way we think about property rights and externalities and has opened up the growing field of law and economics.*

"The question to be decided is: is the value of fish lost greater or less than the value of the product which contamination of the stream makes possible?"

RONALD H. COASE
The Problem of Social Cost

The Issues

As knowledge accumulates, we are becoming more sensitive to environmental externalities. We are also developing more sensitive methods of dealing with them. But all the methods involve a public choice.

Urban smog, which is both unpleasant and dangerous to breathe, forms when sunlight reacts with emissions from the tailpipes of automobiles. Because of this external cost of auto exhaust, we set emission standards and tax gasoline. Emission standards increase the cost of a car, and gasoline taxes increase the cost of the marginal mile traveled. The higher costs decrease the quantity demanded of road transportation and so decrease the amount of pollution it creates. Is the value of cleaner urban air worth the higher cost of transportation? The public choices of voters, regulators, and lawmakers answer this question.

Acid rain, which imposes a cost on everyone who lives in its path, falls from sulfur-laden clouds produced by electric utility smokestacks. This external cost is being tackled with a market solution. This solution is marketable permits, the price and allocation of which are determined by the forces of supply and demand. Private choices determine the demand for pollution permits, but a public choice determines the supply.

As cars stream onto an urban freeway during the morning rush hour, the highway clogs and becomes an expensive parking lot. Each rush hour traveler imposes external costs on all the others. Today, road users bear private congestion costs but do not face a share of the external congestion costs that they create. But a market solution to this problem is now technologically feasible. It is a solution that charges road users a fee similar to a toll that varies with time of day and degree of congestion. Confronted with the social marginal cost of their actions, each road user makes a choice and the market for highway space is efficient. Here, a public choice to use a market solution leaves the final decision about the degree of congestion to private choices.

Now

Today, Lake Erie supports a fishing industry, just as it did in the 1930s. No longer treated as a garbage dump for chemicals, the lake is regenerating its ecosystem. Fertilizers and insecticides are now recognized as products that have potential externalities, and their external effects are assessed by the Environmental Protection Agency before new versions are put into widespread use. Dumping industrial waste into rivers and lakes is now subject to much more stringent regulations and penalties. Lake Erie's externalities have been dealt with by one of the methods available: government regulation.

Then

Chester Jackson, a Lake Erie fisherman, recalls that when he began fishing on the lake, boats didn't carry drinking water. Fishermen drank from the lake. Speaking after World War II, Jackson observed, "Can't do that today. Those chemicals in there would kill you." Farmers used chemicals, such as the insecticide DDT that got carried into the lake by runoff. Industrial waste and trash were also dumped in the lake in large quantities. As a result, Lake Erie became badly polluted during the 1940s and became incapable of sustaining a viable fish stock.

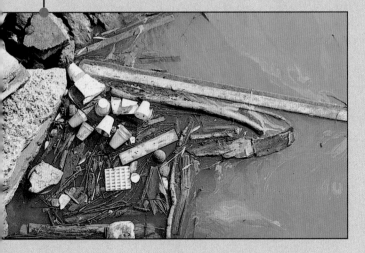

Walter Williams, whom you can meet on the following pages, has done much to improve our understanding of public policy and the problems of government intervention in the economy.

Talking with

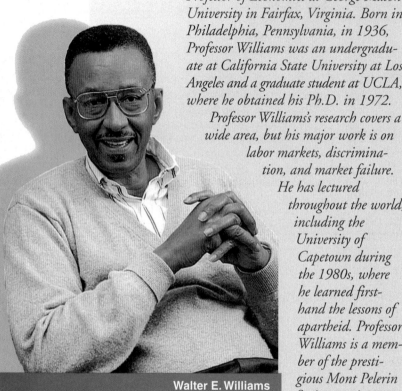

Walter E. Williams *is Professor of Economics at George Mason University in Fairfax, Virginia. Born in Philadelphia, Pennsylvania, in 1936, Professor Williams was an undergraduate at California State University at Los Angeles and a graduate student at UCLA, where he obtained his Ph.D. in 1972.*

Professor Williams's research covers a wide area, but his major work is on labor markets, discrimination, and market failure. He has lectured throughout the world, including the University of Capetown during the 1980s, where he learned firsthand the lessons of apartheid. Professor Williams is a member of the prestigious Mont Pelerin Society, an international organization of free market economists. Its membership includes six Nobel Laureates: Milton Friedman, Friedrich Hayek, George Stigler, James Buchanan, Gary Becker, and Ronald Coase.

Michael Parkin talked with Professor Williams about his work, how it connects with the ideas of other great economists, and the insights they offer us in facing today's problems.

Professor Williams, what attracted you to economics?
Like many undergraduate students of the 1960s, I was concerned with public policy that focused on the betterment of mankind and tackled issues such as urban decay, poverty, unemployment, and discrimination. At the time, it seemed that social sciences like sociology and psychology were the ideal tools to analyze these important social issues. That was until by pure chance a particular sociology class was filled, and so I substituted an introductory economics class. As a consequence of not being good at the deductive logic of economics, plus several classroom disputes with the professor on topics such as income distribution and racial discrimination, I wound up getting a "D." However, I was sufficiently interested in economics that I took two economics classes the following semester, earning an "A" in both. Ultimately, I changed my major to economics and earned a B.A. from California State University at Los Angeles and later earned a Ph.D. in Economics from UCLA.

You and I first met in Capetown, South Africa, in 1980, when we were both visiting professors at the University of Capetown. What are the big economic lessons that the experience of South Africa teaches about the proper role of government in economic life?
When we first met in Capetown, apartheid was very much a part of South Africa. I was very impressed with the economic lessons of apartheid, so much so that I ultimately wrote a book in 1992 entitled *South Africa's War Against Capitalism.* The biggest lesson from South Africa's experience is that the free market does not confer privileges based on race. The free market instead uses economic factors such as prices and productivity. If people wish to indulge their preferences for noneconomic factors

470

such as race, sex, and nationality, the free market exacts a price. South African whites knew this very well and found that if they wanted privileges, they needed the extensive government apparatus of coercion and control that became known as apartheid. Labor laws such as those that reserved certain jobs for whites stand as unambiguous evidence that the market would not discriminate in employment to the extent whites wished. If it would have, there would have been no need for racially restrictive laws.

> The biggest lesson from South Africa's experience is that the free market cannot be trusted to confer privileges based on race. The free market instead uses economic factors such as prices and productivity.

What do you identify as the major sources of market failure that need government action today?

Many alleged instances of "market failure" are the result of ill-defined property rights. That is surely the case in instances of air and water pollution. In those instances, a case can be made for efficient government intervention. Government can ban the polluting activity, assign pollution taxes, or assign pollution rights that can be bought and sold in the market. Many economists agree that the last is a more efficient method of dealing with the external costs of pollution. We should also recognize that government decision makers do not hold property rights to the resources they control. Since they are not residual claimants to either the costs or benefits they create, we cannot expect to see the kinds of forces, such as the threat of bankruptcy, that create the kind of operational efficiency we see in the market. In other words, since a politician's personal wealth is not at stake, when he makes decisions, he will be far more shortsighted than his counterpart in the private sector.

Has deregulation of telecommunications and air transportation done its job? Has deregulation brought problems that were not expected?

By any objective measure, the deregulation of the telecommunications and transportation industries has done its job. Consumers pay lower prices and receive higher quality and a more varied set of services than was the case before deregulation. Deregulation of airlines led to cheaper fares, which in turn led to more Americans traveling by air. To the extent that statistics show that air travel is far safer than highway travel, the deregulation has actually saved thousands of lives. With the deregulation of the telephone industry, we see the greater use of services such as faxes, modems, electronic transactions, and the Internet that would have been impossible with the regulatory heavy hand of government. The remaining problem in these industries is that deregulation has not gone far enough: in the case of transportation, privatization of the airports and air traffic control, and in the case of telecommunications, complete auctioning of the airwaves to new and existing firms in the communications industry.

Do we have a monopoly problem in the new information industries? Microsoft? Intel? The Internet? Why and what do we need to do about it?

Often a monopoly is the most efficient method of organization. Monopolies are not inherently good or bad. After all, the institution of marriage is essentially one of a monopolistic structure: It hopes to limit competition. Obviously, the participants guess there are some gains from limited competition. If you read the Ten Commandments, you will see that the first two, presumably the most important, are: Thou shalt have none other gods before me, and thou shalt not make any graven image. In other words, there cannot be any substitutes for God—surely a monopoly arrangement!

Monopoly is a problem when government creates monopolies, whether the monopoly is private or public. Classic government-created monopolies are those in education, postal services, and rail services that limit consumer choices and are not subject to the corrective forces of the marketplace when they do not serve their customers properly. Such insulation does not apply in the cases of Microsoft and Intel.

What are the main forms of discrimination that economic policy can correct and what is your assessment of the progress made in the United States during the past decade?

First, we need to come up with an operational and useful definition of discrimination. I think discrimination can be best described solely as the act of choice. Scarcity implies choice. When one chooses one activity or person, he or she must necessarily choose against some other activity or person. For example, when the student chooses to major in economics, he or she must necessarily choose—or discriminate—against other majors. When someone chooses a spouse, he or she must discriminate against other potential spouses.

When one modifies the word "discrimination" with the word "sex" or "race," one is merely specifying an attribute upon which a choice is made. What most people call discrimination is more properly called preference indulgence. As such, the preference for Burgundy wine over Bordeaux wine does not conceptually differ from a person's preference for a white spouse, white employee, or white renter. In other words, there are no commonly accepted criteria to say whether the preference for one good or set of physical attributes is better or more righteous than another.

Preference indulgence becomes a moral and economic problem when government is used. For example, any principle of liberty suggests that a person has the right to sell his house to whomever he pleases, but that principle does not allow him to use state coercion to force his neighbor to act likewise. When there is public provision of a good such as schools, libraries, or golf courses, that fact implies that every member of the public has the right to use the good in question. While racial or sexual preference indulgence may be offensive, the true test of one's commitment

to freedom of association does not come when we permit people to associate as we see fit. The true test of that commitment comes when we allow people to associate in ways we deem offensive.

The best thing that government can do in the area of racial or sex discrimination is not to subsidize it through laws that regulate prices such as minimum wages and rent control and other regulatory laws such as occupational and business licensure. Minimum wages deny people the right to bid lower prices for their labor services. Rent control laws deny them the right to bid higher prices for rental services. Licensure laws allow incumbent practitioners to establish arbitrary, capricious, legally binding occupational and business entry standards.

The power to bid lower prices for what one sells or higher prices for what one buys is the most effective way for people deemed less preferred—minorities, women, and foreigners—to compete with others. Price controls prevent that competition. Similarly, voluntary mutually satisfactory exchange permits effective competition with people deemed more preferred.

Who are the great economists of the past who have inspired you most? What principal idea has proved crucial in your own thinking?
Frederic Bastiat's works, *The Law* and *Economic Sophisms*, have been my major sources of inspiration. But Friedrich Hayek's many works have played a major part as well. Both shared the vision that the uglier portions of mankind's history features arbitrary abuse and

control by a powerful government. If liberty is to emerge and survive, government must be limited to the legitimate and moral functions of government. For the most part, those functions lie principally in the areas of protection of the individual from coercion by others and the protection of his property, including his person. Evidence shows that where individuals have a greater measure of liberty, there is a higher level of prosperity and wealth accumulation. But prosperity and wealth should be viewed as a secondary benefit of liberty. Liberty is morally superior, and its primary benefit lies in its respect for the individual.

> Evidence shows that where individuals have a greater measure of liberty, there is a higher level of prosperity and wealth accumulation.

What do you say to an undergraduate who wants to know whether it is worth majoring in economics?
Economics is a way of thinking and, as such, a powerful tool of analysis that has broad application. Economic theory can be usefully applied in any discussion where there is an issue of benefits versus the cost of human action. Economists have a broad range of employment choices from working in business, government, research, and educational institutions. Moreover, among social scientists, economists tend to be the more highly paid.

Chapter 22

Trading with the World

Since ancient times, people have expanded their trading as far as technology allowed. Marco Polo opened up the silk route between Europe and China in the thirteenth century. Today, container ships laden with cars and machines and Boeing 747s stuffed with farm-fresh foods ply sea and air routes, carrying billions of dollars worth of goods. Why do people go to such great lengths to trade with those in other nations? ◆ Low-wage Mexico has entered into a free trade agreement with high-wage Canada and the United States—the North American Free Trade Agreement, or NAFTA. According to Texas billionaire Ross Perot, this agreement has caused a "giant sucking sound" and transferred jobs from Michigan to Mexico. Is Ross Perot right? How can we compete

Silk Routes and Sucking Sounds

with a country that pays its workers a fraction of U.S. wages? Are there any industries, besides perhaps the Hollywood movie industry, in which we have an advantage? ◆ In 1930, Congress passed the Smoot-Hawley Act, which imposed a 45 percent tariff (rising to 60 percent by 1933) on one third of U.S. imports. This move provoked widespread retaliation and a tariff war among the world's major trading countries. After World War II, a process of trade liberalization brought about a gradual reduction of tariffs. What are the effects of tariffs on international trade? Why don't we have completely unrestricted international trade?

◆ In this chapter, we're going to learn about international trade. We'll discover how all nations can gain by specializing in producing the goods and services in which they have a comparative advantage and trading with other countries. We'll discover that *all* countries can compete, no matter how high their wages. We'll also explain why countries restrict trade.

After studying this chapter, you will be able to:

- Describe the patterns in international trade

- Explain comparative advantage and explain why all countries can gain from international trade

- Explain how economies of scale and diversity of taste lead to gains from trade

- Explain why trade restrictions reduce our imports, exports, and consumption possibilities

- Explain the arguments used to justify trade restrictions and show how they are flawed

- Explain why we have trade restrictions

Patterns and Trends in International Trade

THE GOODS AND SERVICES THAT WE BUY FROM people in other countries are called **imports**. The goods and services that we sell to people in other countries are called **exports**. What are the most important things that we import and export? Most people would probably guess that a rich nation such as the United States imports raw materials and exports manufactured goods. Although that is one feature of U.S. international trade, it is not its most important feature. The vast bulk of our exports *and* imports is manufactured goods. We sell foreigners earth-moving equipment, airplanes, supercomputers, and scientific equipment, and we buy televisions, VCRs, blue jeans, and T-shirts from them. Also, we are a major exporter of agricultural products and raw materials. We also import and export a huge volume of services.

Trade in Goods

Manufactured goods account for 50 percent of our exports and for 60 percent of our imports. Industrial materials (raw materials and semimanufactured items) account for 17 percent of our exports and for 20 percent of our imports, and agricultural products account for only 7 percent of our exports and 3 percent of our imports. Our largest individual export and import items are capital goods and autos.

But goods account for only 74 percent of our exports and 83 percent of our imports. The rest of our international trade is in services.

Trade in Services

You may be wondering how a country can "export" and "import" services. Here are some examples.

If you take a vacation in France and travel there on an Air France flight from New York, you import transportation services from France. The money you spend in France on hotel bills and restaurant meals is also a U.S. import of services. Similarly, the vacation taken by a French student in the United States counts as an U.S. export of services to France.

When we import TV sets from South Korea, the owner of the ship that transports them might be Greek and the company that insures them might be British. The payments that we make for the transportation

and insurance are U.S. imports of services. Similarly, when an American shipping company transports California wine to Tokyo, the transportation cost is an American export of a service to Japan. Our international trade in these types of services is large and growing.

Geographical Patterns

The United States has trading links with every part of the world, but Canada is our biggest single trading partner for both exports and imports. We buy 45 percent of our imports from Japan and other Asian countries such as China, Hong Kong, South Korea, and Taiwan, and we sell a similar percentage of our exports to Asia, Europe, Latin America, and Canada.

Trends in the Volume of Trade

In 1960, we exported less than 5 percent of total output and imported 4 1/2 percent of the goods and services that we bought. In 1998, we exported 11 percent of total output and imported 13 percent of the goods and services that we bought.

On the export side, capital goods, automobiles, food, and raw materials have remained large items and held a roughly constant share of total exports, but the composition of imports has changed. Food and raw material imports have fallen steadily. Imports of fuel increased dramatically during the 1970s but fell during the 1980s. Imports of machinery have grown, and today they approach 50 percent of total imports.

Balance of Trade and International Borrowing

The value of exports minus the value of imports is called the **balance of trade.** In 1998, the U.S. balance of trade was a negative $170 billion. Our imports were $170 billion more than our exports. When we import more than we export, as we did in 1998, we borrow from foreigners or sell some of our assets. When we export more than we import, we make loans to foreigners or buy some of their assets.

You will study the *balance* of trade if you take a course in *macroeconomics*. Here, our goal is to understand the factors that influence the *volume* and *directions* of international trade rather than its balance. And the keys to this understanding are the concepts of opportunity cost and comparative advantage.

Opportunity Cost and Comparative Advantage

THE FUNDAMENTAL FORCE THAT GENERATES international trade is *comparative advantage*. And the basis of comparative advantage is divergent *opportunity costs*. You met these ideas in Chapter 3, when we learned about the gains from specialization and exchange between Tom and Nancy.

Tom and Nancy each specialize in producing just one good and then trade with each other. Most nations do not go to the extreme of specializing in a single good and importing everything else. Nonetheless, nations can increase the consumption of all goods if they redirect their scarce resources toward the production of those goods and services in which they have a comparative advantage.

To see how this outcome occurs, we'll apply the same basic ideas we learned in the case of Tom and Nancy to trade among nations. We'll begin by recalling how we can use the production possibility frontier to measure opportunity cost. Then we'll see how divergent opportunity costs bring comparative advantage and gains from trade for countries as well as for individuals even though no country completely specializes in the production of just one good.

Opportunity Cost in Farmland

Farmland (a fictitious country) can produce grain and cars at any point inside or along its production possibility frontier, *PPF*, shown in Fig. 22.1. (We're holding constant the output of all the other goods that Farmland produces.) The Farmers (the people of Farmland) are consuming all the grain and cars that they produce, and they are operating at point *a* in the figure. That is, Farmland is producing and consuming 15 billion bushels of grain and 8 million cars each year. What is the opportunity cost of a car in Farmland?

We can answer that question by calculating the slope of the production possibility frontier at point *a*. The magnitude of the slope of the frontier measures the opportunity cost of one good in terms of the other. To measure the slope of the frontier at point *a*, place a straight line tangential to the frontier at point *a* and calculate the slope of that straight line. Recall that the formula for the slope of a line is the change in the value of the variable measured on the *y*-axis divided by the change in the value of the variable measured on the *x*-axis as we move along the line.

Here, the variable measured on the *y*-axis is billions of bushels of grain, and the variable measured on the *x*-axis is millions of cars. So the slope is the change in the number of bushels of grain divided by the change in the number of cars.

As you can see from the red triangle at point *a* in the figure, if the number of cars produced increases by 2 million, grain production decreases by 18 billion bushels. Therefore the magnitude of the slope is 18 billion divided by 2 million, which equals 9,000. To get one more car, the people of Farmland must give up 9,000 bushels of grain. Thus the opportunity cost of 1 car is 9,000 bushels of grain. Equivalently, 9,000 bushels of grain cost 1 car. For the people of Farmland, these opportunity costs are the prices they face. The price of a car is 9,000 bushels of grain, and the price of 9,000 bushels of grain is 1 car.

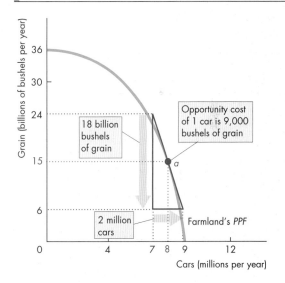

FIGURE 22.1

Opportunity Cost in Farmland

Farmland produces and consumes 15 billion bushels of grain and 8 million cars a year. That is, it produces and consumes at point *a* on its production possibility frontier. Opportunity cost is equal to the magnitude of the slope of the production possibility frontier. The red triangle tells us that at point *a*, 18 billion bushels of grain must be forgone to get 2 million cars. That is, at point *a*, 2 million cars cost 18 billion bushels of grain. Equivalently, 1 car costs 9,000 bushels of grain or 9,000 bushels cost 1 car.

Opportunity Cost in Mobilia

Figure 22.2 shows the production possibility frontier of Mobilia (another fictitious country). Like the Farmers, the Mobilians consume all the grain and cars that they produce. Mobilia consumes 18 billion bushels of grain a year and 4 million cars, at point *a'*.

Let's calculate the opportunity costs in Mobilia. At point *a'*, the opportunity cost of a car is equal to the magnitude of the slope of the red line tangential to the production possibility frontier, *PPF*. You can see from the red triangle that the magnitude of the slope of Mobilia's production possibility frontier is 6 billion bushels of grain divided by 6 million cars, which equals 1,000 bushels of grain per car. To get one more car, the Mobilians must give up 1,000 bushels of grain. Thus the opportunity cost of 1 car is 1,000 bushels of grain, or, equivalently, the opportunity cost of 1,000 bushels of grain is 1 car. These are the prices faced in Mobilia.

FIGURE 22.2
Opportunity Cost in Mobilia

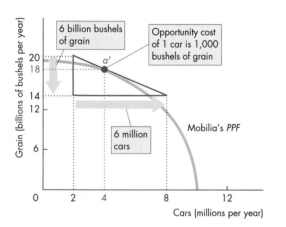

Mobilia produces and consumes 18 billion bushels of grain and 4 million cars a year. That is, it produces and consumes at point *a'* on its production possibility frontier. Opportunity cost is equal to the magnitude of the slope of the production possibility frontier. The red triangle tells us that at point *a'*, 6 billion bushels of grain must be forgone to get 6 million cars. That is, at point *a'*, the opportunity cost of 6 million cars is 6 billion bushels of grain. Equivalently, 1 car costs 1,000 bushels of grain or 1,000 bushels of grain cost 1 car.

Comparative Advantage

Cars are cheaper in Mobilia than in Farmland. One car costs 9,000 bushels of grain in Farmland but only 1,000 bushels of grain in Mobilia. But grain is cheaper in Farmland than in Mobilia—9,000 bushels of grain costs only 1 car in Farmland, while that same amount of grain costs 9 cars in Mobilia.

Mobilia has a comparative advantage in car production. Farmland has a comparative advantage in grain production. A country has a **comparative advantage** in producing a good if it can produce that good at a lower opportunity cost than any other country.

Let's see how opportunity cost differences and comparative advantage generate gains from international trade.

Gains from Trade

IF MOBILIA BOUGHT GRAIN FOR WHAT IT COSTS Farmland to produce it, then Mobilia could buy 9,000 bushels of grain for 1 car. That is much lower than the cost of growing grain in Mobilia, for there it costs 9 cars to produce 9,000 bushels of grain. If the Mobilians can buy grain at the low Farmland price, they will reap some gains.

If the Farmers can buy cars for what it costs Mobilia to produce them, they will be able to obtain a car for 1,000 bushels of grain. Because it costs 9,000 bushels of grain to produce a car in Farmland, the Farmers would gain from such an opportunity.

In this situation, it makes sense for Mobilians to buy their grain from Farmers and for Farmers to buy their cars from Mobilians. But at what price will Farmland and Mobilia engage in mutually beneficial international trade?

The Terms of Trade

The quantity of grain that Farmland must pay Mobilia for a car is Farmland's **terms of trade** with Mobilia. Because the United States exports and imports many different goods and services, we measure the terms of trade in the real world as an index number that averages the terms of trade over all the items we trade.

The forces of international supply and demand determine the terms of trade. Figure 22.3 illustrates these forces in the Farmland-Mobilia international car market. The quantity of cars *traded internationally* is measured on the *x*-axis. On the *y*-axis, we measure the

FIGURE 22.3
International Trade in Cars

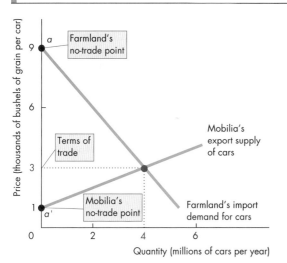

As the price of a car falls, the quantity of imports demanded by Farmland increases—Farmland's import demand curve for cars is downward sloping. As the price of a car rises, the quantity of cars supplied by Mobilia for export increases—Mobilia's export supply curve of cars is upward sloping. Without international trade, the price of a car is 9,000 bushels of grain in Farmland (point *a*) and 1,000 bushels of grain in Mobilia (point *a'*).

With free international trade, the price (terms of trade) is determined where the export supply curve intersects the import demand curve—3,000 bushels of grain per car. At that price, 4 million cars a year are imported by Farmland and exported by Mobilia. The value of grain exported by Farmland and imported by Mobilia is 12 billion bushels a year, the quantity required to pay for the cars imported.

price of a car. This price is expressed as the *terms of trade*—bushels of grain per car. If no international trade takes place, the price of a car in Farmland is 9,000 bushels of grain, its opportunity cost, as indicated by point *a* in the figure. Again, if no trade takes place, the price of a car in Mobilia is 1,000 bushels of grain, its opportunity cost, as indicated by point *a'* in the figure. The no-trade points *a* and *a'* in Fig. 22.3 correspond to the points identified by those same letters in Figs. 22.1 and 22.2. The lower the price of a car (terms of trade), the greater is the quantity of cars that the Farmers are willing to import from the Mobilians. This fact is illustrated by the downward-sloping curve, which shows Farmland's import demand for cars.

The Mobilians respond in the opposite direction. The higher the price of a car (terms of trade), the greater is the quantity of cars that Mobilians are willing to export to Farmers. This fact is reflected in Mobilia's export supply of cars—the upward-sloping line in Fig. 22.3.

The international market in cars determines the equilibrium price (terms of trade) and quantity traded. This equilibrium occurs where the import demand curve intersects the export supply curve. In this case, the equilibrium price is 3,000 bushels of grain per car. Mobilia exports and Farmland imports four million cars a year. Notice that the terms of trade are lower than the initial price in Farmland but higher than the initial price in Mobilia.

Balanced Trade

The number of cars exported by Mobilia—4 million a year—is exactly equal to the number of cars imported by Farmland. How does Farmland pay for its cars? By exporting grain. How much grain does Farmland export? You can find the answer by noticing that for 1 car, Farmland has to pay 3,000 bushels of grain. Hence, for 4 million cars, they have to pay 12 billion bushels of grain. Thus Farmland's exports of grain are 12 billion bushels a year. Mobilia imports this same quantity of grain.

Mobilia is exchanging 4 million cars for 12 billion bushels of grain each year, and Farmland is doing the opposite, exchanging 12 billion bushels of grain for 4 million cars. Trade is balanced between these two countries. The value received from exports equals the value paid out for imports.

Changes in Production and Consumption

We've seen that international trade makes it possible for Farmers to buy cars at a lower price than that at which they can produce them for themselves. Equivalently, Farmers can sell their grain for a higher price. International trade also enables Mobilians to sell their cars for a higher price. Equivalently, Mobilians can buy grain for a lower price. Thus everybody gains. How is it possible for *everyone* to gain? What are the changes in production and consumption that accompany these gains?

An economy that does not trade with other economies has identical production and consumption possibilities. Without trade, the economy can consume only what it produces. But with international trade, an economy can consume different quantities of goods from those that it produces. The production possibility frontier describes the limit of what a country can produce, but it does not describe the limits to what it can consume. Figure 22.4 will help you to see the distinction between production possibilities and consumption possibilities when a country trades with other countries.

First of all, notice that the figure has two parts, part (a) for Farmland and part (b) for Mobilia. The production possibility frontiers that you saw in Figs. 22.1 and 22.2 are reproduced here. The slopes of the two black lines in the figure represent the opportunity costs in the two countries when there is no international trade. Farmland produces and consumes at point *a*, and Mobilia produces and consumes at *a'*. Cars cost 9,000 bushels of grain in Farmland, and 1,000 bushels of grain in Mobilia.

Consumption Possibilities   The red line in each part of Fig. 22.4 shows the country's consumption possibilities with international trade. These two red lines have the same slope, and the magnitude of that slope is the opportunity cost of a car in terms of grain on the world market—3,000 bushels per car. The *slope* of the consumption possibilities line is common to both countries because its magnitude equals the *world* price. But the position of a country's consumption possibilities line depends on the country's production possibilities. A country cannot produce outside its production possibility curve, so its consumption possibility curve touches its production possibility curve. Thus Farmland could choose to consume at point *b* with no international trade or at any point on its red consumption possibilities line with international trade.

Free Trade Equilibrium   With international trade, the producers of cars in Mobilia can get a higher price for their output. As a result, they increase the quantity of car production. At the same time, grain producers in Mobilia get a lower price for their grain, and so they reduce production. Producers in Mobilia adjust their output by moving along their production possibility frontier until the opportunity cost in Mobilia equals the world price (the opportunity cost in the world market). This situation arises when Mobilia is producing at point *b'* in Fig. 22.4(b).

But the Mobilians do not consume at point *b'*. That is, they do not increase their consumption of

cars and decrease their consumption of grain. Instead, they sell some of their car production to Farmland in exchange for some of Farmland's grain. They trade internationally. But to see how that works out, we first need to check in with Farmland to see what's happening there.

In Farmland, producers of cars now get a lower price and producers of grain get a higher price. As a consequence, producers in Farmland decrease car production and increase grain production. They adjust their outputs by moving along the production possibility frontier until the opportunity cost of a car in terms of grain equals the world price (the opportunity cost on the world market). They move to point *b* in part (a). But the Farmers do not consume at point *b*. Instead, they trade some of their additional grain production for the now cheaper cars from Mobilia.

The figure shows us the quantities consumed in the two countries. We saw in Fig. 22.3 that Mobilia exports 4 million cars a year and Farmland imports those cars. We also saw that Farmland exports 12 billion bushels of grain a year and Mobilia imports that grain. Thus Farmland's consumption of grain is 12 billion bushels a year less than it produces, and its consumption of cars is 4 million a year more than it produces. Farmland consumes at point *c* in Fig. 22.4(a).

Similarly, we know that Mobilia consumes 12 billion bushels of grain more than it produces and 4 million cars fewer than it produces. Thus Mobilia consumes at *c'* in Fig. 22.4(b).

Calculating the Gains from Trade

You can now literally see the gains from trade in Fig. 22.4. Without trade, Farmers produce and consume at point *a* (part a)—a point on Farmland's production possibility frontier. With international trade, Farmers consume at point *c* in part (a)—a point *outside* the production possibility frontier. At point *c*, Farmers are consuming 3 billion bushels of grain a year and 1 million cars a year more than before. These increases in consumption of both cars and grain, beyond the limits of the production possibility frontier, are the gains from international trade. Mobilians also gain. Without trade, they consume at point *a'* in part (b)—a point on Mobilia's production possibility frontier. With international trade, they consume at point *c'*—a point outside the

FIGURE 22.4
Expanding Consumption Possibilities

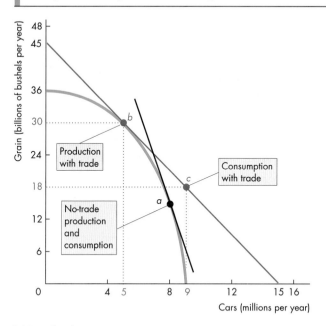

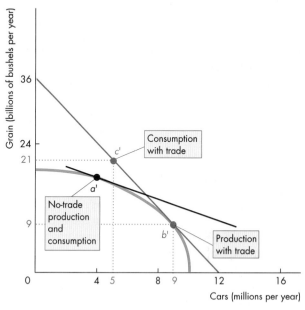

(a) Farmland

With no international trade, the Farmers produce and consume at point *a* and the opportunity cost of a car is 9,000 bushels of grain (the slope of the black line in part a). Also, with no international trade, the Mobilians produce and consume at point *a'* and the opportunity cost of 1,000 bushels of grain is 1 car (the slope of the black line in part b). Goods can be exchanged internationally at a price of 3,000 bushels of grain for 1 car along the red line in each part of the figure. In part (a), Farmland decreases its production of cars and

(b) Mobilia

increases its production of grain, moving from *a* to *b*. It exports grain and imports cars, and it consumes at point *c*. The Farmers have more of both cars and grain than they would if they produced all their own goods—at point *a*. In part (b), Mobilia increases car production and decreases grain production, moving from *a'* to *b'*. Mobilia exports cars and imports grain, and it consumes at point *c'*. The Mobilians have more of both cars and grain than they would if they produced all their own goods—at point *a'*.

production possibility frontier. With international trade, Mobilia consumes 3 billion bushels of grain a year and 1 million cars a year more than without trade. These are the gains from international trade for Mobilia.

Gains for All

Trade between the Farmers and the Mobilians does not create winners and losers. Everyone wins. Sellers add the net demand of foreigners to their domestic demand, and so their market expands. Buyers are faced with domestic supply plus net foreign supply and so have a larger supply available to them.

R E V I E W   Q U I Z

In what circumstances can countries gain from international trade?

- What determines the goods and services that a country will export? What determines the goods and services that a country will import?

- What is a comparative advantage and what role does it play in determining the amount and type of international trade that occurs?.

- How can it be that all countries gain from international trade and that there are no losers?

Gains from Trade in Reality

THE GAINS FROM TRADE THAT WE HAVE JUST studied between Farmland and Mobilia in grain and cars occur in a model economy—in a world economy that we have imagined. But these same phenomena occur every day in the real global economy.

Comparative Advantage in the Global Economy

We buy TVs and VCRs from Korea, machinery from Europe, and fashion goods from Hong Kong. In exchange, we sell machinery, grain and lumber, airplanes, computers and financial services. All this international trade is generated by comparative advantage, just like the international trade between Farmland and Mobilia in our model economy. All international trade arises from comparative advantage, even when trade is in similar goods such as tools and machines. At first thought, it seems puzzling that countries exchange manufactured goods. Why doesn't each developed country produce all the manufactured goods its citizens want to buy?

Trade in Similar Goods

Why does the United States produce automobiles for export and at the same time import large quantities of them from Canada, Japan, Korea, and Western Europe? Wouldn't it make more sense to produce all the cars that we buy here in the United States? After all, we have access to the best technology available for producing cars. Autoworkers in the United States are surely as productive as their fellow workers in Canada, Western Europe, and Asian countries. So why does the United States have a comparative advantage in some types of cars and Japan and Europe in others?

Diversity of Taste and Economies of Scale

The first part of the answer is that people have a tremendous diversity of taste. Let's stick with the example of cars. Some people prefer a sports car, some prefer a limousine, some prefer a regular, full-size car, and some prefer a minivan. In addition to size and type of car, there are many other dimensions in which cars vary. Some have low fuel consumption, some have high performance, some are spacious and comfortable, some have a large trunk, some have four-wheel drive, some have front-wheel drive, some have a radiator grill that looks like a Greek temple, and others look like a wedge. People's preferences across these many dimensions vary. The tremendous diversity in tastes for cars means that people value variety and are willing to pay for it in the marketplace.

The second part of the answer to the puzzle is *economies of scale*—the tendency for the average cost to be lower, the larger the scale of production. In such situations, larger and larger production runs lead to ever lower average costs. Many goods, including cars, experience economies of scale. For example, if a car producer makes only a few hundred (or perhaps a few thousand) cars of a particular type and design, the producer must use production techniques that are much more labor-intensive and much less automated than those employed to make hundreds of thousands of cars in a particular model. With short production runs and labor-intensive production techniques, costs are high. With very large production runs and automated assembly lines, production costs are much lower. But to obtain lower costs, the automated assembly lines have to produce a large number of cars.

It is the combination of diversity of taste and economies of scale that determines opportunity cost, produces comparative advantages, and generates such a large amount of international trade in similar commodities. With international trade, each car manufacturer has the whole world market to serve. Each producer can specialize in a limited range of products and then sell its output to the entire world market. This arrangement enables large production runs on the most popular cars and feasible production runs even on the most customized cars demanded by only a handful of people in each country.

The situation in the market for cars is also present in many other industries, especially those producing specialized equipment and parts. For example, the United States exports computer central processor chips but imports memory chips, exports mainframe computers but imports PCs, exports specialized video equipment but imports VCRs. Thus international exchange of similar but slightly differentiated manufactured products is a highly profitable activity.

Let's next see what happens when governments restrict international trade. We'll see that free trade brings the greatest possible benefits. We'll also see why, in spite of the benefits of free trade, governments sometimes restrict trade.

Trade Restrictions

GOVERNMENTS RESTRICT INTERNATIONAL TRADE to protect domestic industries from foreign competition by using two main tools:

1. Tariffs
2. Nontariff barriers

A **tariff** is a tax that is imposed by the importing country when an imported good crosses its international boundary. A **nontariff barrier** is any action other than a tariff that restricts international trade. Examples of nontariff barriers are quantitative restrictions and licensing regulations that limit imports. First, let's look at tariffs.

The History of Tariffs

U.S. tariffs today are modest compared with their historical levels. Figure 22.5 shows the average tariff rate—total tariffs as a percentage of total imports.

You can see in this figure that this average reached a peak of 20 percent in 1933. In that year, three years after the passage of the Smoot-Hawley Act, one third of imports was subject to a tariff, and on those imports, the tariff rate was 60 percent. (The average tariff in Fig. 22.5 for 1933 is 60 percent multiplied by 0.33, which equals 20 percent.) Today, the average tariff rate is only 4 percent.

The reduction in tariffs since World War II followed the signing in 1947 of the **General Agreement on Tariffs and Trade** (GATT). Since its formation, the GATT has organized several rounds of negotiations that have resulted in tariff reductions. One of these, the Kennedy Round, which began in the early 1960s, resulted in large tariff cuts starting in 1967. Another, the Tokyo Round, resulted in further tariff cuts in 1979. The most recent, the Uruguay Round, which started in 1986 and was completed in 1994, was the most ambitious and comprehensive of the rounds. The Uruguay Round also led to the creation of a new **World Trade Organization** (WTO). Membership of the WTO brings greater obligations on countries to observe the GATT rules.

FIGURE 22.5

U.S. Tariffs: 1930–1998

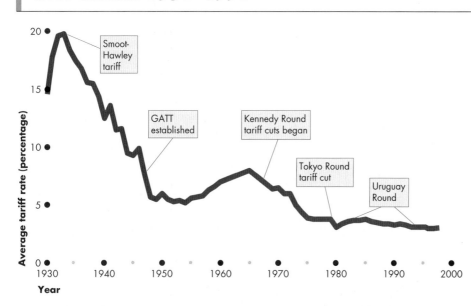

The Smoot-Hawley Act, which was passed in 1930, took U.S. tariffs to a peak average rate of 20 percent in 1933. (One third of imports was subject to a tariff rate of 60 percent.) Since the establishment of GATT in 1947, tariffs have steadily declined in a series of negotiating rounds, the most significant of which are identified in the figure. Tariffs are now as low as they have ever been.

Sources: U.S. Bureau of the Census, *Historical Statistics of the United States, Colonial Times to 1970*, Bicentennial Edition, Part 1 (Washington, D.C., 1975), Series U-212: *Statistical Abstract of the United States: 1986*, 106th edition (Washington, D.C., 1985); and *Statistical Abstract of the United States: 1998*, 118th edition (Washington, D.C., 1998).

In addition to the agreements under the GATT and the WTO, the United States is a party to the **North American Free Trade Agreement** (NAFTA), which became effective on January 1, 1994, and under which barriers to international trade between the United States, Canada, and Mexico will be virtually eliminated after a 15-year phasing-in period.

In other parts of the world, trade barriers have virtually been eliminated among the member countries of the European Union, which has created the largest unified tariff-free market in the world. In 1994, discussions among the Asia-Pacific Economic group (APEC) led to an agreement in principle to work toward a free-trade area that embraces China, all the economies of East Asia and the South Pacific, and the United States and Canada. These countries include the fastest-growing economies and hold the promise of heralding a global free-trade area.

The effort to achieve freer trade underlines the fact that trade in some goods is still subject to extremely high tariffs. The highest tariffs faced by U.S. buyers are those on textiles and footwear. A tariff of more than 10 percent (on the average) is imposed on almost all our imports of textiles and footwear. For example, when you buy a pair of blue jeans for $20, you pay about $5 more than you would if there were no tariffs on textiles. Other goods protected by tariffs are agricultural products, energy and chemicals, minerals, and metals. The meat, cheese, and sugar that you consume cost significantly more because of protection than they would with free international trade.

The temptation on governments to impose tariffs is a strong one. First, tariffs provide revenue to the government. Second, they enable the government to satisfy special interest groups in import-competing industries. But, as we'll see, free international trade brings enormous benefits that are reduced when tariffs are imposed. Let's see how.

How Tariffs Work

To analyze how tariffs work, let's return to the example of trade between Farmland and Mobilia. Figure 22.6 shows the international market for cars in which these two countries are the only traders. The volume of trade and the price of a car are determined at the point of intersection of Mobilia's export supply curve of cars and Farmland's import demand curve for cars.

FIGURE 22.6

The Effects of a Tariff

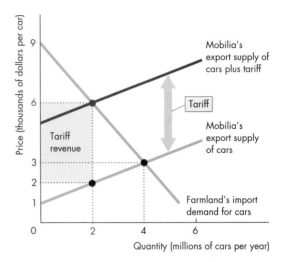

Farmland imposes a tariff on car imports from Mobilia. The tariff increases the price that Farmers have to pay for cars. It shifts the supply curve of cars in Farmland leftward. The vertical distance between the original supply curve and the new one is the amount of the tariff, $4,000 per car. The price of cars in Farmland increases, and the quantity of cars imported decreases. The government of Farmland collects a tariff revenue of $4,000 per car—a total of $8 billion on the 2 million cars imported. Farmland's exports of grain decrease because Mobilia now has a lower income from its exports of cars.

In Fig. 22.6, these two countries trade cars and grain in exactly the same way that we saw in Fig. 22.3. Mobilia exports cars, and Farmland exports grain. The volume of car imports into Farmland is 4 million a year, and the world market price of a car is 3,000 bushels of grain. Fig. 22.6 expresses prices in dollars rather than in units of grain and is based on a money price of grain of $1 a bushel. With grain costing $1 a bushel, the money price of a car is $3,000.

Now suppose that the government of Farmland, perhaps under pressure from car producers, decides to impose a tariff on imported cars. In particular, suppose that a tariff of $4,000 per car is imposed. (This is a huge tariff, but the car producers of Farmland are pretty fed up with competition from Mobilia.) What happens?

- The supply of cars in Farmland decreases.
- The price of a car in Farmland rises.
- The quantity of cars imported by Farmland decreases.
- The government of Farmland collects the tariff revenue.
- Resource use is inefficient.
- The *value* of exports changes by the same amount as the *value* of imports and trade remains balanced.

Change in the Supply of Cars   Farmland cannot buy cars at Mobilia's export supply price. It must pay that price plus the $4,000 tariff. So the supply curve in Farmland shifts leftward. The new supply curve is that labeled "Mobilia's export supply of cars plus tariff." The vertical distance between Mobilia's export supply curve and the new supply curve is the tariff of $4,000 a car.

Rise in Price of Cars   A new equilibrium occurs where the new supply curve intersects Farmland's import demand curve for cars. That equilibrium is at a price of $6,000 a car, up from $3,000 with free trade.

Fall in Imports   Car imports fall from 4 million to 2 million cars a year. At the higher price of $6,000 a car, Farmland's car producers increase their production. Grain production in Farmland decreases as resources are moved into the expanding car industry.

Tariff Revenue   Total expenditure on imported cars by the Farmers is $6,000 a car multiplied by the 2 million cars imported ($12 billion). But not all of that money goes to the Mobilians. They receive $2,000 a car, or $4 billion for the 2 million cars. The difference—$4,000 a car, or a total of $8 billion for the 2 million cars—is collected by the government of Farmland as tariff revenue.

Inefficiency   The people of Farmland are willing to pay $6,000 for the marginal car imported. But the opportunity cost of that car is $2,000. So there is a gain from trading an extra car. In fact, there are gains—willingness to pay exceeds opportunity cost—all the way up to 4 million cars a year. Only when 4 million cars are being traded is the maximum price that a Farmer is willing to pay equal to the minimum price that is acceptable to a Mobilian. Thus restricting trade reduces the gains from trade.

Trade Remains Balanced   With free trade, Farmland was paying $3,000 a car and buying 4 million cars a year from Mobilia. Thus the total amount paid to Mobilia for imports was $12 billion a year. With a tariff, Farmland's imports have been cut to 2 million cars a year and the price paid to Mobilia has also been cut to only $2,000 a car. Thus the total amount paid to Mobilia for imports has been cut to $4 billion a year. Doesn't this fact mean that Farmland now has a balance of trade surplus?

It does not. The price of cars in Mobilia has fallen. But the price of grain remains at $1 a bushel. So the relative price of cars has fallen, and the relative price of grain has increased. With free trade, the Mobilians could buy 3,000 bushels of grain for one car. Now they can buy only 2,000 bushels for a car. With a higher relative price of grain, the quantity demanded by the Mobilians decreases and Mobilia imports less grain. But because Mobilia imports less grain, Farmland exports less grain. In fact, Farmland's grain industry suffers from two sources. First, there is a decrease in the quantity of grain sold to Mobilia. Second, there is increased competition for inputs from the now expanded car industry. Thus the tariff leads to a contraction in the scale of the grain industry in Farmland.

It seems paradoxical at first that a country imposing a tariff on cars hurts its own export industry, decreasing its exports of grain. It may help to think of it this way: Mobilians buy grain with the money they make from exporting cars to Farmland. If they export fewer cars, they cannot afford to buy as much grain. In fact, in the absence of any international borrowing and lending, Mobilia must cut its imports of grain by exactly the same amount as the loss in revenue from its export of cars. Grain imports into Mobilia are cut back to a value of $4 billion, the amount that can be paid for by the new lower revenue from Mobilia's car exports. Thus trade is still balanced. The tariff cuts imports and exports by the same amount. The tariff has no effect on the *balance* of trade, but it reduces the *volume* of trade.

The result that we have just derived is perhaps one of the most misunderstood aspects of international economics. On countless occasions, politicians and others call for tariffs to remove a balance of trade deficit or argue that lowering tariffs would produce a balance of trade deficit. They reach this conclusion by failing to work out all the implications of a tariff.

Let's now turn our attention to the other tool for restricting trade: nontariff barriers.

Nontariff Barriers

The two main forms of nontariff barriers are:

1. Quotas
2. Voluntary export restraints

A **quota** is a quantitative restriction on the import of a particular good, which specifies the maximum amount of the good that can be imported in a given period of time. A **voluntary export restraint** (VER) is an agreement between two governments in which the government of the exporting country agrees to restrain the volume of its own exports.

Quotas are especially prominent in textiles and agriculture. Voluntary export restraints are used to regulate trade between Japan and the United States.

How Quotas and VERs Work

To see how a quota works, suppose that Farmland imposes a quota that restricts its car imports to 2 million cars a year. Figure 22.7 shows the effects of this action. The quota is shown by the vertical red line at 2 million cars a year. Because it is illegal to exceed the quota, car importers buy only that quantity from Mobilia, for which they pay $2,000 a car. But because the import supply of cars is restricted to 2 million cars a year, people in Farmland are willing to pay $6,000 per car. This is the price of a car in Farmland.

The value of imports falls to $4 billion, exactly the same as in the case of the tariff. So with lower incomes from car exports and with a higher relative price of grain, Mobilians cut back on their imports of grain in exactly the same way that they did under a tariff.

The key difference between a quota and a tariff lies in who collects the gap between the import supply price and the domestic price. In the case of a tariff, it is the government of the importing country. In the case of a quota, it goes to the person who has the right to import under the import quota regulations.

A voluntary export restraint is like a quota arrangement in which quotas are allocated to each exporting country. The effects of voluntary export restraints are similar to those of quotas but differ from them in that the gap between the price in the importing country and the export price is captured not by domestic importers but by the foreign exporter. The government of the exporting country has to establish procedures for allocating the restricted volume of exports among its producers.

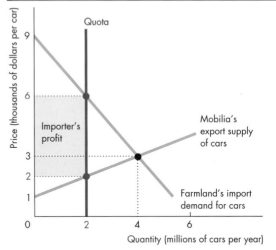

FIGURE 22.7

The Effects of a Quota

Farmland imposes a quota of 2 million cars a year on car imports from Mobilia. That quantity appears as the vertical line labeled "Quota." Because the quantity of cars supplied by Mobilia is restricted to 2 million, the price at which those cars will be traded increases to $6,000. Importing cars is profitable because Mobilia is willing to supply cars at $2,000 each. There is competition for import quotas.

REVIEW QUIZ

- What happens to a country's consumption possibilities when it opens itself up to international trade and trades freely at world market prices?
- What do trade restrictions do to the gains from international trade?
- What is best for a country: restricted trade, no trade, or free trade?
- What does a tariff on imports do to the volume of imports and the volume of exports?
- In the absence of international borrowing and lending, how do tariffs and other trade restrictions influence the total value of imports and exports and the balance of trade—the value of exports minus the value of imports?

Let's now look at some commonly heard arguments for restricting international trade.

The Case Against Protection

FOR AS LONG AS NATIONS AND INTERNATIONAL trade have existed, people have debated whether a country is better off with free international trade or with protection from foreign competition. The debate continues, but for most economists, a verdict has been delivered and is the one you have just seen. Free trade promotes prosperity for all; protection is inefficient. We've seen the most powerful case for free trade in the example of how Farmland and Mobilia both benefit from their comparative advantage. But there is a broader range of issues in the free trade versus protection debate. Let's review these issues.

Three arguments for restricting international trade are:

- The national security argument
- The infant-industry argument
- The dumping argument

Let's look at each in turn.

The National Security Argument

The national security argument for protection is that a country must protect industries that produce defense equipment and armaments and those on which the defense industries rely for their raw materials and other intermediate inputs. This argument for protection does not withstand close scrutiny.

First, it is an argument for international isolation, for in a time of war, there is no industry that does not contribute to national defense. Second, if the case is made for boosting the output of a strategic industry, it is more efficient to achieve this outcome with a subsidy to the firms in the industry financed out of taxes. Such a subsidy would keep the industry operating at the scale judged appropriate, and free international trade would keep the prices faced by consumers at their world market levels.

The Infant-Industry Argument

The so-called **infant-industry argument** for protection is that it is necessary to protect a new industry to enable it to grow into a mature industry that can compete in world markets. The argument is based on the idea of *dynamic comparative advantage*, which can arise from *learning-by-doing* (see Chapter 3).

Learning-by-doing is a powerful engine of productivity growth, and comparative advantage evolves and changes because of on-the-job experience. But these facts do not justify protection.

First, the infant-industry argument is valid only if the benefits of learning-by-doing *not only* accrue to the owners and workers of the firms in the infant industry but also *spill over* to other industries and parts of the economy. For example, there are huge productivity gains from learning-by-doing in the manufacture of aircraft. But almost all of these gains benefit the stockholders and workers of Boeing and other aircraft producers. Because the people making the decisions, bearing the risk, and doing the work are the ones who benefit, they take the dynamic gains into account when they decide on the scale of their activities. In this case, almost no benefits spill over to other parts of the economy, so there is no need for government assistance to achieve an efficient outcome.

Second, even if the case is made for protecting an infant industry, it is more efficient to do so by a subsidy to the firms in the industry, with the subsidy financed out of taxes.

The Dumping Argument

Dumping occurs when a foreign firm sells its exports at a lower price than its cost of production. Dumping might be used by a firm that wants to gain a global monopoly. In this case, the foreign firm sells its output at a price below its cost to drive domestic firms out of business. When the domestic firms have gone, the foreign firm takes advantage of its monopoly position and charges a higher price for its product. Dumping is usually regarded as a justification for temporary countervailing tariffs.

But there are powerful reasons to resist the dumping argument for protection. First, it is virtually impossible to detect dumping because it is hard to determine a firm's costs. As a result, the test for dumping is whether a firm's export price is below its domestic price. But this test is a weak one because it can be rational for a firm to charge a low price in markets in which the quantity demanded is highly sensitive to price and a higher price in a market in which demand is less price-sensitive.

Second, it is hard to think of a good that is produced by a natural *global* monopoly. So even if all the domestic firms were driven out of business in some industry, it would always be possible to find several and usually many alternative foreign sources of supply and to buy at prices determined in competitive markets.

Third, if a good or service were a truly global natural monopoly, the best way of dealing with it would be by regulation—just as in the case of domestic monopolies. Such regulation would require international cooperation.

The three arguments for protection that we've just examined have an element of credibility. The counter-arguments are in general stronger, so these arguments do not make the case for protection. But they are not the only arguments that you might encounter. The many other arguments that are commonly heard are quite simply wrong. They are fatally flawed. The most common of them are that protection:

- Saves jobs
- Allows us to compete with cheap foreign labor
- Brings diversity and stability
- Penalizes lax environmental standards
- Protects national culture
- Prevents rich countries from exploiting developing countries

Saves Jobs

The argument is: When we buy shoes from Brazil or shirts from Taiwan, U.S. workers lose their jobs. With no earnings and poor prospects, these workers become a drain on welfare and spend less, causing a ripple effect of further job losses. The proposed solution to this problem is to ban imports of cheap foreign goods and protect U.S. jobs. The proposal is flawed for the following reasons.

First, free trade does cost some jobs, but it also creates other jobs. It brings about a global rationalization of labor and allocates labor resources to their highest-value activities. Because of international trade in textiles, tens of thousands of workers in the United States have lost jobs because textile mills and other factories have closed. But tens of thousands of workers in other countries have gotten jobs because textile mills have opened there. And tens of thousands of U.S. workers have gotten better-paying jobs than textile workers because other export industries have expanded and created more jobs than have been destroyed.

Second, imports create jobs. They create jobs for retailers that sell imported goods and firms that service those goods. They also create jobs by creating incomes in the rest of the world, some of which are spent on imports of U.S.-made goods and services.

Although protection does save particular jobs, it does so at inordinate cost. For example, textile jobs are protected in the United States by quotas imposed under an international agreement called the Multifiber Arrangement. It has been estimated by the U.S. International Trade Commission (ITC) that because of quotas, 72,000 jobs exist in textiles that would otherwise disappear and annual clothing expenditure in the United States is $15.9 billion, or $160 per family higher than it would be with free trade. Equivalently, the ITC estimates that each textile job saved costs $221,000 a year.

Allows Us to Compete with Cheap Foreign Labor

With the removal of protective tariffs in U.S. trade with Mexico, Ross Perot said we would hear a "giant sucking sound" of jobs rushing to Mexico (one of which is shown in the cartoon). Let's see what's wrong with this view.

The labor cost of a unit of output equals the wage rate divided by labor productivity. For example, if a U.S. auto worker earns $30 an hour and produces 15

"I don't know what the hell happened—one minute I'm at work in Flint, Michigan, then there's a giant sucking sound and suddenly here I am in Mexico."

Drawing by M. Stevens; © 1993
The New Yorker Magazine, Inc.

units of output an hour, the average labor cost of a unit of output is $2. If a Mexican auto assembly worker earns $3 an hour and produces 1 unit of output an hour, the average labor cost of a unit of output is $3. Other things remaining the same, the higher a worker's productivity, the higher is the worker's wage rate. High-wage workers have high productivity. Low-wage workers have low productivity.

Although high-wage U.S. workers are more productive, on the average, than low-wage Mexican workers, there are differences across industries. U.S. labor is relatively more productive in some activities than in others. For example, the productivity of U.S. workers in producing movies, financial services, and customized computer chips is relatively higher than in the production of metals and some standardized machine parts. The activities in which U.S. workers are relatively more productive than their Mexican counterparts are those in which the United States has a *comparative advantage*. By engaging in free trade, increasing our production and exports of the goods and services in which we have a comparative advantage and decreasing our production and increasing our imports of the goods and services in which our trading partners have a comparative advantage, we can make ourselves and the citizens of other countries better off.

Brings Diversity and Stability

A diversified investment portfolio is less risky than one that has all the eggs in one basket. The same is true for an economy's production. A diversified economy fluctuates less than an economy that produces only one or two goods.

But big, rich, diversified economies like those of the United States, Japan, and Europe do not have this type of stability problem. Even a country like Saudi Arabia that produces almost only one good (oil) can benefit from specializing in the activity at which it has a comparative advantage and then investing in a wide range of other countries to bring greater stability to its income and consumption.

Penalizes Lax Environmental Standards

A new argument for protection is that many poorer countries, such as Mexico, do not have the same environment policies that we have and, because they are willing to pollute and we are not, we cannot compete with them without tariffs. So if they want free trade with the richer and "greener" countries, they must clean up their environments to our standards.

This argument for trade restrictions is weak. First, not all poorer countries have significantly lower environmental standards than the United States has. Many poor countries and the former Communist countries of Eastern Europe do have bad environment records. But some countries enforce strict laws. Second, a poor country cannot afford to be as concerned about its environment as a rich country can. The best hope for a better environment in Mexico and in other developing countries is rapid income growth through free trade. As their incomes grow, developing countries will have the *means* to match their desires to improve their environment. Third, poor countries have a comparative advantage at doing "dirty" work, which helps rich countries achieve higher environment standards than they otherwise could.

Protects National Culture

The national culture argument for protection is not heard much in the United States, but it is a commonly heard argument in Canada and Europe.

The expressed fear is that free trade in books, magazines, movies, and television programs means U.S. domination and the end of local culture. So, the reasoning continues, it is necessary to protect domestic culture industries from free international trade to ensure the survival of a national cultural identity.

Protection of these industries is common and takes the form of nontariff barriers. For example, local content regulations on radio and television broadcasting and in magazines is often required.

The cultural identity argument for protection has no merit, and it is one more example of rent seeking (see Chapter 13, p. 272). Writers, publishers, and broadcasters want to limit foreign competition so that they can earn larger economic profits. There is no actual danger to national culture. In fact, many of the creators of so-called American cultural products are not Americans, but the talented citizens of other countries, ensuring the survival of their national cultural identities in Hollywood! Also, if national culture is in danger, there is no surer way of helping it on its way out than by impoverishing the nation whose culture it is. And protection is an effective way of doing just that.

Prevents Rich Countries from Exploiting Developing Countries

Another new argument for protection is that international trade must be restricted to prevent the people of the rich industrial world from exploiting the poorer people of the developing countries, forcing them to work for slave wages.

Wage rates in some developing countries are indeed very low. But by trading with developing countries, we increase the demand for the goods that these countries produce, and, more significantly, we increase the demand for their labor. When the demand for labor in developing countries increases, the wage rate also increases. So, far from exploiting people in developing countries, trade improves their opportunities and increases their incomes.

We have reviewed the arguments that are commonly heard in favor of protection and the counter-arguments against them. There is one counter-argument to protection that is general and quite overwhelming. Protection invites retaliation and can trigger a trade war. The best example of a trade war occurred during the Great Depression of the 1930s when the Smoot-Hawley Tariff was introduced. Country after country retaliated with its own tariff, and in a short period, world trade had almost disappeared. The costs to all countries were large and led to a renewed international resolve to avoid such self-defeating moves in the future. They also led to the creation of GATT and are the impetus behind NAFTA, APEC, and the European Union.

REVIEW QUIZ

- Is there any merit to the view that we should restrict international trade to achieve national security goals, to stimulate the growth of new industries, or to restrain foreign monopoly?
- Is there any merit to the view that we should restrict international trade to save jobs, compensate for low foreign wages, make the economy more diversified, compensate for costly environmental policies, protect national culture, or protect developing countries from being exploited?
- Is there any merit to the view that we should restrict international trade for any reason? What is the main argument against trade restrictions?

Why Is International Trade Restricted?

WHY, DESPITE ALL THE ARGUMENTS AGAINST protection, is trade restricted? There are two key reasons:

- Tariff revenue
- Rent seeking

Tariff Revenue

Government revenue is costly to collect. In the developed countries such as the United States, a well-organized tax-collection system is in place that can generate billions of dollars of income tax and sales tax revenues. This tax-collecting system is made possible by the fact that most economic transactions are done by firms that must keep properly audited financial records. Without such records, the revenue collection agencies (the Internal Revenue Service in the United States) would be severely hampered in the work. Even with audited financial accounts, some proportion of potential tax revenue is lost. Nonetheless, for the industrialized countries, the income tax and sales taxes are the major sources of revenue and the tariff plays a very small role.

But governments in developing countries have a difficult time collecting taxes from their citizens. Much economic activity takes place in an informal economy with few financial records. So only a small amount of revenue is collected from income taxes and sales taxes in these countries. The one area in which economic transactions are well recorded and audited is in international trade. So this activity is an attractive base for tax collection in these countries and is used much more extensively than in the developed countries.

Rent Seeking

The major reason why international trade is restricted is because of rent seeking. Free trade increases consumption possibilities *on the average,* but not everyone shares in the gain and some people even lose. Free trade brings benefits to some and imposes costs on others, with total benefits exceeding total costs. It is the uneven distribution of costs and benefits that is the principal source of impediment to achieving more liberal international trade.

Returning to our example of trade in cars and grain between Farmland and Mobilia, the benefits to Farmland from free trade accrue to all the producers of grain and those producers of cars who would not have to bear the costs of adjusting to a smaller car industry. These costs are transition costs, not permanent costs. The costs of moving to free trade are borne by those car producers and their employees who have to become grain producers. The number of people who gain will, in general, be enormous compared with the number who lose. The gain per person will therefore be rather small. The loss per person to those who bear the loss will be large. Because the loss that falls on those who bear it is large, it will pay those people to incur considerable expense to lobby against free trade. On the other hand, it will not pay those who gain to organize to achieve free trade. The gain from trade for any one individual is too small for that individual to spend much time or money on a political organization to achieve free trade. The loss from free trade will be seen as being so great by those bearing that loss that they *will* find it profitable to join a political organization to prevent free trade. Each group is optimizing—weighing benefits against costs and choosing the best action for themselves. The anti-free-trade group will, however, undertake a larger quantity of political lobbying than the pro-free-trade group.

Compensating Losers

If, in total, the gains from free international trade exceed the losses, why don't those who gain compensate those who lose so that everyone is in favor of free trade? To some degree, such compensation does take place. When Congress approved the NAFTA deal with Canada and Mexico, it set up a $56 million fund to support and retrain workers who lost their jobs because of the new trade agreement. During the first six months of the operation of NAFTA, only 5,000 workers applied for benefits under this scheme.

The losers from freer international trade are also compensated indirectly through the normal unemployment compensation arrangements. But only limited attempts are made to compensate those who lose from free international trade. The main reason why full compensation is not attempted is that the costs

of identifying all the losers and estimating the value of their losses would be enormous. Also, it would never be clear whether a person who has fallen on hard times is suffering because of free trade or for other reasons, perhaps reasons that are largely under the control of the individual. Furthermore, some people who look like losers at one point in time may, in fact, wind up gaining. The young auto worker who loses his job in Michigan and becomes a computer assembly worker in Minneapolis resents the loss of work and the need to move. But a year or two later, looking back on events, he counts himself fortunate. He has made a move that has increased his income and given him greater job security.

It is because we do not, in general, compensate the losers from free international trade that protectionism is such a popular and permanent feature of our national economic and political life.

R E V I E W Q U I Z

- What are the two main reasons for imposing a tariff on imports?
- What type of country benefits most from the revenue that tariffs generate? Does the United States need to use tariffs to raise revenue for the government?
- If trade restrictions are costly, why do we use them? Why don't the people who gain from trade organize a political force that is strong enough to ensure that their interests are protected?

◆ You've now seen how free international trade enables all nations to gain from specialization and trade. By producing goods in which we have a comparative advantage and trading some of our production for that of others, we expand our consumption possibilities. Placing impediments on that trade restricts the extent to which we can gain from specialization and trade. Opening our country up to free international trade expands the market for the things that we sell and raises their relative price. The market for the things that we buy also expands, and the relative price falls. *Reading Between the Lines* on pp. 490– 491 looks at a recent example of an international trade dispute between the United States and Europe.

Tariffs in Action

THE NEW YORK TIMES, MARCH 4, 1999

Miffed at Europe, U.S. Raises Tariffs for Luxury Goods

By DAVID E. SANGER

The United States heated up two politically contentious trade disputes with Europe today, slapping 100 percent tariffs on $520 million in European products and threatening to ban Europe's supersonic pride, the Concorde, from landing in the United States.

The tariffs imposed by the Clinton Administration on goods such as Louis Vuitton handbags, Parma ham, pecorino cheese and Scottish cashmere sweaters, which essentially double their price and make it much harder for European exporters to sell them in this country, are part of a six-year battle over trade in bananas.

The threat to ban the Concorde is in a bill passed overwhelmingly in the House of Representatives today, in retaliation for a European ruling that would ban many older American airplanes from landing in Europe. American officials say Europe's restriction is designed to promote the sale of new engines and aircraft made by European manufacturers.

But both battles are really about the enormous tensions that have erupted between the United States and a Europe newly unified by a common currency. On both continents, politicians are feeling the heat from slowing exports, and fear a slowdown in economic growth later this year. And Washington and the European Union find themselves unable to resolve seemingly ordinary economic disputes, with each accusing the other of defying the World Trade Organization, the four-year-old court of international trade.

The court has stepped in to arbitrate the banana dispute, which involves European limits on imports, and has become the battleground over other politically sensitive issues, including Europe's ban on imported beef from cattle raised with hormones. ...

The trade fight with Europe has become a major issue at the White House, with President Clinton becoming directly involved in some of the negotiations, most recently with French President Jacques Chirac. But the economic impact is relatively modest: The United States imported $176.3 billion in goods from nations in the European Union last year, meaning that today's sanctions apply to one-quarter of 1 percent of goods imported from Europe. ...

© 1999 *The New York Times.* Reprinted with permission.
Further reproduction prohibited.

Essence of the Story

■ The United States imposed a 100 percent tariff on $520 million of European products such as Louis Vuitton handbags, Parma ham, pecorino cheese, and Scottish cashmere sweaters in a six-year battle over trade in bananas.

■ The United States also threatened to ban the Concorde (the supersonic airplane) from landing in the United States in retaliation for a European ruling that would ban many older American airplanes from landing in Europe.

■ The economic impact of the tariff is relatively modest because it applies to one quarter of 1 percent of the goods imported from Europe.

Economic Analysis

■ Figure 1 shows the U.S. market for a luxury good such as a high-quality handbag or a cashmere sweater.

■ The demand curve of U.S. buyers of this luxury good is D.

■ There are two supply curves: the supply curve of the European producers, S_E, and the supply curve of U.S. producers, S_{US}.

■ With no tariff, the quantity of this luxury good bought in the United States is QC_0. Of these, QP_0 are produced in the United States and the rest are imported, as shown by the arrow in Fig. 1.

■ Now the United States puts a 100 percent tariff on the imports of these items. The foreign good is now supplied to the U.S. market at the original supply price, $100, plus the tariff, $100, so the supply curve of this luxury good from Europe shifts to become $S_E + tariff$.

■ With the tariff, the quantity of the good bought in the United States is QC_1. Of these, QP_1 are produced in the United States and the rest are imported from Europe, as shown by the arrow in Fig. 1.

■ The tariff decreases U.S. consumption and imports and increases U.S. production.

■ Figure 2 shows the winners and the losers in the United States.

■ The winners include U.S producers who gain additional economic profit, which is shown by the blue area in Fig. 2.

■ Another winner is the U.S. government, which collects additional revenue shown by the purple area in Fig. 2.

■ The losers are the U.S. consumers. The consumers' loss equals the producers' gain plus the government's gain plus two other losses. One is an increase in the opportunity cost of producing the good in the United States, which is shown by the red area. Another is deadweight loss, which is shown by the gray area.

■ The sum of the blue, red, purple, and gray areas is the loss of consumer surplus that results from the tariff.

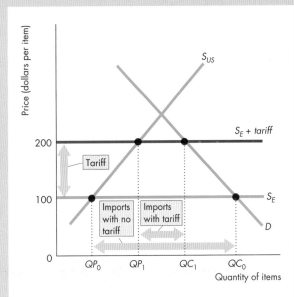

Figure 1 Tariffs and imports

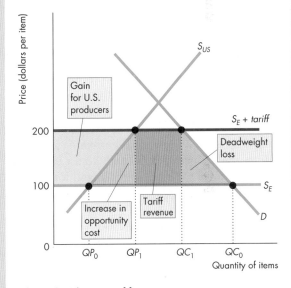

Figure 2 Winners and losers

You're The Voter

■ Are you for or against the tariff on luxury goods from Europe?

■ Write a report to your member of Congress explaining why you favor or oppose the luxury good tariff.

SUMMARY

KEY POINTS

Patterns and Trends in International Trade (p. 474)

- Large flows of trade take place between countries, most of which is in manufactured goods exchanged among rich industrialized countries.
- Since 1960, the volume of U.S. trade, as a percentage of total output, has more than doubled.

Opportunity Cost and Comparative Advantage (pp. 475–476)

- When opportunity costs between countries diverge, comparative advantage enables countries to gain from international trade.

Gains from Trade (pp. 476–479)

- By increasing its production of goods in which it has a comparative advantage and then trading some of the increased output, a country can consume at a point outside its production possibility frontier.
- In the absence of international borrowing and lending, trade is balanced as prices adjust to reflect the international supply of and demand for goods.
- The world price balances the production and consumption plans of the trading parties. At the equilibrium price, trade is balanced.

Gains from Trade in Reality (p. 480)

- Comparative advantage explains the international trade that takes place in the world.
- But trade in similar goods arises from economies of scale in the face of diversified tastes.

Trade Restrictions (pp. 481–484)

- Countries restrict international trade by imposing tariffs and quotas.
- Trade restrictions raise the domestic price of imported goods, lower the volume of imports, and reduce the total value of imports.
- Trade restrictions also reduce the total value of exports by the same amount as the reduction in the value of imports.

The Case Against Protection (pp. 485–488)

- Arguments that protection is necessary for national security, to allow infant industries the chance to grow, and to prevent dumping are weak.
- Arguments that protection saves jobs, allows us to compete with cheap foreign labor, makes the economy diversified and stable, protects national culture, and is needed to offset the costs of environmental policies are fatally flawed.

Why Is International Trade Restricted? (pp. 488–489)

- Trade is restricted because tariffs raise government revenue and because protection brings a small loss to a large number of people and a large gain per person to a small number of people.

KEY FIGURES

KEY TERMS

PROBLEMS

*1. The table provides information about Virtual Reality's production possibilities.

TV sets (per day)		Computers (per day)
0	and	36
10	and	35
20	and	33
30	and	30
40	and	26
50	and	21
60	and	15
70	and	8
80	and	0

a. Calculate Virtual Reality's opportunity cost of a TV set when it produces 10 sets a day.
b. Calculate Virtual Reality's opportunity cost of a TV set when it produces 40 sets a day.
c. Calculate Virtual Reality's opportunity cost of a TV set when it produces 70 sets a day.
d. Using the answers to parts (a), (b), and (c), sketch the relationship between the opportunity cost of a TV set and the quantity of TV sets produced in Virtual Reality.

2. The table provides information about Vital Signs' production possibilities.

TV sets (per day)		Computers (per day)
0	and	18.0
10	and	17.5
20	and	16.5
30	and	15.0
40	and	13.0
50	and	10.5
60	and	7.5
70	and	4.0
80	and	0

a. Calculate Vital Signs' opportunity cost of a TV set when it produces 10 sets a day.
b. Calculate Vital Signs' opportunity cost of a TV set when it produces 40 sets a day.
c. Calculate Vital Signs' opportunity cost of a TV set when it produces 70 sets a day.
d. Using the answers to parts (a), (b), and (c), sketch the relationship between the opportunity cost of a TV set and the quantity of TV sets produced in Vital Signs.

*3. Suppose that with no international trade, Virtual Reality in problem 1 produces and consumes 10 TV sets a day and Vital Signs produces and consumes 60 TV sets a day. Now suppose that the two countries begin to trade with each other.
a. Which country exports TV sets?
b. What adjustments are made to the amount of each good produced by each country?
c. What adjustments are made to the amount of each good consumed by each country?
d. What can you say about the terms of trade (the price of a TV set expressed as computers per TV set) under free trade?

4. Suppose that with no international trade, Virtual Reality in problem 1 produces and consumes 50 TV sets a day and Vital Signs produces and consumes 20 TV sets a day. Now suppose that the two countries begin to trade with each other.
a. Which country exports TV sets?
b. What adjustments are made to the amount of each good produced by each country?
c. What adjustments are made to the amount of each good consumed by each country?
d. What can you say about the terms of trade (the price of a TV set expressed as computers per TV set) under free trade?

*5. Compare the total quantities of each good produced in problems 1 and 2 with the total quantities of each good produced in problems 3 and 4.
a. Does free trade increase or decrease the total quantities of TV sets and computers produced in both cases? Why?
b. What happens to the price of a TV set in Virtual Reality in the two cases? Why does it rise in one case and fall in the other?
c. What happens to the price of a computer in Vital Signs in the two cases? Why does it rise in one case and fall in the other?

6. Compare the international trade in problem 3 with that in problem 4.
a. Why does Virtual Reality export TV sets in one of the cases and import them in the other case?
b. Do the TV producers or the computer producers gain in each case?
c. Do consumers gain in each case?

*7. The figure depicts the international market for soybeans.

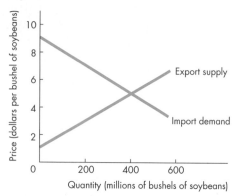

a. If the two countries did not engage in international trade, what would be the prices of soybeans in the two countries?
b. What is the world price of soybeans if there is free trade between these countries?
c. What quantities of soybeans are exported and imported?
d. What is the balance of trade?

8. If the country in problem 7(b) that imports soybeans imposes a tariff of $2 per bushel, what is the world price of soybeans and what quantity of soybeans gets traded internationally? What is the price of soybeans in the importing country? Calculate the tariff revenue.

*9. The importing country in problem 7(b) imposes a quota of 300 million bushels on imports of soybeans.
a. What is the price of soybeans in the importing country?
b. What is the revenue from the quota?
c. Who gets this revenue?

10. The exporting country in problem 7(b) imposes a VER of 300 million bushels on its exports of soybeans.
a. What is the world price of soybeans now?
b. What is the revenue of soybean growers in the exporting country?
c. Which country gains from the VER?

CRITICAL THINKING

1. Study *Reading Between the Lines* on pp. 490–491 and then answer the following questions:
a. Why did the United States impose a tariff on luxury goods from Europe?
b. What are the effects of the tariff on these goods? Explain your answer.
c. Who are the winners and who are the losers from the tariff?
d. Why do you think that the government cares about banana growers? (Hint: Think about where bananas grow and think about who owns the firms that produce bananas.)
e. The news article talks about a U.S. ban on Concorde landings in retaliation for the European ban on some older U.S aircraft types. How would you go about analyzing the effects of this action? Who gains and who loses?

2. Visit the Parkin Web site and study the *Web Reading Between the Lines* on steel dumping. Then answer the following questions:
a. What is the argument in the news article for limiting steel imports?
b. Evaluate the argument. Is it correct or incorrect in your opinion? Why?
c. Would you vote to limit steel imports? Why or why not?
d. Would you vote differently if you lived in another steel-producing country? Why or why not?

3. Use the links on the Parkin Web site to visit the Public Citizen Global Trade Watch and the State of Arizona Department of Commerce Web sites. Review the general message provided by the two sites about NAFTA and then answer the following questions:
a. What is the message that the Public Citizen Global Trade Watch wants to give?
b. What is the basic message of the Arizona Commerce Department?
c. Which message do you think is the correct one and why?
d. Would you vote to maintain NAFTA? Why or why not?

The scale of international trade, borrowing, and lending, both in absolute dollar terms and as a percentage of total world production, expands every year. One country, Singapore, imports and exports goods and services in a volume that exceeds its gross domestic product. The world's largest nation, China, returned to the international economic stage during the 1980s and is now a major producer of manufactured goods. ◆ International economic activity is large because today's economic world is small and because communication is so incredibly fast. But today's world is not a new world. From the beginning of recorded history, people have traded over large and steadily increasing distances. The great Western civilizations of Greece and Rome traded not only around the Mediterranean but also into the Gulf of Arabia. The great Eastern civilizations traded around the Indian Ocean. By the Middle Ages, the East and the West were trading routinely overland on routes pioneered by Venetian traders and explorers such as Marco Polo. When, in 1497, Vasco da Gama opened a sea route between the Atlantic and Indian Oceans around Africa, a new trade between East and West began, which brought tumbling prices of Eastern goods in Western markets. ◆ The European discovery of America and the subsequent opening up of Atlantic trade continued the process of steady globalization. So the developments of the 1990s, amazing though many of them were, represent a continuation of an ongoing expansion of human horizons. ◆ Chapter 22 studies the interaction of nations in today's global economy. ◆ It describes and explains international trade in goods and services. In this chapter, you have come face to face with one of the biggest policy issues of all ages, free trade versus protection. You have learned how all nations can benefit from free international trade. And you have seen how protection from competition brings big benefits to a few and small losses to the many. The total gains from protection are dwarfed by the losses, but because the losses are spread thinly and the gains thickly, protectionism always has its supporters and political backers. ◆ Chapter 22 does not explain international deficits and surpluses and borrowing and lending. You will lean about these aspects of the international economy in a course in *macroeconomics*. In such a course, you will learn that our international deficit depends not on how efficient we are, but on how much we save relative to how much we invest. Nations with low saving rates, everything else being the same, have international deficits. ◆ The global economy is big news these days. And it has always attracted attention. On the next page, you can meet the economist who first understood comparative advantage: David Ricardo. And you can meet one of today's leading international economists, Stanley Fischer, formally a professor at MIT and now Deputy Managing Director of the International Monetary Fund.

It's a Small World

Gains from International Trade

The Economist

David Ricardo *(1772–1832) was a highly successful 27-year-old stockbroker when he stumbled on a copy of Adam Smith's* Wealth of Nations *(see p. 56) on a weekend visit to the country. He was immediately hooked and went on to become the most celebrated economist of his age and one of the all-time great economists. One of his many contributions was to develop the principle of comparative advantage, the foundation on which the modern theory of international trade is built. The example he used to illustrate this principle was the trade between England and Portugal in cloth and wine.*

The General Agreement on Tariffs and Trade was established as a reaction against the devastation wrought by beggar-my-neighbor tariffs imposed during the 1930s. But it is also a triumph for the logic first worked out by Smith and Ricardo.

"Under a system of perfectly free commerce, each country naturally devotes its capital and labor to such employments as are most beneficial to each."

DAVID RICARDO
The Principles of Political Economy and Taxation,
1817

The Issues

Until the mid-eighteenth century, it was generally believed that the purpose of international trade was to keep exports greater than imports and pile up gold. If gold was accumulated, it was believed, the nation would prosper; if gold was lost through an international deficit, the nation would be drained of money and impoverished. These beliefs are called *mercantilism,* and the *mercantilists* were pamphleteers who advocated with missionary fervor the pursuit of an international surplus. If exports did not exceed imports, the mercantilists wanted imports restricted.

In the 1740s, David Hume explained that as the quantity of money (gold) changes, so also does the price level, and the nation's *real* wealth is unaffected. In the 1770s, Adam Smith argued that import restrictions would lower the gains from specialization and make a nation poorer. Thirty years later, David Ricardo proved the law of comparative advantage and demonstrated the superiority of free trade. Mercantilism was intellectually bankrupt but remained politically powerful.

Gradually, through the nineteenth century, the mercantilist influence waned and North America and Western Europe prospered in an environment of increasingly free international trade. But despite remarkable advances in economic understanding, mercantilism never quite died. It had a brief and devastating revival in the 1920s and 1930s when tariff hikes brought about the collapse of international trade and accentuated the Great Depression. It subsided again after World War II with the establishment of the General Agreement on Tariffs and Trade (GATT).

But mercantilism lingers on. The often expressed view that the United States should restrict Japanese imports and reduce its deficit with Japan and fears that NAFTA will bring economic ruin to the United States are modern manifestations of mercantilism. It would be interesting to have David

Hume, Adam Smith, and David Ricardo commenting on these views. But we know what they would say—the same things that they said to the eighteenth-century mercantilists. And they would still be right today.

Then

In the eighteenth century, when mercantilists and economists were debating the pros and cons of free international exchange, the transportation technology that was available limited the gains from international trade. Sailing ships with tiny cargo holds took close to a month to cross the Atlantic Ocean. But the potential gains were large, and so was the incentive to cut shipping costs. By the 1850s, the clipper ship had been developed, cutting the journey from Boston to Liverpool to only 12¼ days. Half a century later, 10,000-ton steamships were sailing between America and England in just 4 days. As sailing times and costs declined, the gains from international trade increased and the volume of trade expanded.

Now

The container ship has revolutionized international trade and contributed to its continued expansion. Today, most goods cross the oceans in containers—metal boxes—packed into and piled on top of ships like this one. Container technology has cut the cost of ocean shipping by economizing on handling and by making cargoes harder to steal, lowering insurance costs. It is unlikely that there would be much international trade in goods such as television sets and VCRs without this technology. High-value and perishable cargoes such as flowers and fresh foods, as well as urgent courier packages, travel by air. Every day, dozens of cargo-laden 747s fly between every major U.S. city and to destinations across the Atlantic and Pacific oceans.

As the world economy has become more integrated, new international institutions have evolved. One of these institutions is the International Monetary Fund, or IMF. Let's talk with one of today's outstanding economists who now plays a leading role at the IMF and has become a household name during the Asia crisis, Stanley Fischer.

Stanley Fischer *has served as the First Deputy Managing Director of the International Monetary Fund (The IMF) since 1994. Born in Zambia in 1943, he received a B.S. and an M.S. from the London School of Economics in 1965 and 1966, respectively, and a Ph.D. from MIT in 1969. Professor Fischer has taught at the University of Chicago and MIT. He served as Vice President of Development Economics and Chief Economist at the World Bank from 1988 to 1992. Michael Parkin talked with Stanley Fischer about his work at the IMF, the goals of that institution, and the lessons that we've learned from the Asian financial crisis.*

Stanley Fischer

How did you get into economics?

I was at high school in Zimbabwe (then Rhodesia) and in the sixth form I began to specialize in physics, chemistry, and math. Then I heard about economics. I switched one of my science courses to economics and I loved it.

This was the perfect field, one that provided an analytic way of understanding an important part of how societies work and also one in which I could use my quantitative skills. I went to the London School of Economics for my bachelor's and master's degrees and then to MIT for my Ph.D. My first appointment was at the University of Chicago

at a time when Milton Friedman was still the dominant influence there.

Can we talk first about the amazing liberalization and growth of world trade during the post–World War II years? Has this growth of world trade brought economic growth for all countries? Or have some gained more than others?

If you were to look at what has happened in the postwar period to the industrialized countries—which, despite some slowing since the 1960s, have grown faster, more consistently, and with less disruption than in any period of similar length in history—you would have to say that the architecture of the postwar economy has been very successful. And then if you look at the developing countries, you will find that, on the average, they have grown faster yet. In the most populous part of the globe, namely, East Asia, China, and, to some extent, India, we have had absolutely unprecedented growth. Every one of the successful East Asian countries has succeeded by integrating with the world economy, by promoting exports and increasing imports, especially of capital and intermediate goods. This process of opening up and using world markets for exports and imports has been absolutely critical. This outcome is what most economists from Adam Smith and David Ricardo on would have predicted.

The one part of the world where progress has, on the average, been most disappointing, is Africa. But there are countries in Africa that have done well. The countries that have been serious about trying to trade in the global economy and about implementing market-friendly policies have done better on the whole. We have seen significant growth

Every one of the successful East Asian countries has succeeded by integrating with the world economy.

in per capita income in Africa in the last few years. The prospects for South Africa look good, and that could be very important for a large part of the continent. In addition, countries such as Mozambique and Uganda have begun growing very fast after terrible civil wars, and Botswana has been one of the fastest-growing economies in the world for the past two decades.

What is the role of the IMF and what are the main problems that it seeks to address?

The IMF has several main functions. The first is *surveillance:* It is an institution in which countries discuss problems of the international economy, as well as each other's economies. Twice a year, the Fund staff presents its survey of the world economy, the *World Economic Outlook.*

In addition, Fund staff presents an annual report—the Article IV report—on the economy of each member country. The Article IV reports are based on the staff's analysis and discussions with the economic policy makers in each country.

Another function of the Fund is to *make loans to countries* in economic trouble. These loans typically provide balance of payments support to countries in crisis and countries to which the private capital markets are reluctant to lend.

One such crisis began in 1997—the financial crisis of Asia, Russia, Brazil, and other countries. What was its central feature?

Financial system weakness was a feature of almost all the crisis countries except Brazil. All the crises were driven and worsened by rapid international movements of capital. Investors pushed money into the crisis countries and then pulled it out, very rapidly, as the crisis approached its peak. The crisis featured *contagion*, spreading fast from one country to another.

What are the lessons of this episode of financial crisis?

The main lesson is that individual countries and the international financial system must adapt to the new circumstances of globally integrated financial markets. We must reduce the volatility of international capital flows and improve the capacity of financial systems and economies to cope with shifts in market confidence and investor sentiment that will inevitably occur in future.

Work is now under way in the emerging market economies, industrialized countries, and international institutions, to identify the polices and reforms that are needed.

For the *emerging market countries*, the list of items that need attention is a long one. Efforts

... Countries and the international financial system must adapt to the new circumstances of globally integrated financial markets.

must focus on sound macroeconomic policies, which include avoiding operating fixed exchange rate systems, which have been crisis-prone. Banking systems must be restructured, and the supervision and regulation of banks must be improved. Better economic and financial information on private and public sector activities must be provided. Business financial practices and bankruptcy laws must be improved. And these countries need to find ways of dealing with rapid and large reversals in international capital flows.

Countries need to think carefully about how fast and in what order to free capital account transactions and to make sure their borrowing is not too short term. They also need adequate reserves and, possibly, lines of credit that will give them access to liquidity when they need it.

The *advanced industrialized countries* need to pursue macroeconomic policies that bring sustainable growth. When these countries are not expanding, developing countries, too, find it difficult to grow. The advanced countries also need to maintain healthy financial systems and to regulate their own financial institutions to minimize potential disruptive capital flows to emerging market countries.

The *international financial institutions*, the IMF among them, must act as well. One example of an important initiative is the design and adoption of international standards for bank operation and supervision and for reporting fiscal and monetary data. Another is the effort to encourage the provision of better economic and financial data to the public by emerging market economies. A third is the effort to strengthen *surveillance* by the IMF. The IMF reports regularly on each country's economy, assessing its policies and practices, thereby encouraging the country to do better. Fourth, IMF member countries are gradually coming to the view that IMF reports, the Article IV reports, should be published so that the general public and investors can share information that so far has been available only to governments. Fifth, we are finding ways of making sure that private investors do their share in solving crises. One important criticism of IMF programs has been that the official sector bails out the private sector, providing loans so that the private sector can take its money out of a country in trouble. This is a very complicated issue, but we are definitely making progress on what is known as "bailing in" the private sector, finding ways of discouraging the private sector from taking its money out when a crisis hits.

What big conclusions should we draw from the special features of Russia's economic and financial condition?
A key question that has been asked since the onset of Russia's crisis in 1999 is: Was the reform strategy of the previous Russian government wrong? My conclusion is, fundamentally, no. The problem was not that the basic strategy was wrong, but that it was not pursued vigorously or deeply enough. What has been necessary in Russia

for some time has been a comprehensive strategy for moving boldly to tackle a large fiscal imbalance and to deal with important structural problems related to the way its economy operates—in particular, the nonpayment problem. Such a strategy was at the heart of the July 1998 program agreed on with the IMF. But by then, the financial situation and market confidence were too precarious and vulnerable to any missteps in implementation, which indeed happened and quickly led to the August collapse.

Put differently, the conclusion is that stabilization is not enough. Russia stabilized its economy extremely successfully from about the middle of 1995, with an appropriate degree of monetary discipline accompanied by a fixed exchange rate regime, which stabilizes inflationary expectations following a prolonged period of high inflation. However, the fiscal adjustment needed was not forthcoming, so there was a massive and rapid buildup in public debt. Ultimately, the government was not able to service its debt out of its own resources and could not convince investors to continue financing its ongoing deficit. This led to both the devaluation of the ruble and the government default on its treasury bills in August 1998.

Moreover, a critical reason why the fiscal adjustment could not be implemented was the lack of progress in industrial restructuring and other structural reforms; thus the stabilization was not sustainable. A very large part of the Russian economy remains

> So the failure of structural reforms underlies the fiscal problem in Russia.

unreformed, has not been part of the monetary economy, and is conducting its operations largely through barter—not only literally barter of goods against goods, but in many cases barter through very sophisticated financial mechanisms that do not involve the use of money. This situation has arisen because of a vast number of factors, including poor enforcement of tax obligations, an unfair tax system, weak bankruptcy laws, poor lending practices by banks, and corrupt business practices. Thus, much of the productive sector was either losing money in real terms or not paying a fair share of taxes. So the failure of structural reforms underlies the fiscal problem in Russia. Without these reforms, the budget will not balance, growth will not materialize, and eventually financial stability will be compromised.

Why do you believe that the IMF can play a role as the lender of last resort?
The IMF already is increasingly playing that role, both as crisis lender and as crisis manager. As crisis lender, the IMF, whose financial structure is similar to that of a credit union, has access to a pool of resources. As crisis manager, it has been taking the lead in negotiating with its member countries that are experiencing a financial crisis. It also has played an important coordinating and

Should the IMF function as an international lender of last resort? I believe that there is a need for an agency that will act as such a lender to countries facing a crisis.

advisory role in arranging financing packages to help countries work out their debt problems with their foreign creditors.

Some have asked whether the IMF has enough resources to act as crisis lender. While the resources available have grown less than the size of the world economy since the IMF's inception in 1945, the IMF can still assemble a sizable financial package in response to a crisis, including, in special circumstances, by borrowing from members' central banks and by creating additional reserves for its members through the issuance of Special Drawing Rights (SDRs).

Should the IMF function as an international lender of last resort? I believe that there is a need for an agency that will act as such a lender to countries facing a crisis. The need arises because international capital flows are both extremely volatile and contagious, exhibiting the classic signs of financial panics, and an international lender of last resort can help to mitigate the effects of this instability and perhaps even help prevent the instability itself. Again, the IMF has already been acting in many ways as such a lender, and there is ongoing work to help make the IMF more effective in that capacity.

Of the main criticisms leveled at the IMF during the Asian crisis, which are the easiest to dismiss, and which, if any, should we take more seriously?

This is a complex question that cannot be easily answered in a few words. While I will try, I should say that the IMF has taken all the criticisms seriously and indeed has produced a comprehensive study of the experience in Indonesia, Korea, and Thailand, which I would encourage those interested to read.

The programs in the Asian crisis countries supported by the IMF sought to restore macroeconomic stability and the conditions for growth while addressing deep-rooted structural weaknesses that lay at the heart of the crisis in each country. These programs have been attacked from a number of angles, but here again I believe that, particularly in the highly fluid and uncertain circumstances, the approach taken and choices made were basically correct.

A frequent criticism is that the policy of high interest rates worsened financial problems being experienced by corporations and therefore made the recessions worse in these countries. However, their currencies were collapsing, and it was critical to avoid a depreciation-inflation spiral. Indeed, the critics fail to recognize that, in addition to the well-known negative effects on growth of high inflation, in a situation where companies and banks had borrowed heavily abroad, the further depreciations implied by lower interest rates would have exacerbated financial problems by

increasing the burden of servicing dollar-denominated debts.

Another criticism is that the programs entailed unduly contractionary fiscal policies. The original programs in these countries, formulated in the initial stages of the crisis, included some degree of fiscal adjustment to lessen the burden that might be placed on the private sector in the face of the large adjustment in the current account of the balance of payments that was needed. The truth is that, even then, the fiscal adjustment that was planned was rather small in both Korea and Indonesia and was substantial only in Thailand, where the initial fiscal imbalance was larger. Moreover, as economic activity deteriorated over the course of the programs, fiscal policy was progressively allowed to become more expansionary. In fact, our study concluded that fiscal policy was not a major factor accounting for the output decline in these countries.

The inclusion of structural measures in our programs also has drawn criticism. Financial and corporate sector inefficiencies were at the heart of these crises, and it was clear from the start that the restoration of durable growth required financial and corporate restructuring. Still, some argued that these reforms, while sensible over the medium term, impose large costs in the short term, and therefore it was a mistake to put them in place when economic activity was already so weak. While this is a valid concern, I think that attempting to stabilize the situation without attempting to address the underlying causes of the crisis would have been akin to treating the symptom without addressing the real cause of the disease. And delay does not make the structural problem any easier to deal with; indeed, as the problem of the Japanese banking sector in the 1990s clearly demonstrates, it makes it worse.

All this said, why did the programs work less well than we all hoped? Why was the economic downturn worse than initially foreseen? Clearly, the projections embodied in the original programs were somewhat more optimistic than the consensus view. However, very few observers foresaw the severity of the downturn—neither the governments, private forecasters, nor academic observers. A number of factors conspired to make matters worse than foreseen. First, the external environment for the crisis countries worsened markedly. In particular, the Japanese recession has been deeper and more prolonged than anticipated, hurting the exports of the crisis countries. Second, several factors—an initial reluctance by governments to implement the programs, political uncertainties, and lack of public support for the programs—made it much more difficult for market confidence to be restored than had been assumed. This led to greater

> The Japanese recession has been deeper and more prolonged than anticipated, hurting the exports of the crisis countries.

capital outflows and put additional upward pressure on interest rates and downward pressure on exchange rates, and forced a larger downward adjustment of domestic demand.

While I believe the basic approach of the programs was right, that doesn't mean that we shouldn't try to do better. As I already discussed, the recent financial crises have revealed weaknesses in the international financial system that we must try to deal with. As briefly described above, the IMF and other international institutions are doing their part to help in that endeavor.

What kinds of jobs do economics graduates get in organizations such as the IMF and the World Bank? What should students be doing as undergraduates to prepare themselves for such positions?

People who want to work in the Fund and the Bank should take courses in macroeconomics, international trade and finance, development, monetary economics, and public finance. From the viewpoint of the Bank, it would also be useful to study micro-oriented policy issues. The Fund and the Bank have entry programs for people who may be destined for their professional ranks. The World Bank's is called Young Professionals, and the IMF's is called the Economist Program.

The IMF and the World Bank are terrific places to work. You use your analytic skills all the time, in the real world. You have to decide what really matters, you have to be sure that what you're recommending will improve the lives of people. Then if you work in the operational parts of the Fund or Bank, you have to persuade the countries with which you're working that you're right. If you are right and you succeed, you have the satisfaction of having done something useful.

In the process, you'll have had the benefit of learning some diplomacy. You are also likely to learn some humility—for you will realize that the really hard work of implementing policies is done by the politicians and officials of the countries that undertake them. Your job is to help them do their own jobs better, always bearing in mind that the benefits or costs are borne by their people.

Solutions to Odd-Numbered Problems

CHAPTER 1

1. The opportunity cost of going to school is $9,600 of goods and services.

   The opportunity cost of going to school this summer is the highest-valued activity that you will give up so that you can go to summer school. In going to summer school, you will forgo all the goods and services that you could have bought with the income from your summer job ($6,000) plus the expenditure on tuition ($2,000), textbooks ($200), and living expenses ($1,400).

3. No, parking at this mall is not free. Yes, you did impose a cost on Harry.

   Finding a parking space takes about 30 minutes, so you incur an opportunity cost when you park your car. The opportunity cost is the highest-valued activity that you forgo by spending 30 minutes parking your car. If you would have spent those 30 minutes studying, then the opportunity cost of parking at this mall is 30 minutes of studying.

   The cost that you imposed on Harry is the additional 30 minutes that Harry will have to spend searching for a parking space.

CHAPTER 2

1a. To make a time-series graph, plot the year on the x-axis and the inflation rate on the y-axis. The graph will be a line joining all the points.

1b. (i) 1980 (ii) 1986 (iii) 1984, 1987–1990, 1995–1996 (iv) 1981–1983, 1985–1986, 1991–1992, 1994, 1997–1998 (v) 1987 (vi) 1982

1c. Inflation has had a downward trend. The line tends to slope down to the right.

3. To make a scatter diagram, plot the inflation rate on the x-axis and the interest rate on the y-axis. The graph will be a set of dots. The pattern made by the dots tells us that as the inflation rate increases, the interest rate usually increases.

5a. To make a graph that shows the relationship between x and y, plot x on the x-axis and y on the y-axis. The relationship is positive because x and y move together: As x increases, y increases.

5b. The slope increases as x increases. Slope is equal to the change in y divided by the change in x as we move along the curve. When x increases from 1 to 2 (a change of 1), y increases from 1 to 4 (a change of 3), so the slope is 3. But when x increases from 7 to 8 (a change of 1), y increases from 49 to 64 (a change of 15), so the slope is 15.

5c. The taller the building, the bigger is the cost of building it. The higher the unemployment rate, the higher is the crime rate. The longer the flight, the larger is the amount of fuel used.

   The slope equals 8.

   The slope of the curve at the point where x is 4 is equal to the slope of the tangent to the curve at that point. Plot the relationship and then draw the tangent line at the point where x is 4 and y is 16. Now calculate the slope of this tangent line. To do this, you must find another point on the tangent. The tangent line will cut the x-axis at 2, so another point is x equals 2 and y equals 0. Slope equals rise/run. The rise is 16 and the run is 2, so the slope is 8.

   The slope is 7.

   The slope of the relationship across the arc when x increases from 3 to 4 is equal to the slope of the straight line joining the points on the curve at x equals 3 and x equals 4. In the graph, draw this straight line. When x increases from 3 to 4, y increases from 9 to 16. Slope equals rise/run. The rise is 7 (16 minus 9) and the run is 1 (4 minus 3), so the slope across the arc is 7.

   The slope is –5/4.

   The curve is a straight line, so its slope is the same at all points on the curve. Slope equals the change in the variable on the y-axis divided by the change in the variable on the x-axis. To calculate the slope, you must select two points on the line. One point is at 10 on the y-axis and 0 on the x-axis, and another is at 8 on the x-axis and 0 on the y-axis. The change in y from 10 to 0 is associated with the change in x from 0 to 8. Therefore the slope of the curve equals –10/8, which equals –5/4.

13a. The slope at point a is –2, and the slope at point b is –0.75.

   To calculate the slope at a point on a curved line, draw the tangent to the line at the point. Then find a second point on the tangent and calculate the slope of the tangent.

   The tangent at point a cuts the y-axis at 10. The slope of the tangent equals the change in y divided by the change in x. The change in y equals 4 (10 minus 6) and the change in x equals –2 (0 minus 2). The slope at point a is 4/–2, which equals –2.

   Similarly, the slope at point b is –0.75. The tangent at point b cuts the x-axis at 8. The change in y equals 1.5, and the change in x equals –2. The slope at point b is –0.75.

13b. The slope across the arc ab is –1.125.

   The slope across an arc ab equals the change in y, which is 4.5 (6.0 minus 1.5) divided by the change in x, which equals –4 (2 minus 6). The slope across the arc ab equals 4.5/–4, which is –1.125.

15a. A set of curves, one for each different temperature.

   To draw a graph of the relationship between the price and the number of rides, keep the temperature at 50°F and

503

plot the data in that column against the price. The curve that you draw is the relationship between price and number of rides when the temperature is 50°F. Now repeat the exercise but keep the temperature at 70°F. Then repeat the exercise but keep the temperature at 90°F.

15b. A set of curves, one for each different price.

To draw a graph of the relationship between the temperature and the number of rides, keep the price at $5.00 a ride and plot the data in that row against the temperature. The curve shows the relationship between temperature and the number of rides when the price is $5.00 a ride. Now repeat the exercise but keep the price at $10.00 a ride. Repeat the exercise again and keep the price at $15.00 a ride and then at $20.00 a ride.

15c. A set of curves, one for each different number of rides.

To draw a graph of the relationship between the temperature and price, keep the number of rides at 32 and plot the data along the diagonal in the table. The curve is the relationship between temperature and price at which 32 rides are taken. Now repeat the exercise and keep the number of rides at 27. Repeat the exercise again and keep the number of rides at 18 and then at 40.

CHAPTER 3

1a. Wendell's opportunity cost is 5 percentage points.

When Wendell increases the time he plays tennis from 4 hours to 6 hours, his grade in economics falls from 75 percent to 70 percent. His opportunity cost is 5 percentage points.

1b. Wendell's opportunity cost is 10 percentage points.

When Wendell increases the time he plays tennis from 6 hours to 8 hours, his grade in economics falls from 70 percent to 60 percent. His opportunity cost is 10 percentage points.

3. Wendell's opportunity cost of playing tennis increases as he spends more time on tennis.

When Wendell increases the time he plays tennis from 4 hours to 6 hours, his opportunity cost is 5 percentage points. But when he increases the time he plays tennis from 6 hours to 8 hours, his opportunity cost is 10 percentage points. Wendell's opportunity cost of playing tennis increases as he spends more time on tennis.

5a. Wendell's grade in economics is 66 percent.

When Wendell increases the time he plays tennis from 4 hours to 6 hours, his opportunity cost of the additional 2 hours of tennis is 5 percentage points. So his opportunity cost of an additional 1 hour is 2.5 percentage points. But when he increases the time he plays tennis from 6 hours to 8 hours, his opportunity cost of the additional 2 hours of tennis is 10 percentage points. So his opportunity cost of the additional 1 hour of tennis is 5 percentage points. Wendell's opportunity cost of playing tennis increases as he spends more time on tennis. Opportunity cost is plotted at the midpoint of the range. This curve is Wendell's marginal cost of a additional hour of tennis.

Wendell uses his time efficiently if he plays tennis for 7 hours a week—marginal benefit from tennis equals its

marginal cost. Wendell's marginal benefit is 5 percentage points and his marginal cost is 5 percentage points. When Wendell plays 7 hours of tennis, his grade in economics (from his *PPF*) is 66 percent.

5b. If Wendell studied for enough hours to get a higher grade, he would have fewer hours to play tennis. Wendell's marginal benefit from tennis would be greater than his marginal cost, so he would be more efficient if he played more hours of tennis and took a lower grade.

7a. Leisureland's *PPF* is a straight line.

To make a graph of Leisureland's *PPF* measure the quantity of one good on the *x*-axis and the quantity of the other good on the *y*-axis. Then plot the quantities in each row of the table and join up the points.

7b. The opportunity cost of 1 pound of food is 1/2 gallon of sunscreen.

The opportunity cost of the first 100 pounds of food is 50 gallons of sunscreen. To find the opportunity cost of the first 100 pounds of food, increase the quantity of food from 0 pounds to 100 pounds. In doing so, Leisureland's production of sunscreen decreases from 150 gallons to 100 gallons. The opportunity cost of the first 100 pounds of food is 50 gallons of sunscreen. Similarly, the opportunity costs of producing the second 100 pounds and the third 100 pounds of food are 50 gallons of sunscreen.

The opportunity cost of 1 gallon of sunscreen is 2 pounds of food. The opportunity cost of producing the first 50 gallons of sunscreen is 100 pounds of food. To calculate this opportunity cost, increase the quantity of sunscreen from 0 gallons to 50 gallons. Leisureland's production of food decreases from 300 pounds to 200 pounds. Similarly, the opportunity cost of producing the second 50 gallons and the third 50 gallons are 100 pounds of food.

9a. The marginal benefit curve slopes downward.

To draw the marginal benefit from sunscreen, plot the quantity of sunscreen on the *x*-axis and the willingness to pay for sunscreen (that is, the number of pounds of food that they are willing to give up to get a gallon of sunscreen) on the *y*-axis.

9b. The efficient quantity is 75 gallons a month.

The efficient quantity to produce is such that the marginal benefit from the last gallon equals the opportunity cost of producing it. The opportunity cost of a gallon of sunscreen is 2 pounds of sunscreen. The marginal benefit of the 75th gallon of sunscreen is 2 pounds of food. And the marginal cost of the 75th gallon of sunscreen is 2 pounds of food.

Busyland's opportunity cost of a pound of food is 2 gallons of sunscreen, and its opportunity cost of a gallon of sunscreen is 1/2 pound of food.

When Busyland increases the food it produces by 50 pounds a month, it produces 100 gallons of sunscreen less. The opportunity cost of 1 pound of food is 2 gallons of sunscreen. Similarly, when Busyland increases the sunscreen it produces by 100 gallons a month, it produces 50 pounds of food less. The opportunity cost of 1 gallon of sunscreen is 1/2 pound of food.

13a. Leisureland sells food and buys sunscreen.

Leisureland sells the good in which it has a comparative advantage and buys the other good from Busyland. Leisureland's opportunity cost of 1 pound of food is 1/2 gallon of sunscreen, while Busyland's opportunity cost of 1 pound of food is 2 gallons of sunscreen. Leisureland's opportunity cost of food is less than Busyland's, so Leisureland has a comparative advantage in producing food.

Leisureland's opportunity cost of 1 gallon of sunscreen is 2 pounds of food, while Busyland's opportunity cost of 1 gallon of sunscreen is 1/2 pound of food. Busyland's opportunity cost of sunscreen is less than Leisureland's, so Busyland has a comparative advantage in producing sunscreen.

13b. The gains from trade for each country are 50 pounds of food and 50 gallons of sunscreen.

With specialization and trade, together they can produce 300 pounds of food and 300 gallons of sunscreen. So each will get 150 pounds of food and 150 gallons of sunscreen—an additional 50 pounds of food and 50 gallons of sunscreen.

CHAPTER 4

1a. The price of a tape will rise, and the quantity of tapes sold will increase.

CDs and tapes are substitutes. If the price of a CD rises, people will buy more tapes and fewer CDs. The demand for tapes will increase. The price of a tape will rise, and more tapes will be sold.

1b. The price of a tape will fall, and fewer tapes will be sold.

Walkmans and tapes are complements. If the price of a Walkman rises, fewer Walkmans will be bought. The demand for tapes will decrease. The price of a tape will fall, and people will buy fewer tapes.

1c. The price of a tape will fall and fewer tapes will be sold.

The increase in the supply of CD players will lower the price of a CD player. With CD players cheaper than they were, some people will buy CD players. The demand for CDs will increase, and the demand for tapes will decrease. The price of a tape will fall, and people will buy fewer tapes.

1d. The price of a tape will rise, and the quantity sold will increase.

An increase in consumers' income will increase the demand for tapes. As a result, the price of a tape will rise and the quantity bought will increase.

1e. The price of a tape will rise, and the quantity sold will decrease.

If the workers who make tapes get a pay raise, the cost of making a tape increases and the supply of tapes decreases. The price will rise, and people will buy fewer tapes.

1f. The quantity sold will decrease, but the price might rise, fall, or stay the same.

Walkmans and tapes are complements. If the price of a Walkman rises, fewer Walkmans will be bought and so the demand for tapes will decrease. The price of a tape will fall, and people will buy fewer tapes. If the wages paid to workers who make tapes rise, the supply of tapes decreases. The quantity of tapes sold will decrease, and the price of a tape will rise. Taking the two events together, the quantity sold will decrease, but the price might rise, fall, or stay the same.

3a. (ii) and (iii)

If the price of crude oil (the resource used to make gasoline) rises, the supply of gasoline decreases. The demand for gasoline does not change, so the price of gasoline rises and there is a movement along the demand curve. The quantity demanded of gasoline decreases.

3b. (i) and (iv)

If the price of a car rises, the quantity of cars bought decreases. So the demand for gasoline decreases. The supply of gasoline does not change, so the price of gasoline falls and there is a movement down the supply curve of gasoline. The quantity supplied of gasoline decreases.

3c. (i) and (iv)

If all speed limits on highways are abolished, people will drive faster and use more gasoline. The demand for gasoline increases. The supply of gasoline does not change, so the price of gasoline rises and there is a movement up along the supply curve. The quantity supplied of gasoline increases.

3d. (i) and (iv)

If robot production plants lower the cost of producing a car, the supply of cars will increase. With no change in the demand for cars, the price of a car will fall and more cars will be bought. The demand for gasoline increases. The supply of gasoline does not change, so the price of gasoline rises and the quantity of gasoline supplied increases.

5a. The demand curve is the curve that slopes down toward the right. The supply curve is the curve that slopes up toward the right.

5b. The equilibrium price is $14 a pizza, and the equilibrium quantity is 200 pizzas a day.

Market equilibrium is determined at the intersection of the demand curve and supply curve.

7a. The equilibrium price is 50 cents a pack, and the equilibrium quantity is 120 million packs a week.

The price of a pack adjusts until the quantity demanded equals the quantity supplied. At 50 cents a pack, the quantity demanded is 120 million packs a week and the quantity supplied is 120 million packs a week.

7b. At 70 cents a pack, there will be a surplus of gum and the price will fall.

At 70 cents a pack, the quantity demanded is 80 million packs a week and the quantity supplied is 160 million pack a week. There is a surplus of 80 million packs a week. The price will fall until market equilibrium is restored—50 cents a pack.

The supply curve has shifted leftward.

As the number of gum-producing factories decreases, the supply of gum decreases. There is a new supply schedule, and the supply curve shifts leftward.

9b. There has been a movement along the demand curve.

The supply of gum decreases, and the supply curve shifts leftward. Demand does not change, so the price rises along the demand curve.

9c. The equilibrium price is 60 cents, and the equilibrium quantity is 100 million packs a week.

Supply decreases by 40 millions packs a week. That is, the quantity supplied at each price decreases by 40 million packs. The quantity supplied at 50 cents is now 80 million packs, and there is a shortage of gum. The price rises to 60 cents a pack, at which the quantity supplied equals the quantity demanded (100 million packs a week).

11. The new price is 70 cents a pack, and the quantity is 120 million packs a week.

The demand for gum increases, and the demand curve shifts rightward. The quantity demanded at each price increases by 40 million packs. The result of the fire is a price of 60 cents a pack. At this price, there is now a shortage of gum. The price of gum will rise until the shortage is eliminated.

CHAPTER 5

1a. The price elasticity of demand is 1.25.

The price elasticity of demand equals the percentage change in the quantity demanded divided by the percentage change in the price. The price rises from $4 to $6 a box, a rise of $2 a box. The average price is $5 a box. So the percentage change in the price equals $2 divided by $5, which equals 40 percent.

The quantity decreases from 1,000 to 600 boxes, a decrease of 400 boxes. The average quantity is 800 boxes. So the percentage change in quantity equals 400 divided by 800, which equals 50 percent.

The price elasticity of demand for strawberries equals 50 divided by 40, which is 1.25.

1b. The price elasticity of demand exceeds 1, so the demand for strawberries is elastic.

3a. The price elasticity of demand is 2.

When the price of a videotape rental rises from $3 to $5, the quantity demanded of videotapes decreases from 75 to 25 a day. The price elasticity of demand equals the percentage change in the quantity demanded divided by the percentage change in the price.

The price increases from $3 to $5, an increase of $2 a videotape. The average price is $4 a videotape. So the percentage change in the price equals $2 divided by $4, which equals 50 percent.

The quantity decreases from 75 to 25 videotapes, a decrease of 50 videotapes. The average quantity is 50 videotapes. So the percentage change in quantity equals 50 divided by 50, which equals 100 percent.

The price elasticity of demand for videotape rentals equals 100 divided by 50, which is 2.

3b. The price elasticity of demand equals 1 at $3 a videotape. The price elasticity of demand equals infinity at $6 a videotape. The price elasticity of demand equals zero at $0 a videotape.

The price elasticity of demand equals 1 at the price halfway between the origin and the price at which the demand curve hits the y-axis. That price is $3 a videotape.

The price elasticity of demand equals infinity at the price at which the demand curve hits the y-axis. That price is $6 a videotape.

The price elasticity of demand equals zero at the price at which the demand curve hits the x-axis. That price is $0 a videotape.

5. The demand for dental services is unit elastic.

The price elasticity of demand for dental services equals the percentage change in the quantity of dental services demanded divided by the percentage change in the price of dental services.

The price elasticity of demand equals 10 divided by 10, which is 1. The demand is unit elastic.

7a. Total revenue increases.

When the price of a chip is $400, 30 million chips are sold and total revenue equals $12,000 million. When the price of a chip falls to $350, 35 million chips are sold and total revenue is $12,250 million. Total revenue increases when the price falls.

7b. Total revenue decreases.

When the price is $350 a chip, 35 million chips are sold and total revenue is $12,250 million. When the price of a chip is $300, 40 million chips are sold and total revenue decreases to $12,000 million. Total revenue decreases as the price falls.

7c. Total revenue is maximized at $350 a chip.

When the price of a chip is $300, 40 million chips are sold and total revenue equals $12,000 million. When the price is $350 a chip, 35 million chips are sold and total revenue equals $12,250 million. Total revenue increases as the price rises from $300 to $350 a chip. When the price is $400 a chip, 30 million chips are sold and total revenue equals $12,000 million. Total revenue decreases as the price rises from $350 to $400 a chip. Total revenue is maximized when the price is $350 a chip.

7d. The quantity will be 35 million chips a year.

The demand schedule tells us that when the price is $350 a chip, the quantity of chips demanded is 35 million chips a year.

7e. The demand for chips is unit elastic.

The total revenue test says that if the price changes and total revenue remains the same, the demand is unit elastic at the average price. For an average price of $350 a chip, cut the price from $400 to $300 a chip. When the price of a chip falls from $400 to $300, total revenue remains at $12,000 million. So at the average price of $350 a chip, demand is unit elastic.

9. The demand for chips is inelastic.

The total revenue test says that if the price falls and total revenue falls, the demand is inelastic. When the price falls from $300 to $200 a chip, total revenue decreases from $12,000 million to $10,000 million. So at an average price of $250 a chip, demand is inelastic.

11. The cross elasticity of demand between orange juice and apple juice is 1.17.

The cross elasticity of demand is the percentage change in the quantity demanded of one good divided by the percentage change in the price of another good. The rise in the price of orange juice resulted in an increase in the quantity demanded of apple juice. So the cross elasticity of demand is the percentage change in the quantity demanded of apple juice divided by the percentage change in the price of orange juice. The cross elasticity equals 14 divided by 12, which is 1.17.

13. Income elasticity of demand for (i) bagels is 1.33 and (ii) donuts is −1.33.

Income elasticity of demand equals the percentage change in the quantity demanded divided by the percentage change in income. The change in income is $2,000 and the average income is $4,000, so the percentage change in income equals 50 percent.

(i) The change in the quantity demanded is 4 bagels and the average quantity demanded is 6 bagels, so the percentage change in the quantity demanded equals 66.67 percent. The income elasticity of demand for bagels equals 66.67/50, which is 1.33.

(ii) The change in the quantity demanded is −6 donuts and the average quantity demanded is 9 donuts, so the percentage change in the quantity demanded is −66.67. The income elasticity of demand for donuts equals −66.67/50, which is −1.33.

15a. The elasticity of supply is 1.

The elasticity of supply is the percentage change in the quantity supplied divided by the percentage change in the price. When the price falls from 40 cents to 30 cents, the change in the price is 10 cents and the average price is 35 cents. The percentage change in the price is 28.57.

When the price falls from 40 cents to 30 cents, the quantity supplied decreases from 800 to 600 calls. The change in the quantity supplied is 200 calls, and the average quantity is 700 calls, so the percentage change in the quantity supplied is 28.57.

The elasticity of supply equals 28.57/28.57, which equals 1.

15b. The elasticity of supply is 1.

The formula for the elasticity of supply calculates the elasticity at the average price. So to find the elasticity at 20 cents, change the price such that 20 cents is the average price—for example, a fall in the price from 30 cents to 10 cents.

When the price falls from 30 cents to 10 cents, the change in the price is 20 cents and the average price is 20 cents. The percentage change in the price is 100. When the price falls from 30 cents to 10 cents, the quantity supplied decreases from 600 to 200 calls. The change in the quantity supplied is 400 calls and the average quantity is 400 calls, so the percentage change in the quantity supplied is 100.

The elasticity of supply is the percentage change in the quantity supplied divided by the percentage change in the price. The elasticity of supply is 1.

CHAPTER 6

1a. Equilibrium price is $1.00 a floppy disk, and the equilibrium quantity is 3 floppy disks a month.

1b. Consumer surplus is $2.25.

The consumer surplus is the area of the triangle under the demand curve above the price. The price is $1.00 a disk. The area of the triangle equals (2.50 − 1.00)/2 multiplied by 3, which is $2.25.

1c. Producer surplus is $0.75.

The producer surplus is the area of the triangle above the supply curve below the price. The price is $1.00 a disk. The area of the triangle equals (1.00 − 0.50)/2 multiplied by 3, which is $0.75.

1d. The efficient quantity is 3 floppy disks a month.

The efficient quantity is the quantity that makes the marginal benefit from the last disk equal to the marginal cost of producing the last disk. The demand curve shows the marginal benefit and the supply curve shows the marginal cost. Only if 3 floppy disks are produced is the quantity produced efficient.

3a. The maximum price that consumers will pay is $3.

The demand schedule shows the maximum price that consumers will pay for each sandwich. The maximum price that consumers will pay for the 250th sandwich is $3.

3b. The minimum price that producers will accept is $5.

The supply schedule shows the minimum price that producers will accept for each sandwich. The minimum price that producers will accept for the 250th sandwich is $5.

3c. Greater than the efficient quantity.

The efficient quantity is such that marginal benefit from the last sandwich equals the marginal cost of producing it. The efficient quantity is the equilibrium quantity—200 sandwiches an hour.

3d. Consumer surplus is $400.

The equilibrium price is $4. The consumer surplus is the area of the triangle under the demand curve above the price. The area of the triangle is (8 − 4)/2 multiplied by 200, which is $400.

3e. Producer surplus is $400.

The producer surplus is the area of the triangle above the supply curve below the price. The price is $4. The area of the triangle is (4 − 0)/2 multiplied by 200, which is $400.

3f. The deadweight loss is $50.

Deadweight loss is the sum of the consumer surplus and producer surplus that is lost because the quantity produced is not the efficient quantity. The deadweight loss equals the quantity (250 − 200) multiplied by (5 − 3)/2, which is $50.

5a. Ben's consumer surplus is $122.50. Beth's consumer surplus is $22.50, and Bo's consumer surplus is $4.50.

Consumer surplus is the area under the demand curve above the price. At 40 cents, Ben will travel 350 miles, Beth will travel 150 miles, and Bo will travel 30 miles. To find Ben's consumer surplus extend his demand schedule until you find the price at which his demand curve cuts the *y*-axis. This price is 110 cents. So Ben's consumer surplus equals (110 − 40)/2 multiplied by 350, which equals $122.50. Beth's consumer surplus equals (70 − 40)/2 multiplied by 150, which equals $22.50. And Bo's consumer surplus equals (70 − 40)/2 multiplied by 30, which equals $4.50.

5b. Ben's consumer surplus is the largest because he places a higher value on each unit of the good than the other two do.

5c. Ben's consumer surplus falls by $32.50. Beth's consumer surplus falls by $12.50, and Bo's consumer surplus falls by $2.50.

At 50 cents a mile, Ben travels 300 miles and his consumer surplus is $90, a decrease of $32.50. Beth travels 100 miles and her consumer surplus is $10, a decrease of $12.50. Bo travels 20 miles and her consumer surplus is $2.00, a decrease of $2.50.

CHAPTER 7

1a. Equilibrium price is $200 a month and the equilibrium quantity is 10,000 housing units.

1b. The quantity rented is 5,000 housing units.

The quantity of housing rented is equal to the quantity supplied at the rent ceiling.

1c. The shortage of housing is 10,000 housing units.

At the rent ceiling, the quantity of housing demanded is 15,000 but the quantity supplied is 5,000, so there is a shortage of 10,000 housing units.

1d. The maximum price that someone is willing to pay for the 5,000th unit available is $300 a month.

The demand curve tells us the maximum price that someone is willing to pay for the 5,000th unit.

3a. The equilibrium wage rate is $4 an hour, and employment is 2,000 hours a month.

3b. Unemployment is zero. Everyone who wants to work for $4 an hour is employed.

3c. They work 2,000 hours a month.

A minimum wage rate is the lowest wage rate that a person can be paid for an hour of work. Because the equilibrium wage rate exceeds the minimum wage rate, the minimum wage is ineffective. The wage rate will be $4 an hour and employment is 2,000 hours.

3d. There is no unemployment.

The wage rate rises to the equilibrium wage—the quantity of labor demanded equals the quantity of labor supplied. So there is no unemployment.

3e. At $5 an hour, 1,500 hours a month are employed and 1,000 hours a month are unemployed.

The quantity of labor employed equals the quantity demanded at $5 an hour. Unemployment is equal to the quantity of labor supplied at $5 an hour minus the quantity of labor demanded at $5 an hour. The quantity supplied is 2,500 hours a month, and the quantity demanded is 1,500 hours a month. So 1,000 hours a month are unemployed.

3f. The wage rate is $5 an hour, and unemployment is 500 hours a month.

At the minimum wage of $5 an hour, the quantity demanded is 2,000 hours a month and the quantity supplied is 2,500 hours a month. So 500 hours a month are unemployed.

5a. With no tax on brownies, the price is 60 cents a brownie and 4 million a day are consumed.

5b. The price is 70 cents a brownie, and 3 million brownies a day are consumed. Consumers and producers each pay 10 cents of the tax on a brownie.

The tax decreases the supply of brownies and raises the price of a brownie. With no tax, producers are willing to sell 3 million brownies a day at 50 cents a brownie. But with a 20 cent tax, they are willing to sell 3 million brownies a day only if the price is 20 cents higher at 70 cents a brownie.

7a. Inventory holders sell 500 boxes of rice.

Inventory holders sell rice from inventory because otherwise the storm will cause the price to rise above $1.40 a box.

7b. The price is $1.40 a box, and farm revenue is $2,800 a week.

The storm reduces the quantity grown by 500 boxes to 2,000 boxes. The action of the inventory holders maintains the price at $1.40 a box, so farm revenue equals $1.40 multiplied by 2,000 boxes.

CHAPTER 8

1a. To draw a graph of Jason's total utility from rock CDs, plot the number of CDs on the *x*-axis and Jason's utility from CDs on the *y*-axis. The curve will look similar to Fig. 9.2(a). To draw a graph of Jason's total utility from spy novels, repeat the above procedure but use the spy novel data.

1b. Jason gets more utility from any number of rock CDs than he does from the same number of spy novels.

1c. To draw a graph of Jason's marginal utility from rock CDs plot the number of CDs on the *x*-axis and Jason's marginal utility from CDs on the *y*-axis. The curve will look similar to Fig. 9.2(b). To draw a graph of Jason's marginal utility from spy novels, repeat the above procedure but use the spy novel data.

Jason's marginal utility from rock CDs is the increase in total utility he gets from one additional rock CD. Similarly, Jason's marginal utility from spy novels is the increase in total utility he gets from one additional spy novel.

1d. Jason gets more marginal utility from an additional rock CD than he gets from an additional spy novel when he has the same number of each.

3a. To draw a graph of Max's budget line, plot the hours spent on one activity (say, windsurfing) on the *x*-axis and the hours spent on the other activity of the *y*-axis. The budget line is a straight line running from 3.5 hours of windsurfing on the *x*-axis to 7 hours of snorkeling on the *y*-axis.

If Max spends all of his $35 on windsurfing, he can rent the windsurfing equipment for $35/$10 an hour, which is 3.5 hours. If Max spends all of his $35 on snorkeling, he can rent the snorkeling equipment for $35/$5 an hour, which is 7 hours.

3b. To maximize his utility, Max windsurfs for 3 hours and snorkels for 1 hour.

Max will spend his $35 such that all of the $35 is spent and that the marginal utility per dollar spent on each activity is the same. When Max windsurfs for 3 hours and snorkels for 1 hour, he spends $30 renting the windsurfing equipment and $5 renting the snorkeling equipment—a total of $35.

The marginal utility from the third hour of windsurfing is 80 and the rent of the windsurfing equipment is $10 an hour, so the marginal utility per dollar spent on windsurfing is 8. The marginal utility from the first hour of snorkeling is 40 and the rent of the snorkeling equipment is $5 an hour, so the marginal utility per dollar spent on snorkeling is 8. The marginal utility per dollar spent on windsurfing equals the marginal utility per dollar spent on snorkeling.

5a. Max's budget line is the straight line running from 5.5 hours of windsurfing and no snorkeling to 11 hours of snorkeling and no windsurfing.

5b. To maximize his utility, Max windsurfs for 4 hours and snorkels for 3 hours.

Max will spend his $55 such that all of the $55 is spent and that the marginal utility per dollar spent on each activity is the same. When Max windsurfs for 4 hours and snorkels for 3 hours, he spends $40 renting the windsurfing equipment and $15 renting the snorkeling equipment—a total of $55.

The marginal utility from the fourth hour of windsurfing is 60 and the rent of the windsurfing equipment is $10 an hour, so the marginal utility per dollar spent on windsurfing is 6. The marginal utility from the third hour of snorkeling is 30 and the rent of the snorkeling equipment is $5 an hour, so the marginal utility per dollar spent on snorkeling is 6. The marginal utility per dollar spent on windsurfing equals the marginal utility per dollar spent on snorkeling.

7. To maximize his utility, Max windsurfs for 6 hours and snorkels for 5 hours.

Max will spend his $55 such that all of the $55 is spent and that the marginal utility per dollar spent on each activity is the same. When Max windsurfs for 6 hours and snorkels for 5 hours, he spends $30 renting the windsurfing equipment and $25 renting the snorkeling equipment—a total of $55.

The marginal utility from the sixth hour of windsurfing is 12 and the rent of the windsurfing equipment is $5 an hour, so the marginal utility per dollar spent on windsurfing is 2.4. The marginal utility from the fifth hour of snorkeling is 12 and the rent of the snorkeling equipment is $5 an hour, so the marginal utility per dollar spent on snorkeling is 2.4. The marginal utility per dollar spent on windsurfing equals the marginal utility per dollar spent on snorkeling.

9. To maximize his utility, Max windsurfs for 5 hours and snorkels for 1 hour.

Because the equipment is free, Max does not have to allocate his *income* between the two activities; instead, he allocates his *time* between the two activities. Max spends 6

hours on these activities. Max allocates the 6 hours such that the marginal utility from each activity is the same. When Max windsurfs for 5 hours and snorkels for 1 hour, he spends 6 hours. His marginal utility from the fifth hour of windsurfing is 40 and his marginal utility from the first hour of snorkeling is 40—so the marginal utilities are equal.

11. The market demand curve passes through the following points: 90 cents and 3 cartons; 70 cents and 6 cartons; 50 cents and 10 cartons; 30 cents and 14 cartons; and 10 cents and 18 cartons.

At each price, the quantity demanded by the market is equal to the sum of the cartons of popcorn that Shirley demands and the cartons of popcorn that Dan demands. For example, at 50 cents a carton, the quantity demanded by Shirley and Dan is 10, the sum of Shirley's 6 and Dan's 4.

CHAPTER 9

1a. Sara's real income is 4 cans of cola.

Sara's real income in terms of cans of cola is equal to her money income divided by the price of a can of cola. Sara's money income is $12, and the price of cola is $3 a can. Sara's real income is $12 divided by $3 a can of cola, which is 4 cans of cola.

1b. Sara's real income is 4 bags of popcorn.

Sara's real income in terms of popcorn is equal to her money income divided by the price of a bag of popcorn, which is $12 divided by $3 a bag or 4 bags of popcorn.

1c. The relative price of cola is 1 bag per can.

The relative price of cola is the price of cola divided by the price of popcorn. The price of cola is $3 a can and the price of popcorn is $3 a bag, so the relative price of cola is $3 a can divided by $3 a bag, which equals 1 bag per can.

1d. The opportunity cost of a can of cola is 1 bag of popcorn.

The opportunity cost of a can of cola is the quantity of popcorn that must be forgone to get a can of cola. The price of cola is $3 a can and the price of popcorn is $3 a bag, so to buy one can of cola Sara must forgo 1 bag of popcorn.

1e. The equation that describes Sara's budget line is

$Q_P = 4 - Q_C$.

Call the price of popcorn P_P and the quantity of popcorn Q_P, the price of cola P_C and the quantity of cola Q_C, and income y. Sara's budget equation is

$P_P Q_P + P_C Q_C = y$.

If we substitute $3 for the price of popcorn, $3 for the price of cola, and $12 for the income, the budget equation becomes

$3 \times Q_P + \$3 \times Q_C = \$12$.

Dividing both sides by $3 gives

$Q_P + Q_C = 4$.

Subtract Q_C from both sides to give

$Q_P = 4 - Q_C$.

1f. To draw a graph of the budget line, plot the quantity of cola on the *x*-axis and the quantity of popcorn on the *y*-axis. The budget line is a straight line running from 4 cans on the *y*-axis to 4 bags on the *x*-axis.

1g. The slope of the budget line, when cola is plotted on the *x*-axis is minus 1. The magnitude of the slope is equal to the relative price of cola.

The slope of the budget line is "rise over run." If the quantity of cola decreases from 4 to 0, the quantity of popcorn increases from 0 to 4. The rise is 4 and the run is −4. Therefore the slope equals 4/−4, which is −1.

3a. Sara buys 2 cans of cola and 2 bags of popcorn.

Sara buys the quantities of cola and popcorn that gets her onto the highest indifference curve, given her income and the prices of cola and popcorn. The graph shows Sara's indifference curves. So draw Sara's budget line on the graph. The budget line is tangential to indifference curve I_0 at 2 cans of cola and 2 bags of popcorn. The indifference curve I_0 is the highest indifference curve that Sara can get onto.

3b. Sara's marginal rate of substitution is 1.

The marginal rate of substitution is the magnitude of the indifference curve at Sara's consumption point, which equals the magnitude of the slope of the budget line. The slope of Sara's budget line is −1, so the marginal rate of substitution is 1.

5a. Sara buys 6 cans of cola and 1 bag of popcorn.

Draw the new budget line on the graph with Sara's indifference curves. The budget line now runs from 8 cans of cola on the *x*-axis to 4 bags of popcorn on the *y*-axis. The new budget line is tangential to indifference curve I_1 at 6 cans of cola and 1 bag of popcorn. The indifference curve I_1 is the highest indifference curve that Sara can now get onto.

5b. Two points on Sara's demand for cola are the following: At $3 a can of cola, Sara buys 2 cans of cola. At $1.50 a can of cola, Sara buys 6 cans.

5c. The substitution effect is 2 cans of cola and −1.5 bags of popcorn.

To divide the price effect into a substitution effect and an income effect, take enough income away from Sara and gradually move her new budget line back toward the origin until it just touches Sara's indifference curve I_0. The point at which this budget line just touches indifference curve I_0 is 4 cans of cola and 0.5 bag of popcorn. The substitution effect is the increase in the quantity of cola from 2 cans to 4 cans and the decrease in the quantity of popcorn from 2 bags to 0.5 bag along the indifference curve I_0. The substitution effect is 2 cans of cola and −1.5 bags of popcorn.

5d. The income effect is 2 cans of cola and 0.5 bag of popcorn.

The income effect is the change in the quantity of cola from the price effect minus the change from the substitution effect. The price effect is 4 cans of cola (6 cans minus the initial 2 cans) and −1 bag of popcorn (1 bag minus the initial 2 bags). The substitution effect is an increase in the quantity of cola from 2 cans to 4 cans and the decrease in the quantity of popcorn from 2 bags to 0.5 bag of popcorn. So the income effect is 2 cans of cola and 0.5 bag of popcorn.

5e. Cola is a normal good for Sara because the income effect is positive. An increase in income increases the quantity of cola she buys from 4 to 6 cans.

5f. Popcorn is a normal good for Sara because the income effect is positive. An increase in income increases the quantity of popcorn she buys from 0.5 bag to 1 bag.

7a. Pam can still buy 30 cookies and 5 comic books.

When Pam buys 30 cookies at $1 each and 5 comic books at $2 each, she spends $40 a month. Now that the price of a cookie is 50 cents and the price of a comic book is $5, 30 cookies and 5 comic books will cost $40. So Pam can still buy 30 cookies and 5 comic books.

7b. Pam will not want to buy 30 cookies and 5 comic books because the marginal rate of substitution does not equal the relative price of the goods. Pam will move to a point on the highest indifference curve possible where the marginal rate of substitution equals the relative price.

7c. Pam prefers cookies at 50 cents each and comic books at $5 each because she can get onto a higher indifference curve than when cookies are $1 each and comic books are $2 each.

7d. Pam will buy more cookies and fewer cans of cola.

The new budget line and the old budget line pass through the point at 30 cookies and 5 comic books. If comic books are plotted on the *x*-axis, the marginal rate of substitution at this point on Pam's indifference curve is equal to the relative price of a comic book at the original prices, which is 2. The new relative price of a comic book is $5/50 cents, which is 10. That is, the budget line is steeper than the indifference curve at 30 cookies and 5 comic books. Pam will buy more cookies and fewer comic books.

7e. There will be a substitution effect and an income effect.

A substitution effect arises when the relative price changes and the consumer moves along the *same* indifference curve to a new point where the marginal rate of substitution equals the new relative price. An income effect arises when the consumer moves from one indifference curve to another, keeping the relative price constant.

CHAPTER 10

Explicit costs are $30,000. Explicit costs are all the costs for which there is a payment. Explicit costs are the sum of the wages paid ($20,000) and the goods and services bought from other firms ($10,000).

Implicit costs are the sum of the costs that do not involve a payment. Implicit costs are the sum of the interest forgone on $50,000 put into the firm; the $30,000 income forgone by Jack not working at his previous job; $15,000, which is the value of 500 hours of Jill's leisure (10 hours a week for 50 weeks); and the economic depreciation of $2,000 ($30,000 minus $28,000).

3a. All methods other than "pocket calculator with paper and pencil" are technologically efficient.

To use a pocket calculator with paper and pencil to complete the tax return is not a technologically efficient method because it takes the same number of hours as it would with a pocket calculator but it uses more capital.

3b. The economically efficient method is to use (i) a pocket calculator, (ii) a pocket calculator, (iii) a PC.

The economically efficient method is the technologically efficient method that allows the task to be done at least cost.

When the wage rate is $5 an hour: Total cost with a PC is $1,005, total cost with a pocket calculator is $70, and total cost with paper and pencil is $81. Total cost is least with a pocket calculator.

When the wage rate is $50 an hour: Total cost with a PC is $1,050, total cost with a pocket calculator is $610, and the total cost with paper and pencil is $801. Total cost is least with a pocket calculator.

When the wage rate is $500 an hour: Total cost with a PC is $1,500, total cost with a pocket calculator is $6,010, and total cost with pencil and paper is $8,001. Total cost is least with a PC.

5a. Methods *a*, *b*, *c*, and *d* are technologically efficient. Compare the amount of labor and capital used by the four methods. Start with method *a*. Moving from *a* to *b* to *c* to *d*, the amount of labor increases and the amount of capital decreases in each case.

5b. The economically efficient method is (i) method *d* (ii) methods *c* and *d* (iii) method *a*.

The economically efficient method is the technologically efficient method that allows the 100 shirts to be washed at least cost.

(i) Total cost with method *a* is $1,001, total cost with method *b* is $805, total cost with method *c* is $420, and total cost with method *d* is $150. Method *d* has the lowest total cost.

(ii) Total cost with method *a* is $505, total cost with method *b* is $425, total cost with method *c* is $300, and total cost with method *d* is $300. Methods *c* and *d* have the lowest total cost.

(iii) Total cost with method *a* is $100, total cost with method *b* is $290, total cost with method *c* is $1,020, and total cost with method *d* is $2,505. Method *a* has the lowest total cost.

7a. The four-firm concentration ratio is 60.49.

The four-firm concentration ratio equals the ratio of the total sales of the largest four firms to the total industry sales expressed as a percentage. The total sales of the largest four firms is $450 + $325 + $250 + $200, which equals $1,225. Total industry sales equal $1,225 + $800, which equals $2,025. The four-firm concentration ratio equals ($1,225/$2,025) × 100, which is 60.49 percent.

7b. This industry is highly concentrated because the four-firm concentration ratio exceeds 60 percent.

9a. The Herfindahl-Hirschman Index is 1,700.

The Herfindahl-Hirschman Index equals the sum of the squares of the market shares of the 50 largest firms or of all firms if there are less than 50 firms. The Herfindahl-Hirchman Index equals $15^2 + 10^2 + 20^2 + 15^2 + 25^2 + 15^2$, which equals 1,800.

9b. This industry is moderately competitive because the Herfindahl-Hirschman Index lies in the range 1,000–1,800.

CHAPTER 11

1a. To draw the total product curve measure labor on the *x*-axis and output on the *y*-axis. The total product curve is upward sloping.

1b. The average product of labor is equal to total product divided by the quantity of labor employed. For example, when 3 workers are employed, they produce 6 boats a week, so the average product is 2 boats per worker.

The average product curve is upward sloping when the number of workers is between 1 and 8, but it becomes downward sloping when 9 and 10 workers are employed.

1c. The marginal product of labor is equal to the increase in total product when an additional worker is employed. For example, when 3 workers are employed, total product is 6 boats a week. When a fourth worker is employed, total product increases to 10 boats a week. The marginal product of going from 3 to 4 workers is 4 boats.

The marginal product curve is upward sloping when the number of workers is between 1 and 6, but it becomes downward sloping when 7 or more workers are employed.

1d. (i) When Rubber Duckies produces fewer than 30 boats a week, it employs fewer than 8 workers a week. With fewer than 8 workers a week, marginal product exceeds average product and average product is increasing. Up to an output of 30 boats a day, each additional worker adds more to output than the average. Average product increases.

When Rubber Duckies produces more than 30 boats a week, it employs more than 8 workers a week. With more than 8 workers a week, average product exceeds marginal product and average product is decreasing. For outputs greater than 30 boats a week, each additional worker adds less to output than average. Average product decreases.

3a. Total cost is the sum of the costs of all the inputs that Rubber Duckies uses in production. Total variable cost is the total cost of the variable inputs. Total fixed cost is the total cost of the fixed inputs.

For example, the total variable cost of producing 10 boats a week is the total cost of the workers employed, which is 4 workers at $400 a week, which equals $1,600. Total fixed cost is $1,000, so the total cost of producing 10 boats a week is $2,600.

To draw the short-run total cost curves, plot output on the *x*-axis and the total cost on the *y*-axis. The total fixed cost curve is a horizontal line at $1,000. The total variable cost curve and the total cost curve have shapes similar to those in Fig. 11.4, but the vertical distance between the total variable cost curve and the total cost curve is $1,000.

3b. Average fixed cost is total fixed cost per unit of output. Average variable cost is total variable cost per unit of output. Average total cost is the total cost per unit of output.

For example, when the firm makes 10 boats a week: Total fixed cost is $1,000, so average fixed cost is $100 per boat; total variable cost is $1,600, so average variable cost is $160 per boat; and total cost is $2,600, so average total cost is $260 per boat.

Marginal cost is the increase in total cost divided by the increase in output. For example, when output increases from 3 to 6 boats a week, total cost increases from $1,800 to $2,200, an increase of $400. That is, the increase in output of 3 boats increases total cost by $400. Marginal cost is equal to $400 divided by 3 boats, which is $133.33 a boat.

The short-run average and marginal cost curves are similar to those in Fig. 11.5.

5. The increase in total fixed cost increases total cost but does not change total variable cost. Average fixed cost is total fixed cost per unit of output. The average fixed cost curve shifts upward. Average total cost is total cost per unit of output. The average total cost curve shifts upward. Marginal cost and average variable cost do not change.

7a. Total cost is the cost of all the inputs. For example, when 3 workers are employed they now produce 12 boats a week. With 3 workers, the total variable cost is $1,200 a week and the total fixed cost is $2,000 a week. The total cost is $3,200 a week. The average total cost of producing 12 boats is $266.67.

7b. The long-run average cost curve is made up of the lowest parts of the firm's short-run average total cost curves when the firm operates 1 plant and 2 plants. The long-run average cost curve is similar to Fig. 11.8.

7c. It is efficient to operate the plant that has the lower average total cost of a boat. It is efficient to operate one plant when output is less than 27 boats a week, and it is efficient to operate two plants when the output is more than 27 boats a week.

Over the output range 1 to 27 boats a week, average total cost is less with one plant than with two, but if output exceeds 27 boats a week, average total cost is less with two plants than with one.

9a. For example, the average total cost of producing a balloon ride when Bonnie rents 2 balloons and employs 4 workers equals the total cost ($1,000 rent for the balloons plus $1,000 for the workers) divided by the 20 balloon rides produced. The average total cost equals $2,000/20, which is $100 a ride.

The average total cost curve is U-shaped, as in Fig. 11.5.

9b. The long-run average cost curve is similar to that in Fig. 11.8.

9c. Bonnie's minimum efficient scale is 13 balloon rides when Bonnie rents 1 balloon.

The minimum efficient scale is the smallest output at which the long-run average cost is a minimum. To find the minimum efficient scale, plot the average total cost curve for each plant and then check which plant has the lowest minimum average total cost.

9d. Bonnie will choose the plant (number of balloons to rent) that gives her minimum average total cost for the normal or average number of balloon rides that people buy.

CHAPTER 12

1a. Quick Copy's profit-maximizing quantity is 80 pages an hour.

Quick Copy maximizes its profit by producing the quantity at which marginal revenue equals marginal cost. In perfect competition, marginal revenue equals price, which is 10 cents a page. Marginal cost is 10 cents when 80 pages an hour are produced.

1b. Quick Copy's profit is $2.40 an hour.

Profit equals total revenue minus total cost. Total revenue equals $8.00 an hour (10 cents a page multiplied by 80 pages). The average total cost of producing 80 pages is 7 cents a page, so total cost equals $5.60 an hour (7 cents multiplied by 80 pages). Profit equals $8.00 minus $5.60, which is $2.40 an hour.

1c. The price will fall in the long run to 6 cents a page.

At a price of 10 cents a page, firms make economic profit. In the long run, the economic profit will encourage new firms to enter the copying industry. As they do, the price will fall and economic profit will decrease. Firms will enter until economic profit is zero, which occurs when the price is 6 cents a copy (price equals minimum average total cost).

3a. Pat's profit-maximizing output is 4 pizzas an hour. Pat's profit is $2 an hour.

Pat maximizes its profit by producing the quantity at which marginal revenue equals marginal cost. In perfect competition, marginal revenue equals price, which is $14 a pizza. Marginal cost is the change in total cost when output is increased by 1 pizza an hour. The marginal cost of increasing output from 3 to 4 pizzas an hour is $13 ($54 minus $41). The marginal cost of increasing output from 4 to 5 pizzas an hour is $15 ($69 minus $54). So the marginal cost of the fourth pizza is half-way between $13 and $15, which is $14. Marginal cost equals marginal revenue when Pat produces 4 pizzas an hour.

Economic profit equals total revenue minus total cost. Total revenue equals $56 an hour ($14 a pizza multiplied by 4 pizzas). Total cost of producing 4 pizzas is $54. Economic profit equals $56 minus $54, which is $2 an hour.

3b. Pat's shutdown point occurs at a price of $10 a pizza.

The shutdown point is the price that equals minimum average variable cost. To calculate total variable cost, subtract total fixed cost ($10, which is total cost at zero output) from total cost. Average variable cost equals total variable cost divided by the quantity produced. For example, the average variable cost of producing 2 pizzas is $10 a pizza. Average variable cost is a minimum when marginal cost equals average variable cost. The marginal cost of producing 2 pizzas is $10. So the shutdown point is a price of $10 a pizza.

3c. Pat's supply curve is the same as the marginal cost curve at prices equal to or above $10 a pizza and the y-axis at prices below $10 a pizza.

3d. Pat will leave the industry if in the long run the price is less than $13 a pizza.

Pat's Pizza Kitchen will leave the industry if it incurs an economic loss in the long run. To incur an economic loss, the price will have to be below minimum average total cost. Average total cost equals total cost divided by the quantity produced. For example, the average total cost of producing 2 pizzas is $15 a pizza. Average total cost is a minimum when it equals marginal cost. The average total cost of 3 pizzas is $13.67, and the average total cost of 4 pizzas is $13.50. Marginal cost when Pat's produces 3 pizzas is $12 and marginal cost when Pat's produces 4 pizzas is $14. At 3 pizzas, marginal cost is less than average total cost; at 4 pizzas, marginal cost exceeds average total cost. So minimum average total cost occurs between 3 and 4 pizzas—$13 at 3.5 pizzas an hour.

3e. Firms with costs identical to Pat's will enter at any price above $13 a pizza.

Firms will enter an industry when firms currently in the industry are making economic profit. Firms with costs identical to Pat's will make economic profit when the price exceeds minimum average total cost, which is $13 a pizza.

3f. The price in the long run is $13 a pizza. This is the price that makes economic profit zero.

5a. The market price is $8.40 a cassette.

The market price is the price at which the quantity demanded equals the quantity supplied. The firm's supply curve is the same as its marginal cost curve at prices above minimum average variable cost. Average variable cost is a minimum when marginal cost equals average variable cost. Marginal cost equal average variable cost at the quantity 250 cassettes a week. So the firm's supply curve is the same as the marginal cost curve for the outputs equal to 250 cassettes or more. When the price is $8.40 a cassette, each firm produces 350 cassettes and the quantity supplied by the 1,000 firms is 350,000 cassettes a week. The quantity demanded at $8.40 is 350,000 a week.

5b. The industry output is 350,000 cassettes a week.

5c. Each firm produces 350 cassettes a week.

5d. Each firm makes an economic loss of $581 a week.

Each firm produces 350 cassettes at an average total cost of $10.06 a cassette. The firm can sell the 350 cassettes for $8.40 a cassette. The firm incurs a loss on each cassette of $1.66 and incurs an economic loss of $581a week.

5e. In the long run, some firms exit the industry because they are incurring economic losses.

5f. The number of firms in the long run is 750.

In the long run, as firms exit the industry, the price rises. In long-run equilibrium, the price will equal the minimum average total cost. When output is 400 cassettes a week, marginal cost equals average total cost and average total cost is a minimum at $10 a cassette. In the long run, the price is $10 a cassette. Each firm remaining in the industry produces 400 cassettes a week. The quantity demanded at $10 a cassette is 300,000 a week. So the number of firms is 300,000 cassettes divided by 400 cassettes per firm, which is 750 firms.

7a. The market price is $7.65 a cassette.

When the price is $7.65 a cassette, each firm produces 300 cassettes and the quantity supplied by the 1,000 firms is 300,000 cassettes a week. The quantity demanded at $7.65 is 300,000 a week.

7b. The industry output is 300,000 cassettes a week.

7c. Each firm produces 300 cassettes a week.

7d. Each firm makes an economic loss of $834 a week.

Each firm produces 300 cassettes at an average total cost of $10.43 a cassette. The firm can sell the 300 cassettes for $7.65 a cassette. The firm incurs a loss on each cassette of $2.78 and incurs an economic loss of $834 a week.

7e. In the long run, some firms exit the industry because they are incurring economic losses.

7f. The number of firms in the long run is 500.

In the long run, as firms exit the industry, the price rises. Each firm remaining in the industry produces 400 cassettes a week. The quantity demanded at $10 a cassette is 200,000 a week. So the number of firms is 200,000 cassettes divided by 400 cassettes per firm, which is 500 firms.

CHAPTER 13

1a. Minnie's total revenue schedule lists the total revenue at each quantity sold. For example, Minnie's can sell 1 bottle for $8 a bottle, which gives it a total revenue of $8 at the quantity 1 bottle.

1b. Minnie's marginal revenue schedule lists the marginal revenue that results from increasing the quantity sold by 1 bottle. For example, Minnie's can sell 1 bottle for a total revenue of $8. Minnie's can sell 2 bottles for $6 each, which gives it a total revenue of $12 at the quantity 2 bottles. So by increasing the quantity sold from 1 bottle to 2 bottles, marginal revenue is $4 a bottle ($12 minus $8).

3a. Minnie's profit-maximizing output is 1.5 bottles.

The marginal cost of increasing the quantity from 1 bottle to 2 bottles is $4 a bottle ($7 minus $3). That is, the marginal cost of the 1.5 bottles is $4 a bottle. The marginal revenue of increasing the quantity sold from 1 bottle to 2 bottles is $4 ($12 minus $8). So the marginal revenue from 1.5 bottles is $4 a bottle. Profit is maximized when the quantity produced makes the marginal cost equal to marginal revenue. The profit-maximizing output is 1.5 bottles.

3b. Minnie's profit-maximizing price is $7 a bottle.

The profit-maximizing price is the highest price that Minnie's can sell the profit-maximizing output of 1.5 bottles. Minnie's can sell 1 bottle for $8 and 2 bottles for $6, so it can sell 1.5 bottles for $7 a bottle.

3c. Minnie's marginal cost is $4 a bottle.

3d. Minnie's marginal revenue is $4 a bottle.

3e. Minnie's economic profit is $5.50.

Economic profit equals total revenue minus total cost. Total revenue equals price ($7 a bottle) multiplied by quantity (1.5 bottles), which is $10.50. Total cost of producing 1 bottle is $3 and the total cost of producing 2 bottles is $7, so the total cost of producing 1.5 bottles is $5. Profit equals $10.50 minus $5, which is $5.50.

3f. Minnie's is inefficient. Minnie's charges a price of $7 a bottle, so consumers get a marginal benefit of $7 a bottle. Minnie's marginal cost is $4 a bottle. That is, the marginal benefit of $7 a bottle exceeds Minnie's marginal cost.

5a. The profit-maximizing output is 150 newspapers a day.

Profit is maximized when the firm produces the output at which marginal cost equals marginal revenue. Draw in the marginal revenue curve. It runs from 100 on the *y*-axis to 250 on the *x*-axis. The marginal revenue curve cuts the marginal cost curve at the quantity 150 newspapers a day.

5b. The price charged is 70 cents a paper.

The highest price that the publisher can sell 150 newspapers a day is read from the demand curve.

5c. The daily total revenue is $105 (150 papers at 70 cents each).

5d. Demand is elastic.

Along a straight-line demand curve, demand is elastic at all prices above the midpoint of the demand curve. The price at the midpoint is 50 cents. So at 70 cents a paper, demand is elastic.

7a. The efficient quantity is 250 newspapers—the quantity that makes marginal benefit (price) equal to marginal cost. With 250 newspapers available, people are willing to pay 50 cents for a paper. To produce 250 newspapers, the publisher incurs a marginal cost of 50 cents a paper.

7b. The consumer surplus is $22.50 a day.

Consumer surplus is the area under the demand curve above the price. The price is 70 cents, so consumer surplus equals (100 cents minus 70 cents) multiplied by 150/2 papers a day, which is $22.50 a day.

7c. The deadweight loss is $15 a day.

Deadweight loss arises because the publisher does not produce the efficient quantity. Output is restricted to 150, and the price is increased to 70 cents. The deadweight loss equals (70 cents minus 40 cents) multiplied by 100/2.

9. The maximum that will be spent on rent seeking is $5.50 a day—an amount equal to Minnie's economic profit. The total social cost equals the deadweight loss plus the amount spent on rent seeking. To calculate the deadweight loss, first calculate the efficient output—the intersection point of the demand curve (marginal benefit curve) and the marginal cost curve. Do this by finding the equations to the two curves and solving them. The efficient output is 2.25 bottles. The deadweight loss equals $1.125. The loss to society is $6.625 ($5.50 plus $1.125).

11a. The firm will produce 2 cubic feet a day and sell it for 6 cents a cubic foot. Deadweight loss will be 4 cents a day.

Draw in the marginal revenue curve. It runs from 10 on the *y*-axis to 2.5 on the *x*-axis. The profit-maximizing output is 2 cubic feet at which marginal revenue equals marginal cost. The price charged is the highest that people will pay for 2 cubic feet a day, which is 6 cents a cubic foot. The efficient output is 4 cubic feet, at which marginal cost equals price (marginal benefit). So the deadweight loss is (4 minus 2 cubic feet) multiplied by (6 minus 2 cents)/2.

11b. The firm will produce 3 cubic feet a day and charge 4 cents a cubic foot. Deadweight loss is 1 cent a day.

If the firm is regulated to earn only normal profit, it produces the output at which price equals average total cost—at the intersection of the demand curve and the *ATC* curve.

11c. The firm will produce 4 cubic feet a day and charge 2 cents a cubic foot. There is no deadweight loss.

If the firm is regulated to be efficient, it will produce the quantity at which price (marginal benefit) equals marginal cost—at the intersection of the demand curve and the marginal cost curve.

CHAPTER 14

1a. Lite and Kool produces 100 pairs a week.

To maximize profit, Lite and Kool produces the quantity at which marginal revenue equals marginal cost.

1b. Lite and Kool charges $20 a pair.

To maximize profit, Lite and Kool charges the highest price for the 100 pairs of shoes, as read from the demand curve.

1c. Lite and Kool makes a profit of $500 a week.

Economic profit equals total revenue minus total cost. The price is $20 and the quantity sold is 100 pairs, so total revenue is $2,000. Average total cost is $15, so total cost equals $1,500. Economic profit equals $2,000 minus $1,500, which is $500 a week.

3a. The firm produces 100 pairs and sells them for $60 a pair.

To maximize profit, the firm produces the quantity at which marginal cost equals marginal revenue. Marginal cost is $20 a pair. The firm can sell 200 pairs at $20 a pair, so the marginal revenue is $20 at 100 pairs. (Marginal revenue curve lies halfway between the *y*-axis and the demand curve.)

The firm sells the 100 pairs at the highest price that consumers will pay, which is read from the demand curve. This price is $60 a pair.

3b. The firm's economic profit is zero.

The firm produces 100 pairs and sells them for $60 a pair, so total revenue is $6,000. Total cost is the sum of total fixed cost plus total variable cost of 100 pairs. Total cost equals $4,000 plus ($20 multiplied by 100), which is $6,000. The firm's profit is zero.

3c. The firm produces 200 pairs and sells them for $60 a pair.

To maximize profit, the firm produces the quantity at which marginal cost equals marginal revenue. Marginal cost is $20 a pair. At $20 a pair, the firm can sell 400 pairs (twice the number with no advertising), so the marginal revenue is $20 at 200 pairs. (The marginal revenue curve lies halfway between the *y*-axis and the demand curve.)

The firm sells the 200 pairs at the highest price that consumers will pay—read from the demand curve. This price is $60 a pair.

3d. The firm makes an economic profit of $1,000.

The firm produces 200 pairs and sells them for $60 a pair, so total revenue is $12,000. Total cost is the sum of total fixed cost plus the advertising cost plus total variable cost of 200 pairs. Total cost equals $4,000 plus $3,000 plus ($20 multiplied by 200), which is $11,000. The firm makes an economic profit of $1,000.

3e. The firm will spend $3,000 advertising because it makes more economic profit than when it does not advertise.

3f. The firm will not change the quantity it produces or the price it charges. The firm makes less economic profit.

5. The firm will not change the quantity it produces or the price it charges. The firm makes less economic profit.

   The firm maximizes profit by producing the output at which marginal cost equals marginal revenue. An increase in fixed cost increases total cost, but it does not change marginal cost. So the firm does not change its output or the price it charges. The firm's total costs have increased and its total revenue has not changed, so the firm makes less economic profit.

7a. The price rises, output increases, and economic profit increases.

   The dominant firm produces the quantity and sets the price such that it maximizes its profit. When demand increases, marginal revenue increases, so the firm produces a larger output. The highest price at which the dominant firm can sell its output increases. Because price exceeds marginal cost, economic profit increases.

7b. The price rises, output increases, and economic profit increases.

   The small firms are price takers, so the price they charge rises. Because these firms are price takers, the price is also marginal revenue. Because marginal revenue increases, the small firms move up along their marginal cost curves (supply curves) and increase the quantity they produce. Because price exceeds marginal cost, economic profit increases.

9a. The game has 2 players (A and B), and each player has 2 strategies: to answer honestly or to lie. There are 4 payoffs: Both answer honestly; both lie; A lies, and B answers honestly; and B lies, and A answers honestly.

9b. The payoff matrix has the following cells: Both answer honestly: A gets $100, and B gets $100; both lie: A gets $50, and B gets $50; A lies and B answers honestly: A gets $500, and B gets $0; B lies and A answers honestly: A gets $0, and B gets $500.

9c. Equilibrium is that each player lies and gets $50.

   If B answers honestly, the best strategy for A is to lie because he would get $500 rather than $100. If B lies, the best strategy for A is to lie because he would get $500 rather than $0. So A's best strategy is to lie, no matter what B does. Repeat the exercise for B. B's best strategy is to lie, no matter what A does.

11a. Each firm makes a zero economic profit or normal profit.

   If both firms cheat, each firm will lower the price in an attempt to gain market share from the other firm. In the process, the price will be driven down until each firm is making normal profit.

11b. The payoff matrix has the following cells: Both abide by the agreement: Soapy makes $1 million profit, and Sudsies makes $1 million profit; both cheat: Soapy makes $0 profit, and Sudsies makes $0 profit; Soapy cheats and Sudsies abides by the agreement: Soapy makes $1.5 million profit, and Sudsies incurs a $0.5 million loss; Sudsies cheats and Soapy abides by the agreement: Sudsies makes $1.5 million profit, and Soapy incurs a $0.5 million loss.

11c. The best strategy for each firm is to cheat.

   If Sudsies abides by the agreement, the best strategy for Soapy is to cheat because it would make a profit of $1.5

million rather than $1 million. If Sudsies cheats, the best strategy for Soapy is cheat because it would make a profit of $0 (the competitive outcome) rather than incur a loss of $0.5 million. So Soapy's best strategy is to cheat, no matter what Sudsies does. Repeat the exercise for Sudsies. Sudsies's best strategy is to cheat, no matter what Soapy does.

11d. The equilibrium is that both firms cheat and each makes normal profit.

11e. Each firm can adopt a tit-for-tat strategy or a trigger strategy. Pages 301-302 give descriptions of these strategies.

CHAPTER 15

1a. The wage rate is $6 an hour. The wage rate adjusts to make the quantity of labor demanded equal to the quantity supplied.

1b. The number of pickers hired is 400 a day. At a wage rate of $6 an hour, 400 pickers a day are hired.

1c. The income received is $2,400 an hour. Income equals the wage rate ($6 an hour) multiplied by the number of pickers (400).

3a. Marginal product of labor is the increase in total product that results from hiring one additional student. For example, if Wanda increases the number of students hired from 2 to 3, total product (the quantity of fish packed) increases from 50 to 90 pounds. The marginal product of hiring the third student is 40 pounds of fish.

3b. Marginal revenue product of labor is the increase in total revenue that results from hiring one additional student. For example, if Wanda hires 2 students, they produce 50 pounds of fish and Wanda sells fish for 50 cents a pound. Total revenue is $25. If Wanda increases the number of students hired from 2 to 3, total product increases to 90 pounds. Total revenue from the sale of this fish is $45. Marginal revenue product resulting from hiring the third student is $20 ($45 minus $25). Alternatively, marginal revenue product equals marginal product multiplied by marginal revenue (price). Marginal revenue product of hiring the third student is $20, which is 40 pounds of fish she sells at 50 cents a pound.

3c. One point on Wanda's demand for labor curve: At a wage rate of $20 an hour, Wanda will hire 3 students. The demand for labor curve is the same as the marginal revenue product curve.

3d. Wanda hires 7 students.

   Wanda hires the number of students that makes the marginal revenue product equal to the wage rate of $7.50 an hour. When Wanda increases the number of students from 6 to 7, marginal product is 15 pounds of fish an hour, which Wanda sells for 50 cents a pound. Marginal revenue product is $7.50—the same as the wage rate.

5a. Marginal product does not change. Marginal product that results from hiring the third student is still 40 pounds of fish.

5b. Marginal revenue product decreases.

   If Wanda hires the third student, marginal product is 40 pounds of fish. But now Wanda sells the fish for 33.33

cents, so marginal revenue product is now $13.33, down from $20.

5c. Wanda's demand for labor decreases, and her demand for labor curve shifts leftward. Wanda is willing to pay the students their marginal revenue product, and the fall in the price of fish has lowered their marginal revenue product.

5d. Wanda will hire fewer students. At the wage rate of $7.50, the number of students Wanda hires decreases as the demand for labor curve shifts leftward.

7a. Marginal revenue product does not change. If Wanda hires the third student, marginal product is 40 pounds of fish and Wanda sells the fish for 50 cents a pound, so marginal revenue product remains at $20.

7b. Wanda's demand for labor remains the same because marginal revenue product has not changed.

7c. Wanda will hire fewer students. At the wage rate of $10 an hour, Wanda hires the number of students that makes marginal revenue product equal to $10 an hour. Wanda now hires 6 students—down from 7. The marginal product that results when Wanda hires the sixth student is 20 pounds of fish an hour, and Wanda sells this fish for 50 cents a pound. Marginal revenue product of the sixth student is $10 an hour.

9. Wanda maximizes her profit when marginal revenue product equals the wage rate and when marginal revenue equals marginal cost.

When the wage rate is $7.50 an hour, Wanda hires 7 students. Marginal revenue product is marginal product (15 pounds of fish an hour) multiplied by the price of fish (50 cents a pound), which equals $7.50 an hour.

Marginal revenue resulting from selling an additional pound of fish is 50 cents. The seventh student costs $7.50 an hour and has a marginal product of 15 pounds of fish. So the marginal cost of an additional pound of fish is $7.50 an hour divided by 15 pounds of fish, which is 50 cents. So when Wanda hires 7 students, marginal revenue equals marginal cost and profit is maximized.

11. Venus installs three production lines.

With one production line: The present value of the marginal revenue product in the first year is $590,000/1.05, which is $561,904.76. The present value of the marginal revenue product in the second year is $590,000/(1.05)^2, which is $535,147.39. So the present value of the flow of marginal revenue product is $1,097,052.15. The cost of one production line is $1 million. The net present value is $97,052.15, so Venus buys the production line.

Similar calculations for 2 and 3 production lines give positive net present values, so Venus installs 3 production lines.

13. To answer this problem, we need to know the interest rate and the price that Greg expects next year. If he expects the price to rise by a bigger percentage than the interest rate, he pumps none and waits for the higher price. If he expects the price to rise by a smaller percentage than the interest rate, he pumps it all now. If he expects the price to rise by a percentage equal to the interest rate, he doesn't mind how much he pumps.

15a. Income of $2,400 a day is divided between opportunity cost and economic rent. Economic rent is the area above

the supply curve below the wage rate. To show the economic rent on the graph, extend the supply curve until it touches the y-axis. Shade in the area above the supply curve up to the wage rate $6 an hour.

15b. Opportunity cost is the area under the supply curve. To show the opportunity cost on the graph, shade in the area under the supply curve up to 400 pickers on the x-axis.

CHAPTER 16

1a. The wage rate of low-skilled workers is $5 an hour.

The wage rate adjusts to make the quantity of labor demanded equal to the quantity supplied.

1b. Firms employ 5,000 hours of low-skilled workers a day. At a wage rate of $5 an hour, 5,000 hours are employed each day.

1c. The wage rate of high-skilled workers is $8 an hour.

Because the marginal product of high-skilled workers is twice the marginal product of low-skilled workers, firms are willing to pay high-skilled workers twice the wage rate that they are willing to pay low-skilled workers. For example, the demand curve for low-skilled workers tells us that firms are willing to hire 6,000 hours of low-skilled workers at a wage rate of $4 an hour. So with high-skilled workers twice as productive as low-skilled workers, firms are willing to hire 6,000 hours of high-skilled workers at $8 an hour. That is, the demand curve for high-skilled labor lies above the demand curve for low-skilled workers such that at each quantity of workers the wage rate for high-skilled workers is double that for low-skilled workers.

The supply of high-skilled workers lies above the supply of low-skilled workers such that the vertical distance between the two supply curves equals the cost of acquiring the high skill—$2 an hour. That is, high-skilled workers will supply 6,000 hours a day if the wage rate is $8 an hour.

Equilibrium in the labor market for high-skilled workers occurs at a wage rate of $8 an hour.

1d. Firms employ 6,000 hours of high-skilled workers a day.

3a. The wage rate is $10 an hour.

With the amount of high-skilled workers equal to 5,000 hours a day, the demand for labor curve tells us that firms are willing to pay the $10 an hour to hire high-skilled workers.

3b. The wage differential is $5 an hour.

The demand for labor curves tells us that firms are willing to pay the $10 an hour to hire high-skilled workers and $5 an hour to hire low-skilled workers.

5a. The wage rate is $6 an hour.

A minimum wage is the lowest wage rate that a low-skilled worker can be paid.

5b. Firms hire 4,000 hours of low-skilled workers a day.

At the minimum wage of $6 an hour, the demand for low-skilled labor tells us that firms will hire only 4,000 hours of low-skilled workers a day.

7a. The wage rate is $10 a day.

The monopsony firm maximizes its profit by hiring the quantity of labor that makes the marginal cost of labor equal to the marginal revenue product of labor (see Fig. 16.5). The marginal product of the fifth worker is 10 grains per day. Gold sells for $1.40 per grain, so the marginal revenue product of the fifth worker is $14 a day. The marginal cost of the fifth worker a day equals the total labor cost of 5 workers a day minus the total labor cost of 4 workers a day. The supply of labor tells us that to hire 5 workers a day, the gold company must pay $10 a day, so the total labor cost is $50 a day. The supply of labor also tells us that to hire 4 workers a day, the gold company must pay $9 a day, so the total labor cost is $36 a day. So the marginal cost of the fifth worker is $14 a day ($50 minus $36).

The profit-maximizing quantity of labor is 5 workers because the marginal cost of the fifth worker equals the marginal revenue product of the fifth worker. The monopsony pays the 5 workers the lowest wage possible: the wage rate at which the 4 workers are willing to supply their labor. The supply of labor schedule tells us that 5 workers are willing to supply their labor for $10 a day.

7b. The gold company hires 5 workers a day.

7c. The marginal revenue product of the fifth worker is $14 a day.

A court-enforced wage rate above $10 a day will increase the wage rate. The quantity of labor supplied will increase, and employment will increase. Marginal revenue product of the monopsony will decrease as more labor is hired.

9. A court-enforced wage rate above $10 a day will increase the wage rate. The quantity of labor supplied will increase, and employment will increase. Marginal revenue product of the monopsony will decrease as more labor is hired.

CHAPTER 17

1a. To draw the Lorenz curve, plot the cumulative percentage of households on the x-axis and the cumulative percentage of income on the y-axis. Make the scale on the two axes the same. The Lorenz curve will pass through the following points: 20 percent on the x-axis and 5 percent on the y-axis; 40 percent on the x-axis and 16 percent on the y-axis; 60 percent on the x-axis and 33 percent on the y-axis; 80 percent on the x-axis and 57 percent on the y-axis; and 100 percent on the x-axis and 100 percent on the y-axis.

1b. U.S. income is distributed less equally than the income in the economy in this problem.

The line of equality shows an equal distribution of income. The closer the Lorenz curve is to the line of equality, the more equal is the income distribution. The Lorenz curve for this economy lies between the U.S. Lorenz curve and the line of equality.

3a. The distributions of income and wealth are the same. Every 45-year-old person has income of $30,000 a year and wealth of $255,000.

Each 45-year-old person has earned $30,000 a year for 31 years, a total of $930,000. The lifetime income will be $1,050,000 (35 multiplied by $30,000). Because total income is consumed over the lifetime and at a constant

rate, consumption is $15,000 a year ($1,050,000 divided by 70). Total consumption of a 45-year-old person is $675,000 (45 multiplied by $15,000). So the accumulated savings (wealth) at 45 years of age is $255,000 ($930,000 minus $675,000).

3b. Income is $30,000 a year for the people aged 25, 35, and 45 and zero for the people aged 55 and 65. Wealth is distributed unequally. Wealth is −$45,000 for the 25-year-old; $105,000 for the 35-year-old; $255,000 for the 45-year-old; $225,000 for the 55-year-old; and $75,000 for the 65-year-old. (Each calculation is similar to that in answer 3a.)

Case (a) shows greater equality than case (b). The distributions of wealth and income are equal in case (a) but unequal in case (b).

5a. The average wage rate is $3 an hour.

In an hour, the 10 people earn a total of $30. So the average wage rate is $3 an hour.

5b. The ratio of the highest to the lowest wage is 5/1 ($5/$1).

5c. Average daily income is $14.50 an hour.

To calculate the total income earned, start with a wage rate and find the number of hours each will work at that wage rate (first table); then find the number of people who work at that wage rate (second table). For example, if the wage rate is $3 an hour, the people who work at wage rate will work for 4 hours a day and the number of people who will work at $3 an hour is 4 people. The total daily income of these 4 people is $48 ($3 multiplied by 4 multiplied by 4).

Total income of the 10 people is $145 a day. Average daily income is equal to $14.50.

5d. The ratio of the highest to the lowest daily income is 40/1.

The highest daily income earned is $40. At $5 an hour, 1 person works and that person works for 8 hours a day. The lowest daily income is $1. At $1 an hour, 1 person works and that person works for 1 hour a day. The ratio of highest to lowest daily income is $40/$1.

5e. The distribution of hourly wage rates is symmetrically around the average wage rate of $3.00 an hour. At $1 an hour, 10 percent of people (1 person) work; at $2 an hour, 20 percent of people (2 people) work; at $3 an hour, 40 percent of people (4 people) work; at $4 an hour, 20 percent of people (2 people) work; at $5 an hour, 10 percent of people (1 person) work.

5f. The distribution of daily incomes is skewed to the left: $1 a day is earned by 10 percent of people (1 person); $4 a day is earned by 20 percent of people (2 people); $12 a day is earned by 40 percent of people (4 people); $24 a day is earned by 20 percent of people (2 people); $40 a day is earned by 10 percent of people (1 person). The most common income ($12 a day) is less than the average income ($14.50 a day).

5g. The distribution of income is skewed despite the equal distribution of abilities (as indicated by the distribution of wage rates). The distribution of income is influenced by the choices people make about how many hours to work.

7a. To draw the Lorenz curve, plot the cumulative percentage of households on the x-axis and the cumulative percentage of income after taxes and benefits on the *y*-axis. Make the scale on the two axes the same. The Lorenz curve passes through the following points: 20 percent on the *x*-axis and 15.0 percent on the *y*-axis; 40 percent on the *x*-axis and 32.0 percent on the *y*-axis; 60 percent on the *x*-axis and 50.3 percent on the *y*-axis; 80 percent on the *x*-axis and 72.7 percent on the *y*-axis; and 100 percent on the *x*-axis and 100 percent on the *y*-axis.

The income for each 20 percent of households equals market income minus taxes plus benefits. For example, for the third 20 percent income after taxes and benefits equals $18 million minus taxes of $2.7 million (15 percent of 18 million) plus benefits of $3 million, which equals $18.3 million.

7b. The government of this economy redistributes income by less than the U.S. government does. Plot the original and new Lorenz curves for the economy in this problem on Fig. 17.5 and compare the amounts of redistribution in this economy with that in the U.S. economy.

CHAPTER 18

1a. The capacity that achieves maximum net benefit is 2.5 million gallons a day.

Net benefit of the last million gallons of capacity equals marginal benefit minus marginal cost. The capacity that maximizes net benefit is the capacity at which net benefit is zero. So the capacity that maximizes net benefit is the cone at which marginal benefit equals marginal cost, which is 2.5 million gallons a day.

1b. $62.50 per person.

The efficient capacity is the one that maximizes net benefit. Total cost of the sewerage system is the sum of the marginal cost of each additional gallon of capacity. That is, total cost is the area under that marginal cost curve up to 2.5 million gallons, which equals $62.5 million. The population is 1 million, so each person will have to pay $62.50.

1c. The political equilibrium will be a sewerage system that has a capacity of 2.5 million gallons.

If voters are well informed, the political equilibrium will be the efficient capacity.

1d. Bureaucrats will provide a capacity of 5 million gallons.

With voters rationally ignorant, bureaucrats will maximize the budget. That is, they will increase the capacity until net benefit is zero. The total benefit from a capacity of 5 million gallons is $250 million. The total cost of a capacity of 5 million gallons is $250 million. So the net benefit from a capacity of 5 million gallons is zero.

3a. Taxes will be progressive: *B*-type people will pay a higher tax rate than *A*-type people.

The median voter theorem tells us the tax arrangement will be that which minimizes the taxes of the median voter. The median voter is an *A*-type person.

3b. The before-tax wage rate of *A*-type people will rise by the amount of the tax, and fewer *A*-type people will be employed. The after-tax wage rate will remain at $10 an hour. The before-tax wage rate of *B*-type people will

remain at $100, and employment of *B*-type people will not change. The after-tax wage rate will fall by the amount of the tax.

5a. The equilibrium wage rate is $12 an hour, and 30 hours of work are done each week.

Equilibrium wage rate is such that the quantity of labor demanded equals the quantity of labor supplied. Hours of work done equal the equilibrium quantity of labor hired.

5b. (i) The new wage rate is $13.60 an hour. (ii) The new number of hours worked is 24 a week. (iii) The after-tax wage rate is $9.60 an hour. (iv) The tax revenue is $96.00 a week. (v) Deadweight loss is $12 a week.

To work this problem either draw an exact graph (like Fig. 18.8b) or use equations. The equation for the pre-tax demand for labor curve is $W = -(8/30)L + 20$, where W is the wage rate and L is hours of labor. The equation for the demand for labor curve once the Social Security tax is imposed on employers is $W = -(8/30)L + 16$. The equation for the supply of labor curve is $W = (12/30)L$. So the equilibrium employment is 24 hours a week. To find the cost of labor, substitute 24 for L in the demand for labor curve. To find the after-tax wage rate, substitute 24 for L in the demand for labor curve after the tax is imposed. The tax revenue is $4 an hour multiplied by the 24 hours employed. The deadweight loss equals the tax multiplied by half the cut in employment—that is, $4 multiplied by $(30 - 24)/2$.

7a. The equilibrium price is $3 a pound, and the equilibrium quantity is 14 pounds a month.

To work this problem either draw an exact graph (like Fig. 18.9) or use equations. The equation for the demand curve is $P = -(1/2)Q + 10$. The equation for the supply curve before the tax is imposed is $P = (1/2)Q - 4$. Solving these equations gives an equilibrium price of $3 a pound and an equilibrium quantity of 14 pounds a month.

7b. (i) The new price is $4 a pound. (ii) The new quantity is 12 pounds a month. (iii) Tax revenue is $24 a month. (iv) Deadweight loss is $2 a month.

With the $2 a pound tax, the supply curve becomes $P = (1/2)Q - 2$. Solving the new supply curve and the demand curve gives a price of $4 a pound, and 12 pounds a month are bought. The tax revenue is $2 a pound multiplied by the 12 pounds bought. The deadweight loss equals the tax multiplied by half the cut in the quantity bought—that is, $2 multiplied by $(14 - 12)/2$.

CHAPTER 19

1a. The price is 30 cents a bottle.

Elixir Springs is a natural monopoly. It produces the quantity that makes marginal revenue equal to marginal cost, and it charges the highest price it can for the quantity produced. The marginal revenue curve is twice as steep as the demand curve, so it runs from 50 on the *y*-axis to 1.25 on the *x*-axis. Marginal revenue equals marginal cost at 1 million bottles a year. The highest price at which Elixir can sell 1 million bottles a year is 30 cents a bottle, read from the demand curve.

1b. Elixir Springs sells 1 million bottles a year.

1c. Elixir maximizes producer surplus.

If Elixir maximizes total surplus, it would produce the quantity that makes price equal to marginal cost. That is, it would produce 2 million bottles a year and sell them for 10 cents a bottle. Elixir is a natural monopoly, and it maximizes its producer surplus.

3a. The price is 10 cents a bottle.

Marginal cost pricing regulation sets the price equal to marginal cost, 10 cents a bottle.

3b. Elixir sells 2 million bottles.

With the price set at 10 cents, Elixir maximizes profit by producing 2 million bottles—at the intersection of the demand curve (which shows price) and the marginal cost curve.

3c. Elixir incurs an economic loss of $150,000 a year.

Economic profit equals total revenue minus total cost. Total revenue is $200,000 (2 million bottles at 10 cents a bottle). Total cost is $350,000 (total variable cost of $200,000 plus total fixed cost of $150,000). So Elixir incurs an economic loss of $150,000 (a profit of $200,000 minus $350,000).

3d. Consumer surplus is $400,000 a year.

Consumer surplus is the area under the demand curve above the price. Consumer surplus equals 40 cents a bottle (50 cents minus 10 cents) multiplied by 2 million bottles divided by 2, which is $400,000.

3e. The regulation is in the public interest because total surplus is maximized. The outcome is efficient.

The outcome is efficient because marginal benefit (or price) equals marginal cost. When the outcome is efficient, total surplus is maximized.

5a. The price is 20 cents a bottle.

Average cost pricing regulation sets the price equal to average total cost. Average total cost equals average fixed cost plus average variable cost. Because marginal cost is constant at 10 cents, average variable cost equals marginal cost. Average fixed cost is total fixed cost ($150,000) divided by the quantity produced. For example, when Elixir produces 1.5 million bottles, average fixed cost is 10 cents, so average total cost is 20 cents. The price at which Elixir can sell 1.5 million bottles a year is 20 cents a bottle.

5b. Elixir sells 1.5 million bottles.

5c. Elixir makes zero economic profit.

Economic profit equals total revenue minus total cost. Total revenue is $300,000 (1.5 million bottles at 20 cents a bottle). Total cost is $300,000 (1.5 million bottles at an average total cost of 20 cents). So Elixir makes zero economic profit.

5d. Consumer surplus is $225,000 a year.

Consumer surplus is the area under the demand curve above the price. Consumer surplus equals 40 cents a bottle (50 cents minus 20 cents) multiplied by 1.5 million bottles divided by 2, which is $225,000.

5e. The regulation creates a deadweight loss, so the outcome is inefficient. The regulation is not in the public interest.

7a. The price is $500 a trip, and the quantity is 2 trips a day.

Regulation in the public interest is marginal cost pricing.

Each airline charges $500 a trip and produces the quantity at which price equals marginal cost. Each airline makes 1 trip a day.

7b. The price is $750 a trip, and the number of trips is 1 trip a day (one by each airline on alternate days).

If the airlines capture the regulator, the price will be the same as the price that an unregulated monopoly would charge. An unregulated monopoly produces the quantity and charges the price that maximizes profit—that is, the quantity that makes marginal revenue equal to marginal cost. This quantity is 1 trip a day, and the highest price that the airlines can charge for that trip (read from the demand curve) is $750.

7c. Deadweight loss is $125 a day.

Deadweight loss arises because the number of trips is cut from 2 to 1 a day and the price is increased from $500 to $750. Deadweight loss equals (2 minus 1) trip multiplied by ($750 minus $500) divided by 2. Deadweight loss is $125 a day.

7d. The regulation is in the public interest if total surplus is maximized. That is, the outcome is efficient. A regulation that is inefficient is a regulation in the producer interest.

Government agencies regulate economic activity by setting prices, product standards and types, and entry conditions into markets. Antitrust laws are rules concerning certain types of market behavior.

Regulation is used when a natural monopoly exists and is used to make the market in which the natural monopoly exists more efficient. Examples include the setting of prices for local utilities and transit systems. Antitrust laws are used to prevent producers from acting to reduce the amount of competition between them. Examples include producers agreeing to fix the price and producers attempting to create a monopoly.

CHAPTER 20

1a. The efficient amount of waste is 3 tons a week.

The efficient amount of waste is the quantity that makes the marginal cost equal to marginal benefit. When the pesticide factory dumps 2 tons of waste, the trout farm's profit is $875 per week. When the pesticide factory dumps 3 tons of waste, the trout farm's profit is $775 per week. The loss of profit from the third ton of waste is $100. The marginal benefit to the pesticide factory of dumping the waste (the cost cut by not trucking the waste) is $100 a ton. That is, the marginal cost of the third ton to the trout farm equals the marginal benefit of the third ton to the pesticide factory.

1b. If the trout farm owns the lake, the amount of waste is 3 tons a week.

The pesticide factory pays the trout farm $100 a ton for the right to dump 3 tons of waste a week.

1c. If the pesticide factory owns the lake, the amount of waste is 3 tons a week.

The trout farm pays the pesticide factory $300 a week for farming rights and for an agreement that the dumping of waste will not exceed 3 tons a week.

3a. A tax of $100 a ton will achieve an efficient quantity of waste dumped into the lake.

The cost of dumping the waste is zero, so the pesticide factory will dump all its waste. A tax of $100 a ton will increase the marginal cost of dumping and reduce the amount of waste dumped to 3 tons a week.

3b. If no one owns the lake (that is, property rights do not exist), the efficient amount of dumped waste can be achieved by imposing the appropriate tax on the polluter.

5a. The quantity that may be dumped is 3 tons a week—the efficient quantity.

5b. The market price of a permit is $150 (or $100 a ton). The trout farm sells its permit to the factory.

The factory and the farm share equally the permits to dump 3 tons of waste. That is, each has a permit to dump 1.5 tons of waste. The efficient amount of waste is 3 tons, so the farm sells its permit to pollute to the factory for $100 a ton.

5c. The cost of dumping the waste is zero, so the pesticide factory will dump all its waste. A tax of $100 a ton will increase the marginal cost of dumping and reduce the amount of waste dumped to 3 tons a week. In this problem, the factory has a permit to dump 1.5 tons of waste a week. To be able to dump another 1.5 tons a week, the factory must buy the permit from the trout farm. The alternative to dumping the 1.5 tons is to truck it at a cost of $100 a ton. So the opportunity cost of buying the permit is $150.

7a. If schools are competitive, 30,000 students enroll and tuition is $4,000 a year.

In a competitive market, schools maximize profit. They produce the quantity at which the marginal benefit of the last student enrolled equals the marginal cost of educating the last student enrolled. Tuition is $4,000 a student.

7b. Efficient number of places is 50,000, and tuition is $4,000 a student.

The efficient number of places is such that the marginal social benefit of education equals the marginal cost of education. The marginal social benefit equals the marginal private benefit plus the external benefit. For example, the marginal social benefit of 50,000 places equals the marginal private benefit of $2,000 plus the external benefit of $2,000, which is $4,000.

CHAPTER 21

1a. Expected income is $2,000 a month.

Lee expects to make $4,000 with a 50 percent probability and nothing with a 50 percent probability. Lee's expected income is $4,000 multiplied by 0.5 plus $0 multiplied by 0.5, which is $2,000 a month.

1b. Expected total utility is 50 units.

Lee expects to make $4,000 and get 100 units of utility with a 50 percent probability and no income and get zero utility with a 50 percent probability. Lee's expected utility is 100 units multiplied by 0.5 plus 0 units multiplied by 0.5, which is 50 units a month.

1c. Another firm would have to offer about $1,250 a month for Lee not to take the risky job.

Lee would get 50 units of total utility from a certain income of about $1,250 a month (read from the utility of wealth curve at a total utility of 50 units).

3. Zenda is more risk averse.

The more rapidly a person's marginal utility of wealth diminishes, the more risk averse that person is. As wealth increases by 100, Jimmy's marginal utility decreases from 200 to 100 to 50. That is, Jimmy's marginal utility halves as his wealth increases by 100. As wealth increases by 100, Zenda's marginal utility decreases from 512 to 128 to 32. That is, Zenda's marginal utility falls to a quarter as her wealth increases by 100.

5. Lee is willing to pay $4,500 for house insurance.

With no insurance, Lee's expected wealth is $5,000 multiplied by 0.25 plus $0 multiplied by 0.75. Lee's expected wealth is $1,250, and her expected utility of (about) 25 units. But her guaranteed utility is 25 units with wealth of $500. Lee is willing to pay up to $4,500 ($5,000 minus $500) for insurance that pays out $5,000 if the house is washed away.

7. Lee will implement the optimal-search rule explained on pp. 455-456.

CHAPTER 22

1a. 0.10 computer per TV set at 10 TV sets.

1b. 0.40 computer per TV set at 40 TV sets.

1c. 0.70 computer per TV set at 70 TV sets.

1d. The graph shows an upward-sloping line that passes through the three points described in solutions 1a, 1b, and 1c.

The opportunity cost of a TV set is calculated as the decrease in the number of computers produced divided by the increase in the number of TV sets produced as we move along the *PPF*. The opportunity cost of a TV set increases as the quantity of TV sets produced increases.

3a. Virtual Reality exports TV sets to Vital Signs.

At the no-trade production levels, the opportunity cost of a TV set is 0.10 computer in Virtual Reality and 0.30 computer in Vital Signs. Because it costs less to produce a TV set in Virtual Reality, Vital Signs can import TV sets for a lower price than it can produce them. And because a computer costs less in Vital Signs than in Virtual Reality, Virtual Reality can import computers at a lower cost than it can produce them.

3b. Virtual Reality increases the production of TV sets and Vital Signs decreases the production of TV sets. Virtual Reality decreases the production of computers and Vital Signs increases the production of computers.

Virtual Reality increases production of TV sets to export some to Vital Signs and Vital Signs decreases production of TV sets because it now imports some from Virtual Reality.

3c. Each country consumes more of at least one good and possibly of both goods.

Because each country has a lower opportunity cost than the other at producing one of the goods, total production of both goods can increase.

3d. The price of a TV set is greater than 0.10 computer and less than 0.30 computer.

The price will be higher than the no-trade opportunity cost in Virtual Reality (0.10 computer) and lower than the no-trade opportunity cost in Vital Signs (0.30 computer).

5a. Free trade increases the production of at least one good (but not necessarily both goods) in both cases because each country increases the production of the good at which it has a comparative advantage.

5b. In problem 3, the price of a TV set rises in Virtual Reality. In problem 4, it falls.

The reason is that in problem 3, Virtual Reality produces a small number of TV sets with no trade and has the lower opportunity cost per TV set. But in problem 4, Virtual Reality produces a large number of TV sets with no trade and has the higher opportunity cost per TV set. So in problem 3, Virtual Reality becomes an exporter and increases production. The price of a TV set rises. In problem 4, Virtual Reality becomes an importer and decreases production, and the price of a TV set falls.

5c. In problem 3, the price of a computer rises in Vital Signs. In problem 4, it falls.

The reason is that in problem 3, Vital Signs produces a small number of computers with no trade and has the lower opportunity cost per computer. But in problem 4, Vital Signs produces a large number of computers with no trade and has the higher opportunity cost per computer.

So in problem 3, Vital Signs becomes an exporter of computers and increases production. The price of a computer rises. In problem 4, Vital Signs becomes an importer of computers and decreases production, and the price of a computer falls.

7a. $9 per bushel in the importing country and $1 per bushel in the exporting country.

These are the prices at which each country wishes to import and export a zero quantity.

7b. $5 per bushel.

This is the price at which the quantity demanded by the importer equals the quantity supplied by the exporter.

7c. 400 million bushels.

This is the quantity demanded and supplied at the equilibrium price.

7d. Zero.

The balance of trade is zero because the value imported equals the value exported.

9a. $6 per bushel.

The quantity demanded by the importer equals the quantity available under the quota of 300 million bushels at this price.

9b. $600 million.

The price at which the exporters are willing to sell 300 million bushels is $4 a bushel. So there is a profit of $2 a bushel. The total revenue from the quota is 300 million multiplied by $2.

9c. The importing agents to whom the quota is allocated.

Glossary

Absolute advantage A person has an absolute advantage in the production of two goods if by using the same quantities of inputs, that person can produce more of both goods than another person; a country has an absolute advantage if its output per unit of inputs of all goods is larger than that of another country.

Adverse selection The tendency for people to enter into agreements in which they can use their private information to their own advantage and to the disadvantage of the less-informed party.

Antitrust law A law that regulates and prohibits certain kinds of market behavior, such as monopoly and monopolistic practices.

Average cost pricing rule A rule that sets price equal to average total cost.

Average fixed cost Total fixed cost per unit of output—total fixed cost divided by output.

Average product The average product of a resource. It equals total product divided by the quantity of the resource employed.

Average tax rate The percentage of income that is paid in tax.

Average total cost Total cost per unit of output.

Average variable cost Total variable cost per unit of output.

Balance of trade The value of exports minus the value of imports.

Barriers to entry Legal or natural constraints that protect a firm from potential competitors.

Big tradeoff The conflict between equity and efficiency.

Bilateral monopoly A situation in which there is a single seller (a monopoly) and a single buyer (a monopsony).

Black market An illegal trading arrangement in which the price exceeds the legally imposed price ceiling.

Budget line The limits to a household's consumption choices.

Capacity output The output at which average total cost is a minimum—the output at the bottom of the U-shaped ATC curve.

Capital The equipment, buildings, tools, and manufactured goods that we use to produce other goods and services.

Capital accumulation The growth of capital resources.

Capture theory A theory of regulation that states that the regulations are supplied to satisfy the demand of producers to maximize producer surplus—to maximize economic profit.

Cartel A group of firms that has entered into a collusive agreement to restrict output and increase prices and profits.

Ceteris paribus Other things being equal—all other relevant things remaining the same.

Change in demand A change in buyers' plans that occurs when some influence on those plans other than the price of the good changes. It is illustrated by a shift of the demand curve.

Change in supply A change in sellers' plans that occurs when some influence on those plans other than the price of the good changes. It is illustrated by a shift of the supply curve.

Change in the quantity demanded A change in buyers' plans that occurs when the price of a good changes but all other influences on buyers' plans remain unchanged. It is illustrated by a movement along the demand curve.

Change in the quantity supplied A change in sellers' plans that occurs when the price of a good changes but all other influences on sellers' plans remain unchanged. It is illustrated by a movement along the supply curve.

Coase theorem The proposition that if property rights exist and transactions costs are low, private transactions are efficient. Equivalently, with property rights and low transaction costs, there are no externalities.

Collective bargaining A process of negotiation between representatives of employers and unions.

Collusive agreement An agreement between two (or more) producers to restrict output so as to increase prices and profits.

Command system A system in which some people give orders and other people obey them.

Comparative advantage A person or country has a comparative advantage in an activity if that person or country can perform the activity at a lower opportunity cost than anyone else or any other country.

Complement A good that is used in conjunction with another good.

Constant returns to scale Features of a firm's technology that leads to constant long-run average cost as output increases. When constant returns to scale are present, the LRAC curve is horizontal.

Consumer equilibrium A situation in which a consumer has allocated his or her income in the way that maximizes his or her utility.

Consumer surplus The value that the consumer gets from each unit of a good minus the price paid for it.

Contestable market A market in which one firm (or a small number of firms) operates but in which entry and exit are free, so the firm (or firms) in the industry faces competition from potential entrants.

Cooperative equilibrium The outcome of a collusive agreement between players when the players make and share the monopoly profit.

Copyright A government-sanctioned exclusive right granted to the inventor of a good, service, or productive process to produce, use, and sell the invention for a given number of years.

Craft union A group of workers who have a similar range of skills but work for many different firms in many different industries and regions.

Cross elasticity of demand The responsiveness of the demand for a good to the price of a substitute or complement, other things remaining the same. It is calculated as the percentage change in the quantity demanded of the good divided by the percentage change in the price of the substitute or complement.

Cross-section graph A graph that shows the values of an economic variable for different groups in a population at a point in time.

Deadweight loss A measure of inefficiency. It is equal to the loss in total surplus (consumer surplus plus producer surplus) when output is below or above its efficient level.

Demand The relationship between the quantity of a good that consumers plan to buy and the price of the good when all other influences on buyers' plans remain the same. It is described by a demand schedule and illustrated by a demand curve.

Demand curve A curve that shows the relationship between the quantity demanded of a good and its price when all other influences on consumers' planned purchases remain the same.

Derived demand Demand for a productive resource which is derived from the demand for the goods and services produced by the resource.

Diminishing marginal rate of substitution The general tendency for the marginal rate of substitution of one good for another to diminish as a consumer moves along an indifference curve increasing consumption of the first good.

Diminishing marginal returns The tendency for the marginal product of an additional resource eventually to be less than the marginal product of the previous unit of the resource.

Diminishing marginal utility The marginal utility that a consumer gets from a good decreases as more of the good is consumed.

Direct relationship A relationship between two variables that move in the same direction.

Discounting The conversion of a future amount of money to its present value.

Diseconomies of scale Features of a firm's technology that leads to rising long-run average cost as output increases.

Dominant strategy equilibrium The outcome of a game in which there is a single best strategy (a dominant strategy) for each player, regardless of the strategy of the other players.

Dumping The sale of a good or service to a foreign country at a price that is less than the cost of producing the good or service.

Duopoly A market structure in which two producers of a good or service compete.

Dynamic comparative advantage A comparative advantage that a person or country possesses as a result of having specialized in a particular activity and then, as a result of learning-by-doing, having become the producer with the lowest opportunity cost.

Economic depreciation The change in the market price of a piece of capital over a given period.

Economic efficiency A situation that occurs when the cost of producing a given output is as low as possible.

Economic growth The expansion of production possibilities that results from capital accumulation and technological change.

Economic information Data on prices, quantities, and qualities of goods and services and factors of production.

Economic model A description of some aspect of the economic world that includes only those features of the world that are needed for the purpose at hand.

Economic profit A firm's total revenue minus its opportunity cost.

Economic rent The income received by the owner of a resource over and above the amount required to induce that owner to offer the resource for use.

Economics The science that explains the choices we make and how those choices change as we cope with scarcity.

Economic theory A generalization that summarizes what we think we understand about the economic choices that people make and the performance of industries and entire economies.

Economies of scale Features of a firm's technology that leads to a falling long-run average cost as output increases.

Economies of scope Decreases in average total cost that occur when a firm uses specialized resources to produce a range of goods and services.

Efficient Resource use is efficient when we produce the goods and services that we value most highly.

Efficient market A market in which the actual price embodies all currently available relevant information. Resources are sent to their highest-valued use.

Elastic demand Demand with a price elasticity greater than 1; other things remaining the same, the percentage change in the quantity demanded exceeds the percentage change in price.

Elasticity of demand The responsiveness of the quantity demanded of a good to a change in its price, other things remaining the same.

Elasticity of supply The responsiveness of the quantity supplied of a good to a change in its price, other things remaining the same.

Entrepreneurship The resource that organizes the other three factors of production: labor, land, and capital. Entrepreneurs come up with new ideas about what, how, when, and where to produce, make business decisions, and bear the risk that arises from their decisions.

Equilibrium price The price at which the quantity demanded equals the quantity supplied.

Equilibrium quantity The quantity bought and sold at the equilibrium price.

Excise tax A tax on the sale of a particular commodity.

Exhaustible natural resources Natural resources that can be used only once and that cannot be replaced once they have been used.

Expected utility The average utility arising from all possible outcomes.

Expenditure The price of a good multiplied by the quantity of the good that is bought is the expenditure on a good.

Exports The goods and services that we sell to people in other countries.

External benefits Benefits that accrue to people other than the buyer of the good.

External costs Costs that are not borne by the producer of the good but by someone else.

External diseconomies Factors outside the control of a firm that raise the firm's costs as the industry produces a larger output.

External economies Factors beyond the control of a firm that lower the firm's costs as the industry produces a larger output.

Externality A cost or a benefit that arises from an economic transaction and that falls on people who do not participate in the transaction.

Firm An institution that hires productive resources and that organizes those resources to produce and sell goods and services.

Four-firm concentration ratio A measure of market power that is calculated as the percentage of the value of sales accounted for by the four largest firms in an industry.

Free rider A person who consumes a good without paying for it.

Game theory The main tool that economists use to analyze strategic behavior—behavior that takes into account the expected behavior of others and the mutual recognition of independence.

General Agreement on Tariffs and Trade (GATT) An international agreement designed to reduce tariffs on international trade.

Goods and services All the things that people are willing to pay for.

Herfindahl-Hirschman Index A measure of market power that is

calculated as the square of the market share of each firm (as a percentage) summed over the largest 50 firms (or over all firms if there are fewer than 50) in a market.

Human capital The skill and knowledge that people obtain from education and on-the-job training.

Implicit rental rate The rent that a firm pays to itself for the use of its own assets.

Imports The goods and services that we buy from people in other countries.

Incentive An inducement to take a particular action.

Incentive regulation scheme A regulation that gives a firm an incentive to operate efficiently and keep costs under control.

Incentive system A method of organizing production that uses a market-like mechanism inside the firm.

Income The amount of money that someone earns by working.

Income effect The change in consumption that results from a change in the consumer's income, other things remaining the same.

Income elasticity of demand The responsiveness of demand to a change in income, other things remaining the same. It is calculated as the percentage change in the quantity demanded divided by the percentage change in income.

Indifference curve A line that shows combinations of goods among which a consumer is indifferent.

Industrial union A group of workers who have a variety of skills and job types but work for the same industry.

Inelastic demand A demand with a price elasticity between 0 and 1; the percentage change in the quantity demanded is less than the percentage change in price.

Infant-industry argument The argument that protection is necessary to enable an infant industry to grow into a mature industry that can compete in world markets.

Inferior good A good for which demand decreases as income increases.

Inflation A process of rising prices.

Information cost The opportunity cost of economic information—the cost of acquiring information on prices, quantities, and qualities of goods and services and resources.

Intellectual property rights Property rights for discoveries owned by the creators of knowledge.

Inverse relationship A relationship between variables that move in opposite directions.

Labor The time and effort that people allocate to producing goods and services.

Labor union An organized group of workers whose purpose is to increase wages and to influence other job conditions.

Land All the gifts of nature that we use to produce goods and services.

Law of diminishing returns As a firm uses more of a variable input with a given quantity of other inputs (fixed inputs), the marginal product of the variable input eventually diminishes.

Learning-by-doing People become more productive in an activity (learn) just by repeatedly producing a particular good or service (doing).

Legal monopoly A market structure in which there is one firm and entry is restricted by the granting of a public franchise, government license, patent, or copyright.

Limit pricing The practice of charging a price below the monopoly profit-maximizing price and producing a quantity greater than that at which marginal revenue equals marginal cost so as to deter entry.

Linear relationship A relationship between two variables that is illustrated by a straight line.

Local public good A public good that is consumed by all the people who live in a particular area.

Long run A period of time in which a firm can vary the quantities of all its inputs.

Long-run average cost curve The relationship between the lowest attainable average total cost and output when both capital and labor are varied.

Long-run industry supply curve A curve that shows how the quantity supplied by an industry varies as the market price varies after all the possible adjustments have been made, including changes in plant size and the number of firms in the industry.

Lorenz curve A curve that graphs the cumulative percentage of income or wealth against the cumulative percentage of families or population.

Macroeconomics The study of the national economy and the global economy, the way in which economic aggregates grow and fluctuate, and the effects of government actions on them.

Margin When a choice is changed by a small amount or by a little at a time, the choice is made at the margin.

Marginal benefit The benefit that a person receives from consuming one more unit of a good or service. It is measured as the maximum amount that a person is willing to pay for one more unit of the good or service.

Marginal cost The opportunity cost of producing one more unit of a good or service. It is the best alternative forgone. It is calculated as the increase in total cost divided by the increase in output.

Marginal cost pricing rule A rule that sets the price of a good or service equal to the marginal cost of producing it.

Marginal product The extra output produced as a result of a small increase in the variable input. It is calculated as the increase in total product divided by the increase in the variable input employed, when the quantities of all other resources are constant.

Marginal rate of substitution The rate at which a person will give up good y (the good measured on the y-axis) to get more of good x (the good measured on the x-axis) and at the same time remain indifferent (remain on the same indifference curve).

Marginal revenue The change in total revenue received from selling one additional unit of the good or service. It is calculated as the change in total revenue divided by the change in quantity sold.

Marginal revenue product The change in total revenue that results from employing one more unit of a resource while the quantity of all other resources remains the same. It is calculated as the increase in total revenue divided by the increase in the quantity of the resource.

Marginal social benefit The marginal benefit received by the buyer of a good (marginal private benefit) plus the marginal benefit received by others (external benefit).

Marginal social cost The marginal cost incurred by the producer of a good (marginal private cost) plus the marginal cost imposed on other members of society (external cost).

Marginal tax rate The percentage of an additional dollar of income that is paid in tax.

Marginal utility The change in total utility resulting from a one-unit increase in the quantity of a good consumed.

Marginal utility per dollar spent The marginal utility obtained from the last unit of a good consumed divided by the price of the good.

Market Any arrangement that enables buyers and sellers to get information and to do business with each other.

Market demand The relationship between the quantity demanded of a good or service by everyone in the population and its price. It is illustrated by the market demand curve.

Market failure A state in which the market does not use resources efficiently.

Market power The ability to influence the market, and in particular the market price, by influencing the total quantity offered for sale.

Microeconomics The study of the decisions of people and businesses, the interactions of those decisions in markets, and the effects of government regulation and taxes on the prices and quantities of goods and services.

Minimum efficient scale The smallest quantity of output at which the long-run average cost curve reaches its lowest level.

Minimum wage law A regulation that makes the hiring of labor below a specified wage rate illegal.

Monopolistic competition A market in which a large number of firms compete by making similar but slightly different products.

Monopoly An industry that produces a good or service for which no close substitute exists and in which there is one supplier that is protected from competition by a barrier preventing the entry of new firms.

Monopsony A market in which there is a single buyer.

Moral hazard A situation in which one of the parties to an agreement has an incentive after the agreement is made to act in a manner that brings additional benefits to himself or herself at the expense of the other party.

Nash equilibrium The outcome of a game that occurs when player A takes the best possible action given the action of player B and player B takes the best possible action given the action of player A.

Natural monopoly A monopoly that occurs when one firm can supply the entire market at a lower price than two or more firms can.

Negative income tax A redistribution scheme that gives every family a guaranteed minimum annual income and taxes all income above the guaranteed minimum at a fixed marginal tax rate.

Negative relationship A relationship between variables that move in opposite directions.

Net present value The present value of the future flow of marginal revenue product generated by capital minus the cost of the capital.

Nonexhaustible natural resources Natural resources that can be used repeatedly without depleting what is available for future use.

Nontariff barrier Any action other than a tariff that restricts international trade.

Normal good A good for which demand increases as income increases.

Normal profit The expected return for supplying entrepreneurial ability.

North American Free Trade Agreement An agreement signed in 1994 between the United States, Canada, and Mexico to virtually eliminate all barriers to international trade between them in 15 years.

Oligopoly A market in which a small number of firms compete.

Opportunity cost The opportunity cost of an action is the highest-valued alternative forgone.

Patent A government-sanctioned exclusive right granted to the inventor of a good, service, or productive process to produce, use, and sell the invention for a given number of years.

Payoff matrix A table that shows the payoffs for every possible action by each player for every possible action by each other player.

Perfect competition A market in which there are many firms each selling an identical product; there are many buyers; there are no restrictions on entry into the industry; firms in the industry have no advantage over potential new entrants; and firms and buyers are well informed about the price of each firm's product.

Perfectly elastic demand Demand with an infinite price elasticity; the quantity demanded changes by a large percentage in response to a tiny price change.

Perfectly inelastic demand Demand with a price elasticity of zero; the quantity demanded remains constant when the price changes.

Perfect price discrimination Price discrimination that extracts the entire consumer surplus.

Political equilibrium The outcome that results from the choices of voters, politicians, and bureaucrats.

Positive relationship A relationship between two variables that move in the same direction.

Poverty A state in which a family's income is too low to be able to buy the quantities of food, shelter, and clothing that are deemed necessary.

Present value The amount of money that, if invested today, will grow to be as large as a given future amount when the interest that it will earn is taken into account.

Price ceiling A regulation that makes it illegal to charge a price higher than a specified level.

Price discrimination The practice of selling different units of a good or service for different prices or of charging one customer different prices for different quantities bought.

Price effect The change in consumption that results from a change in the price of a good or service, other things remaining the same.

Price elasticity of demand A measure of the responsiveness of the quantity demanded of a good to a change in its price, all other influences on buyers' plans remaining the same.

Price taker A firm that cannot influence the price of the good or service it produces.

Principal-agent problem The problem of devising compensation rules that induce an agent to act in the best interest of a principal.

Principle of minimum differentiation The tendency for competitors to make themselves identical as they try to appeal to the maximum number of clients or voters.

Private information Information that is available to one person but is too costly for anyone else to obtain.

Producer surplus The price a producer gets for a good or service minus the opportunity cost of producing it.

Product differentiation Making a good or service slightly different from that of a competing firm.

Production efficiency A situation in which the economy cannot produce more of one good without producing less of some other good.

Production possibility frontier The boundary between those combinations of goods and services that can be produced and those that cannot.

Productivity Production per unit of resource used in the production of goods and services.

Progressive income tax A tax on income at a marginal rate that increases with the level of income.

Property rights Social arrangements that govern the ownership, use, and disposal of resources, goods, and services.

Proportional income tax A tax on income that remains at a constant rate, regardless of the level of income.

Public good A good or service that can be consumed simultaneously by everyone, even if they don't pay for it.

Public interest theory A theory of regulation that states that regulations are supplied to satisfy the demand of consumers and producers to maximize total surplus—that is, to attain efficiency.

Quantity demanded The amount of a good or service that consumers plan to buy during a given time period at a particular price.

Quantity supplied The amount of a good or service that producers plan to sell during a given time period at a particular price.

Quota A quantitative restriction on the import of a particular good, which specifies the maximum amount that can be imported in a given time period.

Rate of return regulation A regulation that determines a regulated price by setting the price at a level that enables the regulated firm to earn a specified target percent return on its capital.

Rational ignorance The decision not to acquire information because the cost of doing so exceeds the expected benefit.

Real income A household's income expressed not as money but as a quantity of goods that the household can afford to buy.

Regressive income tax A tax on income at a marginal rate that decreases with the level of income.

Regulation Rules administered by a government agency to influence economic activity by determining prices, product standards and types, and conditions under which new firms may enter an industry.

Relative price The ratio of the price of one good or service to the price of another good or service. A relative price is an opportunity cost.

Rent ceiling A regulation that makes it illegal to charge a rent higher than a specified level.

Rent seeking Any activity that attempts to capture a consumer surplus, a producer surplus, or an economic profit.

Reservation price The highest price that a buyer is willing to pay for a good.

Risk A situation in which more than one outcome might occur and the probability of each possible outcome can be estimated.

Scarcity The state in which the resources available are insufficient to satisfy people's wants.

Scatter diagram A diagram that plots the value of one economic variable against the value of another.

Search activity The time spent looking for someone with whom to do business.

Short run The short run in microeconomics has two meanings. For the firm, it is the period of time in which the quantity of at least one input is fixed and the quantities of the other inputs can be varied. The fixed input is usually capital—that is, the firm has a given plant size. For the industry, the short run is the period of time in which each firm has a given plant size and the number of firms in the industry is fixed.

Short-run industry supply curve A curve that shows the quantity supplied by the industry at each price varies when the plant size of each firm and the number of firms in the industry remain the same.

Shutdown point The output and price at which the firm just covers its total variable cost. In the short run, the firm is indifferent between producing the profit-maximizing output and shutting down temporarily.

Signal An action taken outside a market that conveys information that can be used by that market.

Single-price monopoly A monopoly that sells each unit of its output for a same price.

Slope The change in the value of the variable measured on the y-axis divided by the change in the value of the variable measured on the x-axis.

Strategies All the possible actions of each player in a game.

Subsidy A payment made by the government to producers that depends on the level of output.

Substitute A good that can be used in place of another good.

Substitution effect The effect of a change in price of one good or service on the quantity bought when the consumer remains indifferent between the original and the new consumption situations—that is, the consumer remains on the same indifference curve.

Sunk cost A cost that has been incurred in the past and cannot be reversed now.

Supply The relationship between the quantity of a good that producers plan to sell and the price of the good when all other influences on sellers' plans remain the same. It is described by a supply schedule and illustrated by a supply curve.

Supply curve A curve that shows the relationship between the quantity supplied and the price of a good when all other influences on producers' planned sales remain the same.

Symmetry principle A principle that states that people in similar situations be treated similarly.

Tariff A tax that is imposed by the importing country when an imported good crosses its international boundary.

Technological change The development of new goods and better ways of producing goods and services.

Technological efficiency A situation that occurs when it is not possible to increase output without increasing inputs.

Technology Any method of producing a good or service.

Terms of trade The quantity of goods and services that a country exports to pay for its imports of goods and services.

Time-series graph A graph that measures time (for example, months or years) on the x-axis and the variable or variables in which we are interested on the y-axis.

Total cost The cost of all the productive resources that a firm uses.

Total fixed cost The cost of the fixed inputs.

Total product The total output produced by a firm in a given period of time.

Total revenue The value of a firm's sales. It is calculated as the price of the good multiplied by the quantity sold.

Total revenue test A method of estimating the price elasticity of demand by observing the change in total revenue that results from a change in the price, when all other influences on the quantity sold remain the same.

Total utility The total benefit that a person gets from the consumption of goods and services.

Total variable cost The cost of all the variable inputs.

Tradeoff A constraint that involves giving up one thing to get something else.

Transactions costs The costs incurred in searching for someone with whom to do business, in reaching an agreement about the price and other aspects of the exchange, and in ensuring that the terms of the agreement are fulfilled.

Trend The general direction (rising or falling) in which a variable is moving over the long term.

Uncertainty A situation in which more than one event might occur but it is not known which one.

Unemployment Resources that are available but are not being used.

Unit elastic demand Demand with a price elasticity of 1; the percentage change in the quantity demanded equals the percentage change in price.

Utilitarianism A principle that states that we should strive to achieve "the greatest happiness for the greatest number of people."

Utility The benefit or satisfaction that a person gets from the consumption of a good or service.

Utility of wealth The amount of utility that a person attaches to a given amount of wealth.

Value The maximum amount that a person is willing to pay for a good. The value of one more unit of the good or service is its marginal benefit.

Value of production The value of the goods and services produced.

Voluntary exchange A transaction between people, businesses, or countries that is undertaken voluntarily.

Voluntary export restraint An agreement between two countries in which the government of the exporting country agrees to reduce the volume of its own exports to the other country.

World Trade Organization An international organization that places obligations on its member countries to observe the GATT rules.

Index

Key terms and pages on which they are
defined appear in **boldface type**.